INTERNATIONAL POLITICAL ECONOMY SERIES

General Editor: Timothy M. Shaw, Professor of Political Science and International Development Studies, and Director of the Centre for Foreign Policy Studies, Dalhousie University, Nova Scotia, Canada

Recent titles include:

Pradeep Agrawal, Subir V. Gokarn, Veena Mishra, Kirit S. Parikh and Kunal Sen
ECONOMIC RESTRUCTURING IN EAST ASIA AND INDIA: Perspectives on Policy Reform

Solon L. Barraclough and Krishna B. Ghimire
FORESTS AND LIVELIHOODS: The Social Dynamics of Deforestation in Developing Countries

Jerker Carlsson, Gunnar Köhlin and Anders Ekbom
THE POLITICAL ECONOMY OF EVALUATION: International Aid Agenicies and the Effectiveness of Aid

Steve Chan (*editor*)
FOREIGN DIRECT INVESTMENT IN A CHANGING GLOBAL POLITICAL ECONOMY

Edward A. Comor (*editor*)
THE GLOBAL POLITICAL ECONOMY OF COMMUNICATION

Paul Cook and Frederick Nixson (*editors*)
THE MOVE TO THE MARKET? Trade and Industry Policy Reform in Transitional Economies

O. P. Dwivedi
DEVELOPMENT ADMINISTRATION: From Underdevelopment to Sustainable Development

John Healey and William Tordoff (*editors*)
VOTES AND BUDGETS: Comparative Studies in Accountable Governance in the South

Noeleen Heyzer, James V. Riker and Antonio B. Quizon (*editors*)
GOVERNMENT–NGO RELATIONS IN ASIA: Prospects and Challenges for People-Centered Development

George Kent
CHILDREN IN THE INTERNATIONAL POLITICAL ECONOMY

The World Bank and Non-Governmental Organizations

The Limits of Apolitical Development

Paul J. Nelson

Associate Director for Development Policy
Church World Service and Lutheran World Relief
Washington, DC

First published in Great Britain 1995 by
MACMILLAN PRESS LTD
Houndmills, Basingstoke, Hampshire RG21 6XS
and London
Companies and representatives
throughout the world

A catalogue record for this book is available
from the British Library.

ISBN 0–333–64577–4

First published in the United States of America 1995 by
ST. MARTIN'S PRESS, INC.,
Scholarly and Reference Division,
175 Fifth Avenue,
New York, N.Y. 10010

ISBN 0–312–12620–4

Library of Congress Cataloging-in-Publication Data
Nelson, Paul J, 1956–
The World Bank and non-governmental organizations : the limits of
apolitical development / Paul J. Nelson.
p. cm.
Includes bibliographical references and index.
ISBN 0–312–12620–4
1. World Bank. 2. Non-governmental organizations. I. Title.
II. Series.
HG3881.5.W57N45 1995
332.1'532—dc20 95–7825
CIP

10 9 8 7 6 5
04 03 02 01

Printed and bound in Great Britain by
Antony Rowe Ltd, Chippenham, Wiltshire

Contents

List of Tables and Figures

Tables

Figures

Preface

The fiftieth anniversary year of the Bretton Woods organizations has been a turbulent one for the World Bank. 1995 has already been marked by a political shift in the Congress of its largest financial contributor, a major financial crisis in Mexico, the resignation of the late Lewis Preston and the nomination and appointment of James D. Wolfensohn to become its new President in June of 1995.

It is difficult to predict the significance of any of these events and changes for the Bank. Internal and external reformers, including NGOs, have pressed for reforms in environmental policy, changes in policy and practice with respect to structural adjustment and popular participation, freer access to information and channels for complaints about Bank-financed projects. Reforming efforts found some support at the top during Preston's presidency. A new, somewhat less secretive information disclosure policy was enacted and an independent inspection panel created to hear complaints. Preston emphasized poverty reduction and the environment in speeches and policy documents throughout his tenure.

The incoming President has announced his intention to reshape the Bank. Wolfensohn's long-time interest in environmental and social development issues has raised hopes and expectations among many observers. But he takes over a large and conservative bureaucracy whose entrenched interests, myths and organizational dynamics have resisted and reshaped changes promulgated by previous leaders.

How the new President's agenda will take shape, and how it will intersect and interact with NGO and social movements' agendas and with the changing politics of multilateral cooperation, remain to be seen. The research on Bank-NGO relations reported here, together with a review of policy changes in the 1970s and 1980s, points to some of the organizational features that have resisted change. These same features – including a relatively rigid project cycles, the protective organizational myth of apolitical development, and a hierarchical and insular information management system – should be among the targets for determined leadership within the Bank. They also suggest indicators by which reformers and observers can assess the response.

NGOs and social movements that have targeted the Bank appear prepared to continue pressing for changes in policy and practice at the

Bank. The present political turn in Washington threatens to reduce drastically US participation in most multilateral and international cooperation, and has slowed the momentum of critique and reform momentarily. But interaction between the Bank and nongovernmental bodies, both cooperative and conflictive, continues to grow. And as networks of NGOs seek influence over the Bank, NGOs themselves are inevitably reshaped by their relations with World Bank programs and practice.

PAUL J. NELSON

Acknowledgements

The research and writing of this book has spanned seven years, beginning as a Ph.D dissertation and ending as a focus of four years of activist research in Washington, DC. I hope that I have recognized specific intellectual debts clearly along the way, but there are a few people to whom I wish to give particular thanks.

At the University of Wisconsin-Madison, Russ Middleton, Bill Thiesenhusen, David Stark, David Trubek and Joanne Csete offered instruction and encouragement. Doug Hellinger and his colleagues at the Development GAP were generous with advice and office hospitality during research in Washington, as was Bill Rau. The Mennonite Central Committee program in the Philippines gave much-needed hospitality and guidance during a visit there.

Many NGO colleagues have made the work enjoyable and rewarding. Marcos Arruda, Steve Commins, Nancy Alexander, Marijke Torfs, Chad Dobson, Rajesh Tandon, Paul Spray, Lisa McGowan, Ross Hammond, Veena Siddharth, Jo Marie Griesgraber and Alex Rondos have inspired through their energy and selfless work, and reminded by example that even serious work should be fun.

Church World Service and Lutheran World Relief, and my colleagues in their Office on Development Policy, have supported continued engagement with the World Bank, and this writing owes much to my experience as a part of that advocacy effort. The research and writing, however, have been done in my individual capacity, and the book and the views expressed are neither a project of nor attributable to any agency.

James Riker and Kathryn Sikkink offered valuable advice in a research working group, and I have benefitted from conversations with Gerald Schmitz, David Williams and David Gillies. The dissertation research was funded by the John D. And Catherine T. MacArthur Foundation, which has also supported continuing conversation among researchers on international conflict and cooperation. Thanks to Series Editor Tim Shaw for probing comments on the manuscript, and for his commitment to exchange among participants in and scholars of international affairs, across boundaries of the university, government and NGO.

Many staff and consultants at the World Bank have helped clarify issues, pointed the way to documents or individual sources, and given their time for interviews. Most of these will remain unnamed, but among those who helped in official capacities are David Beckmann, John Clark, Chris Hennin, Carmen Malena, Kris Martin and Aubrey Williams.

None of these colleagues from NGOs, universities or the Bank bears any responsibility for the books's remaining shortcomings.

Thanks to friends and family who have provided companionship and hospitality along the way: Wayne Sigelko and Nancy Didion, the La Samaritaine Community in Madison, Joanne Csete, Brian Best and Jane Lincoln, Carol Bradford and Robert Laslett, Craig and Edith Eder, Margaret and Paul McNamara, Wally and Demaris Nelson and Tony and Lill Scommegna.

Paola Scommegna, my partner in the home economy, knows the impositions of this project better than anyone. Thanks to her for editorial advice and untold other forms of support, and to Renata and Ted for interrupting my work as often, delightfully and imaginatively as possible.

Mount Rainier, Maryland   PAUL J. NELSON

Acronyms and Abbreviations

ADF	African Development Foundation
AKF	Aga Khan Foundation
APRODEV	Association of Protestant Development Organizations in Europe
BRAC	Bangladesh Rural Advancement Committee
CARE	Cooperative for American Relief Everywhere
CBO	Community-based organization
CCIC	Canadian Council for International Cooperation
CGAPP	Consultative Group to Assist the Poorest of the Poor
CGIAR	Consultative Group on International Agricultural Research
CIDA	Canadian International Development Agency
CIDSE	Cooperation Internationale pour le Developpement et la Solidarité
CLUSA	Cooperative League of the USA
CRS	Catholic Relief Services
Development GAP	Development Group for Alternative Policies
ED	Executive Director
EDI	Economic Development Institute, a World Bank-managed institute for training government officials of borrowing countries.
EIA	Environmental Impact Assessment
EMENA	The World Bank's Europe, Middle East and North Africa Region. The EMENA grouping was eliminated in a recent reconfiguration of the regional Vice Presidencies, but is retained here for regional comparisons.
EXTIE	The International Economics Relations unit of the External Relations department, responsible for NGO relations. SPRIE was moved to External Relations early in 1990, and renamed EXTIE. In 1992 it was shifted to Operations Division and renamed OPRIE.
FDC	Fundacion del Centavo, Guatemala
FY	Fiscal Year

GEF	Global Environmental Facility
IAF	Inter-American Foundation
IBRD	International Bank for Reconstruction and Development, the World Bank's main lending window
ICVA	International Council of Voluntary Agencies
IDA	International Development Association, the concessional lending arm of the World Bank
IDA-10	The tenth three-year replenishment by donor countries ('Part I Members') of IDA's lending funds
IFAD	International Fund for Agricultural Development
IFC	International Finance Corporation, affiliate of the World Bank, part of the World Bank Group.
IMF	International Monetary Fund
INGI	International NGO Forum on Indonesia
LAC	The World Bank's Latin America and Caribbean region
MIGA	Multilateral Investment Guarantee Agency
NAM	Non-Aligned Movement
NGO	Non-governmental organization
NIC	Newly industrialized country
NRECA	National Rural Electrification Association
OD	Operational Directive. Formal written guidance for World Bank staff on operations and procedures. Formerly called Operational Manual Statements (OMS).
OECD	Organization for Economic Co-operation and Development
OED	Operations Evaluation Department of the World Bank
OMS	Operational Manual Statement. See OD.
OPRIE	The International Economic Relations unit within the Bank's Operations complex. Responsibility for NGO policy has rested in Operations since 1992.
ORT	Organization for Rehabilitation through Training
PCR	Project Completion Report, done for each project at the end of disbursements from the Bank
PRIA	Society for Participatory Research in Asia
PVO	Private voluntary organization
SAL	Structural adjustment loan
SAP	Structural adjustment plan
SDA	Social Dimensions of Adjustment

SECAL	Sectoral adjustment loan
SPR	The World Bank's Strategic Planning and Review unit
SPRIE	The International Economic Relations unit within Strategic Planning and Review. SPRIE's personnel and function were moved in 1990 to External Affairs, then in 1992 to Operations Division.
TFAP	Tropical Forest Action Plan
UN	United Nations
UNCED	United Nations Conference on Environment and Development, held in Rio de Janeiro in 1992
UNDP	United Nations Development Program
UNICEF	United Nations Children's Fund
USAID	United States Agency for International Development
WDR	*World Development Report*, published annually by the World Bank

1 Introduction and Overview

The World Bank's 1990 *Annual Report* (World Bank, 1990a, pp. 95–6) includes two pages of text and charts detailing its operational relations with non-governmental organizations (NGOs). The new, high-profile presentation (a format followed in subsequent Annual Reports) highlights a growing number of World Bank-financed projects in which NGOs have a role and reports a 'deepening' of these operational relationships: NGOs are involved more frequently, it is reported, in the design of projects and in programs to 'mitigate the adverse social costs of structural adjustment.' Finally, an expanded policy dialogue with NGOs is reported, 'on important development policy issues of common concern.'

The World Bank has climbed onto the NGO bandwagon in a big way. The Bank's public reports note expanded collaboration with private agencies and grassroots groups in projects, a growing policy dialogue with NGOs, and an important role for NGOs in 'mitigating the adverse costs of structural adjustment' (World Bank 1990a, p. 96).

This study reports on several years of observation of, and participation in, the relationship between the World Bank and NGOs, interpreting them in light of evidence from other cases of policy change at the Bank. Its primary purpose is to understand the World Bank better by:

1. evaluating its claims and performance in relating to NGOs;
2. analyzing its implementation of poverty- and NGO-related policies, through the lens of its organizational dynamics and culture;
3. assessing the potential for more systematic and responsive interaction with NGOs, and for policy change in line with a broadly shared NGO agenda; and
4. assessing the significance of the engagement for the Bank and for NGOs.

In addition, the study reports on the varied postures of NGOs toward the Bank and on the effectiveness of various NGO strategies to date, and suggests guidelines for planning and assessing future interaction.

The issue has important implications for pressing policy issues, and for theoretical debates that underlie them. What are we to make of the World Bank's commitments to refocus on poverty and environmental protection? How do its mandate, organizational form and financial and intellectual resources dispose it to address the changing world of globalized production and capital, weakened national governments and degraded natural resources? Is the policy conditionality associated with structural reform a suitable basis for global development that is economically, environmentally and ethically 'sustainable'? How does NGO engagement with the Bank affect NGOs' role in developing articulate and representative institutions in civil society?

The Bank's record on issues related to NGOs' concerns does not offer much basis for optimism. Rather, it suggests that:

1. Deeply-rooted organizational characteristics reflect the Bank's mandate and the interests of its powerful members and of financial markets.
2. These organizational traits – structural, intellectual, cultural – limit change and promote stability at the Bank. They are key factors to watch for indications of fundamental change.
3. While the Bank's relations with NGOs put pressure on several of these organizational traits – its imperative to 'move money,' its myth of apolitical development, and the insular information system of its organizational culture – there has been little change at these key pressure points.
4. NGO agendas, strategies and impact have been inconsistent and uneven. They have won policy concessions, but often lack the political and institutional clout to secure their implementation. Further progress will require expanded and coordinated efforts.

At the same time, the Bank's engagement with NGOs has broken some new ground for international agencies. The Bank's approach is pragmatic, informal and often *ad hoc*. While its formal governance bodies are less open to NGOs than those of many UN bodies, it is also less caught up in the formalities of NGOs' legal relations to its operations, and has been quite willing to allow experiments and minor innovations to facilitate operational engagement. If the World Bank has been less accessible than the Inter-American or Asian Development Banks to NGOs in those regions, it has none the less not stifled a small but energetic internal effort to encourage greater access.

THE NGO PHENOMENON AT THE WORLD BANK: CLAIMS AND PERCEPTIONS

The World Bank's relationship to NGOs is intrinsically important for project performance and for the impact it can have on the development of national civil societies. The Bank's considerable intellectual and financial influence with borrowing governments means that its approach to NGOs can also shape their evolving views of NGOs in their own societies. The intrinsic importance is heightened by the public relations campaign the Bank has built around it, advertizing the engagement of NGOs in World Bank-financed projects while seeking to minimize the damage from NGO criticism.

Since 1988 a series of Annual Reports, a World Bank-published book (Paul and Israel, 1991), articles in the World Bank/IMF journal *Finance and Development*, and speeches by various Bank executives have all highlighted the Bank's 'NGO work.' This ongoing promotion reached a fever pitch in the materials prepared for the 50th Anniversary of the Bretton Woods agreements. The widely-distributed press packet includes the expected pamphlets ('Making a Difference in People's Lives,' 'What Others Say About Us'), plus an entire 29-page booklet featuring work with NGOs (World Bank, 1994c). From a nearly unmentioned liaison ten years ago, the Bank-NGO connection has grown to take a place on the Bank's official 50-year timeline of its history. The establishment of the Bank-NGO Committee appears there along with McNamara's presidency, the creation of the International Development Association (IDA), the first structural adjustment loan and the creation of the Multilateral Investment Guarantee Agency (MIGA) (*World Bank News* 13, p. 29, 21 July 1994).

The perception that the Bank is deeply engaged with NGOs has also made its way into recent outside commentaries. The 'NGO work' wins positive comments from mass-circulation magazines (*US News and World Report*), global policy journals (*National Journal*), research foundations (the Esquel Group Foundation, 1993, p. 18) and donor governments. A *US News and World Report* article (1989, p. 47) closes a stinging critique of some notorious Bank-financed projects by noting that the Bank 'is moving to address the problems' by 'sharply increasing the involvement of native community groups . . . and farmers' clubs.' And the *National Journal*, widely read among US government policy makers, reported at the end of 1988 that the World Bank had been 'dragged' by NGOs into 'participatory-public-interest politics and may never be the same' (Stokes, 1988, p. 3250).

These and other references, along with World Bank policy statements, give the impression that the Bank, once tied exclusively to governments and official donors, is now opening itself to a systematic and open-ended collaboration with grassroots, national and international non-governmental agencies.

WORLD BANK POLICY AND NGOs

The World Bank and NGOs may be thought of as opposite poles of a continuum of organizations involved in development assistance. Their operations differ in many ways that present formidable challenges to collaboration. Differences in size, access to resources, location, constituencies, charters, and operating styles are seen by some as obstacles, by others as the complementary strengths that argue for cooperation. Some at the Bank, and a few NGOs, have tried to collaborate operationally in the face of these differences, with varied results. The record of such collaborations is now extensive enough that some preliminary conclusions can be drawn about its nature and significance. Chapter 4 of this study reviews the record.

But I have not focused primarily on these obstacles to or arguments for cooperation. Beyond the logistical and managerial difficulties lies a more fundamental question: Are NGOs becoming tools of a development paradigm most do not support? Or can NGOs shift the World Bank's practice and performance in the areas of environmental impact, popular participation and structural adjustment? What aspects of NGO strategy and NGO and government policy are the most important in achieving such changes in policy and performance?

This study's findings are not optimistic: political-economic commitments and interests and deep-seated organizational characteristics affect the World Bank's capacity to cooperate systematically and responsively with NGOs, notwithstanding the intentions of individuals. NGOs' tendencies to process-oriented programming, emphasis on participation, and partisanship in support of poor people – the very virtues that are said to argue for cooperation – contradict the interests and organizational characteristics of the Bank so directly that systematic, collaborative relations are extremely difficult. Policymakers, NGOs and supportive World Bank staff need to understand the potential and limitations clearly, or they will find themselves engaged in a process that undercuts the potential significance of NGOs without fundamentally altering the Bank's impact.

The World Bank's record of collaboration with NGOs is best interpreted in the context of the broader policy and direction of the Bank itself. The 1980s was a period of expanded activity for the Bank, as it initiated policy-based, non-project lending. Attaching policy conditions to loans opened a larger role for the Bank in managing and shaping countries' participation in the global economy.

NGOs, on the other hand, are associated with a constellation of issues that, with the exception of the environment, had a lower profile at the Bank in the 1980s: poverty alleviation, popular participation, small-farmer agriculture, environmentally sustainable development. Issues related to poverty alleviation and income distribution were given much less frequent mention by the World Bank than they received under the presidency of Robert McNamara (1968–81). Their return to a higher profile in Bank publications was signalled by the 1990 *World Development Report* (WDR), focused, as was the 1980 WDR, on poverty.

The World Bank's environmental policies and the environmental impact of some Bank-financed projects were sharply criticized by international environmental NGOs in the 1980s. Its response to this environmental criticism and its engagement with NGOs have led some to hope for a 'greening' of the World Bank (Holden, 1987). A new emphasis on the environment, human resources and poverty in former President Barber Conable's public addresses and the 1990 WDR reinforced this hope, as did President Lewis Preston's re-emphasis of poverty alleviation as 'the overarching goal' of all lending. But the Bank remains the leading proponent of orthodox, export-oriented adjustment and debt-management policies; its internal review of lending performance shows a strong tendency to retreat to financial appraisal as the central indicator of programmatic 'success;' and many critics and NGOs are skeptical of its commitment to the 'softer' environmental and social issues.

One measure of the World Bank's orientation will be how it handles the dialogue and collaboration with NGOs. How open and responsive the Bank is in its relationship with NGOs and what organizational and policy changes it makes in response to its dialogue with them are indicators of its willingness and ability to listen and respond to new constituencies and interests.

CONTRASTING VISIONS OF 'DEVELOPMENT'

The dialogue and working relations between the Bank and NGOs are the setting for an important debate over the shape and direction of 'development.' The contrasting visions of development are manifest in their styles of operation. The World Bank raises capital from member governments and major financial markets. Its projects and loans are planned, negotiated, supervised and evaluated by Washington-based staff together with national governments and consultants. The key criteria by which success is measured are production and productivity gains and financial returns on the investment. In the course of lending to support projects and policies in a country, Bank staff are likely to develop working relationships with high- and mid-level government officials in the relevant ministries. Through macro-economic policy conditionality it has gained influence and direct financial leverage over major national economic policies.

NGOs – or a widely held image of NGOs – challenge this model by example. NGOs that are organized 'above' the local, grassroots level generally collect funds from non-government constituencies and often from government aid programs, and they are said to operate effectively because of the small scale of the development initiatives they support. Staff often work out of a regional city or a town or village, and plan projects in the field in consultation with local leaders and groups. The NGO's evaluation of a program is more likely than the World Bank's to depend in part on assessment by intended beneficiaries and on direct indicators of people's welfare. NGO staff are likely to develop working relationships with leaders of cooperatives, farmers' and women's associations, religious and civic groups.

The 'NGO model' (generalizing and idealizing) differs from that of the World Bank by being partisan, process-oriented, and participatory. NGOs' partisan character derives from overtly taking the side of poor people and communities. 'Process-oriented' refers to a willingness to have project activities evolve in response to changing conditions or perceptions of local people. And many NGOs are 'participatory' in that they take active participation by local communities to be a virtue in itself, as well as a means to successful project implementation.

The two styles do represent, in part, two approaches with distinct 'comparative advantages' in supporting economic change. But they suggest a more important distinction as well. The World Bank's operations suggest that 'development' is fundamentally about amassing capital through investment, borrowing and savings, creating the right incentives, adopting the right policies, introducing the right technologies and building the right institutions and infrastructure, where 'right' is defined by agreement between the national government and World Bank experts. The image of NGO operations outlined here suggests that 'development' is fundamentally about people's articulation of needs, priorities and wishes, and about organizing and marshalling resources to facilitate their fulfillment.

The World Bank's version of 'development' is the domain of governments; it follows from plans, and benefits the population at large, although groups may be 'targeted.' NGOs' 'development' emerges, in some measure at least, from a process of discussion and planning by the people affected by the project. Projects are often specifically planned to respond to the needs of poor groups in an area, whose interests may be in conflict with those of others.

The World Bank, chartered and owned by its member governments, has historically had rather little contact with NGOs. The vast differences in scale and in the resources they offer to support programs and projects sometimes leads to the assumption of a disjuncture between the 'kinds' of development they promote. The World Bank mobilizes resources and expertise for national-level economic programs, while NGOs organize local self-help efforts, meet acute emergency needs, and are sometimes a proving ground for innovative approaches that may be adapted and expanded by governments and international agencies.

But some NGOs insist that this is a false dichotomy. Large-scale investments and programs, they argue, can and should take advantage of the same sources of local and community organization and energy as do smaller programs, and should be subject to mechanisms of popular control and accountability. The wide variety of non-state and non-corporate social groupings referred to as NGOs are proposed as the vehicle for connecting the planning and implementation of World Bank investments with the dynamics of popular participation.

This proposal implicitly offers accountability via various organs of civil society (NGOs) to affected populations as an addition to the World Bank's formal accountability to governments. It has implications for the role of NGOs in the politics of economic and social change in the poor countries, and implies that the institutions of a kind of global civil society have some standing in shaping World Bank policy. And, if its implications for accountability were fully accepted, it would challenge the foundations of the World Bank's operations.

OVERVIEW

Development economist Hans Singer (1989) poses two questions about World Bank policy toward NGOs in his review of the Bank's 1987

Annual Report. What is the nature and intensity of the reported cooperation with NGOs in Bank-financed projects? And is the World Bank establishing an internal capacity for 'genuine two-way collaboration'? These two questions remain central seven years later, and form the kernel of this inquiry.

Chapters 2 and 3, devoted to the World Bank and to NGOs, respectively, set the stage by outlining the key issues facing the Bank and NGOs, and reviewing the history of the dialogue between them. Chapter 4 begins the review of World Bank-NGO experience by examining 304 projects reported to have involved NGOs. The project review focuses on three sets of questions:

1. How are NGOs involved? At what stage, with how much input?
2. What kinds of NGOs are involved? Are local, national or international groups most frequently involved? Professional 'development NGOs' or interest-based associations? Are different sorts of NGOs equally likely to be influential in shaping World Bank projects?
3. How have these patterns changed over time, especially since 1988, which the Bank calls a turning point in its interaction with NGOs?

NGO implementation of a component of a government- and World Bank-planned scheme is the dominant mode of project collaboration. In most projects reported to involve an NGO, the NGO is an implementing agent mobilizing people to carry out pre-designed changes.

While implementation is the dominant NGO role, there is good reason to focus on the minority (one quarter) of World Bank-NGO projects in which NGO roles have gone beyond implementation. In these cases – involving NGO participation in project design, direct funding of NGO activities, or significant conflict with project authorities – the potential and limitations for collaboration can be seen most clearly.

Such 'major' roles have occurred most often when grassroots, national and international NGOs are all involved. The quality of NGO involvement has varied by region: Africa dominates the roster of projects numerically, but major NGO roles have been relatively rare in Africa. Reported gains in NGO involvement in project design in the late 1980s and early 1990s appear to rest largely on zealous reporting and generous standards for what constitutes 'design,' and on increased NGO involvement in social service programs to cushion the effects of structural adjustment.

The remaining chapters present evidence from documents, interviews, more detailed reviews of some projects, and from NGOs, to assess the potential and the limitations of an institutionalized 'genuine two-way collaboration.' Each chapter focuses on a contradiction inherent in the Bank's efforts and claims.

Chapter 5 argues that the imperatives of organizational survival and of lending large amounts of capital quickly limit the World Bank's capacity for concerted collaboration with NGOs. This 'disbursement imperative' dominates policy at the organizational level and pervades individual incentive and motivation. It is driven by external political pressures to manage Third World debt and promote global integration, and although Bank management has become sensitive to the problem, it remains enshrined in an organizational structure that promotes the kind of planning and disbursement required for capital-driven, growth-oriented lending. These structures and procedures are ill-suited to collaboration with NGOs. Indeed, the Bank tends to protect its standard operating procedures against the kind of uncertainty and spontaneity that NGOs promote.

'Sovereignty' and 'development' are introduced in Chapter 6 as two 'myths' that underpin and justify the World Bank's operations. These myths not only define the World Bank's mission and establish formal ground rules for its relations with borrowing countries, they also shape thinking about development in many circles. Both myths rest on the notion that the Bank and its work are apolitical, an image it carefully maintains. Paradoxically, the myths enable the Bank to exert influence over highly political issues through methods including aid coordination, policy-based lending, and training. Their influence is observed in the self-evaluation and perpetuation of structural adjustment programs and lending, and in the limits placed on NGO roles.

The World Bank's organizational culture (Chapter 7) is hierarchical and assigns great value to specialization, technical expertise and control of Bank-supported operations. This culture, I argue, is incompatible with the participatory, flexible operation that many NGOs require. As with any organizational culture, it systematically selects and processes information to maintain a consistent view of the world and of its role in that world. This 'information bias' is examined in the processing of information from 'rural development' lending in the 1970s, in the genesis and internal evaluation of structural adjustment policies, in policy dialogues with NGOs in the 1980s, and in the financing of energy and major dam projects in India, including the controversial Sardar Sarovar project. Selectivity in handling information lends stability to the World Bank's view of the world and, together with other features, limits its ability to learn as an organization.

The concluding chapter reviews the findings and outlines policy issues and recommendations for NGOs; touches on implications for more general debates about democratization, multilateralism, and possible directions of the economic 'world order;' and raises questions for further monitoring and study.

STUDYING THE WORLD BANK: ORGANIZATIONAL THEORY AND METHODOLOGY

The three organizational contradictions that shape the Bank's relations with NGOs are examined through interviews of World Bank staff, readings of internal and public documents, review of selected experiences of project collaboration, and analysis of the course of other policy changes at the Bank in recent years.

Combining sociological theories of complex organizations and political economy offers a valuable perspective, different from that of either approach taken alone. The political economy perspective has stressed the interests to which the Bank responds (industrialized country governments, foreign and local capital) in promoting national development strategies that open economies to international investment on virtually any terms.

When organizational considerations – structural, procedural, ideological and professional dynamics – are systematically added to the analysis, a fuller picture emerges of the factors that drive policy and practice in the Bank, and that reinforce and constrain its influence. Five principles from organizational theories are the basis for understanding how these factors shape relations with NGOs and performance on related issues:

1. *The World Bank is an entity with imperatives, priorities, and strategies of its own, not merely a creation and servant of states and financial institutions.* Like other organizations, it protects its standard operations – the essential processes for production – from sources of uncertainty in its working environment.
2. *The World Bank conforms to and shapes social myths that establish expectations and standards for evaluating its work.* In any field of work, and especially fields where standards of 'success' are not widely agreed, organizations strive to conform to and shape the expectations that add up to a standard for evaluation. The myths, important sources of stability for the organization, are usually carefully upheld and protected.

3. *Organizational cultures systematically select and screen the information to be considered in organizational decision making.* The World Bank's highly hierarchical culture fosters organizational stability but inhibits organizational learning by defining the kinds of information that are considered relevant for decision making, and filtering data to match these standards.
4. *Organizational learning, which entails consideration of basic premises in light of new experience, is almost impossible in such a culture.*
5. *These organizational features are not bureaucratic foibles or maladaptive managerial strategies. They interact with, reinforce and institutionalize the interests, pressures and influences that shape World Bank policy and priorities.*[1]

This perspective guides the strategy and methodology of the study. The structural, ideological and social-psychological variables suggest both points of resistance to policy change, and indicators to distinguish important changes from cosmetic reforms. The choice to rely on such indicators, rather than primarily on official statements, budgetary trends, or the views of organizational leaders, calls for a methodology focused on the standard operations used in planning, policy-making and lending, on beliefs and assumptions that underpin these standard operations, and on the management of information and learning.

The study focuses on a minority of projects and staff that are in the forefront of interaction with NGOs. It is fairly easy to show that significant NGO involvement in Bank-financed projects is the exception, and that many staff are uninterested in NGOs. What is more revealing is what can be learned from activities with the most substantial NGO involvement: participation in design, receipt of funds from a World Bank-financed fund, NGO-Bank conflict over the course of a project, or broader policy dialogue. By examining Bank staff's most advanced efforts, I identify the extent of the collaboration to date and the factors that limit it now and in the future.

To avoid the excessively narrow focus that strategy might promote, I have also paid attention to a range of issues closely associated with NGOs but not strictly tied to the World Bank's interaction with them. The 'NGO issue' in the Bank is part of a complex of issues including poverty reduction, gender equity, popular participation in projects, aboriginal peoples' rights and the protection and management of the environment. Each of these has ties to the Bank-NGO interaction, but has broader significance for the Bank and its borrowers as well. Evidence from discussions of participation, environmental policy and anti-poverty lending illustrate the tendencies and characteristics of the Bank that affect its relations with NGOs.

Research conducted at the World Bank during 1989 and 1990 was carried out with the understanding that documents and interviews would not be cited in a way that would compromise relations with a member government, or reflect personally on any staff member. Under this agreement no limitations were placed on my interviews. To ensure the anonymity of some staff interviewed who asked not to be quoted by name, all staff interviews are cited by their department or regional position. I have participated extensively in subsequent discussions with Bank officials, as an NGO representative. Statements made in these meetings, for which there is a public record, are attributed by name. A list of interviews is included in Appendix 1, and further details on the study's methodology are outlined in Appendix 2.

2 The World Bank Takes Center Stage

The debt crisis and the World Bank's entry into policy-based structural adjustment lending boosted its global profile and influence in the 1980s, and the collapse of the Soviet bloc and new membership of more than a dozen governments in 1991 and 1992 made the Bank a truly global financial institution. At the same time, an array of issues and pressures for change are creating apparent opportunities for NGO influence at the World Bank. Dissatisfaction with government implementation of donor-funded projects, commitment to structural adjustment and to minimizing the reforms' social and political costs, pressure from environmental advocates, desire for greater cost recovery in irrigation and social service programs, pressure on human rights issues – all these create an environment in which NGOs are an increasingly relevant actor for the Bank.

This chapter discusses some of these issues and trends. The perspective developed here – of an institution closely tied to industrial country and major bank economic interests, committed to global integration and bound to a economic adjustment strategy that has become indefensible in the low-income countries – will be the foundation for an organizational analysis in later chapters.

THE WORLD BANK: STRUCTURE, FINANCE AND OPERATIONS

Created in 1945 by the Bretton Woods Agreements, the World Bank is owned by its 178 member governments. The International Bank for Reconstruction and Development (IBRD) makes loans at commercial rates, with 5 or 10 year grace periods on repayment of principal, to finance projects and programs of member governments. The International Development Association (IDA), established in 1959, lends with only a 0.75 per cent service charge to governments of some 70 countries with per capita income less than $765. The IBRD and IDA share a common staff, and IDA credits and IBRD loans are here referred to collectively as loans, unless otherwise specified.

13

Table 2.1 Top Five Voting Powers, IBRD, 1947, 1971 and 1993

1947	%	*1971*	%	*1993*	%
US	35.07	US	23.82	US	17.18
UK	14.52	UK	9.81	Japan	6.64
China	6.85	West Germany	5.19	Germany	5.13
France	6.03	France	4.02	UK	4.92
India	4.66	Japan	3.92	France	4.92

Sources: (1947, 1971) Mason and Asher 1973, pp. 800–2.
(1993) World Bank, *Annual Report* 1993, pp. 199–202.

A third member of the World Bank Group, the International Finance Corporation (IFC), was established in 1956 to finance and insure corporate investment in poor countries. In 1988 a Multilateral Investment Guarantee Agency (MIGA) was created to promote foreign investment in poor countries by 'mitigating non-commercial risk' to investors through insurance and policy dialogue with member governments (World Bank, *Annual Report*, 1989, p. 3).

IBRD and IDA are governed by a shared Board of Governors and Board of Executive Directors. Governors, one per member country, meet annually to handle certain aspects of World Bank governance, but oversight of day-to-day operations is delegated to the Executive Directors (EDs). Member countries are assigned voting power in the governing bodies proportional to their payments (capital subscriptions) under a formula that slightly over-represents small subscribers. The United States is the largest voting power, although US dominance has diminished since the original capital subscriptions in 1947, as Table 2.1 shows.

The concentration of voting power has fallen somewhat: the top five members held more than two-thirds of all votes in 1947, fewer than 40 per cent in 1992. Each of the five largest subscribers is represented by an ED; others are represented in groups (e.g. the Scandinavian countries have a single ED). (For more detail on formal governance, see Osieke (1984), Lister (1984), and Gerster (1993)).

IBRD lending is financed primarily through sale of bonds on international financial markets. Member governments' financial support to the IBRD is primarily in callable capital, backing for IBRD loans, available but not appropriated. Ten per cent of government subscriptions to the IBRD are actually paid up.

In 1993 the IBRD borrowed $12.67 billion on international markets (*Annual Report*, 1993, p. 69), and had a net income of $1.13 billion. IBRD profits are divided among the IDA, the Consultative Group on International Agricultural Research (CGIAR) institutions, and reinvestment. The IDA is financed in part by IBRD profits, but some 90 per cent of IDA capital is provided in triennial replenishments by its member governments.

Lending for Global Integration

In fiscal year 1993 loans totalled $23.7 billion: $16.9 billion in IBRD loans, and $6.7 billion in IDA credits (*Annual Report.* 1993, p. 11). Cumulative lending since 1948 (IBRD) and 1961 (IDA) amounts to $312.9 billion, of which concessional IDA lending makes up $77.8 billion (World Bank, *Annual Report*, 1993, pp. 168–9).

Loans are either to governments or guaranteed by governments, and lending has been dominated by a relatively small group of major borrowers. After early reconstruction loans to Europe and Japan, lending shifted almost exclusively to Third World countries. The concentration of lending among its top 20 borrowers increased from 66.5 per cent to 76.5 per cent between 1971 and 1993 (Mason and Asher, 1973, pp. 830–1; World Bank *Annual Report*, 1993, pp. 166–7). The sectoral makeup of loans has also changed over the years, as Table 2.2 shows.

Regardless of sectoral emphases, the World Bank has pursued the integrative role in the world economy that its Articles of Agreement prescribe. Promoting foreign capital investment in member countries is emphasized in three of the IBRD's five statements of purpose (Article I, p. 1), and has remained central through its 45 years. The annual *World Development Report* (WDR), for example, highlights the importance of integration into the world economy every year, from the 1980 WDR on basic needs and poverty, to the 1987 Report, perhaps the World Bank's strongest manifesto on economic integration and adjustment (World Bank, WDR 1980, chs 2 and 3; World Bank, WDR, 1987, ch. 5). The integration of borrowing members' economies into global markets is reinforced and assisted by the IFC, which finances corporate investment and provides advisory, risk management, and technical assistance services to international investors and to its member governments.

In agriculture, the world food crisis of 1972–74 stimulated a surge of investment by the World Bank in rural infrastructure, credit, livestock production and research and extension on high-yielding seed

Table 2.2   World Bank Lending by Sector, 1961–65, 1975–79, and 1989–93
(amounts in millions of US dollars)

Sector	1961–65 amount	%	1975–79 amount	%	1989–93 amount	%
Agriculture	466.6	9.0	12 542	29.6	10 014	15.8
Education	65.9	1.3	1 835	4.3	8 592	7.6
Energy/Power	1 622.6	31.5	5 986	14.1	21 489	18.9
Industry	566.7	10.9	7 589	17.9	6 610	5.8
Non-Project	219.7	4.3	1 963	4.6	15 340	13.4
Pop., Health, Nut.*	0	0	302	0.7	5 824	5.2
Technical Asstc.	0	0	120	0.3	1 266	1.1
Tourism	0	0	371	0.9	0	0
Transp/Comm.[†]	2115.6	41.1	8 155	19.2	13 183	11.6
Urban	n.a.	n.a.	1 123	2.7	6 800.8	5.9
Water/Sewerage	93.4	1.8	2 349	5.5	5 013.7	4.4
Dev. Fin. Corps.¯	n.a.		n.a.		7 637.3	6.8
Pub. Sect. Mgmt.[§]	n.a.		n.a.		2 877.6	2.5
Sm-Scale Ents.[¶]	n.a.		n.a.		1 103.5	1.0
Total	5 150.5	99.9	42 435	99.8	105 750	100.0

* Population, Health and Nutrition
[†] Transportation and Communication
¯ Development Finance Corporations
[§] Public Sector Management
[¶] Small Scale Enterprises

Percentages do not total 100 due to rounding

Sources: 1961–65: Mason and Asher, 1973, pp. 833–43.
1975–79: Sanford, 1980.
1989–93: *Annual Report*, 1993 pp. 106, 114, 120, 126, 134, 140, 165.

varieties and farming input packages. James Cypher credits the Bank with leading 'the latest phase of capitalist expansion, in which the resource-rich Third World is fully incorporated into the capitalist world economy' (Cypher, 1989a).

The emphasis on economic integration through investment and trade extends to local and national economies as well. World Bank staffer Robert Ayres (1983) describes rural anti-poverty lending as based on the premise that participation in national markets is the road to prosperity for poor farmers. Whether this integrative role is progressive or exploitative is a central issue in the literature on the Bank.

Coordinating the Aid Regime

The World Bank's financial role is supported by leadership in publishing, training and an expanding coordinating role among donors that has led Bonné (1989) and Gibbon (1992) to describe a new 'aid regime.' Its research, economic forecasting and modeling work is disseminated widely through the *World Debt Tables, The World Bank Economic Review* and *The World Bank Research Observer*, the journal *Finance and Development*, and series of Staff Working Papers and other informal papers. Staff economists develop and publish models and projections of international markets, prospects for growth and other indicators, projections that are often a basis for planning by national policy makers (Cole, 1987).

Training through the Economic Development Institute (EDI) also promotes the Bank's perspective on development. Between 1985 and 1989 the EDI averaged 167 training 'activities' per year for middle- and senior-level policy makers from borrowing countries (De Lusignan, 1986, p. 31). In 1993 a total of 152 were held, continuing the EDI 'strategic objective' of mobilizing 'knowledge and experience accumulated in the World Bank' to improve member governments' 'development decisionmaking' (*Annual Report*, 1993, p. 87). EDI's director observes that a newly trained team from a government ministry can be '. . . a dynamic cadre capable of reinforcing each other in the application – and further propagation – of their new skills' (De Lusignan, 1986, p. 29).

The Bank also convenes and chairs coordinating meetings of donors on specific countries and regions (17 in fiscal 1993) (*Annual Report*, 1993, p. 20). It also promotes coordination with commercial banks and international and bilateral donor agencies by co-financing projects. In fiscal 1993 more than half (118) of new World Bank-financed projects involved co-financing, the Bank providing $11.1 billion of their $35.5 billion total value (*Annual Report*, 1993, p. 71).

The World Bank's 6800 professional staff have undergone several reorganizations since the mid-1980s, including a major shake-up in 1987. Most recently, President Lewis Preston located three influential Managing Directors in the Executive Office. Under the Executive Office, the bulk of Bank staff are organized under sixteen vice presidencies. Six of these have responsibility for regional lending and policy, three for Bank finance and accounting functions, three deal with cross-cutting policy areas, and four others are responsible for economic policy direction, co-financing, personnel and evaluation.

The regional units (formerly grouped in an Operations complex), along with the Vice President for Development Economics and the three new Vice Presidencies for Human Resources Development, Private Sector Development and Environmentally Sustainable Development, have the greatest role in formulating lending policy and in identifying, designing and implementing projects. The centralization of staff has been a constant through the Bank's reorganizations: more than 95 per cent of professional staff work in the Washington, DC headquarters.

POVERTY, ADJUSTMENT AND POLITICS

A plethora of articles, pamphlets and books by NGO activists have attacked the World Bank over the last decade on topics ranging from environmental impact, forced resettlement to public information policy, structural adjustment and debt management (among many others, see Abugre, 1992; Bello, Kinley and Elinson, 1982; Clark, 1990; NGO Working Group on the World Bank, 1989; Woodward, 1992; Rau, 1991; Rich, 1990; Bello, 1992; Rich, 1994; George and Sabelli, 1994; Danaher, ed., 1994).

As this storm of criticism suggests, the World Bank is at the center of several pivotal issues for NGOs. Among them are income distribution, structural adjustment and debt management, issues where the Bank's role has been largely inegalitarian, defined by its own organizational interests and closely identified with the interests of the major industrial countries and banks.

The Ebb and Flow of 'Poverty Lending'

The World Bank's official position on the relationship between growth and poverty reduction, and on the appropriate strategies for pursuing both, has varied considerably since the beginning of the McNamara presidency. Comments such as those of a past External Relations Vice President ('. . . there isn't a project that doesn't help the poor [in poor West African countries]. Are these people rich?') (in Ayres, 1983) are the exception to a pattern of carefully phrased statements that aim to balance and render compatible the needs for economic growth and attention to the particular needs of the poor.

The McNamara presidency (1969–82) placed strong rhetorical emphasis on poverty alleviation, stressing the 'large areas of complementarity between the two objectives of growth and poverty alleviation' (World Bank, 1982, p. 2). The 1982 task force on poverty summarized the Bank's approach: 'A balanced strategy of growth combined with poverty alleviation provides the best general framework for development in the 1980s. . . . This policy . . . conforms to the stated priorities of many lenders, of most borrowers, and of the United Nations system' (World Bank, 1982, p. 22). The 'balanced strategy' is rearticulated in the 1990 WDR, after a decade of relative quiet on poverty issues. The WDR (1990, p. 56) advocates 'the adoption of appropriate economy-wide and sectoral policies and of measures to help the poor grasp new income-earning opportunities.'

In agriculture, for example, the WDR (1990, p. 59) argues that better infrastructure 'can lead to increased productivity, technical change, and strengthened market linkages.' New higher yielding varieties of food crops benefit landowners the most in absolute terms, but 'income gains from infrastructure can be widely dispersed.' Studies of rural Bangladesh are cited to show that all households, 'including the poor and landless,' enjoyed some income gains from infrastructure investments. The evidence cited focuses exclusively on average incomes in a community, and the writers seem satisfied with any income gain for those in lower deciles, regardless of the change in their relative status and ability to command food and other commodities in the market, or of gains and losses within households.

For Ayres (1983, p. 106), the 1970s New Directions campaign in the Bank succeeded in isolating the greater part of its lending program from the poverty debate. The split allows the Bank to measure its commitment and performance in poverty reduction by the amount of its targeted 'poverty lending.' Such 'poverty lending' has been modest: the 184 rural development projects funded in the 1970s cost roughly as much as the Bank's investment in one Brazilian steel mill ($2.1 billion) during the period (Ayres, p. 106).

The comparison puts the poverty-lending campaign in context, but it also illustrates the prevalent acceptance of the Bank's historic segmentation of 'kinds' of development and of development lending. The steel mill's relation to poverty is not carefully probed, and such industrial and infrastructure lending has a kind of happy, unproblematic relation to anti-poverty lending. The alternative – analyzing the new steel mill's impact on the poor and the measures needed (labor rights, environmental protection, destination of profits, etc.) for a positive benefit to the poor – is avoided by the segmentation that the World Bank offers and Ayres (and others) accept.

The World Bank now distinguishes a 'core poverty program' of agricultural and social sector lending that aims specifically to benefit the poor. Even loans that are not part of the core poverty program, however, are beneficial to the poor (World Bank, *Annual Report*, 1990, p. 57). For fiscal years 1990 and 1991 combined, the Bank lent $3.8 billion for 'operations whose primary objective is to reduce poverty.' These 44 loans made up 15 per cent of total lending. In fiscal 1992 the figure remained at 14 per cent (World Bank, 'Implementing the World Bank's Strategy to Reduce Poverty,' 1993), rising to 21 per cent in 1993 (World Bank, 1994d).

Much of the discussion of the World Bank's role in poverty alleviation accepts statements of policy at face value, as indicative of priorities and commitments shared bank-wide. But John Clark, then at Oxfam-UK (1988) suggests that the Bank's publications on poverty be read in context. In reviewing policy papers from the late 1980s, he asks which is the 'real World Bank': the few specialists who produce insightful analyses of poverty, gender and other issues for a small audience, or the apparent majority of the institution whose programming seemingly continues to be based strictly on orthodox economic theories of growth, adjustment and fiscal discipline.

Managing Debt and Adjustment: The Bank Takes Center Stage

At the Bank's 1979 annual meetings McNamara announced a new kind of lending for 'structural adjustment.' Adjustment loans are offered in exchange for commitments to change certain macro-economic policies (Structural Adjustment, SAL) or policy at the sectoral level (Sectoral Adjustment, SECAL), rather than to finance specific development projects. Between 1979 and 1991, 258 adjustment loans were made to 75 countries, totaling $41.5 billion. Adjustment lending made up 16 per cent of commitments in FY 1993, down from the 25 per cent mark in 1991. The percentage has been consistently higher for lending to middle-income highly indebted countries of Latin America and the Caribbean (39 per cent of lending) and to low-income Sub-Saharan Africa (45 per cent of lending) (Country Economics Department, 1988, p. 10).

The World Bank sees institutional and policy changes that remove non-market restraints from economies as the essential complement to external funding for adjustment to economic crisis. Improving policies means removing 'sources of inefficiency' in public spending and employment, agricultural policy, the state role in markets, fiscal and monetary policy including currency valuation, and tariff reductions and export promotion (Country Economics Department, 1988, p. 12; Nicholas, 1988, p. xi).

Adjustment lending allowed the Bank to pursue two objectives at once: lend to cover debt servicing costs, and remove policies that obstructed progress toward its vision of growth through integration with the global economy. Non-project lending was superior to projects for these purposes, in that it allows loans to match the broad nature of the economic issues, facilitates cutting back on new projects and new government spending, and allows quick disbursement (Nicholas, 1988, p. 12). The loans are to help in designing national adjustment programs, underwrite some of the changes required, and encourage further lending from donors and commercial banks.

The World Bank's entry into policy-based lending raised its profile and stimulated debate about its role in the world economy. Much of the debate involving NGOs has addressed the 'social dimensions' of adjustment, but some NGO participants are increasingly aware that broader economic issues need to be addressed, in order to prevent the debate from focusing solely on social sector spending and compensatory safety net programs. In addition to poverty and income distribution issues, adjustment lending has largely failed by its own macro-economic standards in the low-income countries; it has failed to elicit the anticipated flow of external and domestic investment; it directs countries into already over-supplied 'niches' in the global economy; it takes decisions about basic development strategies largely out of the hands of affected citizens; and it lacks a fair and coherent policy toward debt burdens and imbalances in the global economy.

The following sections summarize some major lines of criticism, and trace the evolving World Bank response.

Poverty and income distribution

The United Nations Children's Fund's (UNICEF) call for 'adjustment with a human face,' (Jolly, 1985; Cornia *et al.*, 1987; UNICEF, 1986) argues that the short-term impact of adjustment on the poor must be addressed for humanitarian reasons. UNICEF's 'human-face' campaign calls for compensatory measures to soften the effects of adjustment on the poor – notably unemployment among fired state and parastatal employees, rising food prices for net consumers among the poor, and reduced social services as government spending is cut. Protection of certain social expenditures, fair-price shops for urban consumers, job-creation schemes and similar measures are advocated as necessary and neglected components of adjustment. The UNICEF concerns have been reiterated recently (*State of the World's Children*, 1989 and 1992; Cornia, van der Hoeven and Mkandawire (eds), 1992).

The 'human face' campaign began a remarkably unsuccessful decade-long campaign to challenge the legitimacy of the Bank's adjustment program. NGOs, UN agencies and scholars documented and decried the aggravation of poverty by adjustment programs in Latin America, Africa and parts of Asia. Studies in Nigeria (Bangura, 1987), Ivory Coast (Bassett, 1988), Senegal and Ghana (Hodges, 1988), Ghana (Hagan, 1992), The Philippines (Cruz and Repetto, 1992), Jamaica, Pakistan, Ghana and Côte d'Ivoire (Mayatech Corporation, 1991); Mexico (Heredia and Purcell, 1994) have also documented adverse effects on nutrition, infant mortality, employment and health indicators.

The Bank's response to the human-face critique

The Bank has sometimes downplayed the effects on the poor, or argued for their necessity, while selectively adopting the social safety net measures proposed by UNICEF. The most consistent theme in Bank-published papers on the social effects of adjustment is that regardless of the transitional costs, adjustment is a prerequisite to alleviating poverty (Development Committee, 1987, p. 6; Development Committee, 1990, p. 31). Consistent with its position on project lending, the Bank argues that the two objectives are compatible, but that growth, which is expected to follow adjustment, is the fundamental element.

The World Bank advances a variety of other arguments in defense of adjustment programs' impact on the poor. One theme is essentially counterfactual: models and projections are introduced to show that the poor would have suffered as much or more in the absence of adjustment, because of deteriorating economic conditions under pre-reform economic policies. (See, for example, Glewwe (1988) on Peru; *Protecting the Poor during Periods of Adjustment* (Development Committee, 1987; Country Economics Department, 1992, in general.)

An important variant on this counterfactual argument appears in the Bank's ten-year assessment of adjustment lending (Country Economics Department, 1988). The impact of global recession and national economic difficulties is hard to distinguish from the impact of adjustment measures implemented to facilitate recovery. In the absence of conceptual and empirical tools to separate the effects of the two, social dislocations are often blamed on adjustment (p. 30; also Development Committee, 1987, pp. 4–8).

Despite this caveat, World Bank publications accept that adjustment policies have harmed the poor in many situations. This is said to have surprised many staff, who expected adjustment to restore growth and benefit the poor quickly (Nicholas, 1988, p. 36; Zuckerman, 1989, p. 2; Country Economics Department, 1988, p. 10). Early adjustment lending 'focused almost exclusively' on efforts to increase the efficiency of resource allocations, assuming that the poor would quickly benefit from such measures. The World Bank's Elaine Zuckerman (1989, p. 2) says that neglect of social considerations continued 'until recently.' (The Bank's treatment of the differential impact of adjustment on women is discussed in Chapter 7).

In the wake of UNICEF's 'human face' campaign, the World Bank-IMF Development Committee endorsed the analysis of Protecting the Poor as Bank policy in 1987. This document argues that effects on the poor can be softened by three kinds of measures. First, proper design and implementation, including early and orderly adjustment, staged reforms, and generous external finance can reduce social costs. The difficulty of obtaining finance in the face of its declining availability to most countries is noted but not addressed.

Second, government social services can be redirected and refocused more directly on the poor. New fee schedules for social services, for example, allow reduced social services to be focused on the poor, re-covering costs by collecting fees from those better able to pay (Nicholas, 1988, p. 37). Whatever the merits of the emphasis on cost-recovery measures in social services, it is, as Singer (1989) notes, hardly a rallying cry in a campaign to address the needs of the poor.

Third, compensatory services may be provided directly to the poor. The Bank argues that targeted public works employment, local fair-price food shops, and other measures by governments, donor agencies and NGOs have shown in countries such as Chile and Costa Rica that adjustment need not devastate the poor (Zuckerman, 1989; Nicholas, 1988).

Finally, in some quarters there is discussion of the need and opportunity to design adjustment measures that not only protect the poor, but work to increase their access to productive assets. This use of policy conditionality, unfortunately, has never been substantially implemented. The reporting on poverty-related adjustment conditionality in the Bank's annual reports on poverty alleviation reveals how limited the employment of such conditionality has been.

The Bank's 1993 Report on implementing anti-poverty strategies notes that 18 of 32 adjustment loans made in 1992 'contained an explicit poverty focus' (p. 19). The 1994 update notes that the proportion for

1993 was down to six of 17 (World Bank, 1994d, p. 8). But in most cases the 'poverty focus' was either monitoring the effects of adjustment on the poor, or targeting social service spending or supporting compensatory programs.

The 1993 report cites one example of a condition that shifts productive assets to the poor: the transfer of land rights in Mozambique from state farms to private enterprises and smallholders (p. 20). Other 'poverty-related objectives' in 1992 adjustment loans include changes in Zimbabwe's Labor Act 'to provide employers with authority to retrench workers . . .' (p. 54), and deregulation of the labor market in Côte d'Ivoire, to allow formal sector wages to drop (p. 53). These measures to free labor markets are said to 'remove distortions that especially disadvantage the poor' (p. 21), and they may be a route to eventual job growth in the formal sector. But it is difficult to see such restrictions as disadvantaging primarily the poor; it seems likely that employers were most interested in the reforms. It requires a good deal of confidence in unregulated labor markets – more than the experience with market reforms inspires in Africa – to take these seriously as anti-poverty measures.

Recent reviews of adjustment lending

The 1992 (third) review of adjustment lending is the Bank's most spirited defense. The collective findings of the Bank's research are summarized in a highly positive tone, asserting that consumption increases documented in adjustment countries in the late 1980s 'reduced the incidence of poverty in the intensive adjustment lending countries.' Further, 'the distributional effects of well-designed policies often favor the poor' (Country Economics Department, 1992, pp. 19–20).

But having announced these findings, the 1992 review begins to hedge. 'Many of the poor are vulnerable in the transition, especially where recession and declining labor demand are unavoidable. . . .' The overall positive effects depend on the 'structure of the economy and of poverty.' In Costa Rica, where smallholder agriculture is a major employment of the poor, effects were positive. The improvements indicated by overall consumption increases may not really mean that poverty was diminished, because populations grew. And while 'well-designed' macro and sectoral reforms benefit the poor, 'intergroup shifts that favor the poor are not always consistent with political realities, . . . and a balance often has to be struck to make a program feasible' (Country Economics Department, 1992, pp. 20–1).

The World Bank's slowness in recognizing the human and social costs to adjustment mirrors the slow entry of poverty considerations into project lending some twenty years before. As with project lending, the rising tide of growth was at first said to be sufficient to lift all boats. But as the 1980s wore on, the effects of new economic policies and government funding reductions became increasingly difficult to ignore.

Macro-economic performance in low-income countries

World Bank documents have invoked a variety of external and internal factors, particularly for low-income and Sub-Saharan African countries, to explain the weak growth response to a decade and more of fiscal discipline and economic restructuring.

The ten-year evaluation (Country Economics Department, 1988) concludes that the external economic environment in general 'turned out to be substantially worse than was assumed at the start of the 1980s,' and 'made adjustment slower and more difficult than initially expected' (see also Ribe, Carvalho, Liebenthal, Nicholas and Zuckerman, 1990). The 1992 review shifts attention to internal factors. Adjustment measures in Africa have been 'swimming against the tide' of institutional and infrastructure decline. The particular obstacles to successful adjustment read like a catalogue of the woes of low-income countries: ' . . . a weaker human resource base, inadequate and sometimes declining economic infrastructure, less diversified economic structures, and poorly functioning institutions' (Country Economics Department, 1992, p. 25). Were it not for these weaknesses, the review implies, adjustment could have achieved growth rates comparable to the middle-income countries'.

Self-exoneration by pointing to disappointing developments in the global economy – or internal institutional weakness – is hardly a satisfactory response to the severe and extended social dislocations in most low-income SAL countries. Adjustment programs are negotiated with governments on the basis of results the Bank predicts will flow from the changed policies, results drawn from models that specify or predict performance of the variables the Bank later calls exogenous and unpredictable. Global economic performance is, of course, not under the World Bank's control. But models and projections are the basis for SAL negotiations, so the Bank's package should be considered to include not only the loan and conditions, but also its forecasts of conditions essential to adjustment policies' success.

When the obstacles are internal institutions and resources, as in the 1992 review, the argument is even more curious. How could a reform program that requires certain kinds of markets, infrastructure, information, and skills in the workforce be prescribed so regularly for countries that lack these prerequisites? In Africa, where the experience was again evaluated in a 1993 report, adjustment plans have often been incompletely or even intermittently implemented. This leaves the Bank essentially comparing relatively fully-implemented plans with plans that, for a variety of reasons, are not. The most that can be said is that in the few cases where Bank-style adjustment was relatively fully implemented, it worked somewhat better than in the many cases where it was not. *The Economist*, noting this fact, observes that the Bank's confidence about adjustment in Africa 'veers towards complacency' (5 March 1994, p. 22). A corporation would fire a financial advisor whose services ignored prevailing economic and institutional conditions. But most borrowing governments have no alternative to the Bretton Woods institutions as their financial directors.

Simultaneous adjustment and competition

The broad dissemination of export-oriented adjustment strategies adds a further dimension to the Bank's role, as governments are urged essentially to compete for investment and shares of the global productive process by holding the costs of labor and relevant primary commodities lower than their neighbors.

Economists Robin Broad (1988) and Broad and John Cavanagh (1988) show how the changing structure of international production and the World Bank's role in promoting non-traditional export strategies have limited the options for would-be NICs (newly industrialized countries). During the 1970s, as transnational corporate and banking activity expanded and production of apparel, electronics, and other light manufactures was fragmented and globalized, labor-intensive stages of production began to move from the Asian NICs to a second tier of would-be NICs. The character of investment and the division of labor changed: no longer was substantial capital investment or the growth of a lasting industrial base assured.

Broad and Cavanagh argue that the East Asian NIC strategy is not generalizable, and trace the World Bank's role in shaping and promoting the strategy. At least 16 would-be NICs had been encouraged (by 1988) to adopt non-traditional export policies through SALs and SECALs.

Many within the Bank who promote the strategy know that the NIC 'niche' in the global economy is overcrowded, and promote the strategy with unduly optimistic models and forecasts. In so doing the Bank assumes a pivotal role in reorganizing the international division of labor. Questions about economic projections used to sell the SAL packages to governments reinforce this critique. Economist Sam Cole (1987, p. 369, 383) shows that projections of global growth and investment rates are 'biased high' by several percentage points throughout the 1970s and 1980s. He attributes the systematic bias to a variety of factors: flawed methods and models, a volatile global economy, peer group reinforcement and critique among modelers, and the World Bank's need for optimistic projections to leverage national policy changes. The Bank's ten-year review of adjustment loans acknowledges that 'projections of outcomes during the adjustment phase were optimistic. . . . The persistence of negative external shocks [and] lags in implementation and supply response were underestimated' (Country Economics Department, 1988, p. 53).

Adjustment and debt management. Adjustment loans and the World Bank's role in debt-for-equity swaps and other debt buy-out schemes suggest that the Bank manages a creditors' cartel. Eaton and Gersovitz (1981, pp. 35-6) argue that even as World Bank and IMF lending made up a declining portion of total international capital flows in the 1970s, the agencies' importance in international finance grew with their debt management role. They gather and disseminate information for lenders, organize to penalize defaulters, exert political influence in some borrower countries, and protect private loans through austerity and adjustment regimes.

Two contrasting interpretations of the World Bank's debt management role are possible. In Robert Pastor's (1989) view, the Bank (but primarily the IMF) stabilizes and maintains the economic order by restraining creditors from acting alone against debtors. If creditors acted independently to maximize individual utility, the crisis created would shake the international economy. The Bank and IMF facilitate collective action that sustains the status quo. Former World Bank economist Art Van de Laar (1980) sees the Bank as managing the debtor countries' strategies. He argues that for most debtors the strongest strategy would be to negotiate deals individually with creditor institutions and countries. By persuading debtors to negotiate with a central authority rather than employing their strongest strategy, the Bank acts in creditors' favor. Adjustment loans establish and maintain an element of self-enforcement for debt repayment by conditioning further loans or tranches on continued debt servicing. The arrangement serves the Bank's interests nicely, as it maintains its status as a privileged creditor, assured of continuing service payments by all but those few countries who drop of the international finance system altogether.

Whether by influencing creditors' or debtors' strategies, or both, the debt management approach the Bank and IMF have guided has maintained a strong and relatively stable debt management regime (Lehman, 1993). Despite growing calls for more decisive action to relieve the burden of servicing debt owed to the IBRD and IMF, the Bank's management remains determined not to write down obligations to it. Whatever its other effects, Mosley, Harrigan and Toye call Bank adjustment lending an effective safety net under the international financial system. The regime has entailed net capital outflows from the poor countries, debilitating debt burdens on many economies, and a pattern of adjustment whose burden rests almost entirely on debtors.

Adjustment plans have promoted non-traditional export strategies and opening economies to foreign investment on almost any terms, promote investment and reinvestment by foreign capital that ties would-be NICs to a newly structured division of labor in which their sole comparative advantage is the ability to maintain low wages, tax and tariff holidays, and a docile workforce.

Adjustment, politics and governance   This strategy has potent implications for national politics in borrowing countries. World Bank-promoted economic strategies have often been associated with a tendency to authoritarianism in government. John Loxley (1986) argues that 'orthodox models of growth' have 'a very tenuous domestic political base' in many developing countries. 'Without repression it is unlikely that the distributional implications of demand restraint and of correcting the 'bias' in relative prices – the keys to most adjustment programs – could have been constained politically' (p. 38). (See also Pion-Berlin, 1983; McCormack, 1978, on South Korea; Hamilton, 1983, on the Asian NICs; O'Donnell, 1981, on South America.)

But while Bank-style adjustment has often been associated with political repression, it has also been carried out by more open, pluralistic governments. Recent studies find that neither the degree of government repression nor of political instability is closely associated with the character of adjustment programs. (Bratton and van de Walle, 1992; Mosley, Harrington and Toye, 1991; Lafay and Lacaillon, 1993).

A subtler, still pervasive influence – the erosion of domestic political authority over economic policy making – may have more serious and lasting implications in many societies. The effect of an external agency neutralizing powerful interest groups is often considered salutary, as in shifting education or health expenditures away from urban elites, reducing high effective subsidies on energy consumption, or loosening the tight hold of political elites over parastatals, regulatory and licensing agencies, or other government-held bodies.

But this external role puts the Bank's economic program in tension with its growing interest in 'good governance,' especially transparency and broad participation in public life (see *Governance and Development*, World Bank, 1992a). This tension emerged in the 1980s as it became clear that the Bank's structural reform agenda extended beyond fiscal austerity and monetary policy into the redesign of national production, marketing and trade strategies. The tension between structural adjustment and political liberalization has been widely noted (Joan Nelson, 1989a; Healey and Robinson, 1992; Callaghy, 1993). The issue for the Bank and NGOs is explored more fully in Chapter 6. For the present, it is enough to take note of three elements of the politics of World Bank conditionality.

First, under World Bank leadership a single economic strategy has become the program of a united front of donors and financial institutions. 'Donor coordination' has been effective in preventing recalcitrant governments from playing one donor's strategy off against another's. But in the process national policy makers lose a menu of options from which to choose, confronting instead 'a stifling monolithic orthodoxy that bars skeptical questioning . . .' (Levinson, 1992, p. 47). The issue is not whether it makes sense for the Bank to encourage and even insist upon fiscal discipline and adherence to consistent economic plans. It is whether propagation of a single strategy is healthy economically or politically.

Second, the Bank and other donors have generally not sought out and encouraged locally initiated reform movements. Donors' support for domestic political initiatives could be an effective route to economic reform and political accountability. But reform packages have generally been crafted by Bank planners and a small group of likeminded economists and planners in Finance or Planning ministries. Some in the Bank have recognized this: New procedures in the Southern Africa department recognize the need for governments to initiate policy packages, and spell out an alternative approach for the department's nine countries ('Managing Quality', 1994; Denning, 1994).

Third, adjustment plans have been highly selective in their choice of economic 'distortions' to reform, de-emphasizing problems such as ineffective or regressive tax systems, capital flight, maldistribution of land or host countries' difficulties retaining revenues from many varieties of investment. A global reform effort that presented a broader menu of such reforms – a variety of routes by which adjustment could be achieved – would preserve an element of political choice, and make broad social and political commitment to reform plans more feasible.

But the technical requirements of orthodox economic adjustment have overridden domestic political opinion, producing an artificial conformity and uniformity, with the principal variation among countries resulting from the variety of ways governments find to undercut, delay or distort the intentions of external reformers.

The World Bank and the United States: Use and Limits of Power

Many see the World Bank as essentially a tool of US foreign policy. These critics go beyond the view that the Bank promotes 'political stability through defensive modernization' (Ayres, 1983, p. 226), to portray it as part of a 'dovish containment strategy' (Pratt. 1983, p. 57), acting out US foreign policy interests throughout the Cold War era in the Philippines (Bello, Kinley and Elinson, 1982), Vietnam (Kolko, 1975), and elsewhere in the South (Payer, 1982; Bello, 1994). That World Bank lending has risen and fallen where US policy interests have called for it is a matter of record in the Philippines and Vietnam.

A 1982 US Treasury Department report intended to shore up congressional support for the multilateral development banks argued that '. . .we are capable and willing to pursue important policy objectives in the banks by exercising the . . . leverage at our disposal (US Department of Treasury, 1982, p. 47). A close, informal relationship between US government officials and the Bank gives the US influence over lending, especially early in the project preparation process (Schoultz, 1982, p. 543; Hellinger *et al.*, p. 150). The US capacity to influence Bank policy, and enlarge its own leverage over borrowers' economic policies, is a theme that the US executive branch re-emphasized throughout the 1980s, when the need arose to convince the Congress that funds for the Bank or IMF were in the US interest.

But World Bank policy on many important issues cannot be read from the wishes of the US administration; there appears to be substantial autonomy in many policy areas. The sheer volume of loans to be approved taxes the Board of Executive Directors' oversight capacity.

Further, the staff's high level of training and professional status, and their own perception that they are more sophisticated and less politically compromised than staff of national agencies (Thomas, 1980, p. 110; Pratt, 1983, p. 57; Bello, Kinley and Elinson, 1982, p. 205) make them disinclined to submit to pressure from national agencies in operational decisions. Financially the World Bank is less beholden to its members than are other United Nations bodies. Members' capital payments are a relatively small portion of its holdings. And, according to some on the Bank's Board of Executive Directors, frequent US initiatives for changes in environmental policies and for freedom of information policies have weakened support from other donors for US proposals on the Board.

The Bank has been able to balance its obligations to subscribers, commercial banks, borrowers and the development profession, and in so doing has carved out a range of discretion and relative autonomy. It benefits from widely accepted norms of national 'sovereignty' and an apolitical image of 'correct' development policy – discussed in Chapter 6 – in maintaining this degree of freedom and exerting its influence on borrowers' economic policy and institutions.

The significance of the end of the Cold War, and resultant shifts in US foreign policy priorities, remains to be seen. Some Bank staff argue that in the absence of a Soviet threat to contain, US policy toward the Bank will become less intrusive – or at least more benign, focused for example on the environment. But arguably the most important US influence in the Bank in the 1980s has not been over strategic lending priorities but the promotion of a debt management and adjustment strategy. Neither the end of the Cold War nor the change in US administrations with the 1992 elections has substantially changed the US position on these issues at the Bank. It remains to be seen whether the new Republican majority in the US Congress, generally hostile to multilateral programs and initiatives, will significantly change the US posture in the Bank.

PRESSURE ON THE WORLD BANK: ENVIRONMENT, IMPLEMENTATION PERFORMANCE AND HUMAN RIGHTS

The new membership and acute capital needs of the Eastern European and former Soviet countries expand the World Bank's scope and the demands on staff and capital. While global capital requirements stretch its resources, external and internal pressures are straining its capacity to satisfy various constituencies. Responding to government and NGO pressure on environmental issues, the Bank has positioned itself to coordinate and manage several global initiatives for environmental protection. Growing pressure for consideration of human rights issues has gained the attention of some in its legal department. Concerns about the effectiveness and sustainable impact of Bank-financed projects also threaten to put pressure on business as usual.

No area of World Bank policy received public attention in the last decade comparable to that focused on its impact on the environment. Environmental organizations have used case studies, print and electronic media coverage and legislative pressure to mount a highly visible challenge to the Bank's conduct of lending and policy making.

The pressure – often with support from the US Executive Director and resistance by many borrowing governments – has led to the creation of a new environmental division in the Bank, operational divisions within each regional vice presidency, and the elaboration of an environmental impact assessment process now required for many loans. The World Bank has seized the opportunity by seeking to assert leadership in efforts to address global environmental issues. Its coordination of the Global Environment Fund (GEF), role in the Tropical Forest Action Plan (TFAP), and the unsuccessful call for a 5 billion dollar 'earth increment' to its IDA-10 replenishment all illustrate the effort to take a leading role in the emerging global environmental protection regime, a role viewed with skepticism by many NGOs (see Chapter 3).

Human rights advocates have long pressed donor governments and international organizations to use their leverage to secure adherence to internationally adopted standards of political and civil rights. The World Bank and the IMF have historically been the least responsive, but the Bank's own attention to governance issues, focusing largely on government performance in implementing adjustment plans, has given human rights advocates a new lever. The World Bank's handling of governance and human rights, and their impact on its myth of 'apolitical' development, are discussed in Chapter 6.

Internal questions about the effectiveness and implementation of Bank-financed projects gained a new high profile under the presidency of Lewis Preston. Issues have been raised about the lasting impact of investments by the Bank's Operations and Evaluation Division (OED) for some years. For OED, the issue is the economic sustainability of the investments: did loans create changes that outlasted the life of the project?

A 1992 study by retired Bank Vice President Willi Wapenhans raises the question more urgently and publicly, and raises the pressure on management for change to a new level. The Report points to weaknesses in implementation of Bank-financed projects, to country portfolios full of poorly performing projects and to a staff overly concerned with the quantity of lending and ill-equipped to handle important issues that affect the quality of investments. It finds that the Bank has tolerated 'poor performance' in many investments, and that 39 per cent of borrowing countries have 'poorly performing portfolios.' Faced with pressure from the Board over the handling of the Sardar Sarovar project, and needing to inspire confidence to push through the IDA-10 replenishment, Preston signalled in 1992 that the issues would be taken seriously (*Early Warning*, 1992).

But the report itself, as well as management's proposed 'next steps,' consolidate the Bank's definition of 'success' in terms of rates of return on investments and adherence to schedules and legal covenants, rather than social and human indicators of development impact. The Bank's use of this power to define its own 'success' is the subject of Chapter 6.

Competing New Initiatives

In the wake of Wapenhans, several new initiatives have emerged from two of the Bank's three 'central' vice presidencies. Among them are a renewed 'participation fund,' now in place, to encourage participatory initiatives in the Bank's regional divisions by making matching funds available (see Chapter 7); and consultations with operational NGOs on issues in Bank-NGO contracting and collaboration (see Chapter 3). The Operations complex under Vice President Armeane Choksi initiated a Fund for Innovative Social and Human Development, within the Bank. The fund is now to be phased out over three years, as internal budget cuts put pressure on such innovative initiatives.

But one proposal from Vice President Ismail Serageldin, for a microfinance facility and consultative group, has gained a good deal of attention. Serageldin's proposal would establish a donor consultative group for advancing learning, practice and finance of micro-finance assistance. The Bank proposes to supply as much as $30 million to an initial fund of up to $100 million, and to house the secretariat at the Bank. The Bank has convened discussions among major donors, and its board will take up the proposal if sufficient interest emerges from donor discussions.

Some NGO critics of the Bank regard the proposal, which the Bank calls a response to the 1993 conference on Reducing Global Hunger, as a high-profile attempt to address hunger and poverty concerns without responding to the conference's concerns regarding adjustment and participation. The Bank, whose experience in micro-enterprise lending is slender, would benefit in the public eye by associating itself with this popular and highly-regarded form of anti-poverty lending.

But most NGOs involved in the discussions have agreed that the fund would be useful both as a source of finance (although questions of additionality and substitution arise with respect to the bilateral donors' funding), and, potentially, as a forum for discussion of donors' financial sector policies. The draft memorandum does open this possibility, placing discussion of finance sector policy within the consultative group's purview ('Draft Proposal for Establishing a Consultative Group to Assist the Poorest of the Poor (CGAPP)' 1994). Should the proposal be approved and funded, its success in forcing critical reflection on national-level financial policies would be a key measure of its success.

Despite the substantial public relations content in these proposals for the Bank (see the following section), they also do respond to pressure and to new opportunities associated with the Bank's increased contact with NGOs. All but the Participation Fund, however, share a common characteristic: they basically propose to add new initiatives to existing operations and program, rather than to change or transform some aspect of that program.

Many of the Bank's NGO interlocutors accept that change, even eventual transformation, will likely come slowly and in small discrete steps. Some have observed that it may be possible to take advantage of internal dynamics, such as the curious competition between two Vice Presidencies for association with the Bank's NGO agenda, to accelerate the rate of change. But whether individual changes are large-scale or small, the Bank and its governmental and NGO observers should give priority to those that change mechanisms, incentives, priorities and participation for the Bank's existing activities. Chapters 5 through 7 of this study treat past and present changes at the Bank in this light.

Polishing the Image

The Bank's response to internal and external pressures does include substantive policy reviews and changes, but it has also featured a high-level and aggressive public relations effort to improve its image. The minutes of a Vice Presidents' meeting in 1993 signal the high level of concern. Preston notes the Bank's 'increasingly negative external image' and calls for a 'proactive approach' to its image, rather than defending itself 'against criticism from well-organized environmental and human rights groups' (Office Memorandum 23 February 1993).

Upcoming United Nations conferences and the Bretton Woods 50th anniversary are noted as events for a public relations campaign; other strategies are urged, including information dissemination and 'reaching out to under-exploited constituencies in developed countries such as private sector industrialists or major academic centers. . . .' The eighteen months since this meeting have seen the hiring of a top-flight public relations firm and, separately, of a new external affairs director; the production of materials, including an extensive press packet, for the 50th anniversary celebrations; a Bank-sponsored conference on combatting World Hunger; and other events and publications. In all of these, the Bank's liaison with NGOs is an important part of the message.

CONCLUSIONS

The World Bank plays an important role in articulating and coordinating patterns of economic integration in the global economy. Structural adjustment lending has raised this role to new heights, and highlights the World Bank's responsiveness to the interests of commercial banks and the industrialized countries in matters of debt and international finance. In guiding and maintaining a new international division of labor, the Bank smooths relations among the parties to economic change: international investors, host states, and local capital. Its influence rests on its capital and financial leverage, its expertise and intellectual leadership, its apolitical image, its ability to mobilize other donors, and its role in certifying governments' creditworthiness.

But the Bank's critics are less clear on the limitations of these powers, and on the extent of its responsiveness to international capital and the major industrial powers. These limitations, and the Bank's ability to define its own tasks and resist criticism and external influence are better understood by adding to political economy the perspective of organizational analysis.

Such an analysis may be especially enlightening at the present juncture, as the Bank faces pressure for change on issues ranging from the expanding needs of new middle-income members and the economic performance of its investments to environmental policy and human rights. NGOs are important actors on several fronts in shaping this agenda.

3 'Accountable to Whom?' And Other Issues for NGOs

Non-governmental organizations (NGOs) are attracting increased attention and recognition among practitioners and scholars of development and development assistance. Whether because of frustration with frequent government corruption and repression, the failure of major donors' projects substantially to alleviate poverty, or the attraction of smaller scale efforts, NGOs are often touted as a solution to many of the problems that bedevil official development aid. Networks of voluntary associations are seen as a valuable resource for building strong civil societies and accountable governments. This chapter explores some issues in these discussions that have special relevance to the NGOs' engagement with the World Bank.

Much has been written about NGOs in the past decade. They are hailed for their proximity to remote communities and to the poor (Wasserstrom, 1985), their efficiency and the low cost of their operations (USAID, 1986), their promotion of 'sustainable' development (Durning, 1989a), and their potential role as organizing and representative bodies in civil societies (Brown and Korten, 1989). Focusing on issues that confront NGOs in relating to governments and international aid donors, this chapter identifies some of the most fruitful analytic approaches.

The four analytic approaches to NGOs all contribute to the construction of criteria for distinguishing the sorts of NGOs involved in projects collaboration and in policy discussions with the World Bank. One's evaluation of the character of Bank's collaboration depends in part on how one views NGOs, and on what distinctions among them are taken to be most important. In Chapter 4 these distinctions will be employed in weighing the quality and nature of collaboration in the World Bank-financed projects reported to involve NGOs.

Some issues facing NGOs in their contacts with major donors such as the World Bank are reviewed in the latter part of the chapter, as are NGO approaches to the World Bank and several issues particular to US-based NGOs active in lobbying the Bank.

DEFINITION AND DESCRIPTION

'Non-governmental' is an exceedingly broad and imprecise category of social organizations, a residual category generally understood to include organizations that are neither governments nor for-profit firms (Nerfin, 1986). The category includes a vast and varied array of organizations that has defied adequate definition, concise description, and accurate enumeration (Cernea, 1988, p. 9).

The World Bank's working definition is inclusive, specifying only that organizations be:

1. largely or entirely independent of governments;
2. working for humanitarian or cooperative rather than commercial ends, and to relieve suffering, promote the interests of the poor, protect the environment, provide basic social services, or undertake community development (World Bank, Operational Directive 14.70, 1989, p. 1).

The definition (accepted for present purposes) encompasses a wide range of organizations. NGOs include private organizations of international scale whose stated mission is to support development or protect the environment such as CARE, Save the Children Federation, OXFAM, or the National Wildlife Federation. Some 1702 such NGOs are officially registered with the aid agencies of the OECD countries, and perhaps 4000 participate in donor supported activities (OECD, 1988).

National-scale NGOs abound as well in the South; examples include Solidarios of the Dominican Republic, the Bangladesh Rural Advancement Committee (BRAC), Rural Reconstruction Movements of the Philippines and other countries, the Kenyan National Council of Women and Sri Lanka's Sarvodaya Shramadana movement.

But the current enthusiasm for NGOs extends beyond these formal, professional, national-level organizations to local, community-based groups involved in self-help, organizing, collective assistance and advocacy for economic advancement, social change and environmental protection. Worldwatch's Alan Durning calls 'cooperatives, mothers clubs, suburban groundwater committees, peasant farming unions, religious study groups, neighborhood action federations, collective aid societies, tribal nations, and innumerable others . . . an expanding latticework covering the globe' (Durning, 1989a, p. 6). Lester Salamon refers to a 'global associational revolution' that 'may prove as significant as the rise of the nation-state' (1994, p. 109,114).

The broad use of 'NGO' adopted for this study sacrifices precision for inclusiveness. Recent treatments have made some valuable distinctions, and created a welter of new acronyms, for some of the subsets of organizations (Carroll, 1992; Bebbington and Farrington, 1993). Some of these analytic distinctions are treated in this chapter, but I have retained the general and inclusive term 'NGO.'

The enormous variety and number of local organizations makes a brief history of the development of NGOs impossible. Northern-based development NGOs emerged mostly after World War II, and several of the largest were founded during or immediately after the war to provide relief in Europe (OECD, 1988, p. 16). NGOs in the South are much more varied. Some are forms of long-standing local institutions that survived colonialism and the economic transformations that accompanied and followed it (Durning, 1989a, p. 8). Many formed or re-formed since the 1950s, and particularly in the last two decades, responding to frustration with ineffective state action, growing political space for organizing, and increasing impoverishment and natural resource degradation. Some, also, are the efforts of middle class university graduates in Latin America (Macdonald); new career options for professionals denied public employment by government spending cuts (Stiefel and Wolfe, 1994, p. 206); or efforts by young entrepreneurs, with or without commitments to a social program, who create NGOs in order to pursue government and donor funds.

The current fashion for NGOs in the development industry has its basis in important growth and changes among local organizations in the South, and in the national and international networks that increasingly connect and support them. Development and environmental NGOs are increasingly connected by organizational networks, newsletters, and electronic communication. Events even in remote areas cannot be expected to remain isolated and unknown.

But the enthusiasm for NGOs in official circles also has some of the elements of previous 'development decades,' passing emphases such as the decade of children, of women, and emphases on community development, basic needs, or integrated rural development. Each of these has risen to a height of fashion only to disappoint those with high expectations and recede into a modest role in development business as usual (Holdcroft, 1978; Ruttan, 1984).

The new emphasis on NGOs creates the danger that they will be called upon to do more than they in fact can to promote development in the poor countries. Moreover, it fosters myths about NGOs that obscure important problems and distinctions. NGOs' reputed virtues – low cost, ability to benefit the poor, access to local knowledge and awareness of local needs and capacities, flexibility and participatory style, freedom from corruption – are generally believed but largely untested and unproven (Tendler, 1982; Dichter, 1988; Rahmena, 1985; Overseas Development Institute, 1988; Esquel Group Foundation, 1993; for efforts to test these claims see Esman and Uphoff, 1984; USAID, 1986). Robert Shaw of the Aga Khan Foundation stresses the need for NGOs to demonstrate and document their effectiveness, in dialogue with the World Bank and in general (personal correspondence, 14 May 1990).

One contribution the World Bank is offering is the relatively rigorous and critical reviews it has commisioned for its forthcoming sourcebook on participation. A draft chapter by Schmidt and Carroll, which challenges and tests assumptions about intermediary NGOs' promotion of participation, is an unusually probing and critical survey of NGO performance and practice.

Some NGO critics, participants, scholars and aid agencies have made efforts to distinguish NGOs from other sectors of society and draw analytical distinctions among NGOs. The following two sections discuss important distinctions among their diverse operating styles; and explore the proposition that NGOs play an important democratizing role in strengthening civil societies. Distinctions developed in these sections will be an important foundation for analyzing Bank-NGO relations.

SOME ANALYTIC APPROACHES AND CATEGORIES

Some widely-used typologies of NGOs are created for administrative convenience (USAID; World Bank Operational Directive 14.70). But four more analytic approaches offer bases for classifying NGOs in more cohesive sub-groups, and making distinctions relevant to their relations with the World Bank.

1. Pyramidal Networks

The obvious distinction between international, national and local NGOs offer one basis for analysis. NGOs may be seen roughly as a pyramid, with a great number of grassroots or people's organizations at the bottom, a large number of intermediate organizations above them, and fewer international NGOs, acting as coordinators, donors, partners and advisors, at the top. These levels of activity are the distinguishing feature used in analyses of development NGOs by Peruvian scholar Mario Padrón (1987).

Padrón shows that tensions among the three levels must be faced and overcome to maximize the abilities of each to support social change. National level NGOs exist and operate by establishing relations with popular sector organizations and carrying out projects for and with them. Many of these NGOs (and global international development cooperations institutions) do not distinguish themselves clearly from grassroots organizations, as Padrón argues they must. Those that do, seek to work as partners to grassroots groups in development cooperation. Padrón stresses the pivotal role of national NGOs in promoting two-way exchanges that promote development, learning and change in the societies of aid donors and recipient alike.

International NGOs have confronted these tensions in the last decade. Like mission organizations that preceded them in the colonial South, most Northern-based NGOs administered relief and development programs directly through expatriate staff. As counterpart organizations in the South grew in size and sophistication, calls for new relationships between international and national/local NGOs became stronger. Many Southern NGOs and a growing number of those based in the North call for international NGOs to reduce their direct program role and take on supporting roles as mobilizers of funds for Southern partners, and as advocates and educators in their own countries and with donor institutions (UN Economic and Social Council, 1994, p. 7). The Dutch NGO NOVIB, OXFAM-UK and OXFAM-America, Canadian Council for International Cooperation (CCIC), and other European NGOs are among those leading the way in building a new supportive role.

Tim Brodhead (formerly of CCIC) refers to the 'twilight of the Northern NGO era' in this regard (Hellinger, Hellinger and O'Regan, 1988, pp. 102–3), and Sjef Theunis (1988) (formerly of NOVIB) argues for steps to integrate an international non-governmental community of advocacy, education and assistance to sustainable development. Rajesh Tandon of the Society for Participatory Research in Asia (PRIA) argues that such networks, if they strengthen the links among civil societies, could become important to the growth of an 'international civil society' (1991, p. 11). International civil society institutions will be needed to respond to the increasingly internationalized institutions of governance, finance and production.

Not all Northern NGOs have embraced these new roles, nor are they moving at the same pace. Many, including the largest US-based NGOs, continue to fund and administer many of their development and relief programs directly, and are likely to do so in the foreseeable future. But while the new division of labor is not pervasive, the model Padrón advances describes new roles being taken on by a growing number of NGOs.

2. Shared Values, Shared Interests

NGOs may be distinguished from government and commerce by the energy that motivates them, or alternatively, the way they mobilize social energy. The distinctive feature of NGOs, for activist-researchers David Brown and David Korten (1989), is their reliance on shared values as the primary source of 'social energy' that mobilizes action. States and firms, whose distinctive sources of energy are coercion and markets, have advantages in carrying out some kinds of tasks. But shared values and voluntarism contribute to NGOs' ability to promote 'social diversity' and 'democratic pluralism' and to experiment and behave flexibly. NGOs are, in Nerfin's words, 'neither prince nor merchant [but] citizen.'

Brown and Korten place a premium on NGOs' political roles in society. In a paper written for the World Bank, they argue that donor agencies too often see NGOs solely through an economic lens, as providers of certain public goods, correctives in case of market failure, or means of consumer control and efficiency. The more important roles in civil society – as watchdog on the state, training ground for democratic governance, models of accountability and proving ground for new ideas and approaches – are too seldom appreciated. That these capacities may be idealized in NGOs has been noted above. The potential political roles for NGOs is seen here as an important contrast to the vision of NGOs as service deliverers.

The 'shared values' perspective, however, under-emphasizes NGOs' identification with interest groups. Ties to women's associations, peasant movements, trade unions or cooperatives make some NGOs not only values-based partisans of an alternative development, but representatives of concrete interests, and sometimes agendas, of marginalized groups. This distinguishes NGO engagement with the World Bank from, for example, some advocacy on human rights or on biodiversity by values-based NGOs. (See Sikkink, 1993 for a discussion of campaigns by values-based 'issue networks.')

The importance of these values- or interest-based representative roles underlines the political importance of how and when donors enlist NGOs in project cooperation. When donors do involve NGOs, the civil roles should also affect how the NGOs' performance and the success of the collaboration is assessed. If NGOs are not simply contractors for donors' projects, then their services should be engaged and evaluated not on usual contract terms (deadlines, quantitative benchmarks, etc.) but in ways that emphasize the 'distinctive competence' they offer. In particular, donors should ask: Will the arrangement help the NGO uphold voluntarism and its mission and values? Does the arrangement promote 'balanced pluralism and mutual influence' in society (Brown and Korten, 1989, p. 23)? By ignoring this distinctive competence and treating NGOs as contractors, donors lose an essential asset that some NGOs offer in project cooperation. This selective and non-political appreciation and use of NGOs – with potentially profound implications for NGOs' roles in civil society – is a characteristic of World Bank-NGO interaction. Its practice at the Bank is discussed in Chapters 5 and 6.

The emphasis on values suggests a division between NGOs whose work builds on shared values (development catalyst NGOs) and those that operate simply as non-profit service providers. This distinction does not imply that only development catalyst NGOs perform important functions. But the distinction does provide a useful perspective on the World Bank's record: is the Bank simply employing the services of cheap, efficient service deliverers, or opening projects to the input of groups with a claim to speak for affected people?

3. Visions of the Task: Generations and Environments

Korten's (1987) discussion of three 'generations' of NGOs defines three different understandings of the kind of service development NGOs have provided. The three 'generations', relief and welfare, small-scale self-reliant local development, and sustainable systems development, have emerged more or less chronologically. The generations do not necessarily replace each other, and the early generations are not expected to die out. Indeed, some NGOs represent all three generations in different activities.

The first NGO generation delivers services and goods to meet poor people's acute needs, addressing symptoms, not causes of underdevelopment. A second generation of local level community-development style projects aims to build self-reliance and yield benefits that outlast the NGO's programs. Its effects are limited to villages, neighborhoods, or groups of beneficiaries.

A third generation of NGO action, Korten argues, grows out of awareness that local projects will always have restricted impact, and that even these initiatives will endure 'only to the extent that local public and private organizations are linked together into a supportive national development system (p. 149).' The third generation strategy addresses policy and institutional issues at local, sectoral, or national levels. The emphasis for an NGO shifts from delivering services to catalytic roles, promoting learning and change in the sectors in which it works and often engaging in critique of and cooperation with government and international agencies.

Working strategically to change larger institutions by demonstration effect, active cooperation, advocacy or other methods, requires different skills from relief and development projects. Along with new kinds of technical and strategic competence, third-generation work requires patience and a long-term commitment to address systemic issues for years or decades in order to bring about change.

A NGO practitioner in Zimbabwe, Martin DeGraaf (1987) refocuses the issue on how well NGOs recognize and help beneficiaries address the social, cultural, economic and political environment in which they live. Organizations vary in the extent of their cognizance of and interaction with such environments; NGOs have often treated issues such as land distribution, war, and government corruption as 'environmental' issues no more subject to their influence than is the weather. The more an NGO interacts with these environments, the more likely it is to come into contact with state and other institutions, and assume third generation roles as catalyst or advocate for change. NGOs may aim to appreciate the impact of the environment, influence it, or (rarely) control an element of the environment.

4. Blueprint, Broker and Process

Sociologist David Gow's (1979) tripartite division, applicable mainly to intermediate-level groups, is based on NGOs' styles in assisting community-based groups. For Gow, NGOs approach their supportive role in one of three styles: blueprint, broker, or process. The blueprint, adaptable to local conditions, offers an outline of technical or social changes – an irrigation system, latrines, etc. – that the NGO facilitates.

The broker NGO serves as intermediary between a community and regional or national government or an aid donor. It helps the community develop plans or strategies to secure services or resources the community wants. The broker NGO is less service provider, more catalyst, although the plan for change in the community may still originate largely with the NGO.

A process style focuses initially not on providing services or brokering relationships, but on facilitating a community's agreeing to goals and objectives, and to strategies for achieving them. As the label implies, a process-oriented NGO values the growth of community institutions and democratic action in planning as highly as the material results of any project. A process-oriented NGO is likely to develop partnerships with local groups and to devote long periods of time to working in a community. Gow recognizes a fourth category, process-broker, acknowledging that the process approach often leads the NGO to support strategies the community develops to press for policy changes or improved government services.

5. Functional Roles

World Bank staffers Larry Salmen's and Paige Eaves' (1989) study places NGOs on two continua representing their 'function . . . in development work. They categorize NGOs by whether they serve public (common good) versus private (market-oriented) purposes;' and by 'the degree to which the NGO is directed towards the interests of its own membership versus oriented to a constituency beyond itself' (p. 17). A second continuum, from self-interest to service-to-others, produces a two-dimensional field in which, for example, cooperatives are private good/self-interest institutions; while an international relief and development NGO would likely be a public good/service to others institution.

The schema puts aside the usual World Bank classification by sector, irrelevant to many NGOs. The two-dimensional field sometimes conveys more insight about an organization than does a single set of categories. But Salmen and Eaves obscure the political dimension of NGOs' importance in civil society. Political and economic roles are reduced to the economic by reducing all five roles to kinds of economic goods, public or private. This may obscure an NGO's representative role by perceiving its action on behalf of a group's interest to be simply pursuit of a private or public good.

Their schema does not consider the extent of an NGO's connection to local groups or its accountability to those it purports to serve (except in categorizing advocacy NGOs). Salmen's and Eaves' approach is more useful for categorizing the roles of NGOs in particular projects than as a theoretical basis for categorizing NGOs more broadly.

NGOS, CIVIL SOCIETY AND DEMOCRATIZATION

One of the most important claims widely made for NGOs is their capacity to function within a civil society as institutions of democratization or pluralism. Considering the importance of the claim, it is somewhat surprising that it is made so widely with such imprecision. Neither the concept of civil society nor the actual performance of NGOs within civil societies is clearly delineated or tested in much of the discussion of NGOs. Only recently has the claim of NGO enthusiasts begun to attract more systematic attention.

Attention has been drawn to the concept of civil society itself by the economic and political conditions that have beset many states and societies in the 1980s, and a confluence of ideological perspectives on them. In Latin America, civil institutions' role in organizing and energizing the emergence from authoritarian rule has drawn attention from those interested in democratization. The great diversity of NGOs' own political programs makes it possible to see them either as agents of gradual political change, or even of forestalling major structural changes; or as vehicles for seeking 'transformations in the relation of social forces favoring the poor majority' (Macdonald, 1992, p. 16).

In Africa, where administrative collapse and the rigors of internationally-imposed austerity and reform programs have exposed the weakness of many national governments, the importance of networks of non-state institutions has again surfaced. NGOs, as institutional centers within the (re)-emerging civil society, have been treated as 'democratizing development' (Clark, 1991), or, perhaps more accurately, as promoting pluralism in evolving political and social systems (Bebbington and Farrington, 1993; Fowler, 1991).

In both regions, as in some of east and southeast Asia, organized groups of the poor and NGOs have been called on to take another role: cushioning the social shock of economic adjustment programs by delivering services and promoting and supporting coping mechanisms. What the India-based Society for Participatory Research in Asia (PRIA) calls the 'seduction of NGOs' has been observed globally (Steifel and Wolfe, 1994). Stiefel and Wolfe summarize their study of participation in development institutions with a sobering assessment: organized initiatives in the context of adjustment and of other state-sponsored initiatives sometimes secure influence for excluded groups on policies that affect their livelihood, but 'for the most part organized efforts by peasants represent self-defence against development more than participation in development.'

Given NGOs' diversity and the political and economic challenges to which they must respond, what contribution can they be said to offer to poor people's effective influence in their societies? Bebbington and Farrington, skeptical of some general claims on behalf of NGOs, review the record and conclude that NGOs do bring a capacity for methodological innovation; varieties of institutional organization; a superior capacity for implementation of development activities; and a general discontent, variously articulated, with existing distribution of resources and power (1993, pp. 206–7).

Rajesh Tandon (1991) of PRIA outlines the potential NGO roles in strengthening civil society's 'material, institutional and ideological bases.' NGOs could ('and sometimes do') support local communities' claims to land and other resources; encourage and inform an 'active citizenry;' build the capacity to critique 'the existing development paradigm' and construct alternatives; facilitate citizen participation in public policy issues; and, in a variety of ways, 'challeng[e] the continuous attempts to control the minds of people . . .' (p. 11).

How effectively these assets and strategies are in fact deployed to strengthen civil societies depends in good part on how NGOs assess and manage their relations to government agencies and donors. NGOs have also been widely recruited to distribute social services and manage local self-help programs in the context of economic adjustment. Stiefel and Wolfe predict that this trend will continue, and optimistically foresee that both states and NGOs will 'win' in the process. NGOs will gain access to resources for expanded programs; the State will be increasingly challenged by NGO performance and critique to improve its own administration, and in the process will regain some of its authority and legitimacy at the grassroots (pp. 210–11).

Bebbington and Farrington wisely strike a more cautious note. They find within the NGO relation to government and donor a fundamental contradiction: NGOs want expanded influence, and need contact with official institutions to gain it. But the contact or engagement is being offered largely on unattractive terms: implementing government schemes without guarantees of influence, underwriting economic reform policies about which the NGOs have reservations. The task for NGOs is to find the 'room for manoeuvre' in this impasse (p. 215), space which is available but may be surrendered grudgingly.

The search and struggle for this room to manoeuvre is, at best, the story of NGO relations with official agencies. It is also an important portion of the story of NGO engagement with the World Bank. Good judgment and 'a high degree of political insight,' as Stiefel and Wolfe note, will be required of NGOs to ensure that they define their political and public service roles in ways that open up a greater range of choices to the 'excluded' people they aim to serve. The following section outlines some distinctions among NGOs and their organizational and operating approaches to donor agencies that are relevant to understanding their engagement with the World Bank.

NGOs AND AID DONORS

The 1970s and 1980s saw a rapid increase in NGO involvement in official donors' projects. (For a history of donor-NGO relations, see OECD, 1988.) Such engagement presents somewhat different issues for Southern NGOs than it does for international NGOs, some of which (CARE, Catholic Relief Services (CRS), Cooperative League of the USA (CLUSA), National Rural Electrification Association (NRECA), Organization for Rehabilitation through Training (ORT), for example) make project cooperation with official donors a major part of their programs. But for all NGOs, some common issues emerge in maintaining a distinct identity as NGO when cooperating with state or official donors.

Studies of NGOs in development, whether commissioned by major donors (Esman and Uphoff, 1984; USAID, 1986; Brown and Korten, 1989; Salmen and Eaves, 1989) or done by NGO participants, raise issues that confront NGOs in collaborating with government or donor programs. NGOs contemplating cooperative work with the World Bank face an organization with vast staff and financial resources, close relations with governments, a rigid project cycle and calendar, and expectations about the scale of activities to be financed. Most issues are matters of size, independence, accountability, organizational and management style, and strategy as a development promoter. These factors are discussed in turn.

The Question of Scale

The small scale of most NGO projects is an important part of the NGO ethos. Some donors such as USAID, the Canadian International Development Agency (CIDA), the US Inter-American Foundation (IAF) and African Development Foundation (ADF), and the International Fund for Agricultural Development (IFAD) have accommodated the size difference by establishing special windows or offices to fund small-scale

NGO or community development initiatives. But small-scale projects are not a part of other donors' repertoire. IBRD and IDA loans averaged $99.1 million in 1990 (World Bank, *Annual Report*, 1991). The World Bank, like most donors, presumes that if NGOs are to be involved in its projects, they must be able to 'scale up' or handle project activities in more than a local setting (Strategic Planning and Review, 1989, p. 19; see also Donnelly-Roark, 1991).

There is not unanimity about the relation between the size and effectiveness of NGO projects. Tendler (1982) argues for small-scale, more or less single-focus NGO activities, while Esman and Uphoff (1984) suggest that larger-scale integrated NGO activities can be equally effective. Esman's and Uphoff's review of size as a factor in local group's effectiveness produces mixed results. They stress that none of the largest groups reviewed fall into the ranks of least effective on their scale of performance. But without a history of each group, one cannot assume that larger groups fail less often. It is just as likely that only successful groups of any size survive long enough to become large enough and diversified by Esman's and Uphoff's standards.

Whatever the empirical relation, it is widely believed among NGOs that the rapid expansion often required by international donor projects is a threat to the NGO. Brown and Korten (1989, p. 18–19) offer three ways to scale up NGO programs that avoid simply enlarging the populations or geographic areas served. Size and impact can be increased by emphasizing the demonstration effect of NGO projects and promoting adoption of project methods by government; by intensive networking among voluntary and peoples' organizations and by promoting national policies that further enable self-help action. The authors in a collection edited by Edwards and Hulme (1992) outline similar alternatives, and document several NGO efforts. But these constructive suggestions do not change the fact that donor projects often call for capacity to implement a project or component on a scale larger than that of most NGO projects.

Accountability to Whom?

Challenges to NGOs' identity and accountability are often (but not necessarily) related to issues of scale. Most major donor projects involving NGOs enlist them to do community organizing or service delivery as part of an effort to extend benefits into poor or remote rural areas, or into urban or periurban areas where a government has little presence or credibility. But participating in a large-scale donor project can lead to a shift in an NGO's emphasis from community-based to donor-initiated activities, or reinforce that organizational style in an NGO already operating as broker.

NGOs in Guatemala, for example, were offered funding in the late 1980s by USAID for land purchases as part of a market-based land distribution scheme for landless and land-poor peasants. One NGO, Fundación del Centavo (FDC), developed a large land-purchase program, funded almost entirely by USAID, that came to dominate FDC's programming. Already a large-scale, blueprint-oriented NGO, FDC has not been changed fundamentally by the arrangement.

But other Guatemalan NGOs expressed concern about the potential for unwanted transformation of their programs and priorities, and sought assurances that their participation in land-purchase schemes could be on their terms, and in response to initiatives in communities where they work (author's interviews, 1988). In the end, FDC remained the lone Guatemalan NGO carrying out USAID-funded land purchases.

Along with questions of organizational identity come a cluster of issues relating to the degree of independence, accountability and 'privateness.' The challenge to NGO 'independence' is discussed by NGO activists such as Peggy Antrobus (1987, p. 99), and Hendrik van der Heijden (1987, pp. 107, 110). Ernesto Garilao emphasizes the danger of not developing independent financial bases (1987, p. 118). Esman's and Uphoff's (1984, pp. 163–5, 179–82) review concludes that locally-initiated activities are more effective than government- or outside-initiated programs, suggesting that the 'independence' issue has impact even in the most program-oriented evaluation. The International Council of Voluntary Agencies' (ICVA) 1985 guidelines for accepting government funding place the challenge of 'independence' at the top of its list of concerns.

But the issue of 'independence' is better thought of as one of shifting NGO accountability. If NGOs are viewed not as autonomous charitable organizations but as linked and responsive to local people's organizations, then diminished accountability to local partners weakens the NGO's very core. For international NGOs, whose links to local groups in the Third World are inherently difficult, forming close program associations with national and international donors can create tensions between donors' demands and those of Southern partner groups (Dichter, 1988, p. 185). Where competing demands come from the NGO's principal funding source and from the grassroots base it seeks to serve, the links to the community may become, as Brett puts it, 'attenuated' (Brett, 1993, p. 293).

Larry Minear (1987) outlines the extent of government funding for programs of large US-based NGOs (CARE, Catholic Relief Services), and warns that 'P' in PVO could soon be taken to mean not 'private' but 'public' or 'parastatal.' NGOs' responsiveness to increasingly frequent cooperative initiatives by major donors may threaten NGOs' reliance on local input in identifying projects, and compromise their ability to speak openly about problems in development assistance or foreign policy (Hellinger, 1987, p. 137). Even when donors do not intend to manipulate NGOs' agendas or programs, planning and reporting requirements and the scale of donor programs compel a small NGO's operations to become centered around bureaucratic and official procedures, rather than the dynamics of grassroots initiative and critique (LeComte, 1986; Edwards and Hulme, 1992; Bebbington and Farrington, 1993, pp. 207–8).

Alan Fowler's review of NGO-government relations in Eastern and Southern Africa urges donors in the region to take special pains to avoid 'steering' local initiatives by the presence of their project funding. Donor funds, which tend to steer NGOs toward modernization-style development also make organizations vulnerable to governments' withdrawal of permission for the funding, decrease the diversity of NGOs and increase the prevalence of NGOs substituting for government services, rather than providing a distinctive presence in society (p. 70–2).

Risks and Benefits: Choosing to Deal with Donors

These concerns about accountability, independence and organizational style should not be taken to imply a romantic view that NGOs represent and emanate from 'the people' and are subject to corruption by state and donor. A more realistic perspective acknowledges that NGOs already balance the interests of several constituencies (private donors, governments, official donors, partner organizations and intended beneficiaries). From this perspective, an NGO's relation to donors (or, for local NGOs and social movements, their relation to international NGOs), is a critical factor in the NGO's role and orientation in civil society (see Macdonald, 1992). Cooperation with donors does carry risks; but the risk is not an all-or-nothing loss of independence. Rather it is a reordering and distorting of existing relationships and accountabilities.

The potential costs of engagement with the World Bank are balanced, for some, by the opportunity for influence on behalf of populations whose interests they wish to serve. Studies of NGO influence on national and international policy environments have focused primarily on national government policies. BRAC's (1986) efforts to 'unravel webs of corruption' in Bangladesh and Bratton's (1989) exploration of the policy influence of three NGOs in Eastern and Southern Africa show the potential and limits of NGO influence on national government bodies and their policies and programs.

NGO policy engagement with the World Bank sometimes represents a strategic decision to take advocacy outside of national borders. International actors such as the Bank may be more susceptible to criticism on environmental or human rights issues than are some governments, or such actors may be seen as external influences to be swayed or neutralized in struggles over national policy (Rich, 1985; Hellinger, 1987).

Political scientist Jim Riker (1993) shows how Indonesian NGOs used this outward looking strategy as part of a carefully conceived strategy to increase their political space and influence national development priorities. Faced with an authoritarian state that limited political activity, NGOs used discourse on the acceptable area of environmentally sustainable development as a foothold from which to build a critique of state development policy generally. Coalitions with international NGOs and annual meetings of the International NGO Forum on Indonesia (INGI) beginning in 1985, became an integral part of that strategy. The international meetings, which rankled the government, none the less provided both legitimacy and another source of leverage for a campaign to influence politics and economics, social and natural resource policy in Indonesia.

NGO VOICES AND THE WORLD BANK

The greatest part of this study focuses on the World Bank, with little attention to details of NGO activities themselves. This section provides a skeleton outline of NGOs' various approaches to the Bank. Some NGOs have launched concerted campaigns to force policy changes, but the great majority have no dealings with the Bank. Many of the NGOs involved in project collaboration adopt strategies that lie between these two. They accept opportunities to collaborate, seeing participation as a valuable source of funds and as an opportunity for expanded program impact. A few cultivate collaboration deliberately to demonstrate and disseminate methods they have found effective.

NGOs that enter into sustained contact with the World Bank, through project-related interaction or advocacy on some policy issue, are a minority of the vast number of NGOs involved in development. In most parts of Africa, Asia, Latin America and the Caribbean, they are primarily local organizations that make contact with the Bank either because they are recruited to play a role in a project – as is the case with water users' associations as implementers and maintainers of tertiary irrigation schemes – or they actively object to some environmental or economic impact of a policy supported by the Bank. The project-level contact is discussed in Chapter 4. This section profiles some of the policy-level NGO efforts.

For NGOs based in North and South alike, engaging the Bank on policy matters requires an ongoing commitment, including staffing and other resources. For environmental organizations based in the North, and a handful of research or advocacy NGOs with human rights, trade or other development agendas, the strategic choice to address World Bank policy follows from a larger mandate. For Southern NGOs, contact sometimes flows from commitment to work on a policy area. Many of the organizations of the Philippine Freedom from Debt Coalition, for example, see the World Bank and IMF as principal agents behind Philippine government policies toward debt servicing, investment and trade.

The Coalition's 'Unity Statement' of June 1994 attacks government policies such as the Value Added Tax, budgetary priority to debt servicing and funding cuts in national environmental protection programs. But it focuses on the IMF and World Bank, charging that they have exceeded their original authorities. The statement proposes a number of specific steps to render ineffective conditions attached to several loans, and demands greater transparency from the Bank and IMF, reduced debt service obligations on debt owed to them, and that institutional alternatives to them be explored (Freedom from Debt Coalition, 1994).

Organizations and movements of India's vast 'NGO sector' include caste- and class-based organizations, local and national associations concerned with displacement and impoverishment of people resettled during large-scale infrastructure projects; and associations committed to self-reliant, environmentally sustainable development policies. Their engagement with the Bank has ranged from one-time cooperation in implementing a sericulture project, to multi-year organizing to prevent or redress the loss of farmland due to major Bank-financed dam projects. The government's assent to an IMF- and World Bank-supported adjustment program in 1992 has inspired a new surge of anti-Bank and

-IMF sentiment, reminiscent of anti-colonial struggles in the 1940s both in spirit and in language ('World Bank: Quit India!').

'Development' vs 'Environment': Agendas, Constituencies, Styles

Among NGOs based in the industrial countries, the division between 'development' and 'environment' NGOs remains relevant. Despite some successful coalition efforts, the gap between poverty-focused and conservation-focused constituencies, agendas and agencies has not been fully bridged. Their patterns of involvement with the World Bank reflect this disjuncture.

Deliberate project collaboration

Development NGOs have addressed the Bank in a variety of ways, systematic and episodic. The Aga Khan Foundation (AKF), which first invited the World Bank to evaluate its Rural Support Programme in Pakistan in 1986, has continued discussions with the Bank that included a second evaluation. The Bank published its favorable review, and AKF General Manager Robert Shaw believes that the cooperative professional relationships that have developed have 'had a certain influence on the ways in which the Bank does business' (personal letter, 14 May 1990). The contact has also led to further discussions of the participatory approaches used in AKF-sponsored projects, and possibly to further collaborative work in health, education, and agriculture in Pakistan and India. Shaw remains critical of some World Bank programming, but finds many staff now 'willing to learn and to consider the lessons of alternative experiences' (letter, 1990).

The Development Group for Alternative Policies (Development GAP), a Washington-based NGO primarily involved in advocacy on international economic and trade policy, worked with World Bank urban development staff in the early 1980s in an effort to demonstrate the feasibility and effectiveness of working through popularly based NGOs such as federations of credit unions. Managing director Doug Hellinger found Urban Sector staff willing to consider institutional arrangements that facilitated more effective project operation. But he expresses frustration at the apparent lack of integration of the lessons learned into regular urban project programming (interview, 1989). US-based CARE has been involved in reforestation projects that have influenced World Bank-financed projects in Asia and Africa.

Monitoring and country dialogue

NGOs in the northwestern Brazilian state of Rondônia are currently engaged in an exercise of critical collaboration, the World Bank-financed Planofloro project. Planofloro is the successor to the notorious and highly controversial Polonoroeste project, and locally based trade unions, producers' organizations and other associations, together with several regional and national NGOs, are meeting regularly with Bank and government officials and consulting closely in the design, implementation and (it is expected) adjustment and partial redesign of the project. With support from international NGOs, particularly Oxfam UK/Ireland, the Rondônia NGOs are offering both criticism and field collaboration in a project whose initial participatory design gave rise to high hopes. Although highly critical of some national agencies' performance, the NGOs remain engaged in unusually close and frequent exchanges with Bank supervision teams (Patricia Feeney (Oxfam UK/Ireland), 1994).

The Rondônia effort is one of several monitoring efforts, recent or ongoing, of Bank-financed projects by development NGOs. Perhaps inspired by the environmental NGOs' effective project-specific critique, development NGOs have established efforts to monitor specific projects or promote focused national dialogue with the Bank through the NGO Working Group on the World Bank (Sri Lanka, Senegal, Mexico), a steering group following up the Bank's World Hunger Conference (Mali, Nicaragua, Philippines), and under the aegis of the Institute for Development Research (Mexico and India) and through Oxfam UK/Ireland (Bangladesh, Brazil).

Ongoing policy dialogues

Other Northern NGOs have more ongoing discussions with Bank staff, donor governments and their representatives to the World Bank. Several US-based overseas aid agencies have staff or offices that focus on policy advocacy, and whose agendas have included reform or critique of World Bank policy. CARE, World Vision International, Church World Service and Lutheran World Relief are among them. Other advocacy-focused agencies such as Bread for the World, the Friends Committee on National Legislation and RESULTS have also put the World Bank on the agendas of their staffs and membership networks.

In Europe, a variety of agencies and networks have engaged the Bank in advocacy, including Oxfam in the UK and Belgium, Christian Aid, NOVIB, the Coalition of Swiss Development Organizations and the Bern Declaration, and Protestant and Catholic coalitions APRODEV and CIDSE.

Recently, solidarity organizations such as the US-Nicaragua Friendship Network, Religious Task Force on Central America, and Witness for Peace have encouraged their citizen memberships, long involved in advocacy for peace in Central America, to focus on the World Bank and IMF roles in the region. Their apparent success may signal the entry of an important new voice in the debate in the United States.

Environmentalist strategies

Environment-focused organizations, however, have been much more systematic and arguably more successful in their efforts. In 1983 environmental advocacy organizations in the US began to coordinate and expand scattered efforts to highlight environmental effects of World Bank-financed projects through direct lobbying of the Bank, lobbying and hearings in the US Congress, and public education and media campaigns. The campaign, outlined by Bruce Rich (1985) and Rich and Pat Aufderheide (1989), has focused on projects with dramatic environmental impacts and capitalized on the extensive constituency in the US and Europe for environmental conservation issues. Much of the activity has been carried out by the Audobon Society, Environmental Defense Fund, Friends of the Earth, International Rivers Network, Natural Resources Defense Council, and the National Wildlife Federation, involving national affiliates in countries such as the Philippines, Brazil, and Ghana, and independent organizations with whom the US-based groups have formed partnerships.

Their efforts have helped bring the international dimensions of global environmental issues to public attention in the US, and have introduced, however imperfectly, new considerations into the World Bank's rhetoric, organizational structure and loan portfolio. Focusing variously on Bank water policy, energy policy, forestry and infrastructure projects in countries including Brazil, Ecuador, India, the Philippines, Indonesia, Nepal, Zaire, Rwanda and Argentina, environmental NGOs have published popular critiques, produced documentaries, lobbied legislatures and Executive Directors, raised legal challenges and worked with Bank staff in an effort to devise and institutionalize policy changes.

Some development NGOs say they have learned from environmentalists' tactics (Stokes, 1988). Some environmental NGOs' efforts are cited in the chapters that follow, but the review of projects and of dialogue focuses primarily on the efforts of 'development NGOs.'

WORLD BANK-NGO DIALOGUE

Most of the efforts of development and environment NGOs are ongoing, focused on project-, country- or sector-specific issues. Internationally, the most visible episodes of the Bank-NGO dialogue are global gatherings of various kinds. Some of these have become focal points for Bank-NGO interaction, with issues that have surfaced in ongoing country or sectoral discussions gaining international exposure. In all of the fora for interaction the Bank has heard criticism and protest of its economic and environmental policies and programs presented with varying degrees of civility and collegiality.

The NGO-World Bank Committee

The NGO-World Bank Committee, established in 1984, brings representatives of 26 NGOs and several Bank staff together for semi-annual discussions. Agenda items have ranged from proposals for a World Bank fund for NGO projects, policy on disclosure of information to non-government groups, adjustment policies, and participatory development strategies. The NGO members rely increasingly on case studies on participation and adjustment as bases for discussions with Bank country and regional staff. Although sharp criticism is often raised, the discussions are collegial in tone and setting, and meetings are largely funded by the World Bank.

The evolution of discussions in the NGO-World Bank Committee reflects the structural limitations and some of the progress in the dialogue. Three features that limit dialogue in the committee may be in part results of deliberate action by participants, but are largely functions of the diverse nature of NGOs and of the World Bank's structure and culture.

1. *NGO diversity versus World Bank unity*: NGOs on the committee come from five continents and bring to the discussions a variety of agendas and priorities. World Bank representatives appreciate and encourage this diversity. Committee co-chair Alexander Shakow encouraged NGO members not to seek consensus or a unified position in the 1989 committee discussions, stressing that the Bank valued their varied positions.

The Bank's participants, however, come to the meetings with a clear, unified agenda: promote operational collaboration with NGOs, advance the participation learning process and minimize damage from public criticism. The Terms of Reference for representatives to the committee, as well as many informal documents and discussions single out operational collaboration as the Bank's primary interest in the discussions (Terms of Reference, 1981; SPRIE Progress Reports various years). A set of hastily typed memos circulated among the Bank delegation prior to the 1989 discussions orchestrated the response to NGO criticism, assigning themes and counter-points to the various participants. Diversity inherently undercuts the strength of the NGO voice. When some NGOs are silent on subjects such as adjustment and information policy, World Bank representatives are able to report that agitation on these subjects is led by a vocal, policy-oriented minority. The NGOs' persistence in raising policy issues, however, has drawn criticism from Bank participants. Such 'stratospheric' issues, argues the Bank's current co-chair, are not the kind of input the Bank is now seeking from NGOs. What the Bank needs, he asserts, is a focused, pragmatic dialogue on operational issues including popular participation and implementation of the information dissemination policy. NGO members need to facilitate NGOs' operational engagement with the Bank.

2. *Ambiguity in the roles and constituencies of both parties give the dialogue an uncertain footing.* The NGO members have restructured their number over time to assure that two-thirds are from countries of the South. In so doing they strengthen their implicit claim to speak for popular organizations and for people affected by government and World Bank-supported development plans, as well as from their own experience. But as in the wider World Bank-NGO interchange, their legitimacy as a voice for 'the poor' is far from conclusive. The fact that new members are elected by already seated members further weakens the claim to speak for NGOs as a whole, but NGO members' attempts in 1989 to design a more representative form of selection did not succeed.

World Bank participants represent their institution to NGOs, as well as promoting NGO collaboration within the Bank. They frequently articulate this stance, asking for NGO members' patience and understanding, portraying themselves as allies and pleading their limited powers to effect change. They speak sometimes as the official voice of the agency and at other times as beleaguered internal sympathizers.

Recent Committee meetings have seen an improved, more focused agenda and greater exchange with staff from the World Bank's operational offices. The 1992 meetings in Washington, for example, saw discussions of adjustment in Mexico with the Director of the Latin America and Caribbean office; of Indonesian government policy toward

NGOs with the country officer for that country; and of the Sardar Sarovar project with the Country Director for India.

Committee members initiated a national India World Bank-NGO Consultation Committee, with representatives of 23 Indian NGOs and several staff of the World Bank's India Country Department, which met three times a year from late 1988 into 1992. The Indian Committee agreed to consultations between each Bank appraisal mission and 'grassroots NGOs,' and to meetings between World Bank specialists on mission from headquarters and 'NGO representatives concerned with that specialist' (World Bank-NGO Consultation Committee (India) – A Short Report – 1990). Staffing changes in the Bank's resident mission have left the operation of the committee on uncertain footing.

The NGO-World Bank Committee has also sponsored various national and sectoral meetings, bringing together World Bank, government and NGO representatives to discuss sectoral or regional issues. These have included a Regional Workshop on Cooperation for Education and Training in Eastern and Southern Africa (May 1986), a Southern Cone of South America Meeting (December 1989), Urban Sector Meetings in 1981, and national meetings in Honduras (1991) and Indonesia (1989).

Once the Bank's principal site for talks with NGOs, after a decade of NGO-World Bank contacts the Committee is no longer the almost exclusive forum it once was. Both the Bank and some NGOs have become critical of the forum and its NGO participants. Some participants from the Bank now say they need less dialogue on policy issues, more concrete work at facilitating collaboration with NGOs and adoption of participatory methods within the Bank (James Adams, NGO-World Bank Committee Meeting, Geneva, May 1994). The Bank's recent NGO Strategy Paper stresses similar priorities, in at least some of its 11 drafts (Draft 9, pp. 14, 20). Some NGOs, especially in the United States, are critical of the Committee for its failure to support more radical reform proposals and its weak and unsystematic accountability to the larger NGO community.

The NGO participants took a step toward improving this accountability by scheduling a round of regional consultations in Africa, Asia and Latin America and the Caribbean for 1995. Like other NGO networks, the Working Group has noted that neither single-country dialogue with the Bank nor networks built solely on a North-South axis are fully effective. The Working Group is now striving to strengthen continental and subcontinent-wide networks. Another, more advanced initiative in Latin America and the Caribbean has created a regional network with similar goals, with the Instituto del Tercer Mundo in

Uruguay and the US-based Bank Information Center providing staffing and coordination (Kay Treakle, 1994).

Other Settings for NGO-World Bank Dialogue

The Bank recently succeeded in assembling the kind of North American NGO forum, focused on operational collaboration, that its NGO liaison group now emphasizes. A July 1994 'Interaction with NGOs on the Bank's Project Cycle' was initiated by the Bank's Operations Department and planned in cooperation with several Washington-based NGO representatives. In two days' discussions, participants from North American-based NGOs and the Bank's operational offices probed the operational difficulties for NGOs who wish to participate in Bank-financed operations: procurement regulations, delays in advancing currency, resistance from government functionaries, contracting arrangements and the like.

The Bank's Operations Director, James Adams, expressed uncharacteristic enthusiasm for the meetings, saying that the Bank had finally found the kind of dialogue it was looking for with NGOs on operational issues. Similar meetings are being planned for at least two sites in Africa and Asia.

NGO gatherings coinciding with recent World Bank/IMF Annual Meetings have been another, generally more acrimonious, site for Bank-NGO exchanges. At the meetings in Berlin (1988), in Washington, DC (1989, 1990 and 1992), and in Bangkok (1991), NGOs assembled for parallel conferences, public protests of World Bank and IMF policies, and for meetings and discussions with Bank staff and executive directors.

The Berlin meetings were marked by conflicts over the admission of NGO observers, as NGOs from India, the Sudan, Malaysia, Indonesia were rejected when their own governments refused to accept their accreditation (Wirth, letter to World Bank President Conable and IMF Managing Director Camdessus, 4 November 1988). The 1989 meetings saw a more open accreditation process, and featured the publication of 'A Critical Look at World Bank and IMF Policies' by NGO observers. NGOs also produced materials critical of the Bank at the 1990 meetings, including a daily newspaper *Bank Check* (now published as a periodical), which featured criticism of Bank policies and insider stories of dissension and dissatisfaction among staff.

Another NGO forum, focused on responses to World Bank and IMF structural adjustment lending, was held in Washington at the time of the 1992 Annual Meetings. NGOs from 45 countries met to compare experiences in dealing with Bank-supported adjustment programs. Strategy sessions produced coordinated programs of information sharing, national activities, and plans for internationally coordinated activities to coincide with the fiftieth anniversary of the Bretton Woods organizations in 1994. The Madrid meetings themselves drew broad NGO participation in a People's Forum, policy debates, press conferences and other events. The meetings, which also featured demonstrations and acts of civil disobedience by some NGO representatives, provoked angry reactions from some Bank staff. Some threatened that the Bank would segregate NGOs into two groups – those the Bank can work with, and those against which it must simply defend itself.

The United Nations Conference on Environment and Development (UNCED) in 1992 is the best known of the venues where the Bank and NGOs have faced off. Sometimes touted as the international event at which NGOs sharply expanded their international roles and legitimacy (Kakabadse and Burns, 1994), UNCED featured an active, high-profile NGO presence that took on industrial country policies as well as World Bank and IMF lending.

NGOs and the Tenth Replenishment of IDA (IDA-10)

The triennial 'replenishments' of the World Bank's soft loan window are a regular occasion for action by donor governments, NGOs and others who hope to influence Bank policies. As donor governments negotiate the terms and amounts for a new replenishment, NGOs that hope to influence them stake out positions on IDA performance in various sectors or policy areas. Several groups of NGOs, with overlapping membership but only loose coordination, sought to influence the funding process in 1991–92. The three strands of work show the diversity of NGO voices, and some strengths and weaknesses of NGO advocacy with the World Bank.

A coordinated effort, by Washington-based environment and development groups, to develop a set of policy recommendations for IDA-10 and advocate them with US Treasury officials involved in World Bank policy, is one strand. Beginning late in 1991, some 10 NGO staff began to meet to develop a critical paper with concrete policy recommendations for IDA. Agreeing to defer funding questions and focus on a policy agenda, the group produced a paper calling for changes in information policy, poverty and structural adjustment lending, and energy and water sector policies, and secured signatures of more than 40 US agency representatives.

The paper, which took no position on US funding for IDA, received a mixed response in discussions with US Treasury representatives. Generally supportive of at least the spirit of the water and energy sector demands and some changes in information policy, Treasury was unenthusiastic about proposals for further anti-poverty measures and for limiting structural adjustment lending. The negotiations over IDA continued, with a US government position reflecting some of the sectoral policy concerns adapted from the NGO document. NGO participants in the effort monitored the negotiations and waited for a next stage of advocacy, when the US contribution to IDA-10 came before Congress for consideration.

But others were engaged in another, simultaneous effort: the critique of the World Bank's involvement in the notorious Sardar Sarovar dam project in the Narmada river basin of western India. Years of advocacy to reform the project or end its funding, capped by an unprecedented independent review authorized by the World Bank in 1991, prepared many NGOs to make World Bank performance in the project the basis for opposing funding, or calling for reduced allocations, to IDA-10.

NGO involvement in the project centered around treatment of people to be displaced by flooding and irrigation schemes in the river basin. (These issues are reviewed thoroughly in *Sardar Sarovar*, 1992.) The project, and the World Bank's determination to continue funding despite problems, objections, and finally the recommendations of the independent review, became emblematic to some NGOs of its failure to learn and to reform itself, and the failure of years of critique and reform to make a decisive impact. Working with Indian organizations, some US and other NGOs placed a full-page advertisement in *The Financial Times* to announce their conclusion that the Bank was beyond reform and their opposition to funding for IDA-10. US NGOs, including the Environmental Defense Fund, International Rivers Network and Bank Information Center, sought to mobilize support for their position among European NGOs, in hopes of securing a commitment to smaller contributions to IDA-10 and scuttling the World Bank's appeal for an additional $5 billion 'Earth Increment.'

The World Bank, some of whose staff objected to the critique embodied in the US NGO position paper, set in motion a third process of NGO consultation, even as the movement opposing IDA funding was developing. Stimulated by the US NGO critique, World Bank Managing Director Ernest Stern invited six Southern NGO representatives, including four members of the NGO-World Bank Committee, to discuss issues around the IDA replenishment with IDA's governing board (the IDA Deputies).

The six – including an outspoken Indian critic of the Sardar Sarovar project and of the World Bank – were flown to Washington in September 1992. After separate conversations with Bank staff and some Washington-based NGOs, met for several hours with the IDA Deputies on 16 September. The written record reflects a strong critique of Bank policies, couched in an acknowledgement that IDA funding is essential for many governments, and a call for replenishment at least continuing the previous three-year fund, in real terms.

The NGO Working Group on the World Bank followed the lead of the Southern NGO group at their October meetings. The Working Group members voiced their support for continued IDA funding in an open letter to Bank President Lewis Preston, and while they expressed their continued concerns about social, economic and environmental impacts of Bank lending, they reinforced the message of the meeting with IDA deputies on the 'bottom line.'

These episodes in the debate over IDA-10 offer some insights into the NGO voices that address the World Bank. First, the Bank worries and reacts when the NGO community, or a segment thereof, expresses views that threaten its funding. NGOs in the US are considered an important constituency for IDA in a political context where multilateral aid has found few strong supporters. The personal reactions of some World Bank staff and the unprecedented discussions with the IDA deputies demonstrate that the NGO constituency is important to the Bank.

That constituency is also highly varied in its views and priorities. Among Northern NGOs alone, there is an important divide between most environmental NGOs and most development and poverty-focused organizations. Many US development NGOs articulate at least a general critique of World Bank lending and structural adjustment policies. But almost all have none the less supported IDA funding, leaving them, some argue, without serious leverage in trying to shift World Bank performance. Even where the flaws in IDA lending are believed to be serious and the development model destructive, most organizations have not seen fit to urge reduced funding.

The diversity of approaches is partly a function of the nature of US NGOs' associations with Southern NGOs. Environmental NGOs have developed partnerships with organizations threatened by or opposed to particular World Bank-supported projects. Other organizations in IDA borrowing countries, including some development NGOs, church bodies, and research or training institutes, see IDA funding through a different lens. Even some of those who oppose the development strategies the Bank promotes in their countries see reduced IDA concessional funding as disastrous, and their views influence the positions and perhaps reinforce the predispositions of many US NGOs.

US-based NGOs involved in policy advocacy increasingly cite their relations with Southern counterparts as a major source of their authority and credibility. This relationship has come into play in the IDA-10 debate, and some in the World Bank clearly understand that the relationship underlies the Northern groups' advocacy credibility. The Bank's inivitation to the NGO representatives to meet with the IDA deputies was made knowing that, while the deputies were likely to hear a stinging critique of some IDA policies, they would also hear expressions of support for continued funding from Southern NGOs. And such an endorsement from prominent Southern NGO leaders could be a highly effective counterbalance to Northern criticism or opposition.

The 'Problem' of Washington-based NGOs

By the fact of location, Washington-based NGOs have a privileged access to staff and management of the World Bank. Their access to the US Congress makes them doubly worrisome to the Bank, which has never found it easy to win full US funding for its IDA replenishments. (On NGO lobbying of the Congress see Rich, 1994). Because the Washington-based NGOs, especially environmental groups, have also pressed the critique of the Bank the farthest, the Bank and some of its defenders have questioned their standing and challenged their legitimacy in speaking for NGOs more broadly.

There are at least three dimensions to the 'problem' of US-based NGOs: they are said to be un-representative; they drown out more 'legitimate' NGO voices and in so doing alienate borrowing governments of the Bank; and they are too closely tied to the US government in pressing their demands.

The issue of representativeness is the most serious, and is increasingly remarked in a variety of policy circles (Kakabadse and Burns, 1994; Stiefel and Wolfe, 1994; Berg and Sherk, 1994). The Bank's representatives often distinguish between, for example, making information about a Bank investment available to Southern NGOs and to Washington-based NGOs who, they argue, have no particular 'right to know.' It is true that while NGO advocacy agendas are often developed in an effort to represent the concerns of Southern partners, they involve selectivity as to which 'partners' to consider, and are influenced by domestic considerations such as the interests of private supporters and donors and the personal interests of activist staffs.

The charge that the Washington-based NGOs dominate the debate and drown out diverse Southern voices has some basis in fact. It is not unusual for a meeting called by a Bank office director or Vice President with a dozen Washington NGOs to be the extent of the airing that an issue receives. The problem is inherent in the Bank's centralized Washington-based staffing, and if the Bank wants to hear the views of the NGO community more broadly, it will have to work harder at it. NGOs based in the industrial countries, which have staff resources to devote to monitoring the Bank that Southern counterparts lack, need to press themselves and the Bank to do so.

The alienating effects of US-based advocacy on borrowing governments is another element of the Washington NGO 'problem.' Pressure for environmental standards, information disclosure requirements and transparency, galling enough from some governments when they come from official donors, are even more upsetting when the critics are foreign-based NGOs. NGOs' implicit claim that they represent some poor Indians' interests better than the New Delhi government, for example, rankles the Indian government.

Many of the best known 'NGO issues' – resettlement, information disclosure, required environmental impact assessments and poverty assessments – have the effect of strengthening the Bank with respect to its borrowers. Many borrowers would surely be more sanguine about proposals that expand their options and strengthen their bargaining position with the Bank on important issues.

NGOs have missed some opportunities to improve this relationship. There are substantial areas of concern to NGOs where their interests are largely aligned with at least factions in many borrowing governments, and would be perceived as strengthening government positions in relation to the Bank. Debt relief, for example, could unite NGOs and debtor governments. But debt relief has not risen high on the list of priority NGO issues. A strategic approach to structural adjustment that urged more flexibility or room for variation could also provide some common ground with some governments, but adjustment has not been pressed vigorously by most Washington NGOs.[1]

This unbalanced agenda relates to the final 'problem' with Washington NGOs: the portions of their agenda that the US government supports ultimately rise to the highest levels of consideration in the Bank. Environmental Impact Assessments, proposals for an ombudsman, and information disclosure are not the only, or even the dominant subjects of interest to the range of Washington-based NGOs. They have attracted the support of the US government, while concerns about adjustment, the poverty impact of IDA lending, and debt relief have not. The close association of US government representatives with some NGO-favored proposals identifies the proposals with wealthy industrial interests and compromises the NGOs' identity.

One result: even a determined advocate for major changes in the Bank, the Executive Director to the Bank for the Netherlands and a number of Southern and Eastern European countries, Evelyn Herfkens, asserts that while she shares the criticism of the Bank, 'within the institution the US nongovernmental organizations are taken too seriously' (*National Journal* 18, September 1993).

CONCLUSIONS

This survey of NGOs raises important issues for understanding and distinguishing among them, evaluating their role in cooperating with major donors, and for understanding the World Bank's record in collaboration with NGOs. Among the most important:

1. Are the NGOs with which the World Bank collaborates connected to networks of international, national and local NGOs? Such networks have the potential to combine the strengths of grassroots groups with close relations to poor people in the affected area, and of national or international-level groups that can coordinate activities, broker relationships and provide resources.

   Working either with local organizations unconnected to any network, or with national level or international groups not closely tied to local people's organizations, is different in important ways from collaborating with a network of organizations determined to involve community-based groups in decision making, and prepared to use organizational, technical, and political resources on a large scale to support local groups' positions.

2. The reshaped partnership being proposed between Northern and Southern NGOs implies supportive, coordinating and advocacy roles for Northern NGOs. The review of some 300 World Bank-financed projects involving NGOs offers an opportunity to observe how these relationships are operating, and whether the nature of NGO involvement and influence is affected by the dynamics of North-South partnerships among participating NGOs.

3. Is NGO participation in projects structured so as to permit NGOs to act as organs for political participation, representation and

accountability, as well as testing grounds for innovation and local initiative? Few major NGOs are now acting out this role, nor are major donors fully prepared to appreciate and nurture NGOs in this role. One important question about the 300 projects is the extent to which NGOs participate on terms that allow this role to be played and developed.

These issues, and questions suggested by the organizational analysis of the World Bank – questions about the stage and extent of NGO involvement and the relation of NGO projects to Bank adjustment loans – are pursued in the analysis of projects in the chapter that follows.

4 World Bank-NGO Project Cooperation: Less than Meets the Eye?

In an April 1988 speech, (then) World Bank Senior Vice President Moeen A. Qureshi spoke of the World Bank's work with NGOs in these terms:

> In the last few years NGO influence on Bank policies has grown. . . . Where bureaucratic eyes are astigmatic, NGOs provide vivid images of what is really happening at the grassroots. . . . strong organizations of poor people often help public programs respond to the real needs of the poor. . . . I have asked our staff to look for more situations where NGOs could help us elicit the participation of poor people in planning public projects and policies.

Qureshi's speech is frequently quoted by NGO enthusiasts within the World Bank to show the range and depth of the organization's official commitment to working with NGOs. Along with other publications and public statements since 1988, it suggests that the Bank is cooperating with increasing frequency with NGOs, turning especially to local and national organizations in borrowing countries, and opening itself to work in all stages of the project cycle.

This chapter examines the 304 projects that the World Bank cites as involving NGOs between 1973 and 1990, focusing on the nature of NGO involvement, the character of the NGOs involved, and particularly the growth in the number of projects with NGO involvement since 1988. The encouraging growth in the number of Bank-financed projects with NGO involvement, especially in the last years of the 1980s, reflects a determined effort by some in the Bank's Operations Division and its management to expand operational collaboration. The progress, however, is undercut by troubling questions about the quality of the collaboration.

The 304 projects usually involve NGOs in implementing one component of a larger project. One quarter of the projects involve NGOs in project design, direct receipt of funds, or in conflict with the World

Bank. The incidence of these 'major roles' increased slightly after 1988, but reports of a dramatic change in the character of NGO involvement are found to be inflated. A supplementary survey of data available for 151 projects approved in 1991 and 1992 finds NGO 'design' often consists of subprojects to be financed from a project-created fund, or compensatory schemes in the context of structural adjustment plans. Examined over time and across regions with an eye for the quality of the NGO participation, the project record suggests some of the potential and limitations in the collaboration. It also raises questions to be pursued in understanding the World Bank's capacity to expand and systematize the collaboration.

DATA AND CONTEXT

The list of 304 projects involving NGOs has been compiled by the unit responsible for NGO relations, the International Economic Relations unit of the Operations Division (OPRIE) (formerly in Strategic Planning and Review (SPRIE); then in External Affairs (EXTIE)). The one- to three-page summaries of the projects collected by this office have been supplemented with other sources, including Project Completion Reports where available, for roughly half of the projects.

An additional 229 new projects were reported in 1991, 1992 and 1993 as involving NGOs. The 1991 and 1992 projects are reviewed more briefly. (Documentation for the 1993 projects did not permit their integration into the analysis.) The available information for the 1991 and 1992 projects was more limited, and the review focused on understanding the role of adjustment-related projects in the numerical expansion of NGO involvement, and on the nature and extent of NGO participation in 'design' of the projects.

Two weaknesses in the data stand out. First, projects are listed and summarized by World Bank staff, then collected in annual progress reports to management and the Board. There is no guarantee that the list is complete, that it is consistent by region, or that NGO involvement is not overstated. Each year the regional vice presidents ask their staff for a list of projects that involve NGOs. The yearly tally thus depends on staff's response to management's annual memos, and countries with interested staff persons and regions where management stresses reporting of NGO collaboration may be over-represented.

Second, project summaries are derived from Staff Appraisal Reports and reflect the project as designed, not the actual course of project

implementation, so the data used here represent project plans as negotiated by governments and the Bank. The course of several projects'
implementation is discussed in later chapters, but neither the Bank nor
this study has attempted to survey the actual course of implementation
of the reported NGO projects. One staff person close to the NGO effort estimates that perhaps one third of the projects cited in recent
years have 'a significant NGO element.' Another Bank staffer, also a
close observer of policy and practiced toward NGOs, notes that if the
extent of actual (rather than planned) NGO involvement is reviewed
the results will be 'a scandal.'

The 304 projects begun between 1973 and 1990 that the World Bank
reports to have involved NGOs should be kept in perspective. Among
some 5,000 projects financed in the Bank's history, 6.1 per cent involve NGOs. The 304 projects reviewed are a small minority of the
World Bank's operations, and are not at all typical of project lending.
They represent the cutting edge of the Bank's relations with non-governmental groups, and of efforts to encourage popular participation in Bank-
financed activities.

NGO involvement in most cases touches only a small component of
the project. In the $70 million Philippine Health Development III project,
for example, $7.4 million is devoted to community health programs
initiated by NGOs. So the number of projects and their total dollar
value are not accurate measures of the extent of NGO influence on
World Bank lending; in actual dollar terms, NGO involvement is much
smaller.

World Bank engagement with NGOs since the late 1970s has also
coincided with the growth of structural and sectoral adjustment lending. This development has quite properly drawn much wider attention
than have the Bank's overtures to NGOs, and has reshaped the institution and its role in the international economy. Adjustment lending sets
much of the political and organizational context for Bank-NGO relations. In the late 1980s and early 1990s adjustment was also the immediate context for many Bank and government efforts to enlist NGOs'
operational help.

THE VARIABLES: THE NGO PARTICIPANTS AND THEIR
ROLES IN PROJECTS

To explore the nature and quality of the World Bank's project interactions with NGOs, one needs to draw some qualitative distinctions among

the 304 projects surveyed. The simple typology developed here rests on the stage of project development at which NGOs enter into collaboration, and on three distinctions among the types of NGOs involved. The distinctions that result are broad, and classification of individual projects may be open to discussion. But they do provide a basis for some qualitative judgments about the projects and about the character of project interaction.

Community-based, National and International NGOs

Relationships, communication and division of labor among these levels are essential issues in NGO operations. Distinctions between projects with community-based, national NGO and international NGO involvement, and the various combinations of these groups, will be examined closely. For this survey, organizations with local membership are referred to as community-based organizations (CBO); larger-scale umbrella or coordinating organizations (federations of cooperatives, national associations of credit unions, etc.) are national NGOs, as are locally-based development-promoting organizations.)

Professional development NGOs and interest-based organizations

NGOs may be divided, as Salmen and Eaves (1989) note, according to the extent to which they work in support of a common social good versus a private good. But a related distinction is not treated by Salmen and Eaves: NGOs may be divided between those that are professional, charitable, voluntary, or humanitarian organizations expressly promoting 'development' – here called 'professional' – and those that are essentially organized as an expression of common interests: federations of cooperatives, national labor unions, trade associations, etc.

One might expect interest-based NGOs to be more aggressive and more likely to come into conflict with the Bank in protecting the interests of their members or beneficiaries. They may press demands and mobilize people to express objections, rather than confer about the merits of policies over a conference table, and be less readily swayed by the influence the World Bank holds in professional circles. One might also expect Bank staff to be more comfortable working with organizations of development professionals, who know the 'language' and procedures of donor agencies.

The relation to structural adjustment

NGO projects' relation to adjustment loans proved difficult to operationalize in the project survey. The links between NGO participation and World Bank policy conditions are not always clear and explicit. As a result, I have not attempted to test the relationship between NGO collaboration in projects and the growth of adjustment lending, but only to note the rapid growth, after 1988, of NGO participation in compensatory plans explicitly linked to adjustment programs. The politics of NGOs' relation to the World Bank in the broader context of adjustment lending is discussed in Chapter 6.

NGO Roles in Project Collaboration

The project cycle

World Bank discussions of its own work with NGOs recognize the importance of NGO involvement before the project implementation stage. Involvement in design processes is urged so that project designers can learn from the NGOs' knowledge and experience, and design a project or that responds to NGOs' understanding of local needs and priorities.

A major theme in the sociological theory of complex organizations suggests a second reason to give close attention to the stage of NGO participation. Contingency theory (Thompson, 1967) suggests that a large organization will place priority on protecting its 'core technology' from outside disturbance. The 'core technology' or standard operations that are central to production (in this case, of loans and projects) consists in the World Bank of its project cycle and its methods of gathering information, usually through brief missions to member countries.

The project cycle is a series of steps, strictly adhered to in planning loans, which include project identification, pre-appraisal, appraisal, negotiation, implementation and evaluation. The stages that precede implementation (here collectively referred to as 'design') penetrate more deeply into the World Bank's standard operations than does participation in implementing projects. NGO participation in design, direct funding of NGO projects and significant conflict between an NGO and the Bank are the three categories of interaction in which the World Bank's standard operations are most likely to be significantly affected. The 304 projects involving NGOs can be readily divided into three groups, distinguished by the level and nature of NGO involvement. These categories are summarized in Table 4.1 and discussed below.

Table 4.1   NGO Participation in World Bank-Financed Projects, 1973–90
by Type of Involvement

Major Roles	76
Implementation	177
Minor Roles	51
Total	304

Source: calculated from World Bank project summaries.

NGO implementation

NGO implementation of a World Bank-financed project is the typical mode of cooperation, with 177 projects involving NGOs solely in implementing a project component, or involve community groups, cooperatives, or farmers' associations in organizing and delivering some input or service.

Major roles

Seventy-six (76) of the projects feature interaction that is unusual either because it involves NGOs in project design, includes direct funding of NGO projects by a Bank-financed fund, or involves conflict between project managers and NGOs over the actual or potential impact of the project. This group of projects is referred to as major roles, indicating NGO involvement beyond implementation.

Of these 76 projects, 54 feature NGO participation in design. This figure includes cases where NGOs serve on a project design team, are consulted in appraisal or pre-appraisal, or become involved in changes in a project after funding begins. It includes cases of participation by local representative groups, as well as instances of input by NGO staff with technical expertise where relation to local communities' views is less clear.

Salmen and Eaves (1989) distinguish 'advice' from 'design' participation, to identify cases where an NGO may be consulted briefly during project design, but not participate in a sustained way in shaping a project. I have grouped the 'advice' cases with cases of NGO participation in design, ignoring the difference of degree. A more important distinction, not made in the Bank's categorization, is between participation in designing a project, and NGO design of a subproject, to be submitted for support by a fund established by the project. Such arrangements can be a valuable resource for NGO activities, but they do not draw NGOs into shaping a Bank-financed project. Twelve of the 76 projects involve direct funding of NGO activities. In these projects a component of the World Bank's finance is devoted to a fund, usually managed by a committee of government and NGO personnel, for NGO activities in a sector or region.

Finally, 11 of the 76 projects involved conflict between Bank or government officials and an NGO significant enough to be reported in the summaries. It seems likely that more than 11 projects in the last two decades have raised some conflict with an NGO. These cases involve sustained criticism or protest, and have made their way onto the Bank's list of projects with NGO involvement. Several led to an NGO role in redesign of the project.

These 76 projects are the principal focus of this survey, and some are discussed in later chapters as well. Just as the 304 are distinctive among all projects, so these 76 represent the most intensive project interaction to date. Why focus on a subgroup of 'major role' projects? From an organizational analysis perspective, the projects are important because they challenge the World Bank's standard operating procedures. Direct funding, participation in design, and conflict over a project are all likely to penetrate the Bank's standard operations more deeply than does NGO implementation of a project component.

These projects also represent the kind of interaction with NGOs that the World Bank describes as a goal, and examining them is one way to evaluate its claims to be doing more than using NGOs as implementers or cheap contractors. Comparing claims with actual project performance sheds light on the true extent of collaboration, and on the role of public relations in the World Bank's NGO campaign. Loans that finance social services by NGOs in the context of structural adjustment programs may suggest that some of the interest in NGOs is grounded in the Bank's desire to help borrowers make adjustment programs more politically sustainable. The Bank's response to disputes with NGOs in conflictive cases offers insight into its responsiveness to external pressures and politics, and may suggest preferred strategies for NGOs and other reformers.

Minor Roles. Fifty-one projects involve less significant interaction than the NGO-implemented projects above. These include 11 cases in which the project or NGO component was dropped out before appraisal; five in which contact was only in passing; and 35 projects that contracted with NGOs to provide specialized services that did not involve the NGO in direct contact with local populations, or draw on NGO experience and knowledge from such contact. These projects, most from early in the Bank's reported experience with NGOs, are referred to collectively as 'minor role' projects.

Eleven projects where Bank staff initiated plans for NGO participation but either the project was not approved or the NGO component was dropped before appraisal, are included in Bank's report of NGO participation. Government opposition to the NGO role is sometimes the barrier, illustrating one problem faced in Bank-NGO collaboration. In five 'minor' cases NGO participation involved only fleeting contact, as when a volunteer association trained a blacksmith for a regional development program in Niger; or NGO activities that parallel a Bank-financed project, for example NGO volunteers in Liberia building classrooms simultaneous to a Bank-financed school construction project.

The 35 'contractor' projects require more explanation. The point here is not that NGOs are under contract, as a contract is involved in most of the 304 projects. The issue is rather that the NGO either provides a technical service similar to those a for-profit contractor would provide (drilling wells, building facilities, planning a rural electrification scheme or a railway system), without any direct contact with local populations; or provides services solely to the government (usually training) that focus on technical capacities, and do not involve special content relating to contact with local organizations or communities.

NGO PARTICIPATION OVER TIME: A CLOSER LOOK

Figure 4.1 reports the frequency of NGO involvement in Bank-financed projects by year, since 1973. With some fluctuation, the number of projects reported grew steadily through the late 1970s and the 1980s. Between 1976 and 1988 an average of 15 new NGO projects was approved annually. Reporting that 46 and 48 projects involving NGOs were approved in fiscal year 1989 and 1990, the Bank's NGO unit calls 1988 a turning point, signalling a new posture toward NGOs. According to the latest Bank progress report the trend continued in 1991, 1992, 1993 and 1994, with 88, 68, 73 and 114 new projects approved.

The Increasingly Explicit Link to Structural Adjustment Loans

But there are three troubling tendencies in the quality of this recent project engagement with NGOs. First, in 14 of the 94 projects approved in 1989 and 1990, NGOs deliver compensatory services to soften

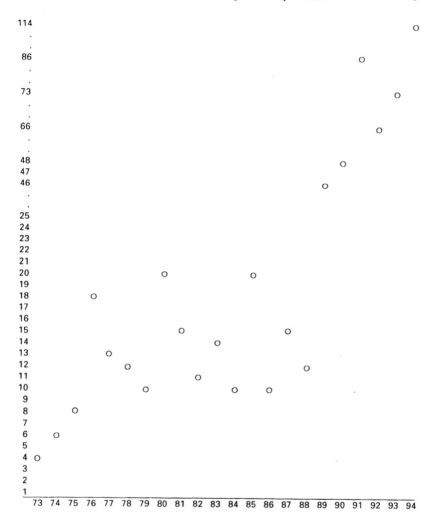

Figure 4.1   World Bank-Financed Projects with NGO Involvement, by
Year of Approval

Source: Salmen and Eaves (1989, p. 9); Strategic Planning and Review
Department (1989); subsequent World Bank Progress Reports on
Cooperation with NGOs.

the effects of an adjustment plan. In Bolivia, Guatemala, Jamaica, Chad, Ghana, Guinea, Guinea Bissau, Madagascar, Mauritania and Uganda, NGOs have been enlisted in special compensatory programs to provide social services to people affected by budget and employment cutbacks or other changes such as the removal of food price subsidies. The World Bank's reports on 1991, 1992 and 1993 project collaboration single out another 14, 9 and 7 newly approved projects as 'adjustment related.' Many NGOs are concerned that this form of interaction amounts to governments and the Bank using NGOs as insurance against the political backlash from harsh adjustment regimes.

NGO involvement in easing the effects of Bank-supported adjustment regimes goes well beyond the cases mentioned here. Some projects in SAL countries have no stated tie to the adjustment program, even though they finance the provision of urban services, housing, and health projects. Such cases – in the Philippines and elsewhere – are more difficult to categorize as adjustment-related.

In other cases NGO compensatory services are not formally part of a World Bank-financed operation. The Catholic Relief Services' (CRS) Compensatory Feeding Program in Morocco was negotiated with the Moroccan government and partially funded by USAID, with only informal participation by Bank staff. In Tanzania, church-related NGOs have been asked by the government to take over the operation of hospitals once run by the government (Interview with Rogate Mshana, 23 September 1992).

Formal NGO participation reflects a wider phenomenon, as NGOs are drawn into Emergency Social Funds and Social Investment Funds and called on to fulfill welfare and relief roles as government agencies retreat under fiscal fire. For some NGOs this has meant increased attention to relief needs, scaled-back development agendas and a greater organizational focus on their role as service providers, rather than as agents of change in civil society.

The trend also sheds light on the politics of the World Bank's increasing project engagement with NGOs. In compensatory programs, the Bank and governments seek NGO assistance in a moment of humanitarian and political need. NGOs become an adjunct to the most important item in the World Bank's agenda: adoption and effective implementation of economic liberalization plans. The significance of this employment of NGOs in politically charged situations by the 'apolitical' World Bank is taken up at length in Chapter 6.

Creating New Community Organizations

A second trend appears in the recent NGO projects: many make farmers' groups, newly organized for purposes of the project, the units for receiving or paying for some input. Establishing new 'beneficiary' groups to play a role in project implementation is not a new tendency, but it is reported more frequently among the most recent NGO projects. Newly created groups are the NGOs involved in 27 of the 94 new projects in 1989–1990 (28.7 per cent), compared to 35 of 210 projects approved through 1988 (16.6 per cent).

In the Eastern Region Agricultural Development Project in the Yemen Arab Republic (1989), for instance, two government agencies will organize 'project beneficiaries' into 'collective units' at the level of tertiary irrigation blocks. The collective units will be responsible for operating and maintaining irrigation canals and for water distribution and water fees. In Bangladesh the BWDB Systems Rehabilitation Project (1990) was to promote the formation of 'Structure Maintenance Groups' and 'Earthworks Maintenance Groups' to do the work of maintaining irrigation structures.

Forming new groups for irrigation systems management and cost recovery undoubtedly has merit on efficiency and financial grounds. But groups created for the project, especially by a national government agency, are neither likely to survive (Oakley and Marsden 1984; OED 1988) nor equipped to play the representative role of existing social organizations. The high incidence of such group formation by project authorities in the newly reported projects suggests that the quality of the Bank's interaction with NGOs has not grown with its frequency since 1988.[1]

What Constitutes an NGO Role in 'Design'?

Third, as noted above, the post-1988 projects do not show the kind of increase in NGO design roles that would indicate a deepening relationship in project collaboration. The Bank's reports about learning from NGOs stress the significance of NGOs' role in project design. So the increase in NGO participation in design, from seven projects annually in the 1980s to 16 in 1988–90, and an impressive 89 in 1991 and 1992 combined, appears to be good news. But when the nature of 'design' involvement is considered, much of the reported surge evaporates. The breakdown of these design projects is summarized in Table 4.2.

Table 4.2   Breakdown of NGO Roles in Project Design, for
World Bank-Financed Projects Reported to Involve NGO Design,
1989–90 and 1991–92

	1989–90	*1991–92*
Reported NGO Design Projects	33	89
Percentage of Total NGO Projects	34%	58%
Sub-projects[a]	11	39[b]
Compensatory Projects	0	23[b]
Reported Total Less Sub-projects and Compensatory Projects	22	35
Percentage of Total NGO Projects	23%	22%

Source: Calculated from World Bank project summaries.

a 'Sub-project' refers not to a project component, but to separate NGO projects that are submitted to a project-financed fund for support.
b Eight of the 23 adjustment 'design' projects are also counted in the 'subproject' category. The double-counting is eliminated in calculating new totals.

Designing NGO sub-projects

In many cases NGOs 'design' only a sub-project, an NGO proposal to be considered and funded by a project-financed authority. NGO design of such proposals should not be conflated with participation in designing World Bank-financed projects or project components. Of the 33 'design' projects report in 1989–90, 12 involve only such sub-projects. (Only one such sub-project arrangement was reported as 'design' before 1989.) The increase in design roles appears to be largely a matter of zealous reporting. If the 12 projects are set aside, the numerical bulge shrinks to annual averages of 7 in 1980–88 and 11 in 1989–90.

Similarly, of 89 'design' projects reported in 1991–92, 39 involve NGO 'design' only of subprojects to be financed by currencies set aside under the project. There is no indication that NGOs influenced the shape of the project, or that the Bank or government opened their planning process to NGO participation.

Designing adjustment-related welfare schemes

The close relation to adjustment programs also produces exaggerated figures for 1991 and 1992. Twenty-three of the 89 'design' projects involve NGOs in adjustment-related programs. NGOs are invited to design not the policy reforms themselves, but food distribution, health care, public employment and other schemes to soften the reforms' impact. More than half (54 of 89) of the vastly expanded number of NGO 'design' projects in 1991 and 1992 involve either no 'design' at all or advice on design of social service or employment programs to mitigate the effects of adjustment conditions. If the sub-project 'design' and adjustment-related projects are subtracted from the 1991 and 1992 'design' projects, 35 of the 156 projects (22 per cent) remain, almost exactly equal to the proportion over the period 1973–1990.

In addition, some of the reported design projects involve NGO advice on tiny components of large sectoral projects. A Ghanaian women's association was consulted in designing a $300,000 pilot scheme as part of a $230 million transportation project. As part of a $410 million primary education program in the Philippines, NGOs designed part of a $300,000 non-formal summer pre-school program. Two ornithological societies were consulted in planning a $623 million energy sector project in Turkey. It appears that some project Task Managers are zealously reporting cases that stretch one's conception of NGO involvement in project design.

Several of the NGOs consulted make no particular claim to represent primarily the interests of the poor.[2] A professional association of veterinarians in Uganda is the NGO involved in promoting privatization of services to farmers. The Chambers of Commerce in Turkey and Sri Lanka, and the Cairo Businessmen's Associations are the NGOs involved in design of three projects, and the Ecuadorian Association of Municipalities is reported as designing training projects for municipal workers.

There are encouraging tendencies in the 1991–92 projects as well. NGO involvement in appraisal and design stages of energy, natural resources management and other environmentally sensitive projects reflects operationalization of the requirements for Environmental Impact Assessments. In several cases governing committees are established to oversee project components, with NGO participation. All of these are to be encouraged. But they do not amount to a major change in the character of project engagement with NGOs.

NGO PARTICIPANTS AND THEIR ROLES

Community-based Groups and NGOs

The World Bank's recent reports on collaboration with NGOs emphasize its increased engagement with national and local, as opposed to
international NGOs. Prominent among these are community-based organizations. Of the 304 projects reviewed here, 137 involved CBOs.
Eighteen of the 137 (13.1 per cent) involved major roles for the NGOs
– design, direct funding or conflict – as do 77 (25.3 per cent) of the
population of 304. There is no marked difference in the tendency of
projects with CBOs to have a major NGO involvement.

Projects in which CBOs *and* intermediary NGOs are involved are
much more likely to involve a major role than are those where CBOs
are involved alone. Only 5 of the 62 projects where CBOs stand alone
involve a major NGO role. (Discounting 16 cases where the project
itself promotes creation of new CBOs, the figure remains modest, 5 of
46.) For projects with joint CBO-intermediary NGO involvement, however, 31 of 75 (41.3 per cent) involve either a role in design (17),
direct funding (9) or conflict with the Bank (5). Table 4.3 reports
these results.

Table 4.3   Major Involvement in World Bank-Financed Projects,
Community-Based Organizations Alone and Community-Based
Organizations and Intermediary NGOs Together

	Type of NGOs Involved	
	Community-Based Alone	*Community-Based With Intermediary NGO*
Total Projects	62	75
Number of Major Roles	5	31
Design	4	17
Direct Funding	1	9
Conflict with World Bank	0	5
Percentage with Major Roles	8.1%	41.3%

Source: Calculated from World Bank Project Summaries.

National and International NGOs

What of the subset of projects that involve NGOs organized above the community level? These consist of all except the projects with CBOs only (62), a total of 242. The World Bank emphasizes its increasing involvement with national – as opposed to international – NGOs (Operational Directive 14.70, 1989, p. 4; Progress Report, 1990, 6; Qureshi, 1988; 'Working with NGOs' in World Bank, 1994c). Its stated emphasis on national organizations may be in part intended to placate borrower governments, who may find domestic NGO involvement less offensive than World Bank engagement with foreign-based NGOs. But cooperating with national-level institutions may also mean working with professionals who are closer to local needs and realities, and may offer an opportunity to help build development institutions in the country itself.

Given the importance the Bank attaches to working with national NGOs, two questions arise about the national and international NGOs involved in projects:

1. How has national NGO participation changed over time? and
2. Do NGOs have major roles more frequently in projects involving either national or international NGOs?

Between 1973 and 1988, newly approved projects involving NGOs relied on national NGOs in 28 per cent of cases, international NGOs in 56 per cent. (Sixteen per cent of cases involved CBOs only). By 1989, 36 per cent of newly-approved projects worked with national NGOs, only 26 per cent with international NGOs. Thirty-eight per cent involved CBOs only (World Bank, 1990 Progress Report, p. 5). Reports from the Bank show this trend toward Southern national NGOs continuing in 1990 and 1991.

These figures also reflect a sharp increase in projects involving only CBOs. CBO involvement without the support of national-level coordinating groups or other supportive NGOs has seldom resulted in more than NGO implementation of Bank-financed schemes.

How important is the involvement of national NGOs for the frequency of major NGO involvement? Table 4.4 summarizes the findings. As anticipated, participation by a national NGO is more likely to be associated with a major role (32.9 per cent of cases) than is an international NGO (17.4 per cent of cases). Even more striking, in 20 of the 32 cases (62.5 per cent) where both national and international

Table 4.4   NGO Involvement in Major Roles in World Bank-Financed Projects, by Involvement of International NGOs, National NGOs, and Both[a]

| | Type of NGO Involved | | |
	International	National	Both
Number of Projects	115	82	32
Number Major Roles	20	27	20
Percentage of Projects with Major Role[b]	17.4%	32.9%	62.5%

Source: Calculated from World Bank Project Summaries.

a Excluding projects involving a CBO only.
b Variation is significant at the 0.01 level.

NGOs are involved, NGOs assume major roles in the project. Several of the 20 are major transportation or energy projects that provoked protest by local unions, peasant's associations, environmental organizations or groups of indigenous people. International organizations, especially environmental organizations, joined the fray, all focusing on the World Bank as a major financer of the projects.

The strong association between combined national and international NGO participation and major NGO roles holds true whether CBOs are involved (13 of 19) or not (7 of 13). Local NGOs with connections to Northern partners or international networks appear to join more readily in contacting local or Washington-based Bank staff about concerns or grievances. Electronic communication networks help move information between project sites, national capitals, and NGO offices in the industrialized countries. Despite the widely shared view that southern NGOs should be the primary participants in an NGO dialogue with the Bank, involvement of northern-based groups is strongly associated with major roles.

Professional Versus Interest Groups

A final distinction among NGOs is between interest-based organizations and professional 'development' NGOs. Interest-based NGOs are involve in a small minority of NGO projects, and their interaction appears not to be qualitatively different from that of development NGOs. Table 4.5 reports the findings.

Table 4.5   Professional and Interest-Based NGOs, and Major Roles in World Bank-Financed Projects

	Interest-based	Professional
Number of Projects	32	186
Number of Major Roles	12	63
Percentage Major Roles	37.5%	35.9%

Source: Calculated from World Bank Project Summaries.

Table 4.6   NGO Involvement in World Bank-Financed Projects, by Region and Year of Approval, 1973–90

	Africa	Asia	Latin America and Caribbean	EMENA[a]
Total World Bank Projects 1947–89	1469	1548	1141	756
Total NGO Projects	160	73	49	22
NGO as % of Total	10.9%	4.7%	4.3%	2.9%

Source: Calculated from World Bank Project Summaries.

a   Europe, Middle East and North Africa.
b   Regional variation is significant at the 0.01 level.

Regional Distribution

The regional distribution of projects presents two anomalies: the numerical dominance of Africa region projects, and the relatively small number of projects in Latin America and the Caribbean. In some ways, the regional distribution reported in Table 4.6 conforms to expectations based on NGO organization and activity in the regions. That the Europe/Middle East/North Africa (EMENA) region should be the lowest, for example, is in keeping with NGOs' relatively minor role in the Middle East, compared to Asia or Africa (Durning, 1989a).[3] The reputations of NGO sectors, however, would not lead one to predict Africa's numerical prominence and the relatively small number of projects in Latin America and the Caribbean.

The regional rankings are unchanged when NGO projects are considered as a proportion of total projects. Africa rates highest with 10.9 per cent of its projects involving NGOs, EMENA lowest at 2.9 per cent.

Table 4.7   World Bank-Financed Projects with NGO Involvement, 1973–90, by Region and Major and Minor Roles

Region	Africa	Asia	Latin Amer./ Caribbean	EMENA[a]
Total NGO Projects	160	73	49	22
Major Roles	32	21	20	4
Major Roles as % NGO Projects	20.0%	28.8%	40.8%	18.2%
Design	26	13	11	4
Direct Funds	5	2	5	0
Conflict	1	6	4	0
Minor Roles	39	9	5	5
Minor Roles as % NGO Projects	24.2%	12.3%	8.2%	22.7%
Aborted	3	4	4	0
Trivial	5	0	0	0
Contracting	31	5	1	5

Source: World Bank, *Annual Report*, 1989, pp. 178–82, and calculations based on World Bank Progress Reports.

a Europe, Middle East and North Africa.

The distribution of major and minor roles, however, deviates from this pattern and offers one explanation for the regional anomalies. Some 40 per cent of all NGO projects in LAC, as shown in Table 4.7, involve NGOs in major roles, while in other regions fewer than 30 per cent of NGO projects are major roles. The character of NGO involvement appears to differ in Latin America from the other regions: Latin American NGOs are reported to participate in projects less often solely as implementers, and more frequently in more influential roles.

The distribution of minor roles is also lopsided: Africa and EMENA each report more than 20 per cent of NGO projects either aborted, trivial, or in contract-style relationships. The EMENA findings, based on a relatively small regional total, reflect the predominance of transport and infrastructure projects in the region's middle-income countries.

In Africa, the large number of contracting projects, particularly in West and Central Africa, implemented exclusively by international NGOs unlinked to local groups, reflects the character of a substantial part of NGO participation in World Bank-financed projects. In several West and Central African countries, NGOs such as the National Rural Electrification Council of America (NRECA) and the British Organization for Rehabilitation through Training (ORT) have been enlisted to provide technical training to government officials and to build roads, railways and schools.

CONCLUSIONS

Much of the work of investigating the real extent of NGO involvement in World Bank lending and interpreting the projects in their political and institutional setting remains to be reported in the next three chapters. A survey of project documents does identify four significant patterns in the involvement of NGOs in Bank-financed projects:

1. The 304 projects are divided among 77 major role projects, 176 where the NGO is solely an implementer, and 51 where NGO involvement is minor. The divisions are based primarily on the depth of potential penetration by an NGO into the World Bank's core technology (design, conflict, direct funding); and the extent to which the NGO involvement offers a chance for NGOs' political roles as representative, watchdog, agent of accountability to be exercised.
2. Projects with major NGO involvement have tended to involve joint participation by community-based, national and international groups. International NGO involvement alone has tended to be less deep, and CBOs alone have rarely engaged in other than implementing and minor roles. Whether this is because of greater political and organizational resources, greater aggressiveness by NGOs affiliated with an international network, or simply the initiative of some Bank staff, is explored in further discussion of project examples (Chapters 5, 6 and 7).
3. NGO involvement has increased gradually since 1981, and beginning in 1989 the number of projects approved annually with some NGO involvement jumped sharply. But problems arise in examining the quality of World Bank-NGO interaction in the new projects, including their close links to structural adjustment programs; the creation of new local organizations to implement project components; the use of 'project design' to describe NGO submission of sub-projects for support by a Bank-financed fund.
4. Africa region projects are dominant, numerically, and relatively few have been approved in Latin America and the Caribbean. But project engagement in Latin America and the Caribbean has tended strongly to involve NGOs in design, direct funding or significant conflict

with the Bank, while implementation and minor contracting roles dominate project cooperation in Africa. Some possible explanations, including varying government capacities, differing proclivities among the Bank's regional divisions, and differing political and policy contexts, are discussed in the remaining chapters.

Categorizing and counting the projects cannot answer the most interesting and important questions about NGO involvement World Bank lending. What is the real extent of NGO participation in project design? How does the combination of national and international NGO involvement come to be associated with very active participation in the projects? Does the growing number of NGO projects reflect a systematic, growing openness in the Bank to more and deeper NGO participation? Is the Bank moving to institutionalize participation of NGOs in project planning and implementation? And how is the trend toward NGO involvement related to the dominant trend in the World Bank during the 1980s, the growth of policy-based structural adjustment lending? These topics are probed through interviews and case studies in the chapters that follow.

5 Moving Money: Organizational Aspects of a Development Model

Introducing organizational theory into the analysis of the World Bank, one risks appearing to excuse its performance as a function of the perversity of large bureaucracies, a quirk of the organizational type. This chapter and the two that follow put forward an organizational analysis that deals not with bureaucratic quirks, but with the form and substance of the World Bank's role in the global economy. The contribution of organizational analysis begins with the premise that organizations are not only created entities and tools of their creators, but also social entities, holding to values and priorities and working to preserve themselves and advance their own interests.

In this chapter I argue that the World Bank promotes and implements a capital-driven development model and investment strategy, and accepts other development mandates only as adjuncts to capital-driven economic growth. This basic mandate and strategy reflect both internal, organizational factors and the interests of powerful actors in the World Bank's political economy. The mandate has led to patterns of staffing, operations and measures of performance that are in contradiction with social and poverty-related objectives that are appended to it. The organizational apparatus that exists to implement a capital- and growth-driven, export-oriented development model is incompatible with the stated goal of working collaboratively and responsively with NGOs.

The capital investment mandate has made efficient disbursement of capital an organizational measure of success at the World Bank, an institutionalized standard of performance that shapes the implementation of new policy initiatives. This effect can be seen in the cases of poverty alleviation policy in the 1970s and the adoption and implementation of structural adjustment lending in the early 1980s. The organizational imperative to 'move money' has implications for NGO involvement in Bank operations and policy formation, as the project record and interviews of World Bank and NGO officials show.

Some Bank officials acknowledge the tension between pressure to disburse funds and the concern for sustainability of investments. But recognizing the tension and adding directives and caveats for staff will not be enough to reorder priorities, without basic changes in the organizational features that are designed to implement those priorities.

THE DISBURSEMENT IMPERATIVE: A PROXY MEASURE OF PERFORMANCE

The imperative of transferring capital has become a principal mandate for the World Bank and for individual staff, who respond in part to institutionalized incentives and priorities. This section argues that the imperative has become the effective standard of success used by the Bank and by many of its observers. The disbursement imperative holds and maintains this standing not simply because of bureaucratic perversity, but because it reflects objectives and interests rooted in the World Bank's role in managing international economic relations. In subsequent sections it is argued that recent reforms of the Bank's portfolio management leave the structures and procedures in which the imperative is institutionalized largely untouched.

The Organizational Mandate

The observation that the World Bank tends to absorb new initiatives into the program of growth-oriented capital investment is not new. Like Mason and Asher (1973), Fatouros (1977, pp. 27–8) notes that policy shifts in the 1970s involved not repudiating former approaches but adding new anti-poverty emphases. Ayres (1983, p. 75) adds that despite the rhetorical emphasis on 'new-style' lending in the 1970s, the 'overwhelming portion of World Bank activities continues to move in the same manner and direction as in the past.'

New issues on the agenda are rendered rhetorically compatible with capital-driven growth, as in 'growth with equity' and 'sustainable development.' But while rhetorical compatibility may suffice for public relations purposes, it has not allowed 'new policies' to be effectively implemented. The 1987 *Annual Report* illustrates this tendency, pledging to integrate 'the core of poverty concerns of the 1970s into the growth and market-oriented concerns that marked the first half of the 1980s.' As Hans Singer (1989, p. 1314) complains in a brief comment on the Annual Report, '. . .there is no recognition of the possibility that the neoliberal pattern of growth advocated may itself preclude such positive action [against poverty].'

The imperative of moving money has made commitment of funds a proxy measure of organizational success and of staff achievement. Sociologist Judith Tendler (1975, p. 90) argues that moving capital comes to 'define organizational output' both for most development agencies and to the outside world. At multilateral development banks especially it 'can cause a quantity-at-any-cost approach . . .' (p. 56).[1]

The institutional tendency to define success in terms of money moved is in keeping with the tendency in official development circles to assess the adequacy of the industrial world's aid effort by reference to amounts of money or per centages of GNP devoted to the cause. At least since the Pearson Commission Report (1969), international authorities have tended to advocate greater amounts of aid and investment, deducing the level needed from GNP growth targets (Tendler, 1975, pp. 91, 124). As Tendler notes, under this standard almost any increase qualifies as a positive step.

Macro-economic development models have softened some of their prescriptions for capital-led development, and some of the economists involved in these theoretical changes have promoted their ideas within the World Bank. But the ensuing changes – modified sectoral priorities, greater emphasis on technical assistance and institutional change, and discussion of social issues – have been appended to Bank operations with the assumption that they can successfully refine and supplement its mandate to promote development through financial intermediation and technical assistance. Sociology advisor Michael Cernea (1989) argues that 'financially induced development' continues to be the norm at the Bank, despite his belief that finance is often the least important of a complex set of inputs needed for widespread improvements in well-being.

The transfer of capital remains a major factor in the World Bank's assessment of aid and development finance. Net transfers from 'the developing countries as a group' in the late 1980s were a source of distress and a sign of the failure of both private and public effort to promote recovery and development (World Bank, *Annual Report* 1990, p. 29). Capital is the World Bank's greatest resource, and capital flows and the amount of its own lending should be indicators of its contribution to development. But recent evidence suggests that the availability of capital and the institutional need to disburse it can drive planning decisions and produce perverse results.

When lending capital is plentiful, as since the 1987 IBRD general capital increase, projects, the primary vehicle for moving capital, become the World Bank's scarcest resource. Supply rather than demand drives the movement of capital. The search for acceptable activities for investment, according to some staff, is energized by the imperative to find projects that conform to government and World Bank priorities, and that can be shown to meet the Bank's economic, financial, social and technical standards (Asia staff no. 3).

The extreme difficulty the World Bank has in withholding loans for even the most problematic projects illustrates the strength of the mandate. Strict procedural standards for financial and economic return of investments, as well as environmental and social measures, are 'finessed' when political and internal pressures require that a loan be made. Worrisome loans are often justified on the grounds that through its involvement the Bank may exert some influence to improve a flawed plan or project. A US Treasury Department official is quoted as saying: '[T]here is no project too destructive, and too costly, that the World Bank will not throw hundreds of millions of dollars at to try to make it better. In fact the worse the project, the more urgent the justification for the Bank's involvement' (in Rich, 1990, p. 321). The Environmental Defense Fund's Bruce Rich argues that this pattern of amelioration through investment has perpetuated destructive projects that might otherwise have withered away for want of foreign financing.[2]

Individual Incentives

Careers at the World Bank have long been built primarily by designing projects that win Board approval. It is commonplace in insider discussions that staff advance primarily by identifying, designing, negotiating and preparing projects that the Board will approve and that further the investment program in a country (Van de Laar, 1980, pp. 236–7; Ayres, 1983; Tendler, 1975; Watson, 1985; Hellinger, Hellinger and O'Regan, 1988).

McNamara introduced management devices that institutionalized this quantity-driven program. Five-year planning documents and 'annual country allocation exercises' set country and sectoral lending targets that are 'benchmark[s] for judging staff performance and individual promotion' (McKitterick, 1986, p. 47). Targets 'put heavy pressure on professional staff to rapidly generate a sufficient volume of projects' (Van de Laar, 1980, p. 222). A former Latin America country economist reports coming under pressure to continue a lending program, despite the staffer's warning that further lending to the country would be unproductive and would almost certainly not be repaid (Finance staff no. 1). The country fell into arrears to the Bank within a year of this episode.

Such resistance to targets by individual staff is by all accounts rare.

Much more common, according to several operational staff, is the tendency to press one's project forward, engaging in advocacy on its behalf under the guise of analytic review and evaluation (Asia staff no. 3). Internal papers by Caroline Moser (1987) and Michael Bamberger (1986) agree that the project cycle, the focus on cost recovery and speedy project preparation, and the requirement that projects be definitively appraised and budgeted before implementation, all limit staff's incentive and ability to finance projects with extensive community participation. In a paper written for the World Bank, Nagle and Ghose (1989, p. 10) cite a 1985 review of participation in World Bank-funded projects in which:

> project staff . . . interviewed contended that there were no incentives for pursuing social and institutional aspects of a project including community participation, except where absolutely necessary. They said that the Bank's norms reward quick development of projects and disbursement of funds.

Nagle and Ghose (1989, p. 11) interviewed a staffer who had:

> worked on three participatory projects in Africa . . . [and] sees the current reward system as the biggest obstacle to developing more participatory projects. He said the Bank does not reward a staffer who wants to spend time and effort to go to project sites to work with beneficiaries to bring about their participation in the project.

For individual staff, as Van de Laar (1980, pp. 236–7) notes, '[n]o amount of exhortation . . . that small, simple and labour-intensive solutions in project design should be sought can overcome what the bureaucracy sees as a major purpose of its own activities: to quickly spend its budget allocations.'

The findings of the 1992 Wapenhans report gave these concerns new official standing (see Chapter 2). And in the period since, Wapenhans the Director of the Operations Evaluation Division has circulated an informal proposal for a new project cycle. A working paper draft acknowledges the problems associated with the present project cycle and argues that the Wapenhans reforms cannot be adequately implemented without a substantial overhaul of the cycle. A new cycle based on four stages – listening, pilot, demonstration, implementation – is proposed.

Some Bank managers argue that less sweeping changes – annual portfolio reviews, marginal increases in time allocated to project supervision – can correct the problems diagnosed by Wapenhans. Short of such a redesigned standard operating procedure, efforts to lessen the disbursement pressure – what Wapenhans refers to as the 'approval culture' – will find itself up against the big issues of the Bank's development model and its debt-management mandate.

Lending to Finance Debt Servicing

The desire to move money is sometimes treated by the World Bank's observers as a function solely of a bureaucratic compulsion (Crane and Finkle, 1981; Ness and Brechin, 1988). Bureaucratic and organizational factors play important roles in establishing and perpetuating the mandate, but capital-based investment in practice rests on profound theoretical and ideological models and programs, and on powerful interests that shape the Bank's management of countries' commercial and official debt.

Major private banks, the US government and leaders of international corporate interests have shaped the Bank's role in transferring capital for debt servicing and repayment, particularly in the early 1980s. A 1982 conference sponsored by the Brookings Institution produced an unusually public record of talks between commercial bankers, corporate leaders and the World Bank. Bankers and leaders of such transnational entities as Bechtel, Inc. who participated in the conference, stressed their keen interest in the Bank's efforts to maintain the solvency and debt servicing schedules of debtor countries and to insure the profitability of private investments to these countries (Fried and Owen, 1982).

US officials involved the World Bank in the development of the Baker and Brady Plans for managing the debt crisis, and have called upon the Bank to play a leading role in the plan. Both plans relied on a basic scheme: transfer enough capital to finance debt servicing and avoid crises between individual debtors and private creditors, while the World Bank encourages new economic policies, more open to foreign investing and marketing (Loxley, 1986; Gibbon, 1992).

The World Bank sought increased capital allotments in order to play these roles while maintaining project lending. Rich argues that the capital increases given the IBRD in 1988 intensified the pressure to build careers by constructing portfolios of large loans. After lobbying for additional lending capital from member countries, the Bank found its lending ability threatened by political and economic crises in three major borrowing countries, China, Brazil and Argentina. These worries seem to have increased the pressure to disburse funds to other borrowers. If adjustment lending (the Bank's least staff-intensive vehicle for disbursing funds) were reduced, the pressure to disburse capital would become even greater (Rich, 1990, p. 318).

REDUCING UNCERTAINTY AND PROTECTING THE MEANS OF PRODUCTION

The organizational impulse to move money and the individual incentives to perform have been widely observed. Insights from the sociological study of major organizations in industry and the service sector help explain why maladaptive processes and organizational structures at the World Bank are so entrenched.

Structural Contingency: Reducing and Managing Uncertainty

Structural contingency theory focuses on the relation between an organization and its environment (primarily other firms and markets). Emphasizing the organization's desire to minimize uncertainty in its environment, and to protect the standard operations that are the core of its productive process, it offers two insights into the World Bank's management of pressure and of new policies.

Every organization copes with a 'task environment,' the markets, individuals and other organizations it deals in the course of doing its work. Sociologist James Thompson showed that the task environment, largely beyond an organization's control, is the chief source of uncertainty and the greatest threat to organizational performance and control.

Organizations' vulnerability to perturbations from the environment can be shown to be central to their behavior (Pfeffer and Salancik, 1978, pp. 24, 34). The organization is a 'market for influence and control' in which internal and external actors put forward their demands and interests. An organization weighs and balances these demands, and interest groups evaluate its effectiveness in terms of their own interests. Actual or perceived dependence on other actors or markets drives much of an organization's behavior.

If coping with uncertainty is the organization's central problem, uncertainty reduction is the basic logic of organizational behavior, strategy and structure. To reduce uncertainty, organizations protect the core of their productive technology, the processes by which raw materials are processed into output, from change in the environment. This core includes machines, skills, knowledge, training, strategies, procedures and special characteristics of inputs and outputs (R. Scott, 1985). Organizations will act to limit uncertainties (variations in supply, demand, inputs), whether their product be automobiles, college graduates or international loans and development projects.

Structural changes are sometimes used to protect the core productive technology. An organization can change its boundaries to embrace a part of the environment that is imposing constraints, as through vertical integration. 'Boundary-spanning units' that handle relations with important actors in the environment are another structural option for protecting the core technology from contingencies. An organization may divide a diverse, heterogeneous environment into homogeneous segments and establish separate units to handle them. A school district's 'tracking' of students into skill levels is an example, as is the division of elementary and secondary schools.

Self-assessment is a final way to reduce uncertainty. How an organization 'keeps score' of its own performance is fundamental when there is ambiguity about standards of desirability in the organization's field of activity, or uncertainty about the cause-effect relationships involved in its activities (Thompson, 1967, pp. 84–5). Each organization seeks to negotiate and establish a clear domain of action, agreed to by actors in its task environment, and to describe and represent their own activities in terms of socially accepted goals. In setting standards for its own work, an organization responds to the most important interests in its task environment, attending especially to the most visible portions of its own work.

Uncertainty, 'Core Technologies' and the World Bank

Applying structural contingency theory to the World Bank requires some reflection about the nature of its key inputs and outputs and its task environment. Capital is a key input, and member states and international capital markets that supply capital can subject the World Bank to political and financial uncertainties. But the supply of projects suitable for World Bank finance may be a greater source of uncertainty than is the supply of capital. Theoretically, the Bank assesses and finances projects proposed by member governments, assisting in design and financing those that its Board approves. But almost as soon as lending began, staff perceived that the flow of suitable project proposals would become a constraint, and began to assume a greater role in identifying and preparing project proposals (LePrestre, 1982; Mason and Asher, 1973). As lending grew in the 1970s, acceptable project proposals became the most critical input (Tendler, 1975; Van de Laar, 1980), and they remain both a key input and a part of the product.

If capital and project proposals are the major inputs, the primary 'output' consists of the packages of financial, technological, social and logistical arrangements that make up projects and program loans. The production process is fraught with uncertainties, requiring cooperation of government officials, other international or bilateral agencies, and, to a greater or lesser degree, the people and communities to be affected by the project. Projects are affected by factors as diverse as electoral politics, commodity prices and the weather.

In principle, strict standards of quality govern the product, defining operationally what are sound investments. The core of these standards is economic and financial: internal rates of return must be acceptable, and borrowers must be acceptable investment risks (Baum, 1978). The processes that guide identification, planning, appraisal and implementation of projects serve to assure the World Bank of the quality of its output. Criteria of economic, financial, technical and social soundness offer standards that define and certify projects' quality. The project cycle provides a prescribed set of steps that guarantee that the project has met these tests. These criteria and the project cycle make up the core of the World Bank's work processes: the skills, knowledge and processes that go into producing loans and development projects. More specifically, the standard operations – 'core technology' – includes the following:

1. *The project cycle guides identification, design, review, approval, implementation and evaluation of all projects.* The consistency of this multi-year process by which projects are identified based on country economic strategies, planned in detail in advance, appraised for economic, financial, institutional and technical soundness, negotiated with the borrower, implemented and evaluated, is a hallmark of World Bank lending (Baum, 1978; OED, 1990).
2. *A highly trained staff of economists, planners, engineers and social scientists is dominated by neoclassically trained economists.* The Bank seeks to build a staff of career employees, minimizing competing loyalties (Van de Laar, 1980, p. 100).
3. *A system of brief missions to borrowing countries which obtain information, assess needs and supervise projects.*
4. *An apparatus for research, publication and review of information elaborates and disseminates its theory and practice of planning and lending.*

5. *A high degree of centralization affects all aspects of its work.* Despite its global operations and impact, the World Bank maintains the vast majority of its staff, information processing, decision-making and analysis in its headquarters.

The organizational imperative to disburse capital depends on the regular and stable operation of this system. The desire to protect it from change and uncertainty therefore has implications for any policy change that affects the amount of staff time or work needed to 'move' a sum of money. The following sections review the very different courses of two major policy initiatives: anti-poverty lending in the 1970s and structural adjustment lending in the 1980s. Adoption of the new anti-poverty initiatives, appended awkwardly to the capital-investment mandate, was not as smooth or complete as the adoption of policy-based adjustment lending, which supports the Bank's development doctrine, facilitates the transfer of capital and increases the organization's leverage.

The Case of 'Poverty Lending'

Much has been written about the extent and limits of the Bank's anti-poverty emphasis under McNamara, and its durability after McNamara's departure in 1981 (Ayres, 1983; OED, 1988; Van de Laar, 1983; Sanford, 1984; Taskforce on Poverty, 1983; Stryker, 1979). Two sources, World Bank staffer Robert Ayres and the Bank's Operations Evaluation Division, draw more directly than most on interviews and internal documentation. They show the poverty alleviation campaign to be a case of adopting a new priority without downgrading existing mandates or making substantial changes in core technology or internal incentives. Further, it exemplifies the World Bank's ability to segregate a sector or category of lending – 'poverty lending' in this case – and protect its larger scale loans from more intensive scrutiny.

The organizational dynamics of poverty lending emerge at three levels: in the ideological and theoretical basis for the poverty policies; the structural and procedural aspects of implementation; and in project appraisal and the World Bank's assessment of its own work. These are discussed in turn in the following sections.

The theory: redistribution with growth

Robert McNamara became President of the World Bank in 1968 determined to address poverty directly and on a grand scale. The mandate for 'poverty orientation,' which contributed to a wave of attempts to articulate anti-poverty strategies in the 1970s, sparked internal debate over its conceptualization and implementation. Two schools competed for approval: Basic Needs and Redistribution with Growth (RWG). Basic Needs theory called for a floor of social services and income-generating aid for the poorest in the population, aimed at redistributing income, a significant reorientation of the Bank's program of capital-led growth.

RWG, the option that prevailed, proposed targeted investment to sectors in which poor people are concentrated, especially agriculture, but left the basic strategy intact. Avoiding income distribution issues, it 'did not represent a paradigm shift' (Ayres, 1983, p. 90). RWG articulated an anti-poverty strategy that shifted investment toward agriculture without challenging the basic concept of development through growth-oriented investment, and without altering the World Bank's basic mechanism for disbursing funds (see, for example, *Focus on Poverty* 1982).

The result, argues Ayres, 'was a rather tenuous gluing together of some markedly divergent approaches. Poverty-oriented emphases sometimes seemed to have been pasted on to the prevalent ideology without . . . altering its fundamental slant. This . . . enabled the Bank to do anything it wanted to do . . .' (p. 75).

'New-style' lending, old-style organization

The new poverty lending priority, even as articulated in RWG, did call for some substantial changes in lending. Stress on poverty and rural development resulted in new sectoral emphases. McNamara persistently emphasized these changes, and his commitment of the Bank to eradicating poverty and 'the worst manifestations of human indignity' suggested a substantially new organization. But while funds flowed to new sectors and to projects that looked unlike most previous World Bank investments, the structural features that shaped how work is done survived largely unaltered.

The OED (1988) summarizes the implementation of 'new-style' rural development lending in these terms: '[Management apparently] assumed that the Bank's operation was suitable for implementing the new strategy. . . .[and] that the Bank's standard project processing procedures were adequate and appropriate.' Standard procedures and assumptions were largely unaltered, reflecting the durability of a core technology that relies on technical expertise and illustrating resistance to change in these key organizational features.

New-style projects were largely designed and overseen by a separate Rural Development unit. Management's early effort to establish rural development units in the regional offices was dropped in the face of regional opposition and a separate central division was established in 1973 (OED, 1988, p. 49). (In contrast, environmental staff were integrated into regional units in the late 1980s, a move the Bank says indicates the high priority now given to environmental policy.) The Rural Development Division's staff were structurally set apart from the mainstream of operational work. According to Schechter (1987, p. 202) the new staff hired to work on RWG strategies 'became something of a parallel staff, working alongside more senior staff, some of whom were not as committed to massive expansion and developmentalism.'

The framework for developing projects within the project cycle was largely unchanged. Ayres (1983, p. 66) attributes a 'lack of imagination' in identifying projects partly to the failure to introduce interdisciplinary teams. Although the need for interdisciplinary work was recognized, sectoral divisions remained unchanged, and taskforce work was not widely used.

Information gathering, supervision and decision making remained highly centralized in Washington (OED, 1988, p. 56). Development needs and project ideas were appraised through brief overseas missions and more lengthy analysis and negotiation in headquarters. 'Bank operational staff and consultants are expensive and are not expected to spend prolonged periods of time in borrowing countries and their outlying project areas,' notes OED (p. 56). Ninety-four per cent of professional staff remained stationed in headquarters, and important decisions were almost all taken there (Ayres, 1983, p. 65).

Critics such as Gran (1988) treat this as evidence of willful ignorance of these aspects of economic life in poor countries that defy explanation under the World Bank's ideology. The persistence of a centralized, narrow information regime is consistent with Thompson's and Wildavsky's (1986) assignment of information selection biases to the hierarchical organizational culture (see Chapter 7). OED and Ayres describe the effects with typical understatement. For OED (1988, p. 56) the highly centralized process resulted in the application of project models to new situations without adequate adaptation. Ayres (1983, p. 65) observes that 'it is difficult for this mission-oriented approach to provide the sustained picture of rural and urban development processes that appeared a requisite for the Bank's decision-making in these areas.'

The project cycle, too, was under pressures that restricted the time available for developing complex rural development projects. The need to allocate sufficient time for project development has been widely recognized, particularly when the project aims to benefit groups that are not already well-organized and prepared to undertake the activities proposed (Bryant and White, 1982; Korten, 1980). Even in project supervision, where new-style lending was fully expected to require more staff time, OED (1988, p. 17) reports that the additional time was not allotted. The scissors effect created by growing amounts of capital to lend and restricted staff resources meant that project staff 'could not afford the luxury of [designing a project] for a slow start-up' (p. 56). Schechter (1987, p. 56) argues that 'staff managing many new-style projects chose to concentrate on putting through the traditional kinds of projects rather than assuming the heavy burden of helping the borrowing countries identify and work out complex, time-consuming new projects.'

Management had evidence from studies by the LAC office that new-style projects were absorbing more staff supervision time than 'conventional' projects (Ayres, 1983, p. 127). Yet in the face of evidence that these time requirements are inherent in the nature of the projects, the 1978 *Annual Report* optimistically asserted that '[d]elays in disbursements can reasonably be expected to fade as borrowers and the Bank gain experience in project execution' (p. 8).

The absence of structural changes to accommodate the new initiative was matched by a paucity of efforts to integrate poverty and rural development concerns into the skills, values and incentive structure of the professional staff. OED (1988, p. 49) notes a failure to 'sell' the new approaches to staff despite widely expressed 'coolness' toward them. Nor was any 'particular effort made to train staff in the finer points of the [rural development] strategy' (p. 48).

This ambiguity with respect to training and promotion of new-style policy, together with implicit messages sent by leaving other aspects of standard procedures intact, left room for uncertainty about management's commitment to a new style of anti-poverty lending. Staff opposition to the change suggests that explicit, energetic promotion through rhetoric, training, and structure would have been required to effect a major change in lending procedures:

The absence of these instead allowed uncertainty about 'the kinds of achievements that would bring rewards to staff members. Sometimes it seemed that poverty alleviation in rural areas took precedence. But other times emphasis seemed to be placed on the aggregate amounts of loans processed or on the aggregate amount of incremental agricultural production likely to occur. . . . Such conflicting signals often contributed to internal controversy' ('Bank official,' quoted in Ayres, 1983, p. 10).

Some important managerial changes did accompany the anti-poverty campaign. Two planning tools, the Country Program paper and the annual country allocation exercise, were introduced as McNamara promoted a programming, planning and budgeting regime developed at Ford Motors and the Pentagon (McKitterick, 1986, p. 47):

> . . . a five-year lending program for the Bank/IDA in a given country [was developed] against a detailed statistical analysis of each sector of the country's economy. The annual country allocation exercise drew on these five-year plans where possible and set targets for the staff for each country and each sector within each country. Attainment of these annual targets became the benchmark for judging staff performance and individual promotion.

The organizational innovations that accompanied the anti-poverty campaign, then, only heightened the focus on the quantity of lending rather than the process of participatory and poverty-oriented lending. Meanwhile the organizational structure, project cycle and information system all remained essentially unchanged in the face of the new identity proclaimed by McNamara. The durability of these features illustrates the strong tendency of a core technology and information system to resist change.

As with anti-poverty lending in general, other social issues encountered considerable ideological, structural and procedural obstacles to integration into the World Bank lending program.[3] In the absence of strong pressure from without, or compelling need to change in order to satisfy and retain an important constituency, these internal organizational obstacles were sufficient to keep social concerns at the margin.

The Case of Adjustment Lending

Adjustment lending was introduced as a short-term, emergency solution to immediate balance of payments problems and the debt crisis (Development Committee, 1990, pp. 14–15). Adjustment lending to any country was to continue for three to five years. Speeches and reports introduced the new policy with an urgency comparable to the launching of anti-poverty lending.

Adjustment lending responded to pressure from the Reagan and Thatcher governments, which controlled 24 per cent of voting power on the Bank board and 'relentlessly attack[ed the Bank] for being insufficiently pro-market' (Cypher, 1989a). Criticism by conservative members of Congress and pressure from the US Administration to participate in the 'Baker Plan' for debt relief also helped motivate management's adoption of policy-based lending (Bacha and Feinberg, 1986, p. 340).

Commercial banks stimulated the adoption of policy-based lending in two ways. First, their retreat from additional lending in the early 1980s helped to create the political and financial crisis that motivated the Baker Plan, and choked off the flow of capital for debt servicing by debtor nations. Second, there is evidence that commercial lenders themselves pressed the World Bank to step into the breach with measures that both financed debt service and motivated policy changes (Hamilton, 1989). For international banks and corporations, adjustment lending represented a more direct approach to opening economies to transnational investment (Cypher, 1989a, p. 61).

Internally, adjustment lending had much to recommend itself. Adjustment's export-oriented program was responsive to the widespread criticism among staff of import-substitution strategies (Bacha and Feinberg, 1986, p. 340). Some staff also consider the 'Asian Miracle' economies of Taiwan, South Korea, Hong Kong and Singapore to be models of free-market development, whose emulation the Bank should encourage (Cypher, 1989a).[4]

Discontent among donors with the impact of project aid also had an influence, and quick-disbursing policy-based loans, especially large loans to major debtor nations, were an attractive vehicle for moving money. SALs have in fact been efficient disbursers of capital: the average amount of adjustment loans was more than 25 per cent larger than the average project loan in 1987 and 1989. (In 1990, SALs and project loans were of roughly equal average size; in 1994 SALs were some 13 per cent larger (calculated from Annual Reports 1987, 1989, 1990).)

Policy-based lending offered new challenges and rewards to staff economists with macro-economic expertise. It was also a flexible tool, adaptable to sectors, and applicable where economy-wide programs could not be negotiated or implemented. Sectoral adjustment loans (SECALs) and 'hybrid loans' made policy-based lending a viable option for many country programs (Development Committee 1990, No. 23, p. 18).

Contingency theory offers a helpful characterization of the policy change. Adjustment lending can be seen as moving the analysis and design of policy at the country and regional level – already part of the core technology – into the forefront of lending activities. Ayres (1983) describes three levels of World Bank activity: participation in the 'international marketplace of ideas' through discussions of macro and sectoral policy; national policy dialogue; and project lending. He notes 'slippage' and compromise with each step away from the abstract (ideas) toward the concrete (project lending). Adjustment lending moves the policy-making apparatus from the background into the center of the core technology by offering loans directly in support of policies the Bank endorses or designs.

Especially when compared to anti-poverty lending, where foot-dragging led to very slow and incomplete adoption, adjustment lending was quickly incorporated into the World Bank's lending program. While organizational and professional factors apparently shaped the pace and extent of adoption of anti-poverty lending, the overriding importance of disbursement and of the Bank's role in debt management led to rapid incorporation of policy-based lending.

I return to both cases in Chapter 6, to discuss how the World Bank's standards of self-assessment influenced the course of policy change. Standards and methods for measuring and certifying its own performance – pre-appraisal of projects and calculation of economic and financial rates of return through cost-benefit analysis – remained stable in the face of new and potentially challenging kinds of lending.

NGOs, DISBURSEMENT AND STAFF TIME

Working with NGOs, unlike adopting anti-poverty lending in the 1970s or adjustment lending in the 1980s, requires that a new set of actors be incorporated into the lending process. The anti-poverty campaign introduced a new priority but made no fundamental change in lending apparatus. Adjustment lending introduced a new kind of loan, and with it new opportunities for disbursement and influence.

The World Bank's engagement with NGOs is related to both poverty lending and adjustment. It gives new rhetorical life to the anti-poverty commitment of the 1970s, as the Bank publicizes its engagement with the development profession's premier poverty fighters. It is tied to adjustment lending by the prominence of NGOs in programs to soften the effects of adjustment on the poor. But the policy of collaboration with NGOs is distinct in that it purports to engage the Bank with a new and different set of actors and interests.

The World Bank has publicized its work with NGOs as part of an effort to demonstrate a continued commitment to poverty-oriented lending. The meteoric rise of adjustment lending provoked questions from several quarters as to the status of anti-poverty lending (Sanford, 1984; Stokes, 1986). Bank documents make it clear that these questions were a matter of concern. The Bank's Operations Evaluation Division (OED, 1988, p. 15) raises the question of whether the 'poverty focus' is waxing, waning or wavering, noting indicators that suggest 'a decline in the share of World Bank activities specifically targeted toward poverty reduction.' The OED concludes that the poverty focus is intact, but cites only research activities, 'positions' and policy statements such as those of a 1986 poverty task force.

As with previous policy emphases, the issue of poverty eradication under structural adjustment, for the Bank, is one of balancing growth, recovery, and protecting the poor (Development Committee, 1987; 1990). The 1987 *Annual Report* commits the Bank to assisting governments in designing adjustment programs 'that to the extent possible . . . protect the poor, notably through improvements in the efficiency and targeting of social expenditures'. Singer (1991, p. 15) worries that this 'ominous' language reflects no 'moral imperative or even high priority for the protection of the poor.'

World Bank reports and public documents on poverty and on NGOs link the NGO effort to its anti-poverty policy both implicitly and explicitly. NGOs, for example, are mentioned repeatedly in Chapter 4 of the 1990 WDR ('Promoting economic opportunities for the poor') and identified as an important option in ending exclusive reliance on government agencies, a change needed for 'successful programs' in rural infrastructure and technology (World Bank, WDR, 1990, pp. 67, 70; see also World Bank, 1990d).

In view of the close relation between anti-poverty and NGO policy in the World Bank's constellation of policy priorities, it is not surprising that the issues raised in interviews about collaboration with NGOs closely parallel those that defined and limited the 1970s anti-poverty campaign: the imperative of moving money, limitations on staff time and energy, the tendency to substitute expertise and effort for listening and learning; and the failure to institutionalize procedures and incentives that would promote the new policy widely and systematically.

'Finessing it'

The pressure of time and money is the most-discussed theme in my interviews with World Bank staff. Many cite what a senior Asia economist called 'the disbursement imperative' as a key limit on innovative lending.

'There is no incentive to innovate,' argues one staffer (Policy staff no. 3), when one rises by moving money quickly. A Finance staffer agrees that the disbursement imperative 'dominates decisions at the Bank,' (Finance staff no. 1), and McKitterick (1986, p. 47) claims that in 200 interviews of Bank staff, not one 'said he got promoted for saying "No.". . . What count[s] is getting the appraisal report done in time to meet the target.'[5]

Limited staff time per project surfaces even more often than the disbursement imperative. Working with NGOs takes time, and senior project staff from Latin America and EMENA stressed that they lack the staff to canvass and build relations with NGOs. Two Operational staff stressed the need to hold down one's 'coefficients,' the work-weeks per project figures reported in Project Completion Reports (LAC staff no. 1; LAC staff no. 2). Frequent complaints of overwork, also noted by Thomas (1980, p. 173), were typified by a senior agriculture specialist's lament about restricted mission size and chronic overstretching of project task managers (Policy staff no. 5). Several Operations staff asked how NGOs might be contacted by someone with more time (NGO experts, Resident staff, consultants) (Africa staff, October 6, 1989; Africa staff no. 3; LAC staff, 6 October 1989).

But Operations staff from Asia, Africa and Latin America regions who described extensive contacts with NGOs consistently said they themselves had spent time in the country meeting and talking with NGO representatives in order to develop relationships with them. Information collected in a central office could be helpful, they argued, but forays by NGO specialists could not substitute for building personal contacts between country staff and local NGOs.

Some frustrated staff say the World Bank lacks the 'agility' needed to work with NGOs, and operations staff from three regions describe cynicism about social requirements, seen as 'baubles' to be hung on 'Christmas tree projects,' a reluctance to 'genuflect' toward new issues (Finance staff no. 1; Policy staff no. 3; Africa staff no. 3; LAC staff no. 2; Asia staff no. 3).

But the most frequent response to the time/money crunch was described by a senior Asia economist as finessing it (Asia staff no.3). 'Finessing it' occurs when too much is required to be done in too little time while preparing a project. One says the right things, proposes (for example) organizing the requisite number of irrigation groups, and does one's best, knowing that the work described would require more than the time allotted. Reluctance to delay or scrap a project was noted by Thomas (1980, p. 174) who found that when a project has been appraised 'it becomes very difficult for the staff to avoid implementing it. "Management puts us under pressure to ignore little problems, but then no one has the guts to say no when the project is a bad one."'

'Finessing it' also describes most staff's response to the time and money crunch faced by the organization as a whole. With staff limited, capital increased and new commitments to staff-intensive environmental, social and NGO measures, most operational staff acknowledge the crunch but finesse it. Official documents often claim to be doing more of all things (for all people) at one time, as in a 1990 publication: '[The World Bank] is focusing more than in the past on economic policies at the national and international levels and, at the same time, on the poverty and environmental aspects of development' (1990d, p. 17).

OED (1988, p. 55) cites the same tendency in reviewing rural development strategies. When 'lending volume remains the main performance measure,' staff are encouraged to 'discount . . . the value of experience in favor of drive and commitment. The latter qualities are conducive to keeping a lending strategy alive . . . in the face of misfortune, but obviously they court serious dangers.'

The 1992 review of project quality and implementation (Wapenhans Report) makes this staff-wide focus on designing new lending, rather than overseeing the quality of existing loans, a matter of official concern. It sees priorities as reversed, with quantity of lending overpowering concerns about quality, and staff pushing internally conceived projects on borrowers. Staff responding to interviews say (71 per cent) that they are 'overwhelmed by responsibilities for which they have little or no pre-Bank experience or in-Bank training' (World Bank, 1992, p. 19).

But in the wake of Wapenhans, and while some Bank managers are asserting that procedural reforms will relieve the pressure to lend, the Bank has announced significant cutbacks in administrative budget for fiscal years 1996 and 1997. The across-the-board 6.5 per cent cuts in internal (not lending) budget respond to member countries' understandable concerns about high costs. But they also make it difficult to be optimistic about the implementation of innovative and participatory methodologies that are demanding of staff time, and thus money.

A great deal of evidence, then, points to a conflict between the mandate to move capital and new issues that place labor-intensive demands on staff. The tension limits the real significance of commitments to social issues. Staff with specific concerns about poverty impact and participatory development process – who identify themselves as a minority – say the effort to involve NGOs in operations depends on the individual efforts of a few highly motivated staff (Africa staff no. 1;

Policy staff no. 6). One Africa staff economist asked with some frustration: 'Is it more important to get resources to poor people, or to move money? Maybe we'll see this changing at the Bank . . . Maybe the Bank will be prepared to do a project without every cent preappraised' (Africa staff, 6 October 1989).

Many NGO sources, including several involved in intensive project collaboration with the Bank, make the same observation. A European NGO executive notes that 'in day-do-day operations, individual staff members, especially the task-managers, have immense freedom of manoeuvre, providing that they deliver the goods.' He observes among some staff great '. . . readiness to cooperate and take account of the views of NGOs, a readiness which would vary from one staff member to another' (G. Meier, letter, 2 July 1990). An NGO staffer in the Philippines engaged in the Philippines Health III project said pointedly that she saw the initiative as coming from the project task manager himself, 'not the World Bank' (interview, 21 November 1989).

Staff do note sub-regional and sectoral exceptions to the time/money crunch. Some social sector project staff noted that the disbursement imperative applies less to health, nutrition and population than to agriculture, industrial and infrastructure loans. Some say that pressure is self-selecting by sector, and that professionals who wish to can choose jobs that put them under relatively little pressure, and find creative ways to use project appraisal resources that build contacts with NGOs (Africa staff no. 2; Africa staff no. 3). An Africa country economist acknowledges that the stereotype of an 'inflexible bureaucracy fixed on moving money' is based in fact, but notes that the organization is not monolithic (Africa staff no. 1).

West Africa staff, for example, had free rein from their regional director in the late 1980s to pursue collaborative projects with NGOs under the Social Dimensions of Adjustment (SDA) program. The Southern Africa Department is the geographic unit that has now moved to the forefront in promoting innovative work. The Department's stated approach to programming, management and policy dialogue calls for resident missions and country staff to consult extensively with interested groups, to slow down operations and dialogue where necessary to allow for government deliberation and initiative, and to apply a variety of assessment methodologies to improve the breadth and depth of the department's information about clients' priorities and needs.

Likewise, the Economic Development Institute's training and capacity-building program with NGOs has been a small exception. Priority is given to 'building trust' through participation in identifying training needs and designing programs. But the EDI programs have the advantage of involving only funds from individual donors' trust funds, not Bank lending resources.

Still, the propensity to commit funds quickly remains a problem for NGO collaboration Bank-wide, even in projects or project components that are small, by World Bank standards, and in the social sectors. The Health Development III Project in the Philippines, with a $7.4 million component to finance NGO primary health care services, aimed to build on progress made in the Aquino government toward a policy of cooperation with NGOs in social sector work. The greatest concern of two experienced UNICEF officials, however, was that the Bank would introduce funds without allowing time for pilot project experimentation and for the training necessary for government regional health personnel to allow working arrangements to grow successfully. Without enough time for a slow start-up, these health officers feared that government-NGO working relationships could not flourish (interview, December 1989).

Budget and time constraints have also been faced more directly in the environmental sector. Kenneth Piddington, then chief of the Bank's environmental office, noted in a 1988 internal memo that the organization had to face 'resource implications of internalizing environmental review to project development.' He noted as well that he was not 'satisfied that the resource implications have been properly worked through. . . .' Regional environmental staff mention funds available for consultants during project preparation, and a perceived flexibility when project preparation is delayed by environmental assessments or debates (SAC staff no. 2; Asia staff no. 5).

Even these exceptions, however, highlight the extreme limitations placed on the World Bank by its treatment of social needs as addenda to the growth imperative. The Bank's NGO liaison office makes a critical distinction between sectors and projects where cultivating participation is 'worth the effort,' and those where it is not. Participation is 'worth the effort' when projects 'are designed to help a specific group of people;' require beneficiaries to pay some costs; or need active beneficiary commitment in order to work (Strategic Planning and Review, 1989, p. 14ff.). In promoting participatory strategies internally, large-scale projects and those thought to produce broadly enjoyed benefits are exempted. Where participation has costs in terms of staff or community residents' time or 'delays and changes in project design, development of community organizations and people-responsive structures . . . benefits may not be as high' (Strategic Planning and Review, 1989, p. 14).

To be sure, thinking among participation advocates within the Bank has advanced a good deal since 1989. It is true, as Stiefel and Wolfe note, that the Bank has conceptualized participation and reviewed its own performance more rigorously than other international organizations, including some of those to whom the rhetoric comes more readily than to the Bank (222–3). Still, in practice, one can only imagine the Bank's lending apparatus adapting to the delays of extensive participation if the practice were limited, by sector or otherwise. The 1989 language expresses the present thinking more candidly than Bank spokespeople would today: participation is 'worth it' in irrigation and probably in other sectors to be determined, and probably 'not worth it' in health and several others.

So these tensions resurfaced in 1991 and 1994 seminars on participation, held as part of the Bank's 'learning process' on participatory development. Bank staff and external participants raised questions about the organization's ability to incorporate more participatory methods when its lending and staff are driven by the mandate to move money. The Bank's review of some 35 participatory projects is seeking to determine whether participation has in fact required more staff time and slowed disbursement. (The content of the workshops and the Learning Process recommendations are discussed in Chapter 7.)

Recognition of this tension by the staff cadre that supports participation, of course, does not resolve the issue. Now that the concern raised by outside critics has been broached by the official review of lending quality – the Wapenhans report – the World Bank will have to choose to confront the tension outlined here. The Bank can re-tool, radically reshaping its lending process and project cycle to meet the challenges, or it can finesse it. The latter option is the ingrained response of a majority of middle level professional staff, according to one staff promoter of participation and NGO strategies. A major contingent of these staffers assume that they can weather the present round of proposed changes as they have previous reforms (interview June 1994). The durability of the Bank's mandates and procedures seem to make the latter more likely. The result will depend in good part on how vigorously and effectively the Bank's NGO critics can press the issue.

'First-level' and 'Second-level' Issues

Some staff complain that the multiple policy directives they receive from management – regarding the environment, poverty, appropriate technology, women in development, NGOs – force them to weigh and discern which are to be taken seriously. Such requirements distract staff from what many consider to be their central mandate, and are sometimes perceived as bureaucratic or politically-inspired requirements that complicate their work and reduce their effectiveness. McKitterick (1986, p. 47), for example, argues that 'under McNamara the Bank . . . became a "development agency" with a multiplicity of purposes. . . . Bank staff lost any coherent sense of institutional purpose. . . .' The Wapenhans report (1992) finds this expanding scope of responsibilities to be a continuing problem for the quality of investments.

Yet no staffer I have spoken with has had any difficulty discerning which issues are to be assigned highest priority. Among the multiplicity of issues to which project staff might give attention, several staff describe a simple hierarchy of issues that they say is generally understood.

Two topics have become 'first-level' issues: national economic and pricing policy and the environment. One ignores these issues in project planning, a senior economist said, only 'at the peril of one's career' (Policy staff no. 7). Their status seems to be recognized by a broad range of staff. Other issues – gender, indigenous peoples, etc. – are 'second rank' issues that may earn 'brownie points' when included in a project, but will not be noticed if they are omitted (Policy staff no. 7; LAC staff no. 2). Operational collaboration with NGOs remains a second-level issue: the Bank's NGO liaison unit acknowledges that although staff are aware of official policy in favor of collaborating with NGOs, most on staff know little about NGOs (SPRIE, 1990, p. 15).

Staff describe two kinds of factors that can boost an issue to first-level status: an issue rises through external pressure or through advances in theoretical and empirical work by Bank staff. Internal expertise and external political pressure were woven together in a sometimes contradictory web of explanations given for policy changes.

One environmental staffer interrupted my question to assert emphatically that pressure from without is what moves an issue along in the World Bank. There are, in this economist's view, staff who recognize themselves the importance of environmental concerns in Bank-financed operations previous to NGO and other public campaigns on the subject. But it is external pressure, from NGOs, the US Congress and the Executive Directors, that elevated the issue.

An economist in private sector operations attributes the rise of the two first-level issues to quite distinct dynamics of change. Environmental issues gained their status, he notes, through outside pressure. Environmentalists seized successfully on 'a few bad projects' and conducted an effective campaign. Macro-economic policy conditionality and cost recovery, on the other hand, became central to Bank lending on their merits, because staff determined that they were 'the right thing to do' (Policy staff no. 7).

Although other staff acknowledged the effectiveness, and some the necessity of external pressure on environmental issues (Policy staff no. 3), World Bank staff tend on the whole to perceive policy change as developed through reasoned deliberation and discussion by their expert colleagues.

The role of environmental NGOs in advocacy with the World Bank has been described in some detail elsewhere (LePrestre, 1986; Rich, 1985; Schwartzman, 1989; Rich, 1994), and my interviews produced no reason to doubt the widely held view that pressure inspired by the reporting and lobbying of national and international environmental NGOs was the key to changes that have been made in environmental policies and regulations at the World Bank.

Environment and the Bank: From Threat to Organizational Asset?

Documentation collected at the Environmental Defense Fund's MDB Information Center, by the Bank Information Center, and in World Bank files chronicle campaigns of correspondence, communication with the media, documentary films and television programs and lobbying of the World Bank and Northern parliaments, largely led by environmental NGOs based in the North, and carried out by networks of international, Southern national and local groups.

The result, an aggressively 'green' World Bank that carves out new responsibilities for itself in the management of international environmental issues, should have been no surprise to observers of the Bank or to students of organizational sociology. Put on the defensive by a vigorous critique, whose demands have included lending slowdowns or moratoriums for large infrastructure projects, the Bank took the initiative, gaining control of the Global Environment Fund (see Chapter 2), then seeking unsuccessfully to augment funds for the tenth replenishment of IDA by proposing a $5 billion 'earth increment' for environment-related projects.

Environmental advocacy and pressure from major donors created a tension with the Bank's overall mandate. As *The Economist* noted, its role as 'a compulsive lender sits uneasily with its new job as custodian of the environment' (2 September 1989, p. 44). An improved environmental policy might call for less rather than more lending. But while carrying out environmental assessments and requiring national environmental action plans, the Bank has successfully turned a potential threat to its disbursement capacity into an asset through the GEF and projects labeled as environment-specific.

The Bank's move into the center of global environmental action is reminiscent of its response in the late 1950s to calls for an institution to meet the capital needs of countries – notably India – that could not borrow from the IBRD. The Bank moved quickly and effectively to put the newly proposed UN fund under its own control, and the IDA was born (see Libby, 1975a). Thirty years later, when global environmental issues became a significant challenge to the Bank's operations, it took advantage of its size, scope and resources to expand its mandate and absorb a troublesome issue into its own structure.

CONCLUSION

Historically, the World Bank has adapted its mandate in order to survive: in so doing it created a development mandate and established a niche for itself among international and national organizations. More recently, the development mandate has proven to be quite stable, and new proposed objectives have been appended to the mandate of financially induced capital-led development. The organizational structure and process that have served capital-induced growth-oriented development strategies do not adapt to the requirements of more process-oriented, participatory operations.

The implications for NGOs and the World Bank are made more explicit in the next chapter, which discusses contradictions within and among the organizational myths that underpin Bank operations.

6 The World Bank and Apolitical Development

Much of the World Bank's influence depends on its success in representing itself, its activities and the 'development' it promotes as 'apolitical.' World Bank officials have long been aware of the importance of the apolitical image: President Eugene Black wrote in 1962 that '[w]e ask a lot of questions and attach a lot of conditions to our loans. . . . [W]e would never get away with this if we did not . . . render the language of economics morally antiseptic. . . .' (in Swedberg, 1986, p. 388).

This chapter explores the apolitical image, shows how this image empowers the World Bank, and argues that the Bank's engagement with NGOs, along with other factors, stretch the image's credibility. Two myths underlie the apolitical image: the myth of the primacy of member countries' sovereignty; and the myth of development as an apolitical, technical process achieved through gradual economic change, political stability, and integration into the global capitalist economic system. These myths constitute a formidable barrier to cooperation with non-governmental organizations. Where the World Bank does engage NGOs, the relations strain its apolitical image and confront the myth of sovereignty and of apolitical development with the highly political nature of the Bank's work and influence.

Engagement with NGOs is one of several ways the myth of apolitical development is being stretched at the World Bank. The Bank's emphasis on 'governance' issues and pressure from without and within for greater attention to civil and political rights in borrowing countries are challenging the Bank's underlying myths (David Gillies, 1993; Jerome Levinson, 1992). In these areas as with NGOs, the realities of a changing world confront myths and structures that have served the Bank through previous changes.

The World Bank is neither apolitical nor a neutral servant of the wishes of its member states, but an organization with a measure of autonomy, considerable power over many of its borrowing members, and a variety of ways to exercise that power. Many of those channels of influence are effective only in the presence of the sovereignty and development myths: development plans with profound political and distributional implications can be promoted forcefully if their basis is agreed to be apolitical and scientific. And when real economic choices are sharply constrained by debt and the absence of financial and institutional alternatives, emphasizing borrowers' formal sovereignty softens the hard realities of power relations in their dealings with the Bank.

Tensions between the apolitical image and a highly political reality, and between the technocratic myth of development and the economic and social realities of poverty in borrowing countries, form a contradictory foundation for liaison with NGOs. As bases for World Bank operations, the sovereignty and development myths are fragile, but have been held together successfully through the Bank's dealings with governments and with quasi-governmental bodies. The tensions and contradictions are sharpened by current efforts to involve NGOs in Bank-funded operations, by a new 'popular participation learning process,' and by the attacks of some of the World Bank's NGO critics.

THE WORLD BANK AND 'APOLITICAL' DEVELOPMENT

The World Bank goes to some lengths to represent its own activity as above politics. This description of dispassionate analysis of technical problems by objective professionals is typical:

> ... a loan proposal or a policy question that reaches the Executive Directors ... has been very thoroughly discussed and analyzed by a group of trained professionals recruited on a broad international basis, with differing points of view, wide international experience, and an ever increasing sensitivity to the individual culture and problems of member countries (World Bank and IDA, Questions and Answers n.d., p. 6).

The claim of freedom from political considerations has been called a 'principal element of the mythology of Bank lending ...' (Ayres, 1983, p. 71). Thomas' interviews of Bank staff show that the mythology also contributes to staff's preference for the Bank as employer over a bilateral aid institution.

The Apolitical Image and Economic Orthodoxy

Legal scholar A.A. Fatorous (1977, pp. 23–5) argues that the apolitical and technical image is the most important dimension of the Bank's operating ideology, the dimension by which it 'frees itself from the common constraints on non-intervention that the international legal order imposes on public actors.' Any remaining constraint is removed 'by the fact that any final action taken . . . is incorporated, or allowed for, in an agreement with the country concerned. [This] consent legitimizes all aspects of the decision the Bank may have successfully imposed.'

This freedom from international legal constraints, along with the breadth of its working mandate, fosters considerable independence, or relative autonomy of action. Not only the World Bank itself, but the 'development' it promotes is represented as apolitical, as progress that will follow from correct policies and institutions. Conversely, the strict separation of the economic and political allows the Bank (and other international financial agencies) to operate without having to 'confront the full implications of their actions within a society' (Levinson, 1992, p. 62). So long as 'country performance' is conceived of overwhelmingly in terms of the Bank's preferred economic indicators, the Bank is free from having to give formal consideration to political and civil rights in borrowing countries.

Sectoral lending patterns have changed since postwar reconstruction, but three factors remained constant in the conceptualization of development. Development is technical, driven by capital investment, and almost always furthered by more contact with the global economy.

Development is treated not as a complex, problematic process where what counts as 'development' depends upon circumstances and on the interests of all groups involved. It is, instead, progress that will proceed in a more-or-less predictable fashion if enough of the missing ingredient – technical skill, capital, correct prices – is supplied. Some NGOs argue that the Bank must 'take the side of the poor' in designing and negotiating policies and projects (Bangkok NGO-World Bank Committee Meetings, 1989; noted in Strategic Planning and Review, 1990, p. 20; Addendum to the Report of the Participatory Development Learning Group, World Bank, 1994g). But 'taking sides' makes no sense if development depends on technically correct measures and on policy guidance that determines scientifically the best route for all participants.

The tendency to de-politicize development is not unique to the World Bank. David Goldsworthy (1988) illustrates the lack of political-mindedness in development theory and practice throughout official and private development agencies, and in much academic discourse. The presence – Goldsworthy would argue the primacy – of values, interests and power considerations in all situations of underdevelopment and social change is inconvenient for World Bank operations, incompatible with the myth of sovereignty, and an obstacle to rapid and effective disbursement of resources.

Politics has no place, formally, because economic science supplies reliable answers to policy questions. Ayres (1983, p. 4) argues that the World Bank relies on 'a dominant ideology' of neoliberalism, emphasizing economic growth through:

... capital accumulation [and]... export expansion and diversification. Ingredients of neoliberalism derivative from these basic goals [are] highly prevalent in Bank documents, publications and interviews with Bank staff and officials. [They] include fiscal and monetary probity; 'getting prices right'...; a sound currency; external economic equilibrium; export dynamism; economic stability; and, through all of these things, a favorable investment climate.

Orthodox theory serves as a sure, scientific basis for policy, and as intellectual and ideological justification for the World Bank's activities. The 'vast majority' of staff interviewed by Ayres:

... reject the notion that these emphases indicate an ideology at all. In their view, as expressed in repeated interviews, all of this is neutral. It is simply sound economic and financial management, technocratically orchestrated and [universally] applicable ... (1983, pp. 74–5).

Economic doctrine helps the Bank shape discourse about development around technique and science rather than values and politics. The presentation of economic theories as scientific formulations shields them from criticism (Sassower, 1988, pp. 167–8), permitting the Bank to exert financial leverage to promote not 'its way,' but a certifiably 'correct way.'

For a generation, officials returning to government posts after training courses at the Bank's Economic Development Institute (EDI) have testified to the status afforded to World Bank development models. A Sudanese official typified the responses to a survey by Ronald Libby (1975b, p. 174), saying that the Bank's '"scientific approach to the problems of development is the best and only way to progress."' EDI participants call the Bank '"the most qualified to assume the general development of a country at any stage of its economic and social growth. Technicians of the World Bank ... are the best the world over"' (Haitian official in Libby, 1975b, p. 174).

Setting the Standards, Defining the Myth of Development

The idea of apolitical development is important to the World Bank for two reasons. One has already been raised: interventions in national economies can be justified if development policy is a matter of correct technical decisions. A second role is more complex. By defining the 'development' it is to support, the World Bank has established standards of success in a field where there is no consensus about what constitutes successful development.

Carlsson, Köhlin and Ekbom, in a study of the organizational and political dimensions of economic evaluation, show that an agency's use of economic analysis follows from its 'ultimate, though often unofficial goals' (p. 185). In the Bank, refinements such as social cost benefit analysis are not used, and traditional cost benefit analysis becomes a tool not for learning more about projects' economic impact, but for certifying their value and facilitating the disbursement of funds. This function of economic analysis is essential because the World Bank must operate both as an international financial institution and a development agency.

Its creditors require evidence that investments meet standards of financial viability. This standard, as measured by economic rates of return, has become part of the Bank's definition of development. World Bank publications acknowledge other dimensions: World Development Reports regularly take up issues such as poverty and human resources (1980, 1990), agriculture (1982), population (1984), and the environment (1992).

Recent sociological theories of organizations, however, suggest that the World Bank's working definition, as embodied in the processes by which it carries out its version of development, may be more important than stated definitions. A pattern of actions that conforms to – or succeeds in establishing – socially accepted standards for organizations, can certify 'success' where consensus on concrete measures of success is elusive. Organizational theorists Dimaggio and Powell write: 'Politics and ceremony . . . pervade much modern organizational life' as organizations compete not only for economic fitness, but for social fitness, 'political power and institutional legitimacy' (1983, p. 150).

The pattern of actions involved in World Bank lending reveal an operational definition of 'development.' As acted out in the lending process, development is marked by three characteristics:

1. It can be planned and managed, as evidenced by the project planning and pre-appraisal process.

2. It is 'bankable,' as evidenced by the apparent bottom-line reliance on internal rates of return and cost-benefit ratios in appraising potential investments.
3. It is 'technical,' achieved by adopting 'right' prices, institutions, and technologies.

The World Bank plans and manages development through a standardized project design process, with each project planned in light of a national development plan and needs assessment. The Bank's Operations Evaluation Department (OED) observed planning procedures in the most poverty-oriented, new-style rural development projects of the 1980s. OED (1988, p. 51) calls the standard process 'definitive appraisal', in which project planning involves a single definitive pre-assessment 'with all that this implies with respect to rigidity . . . and perhaps later slavish adherence to questionable objectives and design.' Appraisals consist of a 'short country visit by a team of staff (and often consultants) followed by a lengthy period of drafting and reviews at headquarters. In some cases follow-up visits were made to complete the appraisal, but most of the work was done at headquarters' (OED, 1988, p. 50).

As the development myth expanded to include explicit attention to equity issues and small farmer production, the project design and development apparatus failed to change with it. In OED's view, the problem with a definitive pre-appraisal or 'blueprint' is that it finds itself 'at odds with some of the realities of sustainable rural development.' Legal, technical and other factors make it difficult to change project plans to respond to changing circumstances, so 'to "live with" the appraisal design is the easiest course. The existence of an appraisal report tends to "cement" the original design in place' (OED, 1988, p. 51).

The definitive appraisal is deeply rooted in the World Bank's management and operating style. It is associated with 'the "bankability" notion of development financing,' in which profitability must be demonstrated conclusively before a planned investment is approved. The appraisal report:

> is in effect the product and chief measure of output for both individuals and units at several levels. Thus in operating units . . . the grey cover appraisal report is an objective in itself, second only to Board approval. . . . The appraisal is thereby seen as an endpoint rather than a beginning. Sometimes after the grey cover stage, staff disengage from an operation, and this adds further discontinuity to the process (OED, 1988, p. 51).

Definitive appraisal and the system of planning and incentives in which it is enshrined is fundamentally out of step with 'sustainable development.' Such social and economic change is a long-term process, but 'the incentive system for staff and the prime measures of their performance are based mainly on convenient short-term measures towards the long-term goals – appraisals, Board approvals and [dollar] amounts committed' (OED, 1988, p. 51).

Some observers attribute these rigidities, and the tendency to formalize and depoliticize development, to the need to tread carefully through the geopolitics and ideologies of the Cold War. Technocratic approaches to theory, planning and assessment were necessary, the theory goes, to make the Bank's intervention as inoffensive as possible to a range of ideologies, among borrowers and donors alike. This view offers the hope that in a post-Cold War era, there may be a loosening and opening at the Bank.

But whether they originated as a kind of protective covering from Cold War pressures or from some other dynamics, these characteristics have taken on a life of their own. They depict, to various interest groups, not only the World Bank's political acceptability, but, as organizational sociologist John Meyer writes of organizations in general, its rationality and its command of its field of activity. Ideas, expectations and ideologies are fleshed out in formal structure and visible work patterns that uphold the principle of rationality, a collective normative principle of modern life that is 'a legitimating moral force external to any particular organization.' Meyer's theoretical description fits the World Bank perfectly: 'Organizations . . . are liturgical structures, celebrating wider principles [technical rationality] in part by ignoring many aspects of experiential reality' (Meyer, 1984, pp. 190–2, 197).

The World Bank's apolitical posture, and the planning and assessment approaches that accompany it offer a mode of operation compatible with industrialized country and banking interests; they are a strategy for organizational survival in a highly uncertain field of work; and, it is argued in the next section, they are a source of power and influence in daily operations.

APOLITICAL DEVELOPMENT AND THE WORLD BANK'S INFLUENCE

The World Bank has successfully promoted its notion of development among bilateral agencies, some development professionals and many borrower government officials. The Bank exerts influence through (1) the 'global marketplace of ideas,' (2) advice and lending that encourages changes in national economic policy, and (3) development projects (Ayres, 1983, pp. 19–22). Intellectually, its reputation for technical competence and its international status give it considerable clout. Publications such as the WDR 'attract . . . worldwide attention,' (Lipton, 1987, p. 200), and the Bank has shaped opinion on issues such as the Green Revolution (Stryker, 1979, p. 331), basic needs strategies (Streeten, 1979) and market-based agricultural pricing (Balassa, 1984; World Bank, 1981).

Intellectual Influence: World Bank as Tutor and Model

Richard Stryker (1979, p. 325) outlines the dimensions of this intellectual leadership, calling the World Bank:

> . . . the leading international institution for development financing and for elaborating new development strategies. [Its] influence . . . extends well beyond any quantitative accounting of its operations. Its country reports, evaluating borrowers' economic and policy performances; its expertise in designing and evaluating development projects; its coordinating role in aid consortia and inter-agency activities . . . ; and the efforts of its President to stake out a broad ranging leadership role, . . . not just as a financial body but as the central and most innovative source for elaborating and operationalizing development strategies – all these, above and beyond its financing weight, make the Bank an increasingly formidable international actor.

Stryker's description, which pre-dated the growth of the Bank's policy-formation role in the 1980s, could be made even stronger today. Policy advice, dispensed through loan conditions, training, informal relationships and employment of national staff at the Bank, secures a working influence in key ministries. The Bank's clout in shaping ideas, policies and institutions would of course be vastly diminished without its financial leverage. But the influence it exerts through means other than financial leverage, while not independent, merits more consideration.

First, the borrower-creditor relationship creates an avenue for ongoing influence on institutions and procedures in government. The ability of lenders to shape institutions and practices has been noted at least since the 1970s. A set of actions explicitly or implicitly called for in relations between Bank and borrower, a 'code of conduct' that includes introducing 'appropriate accounting, disbursing and other business practices,' changing or creating institutions and accepting the authority of 'certain economic policies and laws . . .' (Howard, 1977, pp. 2–3). A cooperative relationship grows out of a loan, 'which establishes a continuing . . . relationship whereby the [lender] can affect . . .the policies of the [borrower] . . .' (Fatouros, 1977, p. 30; see also Libby, 1975).

Through positive working relations, the prestige attached to close contact with Bank personnel, and training programs for borrower government officials, relationships are built that integrate a cadre of state personnel into an international network of financial, economic and other technical experts. British economist Michael Hodd (1987, p. 342) citing Keynes, argues that:

> the power of vested interests [is] vastly exaggerated compared with the gradual encroachment of ideas. For . . . African countries, the prevailing [economic] orthodoxy may have originated with the defunct economists and academic scribblers who developed neo-classical theory. But the more immediate influence is likely to be an African technocrat in continual close contact with the research departments of the IMF and the World Bank.

This ongoing informal contact is reinforced by opportunities for formal training at the World Bank's Economic Development Institute (EDI). The EDI training program helps build a cadre in national ministries sympathetic to the Bank's approach to development and finance (see Chapter 2). The EDI evolves, as its director notes, 'to meet World Bank needs, or needs created by World Bank programming.' At present it focuses on senior policy seminars for 'ministers, deputy ministers and permanent secretaries,' focusing on 'high priority and politically sensitive development issues' (De Lusignan, p. 30), and one- to two-month seminars for mid-level government officials. Some 1,000 government officials participated in training activities in 1983, 3,000 in 1992 (World Bank, *Annual Report*, 1992, p. 91).

Libby's (1975b, p. 198) survey of EDI alumni and a non-EDI control group from the same countries shows the EDI training strategy to be effective. Responses to questionnaires and interviews on subjects such as aid administration, coordination and economic bases for development planning:

> suggest . . . the presence of a World Bank constituency of development administrators in client LDCs. They represent a source of sup-

port for Bank operations . . . , support the autonomy of Bank projects and informally solicit World Bank sponsorship of aid coordination groups for their countries.

Donor Coordination: Managing the Aid Regime

Personal and intellectual influence are reinforced by leverage available to the World Bank through its coordination of donor programs in some countries and its power to certify countries' creditworthiness to commercial lenders (LePrestre, 1982, p. 91). Consultative and Coordinating Groups for national aid programs are a forum for Bank influence on state policies and on bilateral donors (World Bank, *Annual Report*, 1990). The World Bank convened and chaired donor coordinating groups for 26 member countries in 1992 and 1993 (World Bank, *Annual Report*, 1993, p. 20). It promotes coordination with private banks and donor agencies by cofinancing more than half of its new projects (World Bank, *Annual Report*, 1992, p. 91). Cofinancing expands the World Bank's catalytic financial role, but two-thirds of cofinancing in 1992 was by other multilateral and bilateral agencies, suggesting that cofinancing does at least as much to disseminate Bank lending approaches as it does to mobilize resources otherwise not available to finance development. (Another one-quarter of cofinancing in 1992 came from export credit financing.)

Coordinating donor strategies is an important and quiet dimension of the Bank's influence. The World Bank has long asserted more authority than does the OECD, which sometimes plays a similar facilitating role. 'While in theory the Bank's role is "merely" technical and is intended to provide the data on which the donor countries' representatives can base their judgment, in reality it comes very close to making itself judgments and evaluations on behalf of the donors' (Fatouros, 1977, p. 33).

In the 1980s the coordinating role expanded, and its influence increased, through a process that Peter Gibbon (1992, p. 3) describes cogently as part of the rise of a new 'aid regime.' With reduced aid flows and the rise of adjustment lending, aid coordinating bodies took on new roles. They evolved from 'occasional meetings between recipients and bilaterals for purposes of coordinating pledges of new aid with donor lists of new projects,' to serving as 'mechanisms for the . . . review of recipient's [*sic*] progress with policy reforms.'

Bilaterals lacked independent sources of economic data and interpretation, 'the new regime . . . involved a decisive subordination of the bilaterals,' and a more active role for the World Bank as chair. 'Nor was there any real international forum where proposals could be made for revising IMF or World Bank recommendations, even if a will existed to do so' (Gibbon, 1992, p. 3).

In all of these settings the World Bank exerts influence – formal and informal, personal and institutional – that helps to perpetuate its view of development. Conversely, the view that development is a matter of technical expertise, not conflicting values and interests, provides the World Bank with a message that minimizes and legitimizes its intrusiveness.

THE MYTH OF SOVEREIGNTY

The World Bank's myth of sovereignty confronts a real-life problem: The institution does not conduct its affairs in deference to the sovereignty of (some of) its member states. Many borrowing countries are – or perceive themselves to be – in a position of weakness when they meet with the World Bank's representatives. Moreover, the Bank's history of association with the US government challenges the sovereignty myth.

The Appearance of Sovereignty

'Sovereignty' is upheld (and World Bank discretion maintained) by the Bank's formal system of governance, and by important structural and operational features. Four of these features are reviewed here. In each case, formal procedures, which represent the sovereignty myth, are contrasted with the reality of day-to-day operations, in which influence is exerted and the discretion of sovereign members is often limited.

1. *Members' sovereignty in relation to the World Bank is represented by the Governors and Executive Directors (EDs).* Governors delegate authority over day-to-day operations to the EDs, who must also approve each proposed loan. Voting rights, allocated in proportion to countries' capital contributions, set out the formal power relations in the direction of the World Bank. But in reality, it has long been true that 'few, if any, matters of importance are decided by a mere tally of votes.' Management uses 'continuing consultations and informal contacts' to avoid confrontations and reach consensus 'before a loan is

formally submitted for approval' (Fatouros, 1977, p. 114). EDs act only on questions put to them by the President, and expanded lending has eroded EDs' power, making them little more than a rubber stamp in all but exceptional cases (Ascher, 1983, p. 421; LePrestre, 1982, p. 149; McKitterick, 1986, p. 51; Ayres, 1983, p. 66). The Executive Directors have taken more active management roles in several issues in the last two years, asserting themselves on the nature of internal reforms following on the Wapenhans report, and the establishment of an independent appeals panel. But the Bank's formal governance institutions remain, for most members, a forum for acting out rather than asserting sovereignty.

2. *Development policies are publicly promulgated in ways that portray members' sovereignty.* National development plans are ritually presented as government-initiated proposals, even when drafted and negotiated by World Bank staff. The World Bank's role is as creature and servant of the state, which retains control over policy decisions. In Broad's (1988) detailed account of the negotiation of the first Philippine Structural Adjustment Loan in 1980, protracted negotiations and pressure by the World Bank produces a new set of government policy statements, represented solely as the government's initiative. The policy-making role is often subtler and less coercive, but always the ritual of sovereignty is played out. As leader of Consultative Groups for national policy assessment and aid coordination, the Bank works with government officials to prepare development plans. The final product is 'so extensively "processed" by the Bank that they are often perceived by the recipient country's officials as being the Bank's proposals, rather than their own' (Fatouros, 1977, p. 33).

A paper by the Southern Africa division director, proposing measures to restore government initiative and ownership over economic policy, is unusually candid in acknowledging the extent of donor influence. Calling for steps to 'put the government back in the driver's seat,' Director Stephen Denning notes the need for 'creating a space where [g]overnment can think' (1994, pp. 6–7). 'In an environment where donors may be perceived as pressing their own development policies and the services of their own experts on Government, some respite may well be needed for the Government [*sic*] develop its own sectoral policies and priorities' (p. 7). Government officials, Denning notes, 'do not always feel that they are fully in control of donor assisted programs in their ministries,' partly because of 'the major role that donors and donor-funded consultants play in designing, preparing and implementing such assistance' (p. 6).

3. *The procedural fiction that projects are conceived and controlled by borrowing governments is also scrupulously upheld.* Project identification, according to the World Bank staff operating manual, is 'in principle' borrowers' responsibility, but in practice the Bank should be involved (OMS, 2.12, 1978, p. 1). A 1990 paper reminds NGOs that the Bank 'provides financial and technical support to projects, but does not take direct responsibility for their preparation and implementation' (World Bank, 1990d, p. 6).

Other observers, including Swiss economist Bettina Hurni (1980, p. 109), generally friendly to the World Bank, are more candid: '[T]he psychological and material gap between most borrowers and their creditors . . . makes the principle of "borrowers' full responsibility" for projects somewhat theoretical.' Libby (1975b, pp. 115, 120) concludes that 'despite the independent, formal legal status of Bank projects, they are largely conceived, implemented, supervised and protected by the Bank', which retains rights of supervision and review, by contract. A staff economist calls it 'a pity' that, in 1990, Bank staff still develop most projects through most of their stages (Policy Staff no. 7).

The establishment of autonomous government bodies to manage projects was long a favored way to maintain World Bank influence in projects and preserve the projects' autonomy from government ministries. Fatouros notes that autonomous implementing agencies allowed projects to avoid civil service requirements, employ expatriate staff freely, minimize partisan political pressures, and supervise financial accounts and project execution. Lending through intermediary institutions helped make the World Bank 'one of the main external "institution builders" in the Third World' (Hurni, 1980, p. 100). The approach has largely been abandoned (Hellinger, 1987), but recent social service projects in several countries undergoing structural adjustment have created and worked through autonomous agencies.

4. *The Bank assumes a mediating posture.* 'Bank officials . . . see themselves (and their institution) as . . . "in the middle," . . . trying to effect a compromise' between creditor and debtor countries (Ayres, 1983). Political scientist Philippe LePrestre (1982, p. 269) notes that the World Bank 'presents itself as the defender and promoter of Southern interests, appeals for more aid, acts as a go-between, and harnesses its intellectual and financial resources toward alleviating the burden of underdevel-

opment. [It] . . . enjoys, and cultivates, the basic support of its clients.' This mediating posture, however, is a difficult and contradictory one in light of the Bank's role in adjustment and debt management. The Bank is precluded, for example, from advising a client country to repudiate any part of its debt, or to seek to bargain collectively with other debtors for a better 'deal' from creditors. The Bank offers its borrowers debt management arrangements on the creditors' terms, with the promise of continued borrowing as inducement, and no alternatives in sight. The mediating role, then, has built-in limitations. The Bank is positioned in the middle. But while it speaks for the creditors as a group, it cooperates in a strategy to prevent common action by groups of debtors.

The sovereignty myth is rooted in reality: governments do own the World Bank. They repay or guarantee loans, and their representatives approve loans and policy changes. Technically, a country can limit the World Bank's influence by forgoing credit or by honoring agreements selectively. But sovereignty is sharply limited in everyday operations. The emblems of sovereignty in the Bank's structure and procedure discussed above symbolize sovereignty even as they permit the Bank to exercise influence and a measure of autonomy.

The World Bank's relative autonomy of action is widely recognized, although there is not agreement on where the discretion is lodged within the organization. Nathaniel McKitterick (1986, p. 45) believes that the 'President of the World Bank has always been one of the independent leaders in international life; the Bank runs the way he wants it to.'

Much discretion, however, rests with the staff that make up a 'highly qualified technostructure' (Hurni, 1980, pp. 81–2). Hurni notes that when projects are presented to the Board, 'the Executive Directors show great confidence in the ability of the technostructure. . . .the technostructure provides the intellectual and technical inputs necessary . . . and the decision-making process is designed to support it in an objective, nondiscriminatory way' (1980, pp. 81–2). Sovereignty of most members with respect to the World Bank, then, is limited by the weak accountability of staff to the Board and to the nations they represent.

The pressure of debt, reduced capital flows and the lack of organized alternatives make agreement to World Bank policy conditions almost unavoidable for most borrowers. Borrowers' formal control over policy and over project development in reality permits World Bank influence through Consultative Groups and its supervisory role in project implementation. The Bank's apolitical public image, a sign of borrowers' sovereignty, in reality facilitates the exercise of influence over development policy.

Sovereignty and policy-based lending

The myth of an apolitical World Bank serving its sovereign member states was strained when explicitly policy-based lending was initiated in 1980. Structural adjustment loans afforded the Bank a more prominent position in shaping national economic policies that are highly politicized in many countries.

To be sure, the Bank had long exercised influence over policy. As reported by its retired agriculture chief:

Senior Bank officials have ready access to the decision-makers in nearly all countries. . . . [E]conomists and technical staff (backed by a vast information system) provide the material for any ensuing 'dialogues' with governments. . . . [I]ts growing ability to conduct informal dialogues about policy, strategy, programs and projects and to promise financial support for projects that fit into mutually agreed priorities has made the Bank unique (Yudelman, 1985, p. 11).

But quiet 'development diplomacy' became more public and overt with the advent of policy-based lending. Former World Bank economist Elliot Berg and Alan Batchelder argue that structural adjustment loans are 'the price to get the Bank to the "high policy table" in the recipient countries' (quoted in Cypher, 1989a, p. 60). Paul Mosley (1987, p. 6) argues that the Bank offers SALs and promises economic results to persuade governments . . . 'to buy out some of the restrictive practices by which they . . . hold the state together,' typically protective tariffs, exchange rates, quotas and the like, for national industry; patronage and civil service jobs for the middle class; price controls on food and other commodities for consumers; and state marketing systems for commercial agriculture.

Adjustment Lending: The Politics of Conditionality and Implementation

Negotiating and implementing SALs brought the World Bank to a new level of national economic policy making, with two implications for the organization. First, its political profile rises as it is identified with macro policy regimes previously associated principally with the IMF.

Second, supervising policy implementation presents new enforcement challenges to project staff and to management. Because adjustment addresses the structure of production and micro-economic policy, it threatens some groups' interests more fundamentally, and its long duration allows opponents time to organize in opposition (Joan Nelson, 1989, p. 110).

Despite its aversion to public participation in 'political' activity, the World Bank has found it necessary to attend to the volatile political issues that arise in the process of adjustment. The Bank has long enjoyed an image as more benign, less coercive and more generous than the IMF (Broad, 1988; Cypher, 1989b). It was, before the advent of adjustment lending, primarily known as a source of project finance, rather than designer and monitor of economic reform programs.

The political difficulties adjustment schemes confront are reflected in the remarkably weak implementation record of World Bank adjustment loan conditions over the first eight years of adjustment lending. For 51 SALs and 15 Sectoral Adjustment Loans (SECAL) reviewed in the World Bank's 1988 report, an estimated 60 per cent of all conditions were 'fully implemented during the loan disbursement period.' Conditions dealing with energy policy were most likely to be fully implemented, export finance and tax reforms least (Country Economic Department, 1988, pp. 7, 60). The review reports an 80 per cent rate when 'partial implementation' is included, and tries in other ways to present the situation in the best light, but many of the 141 pages are devoted to explaining to the Executive Directors why implementation has been so poor. Mosley's (1987) findings corroborate the Bank's: 60 per cent of conditions have been implemented, in 37 SALs in 21 countries. Mosley, Harrigan and Toye (1991) find similarly weak implementation (54 per cent) in a review supported by case studies (p. 136).

Why is the implementation record of loan conditions so poor? One might expect this powerful representative of international finance to impose its will more effectively on borrowing countries in dire economic straits. In some cases, notably the 1981 SAL to the Philippines, national economic policy and administration has been successfully reworked. But gaps in implementation elsewhere call for explanation.

The implementation and enforcement of SALs is limited by contradictions in the World Bank's bargaining position that render it unable or unwilling to use sanctions to enforce SAL conditions. The Bank has sanctions available to ensure implementation even of politically painful conditions: payment is in tranches, and further payments or new loans may be conditioned on compliance (Development Committee,

1990a, p. 18). SALs have also gained some of the status of IMF Extended Financing Facility agreements, certifying countries' creditworthiness to commercial lenders.

But for a variety of reasons, the World Bank may prefer to give a borrower the benefit of the doubt rather than invoking sanctions for non-compliance. These reasons include the need to move money, geopolitical interests of member states, the desire to cultivate borrower countries' political support, and management's interest in legitimating policy-based lending with their own staff, with industrial country governments and with the financial community. These are among the factors that impede vigorous enforcement of SAL provisions, and that define some of the limits.

Mosley, Harrigan and Toye's case studies of SAP negotiation and implementation confirm some of this. For instance, not only is the Bank reluctant to use non-lending as a sanction for poor implementation, but borrowers wishing to avoid or evade conditionality are 'aware of . . . the Bank's "disbursement dilemma . . ."' (p. 300).

Winning technocratic hearts and minds?

Mosley (1987) speculates that full compliance in most countries is of secondary importance to the World Bank. The long-term impact on the staff of Planning and Finance Ministries, he suggests, may be as important as short-term compliance with specific measures. The Philippine experience supports this hypothesis. By cultivating technocrats within the Philippine state who were sympathetic with its economic program, the Bank won implementation in the 1980s of a program of economic change that had eluded the IMF throughout the 1970s. The national bureaucracy was 'seeded' with a corps of 'young, graduate-educated technocrats,' Western trained, who became 'the World Bank's counterparts on the inside' during negotiation and implementation of the SAL (Broad, 1988, p. 61, 73).

Training at the Economic Development Institute (EDI) has a part in this process. EDI graduates returning to the Philippines can expect a promotion, and there is great demand to be sent, as 'bureaucrats who cannot claim the status of "technocrat" increasingly face job insecurity' (World Bank memo quoted in Broad, 1988, p. 102). The EDI offers the World Bank a source of influence more subtle than financial leverage. In adjustment lending as in other programming, influence among professionals and movement between the Bank and governments is a driving force in shaping administration and economic policy. This trend entails conformity of staffing, policy and sometimes structure of key planning bodies in borrowing countries to that of the Bank. In some countries, adjustment lending allows the Bank to reinforce the objectives of governments already committed to adjustment programs. In others the financial leverage afforded by policy-based loans increases the Bank's influence, especially in the context of indebtedness and decreased capital flows from other sources. And in many countries, the process of negotiations and the opportunities they present for training, influence and persuasion help the Bank build an internal constituency for national policies consistent with its development program. Throughout the process of negotiating and implementing SAL agreements, the doctrine and trappings of sovereignty keep the Bank formally in a subordinate and apolitical role.

The Bank as Governance Institution

This has remained true even as the Bank's negotiation, implementation and supervision of adjustment plans has become increasingly intrusive. Legal scholar Jonathan Cahn (1993) documents the extent of administrative, regulatory and legislative changes required by sectoral and structural adjustment loan agreements. Increasingly detailed conditions have made the Bank 'a governance institution, exercising power through its financial leverage to legislate entire legal regimens and even to alter the constitutional structure of borrowing nations' (p. 160).

Like political theorist Robert Cox, who describes an 'internationalization of the state' through its expanding accountability to the Bretton Woods institutions (1987), Cahn sees the effective sovereignty of nations severely compromised. Less powerful states, he argues, become 'satellites in a new empire, extensions of much broader policy dictates established with only slight reference to territorial boundaries.' The Bank's conditions 'blur the distinction between international and domestic, public and private law, making World Bank influence pervasive at all levels of the law's domain' (p. 187).

Sovereignty and NGOs

While deploying resources to influence government policies and institutions and to privatize whole sectors of state activity, the World Bank takes a gingerly approach to NGOs. From the earliest official statements on NGOs, guidance to staff has been dotted with cautionary references to sovereignty, and with lists of 'weaknesses and disadvantages'

(Ernest Stern, Senior Vice President for Operations, memo to Operational Vice Presidents 27 March 1981). In recent documents staff are repeatedly instructed to safeguard 'the privileged relationship with governments;' they are reminded that 'all overtures to NGOs are with the consent of governments,' and that activities must conform to 'government's policies towards NGOs' (SPR, 1989, p. 3; Qureshi, 1988; Salmen and Eaves, 1989, p. 65; OD 14.70, paragraphs, 1, 7(c), 8 and 10). The earlier Operational Manual Statement (OMS) was revised in 1989 to stress 'the need to proceed in conformity with the relevant governments' (Ducksoo Lee, memo to Vice President for Operations, Moeen Qureshi, 1989). Dropped was the suggestion that labor unions be consulted when a project threatened to close down a factory (Draft OMS, 15 January 1988, p. 7).

Subordinating NGOs' political role to service delivery

NGOs are approached cautiously because their values-oriented and sometimes politicized nature threatens the apolitical expertise on which the World Bank's fundamental myths are based. Many NGOs see development as a matter of values and democracy, of siding with the poor and organizing around political and social issues (Brown and Korten, 1989). Implicitly, through their 'grassroots' ethos, and sometimes explicitly in their advocacy work, NGOs propose accountability to affected groups and communities as an alternative or a complement to sovereignty as the informing principle for World Bank relations to borrowing countries.

This potential as a vehicle for accountability in relations with the World Bank is recognized frequently by NGO leaders (DeGraaf, 1987; Hellinger, 1987; Brodhead, 1989; BRAC, 1989), and some Bank staff whom I interviewed (Policy staff no.3; LAC staff no.2). This dimension of the NGOs' work, rather than the reputation for economic efficiency as service deliverers, is considered of paramount importance by many NGOs. This political role is presented emphatically in one discussion paper written for Bank staff as the key distinctive to be nurtured and appreciated in NGOs (Brown and Korten, 1989), and its importance is recognized in official World Bank statements (Qureshi, 1988; World Bank, 1990d; Strategic Planning and Review, 1989).

But in projects and operations involving NGOs, there is little evidence that staff consider the representative – as opposed to the service-delivery – role. The caution with which staff have approached NGOs is reflected both in the roles assigned to NGOs in Bank-financed projects, and in the kinds of NGOs staff choose to associate with.

The subordinate role assigned to NGOs was typified in the late 1970s and early 1980s by the prominence, especially in Africa, of contractor-style projects in which NGOs were contracted to build roads and schools or supervise railway construction. Bank reports on NGO collaboration argue that in the late 1980s the NGO role grew to be much more substantial. But many examples of projects with minimal, subordinate roles for NGOs may be found in the last few years. Bank reports describe the Kwango-Kwilu technical assistance project in Zaire (1978) as involving NGOs and firms in a mixed capital company created to coordinate and promote rural development efforts. The company, CODAIK, was found by the Project Completion Review (PCR) to be dominated by government representatives, and the role of private sector representatives was, in the end, minimal (PCR, p. 3).

Many other recent projects assign NGOs a minimal role. In the Guinea Education Sector Adjustment Credit, approved in 1990, NGO involvement consists of an ongoing program of school construction by French volunteers. In Honduras, the Agricultural Credit IV project (1988) extends a small line of credit to rural credit unions, which are expected to 'explain the system' to newly formed 'groups of farmers.' In Argentina, the First Housing Sector Project (1988) uses newly formed housing cooperatives as a way to cope with extremely long lines awaiting government housing assistance. Applicants registering together as housing cooperatives receive some priority when assigned places on the waiting list.

Not only are NGOs subordinated to government programs in these project roles, the choice of NGOs for collaboration is also constrained by Bank staff's cautious approach. The concerns encountered in interviews with operational staff were summed up by the concern of an agriculture specialist that NGOs may be 'religiously or politically tainted' (Policy staff no. 5). A senior Africa economist involved in NGO projects warned colleagues in a training session to beware of NGOs with a 'Point of View,' driven by a political agenda or strong value commitment (6 October 1989). NGOs' uneasy relations with some governments is a concern expressed repeatedly in interviews and staff memos (Hans Wyss memo to Moeen Qureshi, 1988; Asia staff no. 3; Policy staff no. 3).

Not only their presumed politics but also NGOs' contrast with familiar, interest- and profit-driven behavior are of concern to some staff economists. An economist working in South Asia worried that NGOs that receive outside support will never 'become entrepreneurial' and self-supporting (Asia staff no. 3). An economist in private sector operations told me he prefers to work with firms because 'we understand firms, they are guided by profits. NGOs are less predictable' (Policy staff no. 7). When NGO members of the NGO-World Bank Committee argued in 1989 for loan conditions to promote participation and 'democracy' in development planning, World Bank staff gave a spirited defense of apolitical lending and respect for diverse political forms (personal observation, NGO-World Bank Committee, Bangkok, 1989).

NGOs and internationalized advocacy campaigns

Staff are particularly uncomfortable with 'advocacy NGOs,' which have in some cases linked Southern and Northern organizations in a network that presses the multilateral development banks (MDB) on issues where they are vulnerable to criticism. A World Bank (1990, p. 4) pamphlet on NGO relations credits environmental NGOs with helping to 'sensitize public opinion and development practitioners, including the Bank,' and indigenous and international NGOs together with focusing 'the attention of the Bank and its member governments to the environmental and social costs of some large-scale projects.' Controversy and conflict between the Bank and NGOs, especially in environmental issues, is reported elsewhere in similarly antiseptic language (World Bank, *Annual Report*, 1987, p. 62; World Bank, *Annual Report*, 1989, p. 95; Strategic Planning and Review, 1990, pp. 9–10).

But staff's opinions of advocacy NGOs and the international networks through which they work are generally less friendly. Although interaction with such cause-oriented groups or networks of international and local NGOs occurs only in a small minority of the World Bank's NGO-related projects, 'advocacy NGOs' are frequently the first subject raised in conversations with operational staff. Some US-based NGOs in particular are accused of practicing an isolated, confrontational style of politics (Policy staff no. 3). An Asia staff economist calls advocacy by policy NGOs 'out of control, out of hand, run amok,' and suggests that advocacy groups are 'unprofessional, not knowledgeable' (Asia staff no. 4). Staff also challenge policy NGOs' knowledge of Bank operations, complaining some of their vocal critics 'don't do their homework' and rely on out-of-date images of World Bank atrocities (LAC staff no. 2; Africa staff no. 2).

Networks of NGOs that extend advocacy on national policy issues beyond national borders raise the political dimension of working with NGOs in a particularly sensitive way. The Sardar Sarovar Dam Project and Singrauli Thermal Energy Project in India, for example, have provoked protest from local groups and national environmental organizations that captured the attention of the Environmental Defense Fund in the United States and other environmental NGOs based in the industrial countries. Their campaigns, through public protests in India, correspondence and meetings with World Bank officials, public information efforts in the United States and Europe and lobbying of donor parliaments, have drawn considerable attention to domestic Indian policies and the World Bank loans that support them (Patkar, 1989; Udall, 1989).

The success of such internationalized campaigns in India, Indonesia, Brazil, the Philippines and elsewhere, has been mixed. Some projects have been modified, and some gains have been made in World Bank policies toward the environment and native peoples' rights, and in staffing for these sensitive areas. The Sardar Sarovar project has become the central test case, with many NGOs charging that the Bank not only failed to implement its own policies for resettlement of displaced persons, but then refused to respond to many of the findings and recommendations of an unprecedented independent review that the Bank itself established. Some made the World Bank's performance in this case grounds for a campaign to reduce government appropriations to IDA-10 (see Chapter 3).

Regardless of the immediate success of the campaigns, however, environmentalists such as Stephan Schwartzman of the Environmental Defense Fund feel that the international networks of information and political activity they have created are lasting achievements (interview, 9 May 1990). In the case of local organizations in the Brazilian Amazon, while influence on the local level has been limited, 'the alliances made . . . have gained an unprecedented voice and influence for Amazonian organizations internationally' (Schwartzman, 1989).

Generally, its close ties to the state and its unwillingness or inability to implement projects through non-government groups that can mobilize participation in projects, distribute benefits equitably and promote lasting and replicable social change render the World Bank unable to assist 'development' as many NGOs see it (Hellinger, 1988; Annis, 1987). But the Bank has not hesitated to embrace and involve NGOs in the implementation of compensatory projects to buffer the political and social effects of Bank-supported structural adjustment plans.

NGOs in Compensatory Projects

The challenge to political stability that sometimes accompanies stabilization and adjustment regimes is also a challenge to the World Bank's sovereignty myth and its apolitical image. Food price and fuel price increases, public sector layoffs and reduced imports have provoked demonstrations and resistance in so many countries under IMF stabilization that the term 'IMF riots' has been coined to describe the phenomenon (Cypher, 1989b).

The World Bank has not adopted its sister organization's stance. Rather than leaving it to cooperating governments to manage social dislocations or political resistance, the Bank has worked with several governments to develop plans to limit the social and political costs of adjustment. These increase the plans' likelihood of success and buoy the World Bank's image as the 'kinder, gentler' lender.

NGOs are a widely-discussed option in designing such plans (Demery and Addison, 1987; Zuckerman, 1989; Joan Nelson, 1989; Ribe, Carvalho, Liebenthal, Nicholas and Zuckerman, 1990). NGOs are not always involved: compensatory plans in Chile, Costa Rica, South Korea, Senegal and elsewhere have entailed little NGO action, as government programs with donor assistance blunt the effects of unemployment, food price increases and currency devaluations (Zuckerman, 1989). Nor are programs financing compensatory services the only measure available to the Bank and borrowing governments. Increased World Bank investment has also accompanied some countries' adjustment programs. Ghana's sustained adjustment program, for instance, helped make it the largest recipient of IDA funds in sub-Saharan Africa, and the third largest in the world, behind only China and India.

But compensatory programs became a more prominent adjunct to adjustment strategies in the late 1980s. In the years 1988–92, the World Bank approved at least 37 new compensatory plans involving NGOs. The Bank cited no project before 1988 where NGO involvement was explicitly 'adjustment-related', but 42 such projects are reported in the years 1988–93.

The spate of new NGO compensatory arrangements seems to have two sources in the World Bank: the reported success of the Bolivian Emergency Social Fund (ESF) and the campaign of research and publication in the Bank's Africa division around the Social Dimensions of Adjustment (SDA). The Bolivian ESF has attracted considerable attention within the Bank. A September 1989 colloquium on the Bolivian experience was well-attended by Latin America region staff, and many staff in training sessions during the following month indicated their region's or country office's interest in similar plans.

Publications of the SDA project highlighted the potential role for NGOs in softening SALs' regressive distributional impact (Serageldin, 1989; Alderman, 1990), and SDA manager Ismail Serageldin, who also directed West Africa operations, reportedly encouraged work with NGOs in his region. Ghana's Program of Action to Mitigate the Social Costs of Adjustment (PAMSCAD), an early example of compensatory measures in Africa, engaged NGO participation, but not without difficulty. The SDA itself has since been absorbed into a technical unit on poverty, and its research program reduced in scope.

Some NGOs have hesitated to get involved in Bank-financed adjustment programs, and the NGO Working Group on the World Bank has suggested conditions for NGO participation in such schemes (NGO Working Group on the World Bank, draft, 1989). But NGOs present no recognizable, unified position on this or almost any other issue, and many have accepted opportunities to use government funds to meet pressing needs that are hoped to be short-term. Bolivia's Emergency Social Fund (ESF), financed by the World Bank and other donors and administered by a semi-autonomous government agency created for the purpose, financed projects proposed and initiated by NGOs and by local governments and firms. Job creation was the principal aim of the ESF and of the Social Investment Fund that has succeeded it.

NGOs play a more prominent role in more recent special compensatory funds in Chad and Guinea. Chad's 'Social Development Action Project,' approved for World Bank finance in 1990, aims to stimulate employment generation through training for unemployed people; to improve poor people's health and living conditions; and to reinforce the government's institutional capacity to design and monitor programs to improve social conditions' (World Bank Project Summary). Volunteers in Technical Assistance (VITA) agreed to provide management training to government officials and manage a micro-credit program. A French NGO (Association Française des Volontaires de Progrès) was to train officials in the Ministry of Labor and Employment. The role of local NGOs in creating and proposing subprojects was not specified.

Guinea's 'Socio-Economic Development Project' was also approved in 1990. The IDA credit, available to NGOs for projects, is to complement an existing government program for local government initiatives. About one-half of the $11.9 million credit finances strengthening the Social Policy Division in the Ministry of Planning. The other half – nearly $6 million – is to be allocated for NGO projects, 'because the

Government did not yet have either the data or the capacity to deal with the various social problems' (World Bank Project Summary). All sub-projects are subject to IDA and government approval. NGO participation in adjustment-related projects has been defined here as narrowly as possible. In some countries other projects are surely related, more or less directly, to adjustment programs. But in most countries the location, timing or sector of NGO projects suggest no particular relation to the SAL. A 1986 Bank-NGO project in Guinea funds livestock improvements, related only in the broadest sense to the country's adjustment program (Guinea Livestock Rehabilitation Project; from World Bank project summary). In other cases the link to adjustment is clearer: while livestock improvement in Guinea had no immediate relation to the adjustment program, projects in health and urban enterprises certainly do (Health Services Project, 1987; Conakry Urban Development Supplemental Finance Project, revised in 1986).

More broadly still, NGO participation in any World Bank-financed operation is relevant to the adoption of adjustment lending in the 1980s. NGOs are part of the 'human face' that the Bank sought to project as it broadened its policy-based lending and defended its environmental record and reputation.

The World Bank's low political profile and carefully cultivated apolitical identity has been called into question by policy-based lending. By raising the level of the Bank's political engagement, adjustment lending has created an opening for NGO involvement, but it is an opening largely defined by the Bank's needs as it seeks to help governments implement adjustment plans.

DEFENDING ADJUSTMENT AND MANAGING INFORMATION: STRAINING THE SOVEREIGNTY MYTH

Discussions between the World Bank and various groupings of NGOs have covered a wide range of topics, from energy, water and forestry policies to adjustment, popular participation and information policy. The Bank's responses to NGOs on two of these – adjustment and information policy – highlight the contradictions between its myths and the reality of its policy and influence.

Unequal Adjustment, Leverage and Sovereignty

NGOs have criticized World Bank adjustment policy for unfairly placing the entire burden of global adjustment on the poor countries who can afford it least; and for promoting strategies that flood the market with export goods as countries desperately try to export and trade their way out of debt.

First, it has been argued that the Bank has helped coordinate a global adjustment regime that has placed all of the burden and hardship of change on the poor, debtor countries. The *NGO Position Paper on the World Bank* (1989), and earlier discussion papers (Clark, 1987; Brodhead, 1989) call on the World Bank to press for adjustment by all nations to deal with problems that are global in scope. Others have noted this 'unbalanced adjustment' as well (Overseas Development Institute, 1986; Griesgraber 1994).

Second, some have argued that the Bank acts in bad faith when it encourages non-traditional export strategies, sometimes focused on producing and marketing the same products, in many highly indebted countries. Two NGO members complained vehemently in the 1989 NGO-World Bank Committee meeting that Bank-supported export promotion policies were moving numerous nations into non-traditional export markets when the market could not absorb their combined production at favorable prices.

World Bank representatives at the meetings responded with three lines of argument; two directed to the 'unequal adjustment' argument; one to the critique of non-traditional export strategies. First, they pointed out that the Bank has indeed called upon the United States to reduce its budget deficits, and upon other industrialized countries to resist protectionist pressures and adopt other measures in keeping with the World Bank's vision of an expanding global economy. Speeches by (then) President Conable were cited, as was a World Bank/IMF Development Committee publication on the subject (Development Committee, 1989; see also Raison, 1986).

NGO discussants, however, argued that these calls for sensitivity to global needs in industrial-country economic policy making were no more than gentle sermons, while adjustment in the poor countries was planned and promoted by Bank staff and backed by the financial leverage of project and policy-based loans.

One World Bank representative then advanced a second line of argument: The Bank cannot be expected, he explained, to criticize too sharply the countries that guarantee or provide the lion's share of its funding. 'These are our bosses,' he noted, and there are limits to what the Bank can do.

The third theme advanced by the Bank representatives was addressed to the critique of export-oriented strategies as flooding limited markets by encouraging similar strategies among many countries aspiring to join the ranks of the 'newly industrialized countries' (NICs). The World Bank's job, one representative argued, is to promote efficiency. If the Bank identifies the strategy that best exploits a country's comparative advantage, the best it can do is help that country to be as efficient as possible in carrying out that strategy and producing those goods and services. If more than one country pursues the same strategy, the benefits will depend on how efficiently each carries it out.

These three responses – present in many Bank statements and discussions – lay bare contradictions embedded in the sovereignty and development myths. Sovereignty, it becomes clear, is mediated and limited by power relations. Adjustment is a joint responsibility of industrialized and underdeveloped countries in theory, but in practice the Bank is powerless to implement the portions of its advice that apply to national economic policies in the North. Left with the option of one-sided adjustment or no adjustment at all, the Bank promotes an adjustment strategy in the South that cannot succeed in the absence of cooperative policies in the industrialized world.

The apolitical, strictly technical nature of World Bank advice is further eroded by the problems of over-used non-traditional export strategies. The Bank's debating strategy is to bring this discussion back to the national level: as advisor and financier, the Bank helps each country implement a plan as efficiently as possible. The size of each market and room for expanded supply may be examined and debated. But the logic of the policy is to encourage each country to produce a product, or to create the environment for international corporations to produce the product within its borders, more efficiently and cheaply than others. This is the nature of competition in the international market, but when competitors' strategies are all guided by a single advisor, the result is a buyers' market where sellers have been directed by non-market forces toward strategies that depress prices.

Privileged Information, Sovereignty and NGOs

NGOs have criticized the World Bank for restricting access to information about projects under consideration. Without early access to project papers as new investment ideas are first considered, NGOs argue, local organizations and communities cannot contribute to the project's development, or react to projects they wish to change or oppose. NGOs in the NGO-World Bank Committee made this demand fundamental to the development of cooperative relations with the Bank, and others, especially US-based environmental NGOs, have pressed the case vigorously. Trust and accountability are impossible, it is argued, when project ideas were kept secret until planning is so far advanced that little influence was possible for NGOs or community groups (NGO-World Bank Committee, 1987 Meeting).

World Bank representatives long responded that the sovereign rights of its member countries required that information remain confidential, held only by government officials and the Bank. The policy implied that the Bank is accountable to citizens solely through their national government. Some NGOs persisted, demanding a more open information policy as a foundation for cooperation, and, in 1987 the Bank agreed to open a considerable amount of project documentation to NGOs. Monthly Operational Statements, listing projects under development and describing briefly any potential for NGO involvement, are available to any NGO. In addition, a 'List of World Bank-Financed Projects with Potential for NGO Involvement' is sent periodically to an extensive mailing list of NGOs in the North and in the South. NGOs are encouraged to review the list and contact World Bank staff about projects in which they are might want to participate.

But most actual project documents remained restricted. NGOs based in Washington developed informal access to documents through sympathetic staff members and Executive Directors who encourage review and comment on proposals. They also mounted a campaign for greater disclosure, often with support from the US government, whose own freedom of information policies make it more sympathetic than some other members.

In 1992, under threat of IDA funds being withheld by a key committee of the US Congress, the Bank's Board agreed to a new information disclosure policy. While the new policy expands the list of documents that are to be routinely available, and makes them available both in Washington and in each Bank office, even this measure falls short of the principle, set forth in the Bank's Operational Directive on the subject, that presumes information to be public in the absence of compelling reason to keep it private.

The most critical shortcoming in the new policy is the substitution of a new summary for public information, called a Project Information Document (PID), for several actual project documents. The working documents remain restricted, and the public gains access to a presentation drafted specifically for public consumption. PIDs, furthermore, are not prepared until the project's development is fairly advanced, rendering them useless to NGOs wishing to be involved in design and pre-design stages.

Despite the limitations, which NGOs continue to attack, these developments in information policy offer a new perspective on the doctrine of the primacy of Bank relations with governments, and on how this 'sovereignty' doctrine is used. First, under pressure, the Bank found a way to modify its governments-only policy. By disseminating some information about projects still under discussion with governments, the Bank acknowledged a legitimate role for NGO comment, and demonstrated that there is room for change in its interpretation of its members' sovereign rights.

Second, the hesitancy with which the Bank approached information-sharing with non-for-profit organizations contrasts with its openness toward private banks and firms that might be interested in a project as potential investors or as bidders to provide services. For such commercial concerns the Bank has long provided information on projects under development, as well as manuals on how to bid on World Bank-financed projects (summarized in World Bank, n.d., *Guide to International Business Opportunities*). The privileged information the Bank hesitated to provide to NGOs was readily available to for-profit firms who wished to invest in projects. (Even the newly-created public information facility was used far more frequently by for-profit companies than by NGOs in its first year.)

Third, the difficulty of obtaining full information, both descriptive and evaluative, extends to the Bank's Board. Proposals for special evaluative units reporting to the Board were made by Executive Directors during the first half of 1993, as the Board seeks to improve the reliability and independence of its own information base.

A final point of contention over information relates to the role of Northern-based NGOs as recipients and users of project and policy planning documents. Bank staff distinguish between making information available to persons likely to be affected by a project, and to Northern-based NGOs (Beckmann, quoted in Stokes, 1988; Policy staff 2; representatives at the 1989 NGO-World Bank Committee meeting). In so doing they echo the reluctance of some governments to have information in the hands of foreign-based NGOs who are critical of their environmental and social policies.

But advocacy NGOs often work most effectively in networks that move information quickly between Washington, the capitals and remote rural areas of the South, and coordinate action based on the information. Affected persons do not frequent resident representatives' offices in their capitals, much less Bank headquarters, and Northern NGOs claim a legitimate role as conduit of information. The Bank remains reluctant to undermine the confidentiality of its relations with borrowing governments by handing documents to NGOs. In information policy as in other matters, the sovereignty myth remains a constraint on the extent of interaction with NGOs.

CONCLUSIONS

The myths of development and sovereignty play three important roles in the World Bank's organizational life. They represent a basis for World Bank activity by defining its goal in terms the Bank is able to meet. Second, by shaping widely-held standards of development, the myths articulate a standard of performance, a way to certify that the Bank is achieving adequate results. Finally, while apparently defining the limits of the World Bank's power and domain by subordinating it to governments and assigning it an 'apolitical' mandate, the myths open avenues of influence and facilitate the exercise of political power.

Growth-oriented lending, policy advice, and technical assistance on project implementation are the primary services the World Bank has to offer. These serve well if 'development' is defined as a function of growth and of objectively 'correct' policies, institutions, prices and technologies. By rendering these choices as engineering, economics and technological problems, the myth of development allows the Bank to promote and finance changes of great political import.

The primacy of state sovereignty is being challenged, both at the World Bank and in the wider world. Advocates within and outside the Bank have made progress in bringing human rights, governance, military spending and other issues into the rhetoric of the Bank. But the myth that its economic advice is apolitical continues to be a significant factor, facilitating the Bank's aggressive intervention in all matters of economic planning and policy, contributing to the Bank's limited vision of the policy options and frustrating NGOs and others in society who require openness and accountability in policy making.

The importance of these myths to World Bank operations means that changes which threaten them, including operational and policy cooperation with NGOs, will be approached with caution. Despite progress in the dialogue and operational collaboration, experience to date confirms the expectation that NGO roles will be shaped to conform to the myths of development and sovereignty.

7 Organizational Culture and Participation in Development

The preceding two chapters review organizational barriers to change – the aversion to uncertainty, the disbursement imperative and the powerful myths of apolitical development – and outline their relations to external interests and pressures that shape World Bank policy. A third set of constraining factors, which together form an organizational culture, are the subject of this chapter. The Bank's organizational culture sharply limits popular participation and NGO involvement in its operations, and constrains the organization's ability to learn from experience. The organizational culture integrates and reinforces elements of the mandate and myths discussed in the previous chapters.

'Organizational culture' is made up of values, ideologies, practices, myths and ceremonies that give an organization internal identity and coherence. Each organizational culture features – and depends upon – a systematic selection and filtering of the information that makes up the organization's picture of its world, and that provides the basis for decision-making. The World Bank's culture is hierarchical and grounded in division of labor, technical expertise and comparative advantage. The culture is pervasive and dominant, but there are small, sometimes vigorous 'undergrounds' working against the grain of the culture. NGO representatives tend to meet the members of these minority groups, often as the dissenters seek external allies. Some of their efforts are documented in this chapter.

Still, the organizational culture dominates and structures thinking and action at the Bank: it filters information thoroughly, limiting the capacity to learn and to practice 'participatory' development. The organizational culture, central to the Bank's operations, contrasts with its publicly espoused image and contradicts and limits efforts and claims to increase the quality and influence of NGO participation in its programs.

The argument is analogous to that of the previous two chapters: a hierarchical and technocratic organizational culture that dominates attitudes and procedures at the World Bank renders the Bank's policies almost impervious to critique – external or internal – that does not begin from accepted organizational and theoretical premises. Despite the efforts and intentions of individuals, this organizational culture makes meaningful growth of NGO influence, and progress on the broad NGO agenda, extremely difficult. The information bias of the culture dominates planning, implementation and evaluation of policies, as this chapter observes in the cases of rural development lending, structural adjustment lending and the ongoing dialogue with NGOs. It promotes intellectual insularity and an emphasis on control of the implementation of investments, and limits the potential for organizational learning.

ORGANIZATIONAL CULTURE

Organizational culture is the internal counterpart of the myths of institutional theory. Conforming to pervasive myths allows an organization to legitimate itself in the view of the larger society. Organizational culture refers to values, ideologies, practices, myths and ceremonies within an organization that give it meaning, identity and coherence internally.

A literature on organizational culture, often strongly applied, proliferated in the 1980s. Peters and Waterman (1982) reflects this applied bent most strongly, but the theme of culture as managers' secret weapon also appears in Schein (1985), and in Deal and Kennedy (1982). 'Culture' has also been used loosely within the Bank, since the 1992 Wapenhans report, to describe the overemphasis on disbursements and project preparation ('approval culture') that Wapenhans criticizes. With its popularity has come ambiguity about the meaning of 'culture.' I distinguish two dimensions of organizational culture.

In its most widely used sense, organizational culture portrays for individuals the organization's basic values, the kinds of people who are most respected in the organization, the kinds of information that are taken seriously in decision-making, and the routes by which one may rise in the organization. Deal and Kennedy (1982, p. 15) treat organizational culture as embracing values that define success for employees, heroes who act out these values; rites, rituals and ceremonies that 'show employees the kind of behavior that is expected of them;' and a cultural network that transmits the culture among participants. This is roughly the meaning of 'culture' in the Bank's current usage.

A second approach to organizational culture highlights systematic biases in how organizations search out and select information. All organizations – firms, voluntary associations and agencies – selectively convert raw data from their environment into information on which decisions and actions are based. Michael Thompson and Aaron Wildavsky (1986) argue that organizational cultures are characterized and sustained by distinct 'information biases' that limit and shape how information is obtained and selected for decision making. As an organization's lower echelons 'filter and compress the data for the higher, detail is removed and order added. The choice of what data are actually transmitted is formally found at the top but informally left to the lower levels' (Thompson and Wildavsky, 1986, p. 275).

Culture, then, is the framework by which data are gathered and constructed into a coherent view of events and circumstances. Each type of organizational culture (hierarchy, market, sectarian or egalitarian) tends toward a distinct kind of information 'search behavior.' The hierarchical culture, for example, typically emphasizes efficiency, specialization and division of labor and justifies inequalities on grounds of efficiency and effectiveness.

A study of the World Bank's organizational culture affords a perspective that contrasts sharply with the organization's official image. Bank officials and many public documents portray the institution as learning, changing and responsive, eager to collaborate with NGOs, including in early stages of project work. Former Vice President Warren Baum (1978, p. 24) praises its ' . . . response to the lessons of experience. . . . Mistakes . . . are not often repeated. The lessons of experience are built into the design and preparation of future projects. The project cycle is working as intended.' Among official documents and papers by senior managers, Yudelman (1985), Israel (1978), and the organization's pamphlet on information disclosure (n.d.) express similar views.

Official documents treat interaction with NGOs as a case of the World Bank's openness and responsiveness. Growing collaboration with NGOs (Strategic Planning and Review, 1989, p. 17), frequent consultation in project design (World Bank, 1990d, p. 8; *Annual Report*, 1989; 1993, pp. 94–5), and learning from dialogue and collaboration with NGOs are stressed: 'NGO input is often crucial in [project] design and implementation' (World Bank, 1990d, p. 11). The Bank's promotional materials for the fiftieth anniversary characterize the Bank as a set of global 'partnerships,' including with NGOs and with 'the worldwide academic and research community' (World Bank, 1994f).

In contrast to official sources, most staff I interviewed (and some internal documents) assess the NGO role more soberly: it depends on individual initiative (Africa region staff no. 1; Finance staff no.1. Policy staff no. 3), is 'still *ad hoc* and dependent on circumstances', and . . . relatively rare[ly involves a] say in the formulation of the project concept and its strategy' (Cernea, 1988, p. 32). ' . . . most Bank staff are still relatively unfamiliar with NGO activities and capabilities,' even according to the unit charged with building Bank-NGO relations (Strategic Planning and Review, 1990, p. 15).

Theories of organizational culture also suggest an alternative view of the culture of the World Bank. Hierarchies emphasize efficiency, specialization and division of labor, justifying inequalities on efficiency grounds. Technical rationality expresses itself in a division of labor, rationalization of work, and emphasis on predictability in the production process. Hierarchies' information search is biased accordingly:

> Hierarchies are concerned with maintaining the existing order. [. . . their legitimacy rests] on science and expertise; the right person in the right job most capable of making the right decision. So hierarchies search for new information to do a better job of holding together the existing social order. [They] are slow to discard old truths, returning to the old until the new can be comfortably accommodated with the existing order (Thompson and Wildavsky, 1986, p. 283).

INFORMATION BIAS AND ORGANIZATIONAL LEARNING: THE CASES OF RURAL DEVELOPMENT AND STRUCTURAL ADJUSTMENT

The information generally selected for consideration in policy-making in the Bank excludes many political and socio-cultural considerations that shape the realities of social and economic change in the countries of the South. Factors that fit the realities defined by the myth of development, and that are susceptible to its influence and control, are treated as the only relevant considerations. Staff's control over information buttresses dominant paradigms by selecting information that is consistent with them.

When a project or national economic policy performs unsatisfactorily, staff appear to choose from a narrow menu of explanations, featuring weak government commitment, poor management, and inappropriate macro-economic policy. Poverty persists and economies languish, in the world of the Bank's culture, for reasons beyond its influence. Other explanations for project failure are generally absent from World Bank papers. One searches in vain for a project or country strategy review that calls a government ministry too corrupt to manage an investment, acknowledges that local power is so skewed that a project cannot benefit the relatively poor, asks whether vital knowledge about coping sustainably with rural conditions resides in sources that the Bank has not tapped, or acknowledges that people did not cooperate in a project that they could not control. These 'answers' are untenable because they undercut the World Bank's mythology. They cannot be embraced within the existing framework, so they go largely unrecognized or unreported. When reported, they are bracketed as extraneous, exogenous, uncontrollable.

The Case of 'Rural Development' and 'Sociological Issues'

A comparison of two series of internal evaluations of rural development projects in the 1970s and 1980s documents this process of information selection (OED, 1988). One set, known as Project Performance Reviews (PPRs) and Project Implementation Reviews (PIRs), are formal parts of the project cycle, sent to senior management. They treat management, financial, disbursement and implementation problems. PIRs are 'selective, both as to projects and general problems. . . . [They] provide good insights into what managers felt were important issues . . .' (OED, 1988, p. 52).

'Lessons Learned' papers, circulated informally among staff, note sociological issues more often, and occasionally criticize World Bank and borrower 'communication and cooperation. . . . In contrast, PIRs largely avoid self-criticism of Bank procedures . . .' (OED, 1988, p. 53). Information is selected to favor technical and administrative problems and to filter out sociological, political and organizational issues.

In rural development lending as in other operations, the information chain's lower strata continued to rely on official views of development needs and priorities. Policy statements stressed involving 'beneficiaries' in project design, but OED (1988, p. 60) concludes that guidelines on participation had 'limited operational impact. Beneficiaries were not assigned a role in the decision-making process, nor was their technological knowledge sought prior to designing project components.'

The Case of Structural Adjustment and the East Asian Miracle

The intellectual history of structural adjustment within the Bank is replete with similar selectivity and purposeful management of information. A major World Bank research project completed in 1993 reinterprets East

Asia's economic successes and provides a window on how the East Asian 'Miracle' has been stylized and presented to support an economic program.

The study's findings are that getting 'the fundamentals' right is indispensable to broadly-based growth, but that in some cases certain state interventions did work in East Asia. The report is distinguished by significant omissions. First, there is not one paragraph about the environmental or natural resource costs or advantages of the strategies reviewed. Although the region's natural resource endowments are mentioned, there is no discussion of real resource costs, sustainability, pollution issues in chemical and steel industries. Even in the review of policy lessons for growth in the present world economy, resource use and costs are unmentioned (pp. 23–4).

Second, the Bank itself is virtually absent as an actor in the study, despite its energetic promotion and finance of the East Asian strategies. The authors' models account for the growth impact of various packages of interventions, but the Bank and other donors are absent from the account, and lessons for growth-producing policies in the 1990s are derived without reference to the major international actors.

But the way the Bank's spokespeople have promoted and interpreted the findings is even more telling. In a *Financial Times* interview the project's research director, John Page, presents as bold and new the central findings: that the Asian economic powers followed varied paths to rapid growth, including, at times, aggressive state intervention and protection of certain domestic industries. "'If we're right", says Mr Page, "the economic policy arsenal has many more weapons than we suspected"' (*The Financial Times*, May 1993, p. 15).

But economists outside the World Bank have argued throughout the 1980s that the Bank's stylized image of the East Asian miracle was distorted. Yale economist Colin Bradford (now Chief Economist at USAID) reviewed the literature in 1986, and argued that the World Bank and IMF misread the East Asian experience, producing a stylized version that supported their adjustment and stabilization models (see, for example, WDR, 1983, pp. 57–63; WDR, 1985, pp. 54–5; Krueger, 1985; Agarwala, 1983.) Bradford cites major published studies of Taiwan, South Korea, Hong Kong and Singapore from the late 1970s and 1980s that highlight the variations the Bank is now 'discovering.'

The Bank not only ignored independent, dissenting research as it created the stylized East Asian experience, but employed its caricature of that experience to justify an approach to structural adjustment that did not succeed, and indeed was never tried, in Asia.[1] Manfred Bienefeld

(1994) considers the East Asia case an example of the 'conflict between the historical record and today's neo-liberal policies.' The Bank's interpretation of the record demonstrates a clear preference for global integration over the 'conscious building of individual, internally coherent economies' (p. 42).

Moseley, Harrigan and Toye (1991) argue that the whole history of Bank-sponsored adjustment in low-income countries has ignored the lessons of East Asia and other industrializing areas. Citing Fei and Ranis, they note that successful postwar industrialization has involved a period of state protection of infant industries, protection that was removed gradually over time. By discouraging protection and state management of investment in the low income countries, Bank-style adjustment is 'a gratuitous obstruction' to the pattern of policy evolution that has produced the very few successful industrializations since World War II.

Similar selectivity is evident in the World Bank's 1988 evaluation of adjustment lending. The global implications of country-based policy recommendations and the domestic political reactions to adjustment both extend beyond the range of factors the Bank wishes to admit into its analysis. But their exclusion means that self-assessment is done in a fictional world that differs sharply from the realities with which client governments must cope.

The evaluation tends to focus solely on the 'correctness' of prescribed policies, given the supply and demand responses forecast by its models, and assuming full implementation. When actual results fail to meet expectations, exogenous factors – slow supply response to new demand for investment, persistent global recession, poor terms of trade – are often invoked to explain the disappointing performance and remove any question of the appropriateness of the adjustment program.

By treating debt and global economic setbacks in this way, rather than as part of an integrated set of domestic and international barriers to development it is possible to segregate economic shocks and explain away the failure of adjustment plans. The alternative would be to recognize such failures as the result of a package of services inappropriate to prevailing conditions.

Assessments of growth-related indicators using computerized general equilibrium models rely heavily on projections of global economic conditions. The systematic optimistic bias of these estimates, documented by Cole (1987), affects SALs and their assessment, as the Bank's ten-year review notes, '. . . projections of outcomes during the adjustment phase were optimistic. Not only the persistence of the negative external shocks but also the lags in implementation and supply response were underestimated' (1988, p. 79). This systematic bias reflects an optimism about economic recovery that can be traced throughout neo-liberal thought and policy on debt management (Corbridge, 1993, pp. 32–4).

An internal memorandum by an analyst in the Policy Analysis and Review Unit (SPRPA) highlights this problem (Earwaker, 1989). Noting that the advent of SALs had made global economic projections central to Bank lending, Earwaker (1989, p. 1) argues that 'to the extent that projections are based upon overly-optimistic assumptions they will exaggerate the likely effectiveness of a proposed package of policy reforms in achieving the targeted adjustment.'

Such estimates have long lacked realism, he argues, because of 'a disposition to favor scenarios' that show the country needs World Bank finance, and that prospects for repayment are satisfactory. But with adjustment lending, where short-term performance is essential to making the case for adopting otherwise unpopular policy measures, economists have employed assumptions that produce 'a rate of GDP growth that is constrained only by the imagination of the task manager and the requirements of the lending program' (Earwaker, 1989, p. 2, 3).

In planning and evaluating adjustment measures as in other programming, the organizational culture carries out a purposeful selection of information. It permits the organization to focus its attention, and the attention of its observers and borrowers, on factors that it officially recognizes, and that are consonant with its myth of development.

Canadian scholar John Mihevc (1993) and Susan George and Fabrizio Sabelli (1994) have both compared the Bank to certain religious institutions in this respect. For Mihevc, the enunciation and pursuit of the basic principles of economic liberalization mirrors the zeal and single-mindedness of fundamentalist theologies and religious bodies, holding certain 'truths' as privileged and reinterpreting and constructing a reality to fit them. George and Sabelli push the metaphor further, 'this supranational, non-democratic institution functions very much like . . . the medieval Church. It has a doctrine, a rigidly structured hierarchy preaching and imposing this doctrine and a quasi-religious mode of self-justification' (p. 5). Religious fundamentalists and admirers of Medieval Catholicism may be troubled by the characterizations, but the observations surely sum up many aspects of the behavior and thinking at the Bank. These tendencies, unfortunately, have strong implications for how and what the organization learns.

CULTURAL, STRUCTURAL AND PROCEDURAL LIMITS ON LEARNING

Hierarchical organizational culture links together many features that limit the World Bank's capacity to listen, change and learn. These features – conceptual, procedural and structural – limit the ability of individual staff and of the organization to establish working relations of collaboration and accountability with NGOs.

The Nature of Organizational Learning

Michael Cernea (1987), World Bank rural sociology advisor, notes that governments and donors find it easier to focus on infusions of capital than to inquire into the causes of failed development strategies and unsuccessful projects. New strategies are launched with fanfare, but Cernea (1987, pp. 9–10) is 'struck by how little interest there has been in learning the true reason for failure . . .' of previous strategies. The factors that impede such systematic organizational learning are explored in this section, and they are shown to limit the World Bank's ability for genuine interaction with NGOs.

Theories of organizational learning stress the role of routines in forming an institutional memory and of common assumptions in underpinning these routines. Barbara Levitt and James March (1988, p. 320) argue that organizations learn 'by encoding inferences from history into routines that guide behavior.' An organization's routines are vehicles that preserve and transmit its experience, a kind of collective memory.

'Routines' as Levitt and March understand them include 'the forms, rules, procedures, conventions, strategies and technologies around which organizations are constructed, and through which they operate,' as well as 'the structure of beliefs, frameworks, paradigms, codes, cultures, and knowledge that buttress, elaborate and contradict the formal routines.' Because routines are independent of individuals, they can survive turnover and the passage of time.

Routines change either through trial and error experimentation or through deliberate organizational search for new methods. But experience gained in either way is always interpreted through actors' own frames of meaning. In drawing lessons from experience:

> the facts are not always obvious, and the causality of events is difficult to untangle. What an organization should expect to achieve, and thus the difference between success and failure, is not always clear. Never-

theless people in organizations form interpretations of events and come to classify outcomes as good or bad (Levitt and March, p. 322).

The common assumptions and understandings that make such judgments possible are extremely difficult for an organization to change or re-learn. Chris Argyris (1987, p. 84) distinguishes two types of learning. One occurs when an error is detected and corrected 'without questioning or altering the underlying values of the system.' The second, systemic learning,[2] goes beyond correcting immediate problems, to confront the values and expectations that guide and drive actions in the organization. Systemic learning involves 'the important issues of competence and justice,' and often raises 'indiscussible' issues.

Here the organization confronts its own myths, by which it defines success for itself, in a field where what 'works' is not self-evident. Systemic learning challenges the factors that provide stability and self-identity in an organization. It calls organizational myths or core technologies into question, and may demand a new kind of information search. All of this is likely to undermine other goals, including those that underlie the organization's system of incentives. Declaring a new policy will probably not be enough to effect the changes required, if actors with informal power bases are not convinced of the merits of the change. In the World Bank, the key variables, valued by individuals and institutionalized in the organization, include neoclassical economics, the doctrine of sovereignty and the supremacy of technocratic policy formation.

Most organizations find systemic learning extremely difficult. Frames of reference and organizational myths create clarity for an organization in the face of the ambiguity of success and failure. These established patterns of perception and analysis reach deep into organizational structures and individual psyches, and it is difficult to build or to accept a case for change when organizational standards and procedures are all based on widely-held standards of success.

Established theories and procedures are often not only encoded in patterns of thought and frames of reference, but also institutionalized in organizational routines and enshrined in professional expectations and norms. Features as general as rational-technical bureaucratic organization and as specific as the use of cost-benefit analysis in appraisal are buttressed by doctrines, myths, habits and expectations in the organization and beyond. Much experience in an organization goes unrecorded or is reported selectively, further strengthening the *status quo*, especially in fields that do not feature strong competitive pressure to change.

These features do not mean that organizations are rigid, allowing no change. On the contrary, the ability to tolerate 'deviant memories' and to admit variance from established procedures, without allowing precedents to be established, is vital to an organization's survival. An organization bolsters the 'short-term flexibility and long-term stability' of its routines if it is able to tolerate such variation (Levitt and March, p. 327).

These theories suggest that learning in an organization is limited in three broad senses.

1. *Learning by the individuals does not equal learning by the organization.* Individual staff or even units within a larger organization may be able to absorb lessons from experience and change behavior in further programming, without the lessons being accepted and 'learned' in the same sense by the organization. The distinction between individual and organization here is critical, because one person or group – outside or within the World Bank – could work for years to reshape a particular investment without any assurance of a broader impact.

2. *Systemic learning is difficult in a hierarchical organizational culture:* a lesson may be appreciated and perhaps acted upon in a particular case, without being 'learned' by examining assumptions, structures and procedures that may require change in order to avoid the errors. Learning in this sense is not just cognitive, it requires systematic action and correction.

3. *Systemic learning is more likely to follow from a new coalition gaining the power to define problems and solution and articulate values, than from a cognitive paradigm shift among individuals* (LePrestre, 1993, p. 16).

Information and Limits on Organizational Learning: Three Cases

How do these problems for organizational learning manifest themselves at the Bank? Three cases illustrate some of the dynamics.

1. *Deliberate manipulation of information as a power base in the organization: program lending in Malaysia.* Management specialist David Hulme (1989) documents learning and 'deliberate non-learning' at the Asian Development Bank (ADB), the World Bank and Malaysian government agencies during a series of rubber estate projects in the 1960s, 1970s and early 1980s. Agencies sometimes fail to learn a lesson because

of inadequate evaluation methodologies, but more often because some participant in the project planning discourse does not want to consider a particular lesson. 'Actively "not learning from experience" is as much a part of organizational process as "learning from experience"' Hulme, 1989, p. 2).

In a series of rubber production schemes in Malaysia, the ADB clearly recorded important lessons about scheme size, site preparation, market adaptation, need for 'settler capital', cropping patterns, the difficulty of procuring land for projects; problems with certain types of settlers; and local staff's management capacity. But while some issues were considered in planning successive projects, others were systematically ignored. The selective learning 'was based not upon an ignorance of certain lessons, but on their avoidance and suppression' (Hulme, 1989, pp. 6–9).

Planners in the government and the banks treated lessons 'not as neutral pieces of information . . . but as strategic resources that are a potential source of power and influence over future planning discourse.' Lending targets and planning agendas were central: lessons that could be incorporated into a rehabilitated and expanded settlement scheme were adopted, while those that threw the project format into question or threatened to delay approval (in this case, land availability, settler selection and management capacity) were ignored or glossed over (Hulme, 1989, pp. 10–11).

Although Hulme focuses primarily on the ADB, the World Bank co-financed the third of the three schemes. An unpublished World Bank report on land-settlement schemes notes that many unsatisfactory land settlement projects initiated since 1975 '"can be faulted on the basis of lessons learnt elsewhere at the time of their commencement"' (Hulme, 1989, p. 12).

In Hulme's case information is suppressed by influential participants. In other instances at the World Bank, not only is information and learning a tool in advancing individual and organizational interests, but some learning is effectively prohibited by beliefs and assumptions that are fundamental to organizational myths and that are maintained by strong information selection biases.

2. *'Learning' without policy change: adjustment and women.* The Bank's evolving awareness of the differential effects of recession and adjustment on women and men shows how understanding can be advanced within the organization without the reappraisal of assumptions and policies that constitutes organizational learning. After the initial period in which

poverty and social effects of adjustment were virtually ignored, the Bank adopted 'protecting the vulnerable' (women, children, the aged) as the substance of its concern for women's welfare under adjustment. Research sponsored within the Bank during the 1980s documented and deepened the understanding of the effects on women. Caroline Moser and others within the Bank confirmed the effects on women's role in the productive system. Women's work typically included both work that conventional national income measures account as productive, and the unpaid work of household and community maintenance.

This documentation helped some within the Bank appreciate the ways in which women's expanded workloads were the central feature of the 'coping strategies' through which communities and households managed the strains of adjustment. But the documentation of the dimensions of the feminization of poverty – informalization, reduced access to health services, resort to cheaper, labor-intensive foodstuffs, family violence, restricted political roles – has not led to the conclusion that gender equity questions inherent in the present pattern of adjustment need to be addressed. Adjustment strategies have not been redesigned to reduce inequities, nor have planning processes been broadened to give women an expanded role in their design. Rather 'coping mechanisms' have been utilized to maintain existing adjustment programs. In effect, the architects of the Bank's adjustment policies have been content to make women 'more efficient beasts of burden' (Nzomo, 1992, p. 107) in bearing the strains of economic adjustment.

3. *Institutional self-deception and the disbursement mandate: infrastructure lending in India.* In recent experience in India, selectivity and suppression of information have contributed to some of the World Bank's most notorious 'problem projects.' Its handling of the independent review of the Sardar Sarovar dam project provoked a high-profile controversy the Bank would surely have preferred to avoid. Behind the controversy lies a history of external protest and internal selectivity in handling information that amounts to a pattern of institutional self-deception.

The Singrauli energy projects, including a thermal power plant, coal mine and the associated energy grid, were supported by three IDA credits and an IBRD loan made between 1977 and 1987. The project provoked criticism, in India and among international environmental NGOs, for its environmental impact and the conditions under which some 20,000 persons were relocated from the project area. Extensive dissent and protest by Indian and other NGOs is documented in letters and petitions collected in the Environmental Defense Fund's MDB Information Center.

Yet the Project Completion Report on the 1977 IDA Credit to support the Singrauli Thermal Power Plant, written in 1987 (Report No. 6784), includes not one word about the relocation issue, nor about the extensive legal and political conflict in India over the project. Instead, after an analysis of project implementation and production and sale of kilowatt-hours of electricity, the report officially closes the books on the investment by judging it 'entirely successful' because the generating units were completed and electric power is being generated and sold to consumers. This treatment, ignoring the issues raised by relocation and environmental impact in its official assessment of the investment, does not inspire confidence that issues of concern to NGOs have been integrated into the Bank's standards of performance and self-assessment.

The storm of protest over the Sardar Sarovar project became impossible to ignore, even in World Bank documents. The Bank-commissioned Independent Review found that the Bank appraised and approved the loan without regard for its own requirements for treatment of displaced populations, and despite technical and planning flaws (*Sardar Sarovar*, 1992).

World Bank support for the massive project began with a $450 million loan in 1985. According to the independent review, World Bank resettlement policies and the Indian government's own environmental requirements were ignored, and information underestimating resettlement needs, misrepresenting hydrological conditions and failing to take into account other projects upstream were not checked by Bank planners. These failings led to widespread displacement, protest, and repression. In the face of these problems, which grew into a human and public relations catastrophe, the Bank remained involved and sought incremental improvement in the Indian state and national governments' performance. The Review judged this strategy unsuccessful and urged the Bank to 'step away' from the project.

In a rare vote, the Executive Directors in October, 1992, approved management's recommendation to disregard the Review's recommendation and continue funding Sardar Sarovar. The Indian government was given six months to rectify certain problems related to forced relocations. In March 1993, the Indian government announced that it would terminate the loan agreement and complete the project without World Bank support.

Finally, after two extraordinary events – the Independent Review and the Board vote – the Bank stood its ground on relocation standards, and provoked the loan's termination. But what is remembered from the nine-year episode was encapsulated in India Program Director Hans Vergin's words to the NGO-World Bank Committee in November, that the Bank was never bound to carry out all of the Review's recommendations. In so saying he added to the list of experiences and lessons the Bank felt free to disregard: previous experience in Brazil during disputes over infrastructure projects; objections from Indian NGOs about improper resettlement, environmental damage and human rights abuses; its own highly touted resettlement policies and environmental procedures; and the history of noncompliance, by two of the Indian states involved, with agreements made by the national government.

The factors at work read like a checklist of the Bank's organizational traits, reluctance to give up on an investment once begun; determination to keep major loans flowing to a major borrower; shortchanging social and environmental considerations in a process driven by 'engineering and economic imperatives' (*Sardar Sarovar*, p. xxiv); citing as justification the Indian government's sovereignty, while manipulating the governing boards that represent sovereign control over Bank investments. The Sardar Sarovar debacle is not unique. According to the independent review, the problems it uncovered 'are more the rule than the exception to resettlement operations supported by the Bank' (*Sardar Sarovar*, 1992, p. 53).

CULTURE, LEARNING AND CHANGE

Selectivity, Socialization and Intellectual Insularity

A powerful socialization of staff and a tendency to intellectual insularity in the World Bank's research and analysis help to reinforce the selectivity in its handling of information. The insular intellectual environment has been noted by friendly and critical sources alike (Mason and Asher, 1973, p. 66; Hellinger, 1988). 'Even by Washington standards,' writes Ayres (1983, p. xiv), the Bank has a reputation as private and reticent.

Self-suppression of dissent

Thomas' research (1980, p. 119) identified the principal sources that staff consult for information or advice. Remarkably few say they turn to external publications (27 per cent) or visit the country involved (28 per cent) when they need information. Many more refer to 'Bank sources' or host country officials (41 per cent each). The inward tendency is even stronger 'in making a difficult decision,' where only 21 per cent name a non-World Bank source (Thomas, 1980, p. 146). This inward orientation and 'remarkable consensus among . . . staff on what information is important to them . . .' reflect socialization 'into a way of looking at the environment which encourages them to focus on specific information' (Thomas, 1980, p. 118).

Staff also act individually to filter and restrict the dissenting views that are aired. Thomas asked professional staff how they react to decisions from which they personally dissent, and elicited a sketch of a hierarchy in which individuals not only readily implement decisions they dislike, but rarely make a sustained effort to record their dissent. 'When I dislike a decision,' 48 per cent of respondents said 'I just implement it' anyway; 29 per cent voice disagreement but implement it, 26 per cent record their dissent formally, 19 per cent appeal to others on the issue, and 7 per cent 'don't participate.'

Respondents stress the need to go along with decisions when 'one agrees with the basic goals' (Thomas, 1980, p. 151). 'People try to understand the Bank's viewpoint, rather than the individual's. Anything is okay if it's consistent with Bank guidelines.' Thomas finds that there is 'overriding support of the staff for Bank operations,' noting comments such as this: 'The Bank provides a systematic way to analyze problems you don't get any other way. It's good exposure to the complete and practical problems of development' (Thomas, 1980, pp. 150, 181). Thomas concludes that staff have a high level of respect for the Bank's privacy and autonomy. But its inward-looking intellectual world, intellectual conformity and relative lack of dissent also reflect a profound socialization of staff.

Socialization

Ayres (1983, p. 39) describes a socialization that promotes continuity, conformity and:

> the norms and ambience of neoclassical economics. . . . Even the socially conscious might in large measure succumb. . . . Too great a concern with poverty in the economic and sector work program would, to some extent at least, have been perceived by many important individuals within the Bank as deviant behavior.

A social services sector officer in LAC sees the Bank as governed by dominant ideas, 'first and foremost, neo-classical economics.' The pervasiveness of economic theory in everyday discussion amused this respondent, as economists in cafeteria lines discuss and frame their choices of menu and service options in terms of marginal gains, preference structures, and other jargon of the trade (LAC staff no. 1). Socialization takes place in all international agencies, but its 'relatively small size, the likely predispositions of persons working for and with it [and] the common influence of the "financial community,"' make the effect particularly potent at the World Bank (Fatorous, 1977, p. 19).

Sociologist Robert Chambers (1987, p. 4) agrees that 'normal professionalism' – a profession's dominant patter of 'thinking, values, methods and behaviour' – adds stability, and resists change at the World Bank. He appeals for change in the 'normal professionalism' of staff through opening new lines of information and experience in making policy.

But powerful organizational and political-economic factors that sustain the professional culture makes such changes unlikely. Arguing that the Bank hires 'only one kind of economist,' neoclassical, Guy Gran (1986, pp. 277–81) charges that 'assumptions, definitions, terms of reference, analytical methods and subjects for discussion in Bank learning and policy formulation are primarily those reflecting the guild behavior of one particular form of Western positivist social science.'

Gran's assertion is no longer completely true: one can now find a few economists in the Bank with decidedly heterodox views on macroeconomics and natural resource economics. But as one social scientist at the Bank noted, the institution resembles an English village in that the only way to be truly accepted there is to be born into it. Midcareer recruits to the Bank are normally hired as 'advisors,' and can ascend to become ever-more senior 'advisors,' but not to management positions. They, like their ideas, are kept institutionally at arm's length.

The impact of criticism on individual staff is mediated by their own intellectual, institutional and professional allegiances, their motivations and the socialization process and internal consensus developed among staff. But the intellectual and institutional power of neoclassical economic theory plays a role as well. As intellectuals and professionals, many staff hold themselves more directly accountable to professional standards than to management's directives and assume responsibility to shape and amend policy as they implement it (Ascher, 1983, p. 427). Economists' credentials and adherence to neoclassical theory give them, within the World Bank, an almost unassailable position from which to judge new mandates.

Insularity

The analytical framework that results suffers from both the lack of cross-disciplinary input within the Bank and from the tendency not to stray far outside its walls. Gran decries the 'insular literary universe' where outside work is rarely cited, and 'any hint of self-critique or irreverence gives way to bureaucratic imperatives' under repeated revision of written work. The selectivity is purposeful; since independent scholars, peasant groups, local NGOs cannot be controlled, 'what they say has no validity. Any other learning method would produce unbearable cognitive dissonance' (Gran, 1986, pp. 277, 285). Several staff interviewed demonstrated this by finding ways to ignore or categorize their critics among the NGOs as ill-informed, attacking outdated images of the Bank (Africa staff no. 2; LAC staff no.2).

Former Bank Vice President Willi Wapenhans (1994), in an essay for the Bretton Woods Commission, criticizes the weak flow of research information into the Bank:

> Relatively little effort is made to engage the intellectual community around the globe . . . The absence of such efforts creates the perception that the Bank's operational research is exclusive, self-serving, and of insufficient objectivity (p. c-297).

Attitudes toward the 1992 internal review 'Effective Implementation' (the 'Wapenhans report') reflect this insularity and the limits of organizational learning. Preston, in a self-congratulatory memo, says the Bank should take pride in 'its willingness and ability to undertake [such a] frank and critical self-evaluation' (memorandum to Executive Directors, 'Portfolio Management: Next Steps,' 31 March 1993). In reality the critique is entirely internal, retrenching and re-applying the traditional standard of 10 per cent rate of return on investment to identify unsatisfactory performance in projects. In so doing it reaffirms the myth of development success as measured by banking standards, sidestepping criticism and pressure on participation, poverty, human rights and environmental issues by redefining the problem in its own terms. Noncompliance with adjustment conditionality becomes an implementation problem, to be solved by more 'client-oriented' implementation and supervision. Project delays and economically unsustainable projects become managerial problems whose solution lies in more supervision time and a broader view of the administrative burdens that country portfolios place on government officials.

The report dwells for two pages on learning processes in the Bank. It identifies three distinct cycles of learning, all narrowly focused on implementing established objectives, rather than on appraising their validity: in-country portfolio performance, distinctive sectoral experience, and 'the professional learning cycle' of training, exposure and dissemination ('Effective Implementation', pp. 23–4).

A few observers are more optimistic about the Bank's capacity to learn. But each of these assessments acknowledges, implicitly or explicitly, that limitations such as those discussed above set boundaries for learning. Montague Yudelman (1985), former head of agricultural programs at the Bank, views the growth of agricultural lending as an evolution of theory and priorities, driven by the work of some staff economists. He notes that agricultural lending increased as distributional issues gained prominence in development theory.

But the belated recognition that income and resource distribution is a critical issue even in the presence of strong economic growth troubled the Bank again two decades later. After the early experience of adjustment lending in the early 1980s, Zuckerman (1989) reports that equity issues associated with adjustment finally became an issue among staff. The lesson that might have been learned in the 1960s seems not to have penetrated the World Bank's basic perspective on its role in development.

Hurni (1980, pp. 65, 82) praises the Bank's internal planning as highly reflective and self-critical. But she observes 'a gap between the World Bank's research and intellectual approach and its practical actions in the field . . .' (Hurni, p. 103). The sophisticated research apparatus is applied almost exclusively to those issues that are tractable for the Bank as an institution.

'Expertise', 'Control' and 'Quality'

Alongside the dominant intellectual role of neoclassical economic theory, two foundations for the organizational culture emerge from interviews of Bank staff. These ideas are the technical expertise and superiority of staff; and 'control' of lending operations to maintain their 'quality.'

Many staff identify the self-image of technical competence and superiority as an important feature of the Bank's culture. Many of the marks of this attitude are impressionistic, and evidence of it anecdotal.

None the less, the prevailing sense of superiority to other donor agencies and to counterparts in borrowing government ministries is widely remarked upon by observers, consultants, and sometimes by staff themselves.

A recent anecdote illustrates the dimensions of this organizational ego. Dr Michael Irwin, who served briefly as Director of Medical Services at the World Bank after 32 years as medical director for the United Nations, resigned early in 1990 in response to what he characterized as a staff 'overconcerned with its prestige, and . . . preoccupied with . . . salaries, benefits, and "grade creep"' (Irwin, 1990, p. 37). In an incident that led to Irwin's resignation, the new medical director suggested in a letter to the Bank's in-house magazine that staff consider giving up the first-class air travel to which they were entitled. The suggested provoked a storm of protest, calling Irwin 'terribly ill-informed or frighteningly insensitive,' dismissing his office as an unproductive burden on the organization, and branding his suggestion as 'unfortunate and damaging to morale in the . . . Bank.' One writer called this perquisite 'the most tangible expression (and some would say the "final expression") of the institution's esteem and consideration [toward staff] . . . ' (Irwin, 1990, pp. 34–6).[3]

The widely-remarked elitism (see Mason and Asher, 1973; Irwin, 1990; Hurni, 1980; Van de Laar 1980) of Bank staff is not simply a function, of course, of well-appointed offices, generous salaries and first-class air travel privileges. The Bank's influence, prestige and other rewards attract technically skilled, highly (if narrowly) qualified professional staff. Professionals who have reached prestigious posts in international development or finance, staff generally share a social and intellectual background that includes advanced training in a handful of American and European universities (van de Laar, 1980). The influence through financial and other clout, the physical and financial perquisites of their employment, and an institutional culture that assigns high status to their intellectual and technical skills, all contribute to a certain lack of humility.

Dimensions of organizational control

The organizational need to control the use of its loans arose early in the World Bank's history, as staff and management sought to balance the notion that projects are initiated and planned by borrowing governments, with the need for project plans that met technical requirements and satisfied the financial institutions from which the World Bank borrowed that its loans would be productive and therefore repayable. Libby (1975b, pp. 45–7) argues that as a World Bank 'development doctrine' was developed in the late 1940s, 'technical assistance' emerged as the concept and tool that reconciled the need for control with borrowers' reluctance to surrender such control. The problem was solved, in Libby's view, by 'subsuming issues of control under the rubric of "technical assistance".'

Former Bank Vice President Wapenhans (1994) details the development of what he considers excessive Bank technical assistance in the design of projects. Wapenhans argues that involvement of Bank staff in project design compromises the Bank's ability to appraise the project and make a credibly disinterested decision as to whether to finance it (p. 296).

The organizational emphasis on 'quality' and 'control' of lending continues to shape staff's interactions with outside actors. A LAC staffer called 'quality' an 'obsession' that degenerates to simple consistency and conformance (LAC staff no. 1). Focused on control and 'quality,' staff find it difficult to delegate control of a project component to an NGO. For this reason one staff economist calls technical expertise the World Bank's greatest strength and weakness (Africa staff no. 3).

QUALITY, CONTROL, UNCERTAINTY AND NGOS

The Problem of 'Certifying' NGOs

Maintaining quality and control also minimizes uncertainty in lending operations, and the threat of uncertainty is an unwelcome implication of cooperating with NGOs. The hundreds of NGOs in most borrowing countries are unknown quantities to most staff, and as a West Africa economist pointed out, there is no easy way to 'certify' NGOs. The absence of a straightforward standard for determining that a NGO is legitimate and acceptable leaves staff with what is widely perceived as a politically risky and time-consuming process of selecting organizations that can be 'effective partners' technically, and inoffensive politically to the borrowing government (Africa staff no. 1).

One result is that staff are likely to contact an NGO that has collaborated on projects with another major donor. In the Philippines, Bank missions contacted two NGOs, Philippine Business for Social Progress and the Davao Medical School Foundation/Institute for Primary Health Care, because of their experience implementing USAID-funded projects

(Asia staff no. 1). This practice of relying on a few NGOs with experience relating to major donors (and comfortable relations with the government) is understandable. But narrowing the range in search of security entails losses, as the Bank misses the experience of other innovative prospective NGO partners.

The risks involved in working with NGOs surface repeatedly in interviews, staff stress the need to distinguish 'serious NGOs' from 'fly-by-night operations' (Policy staff no. 9); to recognize government-based NGO fronts (Africa staff no.1); to distinguish NGOs created solely to respond to a new fund (Policy staff October 6, 1989); and to sort out 'effective partners' for Bank-funded operations (LAC staff, October 6, 1989). The Operational Directive on NGOs, like some other official statements, gives a curiously long recital of NGOs' weaknesses and dangers (OD 14.70, 1989). A staffer in Strategic Policy and Review argues that NGOs must be seen as partners, not risks (Policy staff no. 3). But abhorrence of uncertainty and preference for clear, consistent duties and rewards militates against it.

NGOs, Policy Change and Uncertainty

This resistance to uncertainty is institutionalized in the relative inflexibility of key structural and procedural characteristics of the Bank. The project cycle is the most important of these procedural elements. According to Thomas' (1980, p. 110) interviews, most staff believe the exacting requirements and consistent, reliable process for project development and review are important for 'effective operation'.

Staff have structured and defined outside participation so as to minimize disruption of the process, and to preserve certain stages strictly internal. In India, NGO members of the now defunct national NGO-World Bank consultative body were told that their involvement in discussion of project ideas is welcome and solicited, but that 'appraisal is primarily the responsibility of the World Bank team. . . . this responsibility could not be shared' (Second Meeting of the World Bank-NGO Consultation Committee (India), Summary Record, 1989, p. 7). Exclusive control of appraisal keeps the important stage in which the project's worth is documented and certified within the domain of the Bank, maintaining the primacy of its expertise and its standards of 'quality'.

When popular or NGO input into project design interferes with the pace of project development and information review, it disrupts standard operating procedures that help to define and guarantee successful 'performance' by staff. Interruptions in these processes are widely viewed as risks, disruptions and problems, rather than contributions or opportunities for improved project design (Policy staff no. 3; Policy staff no. 6).[4]

The project cycle's well-defined process for project design, review and implementation assure staff that effort expended to develop a project will yield 'performance,' that is, an approved loan. In the absence of intervening events – a change in government or dramatic economic disturbances – staff have a reasonably consistent guide to satisfactory performance in designing projects. Project approval by the Board remains a *de facto* measure of accomplishment. Under these circumstances, staff are unlikely to resist new policies that enhance the probability of achieving desired outcomes.[5]

But new policies that implicitly redefine performance – guidelines on the environment, poverty, appropriate technology and women in development – can affect staff's perceptions about whether effort expended will yield performance that is agreed to be successful. New policies may be perceived as bureaucratic or politically inspired, slowing project preparation and reducing staff's motivation and satisfaction. New mandates implicitly redefine 'performance' in the organization, giving staff reason to resist or ignore redefinitions of 'performance' or 'success.'

The reluctance of most staff to adopt social measures of welfare in using cost-benefit analysis for project appraisal illustrates this resistance to changes that modify standards of performance. The social weighing of benefits, designed to adjust cost benefit analysis as an evaluative tool to take into account distributional issues, was never widely put into practice. Staff economists argued that it introduced a false precision, because reliable data on the distributional issues were unavailable or impossible to gather. But these same obstacles have not prevented the projection of growth and other macro-economic variables, in order to plan and 'sell' adjustment plans, despite the conjectural nature of much of the data and the (at best) mixed track record of such projections (Earwaker, 1989).

More recently, World Bank anthropologist Lawrence Salmen charged that the staff's failure to adopt a participatory beneficiary assessment methodology – which Salmen has promoted within the Bank – reflects an entrenched organizational culture. He characterizes the intellectual culture as top-down, deductive, favoring economic rather than sociocultural discourse, quantitative, impact- rather than process-oriented, abstract and theoretical. Salmen concludes that 'many Bank staff and borrower-government personnel feel they know what needs to be known regarding a development activity, including the people's perception' (Salmen, 1992, p. 21).

Environmental staff designing procedures for environmental impact assessments (EIA) confront related problems. EIA requirements for projects deemed likely to have environmental impact include consultation with affected organizations in the borrowing country (World Bank, 1990c). But making this requirement effective, and avoiding evasion or perfunctory compliance by appraisal teams is an issue that environmental staff are considering. How many NGOs must be consulted? How extensive is the consultation to be, and what results are required for the project to proceed? (LAC staff no. 2).

Integrating concerns about gender roles and equity has been, as Kardam (1989) concludes, hampered by the absence of a strong internal constituency at the World Bank. One reason is the wide range of issues and techniques involved in assessing and seeking to change the impact of Bank-financed projects. Issues such as intra-household distribution of income and resources and the socio-cultural obstacles to economic opportunity for women are foreign to the economics training of most staff, and incorporating them into project appraisals is not only politically tricky, time-consuming and contrary to the thrust of the development myth, it also undercuts staff's expertise by posing issues they are ill-prepared to address.

Professional socialization, internal and individual motivation and the World Bank's structure and core technology all contribute to the strength of its organizational culture. This culture shapes the interpretation of new input and limits organizational change. In practice, this means that Bank staff who promote change, and advocates from without, face powerful, pervasive resistance.

Exercising 'Control' in World Bank-NGO Experience

The World Bank's need to structure and control the working relationship with NGOs is captured in a small change in the language describing the Operations Manual Statement (OMS) on NGOs. Tentatively entitled 'Operational Collaboration with NGOs' in a 1988 draft, its finalized version is instead 'Involving NGOs in Bank-financed Operations' (OMS draft, 1989; OD 14.70, 1989). The dynamics of individual working relationships vary, but the official policy is not collaborative but tightly controlled, making room for NGO involvement on the World Bank's terms. Other themes encountered in interviews and documents

– 'professionalism,' closely directed 'participation,' government and World Bank formation of local organizations, and careful interpretation of resistance to Bank-supported projects – are all dimensions of the Bank's control of its work with NGOs.

Pervasive attitudes toward professionalism and voluntarism help to set the boundaries for NGO contributions. One Asia staffer summed up the premium placed on professionalism, asserting that '[a]s long as they're based on voluntarism, they'll never be able to do the real development' (Asia staff no. 4). The same staffer argued that the appropriate role for the World Bank was to build on NGO successes, find ways to expand and 'professionalize' NGOs.

Even staff more sympathetic to NGO activities noted that their 'young, idealistic, inexperienced' staff made field collaboration difficult, and found professional consultants to present fewer uncertainties. NGOs' tendency to work 'through their own networks,' sometimes leading to initiatives not prescribed in the project plan, was 'aggravating' even to the most sympathetic staff (Africa staff no. 3). Other staff also singled out 'professionalism' as a key virtue in NGOs they had made contact with (Policy staff no. 5; LAC staff no. 1), and a member of the NGO liaison unit summed up the Bank's goals as seeking a 'more business-like' relation with NGOs (NGO-World Bank Committee Meetings, October 1994).

Prevailing views of participation in the Bank

This premium on professionalism is in keeping with the view I encountered of the basis for NGO participation in design. In general, NGOs were sought out to fill roles much as a consultant might be: their special expertise, not any claim to local knowledge or to represent local peoples' views, was the quality valued. Official guidance on 'involving NGOs in Bank-supported activities' points staff toward NGOs with 'particular professional expertise and managerial capabilities' in a sector or region, or NGOs in 'developed countries' with 'specialized experience . . . in managing foreign assistance . . .' (OD 14.70, 1989, pp. 1–2). If expertise is the sole grounds for participation, then NGO demands for a representative role make little sense. For example, NGOs in the country where one staffer had negotiated a social spending fund objected that they weren't involved in its design. 'I don't see why,' he complained. 'If we produce a project that is satisfactory to them, what's their problem?' (Asia staff no. 3).

This conception of NGOs' role in project design reflects a prevailing, narrow idea of 'participation' in the World Bank that bears little resemblance to that promoted by many NGOs and students of local organizations and social change. Participation is widely discussed outside the Bank as involving people in initiating and shaping plans that affect them (Oakley and Marsden, 1984; Esman and Uphoff, 1984). But at the Bank, participation means mobilizing people to carry out project plans, and projects need 'incentives to elicit participants' contribution to the project objectives' (OMS 2.12, 1978, p. 5). What is sought are not views, priorities and wishes of affected populations but their 'full commitment to the project' (OMS 2.20 1984, p. 10) when it has been sketched out. The Bank's participation learning process, in the end, continued this essentially instrumental view of participation, valuing and encouraging participation for its ability largely as a tool for expanding 'ownership' of Bank-financed activities.

Projects involving NGOs in Laos and in Nigeria illustrate this limitation. The Laos Agricultural Rehabilitation and Development Project (1978) calls for the Ministry of Agriculture to initiate water users groups to coordinate irrigation initiatives, and to train cooperatives (PCR, Report No. 7250, p. 12). 'Few, if any' such groups were formed, even though they were to be assigned 'full responsibility' for maintaining canals and coordinating water distribution. The formation of the groups appears to have been peripheral to the projects' design; it merits only a paragraph's discussion in the Project Completion Report, and no comment in the document's 'Lessons Learned' section.

The Nigeria Multi-State Agricultural Development (II) Project, (1989) involved a similar role for newly-created Water Users Associations and Village Cooperative Societies. The project's predecessor was criticized in the OED Rural Development study for failing to build local institutions and relying too heavily on Bank financing. According to the Bank's project summary, the second project 'will assist local governments in establishing village cooperative societies to raise funds for spares, operational maintenance, and eventual replacement of machinery and equipment for bore holes.' Group formation and contribution of 10 per cent of capital costs are prerequisites for drilling and construction in a community.

In these projects and others, the community organizations involved are newly created by local or national governments and assigned responsibilities for implementing and maintaining the project. In these projects as in most World Bank discussions, participation is not a process of joint planning and accountability but a measure to mobilize those whom the projects' planners aim to benefit. Participation is a measure to improve project performance (Cernea, 1987; Paul, 1988), 'sold' to staff in terms of economic efficiency (Strategic Planning and Review, 1989). In many instances it is employed for its value in promoting cost recovery in irrigation and other projects that involve user maintenance.

Planned participation: managing uncertainty and resistance

Such directed participation, in fact, is proposed as a tool to limit uncertainty and increase efficiency. Staff's guidance on project design calls participation only one option when a 'cooperation problem' arises: 'Measures can be built into the projects to reduce conflicts, strengthen and re-orient traditional local organizations, or adopt a technology that minimizes the need for cooperation' (OMS 2.12, 1978, p. 6).

Planned participation, initiated by project authorities to minimize uncertainty, is the norm: '"spontaneous" participation . . . occurs only rarely. . . ."' (Yudelman, 1985, p. 16). One World Bank document (SPRIE, 1989, p. 1) now defines participation as including 'influence on development decisions . . .', but proactive community participation arises rarely, most often where organized pressure interrupts planning or implementation by demanding changes.

Interpreting and overcoming resistance to projects is another dimension of the Bank's control of lending operations. Projects such as Philippine slum clearance operations in Metro Manila, education policy changes in Bolivia, and numerous resettlement, energy development and other projects in environmentally sensitive areas (road construction in Brazil, resettlement in India and Indonesia) illustrate this tendency.

The conflictive origins of community organizations' roles in many projects illustrates the fact that 'participation' is not necessarily the cooperative grassroots action that aid agencies and project managers desire. Like other development agencies, the Bank assumes that 'participation' implies 'cooperation.' The record of NGO conflict with the World Bank shows that resistance is also a form of participation. As Scott (1985) and Scott and Kerkvliet (1986) show in studies of peasant resistance to other forms of social and economic change, often the 'weapons of the weak' – footdragging, non-cooperation, passive resistance – are the way poor people participate in planned development projects.

In the Malaysia Krian-Sungei Manik Integrated Development Project (1978), project managers resorted to talking with local organizations about the project's design after encountering resistance to initial project plans. The project called for draining local dikes as part of the establishment of new tertiary irrigation systems and introduction of new rice varieties. 'Farmers were reluctant to lower the water in the drains . . . [which] were also used for fishing, etc. It took several years to get the farming community to agree to lowering drain water levels' (Project Completion Report, p. vii).

This resistance – referred to as 'farmer resistance to change' and 'farmer non-acceptability of drainage' – eventually led to action to deal with these 'social problems' of implementation, including extension efforts to 'reach' 388 farmer groups. Farmers' cooperation was gained, and the project implemented, unchanged but delayed by four to five years. The Project Completion Report concludes that cooperation in such a project should be secured through 'close cooperation with local leaders and related agencies, especially the district office,' if implementation delays are to be avoided. Longer implementation periods should be allowed, and pilot and demonstration projects used to secure farmer acceptance of new practices (Project Completion Report, p. x).

Students of local organizations and the OED recognize that organizations imposed by project authorities are ineffective. Yet directed participation remains the norm for participation at the World Bank. The preference for directed community participation is shaped by factors in the organizational culture and by external political interests. Governments' fear of raising expectations is often cited as a reason for caution in involving local groups in early stages of the project cycle (OED, 1988; Paul, 1988; White, 1989; Strategic Planning and Review 1990, p. 6). Some staff acknowledge that Bank project managers' unwillingness to be accountable to affected people is an important reason as well (Policy staff no. 3; Ayres, 1983, p. 225); and the time required and the challenge implied to the all-sufficiency of planning expertise are also cited in interviews (Asia staff no. 3; Policy staff no. 3). Nagle's and Ghose's (1989, p. 3) interviews of staff and review of internal literature on participation led them to conclude that:

> there appears to be a reluctance on the part of Bank staff who have written on the subject to press the application of theory into Bank practice. It is as though such applications might be seen as implicitly critical of the way the Bank goes about its business. It would appear that even non-operational staff see something sacrosanct and immutable about both the procedures and time tables of the project cycle.

A Bank-wide Learning Process on Popular Participation

Until 1990, learning about popular participation in the World Bank was built primarily around the *ad hoc* experience of a few staff. In interviews NGOs and staff alike recognize that most project initiatives reflect individual commitments to participatory development strong enough to overcome organizational pressures and disincentives (Africa staff no. 1; Africa staff no. 2; de los Reyes, November 1989).

But a more deliberate 'learning process on participation' was launched in 1991, in part at the instigation of the NGO-World Bank Committee. The learning process was an effort by supporters of participatory practices to make them more central to the Bank's discourse and practice by interpreting and analyzing staff's experiences with managing participatory projects.

The learning process was a well-conceived and extensive effort to broaden support in the Bank through informal processes. It involved studies of 20 participatory Bank-financed projects; seminars and conferences with practitioners from within and outside the Bank; training and a 'best practices' sourcebook to promote participatory methods. The team directing the learning process recognized and opened for discussion several structural constraints to participation. They also saw the need to press their case vigorously in the Operations division. They recognized the limits in the Bank's institutional commitment and designed a process that relied on informal exchanges to advance their cause.

Believing that participatory development was best promoted in the Bank by demonstrating its economic value, the learning group set out to document this value. The result, in discussions with key managers, seems to be that management will be persuaded of the value of participatory methods on a sector-by-sector basis. The formation of water-users' groups in irrigation schemes, for example, seems to be widely accepted as a cost-effective implementation strategy. As other Bank-sponsored research is completed, operations management say they are prepared to acknowledge other sectors where giving affected people the right to shape Bank-sponsored projects is 'worth the effort' according to the Bank's and borrower's bottom line.

Stiefel and Wolfe, comparing the Bank's participation work to that of other international bodies, consider it 'ironical' that while other agencies efforts are often 'superficial, half-hearted and hypocritical,' the Bank 'seems to have embarked on a relatively systematic effort to come to grips with the interpretation of popular participation and to realize it in its field projects' (pp. 222–3). Their conclusion is a credit to the committed and vigorous efforts of the participation learning group within the Bank, and to the learning group's pragmatic approach to promoting participation within the agency. The Bank is helped, too, in such a comparison, by the high level of rhetoric from many of the UN bodies, and most observers' initial low expectations of the Bank in this field.

In appraising the learning process it is important to keep in view the substantial limitations and obstacles within the Bank. Nothing in the experience to date suggests that the process can overcome the obstacles its leaders recognize: staff's skewed skills mix; the disbursement imperative; government reticence and the sovereignty issue; and a dominant mindset that gives little consideration to socio-cultural issues. The informal promotion strategy is well-chosen given the limited possibilities for full-fledged institutional support. Like other initiatives on socio-cultural issues, the learning process has no funds from the Bank's budget, but is supported by voluntary payments from donors. Staff have no clear mandate from management; training, seminars, and other events and resources are used entirely at staff's discretion.

A change made in the learning group's final report by senior managers highlights a final barrier: the inability or unwillingness to side decisively with poor people. The Bank has historically steered clear of the partisanship that characterizes many NGOs. When poverty reduction is embraced as a priority, it is not in terms of relative poverty or income distribution but of absolute conditions and basic needs. So in the participation discussion, the Bank's management finally rejected a distinction between primary and secondary 'stakeholders' in Bank investments that sought to give precedence to participation by the poor. Over objections from NGO participants (see NGO Annex to World Bank 1994g (Annex VI, p. 5)) and some Bank staff, the learning group's report was tilted subtly away from the pro-poor mandate that some had sought to impart.

The learning group's report and policy recommendations, modified somewhat in a management review, have been accepted by the Bank's Board. Proponents within the Bank have sought NGO support for the most sweeping of the recommendations, a requirement that each loan agreement include a participation framework laying out opportunities for participation surrounding the project.

Implementing the learning group's approach to participation throughout the Bank will confront substantial obstacles. An internal memo notes that most Environmental Assessments – the activity for which staff are already instructed to ensure that local NGOs' and affected people's views are taken into account – have failed to incorporate 'any participation whatever' (James Adams memorandum to Managing Director Sven Sandstrom, 15 January 1993). But promoters in the Bank have devised steps to spread the practices. A small Participation Fund, for example, offers matching support within the Bank to regions or country offices that proposed specific new participatory activities in projects or in economic and sector research.

Assessing the World Bank Dialogue with NGOs

Just as project collaboration is structured to minimize disruption and protect the stability of the Bank's operations, so the dialogue with NGOs and other critics has generally been structured, and the input filtered, to minimize its impact on basic premises and assumptions. The management is most transparent in those fora that are sanctioned by the Bank, where the Bank has some control over agenda and participation. But it is also evident in the Bank's interpretation of NGO and popular issue campaigns.

Staff who manage the NGO consultations are often in a position to limit and define the criticism that will be accepted and heard. Bank staff on the NGO-World Bank Committee said privately in 1989, and many times since, that they had heard and learned enough from the NGOs on adjustment lending and the environment, and wished to move on to discuss participation and details of operational collaboration. More generally, it is now policy to be open to criticism from NGOs 'when it is constructive and valid' (Strategic Planning and Review, 1990, p. 11). Some 'single-issue environmental groups . . . criticize the Bank in ways which often are not constructive' (EXTIE, 1990 Progress Report 20). Qualifying adjectives are a regular reminder that the Bank's participants will judge what subjects, information and criticism are appropriate.

Not only is the character of acceptable criticism defined in advance, the dialogue is often later interpreted to render it collegial and acceptable. After angry protests and confrontations in Berlin at the 1988 IMF/World Bank annual meetings, the Bank's *Annual Report* (1989, p. 95) blandly reports that 'unofficial conferences and NGO events are increasingly prominent during the annual meetings of the Bank and the IMF . . . . NGOs . . . contribute to the Bank's thinking on important development issues in various ways.' The 1987 *Annual Report* (p. 62) similarly renders international conflict over environmental policy and adjustment in the most antiseptic terms: 'Consultations with NGOs . . . have dealt extensively with the concerns of both environmental and poverty-oriented groups. Their views are increasingly taken into consideration in the formulation of appropriate development strategies.'

NGOs have none the less noted positive trends in the dialogue, particularly in substantive discussions of sectoral policies, and the improved access to decision-makers from the Bank's operational divisions. But even as the quality of the dialogue improves, NGOs face an organizational style that threatens to erode the influence they have gained. One concern is that as the dialogue has become more routine, with the routinization of exchanges, NGO input may be losing the sharp edge that captured the Bank's attention in the first place. Several Bank staff say that the dialogue with NGOs no longer needs to be adversarial, because the Bank is now sensitive to NGOs' concerns (Salmen and Eaves, 1989, pp. 43–4). Other staff also view NGOs as moving from an isolated, confrontative style toward negotiations and partnership with the Bank (Policy staff no. 3).

Similarly the Bank characterizes NGO advocacy on environmental issues and tribal people's rights as 'help[ing] to sensitize public opinion and development practitioners, including the Bank . . .' (World Bank, 1990d, p. 14). The successful NGO effort to 'direct the attention of the Bank and its member governments to the environmental and social costs of some large-scale projects' is described in the past tense, carrying the message that the complaints have been heard, taken into consideration, and that the issue is now in the Bank's hands.

A second danger lies in the gap between rhetoric and performance. Theory, policy and intellectual work on 'progressive' themes – women, environment, poverty, impact of adjustment on the poor, involuntary resettlement – are often substituted by World Bank representatives for changes in actual performance.

A 1989 policy paper (Strategic Planning and Review Department 1989) on participation dwells on the evolving history of World Bank *thinking* on the subject. Nagle and Ghose (1989, p. 5) note that Bank literature on participation 'has outdistanced both the policy development and the practice of encouraging participation in Bank projects.' NGO-World Bank Committee co-chair Alexander Shakow emphasized *new articulations* of development goals by President Conable in the 1989 Committee meetings, and discussed the changing, improved, responsive *interpretation* of questions. World Bank staff objected strenuously to the NGOs' Position Paper because it didn't reflect the Bank's *'changing interpretation* of these questions' (NGO-World Bank Committee Meeting, 1 November 1989; emphases added).

Likewise, the legal principle of 'no net losers' for involuntary resettlement in World Bank-funded schemes is touted to academic and NGO audiences as evidence of progressive social science at work in the World Bank (Cernea, 1989; Golan, NGO-World Bank Committee Meeting, 1989). Legal and social principles were carefully worked through in developing a policy for treatment and compensation of displaced populations (Escudero, 1988). But Rich (1990, pp. 313–14) draws on internal reviews and local sources in Zaire, Rwanda, Indonesia, Kenya and India to show that the policy is largely ignored in the field.

John Clark (1988, p. 2), then of OXFAM-UK, argues that special publications on poverty are outside the mainstream of the Bank's operations and research. Poverty is discussed in special documents 'while the central issues remain export promotion, debt service management, control of public spending, reducing parastatals, market liberalization, price de-control. . . .' 'Which,' he asks, 'is the real World Bank? The World Bank which writes special small circulation reports on poverty alleviation? Or the Bank which views poverty as just one of oh-so-many issues to be remembered (on the last page) by those who are responsible for managing the economic affairs of our planet?'

CONCLUSION

The World Bank's organizational culture selects the information that reaches its decision-makers, creating a fictional world in which its analytic, technical and financial resources can be applied impartially and effectively. The information bias isolates the Bank from important input as it protects it from perspectives that challenge its assumptions and myths. Individuals within the Bank experiment and learn, critics speak and receive responses, but a variety of organizational defense mechanisms protect the basic assumptions that guide its operations.

These characteristics shape the Bank's interactions with NGOs. 'Participation' by NGOs and affected people is generally limited to mobilizing communities to carry out their parts of a project. 'Beneficiary groups' are formed to improve project implementation or cost-recovery: this recognizes the need for social organization, but limits its role to consent and mobilization.

Criticism and protest by NGOs and their allies can change World Bank-funded projects. A campaign of protest has also stimulated the creation of an environmental unit, the hiring of regional environmental staff, and a new set of Environmental Impact Assessment procedures that include consultation with local NGOs.

But the dynamics of learning – and of not learning – still present formidable obstacles to reformers within and outside the institution. An organizational culture and information selection mechanism tend to reinforce and perpetuate a lending mandate and organizational myths that define limited roles for NGOs.

8 Conclusions

The *National Journal* speculated in 1988 that the World Bank might 'never be the same' after entering into policy dialogues with US-based environmental and development NGOs (1988, p. 3250). Throughout the 1980s and early 1990s the Bank has, indeed, been the target of pressures from NGOs and others on areas as diverse as human rights, the environment, project performance, debt management and structural adjustment.

But in 1994, at the fiftieth anniversary of the Bank's creation, the variety of changes that are in process in the Bank stop short of any basic change in its operations. Initiatives within the Bank have created more room for innovation and variance by staff in areas such as popular participation and microfinance. And new commitments in environmental policy and a partial opening in information disclosure have marginally increased the ability of groups affected by the Bank's loans to demand a measure of accountability.

But neither its main lending programs nor the organizational factors that have lent stability in the past have been altered. The Bank's influence, through conditionality and its dominant role in donor coordination, has grown faster than the ability of member governments or citizens to demand accountability. This chapter sums up the evidence of change and resistance to change, touches on the significance for some broader theoretical discussions, reviews policy implications for the World Bank and for NGOs, and proposes a program of further monitoring and research.

PROJECTS: THE TERMS OF ENGAGEMENT

NGOs are involved in an increasing number of World Bank-financed projects, and engaged in discussions with the Bank in a larger number of fora than was the case a decade ago. The growing number of project contacts began with the initiative of individual staff members interested in NGOs and the work of the staff unit that promotes NGO collaboration. It has benefited from encouragement by some managers, and increasing interest by some international NGOs in securing contracts from the Bank. While some staff members consider the Bank's

'NGO work' a passing fad, there is no doubt that the number of 'NGO projects' has grown substantially.

But as to the nature of the project interaction – the 'terms of engagement' (Hellinger, 1987) – the record is not as favorable. For most projects, NGO influence is limited to implementing a component of a project designed and negotiated by World Bank staff and government officials. This arrangement, which dominates project collaboration, reflects appreciation by some staff for NGOs' efficiency as service deliverers, but little desire to cultivate NGOs as organizers and agents of accountability.

The implementing role has sometimes grown into more dynamic and potentially influential NGO participation. Implementing NGOs can monitor project impact and help communicate wishes of affected people to government, Bank staff and a wider audience. But this initiative is absent from most NGO-implemented projects, reflecting the caution and narrow mission of many NGOs as well as the reluctance of most Bank staff to enter into such dialogue.

The reported growth in NGO contributions to designing Bank-financed projects since 1988 diminishes under a close review even only of project documents. Much of the reported role in design involved not input to an entire project or even a component of the investment, but NGO design of their own projects, to be submitted for support to a fund financed under the project.

Second, a substantial amount of NGO 'design' work is for projects to provide temporary relief from the adverse effects of Bank-sponsored adjustment plans. NGOs participate not in shaping the adjustment conditions, perhaps by facilitating consultations with organized groups of poor people, but in contributing to plans for social safety net programs. Participation in the design of government programs to be financed by World Bank investments remains an exception to the norm, in which NGOs implement projects and mobilize people's 'participation' in them.

Cooperating groups of international, national and grassroots organizations appear to have been most able and disposed to engage Bank staff and government officials in discussions of sectoral policies, project design and implementation. Whether collaborative or conflictive in tone, these cases, prominent especially in environmental and urban housing and services projects, illustrate the potential for NGO influence and the concerted effort required by NGOs to play this role.

But the much larger number of projects, in which NGOs deliver Bank-financed services for the state, raises the likelihood that the engagement is changing NGOs more than it is the Bank. In the process,

NGOs, the Bank and other donors are allowing the NGOs' potential significance for effective democratization to be compromised.

PROJECTS AND POLICY: ASSESSING THE IMPACT OF THE ENGAGEMENT

The World Bank is a large and complex organization, and assessing the extent and nature of change in policy and practice can be difficult. No approach can remove the ambiguity entirely, but four factors derived from organizational theory are useful indicators of the nature of change in the Bank. Significant changes in policy and practice would likely mean changes in:

1. aspects of the standard operating procedures, including the project cycle, staffing, training and incentives;
2. the organizational myths of sovereignty and apolitical development, and of development impact as measured by economic rate of return;
3. the organizational culture, especially sources of information and its processing within the organization; and
4. patterns of resistance and support from key actors in the environment.

Reviewed against these indicators, the World Bank's record with NGOs points toward the importance and resilience of the structure, procedures and organizational culture of the Bank, the dominance of narrow national, financial, corporate and professional interests, and toward the tendency of these factors to resist change.

Training and experience dispose most Bank staff to see economic, political and social issues through the eyes of elite planners and economists. These inclinations are strongly reinforced by organizational practices and career incentives that discourage spending extra time building relationships with NGOs. The creation of a special unit to handle relations with NGOs offers a convenient and frequently used contact point, but it also puts the liaison in the hands of staff skilled in representing the Bank to outsiders, and in rendering outside input compatible with prevailing thinking and practice.

There are initiatives within the Bank that could be seeds of change: post-Wapenhans concerns with borrower 'ownership' of programs; new, consultative approaches in the Southern Africa department; a group promoting participatory methodologies; and even a proposal that questions the basic framework of the Bank's project cycle.

But these initiatives face a formidable and durable set of organizational interests and mandates. A strong organizational culture sifts and selects information with remarkable consistency. Discourse and innovation are shaped, especially in written work produced in the Bank, in ways that are consonant with the Bank's own understanding of its mission. New mandates are appended to an approach to development finance that rests on the tenets of neo-orthodox economic theory, the myths of apolitical development and of borrower sovereignty, and that squares with the interests of major industrialized countries and international banks.

Has the liaison with NGOs effected any change in these elements of the core technology, myths and organizational culture? Most evidence of NGO impact is not on these systemic factors, but on individual projects. Some urban sector projects have been affected by project experiences involving NGOs; irrigation projects now tend to involve local grassroots groups in cost recovery and maintenance of irrigation systems; the Aga Khan Foundation has had fruitful exchanges in some South Asia operations; and environmental advocates have modified several individual projects, created an environmental impact assessment procedure and initiated a Bank role in national environmental policy planning. These are important accomplishments.

But the evidence of more systematic change is slim. In policy areas where NGOs have been involved – environment, popular participation and adjustment – external pressure is reinterpreted, managed, and responded to in ways that protect or reinforce established assumptions and operations.

Environmental Policy

The most promising products of NGO advocacy are the system of Environmental Impact Assessments (EIA) for projects judged likely to have an adverse environmental impact; mandated National Environmental Action Plans; and an expanded environmental staff in Bank headquarters.

But the promise of these changes is as yet far from fulfilled. EIA procedures, for example, encourage regular participation of concerned NGOs. How the EIAs will work, and how the Bank will manage the conflict between its environmental mandates, growth-based model and the prevailing drive to disburse capital is a matter for close monitoring. The early record, reviewed in an internal 1993 memo, shows participation to be nonexistent in African EIAs, and not much stronger in the other regions. The requirement for EIA, further, extends only to certain projects and not at all to policy-based lending. Excluding projects unlikely to have direct environmental impact is sensible, but setting aside SAPs is tantamount to scrutinizing individual schemes while allowing whole economic plans (including export agriculture, mining, energy development, timber production) to grow without formal regard for resource use or environmental impact.

In sectoral policy areas – water, energy, agriculture – the Bank has sought to involve NGOs in discussions of draft policy papers. While noting certain limitations in the process and content of these consultations, NGO participants recognize the value of the discussions and the candor of participants. But Bank policy with respect to project-related forced resettlement is an example of a regularly observed pattern in social and environmental fields: policy is carefully crafted but not enforced. When governments balk at meeting resettlement standards in full, the Bank has been extremely reluctant or unable to win compliance. Driven by the need to move money and faced with declining influence with some major borrowers, the Bank invokes borrower sovereignty and stops short of using its leverage to protect those ousted by the project.

At its best, World Bank policy should have the exemplary effect claimed by its recent review, changing expectations for all government policy and performance in resettlement associated with major infrastructure works. But given governments' reluctance to bear the financial and political costs of accommodating minority needs, the Bank needs to play a more active role. If the Bank were serious about leading a global change in standards for infrastructure development, it would (1) promote its perspective through training and supervision as vigorously as it has in macro-economic policy; and (2) take seriously the NGO proposals that it shift its priority from monumental infrastructure projects to less centralized, more efficient energy-generation schemes.

The Bank's role in the Global Environment Fund embodies another organizational trait, the capacity to convert pressure for reform into support for new resources by thrusting itself into a leading role in the GEF. NGOs suddenly found the Bank – the target of their critique – in charge of global resources for global environmental protection. As it had three decades before, in the creation of IDA, the Bank managed to neutralize a troublesome new demand (for a concessional lending facility in the IDA case) by absorbing it into its own operations.

The Bank has taken more steps in environmental policy and practice than in any other area in response to NGO concerns and pressure.

But those working for policy change within the Bank are limited by its export- and growth-oriented development model. And it is unprepared to propose and support another paradigm for development, lacking the will and the mandate to devise a new development path and to commit the resources needed to compensate borrowers for the sacrifices the industrial countries want them to make.

This final point was re-emphasized in a highly critical statement by Herman Daly, the Bank's leading environmental economist until he resigned after six years in the Bank's environment department. Daly attacks the assumption of the Bank's basic model that countries' interests are served by inserting them into international production patterns. Without international bodies capable of regulating increasingly internationalized capital, he argues, the Bank's borrowers would be better served by policies that reduce or slow capital's internationalization (Daly, 1994). He charges that the Bank's inability to influence policy in the North renders it 'nearly useless' for dealing with the pressing global issues of consumption, resource use and trade.

Popular Participation

The involvement of NGOs in Bank-funded projects and its learning process on participation reflect the interest of a growing number of individual staff in the possibilities for more participatory operations. Project staff involved with NGOs still characterize their work as mainly individual initiative, requiring the will to bend project design procedures and ignore existing career incentives. Even staff most involved in project collaboration value NGOs mainly as efficient service deliverers, not for any more dynamic, formative role in collaboration.

Discussion and policy papers on participation in World Bank-financed projects deal mostly with techniques for mobilizing and informing local populations, to gain their acceptance and participation in an already planned project activity. The use of water users' associations and other farmer groups to manage local irrigation networks has generally meant that project managers or a government authority encourages the formation of these groups. This process of directed participation through newly-created organizations has little prospect of producing lasting social organization or vehicles for accountability and representation.

The participation learning process has included discussions that correctly diagnose some of these limitations, but lacked the authority to change them. The opening created by the learning process and by pressure on the Bank's 'non-performing' portfolio gives some reason for hope.

Probably the most positive general conclusion to be drawn to date is that the increased interest in NGOs among Bank officials and in the agency's policy statements may help to counterbalance the disincentives that otherwise discourage interested staff from making contact and building working relationships with NGOs.

But the Bank's new focus on 'portfolio management' and on improving financial performance also threatens to make popular participation only an adjunct to the management goal of deepening borrowers' 'ownership' of investments. Participation at the Bank, as at most donor agencies, has more to do with enlisting project stakeholders' support than with building on their input.

Adjustment

Dialogue on participation has been promoted vigorously by some in the Bank but constrained by a variety of limiting factors. On adjustment issues, NGOs have made fewer inroads. The Bank has successfully reduced the varied NGO positions on adjustment to their common element – that adjustment policies are in some way harming poor people – and responded by financing compensatory measures to soften the short-term impact of adjustment. This has in turn focused most Bank-NGO discussions on the adequacy of compensatory measures and safety nets in improving the 'social dimensions' of adjustment.

The Bank's NGO and poverty specialists express interest in 'pro-poor' adjustment and in using conditionality to improve the operating environment for NGOs. But these interests have yet to produce any significant variation from the Bank's program of liberalization and deregulation. And while the Bank's NGO specialists affirm the need to liberalize the operating environment for the NGO sector as much as for private for-profit actors, an effective initiative has yet to materialize. The Bank's modifications of its adjustment package have been measures to improve the implementation record or to cushion short-term impact, not to broaden the options or change the reform agenda. Nor have any but a few NGOs insisted on more fundamental changes, stranding the handful that do call for a new approach without broad support.

The Bank's most recent self-assessment on adjustment makes it clear that its course is set, and that where investment response or other hoped-for results have been slow in coming, what is needed is greater rigor and effort in attracting and reassuring potential external investors. While the Bank remains willing to discuss NGOs' views, it is clear by now that continued dialogue about adjustment plans will not sway the Bank. The mixed record in environmental policy and popular participation and the inflexibility of adjustment policy have frustrated many NGO activists. But the limited impact is not only a function of the Bank's organizational defenses, development myth and ideology. It also reflects the absence of a widespread, concerted effort by NGOs to adopt the representative, innovating and demonstration roles needed to expand their influence.

NGOs AND THE WORLD BANK

Although this study has focused on the World Bank, relations between the Bank and NGOs have important implications for NGOs as well. New patterns of cooperation among Northern and Southern NGOs, and the roles of Southern NGOs in their own societies are being shaped in the interaction with the Bank. For Northern-based NGOs, the effectiveness of networks that include international, national and community-based organizations in gaining influence in Bank-financed projects confirms the potential for Northern NGOs to operate as partners, supporters and advocates for NGOs based in the South. As NGOs based in the industrialized countries face the options and challenges for their identity and their roles, the record of the partnership and advocacy role in these interactions with the World Bank provides some evidence of the expanded impact NGOs can have.

Similarly, international NGOs that have devoted staff and given priority to influencing the Bank through collaboration and example have seen some effect. But such influence requires more than chance collaboration, and few NGOs have committed themselves to a deliberate advocacy and demonstration role. NGO protest and strategies of critical collaboration produce evidence of change only over time. NGOs, like other organizations, prefer to focus on issues and elements of their work environment they can control. For international NGOs, further impact on the World Bank will require commitments of energy and resources to objectives less tangible and immediate than relief or community development projects.

Southern NGOs face different but related choices. Decisions about how to relate to government or intergovernmental bodies such as the Bank affect NGOs' political posture in the immediate term, and the cumulative effect of many such decisions will help define the role of NGOs in civil society. Delivering goods or services for government and Bank-designed programs sets up a tension between constituencies – donors and community-level partners – that is a constant challenge. Many NGOs are seizing the resource of official funding without a strategy and commitment to managing this tension without abandoning their fundamental identification with poor communities.

The tension for NGOs confronts the Bank and other donors in two ways as well. First, if they wish to nurture active NGO movements that support accountability in public and civic institutions, they need to be deliberate in facilitating this connection and accountability to communities and people's organizations. This may mean active facilitation as Alan Fowler argues, encouraging in the process discussions and organizing that is critical of government and Bank policy and practice. The Bank's engagement with NGOs has shown a contrary tendency, encouraging a focus on operational cooperation even in those NGOs most interested in policy debate.

Second, while the Bank emphasizes that its operational engagement is increasingly with local and nationally based NGOs in the borrowing countries, it is probably true that working with such NGOs through appropriate intermediaries is less likely to compromise their relations to their constituencies. The project record to date suggests that NGO networks, rather than community-based organizations alone, are likely to be associated with active, critical NGO involvement in a Bank-financed project.

An Anti-NGO Backlash?

No one should assume that the Bank's enthusiasm for NGOs and its willingness to debate and accommodate them will continue indefinitely. NGOs and other critics hope that each new concession will increase their leverage or the momentum for change at the Bank. But there is limited tolerance in key circles for NGO criticism and the highly political and public nature of their critique.

Resentment of the Bank's concessions to NGOs has simmered among some in management and the board. As criticism reaches the media more effectively, signs of a potential backlash are appearing. The Bank's senior management overturned months of work on a new strategy paper for cooperation with NGOs in August 1994, opting for a less sweeping, 'business as usual' approach.

Public criticism of the Bank in its 1993 forum on Overcoming World Hunger also irked some in the Bank who felt the Bank's spokespeople did too little to defend its record. NGO criticism and demonstrations at the Bank's fiftieth anniversary annual meetings in Madrid heightened the irritation within the Bank. As the criticism broadens and NGOs outside the environmental movement adopt strategies that have won influence for environmentalists, resistance in the Bank will likely grow. The evidence of backsliding on NGO-related issues includes the rejection in August 1994 of staff's NGO strategy paper; the demise of the small, two-year old fund for innovative social and humanitarian initiatives; discussions among senior management of the option of a decisive retreat from rhetorical commitments on poverty and participation, which some feel have given external critics too much leverage over the institution. As James Wolfensohn assumes the presidency of the Bank (in June 1995), his early signals on these issues will help to determine the opportunities for change in the near future.

Will the resistance produce a sharp scaling-back of engagement with development NGOs? While this is possible, what appears more likely is a greater emphasis on the Bank's division between cooperative and 'constructive' NGOs and those whose critique of its policies is more fundamental. Links between such networks, especially environmental networks and most major operational international NGOs, are already tenuous. If the Bank succeeds in strengthening its links to operational groups by providing even very small facilities for grant funding, it will have little difficulty broadening the split. The implications for a strong international voluntary sector would be substantial, and NGOs need to resist such a split. Engagement with external donors provides a legitimacy and protection that strengthens the position of NGOs in many countries. If NGOs allow the donors, led by the Bank, to divide them, it will likely accelerate the trend toward service-delivery NGOs in the South, and weaken the message of the non-governmental movement in the North.

SOME IMPLICATIONS: CIVIL SOCIETY AND NGOs; SUSTAINABLE DEVELOPMENT AND WORLD ORDERS; FUTURE MULTILATERALISM

The Bank's global scale and its economic policy-making role have won it a major role in discussions of future global economic orders. Its engagement with NGOs is also a consideration in current debates over NGOs, civil society and democratization.

Global Civil Society

As production becomes increasingly internationalized and international actors such as the Bank assume larger roles in states' policy-making and administration, a global level of civil society may become increasingly significant. Questions about how such networks function, set agendas and govern themselves are being worked out in *ad hoc* ways, often in the midst of struggles with the Bank and other donors over particular projects and policies. Links among interest groups, social movements, international NGOs and their constituencies in the industrialized countries may become a vehicle for deeper ties of solidarity and mutual interest.

At the national level, the Bank plays a variety of roles in shaping NGO-government relations in the diverse political environments of its borrowing countries. Governments' accountability to international creditors including the Bank, especially on debt and adjustment issues, has often limited state accountability to active groups in civil society. States can, and often do use the international financial institutions as scapegoats, redirecting public resentment toward the Bank and IMF. In areas of social and environmental policy, however, NGOs have often found the Bank and other donors to be a useful ally or lever. Where the Bank is more susceptible to critique (on resettlement, indigenous people's rights, global environmental issues) than is an individual government, NGOs have brought international norms to bear through the Bank's leverage.

The Bank has accepted and played both of these roles. But its institutional focus on project and policy lending means that its appreciation of NGOs will continue to emphasize the instrumental – service delivery – rather than their implicit importance in society. This focus has the salutary effect that the Bank has seldom sought to mobilize NGO opinion to support its policy initiatives with governments. Recent appeals for NGO attention to public expenditure reform may signal a change in this posture. But as the Bank's engagement with national NGOs remains operationally focused, it falls to other actors – international NGO movements and interested donors – to support NGOs in strengthening and maintaining their links and accountability to excluded groups in society. With major projects and social fund money available to NGOs, international NGOs and other donors have an important role to play in encouraging and supporting NGOs' links to popular and community organizations, and links among Southern NGOs and networks.

This building and shaping of international networks may be the most significant outcome of the Bank's relations with NGOs. Observers and participants in the international environmental movement have emphasized the emergence of networks around shared interests or commitments. Equally broad networks exist among development NGOs who relate to the Bank and other donors, principally as sources of program funds. Internationally, these two networks have found relatively little common ground on economic and development policy issues. Their diverse relations to donor funding tend to keep them divided.

NGOs, the Bank and Alternate Economic Futures

After more than a decade of dominance by orthodox adjustment packages and debt management arrangements, some theorists and activists continue to hope for greater openness to alternative strategies and more varied forms of engagement with the global economy. What are their prospects?

There is little in the World Bank's current posture to inspire hope. Despite institutional second thoughts about the East Asia miracle, and discomfort about the record of adjustment in Africa, no paradigm shift appears near. If space is to be made for any alternative economic future – based on regional cooperation or on a renewed emphasis on self-reliance (as suggested by Shaw, 1994) – it will require some loosening of the Bretton Woods institutions' still strong hold on standards and arrangements in development finance. The NGO challenge to the Bank and the IMF could play a role by slowly eroding their credibility and authority on adjustment, debt and the environment. It is even possible that concerted NGO efforts to produce and support alternative economic adjustment packages might compel the Bank to support economic programs that vary somewhat from the present orthodoxy. But it would likely require a significant revolt among the Bank's major shareholders, more decisive than the Japanese dissent to date, to expand the options significantly.

Future Economic Multilateralism

The Bretton Woods organizations' hold on the development finance regime is essentially unchallenged. Although debtor countries continue to have net negative capital flows to the IBRD and the IMF, the G-7 and the institutions themselves have been content with a patchwork of minor debt and finance arrangements. As yet, no significant institutional alternatives have emerged from the fiftieth anniversary discussions.

And despite proposals for a process to consider such alternatives (Helleiner, 1994), no international movement toward a serious debate is in sight.

The Bank, despite its praise for the virtues of market competition, maintains a virtual monopoly as the only player in the marketplace of development strategy with significant finance to back and support its program. Either major bilateral funding in support of divergent strategies, or an institutional change in the Bank's control of both project and policy design, and finance, might provide the Bank and its clients the benefits of a competing service provider. A separate facility to assist governments in preparation of projects independent of Bank staff – without financing capacity – would force the Bank to consider genuinely independent proposals for financing (Turid Sato, personal communication 1994). Neither appears likely.

Still, global political changes in the late 1980s and early 1990s remind us how quickly long-standing features of the global political economy can change. Even if the prospects for major change appear slim, it is incumbent on NGOs to craft policy agendas that encourage reform efforts within the Bank, strengthen Southern networks' ability to influence Bank and government policies, and intensify the pressure on the institution and its major shareholders to justify arrangements that serve the majority in the borrowing countries so poorly. The final section of this study outlines some elements of such an agenda.

STRATEGIC ADVOCACY: AN NGO POLICY AGENDA FOR THE 1990s

NGOs have tended to gain victories on targeted issues within the Bank, modifying or blocking individual projects, influencing a sectoral policy paper or Operational Directive, or provoking a new round of declarations on poverty alleviation as a policy priority. But even as they chalk up victories on these issues, the larger policy direction of the Bank – managing debt repayment and adjustment and controlling funds for global environmental problems, for example – remains beyond their influence. NGOs need a more strategic approach to the Bank, and an agenda that reflects both policy priorities and organizational realities.

The breadth and difficulty of issues, the power of the interests involved, and the organizational complexity of the Bank itself require strategies that identify key issues, recognize organizational roadblocks to change, and identify tangible and verifiable changes to be sought in

World Bank practice. The following is a contribution to such agenda-making. Some of the proposals are already part of the advocacy agendas of some NGOs, notably the '50 Years Is Enough' campaign. Others are more modest proposals of the kind that could surface if more radical initiatives force the Bank toward major reforms. The agenda is by no means exhaustive.

Three Policy Issues for the 1990s

1. *Debt and structural adjustment.* The issues most central to the Bank's global role have been most difficult for NGOs to address. NGOs have helped persuade major creditor countries to adopt more flexible terms in negotiations with debtors in the Paris Club, but more decisive action to relieve the debt burden is needed in this setting and in the World Bank. The IDA Fund for relief of commercial debt of IDA borrowers should be employed quickly to expand its use. But with much of the debt once owed to commercial creditors now converted to debt owed to MDBs, the burden of this debt itself must be addressed, at least for the lowest income, severely indebted countries.

NGOs should articulate a debt relief strategy where relief is based on need and ability to pay, rather than arbitrary percentages and other considerations. The Bank and others have acknowledged that, for the poorest countries, even the most generous debt relief terms under discussion by the G-7 do not lift the debt burden sufficiently to really improve development prospects (World Bank, *World Debt Tables 1992–93* vol. 1, pp. 8–9). The MDBs and creditor governments should be pressed to adopt a new principle: reduce debts sufficiently to shrink service payments to a level of export earnings (perhaps 20 per cent) that permits a country to invest again in its own development. Assent to this principle from the Bank – even if not accompanied immediately by steps to apply it to debt owed to the Bank itself – could help stimulate agreement among the G-7 countries.

Debt relief is a strategic linchpin in the constellation of issues on which NGOs seek to influence the Bank. The debt burden underlies many governments' weak position in negotiating adjustment agreements with the Bank. The debt and finance crisis also makes concessional IDA funds so vital to the lowest-income borrowers that governments and NGOs are constrained from threatening IDA funding, even when this is their most effective source of leverage.

NGO advocacy on adjustment, beyond calling for safety net programs, has been almost entirely ineffective. Southern NGOs and interest groups in borrowing countries have managed to weaken governments' resolves or limit the implementation of adjustment agreements. Northern NGOs seem to have made little headway with the Bank or their governments by documenting the ills of adjustment. Discussions of global adjustment are too general to reach and motivate citizen support in the North. Without mass political support, further NGO input at this global level will not sway the Bank's economists from their models and plans. It is time for alternative strategies.

First, Northern NGOs and NGO networks should focus their critique of adjustment on countries where there is significant resistance and alternatives to orthodox adjustment plans. Major campaigns focused on, for example, Mexico, India, the Philippines, Zimbabwe and Bangladesh could give new energy to the critique of adjustment. It would increase credibility and specificity, strengthen the local basis for global NGO action, and facilitate local political action in support of alternatives. In other cases, NGOs should acknowledge that many governments have accepted liberalization strategies. Where this is the case, the Bank should be urged to focus not on imposing further conditions but on financing the institutions and measures needed to implement the strategy effectively. NGOs could essentially call for 'no new conditionality,' making the reasonable claim that governments not persuaded by the first 15 years of technical advice, policy dialogue and financial pressure are not going to buy the Bank's solution, and that those who have adopted it deserve assistance in implementing it, not further arm-twisting.

A third option, perhaps compatible in some cases with either of the others, is to acknowledge the need for macro-economic adjustment – balanced current accounts and good economic management – and help stimulate development and discussion of concrete, locally-based plans in the national political context.

It is time to recognize that the NGO critique of the World Bank role in adjustment will not carry this issue with donor governments or the Bank. Where strong resistance to anti-egalitarian strategies exists, NGOs should support it. Where it does not, or where a dialogue is called for with donors and the Bank, a strategy that focuses on debt relief and limits on further conditionality is worth trying.

2. *Popular participation.* Both in World Bank-funded activities and as a goal of its policy dialogue with borrowers, participation of broad segments of the population should be a major theme in World Bank practice, and a top strategic priority for NGOs.

Broad, early popular participation in economic and sectoral planning and in project identification, design and implementation could boost the quality and impact of a range of Bank-financed and related activities. The Bank has committed itself to encouraging participation in Poverty Targeted Investments, National Environmental Action Plans, Poverty Assessments, and other planning and policy making processes. The successful promotion of participatory methodologies in the Bank would influence the process and product in each of these, as well as in many Bank-financed projects.

No other single measure would penetrate the Bank's standard operations and its information system as thoroughly as the expanded use of participatory methods. NGOs should capitalize on Bank management's commitments in principle to participation, and work with supporters in the Bank to document its value to Bank investments and to protect it as much as possible from dilution in practice. A concerted effort to promote popular input in Bank-financed activities, coupled with expanded access to Bank documents under a new information policy, is the best tool the NGOs have to change the fundamental operations of the Bank.

Expanded public participation in decisions on matters of policy has implications far beyond the World Bank. The Bank's stated support for NGOs has probably already expanded the space for nongovernmental bodies' participation in national policy deliberations and implementation in some borrowing countries. An earnest effort from the Bank to enlarge that effect, including persistent pressure in policy dialogue with governments, could help level the political and economic playing fields and boost the vitality and effectiveness of public deliberation and action.

But the Bank remains cautious, with senior officials saying that pressure on human rights, administrative and legal issues related to the operating environment for NGOs will not extend beyond the conditions relevant to implementing specific Bank investments (meetings with Canadian human rights advocates, June 1993).

Globally and at Bank headquarters, advocacy on popular participation is complex. There are many fronts on which progress can be made or stymied, and subtle gradations of popular involvement in an agency's decisions and action. NGOs should press for increased participation on as many fronts as possible – NEAPs, poverty assessments, and project loans included – as well for stronger management support for popular participation in overall programming. Policy pressure at headquarters and through the Board needs to be matched by initiatives in the borrowing countries to comment on project plans, discuss sectoral or regional strategies, protest at objectionable projects and jointly evaluate NGO experiences.

Most of the evidence of participation in Bank activities will be widely dispersed and difficult to aggregate. But NGOs can watch for and encourage certain changes at headquarters that would be indicators of organizational progress in promoting participation. More flexible limits and allocation of staff time to project development and implementation would open up room for participatory methods and reduce the incentives to push money. Shifting significant numbers of staff from headquarters to permanent missions would expand the opportunity for contact with local realities. Expanded, accelerated and mandatory training in social science skills related to participatory development would provide important support. And a more flexible approach to the project cycle, downgrading the importance of the definitive pre-appraisal and regularizing the process of feedback and revision during implementation would open opportunities for planning that reflects the dynamics of social change and responds to emerging problems and opportunities.

3. *Reconsidering IDA as institution.* The debate over IDA-10 ended with many NGOs concluding that, in the absence of an alternative channel for funds, they must give IDA at least conditioned support. The fact that neither donors nor borrowers have another viable channel for concessional funding on IDA's scale allows the Bank its pattern of sluggish action or noncompliance in response to official and unofficial demands for change.

This is why the proposal, promoted by the '50 Years is Enough' campaign, to separate the concessional lending function from the World Bank, should be seriously studied. There is no reason why concessional lending funds such as IDA's need to be administered by a bank. Since public tax monies, not financial market proceeds, are being lent, conventional banking standards are not essential. And since IDA concessional loans should fit into the poorest countries' development strategies, it would make more sense for an institution governed by development ministers and directors of national aid agencies, rather than finance ministers, to oversee its operation. In the short term, international consideration of a proposal to remove the multilateral concessional lending function from the Bank would at least give the Bank a strong incentive to take poverty-related demands more seriously. If it failed to do so, the international community could choose to create an institution that might win more widespread and enthusiastic support.

NGO Institutions and Modes of Action

To increase impact and marshall the kind of influence needed to advance their agendas in the coming decade, NGOs need institutions for action that emphasize three priorities: a more integrated agenda and campaign; closer communication among the principal activist networks; and expanded South-South networking and monitoring, and consultations with the World Bank in the borrowing countries.

1. *Integrating NGO agendas*, especially environmental and development agendas, is a priority. NGOs made some progress in the 1980s toward this integration. But the NGO agenda, especially in the North, remains bifurcated, and the differences in priorities, resources and networks are readily exploited by the Bank. Many environmental organizations have taken their agenda well beyond conservation issues, tying the human effects of resource degradation closely to more traditional concerns for wildlife and habitat preservation. Sectoral concerns, however, often dominate environmental agendas, and the Bank has been able to stave off many of its environmental critics with minor concessions on energy, forestry, and water policies.

Still, environmental NGOs, with greater financial resources, a history of advocacy and legal work in the industrialized countries, and a broader constituency among middle class North Americans and Europeans, have had far greater effect on the Bank than poverty-focused NGOs. To take the next step and begin to influence the core policies and practices of the Bank, including adjustment and debt management, an integrated agenda and campaign will be required.

A joint and integrated effort would also require much greater commitment of resources by Northern development NGOs. With fewer staff and resources committed to World Bank work, development NGOs generally cannot match the pace and intensity of environmental NGO advocacy. Nor have most given much attention or support to policy changes promoted by the environmental community on energy and forestry, among other sectors, that have enormous human impact. To implement an agenda that embraces debt, sustainable development, participation and adjustment along with key resource use issues would require a greater commitment to advocacy by the Northern development NGOs, and closer integration of advocacy and program activities.

2. *Greater coordination among NGO advocacy networks* could help to stimulate this broader commitment, and increase the impact of existing

efforts. The most important step would be increased planning and co-ordination among the major nodes of NGO strategizing and information: the cluster of Washington-based environmental NGOs; the Asian NGO coalition ANGOC; the NGO Working Group on the World Bank; the European coalition EURODAD, NGOs such as OXFAM-UK, Community Aid Abroad (Australia), the Third World Network (Malaysia); the new Bank network based in Montevideo, Uruguay; and the US-based development NGOs through InterAction.

Some have called for a global NGO secretariat to coordinate work on the World Bank, or on structural adjustment (Woodward, 1992). The time may come when NGOs conclude that such a body is necessary, but experience suggests that they should concentrate first on thickening, expanding and connecting present networks of communication and action, and on energizing and democratizing present coordinating institutions. The establishment of advocacy offices in Washington by NGO networks based outside the US – now including the Federation of African Voluntary Development Agencies (FAVDO) and the international Oxfam network – should help in this process.

The NGO Working Group on the World Bank could vastly expand its contribution if its NGO participants actively coordinated and facilitated NGO advocacy and monitoring of the Bank in their home countries and regions. This and other imperatives suggest that the Working Group's organization be re-thought. Rather than a NGO forum for sanctioned discussions with the Bank, the Working Group should re-establish itself as a gathering point for NGOs active on key policy issues. Rather than a self-selecting body with a membership list, the Working Group should become a coordinating forum for all organizations seeking cooperative NGO involvement on structural adjustment, debt and popular participation issues.

3. *Expanded South-South regional consultation, coordination and monitoring* would confront the Bank with more frequent and widespread articulation of NGO concerns. The current expansion of monitoring and accountability efforts, especially those with substantial Southern initiative, are an encouraging trend that calls for international cooperation and support. Major Southern networks including the Asian NGO Coalition for Agrarian Reform and Rural Development (ANGOC), PRIA in India, the Center for the Study of Agrarian Change (CECCAM) in Mexico and a Latin American/Caribbean network serviced by Instituto del Tercer Mundo in Uruguay, have attracted international support. As other international groups (Bread for the World Institute and the NGO

Working Group on the World Bank among them) adopt monitoring as a priority, they should work to support and expand existing Southern initiatives.

No amount of effort will produce universal agreement among NGOs, even those already active in advocacy with the Bank, to a full policy agenda. But if a united front could be formed behind some concrete objectives on environmental policy, debt reduction, adjustment, poverty lending and popular participation, a powerful bloc of NGO opinion would be created, a basis for additional work on specialized issues, campaigns, and collaborative efforts.

Unanswered Questions: the Need for Monitoring

It is standard in academic studies to end with a list of questions for further research. But this call for monitoring and further study is integral to the call for action by NGOs and scholars to hold the Bank accountable. Monitoring the nature of World Bank investments, the character of its interaction with NGOs, changes in its internal operations as well as in its policy dialogue with borrowing governments, is vital to effective advocacy. It has been the weakest link in most NGO relations with the Bank.

The World Bank's liaison with NGOs has the potential to open important international financial policies to popular input. But the obstacles are formidable and the effort required by NGOs would be great. Several critical policy questions for the Bank and for NGOs require careful consideration and monitoring. Five such areas are highlighted here as priorities for further monitoring.

1. *Monitoring the actual outcome of proposed project involvement.* Virtually all of the World Bank's claims about NGO involvement in investments are based on projects as documented at the time of appraisal and Board approval. No review of actual implementation of these projects has been undertaken either at the Bank or outside, and a careful survey of a sample would be instructive in two ways. First, it would clarify and evaluate the Bank's actual performance in a field from which it now gains considerable public relations benefits. Even the very limited survey carried out for this study revealed important issues and questions about the actual nature and extent of collaboration.

Second, documenting the varied patterns of collaboration and their results could serve Bank staff who are open to broader contact with the populations affected by Bank policies and projects. Documenting' not only 'best practice' but also pitfalls and issues in contacting and building relations with NGOs could help promote further contact and raise the qualitative issues that have plagued some project collaboration.

2. *Assessing the value and effects of NGO participation in compensatory social service programs under structural adjustment.* There is little evidence now collected as to how NGOs became involved in providing social services to soften the impact of adjustment programs on the poor. The immediate needs of people affected by unemployment, food price increases and reduced social services present compelling reasons for NGO interventions.

NGOs that may oppose new adjustment policies are forced to balance the immediate needs against the need to press for alternative policies. Choosing to participate in compensatory programs may give an NGO greater standing with government and the World Bank. But it may also weaken the NGO's ability to articulate popular needs and serve as an agent of accountability. A review of the World Bank-State-NGO interactions in some of the new cases of adjustment-related NGO programs would afford insight into the costs and advantages of such cooperation with compensatory programs.

3. *Observing the effects of new environmental review procedures on the design of Bank-financed projects.* Do the environmental impact assessments carry enough authority within the Bank to block or significantly slow investment plans when environmental danger signs arise? What role will NGOs assume in the dialogue in this assessment process? Environmental NGOs will need to assess the new EIAs in order to decide on the next steps in their relationship with the Bank.

4. *Monitoring the Bank's work with governments to improve the operating environment for NGOs.* Some staff and observers of the NGO dialogue regard this potential role as the most important aspect of the World Bank's relationship with NGOs. The Bank routinely employs persuasion and financial leverage to support major economic policy changes geared to create an 'enabling environment' for the for-profit private sector. Will the Bank use its influence to support the unleashing of the 'other' private sector in countries where government policies restrict its operation? Government policies, from registration and licensing requirements to active suppression of independent organization by NGOs, limit NGO program and action in many countries.

5. *Documenting World Bank performance in implementing IDA-replenishment agreements.* The agreements on policy and finance negotiated among donor countries stipulate policy directions, emphases and changes. But the Bank's board has generally not assessed implementation of these in any but the most cursory way, noting some progress on each initiative and calling for further action in the next replenishment. NGOs have two options, potentially complimentary. They can monitor the Bank's implementation of the agreements, and lobby their governments to hold the Bank more closely accountable throughout the replenishment, and in negotiating and financing IDA-11 and future replenishments.

But in addition, NGOs should agree to clear standards of their own, against which the next replenishment (IDA-11) will be judged and upon which their position on future replenishments will be decided. The Bank sought out NGO support for IDA-10 vigorously. If broad agreement could be reached on what would constitute satisfactory implementation of IDA-10 and successive replenishments, and if performance could be monitored more closely, NGOs could increase their leverage over the Bank considerably.

Appendix 1 Key to Interviews Cited in Text

World Bank staff and consultant interviews are cited in the text by reference to the region in which operations staff work, or by reference to the division for staff in Finance, Policy, Research and External Affairs Divisions. Citations in the text include a number (e.g. Asia staff no. 1), corresponding to the number used below. Numbers do *not* refer to the numerical system by which the Bank describes countries within each region.

Staff members' remarks in the staff training seminar 'Involving NGOs in Bank-Supported Activities' are also cited in the text. These citations reflect comments and questions of staff members, and were not made in the context of a formal interview. The comments are identified in the text by reference to the division in which they work, and the date 6 October 1989. Many of those whose comments are cited are not among the list of staff interviewed.

Interviews of Bank staff and consultants were conducted in Washington, DC, unless otherwise noted.

Finance staff member, interview 21 May 1990.
Africa region staff no. 1, interview 2 May 1990.
Africa region staff no. 2, interview 4 May 1990.
Africa region staff no. 3, interview 8 May 1990.
Asia region staff no. 1, interview 25 September 1989, telephone; 11 October 1989 interview.
Asia region staff no. 2, interview 25 September 1989, telephone.
Asia region staff no. 3, interview 2 May 1990.
Asia region staff no. 4, interview 4 May 1990.
Asia region staff no. 5, interview 10 May 1990.
Latin America/Caribbean (LAC) staff no. 1, interview 1 May 1990.
Latin America/Caribbean (LAC) staff no. 2, interview 11 October 1990, Madison, Wisconsin.
Policy, Research and External Affairs consultant (staff no. 1), interview 22 September 1988.
Policy, Research and External Affairs staff no. 2, interview 22 September 1988; 27 July 1989; 1 October 1989; 2 May 1990.
Policy, Research and External Affairs staff no. 3, interview 22 October 1988 (by telephone); 11 September 1989; 16 May 1990.
Policy, Research and External Affairs staff no. 4, interview 2 May 1990.
Policy, Research and External Affairs staff no. 5, interview 10 May 1990.
Policy, Research and External Affairs staff no. 6, interview 16 May 1990.
Policy, Research and External Affairs staff no. 7, Private Sector specialist, interview 17 May 1990.
Policy, Research and External Affairs staff no. 8, interview 11 July 1990.
Policy, Research and External Affairs staff no. 9, interview 16 September 1990.

Appendix 2 Methodological Note

I interviewed 30 World Bank staff during 1989 and 1990, including both staff who had already shown interest in NGOs by attending an internal training session on working with NGOs, and other informants chosen irrespective of their views on NGOs. Some 40 NGO informants were interviewed during 1989 and 1990. These interviews have been supplemented by dozens of meetings and conversations during 1992 and 1993.

Documents for most of the 304 projects were reviewed only in one- to three-page summaries produced by the Bank's International Economic Relations Department, the unit responsible for liaison with NGOs. Staff Appraisal Reports, the documents prepared for Board approval before a loan is made, were reviewed in a few cases. More detailed documentation, including Project Completion Reports, was obtained for 22 projects where disbursement has been completed. The data collected on the universe of 304 projects was analyzed and relationships tested with simple bivariate statistical tests.

Because projects involving NGOs since 1989 are more numerous, and because of the World Bank's claims that the new projects are distinguished by their more frequent solicitation of NGO and grassroots group participation in project design, I have also surveyed summary information on 156 projects approved in fiscal 1991 and 1992, and reviewed less complete information on 1993 projects.

In addition to project documents, I reviewed documents and files from the last 15 years of discussions, correspondence and meetings with NGOs. My own involvement with World Bank policy dates from debates in the US Congress and Administration over poverty targeting in the early 1980s, and now continues in research and advocacy work relating to debt management, structural adjustment and poverty and popular participation in World Bank lending. This engagement with Bank policy has exposed me to a collection of sources, documentary and personal, formal and off the record, that underlie much of this research.

My own work with development and environmental NGOs was supplemented by interviews and a mailed questionnaire to NGO leaders involved in recent dialogues with the World Bank. I attended meetings of the NGO-World Bank Committee in 1989 as observer and as 1992, 1993 and 1994 as a participant, and took part in numerous NGO gatherings on structural adjustment, popular participation and the Bank. Seventeen present and past NGO participants in the NGO-World Bank Committee were interviewed or responded to a letter and questionnaire.

NGO perspectives on World Bank operations in the Philippines were gathered during six weeks of field work in that country, November and December of 1989. The Philippines was chosen as the field study country because of the active NGO sector, its government's relatively tolerant and cooperative policy toward many NGO operations, and the substantial record of project collaboration in the Philippines cited by the World Bank.

199

Notes

Introduction and Overview

1. Organizational analysis of the World Bank has sometimes attributed Bank behavior to the perversity of bureaucracy or to its sheer size and scope (Crane and Finkle, 1981; Kardam, 1989). Organizational approaches have rarely been integrated with political economy to show that the World Bank's structural and operational features are consonant with and reinforce the interests that dominate it. Important exceptions, Gran (1986) and Hellinger (1988), are discussed in later chapters.

'Accountable to Whom?' And Other Issues for NGOs

1. Some of the US-based and other Northern NGOs have been persistent and vocal critics of the Bank's structural adjustment policies, most notably the Development Group for Alternative Policies and Oxfam UK/Ireland. Emerging proposals for multilateral debt reduction in the Non-Aligned Movement (NAM), now chaired by the government of Indonesia, have led to consultations between NAM representatives and some US-based NGOs. There is the prospect, even in the next two years, for more cooperative efforts on World Bank- and IMF-held debt, by a governmental and non-governmental coalition.

World Bank-NGO Project Cooperation: Less than Meets the Eye?

1. Data from 1991, 1992 and 1993 projects are not sufficiently detailed to determine which involve newly-created groups.
2. The World Bank makes no claim that NGOs involved in project collaboration necessarily represent the interests of the poor. But in light of the general association of NGOs and poverty alleviation issues, the distinction is worth noting. The issue is particularly relevant where NGOs are consulted on the design of adjustment conditionality, where the Bank's attentiveness to the interests of poor producers and consumers is an issue.
3. EMENA has been reorganized with the Bank's expanded program in Eastern and Central Europe. The former regional breakdown is retained for this review.

Moving Money: Organizational Aspects of a Development Model

1. Hurni (1980), Van de Laar (1983), Hellinger (1988), Rich (1990), Ayres (1983), and McKitterick (1986) have made similar arguments.
2. The Bank's 1994 review of resettlement policy and performance (World Bank 1994h) acknowledges that no Bank-financed project has fully met its own standards for treatment of resettled populations. It defends continued

financing of projects with resettlement components by arguing that projects with Bank financing have a less destructive overall record than other resettlement schemes.

3. Similar arguments have been made, in less detail and less convincingly, for the perceived failure of the Bank to make population planning and 'women in development' concerns integral parts of its lending program. See Crane and Finkle (1981) and Kardam (1989).

4. The experience of the Asian Miracle countries has since been reviewed in detail by a Bank study. Its findings are discussed in Chapter 6.

5. The same concerns are recognized in Preston's memo accompanying the Wapenhans Report. Noting the tension between new lending and 'effective implementation,' Preston hints that change may be needed at least at the level of country programs, and calls for 'understanding' from staff, borrowers and the international financial community (Preston, memorandum to Executive Directors).

Organizational Culture and Participation in Development

1. Economist Michael Lipton documents similarly selective use of information in his analysis of 'pricist' doctrine in the 1987 WDR. While praising the flexibility and openness of some Bank studies, Lipton finds dogmatism most evident on topics that are most central to the Bank's conditionality. Lipton shows that conclusions in the 1987 WDR rest on highly selective use of the World Bank's own research evidence. The selection is the basis for a one-dimensional plea for 'governments to get smaller, let markets work, and thus set prices right' (Lipton, 1987, pp. 197–208).

2. Argyris calls this 'double loop' learning.

3. First class air travel privileges have subsequently been downgraded to business class for most Bank staff.

4. This discussion of individual motivation in organizations draws on the management literature on motivation, particularly Hersey and Blanchard (1988) and Vroom and Yetton (1973).

5. An overhaul of the project cycle such as that being promoted by the director of the Operations Evaluation Division (see Chapter 5) is the kind of fundamental change that could alter this dynamic. Without such a change, the current emphasis on project impact and supervision are unlikely to break through the Bank's durable organizational culture.

Bibliography

Abugre, Charles (1992) 'The Global Environment Facility: perpetuating unsustainable economic models.' *Third World Economics.* 1 (15 April): pp. 14–20.

Adams, James (1992) World Bank Office Memorandum to Sven Sandstrom. 'Participatory Development: Interim Report of the Learning Group: Implementation Status of Recommendations.' Draft, 15 January 1992.

'Africa – A flicker of light.' *The Economist* 5 March 1994, pp. 21–4.

Agarwala, Ramgopal (1983) 'Price Distortions and Growth in Developing Countries.' World Bank Staff Working Paper 575. Washington, DC: World Bank.

Agency for International Development (1986) *Development Effectiveness of Private Voluntary Organizations* (*PVOs*). Report to the Appropriations Committee, U.S. House of Representatives, February.

Alderman, Harold (1990) *Nutritional Status in Ghana and its Determinants.* Working Paper No. 3, Social Dimensions of Adjustment in Sub-Saharan Africa. Washington, DC: The World Bank.

Alexander, Nancy (1992) 'Testimony for the House Select Committee on Hunger on The World Bank and Poverty by Nancy Alexander, Bread for the World, June 4' Typescript.

ANGOC (Asian NGO Coalition) (1988) 'Democratizing Asian Development: A Commitment to Leadership.' ANGOC Monograph Series No. 7, ANGOC, Manila, Philippines.

Annis, Sheldon (1987) 'Can Small-Scale Development be a Large-scale Policy? The Case of Latin America.' *World Development.* 15 (Supplement), pp. 129–34.

Antrobus, Peggy (1987) 'Funding for NGOs: Issues and Options.' *World Development.* 15 (Supplement), pp. 95–102.

Argyris, Chris (1982) *The Applicability of Organizational Sociology.* Cambridge: Cambridge University Press.

Argyris, Chris (1987) 'How Learning and Reasoning Processes Affect Organizational Change.' Pp. 47–86 in *Change in Organizations* edited by Paul S. Goodman and associates. San Francisco: Jossey-Bass.

Arruda, Marcos (1993) 'NGOs and the World Bank: Possibilities and Limits of Collaboration.' Paper based on an oral presentation to the Seminar 'World Bank and NGOs: Operational and Policy Approaches for Collaboration,' Washington DC, 29–30 June.

'Articles of Agreement of the International Bank for Reconstruction and Development (as amended February 16, 1989).' Washington, DC, March 1989.

Ascher, Robert (1983) 'New Development Approaches and the Adaptability of International Agencies: The Case of the World Bank.' *International Organization* 37, pp. 205–29.

Aufderheide, Pat, and Bruce Rich (1988) 'Environmental Reform and the

Multilateral Banks.' *World Policy Review* 5, pp. 301–21.

Ayres, Robert (1983) *Banking on the Poor*. Cambridge, MA: MIT.

Bacha, Edman L., and Richard E. Feinberg (1986) 'The World Bank and Structural Adjustment in Latin America.' *World Development* 14, pp. 333–46.

Balassa, Bela (1984) 'Adjustment Policies in Developing Countries, 1979–83.' World Staff Working Paper No. 675.

Bamberger, Michael (1986) 'The Role of Community Participation in Development Planning and Project Management,' EDI Policy Seminar Report No. 13, Washington, DC: World Bank.

Bangladesh Rural Advancement Committee (1986) 'Unraveling Networks of Corruption.' Pp. 135–55 in *Community Management: Asian Experience and Perspectives*, edited by David C. Korten. West Hartford, CT: Kumarian.

Bangura, Yusuf (1987) 'IMF/World Bank Conditionality and Nigeria's structural adjustment program.' In *The IMF and the World Bank in Africa*, edited by Kjell Havnevik. Uppsala: Scandinavian Institute for African Studies.

Bank Check – Views from the Environment and Development Community (1990) Washington, DC: Bank Check.

Bank Information Center, ed. (1990) *Funding Ecological and Social Destruction: The World Bank and the International Monetary Fund*. Washington, DC: Bank Information Center.

Bassett, Thomas J. (1988) 'Development Theory and Reality: The World Bank in Northern Ivory Coast.' *Review of African Political Economy* 41, pp. 45–59.

Baum, Warren (1978) 'The World Bank Project Cycle.' *Finance and Development* 15, pp. 10–17.

Bebbington, Anthony and John Farrington (1993) 'Governments, NGOs and Agricultural Development: Perspectives on Changing Inter-Organisational Relationships.' *The Journal of Development Studies* 29(2), pp. 199–219.

Beckmann, David (1986) 'The World Bank and Poverty in the 1980s.' *Finance and Development*. September, pp. 26–9.

Bello, Walden, David Kinley and Elaine Elinson (1982) *Development Debacle: The World Bank in the Philippines*. San Francisco: Institute for Food and Development Policy.

Bello, Walden with Shea Cunningham and Bill Rau (1994) *Dark Victory: The United States, Structural Adjustment and Global Poverty*. London: Pluto.

Berg, Elliot and Don Sherk (1994) 'The World Bank and its Environmentalist Critics.' Background Paper in Bretton Woods Commission, *Bretton Woods: Looking to the Future*. Washington, DC: Bretton Woods Commission.

Bhatnagar, Bhuvan and Aubrey C. Williams, eds (1992) *Participatory Development and the World Bank: Potential Directions for Change*. World Bank Discussion Paper 183. Washington, DC, World Bank.

Bienefeld, Manfred (1994) 'The New World Order: echoes of a new imperialism.' *Third World Quarterly* 15(1), pp. 31–48.

Bonné, B. (1989) 'Development Assistance for Policies'. MA Thesis, Roskilde University Centre.

Bowden, Peter (1990) 'NGOs in Asia: issues in development.' *Public Administration and Development* 10, pp. 141–52.

Bradford, Colin I., Jr (1986) 'East Asian Models: Myths and Lessons.' in *Development Strategies Reconsidered*, edited by John P. Lewis and Valeriana

Kallab. Washington, DC: Overseas Development Council, pp. 115–28.

Bratton, Michael (1989) 'The Politics of Government – NGO Relations in Africa,' *World Development* 17, pp. 569–87.

Bratton, Michael (1989a) 'Non-Governmental Organizations in Africa: Can They Influence Public Policy?' *Development and Change* 21, pp. 87–118.

Bratton, Michael (1989b) 'Beyond the State: Civil Society and Associational Life in Africa.' *World Politics*. 41 April, pp. 407–30.

Bratton, Michael and Nicolas van de Walle (1992) 'Toward Governance in Africa: Popular Demands and State Responses' in *Governance and Politics in Africa*, edited by Goren Hyden and Michael Bratton. Boulder, CO: Lynne Rienner, pp. 27–56.

Brett, E.A (1993) 'Voluntary Agencies as Development Organizations: Theorizing the Problem of Efficiency and Accountability.' *Development and Change* 244, pp. 269–303.

Broad, Robin (1988) *Unequal Alliance: The World Bank, The IMF and the Philippines*. Berkeley: University of California Press.

Broad, Robin and John Cavanagh (1988) 'No More NICs.' *Foreign Policy*, Fall, pp. 81–103.

Brodhead, Tim (1989) 'Strings and Things: Does Positive Conditionality Exist? Some Considerations for World Bank Lending.' Unpublished, prepared for the November 1989 meeting of the NGO Working Group on the World Bank.

Brown, L. David and David C. Korten (1989) 'Understanding Voluntary Organizations: Guidelines for Donors.' Working Papers, Public Sector Management and Private Sector Development. Washington, DC: Country Economics Department of The World Bank. WPS 258.

Bryant, C. and L.G. White (1982) *Managing Development in the Third World*. Boulder, CO: Westview Press.

Burki, Shahid Javed (1980) 'Sectoral Priorities for meeting basic needs,' Pp. 13–17 in *Poverty and Basic Needs*. Washington, DC: World Bank.

Cahn, Jonathan (1993) 'Challenging the New Imperial Authority: The World Bank and the Democratization of Development.' *Harvard Human Rights Journal*, 6 (Spring), pp. 159–93.

Callaghy, Thomas M. (1993) 'Political Passions and Economic Interests: Economic Reform and Political Structure in Africa.' In Thomas M. Callaghy and John Ravenhill, eds, *Hemmed In: Responses to Africa's Economic Decline*. New York: Columbia.

Carlsson, Jerker, Gunnar Köhlin and Anders Ekbom (1993) *The Political Economy of Evaluation: International Aid Agencies and the Effectiveness of Aid*. New York: St Martin's.

Carroll, Thomas (1992) *Intermediary NGOs: The Supporting Link in Grassroots Development*. West Hartford, Conn.: Kumarian.

Cavanagh, John, Daphne Wysham and Marcos Arruda, eds (1994) *Beyond Bretton Woods: Alternatives to the Global Economic Order*. Boulder: Pluto Press.

Cernea, Michael M. (1987) 'Farmer Organizations and Institution Building for Sustainable Development.' *Regional Development Dialogue*, 8(2), Summer, pp. 1–19.

Cernea, Michael M. (1988) *Nongovernmental Organizations and Local Development*. World Bank Discussion Papers no. 40. Washington, DC: World Bank.

Chambers, Robert (1987) 'Poverty, Environment and the World Bank: The Opportunity for a New Professionalism.' Prepared for Strategic Planning and Review Department, World Bank.

Charlton, Robert (1993) 'External Debt, Economic Success and Economic Failure: State Autonomy, Africa and the NICs' in Stephen P. Riley, ed., *The Politics of Global Debt.* New York: St Martin's.

Clark, John (1986) 'NGO Perspectives on Debt and Adjustment. Paper for NGO-World Bank Meeting, November, 1986.' October, 1986, Unpublished typewritten manuscript.

Clark, John, *et al.* (1987) 'An NGO Reaction to the World Bank Paper "Protecting the Poor During Periods of Adjustment."' Unpublished typewritten manuscript, 20 February.

Clark, John (1991) *Democratizing Development: The Role of Voluntary Organizations.* West Hartford, Conn: Kumarian Press.

Cohn, Theodore (1973) *Influence of the Less Developed Countries in the World Bank Group.* Ph.D. Diss., University of Michigan.

Colchester, Marcus (1986) 'Banking on Disaster: International Support for Transmigration.' *Ecologist* 16 (2/3), pp. 61–70.

Cole, Sam (1987) 'World Economy Forecasts and the International Agencies.' *International Studies Quarterly* 31, pp. 367–85.

'Cooperation Between the World Bank and NGOs; Progress Report.' Memorandum from Vice President and Secretary to Executive Directors and Alternates. SecM90–290, 8 March 1990.

Corbridge, Stuart (1993) 'Discipline and Punish: The New Right and the Policing of the International Debt Crisis,' in *The Politics of Global Debt,* Stephen P. Riley, ed., New York: St Martin's, 1993, pp. 25–50.

Cornia, Giovanni Andrea, Richard Jolly, Frances Stewart, eds. (1987) *Adjustment with a Human Face: Protecting the Vulnerable and Promoting Growth.* Oxford: Clarendon Press.

Cornia, Giovanni Andrea, Rolf van der Hoeven and Thandika Mkandawire, eds (1992) *Africa's Recovery in the 1990s: From Stagnation and Adjustment to Human Development.* Florence, Italy: UNICEF International Child Development Centre.

Country Economics Department, The World Bank (1988) *Adjustment Lending: An Evaluation of Ten Years of Experience.* Washington, DC: World Bank.

Country Economics Department, The World Bank (1992) *Adjustment Lending and Mobilization of Private and Public Resources for Growth.* Policy and Research Series, No. 22. Washington, DC: World Bank.

Cox, Robert W., and Harold K. Jacobson (1981) 'The Decision-Making Approach to the Study of International Organization.' in *The Concept of International Organization,* edited by Georges Abi-Saab. Paris: UNESCO.

Cox, Robert W. (1987) *Production, Power and World Order: Social Forces in the Making of History.* New York: Columbia.

Cox, Robert W. (1992) 'Multilateralism and World Order.' *Review of International Studies.* 18, April 1992.

Crane, Barbara and Jason L. Finkle (1981) 'Organizational Impediments of Development Assistance: The World Bank's Population Program.' *World Politics* 33, pp. 516–38.

Cruz, Wilfrido and Robert Repetto (1992) *The Environmental Effects of*

Stabilization and Structural Adjustment Programs: The Philippines Case. Washington, DC: World Resources Institute.

Cumings, Bruce (1984) 'The origins and development of the North East Asian Political Economy: Industrial Sectors, Product Cycles, and Political Consequences.' *International Organization* 38, pp. 237–94.

Cypher, James M. (1988) 'The Crisis and the Restructuring of Capitalism in the Periphery' Pp. 43–80 in *Research in Political Economy*, edited by Paul Zarembka, vol 2. Greenwich, Connecticut: JAI Press.

Cypher, James M. (1989a) 'The Debt Crisis as 'Opportunity': Strategy to Revive U.S. Hegemony.' *Latin American Perspectives* 16(1), Winter 1989, pp. 52–78.

Cypher, James M. (1989b) 'Strings Attached: World Bank tightens control of Third World economies.' *Dollars and Sense*, December 1989, pp. 9–11, 19.

Daly, Herman E. (1994) 'Farewell Lecture to the World Bank,' in *Beyond Bretton Woods*, edited by John Cavanagh, Daphne Wysham and Marcos Arruda. London: Pluto Press.

Danaher, Kevin, ed. (1994) *50 Years is Enough: The Case Against the World Bank and the International Monetary Fund.* Boston: South End Press.

DeGraaf, Martin (1987) 'Context, Constraint or Control, Zimbabwean NGOs and their Environment.' *Development Policy Review* 5, pp. 277–301.

De Lusignan, Guy (1986). 'The Bank's Economic Development Institute'. *Finance and Development* 23 (2), pp. 28–31..

Deal, Terrence E. and Allen A. Kennedy (1982) *Corporate Cultures: The Rites and Rituals of Corporate Life.* Reading, MA: Addison-Wesley.

Demery, Lionel and Tony Addison (1987) *The Alleviation of Poverty under Structural Adjustment.* Washington, DC: World Bank.

Denning, Stephen (1994) 'Programme Aid Beyond Structural Adjustment.' Presented to Workshop on New Forms of Programme Aid. Harare, Zimbabwe. 31 January – 1 February.

Development Committee (1987) *Environment, Growth and Development.* Washington, DC, Joint Ministerial Committee of the Boards of Governors of the World Bank and the International Monetary Fund on the Transfer of Real Resources to Developing Countries, Publication 14.

Development Committee (1989) *The Impact of the Industrial Policies of Developed Countries on Developing Countries.* Washington, DC: Joint Ministerial Committee of the Boards of Governors of the World Bank and the International Monetary Fund on the Transfer of Real Resources to Developing Countries, Publication 20.

Development Committee (1990) *Problems and Issues in Structural Adjustment.* Washington, DC: Joint Ministerial Committee of the Boards of Governors of the World Bank and the International Monetary Fund on the Transfer of Real Resources to Developing Countries, Publication 23.

Diamond, Larry (1989) 'Beyond Authoritarianism and Totalitarianism: Strategies for Democratization.' *Washington Quarterly*, Winter, pp. 141–61.

Dichter, Thomas W. (1988) 'The Changing World of Northern NGOs: Problems, Paradoxes, and Possibilities,' pp. 177–88 in *Strengthening the Poor: What Have We Learned?* US-Third World Policy Perspectives No. 10, Overseas Development Council, edited by John P. Lewis. New Brunswick: Transaction.

DiMaggio, Paul J., and Walter W. Powell (1983) 'The Iron Cage Revisited: Institutional Isomorphism and Collective Rationality in Organizational Fields,' *American Sociological Review* 48, pp. 147–60.

Donnelly-Roark, Paula (1991) 'Grassroots Participation: Defining New Realities and Operationalizing New Strategies.' UNDP Discussion Paper. New York: UNDP.

'Draft Proposal for Establishing a Consultative Group to Assist the Poorest of the Poor (CGAPP) – A Micro-finance Program.' Typescript. 26 September 1994.

Durning, Alan B. (1989) *Action at the Grassroots: Foreign Policy*, Winter 1989–90, pp. 66–82.

Early Warning. Vol 1, No.1, December 1992.

Earwaker, Frank (1989) World Bank Office Memorandum, 'Macro-economic Projections and the Appraisal of Adjustment Loans.' 21 September.

Eaton, Jonathan and Mark Gersovitz (1981) 'Poor Country Borrowing in Private Financial Markets and the Repudiation Issue.' *Princeton Studies in International Finance*, no. 47, June.

Edwards, Michael and David Hulme (1992) 'Scaling up NGO Impact on Development: learning from experience.' *Development in Practice* 2 (2): pp. 77–91.

'Effective Implementation: Key to Development Impact.' Report of the World Bank's Portfolio Management Task Force (1992) Washington, DC: World Bank.

Escudero, Carlos R. (1988) *Involuntary Resettlement in Bank – Assisted Projects: An Introduction to Legal Issues.* Washington, DC: World Bank.

Esman, Milton J., and Norman T. Uphoff (1984) *Local Organizations: Intermediaries in Rural Development.* Ithaca: Cornell.

Esquel Group Foundation (1993) 'Civil Society, State and Market: An Emerging Partnership for Equitable Development.' Presented to the Social Forum Convened by the Inter American Development Bank and the United Nations Development Programme. Washington, DC, pp. 10–13, February.

Fatouros, A.A. (1977) 'The World Bank', Pp. 2–79 in *The Impact of International Organizations on Legal and Institutional Change in the Developing Countries.* New York: International Legal Center.

Feeney, Patricia (1994) 'Planofloro: Has the World Bank Learnt its Lesson?' Typescript, Oxfam UK/Ireland.

Freedom from Debt Coalition (Philippines) (1994) 'Unity Statement'.

French, Hilary F. (1994) 'Rebuilding the World Bank.' *State of the World*, Lester R. Brown and others. New York: Norton.

French, J.R.P. and B. Raven (1959) 'The Bases of Social Power,' in *Studies in Social Power* edited by D. Cartwright. Ann Arbor: University of Michigan, Institute for Social Research.

Fried, Edward R. and Henry D. Owen, eds (1982) *The Future of the World Bank.* Conference at the Brookings Institution, 7 January 1982) Washington, DC: Brookings.

Friends of the Earth (1992) *Who Pays the Piper? The Operations of Multilateral Development Banks in Central and Eastern Europe.* Washington, DC: Friends of the Earth.

Garilao, Ernesto D. (1987) 'Indigenous NGOs as Strategic Institutions: Managing the Relationship with Government and Resource Agencies.' *World Development* 15 (Supplement), pp. 113–20.

George, Susan and Fabrizio Sabelli (1994) *Faith and Credit: The World Bank's Secular Empire*. Boulder: Westview.

Gerster, Richard (1993) 'Accountability of Executive Directors in the Bretton Woods Institutions.' *Journal of World Trade*. 27, December, pp. 87–116.

Gibbon, Peter (1992) 'The World Bank and African Poverty, 1973–1991.' *Journal of Modern African Studies* 30(2), pp. 193–220.

Gillies, David (1992) 'Human Rights, Democracy, and 'Good Governance': Stretching the World Bank's Policy Frontiers.' Paper prepared for the President, International Centre for Human Rights and Democratic Development, Montreal.

Glewwe, Paul (1988) 'The Poor in Latin America During Adjustment: A Case Study of Peru.' Washington, DC: World Bank.

Goldsworthy, David (1988) 'Thinking Politically about Development.' *Development and Change* 19, pp. 505–30.

Gow, David D. 1979) *Local Organizations and Rural Development: A Comparative Reappraisal*. Washington, DC: Development Alternatives, 2 vols.

Gran, Guy (1986) 'Beyond African Famines: Whose Knowledge Matters?' *Alternatives* 11, pp. 275–96.

Griesgraber, Jo Marie, ed. (1994) *Rethinking Bretton Woods: Towards Equitable, Sustainable and Participatory Development*. Conference Report and Recommendations, 'Rethinking Bretton Woods,' June 12–17, 1994. Washington, DC: Center of Concern.

Guest, D.E. (1984) 'Social Psychology and Organizational Change,' in *Social Psychology and Organizational Behaviour*, ed. Gruneberg and Wall. Chichester: John Wiley and Sons.

Hagan, Ernestina N. (1992) 'NGO's Women and the Social Dimensions of Adjustment.' Resource Paper Presented at the Roundtable Workshop on NGOs and Structural Adjustment, Accra Ghana, 23–25 March.

Hall, Anthony (1987) 'Social Analysis in Official Foreign Aid.' *Human Organization* 46, pp. 368–72.

Hamilton, Clive (1983) 'Capitalist Industrialisation in East Asia's Four Little Tigers.' *Journal of Contemporary Asia* 13, pp. 35–73.

Hayter, Teresa and Catharine Watson (1985) *Aid: Rhetoric and Reality*. London: Pluto Press.

Healey, John and Mark Robinson (1992) *Democracy, Governance and Economic Policy: Sub-Saharan Africa in Comparative Review*. London: Overseas Development Institute.

Helleiner, Gerald (1994) 'Agendas for the Bretton Woods Institutions.' Notes for Presentation at the Conference 'Fifty Years after Bretton Woods: The Future of the IMF and the World Bank,' 29–30 September, Madrid, Spain. Typescript.

Hellinger, Douglas (1987) 'NGOs and the Large Aid Donors: Changing the Terms of Engagement.' *World Development* 15 (Supplement), pp. 135–43.

Hellinger, Douglas (1988) 'The World Bank's Diminishing Credibility.' Typescript, August.

Hellinger, Stephen and Doug Hellinger (1985) 'Mainlining Major Donor Support for Indigenous NGOs: Guidelines for Constructive Collaboration.' Washington, DC: The Development Group for Alternative Policies.

Hellinger, Stephen, Douglas Hellinger and Fred M. O'Regan (1988) *Aid for Just Development*. Boulder: Lynne Rienner.

Heredia, Carlos A. and Mary E. Purcell (1994) *The Polarization of Mexican Society: A Grassroots View of World Bank Economic Adjustment Policies.* Washington, DC: The Development Group for Alternative Policies.

Hersey, Paul and Kenneth Blanchard (1988) *Management of Organizational Behavior.* Englewood Cliffs, NJ: Prentice-Hall, Fifth edition.

Hodges, Tony (1988) 'Ghana's Strategy for Adjustment with Growth.' *Africa Recovery* 2(3), pp. 16–21, 27.

Holdcroft, Lane E. (1978) 'The Rise and Fall of Community Development in Developing Countries, 1950–65: A Critical Analysis and an Annotated Bibliography.' Washington, DC: USAID.

Holden, Constance (1987) 'The Greening of the World Bank.' *Science* 240, pp. 1610.

Holloway, Richard, ed. (1989) *Doing Development: Government, NGOs and the Rural Poor in Asia.* London: Earthscan.

Howard, John B. (1977) 'General Observations,' pp. 1–12 in *The Impact of International Organizations on Legal and Institutional Change in the Developing Countries.* New York: International Legar Center.

Hulme, David (1989) 'Learning and Not Learning From Experience in Rural Project Planning.' *Public Administration and Development* 9, pp. 1–16.

Hurni, Bettina S. (1980) *The Lending Policy of the World Bank in the 1970s: Analysis and Evaluation.* Boulder: Westview.

Hyden, Goran (1983) *No Shortcuts to Progress: African Development Management in Perspective.* Berkeley: University of California Press.

Irwin, Michael (1990) 'Let Them Eat Honey-Roasted Peanuts – Memos of the Month.' *Washington Monthly*, June, pp. 34–7.

Jacobson, Harold K., William M. Reisinger and Todd Mathers (1986) 'National Entanglements in International Governmental Organizations.' *American Political Science Review* 80, pp. 141–59.

Jazairy, Idriss, Mohiudiin Alamgir and Theresa Panuccio (1992) *The State of World Rural Poverty.* New York: NYU Press (for the International Fund for Agricultural Development).

Jolly, Richard (1985) 'Adjustment with a Human Face.' The Barbara Ward Lecture, 18th Society for International Development Conference, Rome, 1–4 July.

Kahler, Miles (1989) 'International Financial Institutions and the Politics of Adjustment.' Pp. 139–59 in *Fragile Coalitions: The Politics of Economic Adjustment*, edited by Joan M. Nelson. Washington, DC: Overseas Development Council.

Kakabadse, Yolanda N. with Sarah Burns (1994) 'Movers and Shapers: NGOs in International Affairs.' Washington, DC: World Resources Institute. May.

Kanbur, S.M. Ravi (1987) 'Measurement and Alleviation of Poverty with an Application to the Effects of Macro-economic Adjustment.' IMF Staff Papers, vol. 34, Washington, DC: The International Monetary Fund.

Kardam, Nuket (1989) 'Women and Development Agencies.' Pp. 133–54, *The Women and International Development Annual*, edited by Rita S. Gallin. Boulder: Westview.

Kardam, Nüket (1993) 'Development Approaches and the Role of Policy Advocacy: The Case of the World Bank.' *World Development* 21(11), pp. 1773–86.

Khagram, Sanjeev (1993) 'Visions, Coalitions and the State: India's Narmade Valley Projects and Paths of Democratic Development in the Third World.' typescript, Stanford University. 15 August.

Kolko, Gabriel (1975) 'The US Effort to Mobilize World Bank Aid to Saigon.' *Journal of Contemporary Asia* 5(1), pp. 42–52.

Korten, David C. (1980) 'Community Organization and Rural Development: A Learning Process Approach,' *Public Administration Review*, 40, pp. 480–511.

Korten, David C. (1986) 'Unraveling Networks of Corruption: Bangladesh Rural Advancement Committee,' in David C. Korten, ed., *Community Management: Asian Experience and Perspectives*. West Hartford, Conn.: Kumarian Press, pp. 135–55.

Korten, David C. (1987) 'Third Generation NGO Strategies: A Key to People-centered Development.' *World Development* 15 (Supplement), pp. 145–59.

Korten, David C. (1989) 'Social Science in the Service of Social Transformation' in *A Decade of Process Documentation Research*, edited by Cynthia C. Veneracion. Manila: Institute of Philippine Culture, pp. 5–20.

Korten, Frances F. and Robert Y. Siy, Jr., eds (1988) *Transforming a Bureaucracy The Experience of the Philippine National Irrigation Administration*. West Hartford: Kumarian.

Kothari, Smitu (1993) 'Challenging Economic Hegemony: In Search of Sustainability and Justice.' Paper prepared for the conference on 'Sustainable Development with Equity in the 1990s: Policies and Alternatives,' University of Wisconsin, Madison, 13–16 May.

Krasner, Stephen D. (1981) 'Transforming International Regimes: What the Third World Wants and Why.' *International Studies Quarterly* 25, pp. 119–48.

Krasner, Stephen D. (1982) 'Regimes and the Limits of Realism: Regimes as Autonomous Variables.' *International Organization* 36, pp. 499–515.

Krueger, Anne O. (1985) 'Importance of General Policies to Promote Economic Growth.' *World Economy* 8:2, pp. 93–108.

Kydd, J. and A. Hewitt (1986) 'The Effectiveness of Structural Adjustment Lending: Initial Evidence from Malawi.' *World Development* 14, pp. 347–65.

Lafay, Jean-Dominique and Jacques Lecaillon (1993) *The Political Dimension of Economic Adjustment*. Paris: OECD.

Lawyers Committee for Human Rights (1993) *The World Bank: Governance and Human Rights*. New York: Lawyers Committee.

Lecomte, Bernard J. (1986) *Project Aid: Limitations and Alternatives*. Paris: OECD.

Lee, Ducksoo (1989) Memo to Moeen A. Qureshi, the World Bank.

Leff, Nathaniel F. (1985) 'The Use of Policy-Science Tools in Public-Sector Decision Making: Social Benefit-Cost Analysis in the World Bank.' *Kyklos* 38, pp. 60–76.

Leff, Nathaniel F. (1988) 'Disjunction between Policy Research and Practice: social benefit-cost analysis and investment policy at the World Bank.' *Studies in Comparative International Development*, Winter, pp. 77–87.

Lehman, Howard P. (1993) *Indebted Development: Strategic Bargaining and Economic Adjustment in the Third World*. New York: St Martin's.

LePrestre, Philippe (1982) *The Ecology of the World Bank*. Ph.D. dissertation, Indiana University.

LePrestre, Philippe (1986) 'A problematique for international organizations.' *International Social Science Journal* 38, pp. 127–38.

LePrestre, Philippe (1989) *The World Bank and the Environmental Challenge*. Selinsgrove: Susquehanna University Press and London: Associated University Presses.

LePrestre, Philippe (1993) 'Environmental Learning at the World Bank.' Prepared for presentation at the 34th Annual Convention of the International Studies Association, Acapulco, March, pp. 23–27.

Lessard, Donald (1986) *International Financing for Developing Countries: The Unfulfilled Promise*. World Bank Staff Working Papers No. 783, Series on International Capital and Economic Development, No. 2. Washington, DC: World Bank.

Levinson, Jerome (1992) 'Multilateral Financing Institutions: What Form of Accountability?' *The American University Journal of International Law and Policy*. 89(1), pp. 39–64.

Levitt, B. and J.G. March (1988) 'Organizational Learning.' *Annual Review of Sociology* 14, pp. 319–40.

Libby, Ronald T. (1975a) 'International Development Association: A Legal Fiction Designed to Secure an LDC Constituency.' *International Organization* 29, pp. 1065–72.

Libby, Ronald T. (1975b) 'The Ideology of the World Bank.' Ph.D. dissertation, University of Washington.

Lipton, Michael (1987) 'Limits of Price Policy for Agriculture: Which Way for the World Bank?' *Development Policy Review* 5, pp. 197–215.

Lipton, Michael (1988) *The Poor and the Poorest*. World Bank Discussion Papers No. 25. Washington, DC: World Bank.

Lister, Frederick (1984) *Decision-Making Strategies for International Organizations: The IMF Model*. Denver: University of Denver School of International Studies Monograph Series in World Affairs.

Loxley, John (1986) *Debt and Disorder: External Financing for Development*. Boulder: Westview and Ottawa: North-South Institute.

Macdonald, Laura (1992) 'Turning to the NGOs: Competing Conceptions of Civil Society in Latin America.' Presented to the 1992 Annual Meeting of the Latin American Studies Association, Los Angeles, 24–27 September.

McAfee, Kathy (1991) *Storm Signals: Structural Adjustment and Development Alternatives in the Caribbean*. London: Zed.

McCormack, Gavan (1978) 'The South Korean Economy: GNP Versus the People.' pp. 91–111 in *Korea North and South: The Deepening Crisis*, edited by Gavan McCormack and Mark Selden, New York: Monthly Review.

McKitterick, Nathaniel M. 1986) 'The World Bank and the McNamara Legacy.' *The National Interest*, Summer 1986, pp. 45–52.

McNamara, Robert (1973) 'Address to the Board of Governors' (Nairobi, Kenya: 24 September).

'Managing Quality' 1994. Southern Africa Department. World Bank.

March, James G. and J.P. Olsen (1975) 'The Uncertainty of the Past: organizational learning under ambiguity.' *European Journal of Political Research* 3, pp. 147–71.

Martens, Jens (1992) 'NGOs in the UN System: The Participation of Non-Governmental Organizations in Environment and Development Institutions of the United Nations.' Bonn: Projektstelle UNCED, DNR/BUND.

Mason, Edward S. and Robert E. Asher (1973) *The World Bank Since Bretton Woods*. Washington, DC: Brookings Institution.

Mayatech Corporation (1991) *Gender and Adjustment*. Prepared for Office of Women in Development, Bureau for Program and Policy Coordination, USAID.

Meyer, John W. (1984) 'Organizations as Ideological Systems.' Pp. 187–205 in *Leadership and Organizational Culture*, edited by Thomas Sergiovanni and John Corbally. Chicago: University of Illinois.

Meyer, John W. (1986) 'Myths of Socialization and of Personality,' Pp. 187–205 in *Reconstructing Individualism*, edited by T.C. Heller, M. Sosna and E.E. Welbery. Stanford, CA: Stanford.

Meyer, John W., and W. Richard Scott (1983) *Organizational Environments: Ritual and Rationality*. Beverly Hills, CA: Sage.

Meyer, John W. and Brian Rowan (1983) 'Institutionalized Organizations: Formal Structure as Myth and Ceremony,' in Meyer and Scott, eds pp. 21–44.

Miheve, John (1993) 'The Fundamentalist Theology of the World Bank.' Paper delivered to the Canadian Association of African Studies Conference, 14 May 1993.

Mistry, Percy (1991) 'World or Wonderland Bank?' *Banker* 141, October, pp. 39–40, 45–8.

Morgan, Mary (1990) 'Stretching the Development Dollar: The Potential for Scaling-Up,' *Grassroots Development* 14, pp. 1, 2–11.

Moser, Caroline (1987) 'Approaches to Community Participation in Urban Development Programs in Third World Countries,' in EDI, Readings in Community Participation, Vol II. Washington, DC: World Bank.

Mosley, Paul (1985) 'The Politics of Economic Liberalization: USAID and the World Bank in Kenya, 1980–1984.' *African Affairs* 85, pp. 107–19.

Mosley, Paul (1987) 'Conditionality as Bargaining Process: Structural Adjustment Lending, 1980–1986.' *Essays in International Finance*, No. 168, October. Princeton: Princeton University Department of Economics, International Finance Section.

Mosley, Paul and John Toye (1988) 'The Design of Structural Adjustment Programmes.' *Development Policy Review* 6, pp. 395–413.

Mosley, Paul, Jane Harrigan and John Toye (1991) *Aid and Power: The World Bank and Policy-based Lending*. Vol. 1. London: Routledge.

Moulton, Anthony D. (1978) 'On Concealed Dimensions of Third World Involvement in International Economic Organizations.' *International Organization* 32, pp. 1019–35.

NGO Working Group on the World Bank (1989) 'Non-Governmental Development Organisations Guidelines for Possible Collaboration with the World Bank.' Draft for the NGO Working Group on the World Bank, 30 October 1989 in Bangkok.

Nagle, William J., and Sanjoy Ghose (1989) 'Beneficiary Participation in some World Bank Supported Projects.' Prepared for the International Economic Relations Division of the Strategic Planning and Review Department, The World Bank.

Nelson, Joan (1984) 'The Politics of Stabilization,' in *Adjustment Crisis in the Third World*, edited by Richard E. Feinberg and Valeriana Kallab. New Brunswick: Transaction.

Nelson, Joan (1989a) 'The Politics of Long-Haul Economic Reform.' Pp. 3–26 in *Fragile Coalitions: The Politics of Economic Adjustment*, edited by Joan Nelson. Washington, DC: Overseas Development Council.

Nelson, Joan (1989b) 'The Politics of Pro-Poor Adjustment.' Pp. 95–114 in *Fragile Coalitions: The Politics of Economic Adjustment*, edited by Joan M. Nelson. Washington, DC: Overseas Development Council.

Nerfin, Marc (1986) 'Neither Prince nor Merchant: Citizen.' *IFDA Dossier*, pp. 171–95.

Ness, Gayl D., and Steven R. Brechin (1988) 'Bridging the Gap: international organizations as organizations,' *International Organization* 42, 2, Spring, pp. 245–73.

Nicholas, Peter (1988) *The World Bank's Lending for Adjustment: An Interim Report*. World Bank Discussion Papers, 34. Washington, DC: World Bank.

Nyang'oro, Julius E. (1994) 'Reform Politics and the Democratization Process in Africa.' *African Studies Review* 37, 1, pp. 133–49.

Nzomo, Maria (1992) 'Beyond Structural Adjustment Programs: Democracy, Gender, Equity, and Development in Africa, with Special Reference to Kenya.' in *Beyond Structural Adjustment in Africa*, edited by Timothy M. Shaw and Julius Nyang'oro. New York: Praeger.

Oakley, Peter and David Marsden (1984) *Approaches to Participation in Rural Development*. Geneva: ILO.

O'Donnell, Guillermo (1981) 'Reflections on the Patterns of Change in the Bureaucratic-Authoritarian State. *Latin America Research Review* pp. 3–38.

Operations Evaluation Department (1988) *Rural Development: World Bank Experience 1965–86*. Washington, DC: World Bank.

Operations Evaluation Department (1990) *Evaluation Results for 1988: Issues in World Bank Lending Over Two Decades*. Washington, DC: World Bank.

Organisation for Economic Co-operation and Development (1988) *Voluntary Aid for Development: The role of Non-Governmental Organisations*. Paris: OECD.

Osieke, Ebere (1984) 'Majority Systems in the ILO and the IMF.' *International and Comparative Law Quarterly* 33, pp. 381–408.

Overseas Development Institute (1986) 'Adjusting to Recession: Will the Poor Recover?' ODI Briefing Paper.

Overseas Development Institute (1988) 'Development Efforts of NGOs.' *Development* 1988, 4, pp. 41–46.

Padrón, Mario (1987) 'Non-governmental Development Organizations: From Development Aid to Development Cooperation.' *World Development* 15, Supplement, pp. 69–77.

Pastor, Manuel, Jr. (1989) 'Latin America, the Debt Crisis, and the I.M.F.' *Latin American Perspectives* 16, pp. 79–110.

Patkar, Medha (1989) Statement concerning a Critique of the World Bank Financed Sardar Sarovar Dam, before the Subcommittee on Natural Resources, Agricultural Research and Environment, Committee on Science, Space and Technology. US House of Representatives. 24 October.

Paul, Samuel (1987) 'Community Participation in World Bank Projects.' *Finance and Development*, December, pp. 20–3.

Paul, Samuel (1988) 'Governments and Grassroots Organizations: From Co-Existence to Collaboration' pp. 61–71 in *Strengthening the Poor: What Have We Learned?* U.S.-Third World Policy Perspectives No. 10, Overseas Development Council, edited by John P. Lewis. New Brunswick, NJ: Transaction Books.

Paul, Samuel and Arturo Israel, eds (1991) *Nongovernmental Organizations and the World Bank: Cooperation for Development.* Washington, DC: World Bank.

Payer, Cheryl (1982) *The World Bank: A Critical Analysis.* New York: Monthly Review.

Pease, Stanley (1984) *The Hobbled Giant: Essays on the World Bank.* Boulder: Westview.

Perrow, Charles (1986) *Complex Organizations A Critical Essay*, Third Edition. New York: Random House.

Peter, T.J., and R.H. Waterman (1984) *In Search of Excellence: Lessons from America's Best Run Companies.* New York: Warner Books.

Pfeffer, Jeffrey and Gerald R. Salancik (1978) *The External Control of Organizations – A Resource Dependence Perspective.* New York: Harper and Row.

Piddington, Kenneth (1988) Internal Memorandum, World Bank.

Pion-Berlin, David (1983) 'Political Repression and Economic Doctrines.' *Comparative Political Studies* 16, pp. 37–63.

'Portfolio Management: Next Steps' (1993) Memorandum to the Executive Directors, April 5. World Bank.

Powell, Walter W. ed. (1987) *The Nonprofit Sector: A Research Handbook.* New Haven: Yale University Press.

Pratt, R. Cranford (1983) 'The Global Impact of the World Bank.' Pp. 55–66 in *Banking on Poverty*, edited by Jill Torrie. Toronto: Between the Lines.

Preston, P.W. (1985) 'The Ethico-Political Notion of Development: a memorandum on commitments' in P.W. Preston, *New Trends in Development Theory.* London: Routledge.

Project Policy Department of the World Bank (1985) 'Bank/NGO Cooperation: A Successful Case of Cooperation Between the Government of Liberia, CARE International, and the World Bank.' 6 June.

Qureshi, Moeen (1988) 'The World Bank and NGOs: New Approaches.' Speech to Society for Economic Development Conference. 'Learning from the Grassroots,' Washington, DC, 22 April.

Rahnema, Majid (1985) 'NGOs: Sifting the Wheat from the Chaff.' *Development: Seeds of Change* 3, pp. 68–71.

Raison, Timothy (1986) 'Challenges to the International Donor Community.' in *Recovery in the Developing World, The London Symposium on the World Bank's Role.* Washington, DC: World Bank, pp. 3–11.

Rau, Bill (1991) *From Feast to Famine: Official Cures and Grassroots Remedies to Africa's Food Crisis.* London: Zed.

Raven, B.H. and W. Kruglanski (1975) 'Conflict and Power,' in *The Structure of Conflict*, edited by P.G. Swingle. New York: Academic Press, pp. 179–219.

Reid, Walter V., James N. Barnes and Brent Blackwelder (1989) *Bankrolling Successes: A Portfolio of Sustainable Development Projects.* Washington,

DC: Environmental Policy Institute and National Wildlife Federation.

Ribe, Helena, Soniya Carvalho, Robert Liebenthal, Peter Nicholas and Elaine Zuckerman (1990) *How Adjustment Programs Can Help the Poor: The World Bank's Experience*. World Bank Discussion Papers No. 71. Washington, DC: World Bank.

Rich, Bruce (1985) 'The Multilateral Development Banks, Environmental Policy, and the United States.' *Ecology Law Quarterly*. 12, pp. 681–784.

Rich, Bruce (1989) 'Funding Deforestation: Conservation at the World Bank.' *The Nation*, 23 January, 1, pp. 88–91.

Rich, Bruce (1990) 'The Emperor's New Clothes: The World Bank and Environmental Reform.' *World Policy Journal*, Spring, pp. 305–29.

Rich, Bruce (1994) *Mortgaging the Earth: The World Bank, Environmental Impoverishment, and the Crisis of Development*. Boston: Beacon.

Riker, James V. (1993) 'State-NGO Relations and the Politics of Sustainable Development in Indonesia: An Examination of Political Space.' Prepared for presentation at the 1993 Annual Meeting of the American Political Science Association, Washington, DC, 2–5 September.

Ruttan, Vernon W. (1984) 'Integrated Rural Development Programmes: A Historical Perspective.' *World Development* 12(4), pp. 393–401.

Salamon, Lester M. (1994) 'The Rise of the Nonprofit Sector.' *Foreign Affairs* 73(4), pp. 109–22.

Salamon, Lester M. and Helmut K. Anheier (1994) *The Emerging Sector: An Overview*. Baltimore: Institute for Policy Studies, The Johns Hopkins University.

Salmen, Lawrence F. (1987) *Listen to the People*. Oxford: Oxford University Press, for the World Bank.

Salmen, Lawrence F. (1992) *Beneficiary Assessment: An Approach Described*. Working Paper No. 1, Poverty and Social Policy Division, Technical Department, Africa Region, World Bank.

Salmen, Lawrence F. and A. Paige Eaves (1989) 'World Bank Work with Non-governmental Organizations.' World Bank PRE Working Paper 305.

Sanford, Jonathan E. (1984) 'Status of the Poverty Alleviation Focus of the International Development Association'. Washington, DC: Congressional Research Service.

Sardar Sarovar. The Report of the Independent Review. Bradford Morse, Chairman, Thomas R. Berger, Deputy Chairman. Ottawa: Resource Futures International.

Schechter, Michael G. (1987) 'Leadership in International Organizations: systemic, organization and personality factors.' *Review of International Studies* 13, pp. 197–220.

Schein, Edgar H. (1985) *Organizational Culture and Leadership – A Dynamic View*. San Francisco: Jossey-Bass.

Schein, Edgar H. (1987) 'Individuals and Careers,' in *Handbook of Organizational Behavior*, edited by Jay Lorsch. Englewood Cliffs, NJ: Prentice-Hall.

Schoultz, Lars (1982) 'Politics, Economics and US Participation in Multilateral Development Banks.' *International Organization*.

Schwartzman, Stephan (1989) 'Deforestation and Popular Resistance in Acre: From Local Movement to Global Network.' Paper Presented to Symposium,

The Social Causes of Environmental Destruction in Latin America, 88th Annual Meeting of the American Anthropological Association, Washington, DC, 15–19 November.

Scott, James C. (1985) *Weapons of the Weak – Everyday Forms of Peasant Resistance*. New Haven: Yale Press.

Scott, James C. and Benedict J. Tria Kerkvliet (1986) *Everyday Forms of Peasant Resistance*.

Scott, Richard (1985) *Organizations: Rational, Natural and Open Systems*. Englewood Cliff, NJ: Prentice Hall.

Self, Peter (1975) *Econocrats and the Policy Process: The Politics and Philosophy of Cost-Benefit Analysis*. Boulder, CO: Westview.

Serageldin, Ismail (1989) *Poverty, Adjustment and Growth in Africa*. Washington, DC: World Bank.

Serrano, Isagani (1989) 'The Philippine Rural Reconstruction Movement and the Challenges of Development Cooperation.' *Rural Reconstruction Forum* 1, 1, pp. 11–14.

Shaw, Timothy (1993) 'Third World Political Economy and Foreign Policy in the post-Cold War era: Towards a Revisionist Framework with Lessons from Africa.' *Journal of Asian and African Affairs*. 5, Fall, pp. 1–20.

Shields, Elisabeth (1993) 'EDI Expands Its Horizons: A New Role Working with NGOs.' *Bank's World* 12/7–8, pp. 8–10

Shihata, Ibrahim F.I. (1992) 'Human Rights, Development, and International Financial Institutions.' *The American University Journal of International Law and Policy*. 8(1), pp. 27–38.

Sikkink, Kathryn (1993) 'Human rights, principled issue-networks, and sovereignty in Latin America.' *International Organization*. 47(3), pp. 411–41.

Singer, Hans W. (1989) 'The World Bank: Human Face or Facelift? Some Comments in the Light of the World Bank's Annual Report.' *World Development* 17, pp. 1313–16.

Singer, Hans W. (1990) '"Reading between the Lines": A Comment on the World Bank Annual Report 1989.' *Development Policy Review* 8, pp. 203–6.

Smith, Brian H. (1990) *More than Altruism: The Politics of Private Foreign Aid*. Princeton: Princeton University Press.

Squire, Lyn and Herman van der Tak (1975) *Economic Analysis of Projects*. Baltimore: Johns Hopkins, for the World Bank.

Stiefel, Matthias and Marshall Wolfe (1994). *A Voice for the Excluded: Popular Participation in Development*. London: Zed.

Stokes, Bruce (1986) 'Liberals and Conservatives Struggling over the World Bank's Proper Role.' *National Journal*, 8 February, pp. 334–7.

Stokes, Bruce (1988) 'Storming the Bank.' *National Journal* 31 December, pp. 3250–53.

Stokes, Bruce (1993) 'Reinventing the Bank.' *National Journal* September 18, pp. 2232–36.

Strategic Planning and Review Department, The World Bank (1989) *Strengthening Popular Participation in Development: World Bank Experience*. Typescript.

Strategic Planning and Review Department, The World Bank (1990) *The World Bank and Nongovernmental Organizations (NGOs): A Review of Operational Experience*. Typescript, 25 January.

Straw, Barry M. (1982) 'Counterforces to Change,' in *Change in Organizations*, edited by Paul S. Goodman and Associates. San Francisco: Jossey-Bass.

Streeten, Paul (1987) 'A Basic-Needs Approach to Economic Development,' in *Directions in Economic Development*, edited by K. Jameson and C. Wilber. Notre Dame: Notre Dame Press.

Stremlau, Carolyn (1987) 'NGO Coordinating Bodies in Africa, Asia and Latin America. *World Development* 15 (Supplement), pp. 213–25.

Stryker, Richard E. (1979) 'The World Bank and Agricultural Development: Food Production and Rural Poverty.' *World Development* 7, pp. 325–36.

Subramanian, Asok (1985) 'Community Participation in Development Projects.' Public Sector Management Unit, Projects Policy Department, The World Bank. Washington, DC: World Bank.

Swedberg, Richard (1986) 'The Doctrine of Economic Neutrality of the IMF and the World Bank.' *Journal of Peace Research* 23(4), pp. 377–90.

Tandon, Rajesh (1991) 'Civil Society, The State and Roles of NGOs.' IDR Reports 8(3). Boston: Institute for Development Research, August.

Tendler, Judith (1975). *Inside Foreign Aid*. Baltimore: Johns Hopkins.

Tendler, Judith (1982). *Turning Private Voluntary Organizations into Development Agencies: Questions for Evaluation*. Washington, DC: Agency for International Development.

Thenuis, Sjef (1988) 'The Aid Relationship: A New Sound from Donors.' *Development* 4, pp. 26–30.

Thomas, Karen (1980) *Communication and Decision-Making in International Organizations: A Cross-Cultural Perspective on Organizational Behavior in the World Bank*. Ph.D. dissertation, Berkeley.

Thompson, James D. (1967) *Organizations in Action*. New York: McGraw-Hill.

Thompson, Michael and Aaron Wildavsky (1986) 'A Cultural Theory of Information Bias in Organizations.' *Journal of Management Studies* 23, pp. 273–86.

Treakle, Kay (1994) 'Report on the NGO Strategy Meeting on the Multilateral Development Banks, Guadalajara, Mexico, April 8–13.' Typescript, 30 May.

UNICEF (1986) *The State of the World's Children 1986*. Oxford: Oxford University Press (for UNICEF).

UNICEF (1989) *State of the World's Children 1989*. Oxford: Oxford University Press (for UNICEF).

UNICEF (1992) *State of the World's Children 1992*. Oxford: Oxford University Press (for UNICEF).

US Agency for International Development (1986) *Development Effectiveness of Private Voluntary Organizations (PVOs)*. Report to the House Appropriations Committee, February.

US Department of the Treasury (1982) *United States Participation in the Multilateral Development Banks in the 1980s*. Washington, DC: Department of the Treasury.

US News and World Report (1989) 'Bankrolling debacles?' 25 September, 43–7.

Udall, Lori (1989) Statement concerning the Environmental and Social Impacts of the World Bank Financed Sardar Sarovar Dam in India, before the Subcommittee on Natural Resources, Agricultural Research and Environment, Committee on Science, Space and Technology, US House of Representatives. October 24.

United Nations Economic and Social Council (1994) *General Review of Arrangements for Consultations with Non-Governmental Organizations.* Report of the Secretary General (26 May).

Van der Heijden, Hendrik (1987) 'The Reconciliation of NGO Autonomy, Program Integrity and Operational Effectiveness with Accountability to Donors.' *World Development* 15 (Supplement), pp. 103–12.

Van de Laar, Aart (1980) *The World Bank and the Poor.* Boston: Martinus Nijhoff.

Vansant, Jerry (1989) 'Opportunities and Risks for Private Voluntary Organizations as Agents of LDC Policy Change.' *World Development* 17, pp. 1723–31.

Van Wicklin, Warren A. III (1990) 'Private Voluntary Organizations as Agents of Alternative Development Strategies: Existing Constraints and Future Possibilities.' Paper Presented at the International Studies Association Meetings, 10–14 April, Washington, DC.

Vroom, Victor and Philip Yetton (1973) *Leadership and Decision Making.* Pittsburgh: University of Pittsburgh Press.

Wapenhans, Willi A. (1994) 'Efficiency and Effectiveness: Is the World Bank Group Well Prepared for the Task Ahead?' In *Bretton Woods: Looking to the Future,* Commission Report of the Bretton Woods Commission, C289–C304.

Wasserstrom, Robert (1985) *Grassroots Development in Latin America and the Caribbean, Oral Histories of Social Change.* New York: Praeger.

Watson, Catharine (1985) 'Working in the World Bank'. Pp. 268–75 in *Aid: Rhetoric and Reality,* by Teresa Hayter and Catharine Watson, London: Pluto.

White, Howard (1989) 'Community Participation in Development: Problems and Prospects.' Discussion Paper, Strategic Planning and Review Department, World Bank.

Woodward, David (1992) *Debt, Adjustment and Poverty in Developing Countries.* London: Save the Children Federation/Pinter Publishers.

World Bank (annual). *Annual Report.* Washington, DC: The World Bank.

World Bank (annual). *World Development Report.* Oxford: Oxford University Press (for the World Bank).

World Bank (monthly) *Monthly Operation Summary of Bank and IDA Proposed Projects.* SecM90–546, 1 May.

World Bank (1978) Operational Manual Statement 2.12. Project Generation and Design.

World Bank (1981) *Accelerated Development in Sub-Saharan Africa: An Agenda for Action.* Washington, DC: World Bank.

World Bank (1981–90) Internal reports of the World Bank-NGO Committee, unpublished.

World Bank (1982) *Focus on Poverty: A Report of a Task Force of the World Bank.* Washington, DC: World Bank.

World Bank (1983a) *Focus on Poverty.* Washington, DC: World Bank.

World Bank (1983b) *Learning by Doing: World Bank Lending for Urban Development, 1972–1982.* Washington, DC: World Bank.

World Bank (1988a) 'Adjustment Lending.' Report to the Executive Directors, 1 August. Unpublished.

World Bank (1988b) 'Operational Collaboration with Nongovernmental Organizations.' Operational Policy Memorandum, Draft, 15 January.

World Bank (1988c) *Targeted Programs for the Poor during Structural Adjustment.* A Summary of a Symposium on Poverty and Adjustment April. Washington, DC: World Bank.

World Bank (1988d) *The World Bank's Support for the Alleviation of Poverty.* Washington, DC: World Bank.

World Bank (1989a) *Striking a Balance: The Environmental Challenge of Development.* Washington, DC: World Bank.

World Bank (1989b) *Sub-Saharan Africa: From Crisis to Sustainable Growth A Long-term Perspective Study.* Washington, DC: World Bank.

World Bank (1989c) Operational Manual Statement 14.70. 'Involving Non-Governmental Organizations in Bank-Supported Activities.'

World Bank (1990a) *The World Bank Annual Report 1990.* Washington, DC: World Bank.

World Bank (1990b) *Making Adjustment Work for the Poor: A Framework for Policy Reform in Africa.* Washington, DC: World Bank.

World Bank (1990c) *The World Bank and the Environment. First Annual Report Fiscal 1990.* Washington, DC: World Bank.

World Bank (1990d) *How the World Bank Works with Nongovernmental Organizations.* Washington, DC: World Bank.

World Bank (1992a) *Governance and Development.* Washington, DC: World Bank.

World Bank (1992b) *The World Bank and the Environment.* Fiscal. Washington, DC: World Bank.

World Bank (1993) *Implementing the World Bank's Strategy to Reduce Poverty.* Washington, DC: World Bank.

World Bank (1994a) *Governance: The World Bank's Experience.* Washington, DC: World Bank.

World Bank (1994b) *The World Bank Policy on Disclosure of Information.* Washington, DC: World Bank. March.

World Bank (1994c) 'The World Bank: A Global Partnership for Development.' Washington, DC: World Bank.

World Bank (1994d) 'Poverty Reduction and the World Bank: Progress in Fiscal 1993.' Washington, DC: World Bank.

World Bank (1994e) *Adjustment in Africa. Reforms, Results and the Road Ahead.* New York: Oxford (for the World Bank).

World Bank (1994f) 'The World Bank: A Global Partnership for Development.' Pamphlet.

World Bank (1994g) 'The World Bank and Participation.' Operations Policy Department. September.

World Bank (1994h) 'Resettlement Review.' Environment Department.

World Bank (1994i) *Progress Report on the Implementation of Portfolio Management: Next Steps A Program of Actions.* Washington, DC: World Bank Operations Policy Department (September).

World Bank (n.d.) *Guide to International Business Opportunities.* Washington, DC: World Bank.

World Bank (n.d.) 'World Bank and IDA, Questions and Answers'.

World Bank-NGO Consultation India – Short Report (1990).

World Wide Fund for Nature (1993) *The Southern Green Fund: Views from the South on the Global Environment Facility.* Gland, Switzerland: WWF-International.

Wyss, Hans (1987) World Bank Office Memorandum: 'Reorganization and NGOs.' 27 April.

Yudelman, Montague (1985) *The World Bank and Agricultural Development – An Insider's View.* WRI Paper No. 1, Washington DC, World Resources Institute.

Zuckerman, Elaine (1989) *Adjustment Programs and Social Welfare.* World Bank Discussion Paper 44, Washington, DC: World Bank.

Index

MIXED-RACE YOUTH AND SCHOOLING

This timely, in-depth examination of the educational experiences and needs of mixed-race children ("the fifth minority") focuses on the four contexts that primarily influence learning and development: the family, school, community, and society-at-large.

The book provides foundational historical, social, political, and psychological information about mixed-race children and looks closely at their experiences in schools, their identity formation, and how schools can be made more supportive of their development and learning needs. Moving away from an essentialist discussion of mixed-race children, a wide variety of research is included. Life and schooling experiences of mixed-raced individuals are profiled throughout the text. Rather than pigeonholing children into a neat box of descriptions or providing ready-made prescriptions for educators, *Mixed-Race Youth and Schooling* offers information and encourages teachers to critically reflect on how it is relevant to and helpful in their teaching/learning contexts.

Sandra Winn Tutwiler is Professor, Department of Education, Washburn University, USA.

MIXED-RACE YOUTH AND SCHOOLING

The Fifth Minority

Sandra Winn Tutwiler

Routledge
Taylor & Francis Group

NEW YORK AND LONDON

First published 2016
by Routledge
711 Third Avenue, New York, NY 10017

and by Routledge
2 Park Square, Milton Park, Abingdon, Oxon, OX14 4RN

Routledge is an imprint of the Taylor & Francis Group, an informa business

© 2016 Taylor & Francis

Library of Congress Cataloging-in-Publication Data
Tutwiler, Sandra Winn, author.
Title: Mixed-race youth and schooling : the fifth minority / by Sandra Winn Tutwiler.
Description: New York : Routledge, is an imprint of the Taylor & Francis Group, an Informa Business, [2016] | Includes bibliographical references and index.
Identifiers: LCCN 2015028356 | ISBN 9781138021914 (hardback) | ISBN 9781138021938 (pbk.) | ISBN 9781315777429 (ebook)
Subjects: LCSH: Racially mixed children—Education—United States. | Racially mixed youth—Education—United States. | Racially mixed children—United States—Social conditions. | Racially mixed youth—United States—Social conditions. | Multicultural education—United States.
Classification: LCC LC3621 .T87 2016 | DDC 371.829—dc23
LC record available at http://lccn.loc.gov/2015028356

ISBN: 978-1-138-02191-4 (hbk)
ISBN: 978-1-138-02193-8 (pbk)
ISBN: 978-1-315-77742-9 (ebk)

Typeset in Bembo
by Apex CoVantage, LLC

Printed and bound in the United States of America by Publishers Graphics, LLC on sustainably sourced paper.

For Madeleine, William, Charles, Akyra, and Akeenah

CONTENTS

PREFACE

In a recent report on the increase in the number of interracial marriages, researchers proclaimed that race no longer matters (Taylor et al., 2010). According to a report released by the U.S. Department of Education's Office for Civil Rights (2014), racial disparities in the nation's public schools continue to exist in a number of areas critical to the educational success of all children. For example, boys of color continue to be disproportionately affected by school discipline policies, Black and Latino students in general are more likely to be taught by teachers with the least experience, and students of color (with the exception of Asian Americans) generally have limited access to rigorous curricula at the high school level.

Both reports are relevant to the experiences of mixed-race children in schools today. The report on increased interracial marriage portends an increased number of mixed-race children in U.S. schools. The report on the experiences of minority children suggests for mixed-race children who have physical characteristics and/or who socially and/or emotionally identify as children of color, race still matters when it comes to their educational experiences. In fact, educators tend to view mixed-race children as children of color, regardless of how individual children might self-identify racially. However, as Lewis (2004) so poignantly proclaimed, children's educational experiences are influenced by their racial identities ". . . both those assigned . . . and those they choose . . ." (p. 4). Even so, it is plausible that an increased population of mixed-race children will disturb existing school policies and practices and precipitate more focused efforts to understand the impact of race on the learning environment.

This book focuses primarily on conditions that influence the schooling and educational needs of mixed-race children who have at least one parent who is a person of color. It addresses situations experienced by children with minority/ nonminority parents, as well as those with minority/minority parents from different minority races. Regardless of how mixed-race children identify themselves, they are noted as the fifth minority in this book. They are so positioned, not because they have a minority parent, but because as a group they make up a population of youth with distinct attributes and life circumstances that are different from the White majority and the four other major racial minorities (i.e., African American, Asian and Pacific Islanders, Latinos, and Native Americans[1]), which in different combinations constitute their racial heritage.

I recognize the potential risks of this project of essentializing the lives a group of children who share some but not all worldviews and life experiences. As well, I understand the dangers of reifying race as something other than a social construct, albeit a construct with social, economic, and political implications, as I refer to mixed-race children and youth as the fifth minority. I wrestled with how to resolve this conundrum in order to identify a unique group of students in our schools and engage teachers and other school personnel in thoughtful deliberation of the extent to which the educational needs of these children are being addressed. I maintain that the phrase "fifth minority" is useful in that it allows me to talk about a particular group of students, even as I am aware of the multitude of differences among them.

In my view, there is a chasm between teacher knowledge about this highly diverse group of students and the unique educational support they may need. The wave of multicultural educational practices and related texts has been slow to fully address the unique experiences and educational needs of mixed-race children. This oversight leads to an inadequate understanding of mixed-race children, how they come to own a sense of identity, and subsequently how they position themselves within social environments, including schools.

The goal of this book is to provide teachers and other school personnel with background information and strategies that allow them to support learning and development of mixed-race youth within the context of schools. It is not my intent to write, nor would I consider writing, a book as a prescriptive guide to how to work with any group of children, on the basis of their racial makeup. Rather, I want to add to the body of literature that troubles the notion that all children must fit a certain profile in order to successfully learn in our schools. Thus, a major aim of this book is to contribute to efforts to promote multiracial multiculturalism (Thompson, 2012), and encourage educators to embrace mixed-race children as an additional diverse group whose learning and developmental needs must be addressed in learning environments.

Talking Race

Race continues to matter in most areas of public life. Were it not so, mixed-race children would not continue to get stares as onlookers try to figure out their racial identification. They would cease to face overt questions about their racial background, and they would no longer have some experiences similar to children and youth with whom they share a minority heritage, whether they embrace that aspect of their lineage or not. The scrutiny mixed-race children experience is due to the fact that they cross deeply rooted racial boundaries that have historically signaled to onlookers how to treat an individual based on race.

Anticipation of a post-racial United States in the era of a Barack Obama presidency has not been realized. Differences in racial makeup continue to translate into racism that results in differentiated experiences for people of different races in diverse societies. Critical race theorists Delgado and Stefancic (2012) defined racism as the ". . . the practice of discrimination, segregation, persecution or mistreatment based on membership in a race or ethnic group" (p. 171). They suggested that these practices are ". . . ordinary . . . [a] "normal science," the usual way society does business, the common, everyday experience for most people in this country" (p. 7). Even though some may wish to embrace color blindness or racelessness, such positions are contested primarily because of the ways in which racism is deeply ". . . embedded in our thought processes and social structures . . ." (p. 27). Clearly, race is more than skin color, facial characteristics, or hair texture—it is connected to social and historical circumstances that are not easily shaken or forgotten.

Complicating the social and emotional lives of mixed-race children is the fact that we are still a racially stratified society. Mixed-race children may have a White parent in a position of privilege in society and a parent of color from a minority group who does not enjoy the same level of advantages. To be clear, the minority racial group lineage of some mixed-race children is more highly regarded than the minority lineage of others. Still, mixed-race children often wrestle over differences in social status based on race, and what this means for them personally, and may even have concerns over these distinctions in terms of what they mean for their minority parent.

For many mixed-race children, being mixed-race means being of two or more races simultaneously—not, for example, mixed-race but African American, with the latter being the predominant positionality/identity. Their status of being White may not be fully accepted by White peers, and those with whom they share a minority heritage may question the authenticity of their minority lineage. A mixed-race identity may not be salient for all mixed-race youth. A monoracial identity (e.g., Black, Asian, or White) is more comfortable for some mixed-race youth. Alternately, others may feel pressured by peers and adults in their social worlds to be monoracial and not mixed.

Children and youth who embrace the uniqueness of their mixed-race position should not be pressured into performative race, where they try to meet the expected behaviors of one aspect of their heritage or the other. Mixed-race children begin to face race-related questions about themselves and their family from peers as early as preschool. Clearly, schools represent one of many locations where mixed-race children require support from adults who are knowledgeable about how race mediates educational experiences.

Educators must constantly be aware of schools as contested sites, where compromise and change can lead to more flexible settings for children from a broader range of social, cultural, and family background situations. The demographic shift anticipated because of increased numbers of interracial marriages and bonds (and subsequently increased numbers of mixed-race children) will precipitate a period of multiracial pride where individuals with mixed-race backgrounds will no longer be silent regarding their mixed-race lineage. Mixed-race individuals will likely be just as adamant about choosing how they wish to embrace their biraciality or multiraciality.

The Organization of the Book

Racial groups are diverse with distinct histories and cultural proclivities. Attempting to capture the multiple and varied experiences of all mixed-race children (and their families) in one book is simply not possible. For this reason, full "representation" of all groups for all topics will not take place. Overarching themes on mixedness with representative experiences is more a manageable goal than specific histories of all racial/ethnic groups. In some instances, differences among mixed-race individuals will be addressed. Differences in the ways social groups have been racialized have in turn influenced the experiences of their mixed-raced descendants. Even though a tremendous amount of mixed-race literature focuses on the Black-White binary, an attempt is made to include experiences of multiple groups, although these experiences will not be addressed for all issues and themes.

Many, many years ago when I worked in a P-12 setting, a White mother of biracial twins listed the race of one child as White and the other as Black on school records—this well before the 2000 Census afforded mixed-race individuals the opportunity to self-identify. The staff felt she was being contentious, but perhaps this was her way of proclaiming that her children were both. The meanings of being mixed-race and/or living in a multiracial family arrangement are best expressed by mixed-race individuals and individuals who perceive their living arrangement as multiracial. It is for this reason that *Mixed-Race Youth and Schooling* includes biographical excerpts written by and about mixed-race individuals as an essential source of information in the book.

Mixed-Race Youth and Schooling is interdisciplinary and relies primarily on literature from the disciplines of sociology, history, psychology, and cultural studies. To this degree, the book is foundational in approach, with the goal of enhancing educators' knowledge-base in ways that allow them to understand and affirm all students. For this reason, Part I, *Being Mixed-Race in Society,* addresses the broader sociohistorical context for mixed-raceness, which necessarily calls for an exploration of the evolution of race, racism, and privilege in the United States. The eventual impact of these attitudes and practices on multiracialism is addressed through the social and legal positions taken toward multiracialism from both historical and contemporary perspectives. Mixed-race individuals' self-understanding was and continues to be influenced by broader societal attitudes and actions toward mixed-race people. The final chapter of Part I examines how people of more than one race understood themselves in the past, as well as contemporary perspectives on self-understanding in a society where racial categorization persists.

Part II, *Family, Community, and Peers,* attends to the multiple situations mixed-race children encounter in their homes, communities, and schools that potentially affect their schooling experiences. Their families constitute a variety of arrangements, and embrace differing conceptions of what it means to be an interracial family. Further, the extended family plays a heightened role in the lives of mixed-race youth, especially when it comes to children having more in-depth understanding and acceptance of their mixed racial heritage. Mixed-race youth live in communities that range from single-race to highly diverse populations and from low socioeconomic environments to middle class and beyond. Differences in community attributes such as social class and/or the availability of social networks will influence the extent to which mixed-race children are able to execute their identity strategies (Khanna & Johnson, 2010). School personnel who are aware of the variety of ways mixed-race children and youth are influenced by their home and community environments are better able to collaborate with the children's home and communities for the benefit of children's education.

As with any group of children, peers play a significant role in mixed-race children's sense of self and sense of well-being. Peer interactions and friendships are potentially influenced by the child's racial self-identity, as well as how peers racially perceive the mixed-race child. While single-race monoracial youth, for the most part, have ongoing opportunities to interact with same-race peers, this is not the case for many mixed-race youth. Further, mixed-race youth may be accepted or rejected by different peer groups on the basis of race-related values or behaviors they possess when interacting with peers (e.g., they may "act" too Black or too White for a given peer group to which they are exposed and/or desire to join).

It is essential for teachers and other school personnel to know about the inclusion and exclusion practices among children in their classrooms and in the general school environment. Educators will need additional sensitivity to the impact of these practices for mixed-race children in both diverse and more racially homogeneous schools and classrooms. This awareness begins with an understanding of the intricacies of interracial and intraracial (based on their minority group status as mixed-race children) interactions of mixed-race children with their peers.

In the process of being schooled, all children and youth acquire information and develop attitudes about race through what is taught and who teaches it, and the very nature of the location of where it is taught. This knowledge often impacts students' understanding of their positionality within schools. They also learn what to expect in terms of schools' recognition and support of their needs.

The primary emphasis for Part III of the text, *Education and Schooling: People, Places, and Practices,* is mixed-race youths' experiences at school as places where layered learning takes place.

As part of this focus, attention is given to teacher belief systems around race and how these beliefs intersect with school policies and practices to create learning environments that impact schooling experiences of all children, but with specific attention to mixed-race children. At its core, *Mixed-Race Youth and Schooling* encourages teachers and other school personnel to go beyond acquiescence to polices and practice that ostensibly seek to neutralize the impact of diversity in all of its forms, on the process of schooling. In fact, an educator disposition that aims to reframe practices so that they attend to differences will have a positive impact on schools as truly diverse places, which in turn contributes to more positive schooling experiences for mixed-race youth.

Is *Mixed-Race Youth and Schooling* "just another book about race?" Perhaps. To be sure, it is difficult to write about the education and schooling of mixed-race youth without a discussion about race. Though not originally intended as a goal of this book, the enduring influence of race on the schooling experiences of children resurfaces. The fact that mixed-race children straddle the racial divide not only makes this influence even clearer, but as well presents an additional perspective on the intrusion of race on social experiences of the nation's young. Complicating a discussion of the schooling experiences of mixed-race children, however, is the fact that scholarship that centers on children and race is often unclear when mixed-race youth are included as research study participants. The tendency is to identify participants only as monoracial and/or to minimize participation of mixed-race youth. This oversight, in my view, makes this book even more important. Intentionally locating mixed-race youth at the center of an educational discourse makes this population of children and youth more visible and emphasizes the importance of understanding how they experience schooling.

A Note on Terminology

A number of race-related terms associated with mixed-race youth, their families, and their experiences are used interchangeably in the literature. In this book, the term mixed-race is used to include children and youth who may also be referred to as biracial or multiracial. The terms biracial and multiracial to refer to youth of more than one race will be used only when the terms are instrumental to the ideas or constructs presented by scholars contributing to the body of mixed-race literature. Interracial, on the other hand, is used in this text to refer to adults from two different racial backgrounds who join together as a couple, and the family unit they form together. The term multiracial is used to refer to a family unit where the racial backgrounds of the children and parents are different. An example would be two White adults in a family with a White-Native American mixed-race child. I also intentionally stray from using race and ethnicity as interchangeable terms, although I recognize that children can be the progeny of parents from two (or more) ethnic backgrounds. My emphasis here is the impact of race mixture on the experiences of a group children and youth today. Readers should also note that different terms for referencing minority groups are used interchangeably (e.g., Black/African American and Native American/ Indian/American Indian) throughout the text. Shifts in terminology are made most often to align with the use of terms in referenced material.

Note

1. The U.S. Department of Education now requires schools to use reporting of racial categories that separate Asian and Pacific Islanders into Asian and Native Hawaiian or Other Pacific Islanders. The groups (Asian/Pacific Islanders) remain collapsed for this book.

References

Delgado, R. & Stefancic, J. (2012). *Critical race theory: An introduction.* New York: New York University Press.

Khanna, N. & Johnson, C. (2010). Passing as Black: Racial identity work among biracial Americans. *Social Psychology Quarterly,* 73(4), 380–397.

Lewis, A. E. (2004). *Race in the schoolyard: Negotiating the color line in classrooms and communities.* New Brunswick, NJ: Rutgers University Press.

Taylor, P., Passel, J., Wang, W., Kiley, J., Velasco, G., & Dockterman, D. (2010). *Marrying out: One-in-seven new U.S. marriages is interracial or interethnic.* Pew Research Center. From http://pewsocialtrends.org/files/2010/10/755-marrying-out.pdf.

Thompson, D. (2012). Making (mixed-) race: Census politics and the emergence of multiracial multiculturalism in the United States, Great Britain, and Canada. *Ethnic and Racial Studies,* 35(8), 1409–1426.

U.S. Department of Education. (2014, March 21). *Expansive survey of America's public schools reveals troubling racial disparities.* From http://www.ed.gov/news/press-releases/expansive-survey-americas-public-schools-reveals-troubling-racial-disparities.

PART I

Being Mixed-Race in Society

Whether clearly articulated or not, educators attach meaning to the racial makeup of mixed-race children, often without consciously being aware of the theoretical or historical underpinnings for those beliefs. Part I is presented to support educators' understanding of how race, both as a construct and an ideology, has influenced and continues to influence the lives and positionalities of mixed-race people. People who cross racial boundaries have historically challenged social systems based on the separation of people into distinct racial groups. The goal of Part I is to situate mixed-raceness within a society where race continues to play a pivotal role in the social, economic, and political lives of various groups of people according to how they are raced by others and the racial claims they make for themselves.

The focus of Chapter 1 is the evolution of "race" as a tool to separate people into distinct groups—groups that were then subjected to different experiences in society. The theoretical approaches for exploring the meanings of "race" are discussed as a means for illustrating how the separation of people by "race" is motivated by a dominant group's desire to maintain social position and power over others. In Chapter 2, the focus shifts to mixed-raceness from a historical perspective. The emphasis is on the social and legal measures undertaken to ensure that people of more than one race did not disturb a social and economic hierarchy based on separate and distinct races.

Whereas the first and second chapters combine to provide a broader socio-historical context for mixed-raceness, the final chapter of Part I, Chapter 3, addresses how social perceptions of the meanings of race and racial ideology influence individuals' sense of self as well as how they are perceived by others. Theoretical perspectives of racial identity development are addressed and include both historical and more recent views of racial self-understanding and affiliation.

1

THE CONTEXT OF RACE FOR MIXED-RACE PEOPLE

> *. . . My mother filled out my [school] enrollment form . . . she came to the section . . . that asked for my race . . . my mother checked the box marked "Negro" . . . How could I possibly be Black? . . . my aunts, uncles, and cousins were Black . . . But me?*
>
> —E. Lewis (2006, pp. 15–16)

Lewis's understanding of his racial background was obviously different from his mother's beliefs of the appropriate box she was expected to check in order to provide information about his race. That incident occurred prior to the 2000 Census, which was pivotal in the evolution of mixed-race status in the United States. People of more than one race were officially allowed to declare any aspect of their racial heritage they wished to, which in effect enabled them to define themselves. From that point forward, and despite how they may be perceived by the public, mixed-race individuals were able to proclaim a racial identification that more accurately reflected an internal sense of self.

Even so, official and unofficial placement of people into racial categories is important in the United States, in large measure because of the social, economic, and political realities associated with race. Unofficially, for example, people in the United States continue to be treated differently on the basis of assumed racial background. Physical characteristics that do not fit an expected racial category, however, result in confusion as to how one "ought" to be treated. Racial ambiguity often leads to blatant questions such as "What are you?" and/or longer-than-normal stares of mixed-raced individuals from strangers (Kelley, 2007).

Officially, federal statutes, policies, and programs are influenced by race-based census data and, as a result, how race is constructed and counted by the U.S. Census is important to minority groups. Given that mixed-race individuals straddle two or more racial categories, advocates for mixed-race peoples' rights pushed for a separate multiracial category when changes in race designations were being considered for Census 2000. The addition of a multiracial category was met with resistance from civil rights activists who believed this option would lead to a decline in the number of mixed-race individuals declaring a single minority race category. The racial designation option proposed by mixed-race activists could have a negative impact on minority political influence and federal programs designed to help disadvantaged minorities (Shih, Sanchez, Bonam, & Peck, 2007).

The number of mixed-race individuals will likely increase in the coming years, because of shifts in acceptance of interracial marriage and bonds (Taylor et al., 2010). Although it may appear counterintuitive, the increased number of mixed-race individuals will likely heighten rather than diminish a focus on race in the United States. Racial salience (i.e., the extent to which race plays a relevant part of an individual's sense of self) will likely counteract notions that increased interracial marriage/bonds will precipitate a color-blind society where race no longer matters. Further, the diversity with which mixed-race individuals express and embrace their mixed heritage will complicate existing social and institutional practices (including those of schools) with respect to race.

An emerging multiracial multiculturalism (Thompson, 2012) will support a departure from the marginalization of "mixedness," as mixed-race individuals embrace their unique position of being of more than one race (Lopez, 2003, p. 25). In an effort to provide researchers with language more applicable to the experiences of a growing multiracial population, Rockquemore, Brunsma, and Delgado (2009) concluded that the current use of "race" as a construct applied to mixed-race people is not particularly useful. They suggested that racial identity (i.e., the way mixed-race people understand themselves), racial identification (i.e., the way others categorize mixed-race people), and racial category (i.e., the available and chosen racial identities within a particular context) more accurately addresses the complexities of "race" for mixed-race people in societies still encumbered by "race" as a defining and differentiating characteristic.

Nonetheless, it is important to have a framework for understanding how the notion of "race" and racial ideology translated into differentiated life experiences for groups of people for centuries. The discussion that follows is organized around three broad areas of racial theory: race as nation building, race as ethnicity, and race as a reflection of class status (Omi & Winant, 2015). As noted by Omi and Winant, each of these explanations of race has shortcomings and does not fully or adequately explain the formation and impact of race in the United States. Still, each explanation contributes to our understanding of race as a deeply embedded and tenacious reality of the society in which we live. In order to move beyond the shortcomings of each race theory, race as a social construct is given primacy as an overarching concept in the discussion. The chapter then focuses on how beliefs about race shaped differentiated positions and experiences of all people, as well as how mixed-race people impacted and were impacted by this context of race.

Race as a Social Construct

In a book written to pay homage to his mother, McBride (1996) described her as a White woman who raised 12 Black children—and because of the places where the family lived, recalled that she was a "white person in a Black world" (p. 8). Such distinct locations of mother and son in different racial spheres clearly illustrate the pervasiveness of racial division and categorization in the United States and, as will be discussed in depth in later chapters, how such divisions potentially impact internal practices of interracial families. McBride's expression of the social place and racial status of mother and son support the notion of race as a social construction that is mediated by experience and choice—particularly for mixed-race individuals.

Debates over whether race is a social construct or whether there is a biological basis for distinct racial groups persist. Proponents of race as a social construct rely on biological explanations that suggest groups of human beings have more genetic similarity than genetic differences with each other when it comes to racial categories (Shiao, Bode, Beyer, & Sevig, 2012). As a result, they propose that race is a social construction "maintained and contested" (p. 70) for social and political purposes. It is an idea initially made real by acts of "making up people" (Omi & Winant, 2015, p. 106) as different, on the basis of observable physical characteristics (e.g., skin color). Ultimately, racial classification systems were developed so that differential treatment could be assigned to different groups of people in a society.

Shiao et al. (2012) aligned themselves with proponents of biological bases for distinct racial differences. Their support for this position relies on recent improvements in DNA sequencing and the emergence of technologies that enhance genetic analyses. They contended that although researchers in their camp suggested means for providing more concrete biological bases for racial and ethnic categories, they couldn't determine the social consequences for these divisions. To this degree, the debate over the social or biological basis for race and thus racial categories is a specious one when it comes to mixed-race individuals.

According to Shih et al.(2007), mixed-race individuals understand race categories as ". . . arbitrary, subjective, and ultimately meaningless in any biological sense " (p. 125), primarily because there is no single race category in which they can easily be placed. Nonetheless, as critical race theorists Ladson-Billings and Tate (1995) pointed out, "(even) when the concept of race fails to make sense, we continue to employ it" (p. 49). The notion of biologically based monoracial categories is further complicated by the fact that many mixed-race individuals are members of multigenerational mixed-race families where the point of an interracial liaison may be one or two generations removed from the individual embracing a mixed-race identity (Lewis, 2006).

Eubanks (2013), for example, recounted a family history where his mother, who was mixed-race because of a White father and Black mother, was raised as Black. His grandfather was given the opportunity to raise his children as White when his wife died and thus no longer embodied the fact that the children were mixed-race. Because both husband and wife had blond hair and blue eyes, it is likely their children "looked White" enough to be assumed as monoracial White. Even though the family lived in a small town in Alabama, Eubanks's grandfather refused to hide the mixed-race positionality of his children—although they were raised to embrace a Black identity. Eubanks's mother married a Black man. Although Eubanks considers himself Black, he married a White woman and children were born to this union, which further contributes to the multigenerational nature of the family's mixed-race lineage.

Eubanks's mother personifies a situation experienced by many mixed-race individuals—that is, they may be born biracial or multiracial, but come to identify with a minority race by experience (Lewis, 2006). The subjective nature of race for mixed-race individuals is further supported by the fact that in the past, the race designation for mixed-race people could legally change between birth and death. Lewis's father, who was mixed-race as a result of a Black father and White mother, was listed as mulatto on his birth certificate, but as Black on his death certificate. Eubanks's mother was listed as White on her birth certificate; however, in order to marry a Black man, her race had to be legally changed to Black in order to get a marriage license (Eubanks, 2013; Lewis, 2006). Even today, mixed-race people can truthfully claim one racial category during one census, and change that designation when the next census is taken. It is clear that mixed-race individuals complicate official and unofficial practices of naming individuals according to race. In order to fully understand the challenges to these practices, it is important to understand the role played by race in social, political, and economic structures and interactions in the United States.

Constructing Whiteness for Nation Building

A discussion of race from a nation-building perspective necessarily begins with the appropriation and settlement of land by Europeans in areas beyond their homelands (Omi & Winant, 2015). It requires a description of actions employed to preserve these lands as places dominated by White people, actions that collectively translated into processes of whiteness. A discussion of whiteness facilitates our understanding of the function of race in societies where members of the White "race" are in dominant and privileged positions (Bush, 2011).

Kincheloe (1999) described whiteness as a sociohistorical construct that shifts in relation to demographic, political, and economic changes. As a result, whiteness has been discussed and defined from a number of perspectives, to include whiteness as a process, whiteness as an identifying characteristic, and whiteness as an attitude toward self and others. Yoon (2012) summarized the multiple ways whiteness has been addressed to include whiteness as:

- an iterative process that is socially, historically, and culturally constructed;
- a process susceptible to change, depending on people and situational factors;

- a process or system of domination that privileges White people over non-white people;
- invisible and unmarked—and thus normative as the way things are and the way they are supposed to be;
- racial self-identity;
- identification of being White by others;
- synonymous with racism; and
- ideologies, attitudes, and actions of racism in practice.

Bush (2011) further described whiteness as having institutional privileges and ideological components that place its members in positions of dominance in societies, based on notions of European supremacy.

Whiteness as a viable social system emerged during the late seventeenth and early eighteenth centuries, a time when rationality was highly regarded as an approach to wrestling with situations and problems of the time. The capacity to reason was subsequently embodied in the person of White European men as a distinctive trait. As colonization ensued, European colonists used their positions of power and a desire to distinguish themselves from those whom they had conquered to delineate characteristics that defined whiteness and nonwhiteness (Figure 1.1) (Kincheloe, 1999). Kincheloe further proposed that the perception of an inferior nature of conquered nonwhite people provided a moral justification for White racism and colonization.

Convinced of their superiority, European colonists sought to maintain the purity of whiteness by insisting that even one drop of nonwhite blood relegated one to a nonwhite racial category. Hypodescent appears alongside hegemony of whiteness, as perceptions of a biological basis for superiority was perpetuated. Observable physical characteristics of various groups aided in the goal to place some people in subordinate social and political locations and provided easy markers to determine who should be included as White and who should be excluded. Indeed, those deemed to be inferior (e.g., Indian and Black people)

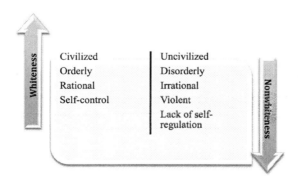

FIGURE 1.1 Characteristics of Whiteness and Nonwhiteness

were reduced to a subhuman positionality. Given this view, nonwhite people did not deserve the same rights as White people—a perspective later transported to the colonies as slavery was established.

Whiteness Disrupted?

Today, it is understood that the U.S. population is increasingly becoming more racially diverse and that there is a steady decrease in the White population. In fact, it is projected that White people will constitute 74 percent of the total population by 2050, down from 81 percent in 2000 (Shrestha & Heisler, 2011). These data alone do not presage a decline in the social and political aspects of whiteness, however. Although the number of individuals who self-identify as or who are identified as being White may decline, whiteness as a process, attitude, or system of domination that privileges White people over other racial groups may prove to be more resistant to comparable change.

Winant (2004) suggested that whiteness has become problematic, as the cloak of biological rationales for White supremacy has fallen away. Social and institutional efforts focused on racial equality have made the notion that one group should have power and status over another on the basis of race seem absurd. Still, according to Winant, purveyors of whiteness have been able to reinterpret, rearticulate, and reinsert the notion of racial equality into the culture and politics of the United States in ways that ensure that large-scale changes in the direction of racial equality will not occur anytime soon. Relatedly, as indicated by the basic premises of critical race theory, whiteness will never fully disappear because of its psychic value to working class and material value to elite White people (Delgado & Stefancic, 2012). Racism that emanates from whiteness may be expressed differently, but it will never disappear (Vaught & Castagno, 2008).

Social and legal events have contributed to a current state of whiteness in flux—so much so that Winant (2004) described whiteness today in terms of "racial dualism" (p. 4). Borrowing from Du Bois's notion of double consciousness that was applied to African Americans, he proposed that White people must reconcile an identity derived from a legacy of White supremacy—one that still reaps social benefits—and the fact that this legacy has been attacked on moral and political grounds. The racial dualism of whiteness presents as a crisis where there exists ". . . allegiances to privilege and equality, to color consciousness and colorblindness, [and] to formally equal justice and to substantive social justice . . ." (p. 5). Moore (2003) discussed the fact that some White people feel an ". . . embattled sense of whiteness . . ." (p. 505), to the point that they feel disadvantaged by institutional change focused on racial equality and besieged by critiques of White privilege by people of color.

White Privilege

The notion established by Europeans that some people were superior to others subsequently translated into institutions and social arrangements that benefited those identified as White (Bush, 2011; Hunter, 2005). In her often-referenced essay on White privilege, McIntosh (1990) described White privilege as the systematically conferred advantages of one group gained through the disadvantage of another. White privilege is neither fully acknowledged nor recognized by some White people, even though they garner unearned social rewards and benefits as a result of being White. Further, some White people do not recognize the pervasive impact of race privilege on the ways in which people interact with each other and may choose to ignore the extent to which White privilege places one group in power or dominance over another.

A number of factors ensure the sustainability of White privilege—first and foremost is the denial that it exists. Solomon, Portelli, Daniel, and Campbell (2005) conducted a study of 200 White Canadian teacher candidates' understanding of whiteness and White privilege as discussed in McIntosh's *White Privilege: Unpacking the Invisible Knapsack.* Candidates tended to circumvent the possibility of White privilege by adopting three distinct positions to contest its existence. Solomon et al. labeled these positions as ideological incongruence, negating White capital, and liberalist notions of individualism and meritocracy.

With respect to ideological incongruence, candidates experienced a mismatch between their expressed beliefs and experiences related to those beliefs. For example, and one that is particularly pertinent from a pedagogical perspective, candidates ". . . reframe[d] information to reinforce their ideological bent . . ." or discount[ed] information that challenge[ed] their beliefs" (Solomon et al., 2005, p. 155). Candidates' expressions under the position of negating White capital denied that White privilege and unearned benefits related to White privilege existed. Solomon et al. reported that emotional responses ranging from anger and aggression to guilt were precipitated by suggestions that candidates possessed unearned benefits as a result of being White. The final position that allowed candidates to avoid addressing the certainty of White privilege was liberalist notions of individualism and meritocracy. Here, candidates expressed beliefs to suggest that everyone has an equal opportunity to achieve and that hard work could overcome obstacles, with little attention to the influence social conditions might have on either individualism or meritocracy.

White privilege, however, is maintained through an interaction between individual beliefs and systemic or structural conditions (Vaught & Castagno, 2008). In an ethnographic study of teachers and administrators in two separate urban districts, Vaught and Castagno determined that the structural dimensions of racism are often overshadowed by a focus on teacher shortcomings as the cause for problematic school situations. Strategies to ameliorate certain negative conditions required improvement in aspects of teacher practice. Thus, efforts to address persistent disparity in test performance between White students and students of color focused on teacher professional development, rather than system-level impediments to student progress.

White privilege is also sustained by the ways in which it is inextricably intertwined with notions of the American way. Whiteness made for cultural norms that came to signify what it meant to be an American (Omi & Winant, 2015). Consequently, whiteness provided the standards against which all other groups were evaluated and defined (Delgado & Stefancic, 2012). It became a property of sorts—something to be owned for its ability to confer rights, privileges, and other advantages (Delgado & Stefancic, 2012; Vaught & Castagno, 2008).

According to a study of attitudes toward equal opportunity and affirmative action among middle and working class White adults conducted by DiTomaso, Parks-Yancy, and Post (2011), White people are often guided by values inherent in a "dominant ideology" of the American way of life. Referencing Kluegel and Smith (1986), DiTomaso et al. suggested White Americans believe that economic opportunity is widespread and that individuals are personally responsible for their state in life, thus, inequalities are fair. These beliefs align closely with the teacher candidates discussed earlier, who believed in individualism and meritocracy. In both instances, contextual factors did not figure into their beliefs.

In the case of the latter study, working class participants used dispositional or personal characteristics (e.g., extended effort) to explain differences in life positions whereas middle class participants tended to use structural explanations (e.g., differences in the quality of neighborhood schools) to account for social differences. Both groups believed in the concept of equal treatment, however, and both believed that institutions or the government should not engage specific policies (e.g., affirmative action) as remedies for inequities.

Again, like the teacher education candidates, participants in this study were oblivious to the fact that they had access to social and material capital not available to some nonwhite individuals. Further, they could not conceive of how any advantages or privileges to which they were privy could contribute to the disadvantages of others. Kaiser and Pratt-Hyatt (2009) listed a number of worldviews or beliefs White people are likely to adopt in order to explain and justify a system of inequities that align with a race-based status hierarchy. These "status-legitimizing worldviews," include ". . . [racial] hierarchy-enhancing myths, . . . [and] system-justifying beliefs" (p. 433).

Race as Ethnicity

The biological nature of race was called into question by the view of race as ethnicity, and given this perspective, culture was given a more central position in attempts to understand differences among people. As Omi and Winant (2015) explained, race discussed as ethnicity focused on issues of ". . . assimilation, cultural pluralism, inclusion, and democracy" (p. 21). Race as conceptualized as ethnicity was subject to a race relations cycle consisting of four stages: contact, conflict, accommodation, and assimilation. Attention to the fact that not all White Europeans have always been accepted as "White" provides an instructive framework for understanding this perspective. As a matter of fact, proponents of this view based their understanding of race on White ethnics, while ignoring the experiences of people of color (i.e., Asian, Native, Latino, and Black people) in the United States (Omi & Winant, 2015).

Southern and eastern Europeans (e.g., Jews, Italians, Poles, and Irish) who entered the United States during the great migration of the 1890s through the 1920s were not initially accepted as unequivocally "White" (Bush, 2011). Roediger (2005) discussed the racial status of the "new immigrants"—a term that carried unspoken connotations of racial difference—as "inbetweeness" (p. 8). They were positioned as being not quite White; however, they were not considered to be nonwhite either. Labels such as "temporary Negroes," "off-white," or "conditionally white" were used to describe immigrants arriving during this period (Bush, 2011, p. 13). The U.S. Census finally counted third-generation descendants of immigrants from these countries as unambiguously White. Initially, both the immigrants and their children were counted as White, but placed in separate categories from White people born in the United States. Once immigrants were counted as White, race distinctions remained only for nonwhite people (Bush, 2011).

Becoming White

Immigrants initially unaccepted as White upon arrival to the United States were able to achieve whiteness by aligning with Whites in power and through participation in strategies and practices that maintained social exclusion and dominance over nonwhite people (e.g., African Americans, Chinese, Native Americans), who were deemed racially inferior. Consequently, White ethnics were eventually able to take advantage of privileges accorded to native born Whites as a mechanism for achieving upward mobility. In the process, many assimilated into U.S. culture, relinquishing allegiance to their ethnic background in order to unify with other "Whites" against disinvited nonwhites. They were no longer Irish or Italians, but "White" (Bush, 2011). At the point of full assimilation, groups previously distinguished by ethnicity were collapsed into one race—the White race—and sometimes referred to as Caucasians (Halley, Eshleman, & Vijaya, 2011; Roediger, 2005). Today, for many White people, ethnicity is symbolized only through celebrations, food, or other cultural activities (Lee & Bean, 2007).

In some instances, aspiring Whites blamed and demonized nonwhites when rewards and privileges of being White did not come quickly enough, despite the lack of economic or political power among these groups (Guglielmo, 2003). In other instances, competition for jobs led to tension between aspiring White people and people of color. Subsequently, aspiring Whites participated in practices that contributed to outright oppression of people of color, even though the former had experienced various forms of oppression (e.g., class-based or race-based) in their homelands and/or in their newly chosen homes in the United States (Guglielmo, 2003; Ignatiev, 2009).

The friction between aspiring White people and people of color was both instigated and sanctioned by Whites in power, who feared collaboration among disparaged groups (i.e., people of color and "new immigrants") might disrupt the social hierarchy created by race-based inequities. Notions of racial inferiority and superiority, along with the promise of social, psychological, and political advantages associated with being White, sufficed to encourage aspiring Whites to engage in projects and practices that served to oppress people of color (Bush, 2011).

Although it is clear that immigrants helped their cause of becoming White by disparaging minorities of color and by willingly assimilating, they were also helped by the fact that the United States began to limit European immigration in the 1920s. As a result, fears about being overrun by perceived racially inferior "not quite whites" dissipated. Restricting the influx of immigrants also helped with the economic incorporation of existing European immigrants and contributed to their economic mobility (Lee & Bean, 2007). In the end, immigrants made the decision that is was far better to assimilate as White, with its associated advantages, than tackle the existing inequitable race-based hierarchy, even when the existence of such a hierarchy was potentially a threat to them as well (Guglielmo, 2003).

Crossing the Color Line

The "color line" rests on notions of superiority-inferiority and designates which racial or ethnic groups are invited to participate in the American way of life as White and which groups are not. The Black-White color line, which is the most frequently cited division between Whites and other racial groups, includes not only African Americans but other racial minorities as well. There is no intent here however to elevate a Black-White binary, which suggests the African American experience is the prototype for understanding the complex and diverse experiences of all minorities in the United States (Delgado & Stefancic, 2012).

On the contrary, some theorists proposed that for African Americans as a group, the Black-White color line ostensibly erects an impenetrable barrier to full access to privileges available to White people, which is not the case for other minority groups. Referencing the work of Gans (1999), Lee and Bean (2007) concluded that regardless of economic and educational advances, progress believed to impact movement into privileges and rewards associated with whiteness, Black people remain last in line among racial groups for whom the color line might fade.

Latinos and Asian Americans may potentially morph into whiteness should the Black-White color line be replaced by a Black-nonblack color line. In this instance, Asians and Latinos would fall into the "nonblack" side of the divide and would be *allowed* to assimilate into whiteness (Lee & Bean, 2007). Similar to southern and eastern European immigrants, they would gain economic mobility as they simultaneously adopt White culture and distance themselves not only from Black people but also from those who marry Black people and the mixed-race children who are born to those unions. Should this prediction come to fruition, history would be repeated as Asian Americans and Latinos would accept, rather than challenge, the existing racial hierarchy, as did European immigrants at the dawn of the twentieth century.

A primary shortcoming of the race-as-ethnicity perspective was the notion that assimilation to whiteness was an end goal for all social groups in the United States. Although proponents attempted to incorporate the experiences of people of color into this model, cultural nationalism movements launched by people of color in the 1960s challenged the notion that all nonwhite people wanted to assimilate (Omi & Winant, 2015). More recently, Kim (2007) questioned assumptions made by sociologists who predict that Asian Americans are purposely moving toward whiteness. She surmised that these conclusions are often made without observing or interviewing Asian Americans in order to understand how race figures in their lives or without analyzing information from surveys of Asian Americans' experience of discrimination and bias. Further, sociologists who propose shifts in Asian Americans' racial status make their predictions without considering connections Asian Americans might have to issues of immigration, global inequality, and other social citizenship issues faced by Asians in other parts of the world.

Sociologists who predict that Asian Americans as a group will soon become White may not be paying attention to perceptions Asian Americans might have of the role played by the United States in situating their homelands into racial hierarchies that exist on global levels. Such sensibilities may deter their desire to become White, particularly when U.S. policies abroad may well impact treatment of Asian Americans here in the United States. Asian Americans continue to be viewed as ". . . forever foreigners . . ." even if they were born in America. This misnomer supports a perception of Asian Americans as "not-American" (Kim, 2007, p. 562). At the same time, they are viewed as model *minorities*. Both beliefs continue to locate Asian Americans outside the boundaries of being White.

That the color line persists for Asian Americans is evident in disparities between Whites and minorities in income, housing, and employment. For example, household income has been discussed as an indication that Asian Americans are moving toward whiteness (their average household income actually exceeds that of Whites on average). Kim (2007) explained that at least some of this reported advantage is due to household incomes that reflect the extended family structure in some Asian American homes, where incomes of multiple adults are counted. Individual incomes, however, are 10 percent and more behind that of individual incomes of Whites. Moreover, Asian Americans, like other minorities, continue to experience the glass ceiling when it comes to upward mobility in the workplace. As another example, Japanese Americans continue to be underrepresented in certain occupational areas (e.g., lawyers and judges), and their level of education is not always reflected in their earnings.

Although Asian Americans and Latinos may have in common the perception that they are shifting toward whiteness, historically they have different routes to acceptance as Americans. The former experienced laws that limited their entry into the United States. The Page Law of 1875 restricted entry of Asians perceived to be undesirable Asians, including women believed to be prostitutes. This legislation was followed by the Chinese Exclusion Act of 1882, which froze immigration for ten years and prohibited Chinese from becoming U.S. citizens until the 1950s (Kim, 2007).

By contrast, Mexican Americans were actually legally granted citizenship following the Mexican American War. As a result of the Treaty of Guadalupe Hidalgo of 1848, Mexico ceded half of its land to the United States, land which is today New Mexico, Arizona, and parts of Wyoming, Nevada, and Colorado. Although the United States wanted the land conquered as a result of the War, they were unsure of what to do with the 115,000 inhabitants that came with the land (Gómez, 2007).

The vast majority of Mexicans, most of whom were located in New Mexico, were mixed-race with Spanish, Indian, and African lineage. Many in the United States believed they should not have the same rights as Whites, particularly the right to own land. Given that there was a distinction between federal and state citizenship, the United States designated New Mexico as a territory rather than a state—a status it held for 64 years—and granted Mexicans federal citizenship. Because all citizens were White, Mexicans were positioned as "off-white—sometimes defined as *legally* white [but] almost always defined as socially non-white" (Gómez, 2007, p. 149). Mexican Americans later shifted to minority status when it appeared pragmatic to do so in order to gain civil rights (Rodriguez, 2007).

According to Gómez (2007), Mexican Americans continue to be unsure of a claim to being White—and may be in a permanent state of off-white, because of resistance among some to obtain White status, even as they pursue social equality. In fact, Lee and Bean (2007) examined the possibility of the emergence of a different type of "color line," one where a population of Latinos would reject American culture and would not be anxious to assimilate as White. With this scenario, the Black-White division as the primary race-based divide would be replaced by Hispanic-White boundaries based on cultural differences. The lines of separation would develop as a result of the increased rate of immigration from Mexico, along with high birth rates among Mexican Americans. In the end, Lee and Bean rejected this proposition on the basis of their assertion that many Latinos are already pursuing whiteness in ways not so unlike Europeans of the early twentieth century.

Racial Minorities and Racial Hierarchies

Race-as-ethnicity theories emphasized the United States' democratic ideal of including all people, regardless of race, creed, or color (Omi & Winant, 2015).

The cultural nationalism movements of the 1960s were disconcerting to race-as-ethnicity proponents, because people of color refuted the idea of assimilation as an end goal for all people in the United States. Further, structural racism (i.e., pervasive race-based economic, educational, social inequities) precluded the assimilation pathway to inclusion for many people of color. Nonetheless, race-as-ethnicity proponents continued to advance the notion of race as a cultural phenomenon—one where beliefs, values, language, and group identification were malleable and a matter of choice (Omi & Winant, 2015). Color blindness and post-racial positions today are sustained by beliefs of ". . . racial status as more voluntary and consequently less imposed . . ." (p. 22). According to this view, the decision to be fully accepted into dominant culture United States is an individual one—it requires only identification with dominant culture beliefs, values, and behaviors (Omi & Winant, 2015).

Color-blind and post-racial positions are based on beliefs in the possibility of equal treatment for all regardless of race. This view ignores the extant nature of White privilege and the tenacious nature of racism and discrimination experienced by people of color. It also disregards the continued propensity in the United States (and indeed of nations globally) to separate people into inferior and superior locations. Minority groups are exposed to different levels of discrimination that reinforce their particular locations within a race-based hierarchy. According to critical race theory, this is a process of differential racialization, whereby ". . . racial and ethnic groups are viewed and treated differently by mainstream society" (Delgado & Stefancic, 2012, p. 160). Moreover, as explained by Delgado and Stefancic, each group ". . . has been racialized in its own individual way and according to the needs of the majority group at particular times in history" (p. 77).

Racial hierarchies are particularly pertinent to discussions of mixed-raceness, given that racial hierarchies were built on notions of inferior and superior positions for monoracial people. Many mixed-race individuals are mixed as a result of White and minority race liaisons, but there are also mixed-race individuals who are mixed as a result of a marriage or partnership between two minority race individuals. Either way, racial hierarchies as status constructions influence their social positions as mixed-race individuals, in part because many in the United States continue to either overtly or covertly adhere to stereotypical notions about race upon which racial hierarchies are built. Moreover, these perspectives, combined with structural inequalities, influence the differential statuses accorded individuals from different minority groups, regardless of dominant cultural values or behaviors they may have adopted.

Among African Americans, Latinos, and Asian Americans, for example, African Americans experience the most discrimination, followed by Latinos, and then Asian Americans. Indeed, as discussed earlier, given the designation of "model minorities," along with the social and economic progress made by Asian Americans as a group, some scholars believe they (along with more recent Latin American immigrants) may follow the path of southern and eastern European immigrants who dropped their ethnic identities as they assimilated into American society (Chong & Kim, 2006).

White prejudice toward Black people contributes to the position of this racial group at the bottom of the racial hierarchy. Kaiser and Pratt-Hyatt (2009) concluded that Black people who strongly identified as being Black were recipients of more racial prejudice than Black people who had a weaker racial identity. The researchers proposed that Black people with stronger minority race identity might be perceived as challenging the in-group values and worldviews of White people, particularly views that legitimize the race status hierarchy. Further, some White people feel that strongly race-identified Black people may possess negative opinions or attitudes about them.

White people may perceive beliefs and attitudes among strongly race-identified Blacks as a threat to their desire to hold onto a belief that the world is fair and that White people deserve any privileges they possess. The prejudice extended to strongly race-identified Black people makes it more difficult for some Blacks to enter the prevailing dominant social system. Mistrustful Whites, in effect, attempt to preserve their values by excluding challenges to them.

Kaiser and Pratt-Hyatt (2009) also noted there is an internal group reaction to weak and strong identification within a minority group. Individuals who are strongly identified with their minority race may mistrust, disparage, and/or reject those who are weakly identified with the race. This may have discouraging implications for mixed-race individuals whose identification with their minority lineage would not be described as strong, but they may nevertheless embrace the minority part of their lineage.

Colorism, Race, and Privilege: Implications for Mixed-Race People

Even though race-as-ethnicity proponents reject the idea of skin color as a marker for treating people differently, colorism persists. In fact, Bonilla-Silva (2004, 2014) theorized that in the United States, we are moving toward a racial stratification structure that is triracial and based on skin color. In this arrangement, a lighter skinned nonwhite group will have access to some but not all privileges available to monoracial White people. In essence, they will have more advantages than monoracial people of color. Lighter skinned nonwhite people in this social location will also tend to interact with White people more so than monoracial people of color.

It is already clear that colorism is at play when it comes to mixed-race individuals and White privilege. As Wise (2008) noted, White privilege is extended to mixed-race people who pass as White, either intentionally or because of misperceptions of their race by others because of their physical characteristics. To date, literature addressing the relationship between White privilege and mixed-race people is limited. Quihuiz (2011), however, studied a group of mixed-race people who could pass for monoracial White and their beliefs regarding access to the social advantages routinely available to monoracial White people. Study participants acknowledged that in general, skin tone influenced access to race group membership, whether the group is White or a minority race group.

Participants in Quihuiz's study also believed they received benefits available to monoracial White people, such as preferential treatment and being perceived as "normal" (normal meaning being left alone or not being questioned), as long as they were perceived as White. Thus, unlike many monoracial White people, the mixed-race respondents in this study were acutely aware of the existence of White privilege. Some respondents were uneasy about the privileges extended to them and felt being perceived as White was a burden. Others, however, felt being perceived and treated as monoracial White provided an avenue for them to educate and advocate around issues of social justice.

Having White or light skin and other features associated with White people (e.g., shape of facial features or hair texture), to some degree, is an advantage to those who are still designated as nonwhite. Hunter (2005) discussed well-documented facts, for example, that among some nonwhites (e.g., African Americans, Mexican Americans) there is a personal preference for lighter skinned individuals as marriage partners. Evidence also shows that color bias exists in multiple areas of life, with darker skinned African Americans tending to earn less money in employment, attain lower levels of education, live more often in segregated neighborhoods, have more punitive interactions with the law, and be less likely to be elected to public office (Hunter 2005; Hochschild & Weaver, 2007).

Differential access to privileges can also exist within interracial families where one parent is White. One parent may have social advantages that are not available to their partner or to their children. Further, when the results of Quihuiz's (2011) study are considered, it is likely that some siblings in interracial families may be perceived as White and thus privy to social benefits not available to their darker skinned siblings.

May-lee Chai (2007) recalled that her White mother understood that their South Dakota town was divided into highly unified ethnic groups (e.g. Norwegians, Germans, Swedes), "tribes" of sort, which served as allies for each other. Given the fact that May-lee's father was Chinese, their status as an interracial family left them without allies. As a White woman, however, May-lee's mother was able to become a member of the Irish "tribe," and in the process, establish allies for her mixed-race family. She was able to gain advantages, which no other member of the family (i.e., Asian American husband or mixed-race son and daughter) was able to accomplish.

Race as Class

Social stratification is one approach used to explain racial differences. In this instance, resources are distributed differently along racial lines, thus accounting for the class location of different racial groups (Omi & Winant, 2015). Reasons for differentiated class location differ, however, among theorists whose views align with this perspective.

Gans (2005), for example, theorized that race substitutes for class in a hierarchical structure that places African Americans as a group at the bottom of the class arrangement in the United States. He proposed that social position and prestige that appear to be based on race allow the United States to distance itself from countries where certain groups of people are permanently located at the bottom of a class hierarchy. According to Gans, ". . . Americans have always used race as a marker or indicator for class and status" (p. 18).

Unlike Gans, Wilson (2011) proposed a closer connection between economic mobility and class affiliation. As discussed earlier, economic mobility improved for southern and eastern European immigrants as they were in the process of "becoming White." For Wilson, there is a connection between economic mobility and access to social class benefits associated with White privilege.

Class—Not Race Hierarchies

Gans (2005) argued that because race is assumed on the basis of skin color and other observable physical characteristics, race has become the face of a hierarchy that is really about class. As evidence, Gans offered that whiteness is becoming equivalent to being middle class—thus, given the median incomes of Hispanics and Asian Americans, they will likely achieve the status of being White. The median wealth of Hispanics, Native Americans, and some Asian American groups, however, continues to be well below that of Whites (Omi & Winant, 2015). Still, in Gans's view, the "whitening" process will never be available to African Americans, poor Mexicans, or Black Hispanics from Puerto Rico or the Dominican Republic and other Caribbean countries, despite any economic achievement they may accomplish.

Gans (2005) also proposed that African Americans and other dark-skinned minorities will retain a lowered class status because of the impact of racism against nonwhite people; a "primeval fear" of darkness that has been transferred to an instinctive fear of dark-skinned people, and a negative reaction to "Negroid" features (p. 20). Further, African Americans are perceived as undeserving of higher social status more so than other groups because of a persistently high poverty rate and the inability of the group as a whole to address the challenges that prevent upward mobility. Even the increasing numbers of African Americans who reach middle class status cannot be trusted as a sign of upward mobility for the race as a whole, because many African Americans ". . . barely have a toehold" into middle class positionality and ". . . some are only a few paychecks away from a return to poverty" (p. 20).

White people, according to Gans, continue to perceive African Americans as ex-slaves who deserve to be discouraged from upward mobility. His views include both biological (e.g., disdain for Negroid features) and social (e.g., African Americans as undeserving of an improved status) explanations for the immutable low-level class status of dark-skinned people in the United States. Race as class stratification explanations such as this one propose that a caste system of sorts exists that constrains mobility on the basis of perceived racial characteristics (Omi & Winant, 2015).

Race, Class, and Occupational Mobility

Wilson (2011) expounded on his views on the intersection between class and race as he addressed research and commentary that, in his view, supported, criticized, and/or misrepresented propositions in his controversial 1980 publication, *The Declining Significance of Race: Blacks and Changing American Institutions.* He reemphasized his belief that economic class became more important than race when it came to life chances for individual African Americans. He contended that jobs from an expanded industrial growth in urban centers in the north and west provided employment opportunities for African Americans who migrated from the south in numbers of approximately six million between 1915 and 1970 (Wilkerson, 2010). During a period labeled as the Great Migration, many African Americans traded unskilled labor and low-paying service and farm jobs for skilled and semi-skilled blue collar and white collar positions. According to Wilson, economic changes (such as availability of jobs spawned from industrial growth) and political changes (such as President Truman's 1948 executive order that called for fair employment policies in federal government civil service jobs) aided in the development of a Black middle class in urban areas in the north.

Gateways to middle class status are different today—as the education and skills for a labor market that reflects growth in corporate and government employment sectors are different from those needed during the industrial expansion. African Americans with limited education and skills are not able to use occupational mobility as a route to middle class status. As Wilson (2011) stated, ". . . the black experience has moved historically from economic racial oppression experienced by virtually all African Americans to economic subordination of the black poor" (p. 57). The result is an "economic schism" in the African American community. Further, economic racial struggles appear to have been supplanted by more racially tinged sociopolitical issues (e.g., better public schools, residential issues). Wilson maintained that if he were writing his well-debated text today, he would place greater emphasis on policies that address both race and class for people of color.

The economic-based class differences between middle class African Americans and those living in poverty should not be taken as a move toward whiteness for middle class African Americans (even though it was assumed by Gans that this would be a difficult, if not impossible, journey). Based on a survey conducted by the Pew Research Center (2007), 61 percent of Blacks responded that values between low income and middle income Black people had become dissimilar over the last decade, and 54 percent of Blacks and 72 percent of Whites responded that values among Black and White people had become more similar. Low income Blacks tended to express beliefs in dissimilarity between low income and middle income Blacks more frequently than middle class and more educated Blacks. The lack of class-based ties, however, does not appear to suggest a desire for separation along personal, familial, or community ties among Black people (Omi & Winant, 2015). Even with this ostensible class divide, 65 percent of Blacks responded on the Pew Research Center Survey that some level of solidarity remains among all Blacks, regardless of class. These data suggest class, at least for Black people, does not present as a compelling explanation of race.

Conflating Race and Class

Some educators assert that the true social division today is based on class more so than race. One way that this line of thinking is represented is to suggest that African Americans, Hispanics/Latinos, and Whites who live in poverty have more in common with each other than they do with their middle to upper class racial counter parts. In reality, there are differences between White people who live in poverty and people of color who live in poverty. Even though the percentage of Whites living in poverty is less than any other racial group (see Chart 1.1), there

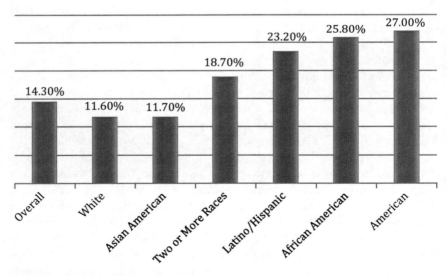

CHART 1.1   Poverty Rates 2007–2011

From Macartney, S., Bishaw, A., & Fontenot, K. (2013). *Poverty rates for selected detailed race and Hispanic groups by state and place: 2007–2011.* https://www.census.gov/prod/2013pubs/acsbr11-17.pdf

are more Whites living in poverty given their percent of the U.S. population. When compared with minorities living in poverty, Whites living in poverty tend to have a higher net worth and more assets, be better able to find affordable housing; be unemployed for shorter periods; and be more likely to attend better high schools (Conley, 2001; Wilson, 2011; Wise, 2008). Further, poverty among people of color tends to span many generations, which is not the case for White people living in poverty. For the latter group, poverty may last only a generation or two (Delgado & Stefancic, 2012).

White dominance associated with whiteness and White privilege remains a reality even for White people living in poverty. Just as the moniker "model minorities" is a marker that situates Asian Americans as minorities acting in ways unexpected of minorities in general, the unpleasant reference to some Whites living in poverty as "white trash" is a marker that locates this group as still White, but living in ways that are not the norm for White people (Halley et al., 2011).

DiAngelo (2006) reflected on her understanding of being White and living in poverty in this way:

> I was acutely aware that I was poor, that I was dirty, that I was not normal, and that there was something "wrong" with me. But I also knew that I was *not* Black . . . As I reflect back on the early messages I received about being poor and being White, I now realize that me and my grandmother *needed* people of color to cleanse and realign us with the dominant White culture that our poverty had separated us from.
>
> *(pp. 53–54)*

Distinctions among Whites by class do not minimize the availability of the status and privileges associated with being White. White dominance and its reliance on disparaging particular groups in a society separate people of different racial backgrounds living in poverty to some degree. As proposed by Halley et al. (2011), "Even though all white people may not be wealthy or have monetary inheritance, they still inherit the knowledge of the "white cultural way of life," which in our society is the right . . . way(s) of life" (p. 112).

Another way of fusing race and class is to conflate the two by overtly talking about class but surreptitiously meaning race. In this way, class becomes a marker for race. For example, on the basis of their analysis of Ruby Payne's (2005) truth claims in her popular book, *A Framework for Understanding Poverty*, Bomer, Dworkin, May, and Semingson (2008) concluded that Payne racialized poverty and, in the process, equated poverty with people of color by using fictional case studies to support her assertions that mainly referenced people of color. It is likely, they concluded, that an audience of primarily White, female, and middle class teachers would read Payne's frameworks as guidance for understanding people of color.

As another example of merging race and class, in an article intended to discuss the value of economically diverse schools and how schools could attend to the needs of poor and affluent students, the discussion soon became one on different learning needs and approaches to teaching Black and White students (Petrilli, 2013). There are also cases where the conflation of race and class is intentional as a means to accomplish race-based desegregation in schools. Socioeconomic desegregation is used as a goal because it is more politically palatable in some school districts—however, the real focus is racial desegregation (Crosnoe, 2009). Class, for instance, substituted for race.

The Intersection of Class and Race

Gans's belief that class substitutes for race in social hierarchies purportedly based only on race or ethnicity ignores the role of the state in intervening in and substantiating racial relations. Racial ideology (i.e., beliefs about race) that forms the bases for policies and practices in a society is transformed into perceptions about race in society, as well as racial interactions (Omi & Winant, 1994). More important, however, race and class (along with other social categories such as gender and sexuality) must be understood simultaneously in order to clearly explain social stratification systems. Any attempt to view them separately overlooks how these categories intersect to form not only social stratification systems, but also ". . . any practice of cultural marginalization . . . inequality or human variation . . ." (Omi & Winant, 2015, p. 106).

We need only be reminded of the major social movements of the twentieth century in order to understand how socially constructed categories of difference affect each other. The Civil Rights, Feminist, Farmworkers, and Gay Rights Movements, for example, were all organized to disrupt the inequality and marginalization perceived to be caused by an independent category (e.g., one's race, gender, or sexual orientation). These organized movements did not always recognize how social positions were impacted by the intersection of socially constructed categories. Nonetheless, a thorough understanding of the Civil Rights and Farmworkers Movements must consider the impact of race, class, and even gender on the social position of the groups seeking change. The Feminist Movement was often tagged as a movement of middle class, heterosexual, White women for not recognizing the race, class, and sexuality implications of their cause. Race does not substitute for class—rather the two must be viewed simultaneously (along with other socially constructed categories) in order to clearly explain social stratification systems.

Alternately, Wilson's economic analysis does not pay enough attention to the role of racism in the United States and the fact that it will likely remain a part of everyday life in society (Delgado & Stefancic, 2012). By his own recognition, Wilson believes his thesis needs a fuller discussion of the intersection of race and class. The pervasiveness of the impact of racism in all aspects of life (e.g., housing, health, education, environment, employment) precludes only an economic response to the social class location of some people of color.

The Impact of Mixedness on Race

Even though diversity is purportedly celebrated in the United States, whiteness dominates as the barometer to evaluate what is good, right, correct, and the way things ought to be. In the past, individuals and groups willingly relinquished or were required to relinquish their culture, language, religion, and even the way they perceived the world in order to be eligible for whiteness. That many groups seek to become White is less certain today than it was at the beginning of the twentieth century. Physical features of racial and ethnic minorities make it more difficult for race-based social boundaries to be crossed, and immigrants today are not as easily absorbed economically and politically into the fabric of the nation, as was the case for southern and eastern Europeans (Qian & Lichter, 2007). More important, however, racial groups will continue to seek social equity, without necessarily becoming White. The competition among racial groups for power, resources, and social standing ensures racial tension for some time to come.

Such is the context of race in which a growing number of mixed-race children will grow, learn, and develop. Children born to interracial unions in the near future will enter a world where complex issues around race continue to exist, even though according to Taylor et al. (2010), six in ten Americans approve of interracial marriage. It has been proposed that increased intermarriage may eliminate barriers that are the bases for social separation among the races (Gans, 2005; Lee & Bean, 2007). Thinking along these lines proposes that social distances will soften and prejudices will decline in ways not so unlike the reduction of prejudices among Whites following intermarriage among White ethnics. The process will be enhanced, it is suggested, by the attenuation of physical differences among races, as mixed-race children are born with less distinctively minority race physical characteristics.

This ethnocentric view of the impact of intermarriage on race relations and race boundaries reflects the classic assimilation theory that accounts only for a one-way movement toward whiteness as a symbol of positive progress. Alternately, Bonilla-Silva and Embrick (2006) argued that skin color will serve as an instrument to further segment groups, such that light-skinned mixed-race individuals will have more privileges than dark-skinned mixed-race individuals in a racial stratification system based on skin tone. In any case, assimilation projections based on the presumption that interracial marriage will reduce differences among various racial and ethnic groups in the U.S. simultaneously minimize the value of diversity and multiculturalism. This perspective implies as well that social equity can only come about for groups who become White.

Concluding Thoughts

Even as the census now allows mixed-race individuals to legally self-identify, the experience of being mixed-race will certainly be affected by the racialized climate that persists in the United States. A major challenge for all social institutions, but particularly for schools, is to ensure that mixed-race children be fully recognized as a group with social experiences that differ in some ways from their monoracial peers. According to the 2010 Census, people reporting more than one race grew by 32 percent from the 2000 Census to the 2010 Census (Jones & Bullock, 2012). Further, 4.4 percent of children under five in 2010 were mixed race, with 3.3 percent of children between the ages of five and 17 falling into this category. In both age categories, the percent of mixed-race children steadily increased over the last ten years (National Center for Education Statistics, 2011).

At this point, it is unclear how the change in census policy will influence public perceptions of mixed-race people as anything other than nonwhite, even when mixed-race people include being White as part of their identity. Based on our understanding of intersectionality, mixed-race people will have ". . . potentially conflicting, overlapping identities, loyalties, and allegiances" owing to the unique mix of their race, class, gender, sexual orientation, and so forth (Delgado & Stefancic, 2012, p. 10). While many mixed-race children will have monoracial identities, schools will need to appreciate the fact that many of these children will have identities that are not available to monoracial children (see Chapter 3). Their needs within schools will reflect this distinction. A value for multicultural education must now attend to multiracial multiculturalism (Thompson, 2012) in all aspects of schooling.

References

Bomer, R., Dworkin, J., May, L., & Semingson, P. (2008). Miseducating teachers about the poor: A critical analysis of Ruby Payne's claims about poverty. *Teachers College Record*, 110(12), 2497–2531.

Bonilla-Silva, E. (2004). From bi-racial to tri-racial: Towards a new system of racial stratification in the U.S.A. *Ethnic and Racial Studies*, 27(6), 931–950.

Bonilla-Silva, E. (2014). *Racism without racists: Color-blind racism and the persistence of racial inequality in America*. New York: Rowman & Littlefield Publishers, Inc.

Bonilla-Silva, E. & Embrick, D. (2006). Black, honorary White, White: The future of race in the United States? In D. Brunsma (Ed.), *Mixed messages: Multiracial identities in the "color blind" era* (pp. 33–48). Boulder, CO: Rienner.

Bush, M. (2011). *Everyday forms of whiteness: Understanding race in a "post-racial" world*. New York: Rowman & Littlefield Publishers, Inc.

Chai, M. (2007). *Hapa girl: A memoir*. Philadelphia: Temple University Press.

Chong, D. & Kim, D. (2006). The experiences and effects of economic status among racial and ethnic minorities. *American Political Science Review*, 100(3), 335–351.

Conley, D. (2001). Decomposing the Black-White wealth gap: The role of parental resources, inheritance, and investment dynamics. *Sociological Inquiry*, 71(1), 39–66.

Crosnoe, R. (2009). Low-income students and the socioeconomic composition of public high schools. *American Sociological Review*, 74(5), 709–730.

Delgado, R. & Stefancic, J. (2012). *Critical race theory: An introduction*. New York : New York University Press.

DiAngelo, R. (2006). My class didn't trump my race: Using oppression to face privilege. *Multicultural Perspectives*, 8(1), 51–56.

DiTomaso, N., Parks-Yancy, R., & Post, C. (2011). White attitudes toward equal opportunity and affirmative action. *Critical Sociology*, 37(5), 615–629.

Eubanks, W. R. (2013). Color line: How DNA ancestry testing can turn our notions of race and ethnicity upside down. *The American Scholar*, 82(2), 20–28.

Gans, H. (1999). The possibility of a new racial hierarchy in the twenty-first century United States. In M. Lamont (Ed.), *The cultural territories of race* (pp. 371–390). Chicago: University of Chicago Press.

Gans, H. (2005). Race as class. *Contexts*, 4(4), 17–21.

Gómez, L. (2007). *Manifest destinies: The making of the Mexican American race*. New York: New York University Press.

Guglielmo, J. (2003). Introduction: White lies, dark truths. In J. Guglielmo & S. Salerno (Eds.), *Are Italians white? How race is made in America* (pp. 1–14). New York: Routledge.

Halley, J., Eshleman, A., & Vijaya, R. (2011). *Seeing White. An introduction to White privilege and race*. Lanham, MD: Rowman & Littlefield Publishers, Inc.

Hochschild, J. L. & Weaver, V. (2007). The skin color paradox and the American racial order. *Social Forces*, 86(2), 643–670.

Hunter, M. (2005). *Race, gender, and the politics of skin tone*. New York: Routledge.

Ignatiev, N. (2009). *How the Irish became White*. New York: Routledge.

Jones, N. & Bullock, J. (2012). *The two or more races population: 2010*. United States Census Bureau. From www.census.gov.

Kaiser, C. & Pratt-Hyatt, J. (2009). Distributing prejudice unequally: Do Whites direct their prejudice toward strongly identified minorities? *Journal of Personality and Social Psychology*, 96(2), 432–445.

Kelley, M. (2007). Conspicuously mixed: The experience of multiracial youth in independent schools. *Independent School*, 67(1), 38–43.

Kim, N. (2007). Critical thoughts on Asian American assimilation in the whitening literature. *Social Forces*, 86(2), 561–574.

Kincheloe, J. (1999). The struggle to define and reinvent whiteness: A pedagogical analysis. *College Literature*, 26(3), 162–194.

Kluegel, J. & Smith, E. (1986). *Beliefs about inequality: Americans' views of what is and what ought to be*. New York: Aldine de Gruyter.

Ladson-Billings, G. & Tate, W. (1995). Toward a critical race theory of education. *Teachers College Record*, 97(1), 47–68.

Lee, J. & Bean, F. (2007). Redrawing the color line. *City & Community*, 6(1), 49–62.

Lewis, E. (2006). *Fade: My journeys in multiracial America*. New York: Carroll & Graf Publishers.

Lopez, A. (2003). Mixed-race school-age children: A summary of Census 2000 data. *Educational Researcher*, 32(6), 25–37.

Macartney, S., Bishaw, A., & Fontenot, K. (2013). *Poverty rates for selected detailed race and Hispanic groups by state and place: 2007–2011*. https://www.census.gov/prod/2013pubs/acsbr11-17.pdf

McBride, J. (1996). *The color of water: A Black man's tribute to his White mother*. New York: Riverhead Books.

McIntosh, P. (1990). White privilege: Unpacking the invisible knapsack. *Independent School*, 49(2), 31–35.

Moore, V. (2003). Kids' approach to whiteness in racially distinct summer day camps. *The Sociological Quarterly*, 44(3), 505–522.

National Center for Education Statistics. (2011). *Digest of education statistics*. From http://nces.ed.gov/programs/digest/d11/tables/dt11_021.asp.

Omi, M. & Winant, H. (1994). *Racial formation in the United States: The 1960s to the 1990s*. New York: Routledge.

Omi, M. & Winant, H. (2015). *Racial formation in the United States* (3rd ed.). New York: Routledge.

Payne, R. (2005). *A framework for understanding poverty: A cognitive approach*. Highland, TX: aha! Process, Inc.

Petrilli, M. (2013). The diversity dilemma. *Educational Leadership*, 70(8), 44–48.

Pew Research Center. (2007). *Optimism about Black progress declines: Blacks see a growing values gap between poor and middle class*. From http://www.pewsocialtrends.org/files/2010/10/Race-2007.pdf.

Qian, Z. & Lichter, D. (2007). Social boundaries and marital assimilation. Interpreting trends in racial and ethnic intermarriage. *American Sociological Review*, 72(1), 68–94.

Quihuiz, S. (2011). *Brown on the inside: Multiracial individuals and White privilege*. From http://ir.library.oregonstate.edu/xmlui/handle/1957/21764?show=full.

Rockquemore, K. A., Brunsma, D., & Delgado, D. (2009). Racing theory or retheorizing race?: Understanding the struggle to build a multiracial identity theory. *Journal of Social Issues*, 65(1), 13–34.

Rodriguez, M. (2007). More than whiteness: Comparative perspectives on Mexican citizenship from law and history. *Berkeley La Raza Law Journal*, 18(1), 79–86.

Roediger, D. (2005). *Working toward whiteness: How America's immigrants became White*. New York: Basic Books.

Shiao, J. L., Bode, T., Beyer, A., & Sevig, D. (2012). The genomic challenge to the social construction of race. *Sociological Theory*, 30(2), 67–88. doi:10.1177/0735275112448053. From http://st.sagepub.com.

Shih, M., Sanchez, D., Bonam, C., & Peck, C. (2007). The social construction of race: Biracial identity and vulnerability to stereotypes. *Cultural and Ethnic Minority Psychology*, 13(2), 125–133.

Shrestha, L. & Heisler, E. (2011). *The changing demographic profile of the United States*. Washington, DC: Congressional Research Service.

Solomon, R. P., Portelli, J., Daniel, B., & Campbell, A. (2005). The discourse of denial: How White teacher candidates construct race, racism, and 'white privilege'. *Race, Ethnicity, and Education*, 8(2), 147–169.

Taylor, P., Passel, J., Wang, W., Kiley, J., Velasco, G., & Dockterman, D. (2010). *Marrying out: One-in-seven new U.S. marriages is interracial or interethnic*. Pew Research Center. From http://pewsocialtrends.org/files/2010/10/755-marrying-out.pdf.

Thompson, D. (2012). Making (mixed-) race: Census politics and the emergence of multiracial multiculturalism in the United States, Great Britain, and Canada. *Ethnic and Racial Studies*, 35(8), 1409–1426.

Vaught, S. & Castagno, A. (2008). "I don't think I'm a racist": Critical race theory, teacher attitudes, and structural racism. *Race, Ethnicity, & Education*, 11(2), 95–113.

Wilkerson, I. (2010). *The warmth of other suns: The epic story of America's great migration*. New York: Random House.

Wilson, W. J. (2011). The declining significance of race: Revised and revisited. *Daedalus,* 140(2), 55–69.

Winant, H. (2004). Behind blue eyes. Whiteness and contemporary U.S. racial politics. In M. Fine, L. Weis, L. Pruitt, & A. Burns (Eds.), *Off-white: Readings on power, privilege, and resistance* (pp. 3–16). New York: Routledge.

Wise, T. J. (2008). *White like me: Reflections on race from a privileged son* (Rev. ed.). Berkeley, CA: Soft Skull Press.

Yoon, I. (2012). The paradoxical nature of whiteness-at-work in the daily life of schools and teacher communities. *Race, Ethnicity and Education,* 15(5), 587–613.

2

MIXED-RACE PEOPLE IN SOCIETY OVER TIME

 All of my experience as a biracial woman has been based on appearance. People will ask me what I am before they ask me what my name is.

—J. Chau (1999, p. 38)[1]

Race categories have historically been used in the United States to separate people for social, economic, political, and ideological purposes. Racial ideology manifested as legalized racism, supported in different historical periods by federal, state, and/or local laws, as well as by social convention. A primary goal was to maintain whiteness as the dominant political, economic, and cultural authority, while at the same time ensuring that White elites maintained power over which groups would be invited to benefit from the advantages of being White, and which groups would remain in a subordinate category of nonwhite.

Mixed-race people historically presented challenges to societies wanting uncomplicated divisions by race. Regulatory practices to prevent situations (e.g., ongoing social contact with subsequent romantic relationships between differently raced people) likely to result in mixed-race progeny existed in societies well before they were evident in the United States (Davis, 2012). Still, as Basson (2008) noted, mixed-race people presented several challenges to the United States in the late nineteenth and early twentieth centuries. The physical appearance of mixed-race people negated the view of a "natural" separation of races; some mixed-race people publically and politically resisted negative responses to their mixed-race status; and, in general, the mere presence of ambiguity regarding race challenged the moral and/or political grounds White elites used as a basis for the privilege and power they possessed. In order to maintain stable racial boundaries, Whites in power sought to ". . . hide, dismiss, or assimilate evidence . . ." of the constructed nature of race boundaries and to deem race mixing an event to be avoided or punished should it occur (p. 10).

In the past, mixed-race people were assigned race categories and accompanying labels that distinguished them from their overtly monoracial ancestors (both White and people of color). From mulatto, octoroon, half-breed, mestizo, hapa, and creole to biracial, an assortment of labels has been meant to not only signify the more-than-one race status of mixed-race people, but also attach to them varying social positions because of their mixed-race status and the particular makeup of their mixed-race lineage. It is noteworthy, however, that today, as it was in the past, variability exists in the extent to which mixed-race people embrace these terms.

Space limitations prohibit in-depth discussion of the diverse experiences and sociohistorical journeys of mixed-raced people from different White-minority and nonwhite-nonwhite racial heritages. The broader goal of the discussion that follows is to examine how race mixing has always existed in the United States, as well as the social, economic, political, and legal impact that mixed-raceness has had on U.S. culture.

Legal Bases for Separation by Race

Mixed-race people have been subjected to state and local laws to control their social status, some of which were principally directed toward their mixed-race, multicultural status and others that were directed toward people of color in general—which during certain historical periods included mixed-race people. For example, a 1662 Virginia law declared a child born to an enslaved woman a slave, regardless of whether the father was a White slave owner or an enslaved Black man. A 1664 Maryland law determined that a child born to a White woman and Black man would be a slave as well (Millward, 2010). These laws directly impacted mixed-race people.

On the other hand, Jim Crow laws that surfaced in southern United States in 1877 were designed to ensure racial segregation in public life between Black and White people. These laws impacted mixed-race individuals as well, regardless of whether they considered themselves Black. Two categories of laws are particularly important for understanding the social and historical evolution of mixed-race people's experiences in the United States: blood quantum laws and miscegenation laws.

Race Designation and Status by Blood Quantum

The notion that mixed-race people should be categorized and identified by the amount of "blood mixture" from their ancestral heritage was popular at different points in history, particularly when it came to people with an African, European, and/or Indian mix. Blood quantum was the mechanism used to determine differences in racial group membership and subsequently the social status for mixed-race people. A race group designation of being neither White nor Black for an individual with European and African ancestry was established well before a mixed-race lineage precipitated specific polices and laws to control the social status of this group of people. The Creoles of New Orleans are an example, however, of how a mixed-race group moved from a position of relatively unconstrained freedom to restrictions imposed by race-based laws.

The Case of New Orleans Creoles

Creoles are people of African and European descent. In the 1500s, French owners of land that was later to become Haiti fathered mixed-race children and often ensured that their offspring were educated and monied land owners. These children were considered neither White nor Black but were often held in disdain by both Black and White people. Still, many identified with the French, and it was not unusual for them to participate in the oppression of monoracial Black people. When the French settled in what is now New Orleans in 1718, they continued the practice of fathering mixed-race children. Early in the land acquisition process, the French imported Africans as slaves in order to bolster the small population of settlers in the newly occupied land. Men made up most of the settlers, as few European women traveled to settlements in the North Americas. As a result, Frenchmen coupled with African and Indian women as wives and concubines, and fathered children as a result of these unions (Davis, 2012).

Out of concern over the fact that slaves eventually outnumbered the French in Louisiana, officials in the Louisiana settlement adopted France's *Code noir* (Black Codes) in 1724 in order to restrict and regulate the behavior and rights not only of slaves, but also slave owners. Endogamy, the rule that one could marry only within their racial group, was included within the *Code*. It provided a way to ensure status and privilege to some people by being able to determine who was White and who was not. Although the law could not do much about sexual relations between White and nonwhite people, it could legislate the living circumstances for offspring of these liaisons by requiring that children of interracial relations follow the lineage and status of the mother, thus making mixed-race children slaves (Davis, 2012).

Prior to implementation of the *Code,* however, White men honored their unions with African women by freeing them from slavery, and/or by leaving them property at the time of the slave owner's death. Eventually, the number of nonwhite people outnumbered White people in the settlement, when counting mixed-race people and African slaves. This situation contributed to the development of a three-tiered racial hierarchy in Louisiana. Whites were at the top and African slaves at the bottom. The in-between group, mixed-race people, had position and privileges beyond those experienced by slaves, but not quite those enjoyed by White people.

The free people of color in Louisiana existed in a social space where they were able to work, buy property, become educated, and develop thriving communities. Creoles viewed themselves as a distinct group with a distinct sense of identity. They deemed slaves as primitive and uncouth. At the same time, they resented White peoples' condescending attitudes, as they believed given their stature and accomplishments, Creoles and Whites should enjoy the similar social positions (Davis, 2012). The population of Creoles in Louisiana increased markedly as a result of the 1804 slave revolt in the French colony of Saint-Dominique in the French West Indies. The approximately 450,000 slaves won their freedom from France and created the Republic of Haiti. Many Whites and Creoles left the islands in the midst of the fighting, some escaping to New Orleans and some to cities along the Atlantic. By this time, France had sold their land in the Americas to the United States through the *Louisiana Purchase,* and the former colony became a state in 1812 (Davis, 2012).

Facing a Hardened Color Line

The United States was not as amenable to a three-tiered racial hierarchy as was the French in Louisiana. Creoles of New Orleans who had become accustomed to the French race-based system were made up of generations of people of mixed European and African descent. They had created one of the wealthiest communities of free people of color in the United States, which included highly literate professionals, plantation owners (some owned slaves), and artisans. While the free people of color in New Orleans felt they deserved full citizenship, the United States pursued a more rigid color line between Whites and nonwhites, with Creoles fitting into the latter race category (Davis, 2012).

Creoles welcomed the end of slavery as a necessary condition important to their desire to be full citizens. Some owned slaves and stood alongside the Confederacy during the Civil War because they did not believe in the abolition of slavery. Others, however, saw benefits to coalescing with former slaves, even though they viewed their issues with White supremacy as patently different from their new collaborators. Although Creoles wanted to maintain their distinction of being neither Black nor White, many felt the need to unite with former slaves for political clout in their effort to attain White privileges.

The Emancipation Proclamation did not eradicate the desire of many in southern United States to maintain social and economic relations as they were prior to the Civil War. Not only was segregation in public life between Whites and nonwhites (i.e., former slaves and Creoles) desired, but southerners also wanted to retain the benefits of free labor provided by slaves. Black Codes were laws passed between 1865 and 1877 in the southern states after the Civil War in order to reestablish civil authority during the period of Reconstruction. These laws were meant to restrict freed Black peoples' activities and ensure their availability as a minimally compensated labor force now that slavery had been abolished. With the enactment of Jim Crow laws in 1877, racial segregation solidified, and the rights given to Blacks in the 13th, 14th, and 15th Amendments were restricted (Wormser, 2003). People suspected of having African ancestry in any degree were considered to be people of color, and thus subjected to these laws.

The Legal Argument against Imposed Race Identification

The outcome of *Plessy v. Ferguson* is well known for allowing racial segregation in schools and other areas of public life under the "separate but equal" doctrine. The U.S. Supreme Court case, however, goes beyond the more basic understanding of a Black man appealing the Louisiana state court decision that upheld the right of a train company to legally refuse to seat Black people in their train's first-class sections. While Plessy's activism was certainly directed toward appeal of the state court decision, the impetus for his action was not the rights of Black people (Avant-Mier & Hasian, 2002).

Many Creoles never embraced the equal rights arguments that had existed since the Civil War and early Reconstruction. Indeed, they did not view equality for all as their issue. Plessy was directed by the Creole community to sit in the restricted area of the train, not to instigate a case against the right of Louisiana's Separate Car Act to exist. Rather, the goal was to challenge the State's right to assign race by physical appearance. Plessy's lawyer argued "The question is not as to the equality of privileges enjoyed, but the right of the State to label one citizen as white and another as colored . . . (Davis, 2012, p. 165).

The *Plessy v. Ferguson* case represents an early effort by a group of mixed-race people to gain the right to self-identify. Plessy was 7/8 Caucasian and 1/8 African, and thus likely *looked* White. The intent of the challenge was to identify Plessy as Creole, and to in effect force Louisiana to recognize the ancestry of Creoles as separate and distinct from White or Black people. In the end, the Supreme Court let stand Louisiana's authority to segregate by race and determined that it was not the role of the Court to rule on states' standards for race. In effect, the Supreme Court left it up to the states to decide one's race (Basson, 2008).

Mixed-Race and Slave by Birth

Unlike the progeny of Creoles, some mixed-race people of White and African descent were automatically legally defined as Black. The desire to associate blackness with slavery triggered a series of vacillating laws that consigned some, but not all, mixed-race White and African children to slavery. Much has been written about the sexual violence and exploitation suffered by Black enslaved women at the hands of White slave owners, and indeed any White man in the antebellum south. Sexual coercion was used not only for sexual gratification, but also to denigrate and control enslaved women. Laws based on *partus sequitur ventrem* meant that children born as a result of these encounters followed the slave status of the mother (Rothman, 2003, pp. 29–30).

Many enslaved women lived in fear that they would be forced into sexual intercourse with White men or beaten and otherwise punished and humiliated should they refuse these reprehensible advances. Stevenson (2013) noted, however, that enslaved women suffered the ". . . gamut from rape and sodomy to romance, chance encounters to obsession, concubinage, and even marriage . . ." (p. 100) at the hands of White men. In some instances, White slave owners and Black female relationships reflected ". . . acknowledged affairs that lasted a lifetime, produced many children, and were familial in every sense but a legally recognized one . . ." (Rothman 2003, p. 15). Hence the sexually based associations between Black women and White men were likely a mixture of coercion and consent.

This notion of coercion and consent is most clearly exemplified in the now-accepted-as-fact 35-year association between Thomas Jefferson and Sally Hemings. Hemings, one of Jefferson's slaves, was in her early teens at the time of her first sexual encounter with Jefferson, then a 46-year-old widower. Given the length of the relationship, it is likely that at some point, regardless of how the relationship began, Hemings willingly remained as Jefferson's concubine.

White men routinely sought mixed-race women who were young and whose physical characteristics were similar to White women (Stevenson, 2013). Consequently, the practice of concubinage was often intergenerational. Grandmothers, mothers, and daughters would serve as concubines because of the mixed-race lineage existing in some families (Rothman, 2003; Stevenson, 2013). Hemings, for example, was the daughter and granddaughter of enslaved women who bore children with White masters. Indeed, her mother, Betty Hemings, had a 12-year sexual association with Jefferson's father-in-law, which made Sally Hemings the half-sister of Jefferson's deceased wife (Rothman, 2003).

Mixed-race children born to White male and enslaved Black female sexual encounters experienced mistreatment from both Blacks and Whites in their communities. The mixed-race child's parentage served as fodder for gossip among slaves, and in general, darker skinned slaves resented the privileges accorded light-skinned slaves. In many instances, mixed-race children lived with their mothers in the slave owner's house, along with other members of his family. They were susceptible to poor treatment, even physical abuse, by slave owner's wives who often bore suppressed anger and resentment based on knowledge of the child's paternity. They were also ill-treated by half-siblings who lived in the same household but who wanted to make sure that the mixed-race child was ever cognizant of his or her status as Black, and thus a slave.

White men mistreated mixed-race children by their tendency to select adolescents for sexual indulgences. Indeed, some young mixed-race girls were purchased for the sole purpose of concubinage. As fathers of mixed-race children, White men tended to ignore children from their relations with Black women, even when these children lived in the same household as their "White family" (Stevenson, 2013).

Sexual intercourse between White men and enslaved women was pervasive and occurred among not only monied "gentlemen" of the antebellum south, but also men with less wealth and property. Stevenson (2013) noted that according to the 1850 Census, 11 percent of the slave population and 37 percent of free

"Blacks" were mixed-race. The substantial percent of the latter likely was due to the tendency of White men to free their children (and sometimes the children's mothers) as the children reached adulthood. Children reared by mixed-race mothers in White households were familiar with the intricacies of White culture. This knowledge was passed on to their children. As in the case with some of the Jefferson–Hemings children, some mixed-race children were able to live as White in adulthood.

Children of White Women and Black Men

Less is generally written about the early interracial liaisons between Black men and White women. Initially, these relationships did not engender an automatic violent response toward or death for Black men. A White woman faced gossip or being ostracized by other Whites for her injudicious decision to couple with a Black man, but the relationship was more or less still tolerated in the pre-emancipation south. Interracial relations were more tolerated for White women living in poverty and Black men, as White women living in poverty were evaluated as depraved and promiscuous enough to make such a relationship plausible. Notions of "female purity" embodied in elite White women made relations between Black men and these White women more dangerous.

The lives of pre–Civil War progeny born as a result of sexual abuse experienced by Black women from White men, and the more intentional sexual liaisons between White women and Black men, differed starkly in most cases. Maryland for example passed a new law in 1681 that allowed freedom status of the child to reflect that of the mother. As result, mixed-race children of European and African descent with White mothers were born free, while those with Black mothers were born slaves (Hodes, 1997). The fact that children with African blood were being born free because of the status of the mother as free eventually became problematic for Whites in the antebellum south. The line between slavery (which was synonymous with being of African descent) and freedom (which was synonymous with being White) was becoming blurred. Even so, the established racial hierarchy was believed to be intact as long as the system of slavery was preserved.

The eradication of slavery as a result of the Civil War and the Emancipation Proclamation, however, left color as the primary basis for maintaining the racial hierarchy embraced by Whites. Interracial relationships between White women and Black men were less tolerated after the War, and efforts to engage in these liaisons meant violence toward and even death for Black men. In the eyes of White supremacists, the economic and political independence now possible for Black men, when combined with the blurring of blackness and whiteness resulting from interracial relationships, presented a considerable challenge to race relations as they had existed prior to the War. As a result, interracial relations became taboo and were subsequently forbidden (Hodes, 1997).

Blood Quantum and the U.S. Census

Plessy's death in 1925 preceded the ability of mixed-race people to legally self-identify their race in the U.S. Census by 75 years. Race designation by blood quantum, however, was a focus for census counts for years. Mixed-race people were counted and discounted in the national census for a period of 80 years on the basis of political, scientific, and ideological motivations, beginning in 1850 and finally ending in 1930. Although the label mulatto was initially attributed to first generation, mixed White and African people, over time, other terms were used to designate the multigenerational nature of mixed-race individuals (Figure 2.1).

From a political perspective, a Congress that made rules for counting people that were whimsical at best controlled the work of census officials. For example, congressmen on either side of the slavery debate sought to sway census information to support their positions. Those in favor of slavery sought to prove that freed former slaves did not fare particularly well on their own. Congressmen against slavery sought census information that would show how much progress former slaves could make once released from the specter of control by slave owners. Consequently, how and why people were counted vacillated—sometimes without much thought given to reasons for the need of the racial categories into which people were placed. With respect to blood quantum, Congress requested that quadroons and octoroons be counted as separate from mulattoes in 1890, even though there was no clear process for determining blood quantum among different mixed-race people. Census officials subsequently reported that data from these efforts were pretty much useless (Hochschild & Powell, 2008).

Congress was not the only group interested in how mixed-race people were counted. Polygenists, race scientists who believed human beings originated from different ancestral types, wanted to know the physical impact of mixing between Whites and various groups of color (e.g., Blacks, Native Americans, and Asians). This information was sought in order to support their beliefs that mixed-race people were physically, mentally, and morally depraved (Hochschild & Powell, 2008). From an ideological perspective, southerners wanted to strengthen a

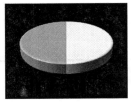

Mulatto –½ Black and ½ White

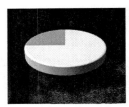

Quadroon – ¼ Black and ¾ White or Mulatto and White

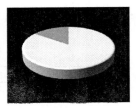

Octoroon –⅛ Black and ⅞ White or Quadroon and White

FIGURE 2.1 Blood Quantum Labels

system of racial stratification based on White supremacy. They wanted to maintain a system of White dominance in the south, despite the outcome of the Civil War. Their efforts were complicated by the fact that mixed-race people spanned the color line. As a result, White supremacists wanted to know the numbers of mixed-race individuals and whether mixed-race people were attempting to move toward whiteness (Hochschild & Powell, 2008).

Solidifying White Dominance through Hypodescent Legislation

By the 1930s, states passed hypodescent, or one-drop rule, legislation, which declared that any amount of nonwhite blood made one not White. Southerners were no longer concerned with the degree to which the number of mixed-race individuals increased or declined, nor whether they were attempting to move toward whiteness. Hypodescent laws, in their view, protected White dominance in the south. Although mulattoes were removed from the 1900 census and reinstated in the 1910 and 1920 censuses, the 1930 census did not include any mixed-race categories of any combination. People were designated as White, Negro, or Indian, and five Asian nationalities were included as well (Hochschild & Powell, 2008).

Blood Quantum and Tribal Membership

Blood quantum figured differently in the lives of Native Americans during the eighteenth and early nineteenth centuries. Natives differed from both Blacks and Chinese in their ability to be counted as White (Basson, 2008; Hochschild & Powell, 2008). Hypodescent legislation did not apply to Natives in the same way it applied to other minority race groups, and thus did not preclude them from joining mainstream White culture. For example, one drop of nonwhite blood excluded mixed-race people with African ancestry from living in society as White. In addition, regardless of whether they were willing to adopt White culture, Chinese who immigrated to the United States were viewed as forever foreigners and perceived as unwilling to become true citizens of their new country. Natives willing to adopt White ways and relinquish their land and claims to sovereignty were able to join White society, and some were eventually racially designated as White.

Unlike the experiences of other people of color in the United States, interracial marriages between Indian and Anglo Americans were encouraged as part of a "civilization" process for Natives. According to Perdue (2003), civilization for southeast Natives meant a shift to ". . . commercial agriculture, English literacy, republican government, patriarchal families, Christianity . . . and love of exclusive property . . ." (p. 52). In the process, Natives would undergo a total deculturalization process that would strip them of their ". . . cultural values, religions, family structures, governments, and economic relationships" (Spring, 1996, p. 4). The ultimate goal was to make use of Native land for an expanding cotton economy. The process to divest Natives of their culture and land was implemented first by schools operated by missionaries and subsequently by physically removing Indians from their land in a migration process referred to as the Trail of Tears (Spring, 1996).

The Racialization of Native People

It was not uncommon for White men who married Native women to abandon White culture, deciding instead to live among Native American tribes (Perdue, 2003; Spring, 1996). Even though offspring of interracial marriages were raised in traditional Indian ways, they were also able to take advantage of education and other benefits of White culture. Like Creoles, mixed-race Indian-White children followed the lineage of the mother. However, this practice was not imposed by legislation outside of tribes, as was the case with Creoles. Rather, matrilineal lineage was a long-standing tradition of Natives in southeastern United States. Blood ties were with the mother and the mother's family. Not only were there no kinship ties with fathers, but also fathers had no parental authority over their children. Raising children was the responsibility of the mother's family, with the primary male influence coming from the mother's brothers (Perdue, 2003).

Still, mixed-race children's fathers were able to get permission to allow their children to study in American schools, where the children learned American culture, language, and political system. Eventually, mixed-race children had an elevated status both within and outside of the tribe and, subsequently, many became tribal leaders (Perdue, 2003). Natives, however, did not use race as a basis to distinguish between full-blooded and mixed-raced Indians. Outsiders imposed this distinction upon Native people. As an example, race differences were inserted into the process of schooling of Indian children. Leaders among the Cherokee, Choctaw, and Chickasaw tribes supported the growth of mission-operated schools to educate all children. Mixed-race children however were disproportionately represented in these schools, given their numbers in their tribes. Race-based practices such as overtly identifying children as mixed-race or full-blooded were used. Further, missionaries tended to evaluate the progress of mixed-race children in becoming civilized as more superior to that of full-blooded Indian children (Perdue, 2003).

The "civilization" process was not as successful as desired, and many intellectuals in the early 1800s began to attribute this lack of success to physical and cultural differences in human beings, differences that were resistant to change. The notion of "savagery" as an "inborn" trait of Native people bourgeoned, alongside suggestions that they could not be civilized by education (Perdue, 2003). Intermarriage was no longer encouraged with Natives, now a disparaged group; indeed, such unions were viewed as "unnatural" or even criminal (p. 85).

Still, mixed-race progeny were placed in a category believed to have characteristics distinct from either parent. Again, similar to the experience of Creoles,

White elites located mixed-race people in the middle of a three-tier racial hierar-chy, with Whites at the top and full-blooded Indians at the bottom. Mixed-race children were assumed to have intelligence superior to their Native peers and Native parent but inferior to that of their White parent. Mixed-race people were viewed as more civilized (and more capable of being civilized) than full bloods with no White ancestry.

The racialization of Natives, that is, the process of creating a social and politi-cal climate where racial heritage began to matter, made it possible for the United States to introduce mistrust within the tribes for their mixed-race members, many of whom were tribal leaders. Mixed-race individuals were portrayed by White elites as ". . . immoral, dishonest, and self-serving . . ." (Perdue, 2003, p. 96). Eventually, state laws were passed in the 1800s that were ostensibly designed to protect Natives from leadership that was potentially corrupt. Once under the control of Anglo laws, however, Natives experienced discrimination and an overall diminution of their civil rights.

By 1830, the United States was able to seize coveted Native land under the Indian Removal Act. The law allowed the government to extend treaties to Natives to release land in southeastern United States for land designated as Indian Territory in what is today Oklahoma. Natives unwilling to sign were forced off their land. Mixed-race Natives tended to oppose the removal process, yet despite their opposition, the relocation process moved forward. For some mixed-race individuals, the advantages available to them in White culture did not supersede tribal loyalties, and they shared the ordeal of reloca-tion with their tribes. Others remained in the southern states and lived among Whites (Perdue, 2003).

Constructing White and Nonwhite Indians

Natives living among Whites were labeled "taxed Indians," and were counted as White in the U.S. Census until 1860, when census takers were required to count them as Indians. By 1870, the Census Office was challenged to count the number of Natives of mixed heritage. They responded by determining that individuals of Native and White ancestry who lived among Whites and who were fully immersed in White culture would be counted as White. Mixed-race individuals of the same descent who lived within tribal communities would not be counted as White (Hochschild & Powell, 2008).

The U.S. practice of using race as a tool to divide Natives continued in the 1890s when it came to allotting land that had been promised to Natives through treaties. Blood quantum was used to determine how much land was allotted to individuals. Although the Anglos had previously sought to denigrate mixed-raced people in the eyes of Natives, when it came to allotting land, Natives believed to have more White blood were initially likely to receive more land (Perdue, 2003). The notion of the amount of White blood was later tied to the issue of competency and intelligence when it came to the ability to handle civic responsibilities. Legislation surfaced in 1896 that allowed the United States to intervene when it came to Natives' decisions to sell allotted land. Initially, mixed-race Indians with one half or less Indian blood were deemed intelligent enough to sell land without governmental approval. The necessary Indian blood quantum to engage in this civic responsibility was later reduced to one quarter or less Indian blood (Basson, 2008).

Indecisiveness and general apprehension around racial categories for Native people was evident in an unrelenting focus on blood quantum for scientific and social purposes. The notion of blood quantum was at the core of vacillating practices of inclusion and exclusion, as attempts were made to determine a social location for Native people. By 1910, census takers were required to delineate the amount of White, Black, and Indian blood of Natives, down to the fraction. Mixed-race individuals who were half or more White were no longer designated Indian. But, by 1934, all individuals with any amount of blood mixture could claim being Indian (Hochschild & Powell, 2008). The practice of claiming Native ancestry by fraction remains today (Perdue, 2003).

Protecting Racial Boundaries through Anti-Miscegenation Laws

The eventual widespread passage of miscegenation laws, particularly in the south, was inextricably woven into White supremacy goals to establish a post–Civil War racial order built on distinct separation of the races. White supremacists determined that a reasonable solution to the confusion mixed-race people presented to the goal of clear divisions by race was to disrupt interaction between the races that might lead to marriage and children as a result of those unions. A propensity to tolerate and/or encourage interracial marriages was consequently replaced by laws forbidding such unions. Miscegenation or mixed-race marriages were illegal in states across the nation until the 1967 Supreme Court ruling in *Loving v. Virginia* that the laws were unconstitutional.

Menchaca (2008) provided a summary of the ideological motivations for anti-miscegenation that can be divided into four categories (see Figure 2.2). Although the social, economic, and political underpinnings of anti-miscegenation laws were evident, these were subordinate to the perception of miscegenation as unnatural (Pascoe, 2009). Fully 96 percent of Whites opposed interracial marriages as late as 1958 (Hollinger, 2003), yet four in ten Americans continue to do so (Taylor et al., 2010).

Laws were passed to regulate marriage not only between Blacks and Whites, but depending on the region of the country, marriage freedom for Mexican Americans, Native Americans, Asian American, and mixed-raced people was also constrained by restrictive marriage laws (Manchaca, 2008). Indeed, Menchaca noted that the dogmatic meticulousness with which White leaders

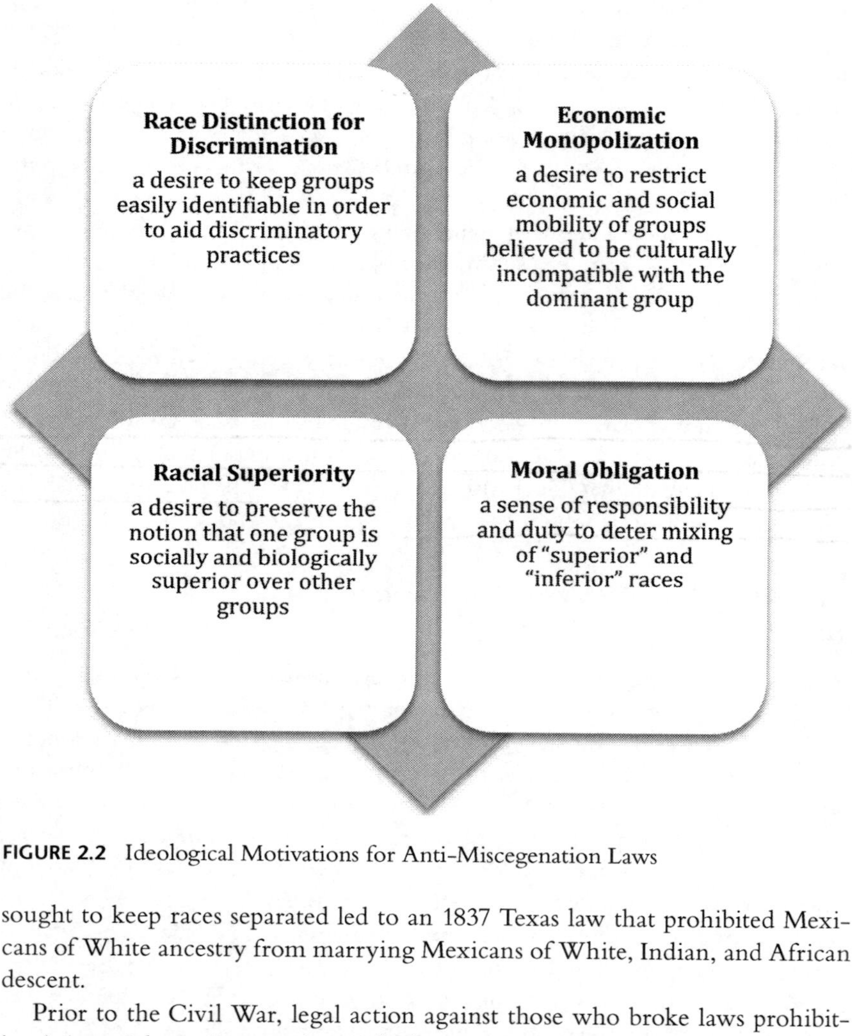

Race Distinction for Discrimination a desire to keep groups easily identifiable in order to aid discriminatory practices	**Economic Monopolization** a desire to restrict economic and social mobility of groups believed to be culturally incompatible with the dominant group
Racial Superiority a desire to preserve the notion that one group is socially and biologically superior over other groups	**Moral Obligation** a sense of responsibility and duty to deter mixing of "superior" and "inferior" races

FIGURE 2.2 Ideological Motivations for Anti-Miscegenation Laws

sought to keep races separated led to an 1837 Texas law that prohibited Mexicans of White ancestry from marrying Mexicans of White, Indian, and African descent.

Prior to the Civil War, legal action against those who broke laws prohibiting interracial marriages and sexual relations was rarely pursued in some states. In Virginia, for example, mixed-race sexual associations ". . . both forced and consensual . . . between blacks and whites were constituent of familial and communal life in the society" (Rothman, 2003, p. 4). A decision to inform authorities about an interracial relationship was just as likely driven by a desire to ". . . humiliate, infuriate, or badger alleged participants" (p. 5), as it was by a deep-seated disdain for sexual and/or affectionate bonds between White and people of color.

The level of pre–Civil War tolerance for interracial marriages is illustrated by Hodes's (1997) description of the 1681 Maryland marriage between "Negro" Charles, a slave, and Irish Nell, a servant. Local White people wondered why a White woman would marry a Black man, because this meant their children would be slaves (note the 1664 Maryland law mentioned earlier). Still, there was no legal sanction against or public condemnation of the marriage. A Catholic priest performed the marriage ceremony that was attended by slave owners, as well as other community members—both White and Black. Hodes's research indicated that:

> Nell "behaved as a bride," and several people wished the couple much joy . . . it was a fine wedding . . . Afterward, Nell and Charles acknowledged themselves as "man and wife," and people knew them as such. Nell called Charles her "old man," and Charles called Nell his "old woman."
>
> *(pp. 20–21)*

Challenges to Anti-Miscegenation Laws

Miscegenation laws were neither stable nor uncontested. During the period prior to the Civil War, laws were passed, repealed, and later reinstated. By the 1880s, however, states were able to develop arguments for miscegenation laws that were solid enough to last until the *Loving v. Virginia* ruling in 1967. The nature of laws restricting marriage between White people and people of color depended on geographic area, politicians in power, and the desire of some states to pass laws that were palatable to the public while at the same time able to withstand constitutionality challenges. Interracial couples had been willing to go to court to establish their right to marry by choice, and they were often able to prevail. Post–Civil War challenges to miscegenation were also successful, as couples argued that marriage was a contract into which they should freely be able to enter, and the right to pick who they chose to marry was a civil right that should have equal protection under the law (Pascoe, 2009).

States were more resolute in their efforts to ban mixed marriages post–Civil War and were determined to find ways to support their view that the right to regulate marriage belonged to states and not the federal government. Their initial strategy was to convict interracial couples of engaging in illicit sex—fornication, which was against the law regardless of the race of the two participants. Courts in southern states, however, allowed for more stringent punishments for interracial couples accused of fornication than same-race couples. Also, courts simply ignored the fact that a marriage existed between two people of different races, and in some cases nullified marriages during court proceedings.

Although same-race couples accused of illicit sex were able to avoid conviction by getting married, interracial marriage was against the law and thus not an option available for interracial couples. Hence many were found guilty of illicit sex, a crime punishable by prison sentences. Pascoe (2009) proposed that the "sexualization of miscegenation" (p. 56) was pivotal in states' ability to thwart efforts of interracial couples' marriage freedom efforts. This, combined with state arguments that marriage was more than a contract, that there was a natural difference between the races, and that the civil rights of interracial couples should not supersede the social disruption caused by mixed marriages eliminated arguments interracial couples were able to use for positive rulings from the courts (Pascoe, 2009).

Miscegenation and Communities of Color

By early twentieth century, in-group marriage was overwhelmingly the preferred marriage arrangement among Whites and people of color in the United States. In fact, the National Association for the Advancement of Colored People (NAACP) observed that during the reign of anti-miscegenation laws, people of different races married so infrequently that such events were a "statistically negligible phenomenon," even in states where no prohibitive law existed (Pascoe, 2009, p. 176). Even though dominant culture anti-miscegenation laws, for the most part, did not prevent people of color from marrying each other, marriage between people of different races was not always embraced in some communities of color either.

Early in the nineteenth century, the Cherokee had laws against interracial marriages that prohibited Cherokees from marrying slaves and free people of color. Later laws were initiated to make marriage between White men and Cherokee women more difficult as well (Yarbrough, 2008). Even after slaves were freed, tribes instituted laws to forbid marriage to Black men or women. The Choctaw, for example, passed an 1888 law that made such a marriage a felony.

Where laws did not yet exist, people of color discouraged miscegenation with Whites and other people of color for cultural, social, and political reasons. For some people of color, mistrust and anger existed toward dominant culture Whites over past treatment. They believed it was not in the best interest of their cultural or ethnic group as a whole to collude with Whites. The Chinese, for example, were hostile to intermarriage with Whites because of White oppression but also because of Chinese "chauvinism" (Spickard, 2001, p. 14).

The Japanese were angry at Whites over internment during World War II and thus were not particularly accepting of mixed marriages with Whites during mid-twentieth century. Some of this anger did not transfer to U.S.-born Japanese, however, who were more open to interracial marriages (Matsumoto, 2010). Further, Asian-White marriages (among White men and Chinese, Japanese, and South Korean women) increased substantially following World War II through the 1970s, as U.S. servicemen returned home with Asian women they married while in the service (Asian-Nation, n.d.). Intergroup marriages among some groups of Asians were also limited prior to the 1960s, constrained by past conflicts between nations (especially Japanese and Chinese) as well as by negative images and prejudices within Asian groups for other Asians. So strong was Japanese prejudice against Filipinos, for example, that Japanese American women who were married to Filipino men were ostracized in the World War II concentration camps (Spickard, 2001).

Socially, racial hierarchies and colorism played a role in miscegenation attitudes among communities of color. The Cherokee did not want to be associated with Black people, because as a group, Blacks appeared to be the least powerful in the United States. Cherokees identified more with Whites ". . . not only because of physical appearance but also [because of] a perceived appearance of power and success" (Yarbrough, 2008, pp. 4–5). Asian American families tended to tolerate White-Asian interracial marriages better than interracial marriages that involved darker skinned partners, as they associated darkness with a lower class of people (Matsumoto, 2010).

Post–Civil War and beyond, Blacks feared men entering into interracial relationships and marriages with White women could lead to the lynching of Black men (Pascoe, 2009). Still, support for miscegenation and anti-miscegenation laws among Blacks was mixed. Many Black men who held public office during Reconstruction supported anti-miscegenation laws as means to prevent White men from preying upon Black women (Pascoe, 2009). Conversely, abolitionist and social reformer Frederick Douglass, mixed-race himself and married at one time to a Black woman and later to a White woman, was staunchly against anti-miscegenation laws. Douglass (1886) believed the survival of Black people was tied to interracial marriage. He wrote:

> . . . it is said that marital alliance between . . . races is unnatural, abhorrent and impossible; . . . If this blending were impossible we should not have at least one-fourth of our colored population composed of persons of mixed blood . . . My strongest conviction as to the future of the negro therefore is, that he will not be expatriated nor annihilated, nor will he forever remain a separate and distinct race from the people around him, but that he will be absorbed, assimilated, and will only appear finally . . . in the features of a blended race.
>
> *(pp. 438–439)*

W.E.B. Du Bois also called for the repeal of anti-miscegenation laws and also challenged the notion of marriage between people of different races as unnatural. Unlike Douglass, however, Du Bois never advocated for interracial marriages. Rather, he viewed the right to marry a partner of whatever race one chose as a matter of racial equality. Initially, the NAACP, the nascent equal rights organization Du Bois helped to found, did not publically support Du Bois's criticism of the laws. The primary focus of civil rights activists was equality in education, work, and housing. The right to marry across racial lines was not a major issue for them. Still, Black leaders and White supporters who sought civil rights for Black people viewed anti-miscegenation laws as an affront to the post–Civil War equality Black people pursued. Even though the NAACP never overtly voiced support for interracial marriage either, they eventually used the disbanding of anti-miscegenation laws as an instrument to further civil rights in general (Pascoe, 2009).

Mixed-Race in Monoracial Communities of Color

Once hypodescent laws were established, some groups of mixed-race people were not welcomed in White communities. Social convention and the law were instrumental, for example, in relegating mixed-race Black-White people to communities populated by their monoracial minority relatives. Mulattoes (mixed people of African and European descent) were subsequently forced to outwardly adopt a Black identity as they were exposed to the same social and legal disadvantages experienced by Black people (Crothers & K'Meyer, 2007; Middleton, 2008).

Mixed-race Black people were similarly excluded from Native American communities. Although Africans were initially freely accepted into Native tribes, by 1830, Natives too owned slaves and wanted to minimize the perception of being in communal relationships with African slaves. When the Cherokee established legal citizenship, for example, the tribe did not legally or socially recognize mixed-race African-Cherokees, thus excluding them from legitimate tribal membership. Even though mixed-race African-Cherokees were able to claim a Cherokee ancestral and cultural identity, those who also embraced their African heritage were soon no longer viewed as mixed and eventually were perceived as being only Black (Yarbrough, 2008).

The Color Line in Black Communities

Du Bois was in favor of Black-White mixed-race people and Black people ignoring past differences and coming together to fight oppression as a unified group (Bernasconi, 2009). In fact, he urged that the census classify all people of African descent as Black in the 1900s, and was thus in favor of eliminating the identification of mulattoes as a distinct group (Hochschild & Powell, 2008). His vision was confounded to some extent by the diverse and complex experiences of Black-White mixed-race people during the early twentieth century. Some were White-looking enough to pass as only White and did so in order to take advantage of the privileges associated with being White while escaping the oppression and discrimination experienced by Black people. Some mixed-race people remained in Black communities even though they could pass as White only. Ross's (2013) description of her grandmother's experience is an example:

> My grandmother Bernice was born in New Orleans in 1918 to a Black mother and a White father at a time when interracial marriage was illegal . . . Grandma Bernice was born with blue eyes, straight hair, and white

skin . . . My grandmother for all outward appearances looked like a White woman, and could have *passed* for White . . . And yet, my grandmother never attempted to leave the Black community.

Still other mixed-race Black-White people were able to live on both sides of the color line. In their narrative of Marguerite Davis Stewart's oral history, Crothers and K'Meyer (2007) wrote that both Stewart, who was born in 1911 in Kentucky, and her mother often intermixed with Whites. Their light skin color made it difficult for them to be identified as Black or even mixed-race. Crothers and K'Meyer stated:

> She *[Marguerite]* attended black schools, used the black branch of the public library, and associated with other black girls. Yet, unlike her classmates and friends, she accompanied her mother to the local, white-only amusement park, upscale shops, theaters, and restaurants. As Stewart entered adulthood she continued to cross the color line and was never completely segregated from white associates and opportunities.
>
> *(p. 28)*

Many mixed-raced people who lived in Black communities chose to emphasize their mixed-race lineage by erecting social structures to distinguish themselves from monoracial Blacks. Leverette (2009) reminded us that the sexual exploitation of Black women during slavery makes for the reality many people who identify as Black have White ancestors, although most in this category do not wish to claim this part of their ancestral lineage. Mixed-race people who embraced their mixed-race status lived in neighborhoods among other mixed-race people, organized social clubs with restricted membership, and attended churches where parishioners were mixed-race. One had to "qualify" in order to be admitted to social structures built by mixed-race people. Qualifications were based on physical characteristics such as skin color, hair texture, and facial features, for example. The blue-vein test (i.e., light-skinned enough so that one veins could be seen); paper bag test (i.e., no darker than a paper bag) and the comb test (i.e., hair could not tangle a comb) were among the requirements to be socially acceptable to some mixed-race people (Khanna, 2011; Leverette, 2009). Khanna also noted that many of these groups practiced endogamy, where marriage outside the mixed-race elite was discouraged.

The colorism that existed in Black communities was the source of tension, resentment, and feelings of disdain among monoracial Blacks for the assumption of superiority exemplified by the distancing practices of mixed-race people. Nonetheless, given the relative position of privilege historically accorded many mixed-race people, it was common for them to be more educated and thus able to work in the professions, more so than others in the Black community. As a result, colorism and class coalesced to create a social hierarchy within the Black community that elevated the status of mixed-race people, which in turn fed a level of mistrust for mixed-race people in the Black community. Many monoracial Blacks (and indeed some mixed-race Blacks who chose a Black identity), however, felt even more contempt for Blacks who chose to avoid the Black community altogether by passing as only White.

Racial Pride and Loyalty

Despite efforts to distinguish themselves from monoracial Blacks, over time mixed-race people of Black-White descent who lived in Black communities were more apt to view themselves as light-skinned Black people over being mixed-race (Daniel, 1992). Even so, the stigma of race-based superiority attributed to mixed-race Black-White people was condemned during the 1960s, an era of heightened racial pride and identity among people of color. Cultural nationalism was instrumental to movements for civil and other rights in the United States and was embodied by expressions of Black, Brown, Red, and Yellow power.

Legitimacy as of person of color was absolute among communities of color, with hints to the contrary likely to result in derisive accusations of being an Oreo, Apple, Banana, or Coconut. Basically one was perceived as being Black, Native American, Asian American, or Latino respectfully on the outside, but culturally White on the inside. Racial identity, political beliefs, and racial group loyalty were all closely aligned (Castagno, 2012). In the Black community, those who wished to claim being mixed-race were accused of internalized racial self-hatred (Leverette, 2009). Even though miscegenation was legal at this point in history, cultural nationalists disparaged interracial marriages and partnerships as signs of racial betrayal and disloyalty (Castagno, 2012). In this instance, we witness the pinnacle of a twentieth century dictate for monoracialism, as imposed by conventions of mixed-race peoples' minority race groups.

Mixed-Race People in Multiethnic Communities of Color

More so than Black (specifically African American) communities, other communities of color consist of multiple ethnic groups, some which did not always view themselves from a single, unified ethnic group perspective (e.g., as Asian Americans). Instead, they embraced separate identities and lived in separate communities. Prior to 1960s, for example, Asian immigrant communities were made up of disparate ethnic Asian groups (i.e., Chinese, Japanese, Korean). Initially, these communities did not accept or recognize interracial couples or their mixed-race offspring. Mixed-race children of Japanese descent in 1940, for example, were disdained to the point of being abandoned to orphanages, or left on the streets to fend for themselves. The Filipino community was an exception to the exclusionary practices of other Asian communities. Interracial marriage with

Whites, probably Mexican Americans (although more research is needed here), and Native American people resulted in communities that were very accepting of mixed-race people (Spickard, 2001).

A common Asian American identity emerged during the Asian American Movement of the 1960s and 1970s. Mixed-race Asian people were able to be a part of this panethnic group on the basis of their willingness to drop their other-race identity and closely affiliate with their Asian ancestry. Today, however, mixed-race people with Asian ancestry are part of an Asian American hierarchy (with Japanese, Chinese, and Koreans as core groups) as a stand-alone group of multiracials, and are not asked to ignore their mixed-raceness in order to be accepted by the Asian American community.

The Hispanic/Latino community, like the Asian American community, consists of intergroup diversity (e.g., Mexican Americans, Puerto Ricans, Cubans, Central or South Americans). These groups differ in terms of their history and experiences in the United States (Qian & Cobas, 2004). Mexican Americans are the largest group and the one with the longest history in the United States. Also, when compared with other Hispanic/Latino groups, Mexican Americans are more likely to marry out. Despite a long history of interracial marriages and subsequent mixed-race populations, Mexican Americans tend to be less accepting of Mexican-Indian and Mexican-Black (Blaxican) people (Ramirez, 2002; Romo, 2011). People with minority-minority mixed-race lineages are often pressured to give up their non-Latino heritage in order to be accepted in the Mexican American community.

Navarro (2012) reported that today, Latinos married to non-Hispanic Whites (particularly Latinos who are fluent in English and have higher levels of education and higher earnings) identify as White, and at least in statistical tracking of Latinos, are not counted as part of Latinos across generations. It is also the case that a number of mixed-race Latino-Blacks and Latino-Asians identify as monoracial Black or Asian. It is likely that mixed-race Latinos who identify as a different monoracial minority do not seek acceptance in Latino communities.

Mixed-raceness plays out differently in Indian communities. Blood quantum remains important to some Indians in determining who is authentically Indian. The federal government facilitates this practice by their continued use of blood quantum to manage tribal enrollments. The federal government, and not the tribes themselves, determines who is an Indian when it comes to federally conferred resources. Still, Natives who adhere to the notion of blood quantum have a preference for full-blooded Indians and evaluate the status of mixed-race Indians on the basis of their fraction of Indian blood. They operate from a "blood hegemony" where ". . . race mixing has become directly associated with cultural loss" (Pack, 2012, p. 179).

In some cases, the racial makeup of mixed-race peoples' mixedness matters. As late as the 1980s, the Cherokee, for example, pursued their mission to exclude mixed-race people with Indian-African lineage from the tribe. Other tribes may be sensitive to claims of Indian ancestry by those seeking possible economic benefits. Hence, DNA fingerprinting may influence some tribes' tribal membership determinations (Montgomery, 2012). Be that as it may, many Indians are swayed by an individual's cultural knowledge and actions in determining who is to be accepted as Indian (Pack, 2012).

The Multiracial Movement

Prior to Census 2000, individuals may have privately claimed a mixed heritage, but legally they were made to list just one race on official forms. This fact, at least in part, was an impetus for the Multiracial Movement. Leverette (2009) argued that an additional reason for the movement was the desire among some mixed-raced people and their families to weaken existing racial categories altogether. According to DaCosta (2007), most groups that organized during the Movement were more interested in public awareness and support of interracial families. The former cause, however, proved to be a more significant one and was animated in a desire for the right to freely declare a mixed heritage. As a result, the issue of mixed-race people's right to racially self-identify reappeared in late twentieth century as a primary focus of a Multiracial Movement.

Although both mixed-race people and their families played instrumental roles in the development of the movement, White mothers of mixed-race children initiated the movement and are often recognized as its "founding mothers" (Castagno, 2012). White mothers of biracial (Black-White) children established Interracial/Intercultural Pride (I-Pride) in 1979, which was the first organization focused on the needs of mixed-race children. A primary goal of I-Pride was to provide a social space for adults in interracial marriages and their children. The first multiracial organization formed for and by multiracial activists, the Association of MultiEthnic Americans (AMEA) emerged in 1988. Their stated mission was to promote awareness of mixed-race people and their families, not only among mixed-race people/interracial families, but also for all society. By 2000, over 60 organizations existed and some, such as Project RACE (Reclassify All Children Equally) organized in 1991, had more political than social motivations.

The forced single-racial classification of mixed-race children on school, medical, and other forms required at the state and/or federal levels was a rallying point for mixed-race organizations, despite the fact that their overall aims often differed. Unlike some of the social support organizations, AMEA, for example, believed the ability to formally identify as multiracial would facilitate more visibility for mixed-race people as a group and allow them to create a forum for interests of the mixed-race community (Williams, 2006). Many social support–focused mixed-race organizations eventually became more political, galvanized by the issue of racial classification of mixed-race children (Castagno, 2012; Williams, 2006).

The Sociopolitical Context of the Multiracial Movement

Even though the Multiracial Movement benefited from the Civil Rights Movement, the Movement's activism threatened to thwart measures used to accomplish gains made by the antecedent movement. According to Williams (2003, 2006), the Multiracial Movement used strategies and symbols that can clearly be attributed to the Civil Rights Movement (e.g., the March on Washington, D.C. organized by the multiracial groups in 1996, boycotts, creating position papers). In fact, the Civil Rights Movement created a social and political climate that made possible the increased participation of a number of groups in the political process, including Asian Americans; Native Americans; Hispanics/Latinos; women; lesbian, gay, bisexual, transgender (LGBT) people; and mixed-race people. Williams (2006) stated: "Multiracial advocates boldly adopted and reframed the tactical tools and ideological arguments of the civil rights movement as they capitalized on the legal precedents established in the context of that earlier set of struggles" (p. 37).

Mixed-race organizations were unified in their determination for federal recognition on the census and other federal forms as a racial group separate from existing race categories. Although a multiracial category was a common objective, some organizations wanted a multiracial category that would then be divided into specific racial heritages, similar to the Hispanic category. Others pushed for a single, stand-alone multiracial category that would be presented alongside existing racial categories (e.g., White, Black, American Indian/Alaska Native, Asian, or Native Hawaiian/Other Pacific Islander, or Hispanic), with no racial heritage distinctions among multiracial people (Castagno, 2012).

As noted earlier, the NAACP found the multiracial category problematic. The civil rights organization felt that such a category would interfere with continued efforts to monitor discrimination efforts as required by law. Compliance under laws such as the Voting Rights Act of 1965 relied on collection of race/ethnic data. Further, the census count was used as a basis for developing programs and services for certain people of color. It would be difficult to have an accurate count of minority Americans if some were listed as multiracial on the census (Williams, 2003, 2006). Other civil rights organizations, including the National Council of American Indians and the National Council of La Raza, joined the NAACP to voice opposition to the multiracial category (Dalmage, 2004).

In arguments directed toward these criticisms, the AMEA suggested that the NAACP should not expect them to set aside the interests of the mixed-race community for those of other racial groups. They maintained that their need for accurate recognition and representation was a civil right and served the same purpose as other groups who were clearly represented by the census (Williams, 2003, 2006). In the end, the Office of Management and Budget returned to earlier U.S. census practices and engaged in studies of racial categories between 1993 and 1997. At the conclusion of their studies, everyone was allowed to indicate as many races as they wished on the census. The 2000 Census was the first time that individuals could self-identity with multiple races (Williams, 2006).

As point of fact, the height of the Multiracial Movement in the 1990s coincided with a diminution in civil rights gains (Dalmage, 2004). Political conservatives embraced the movement in the 1990s, a circumstance welcomed by some but not all multiracial organizations. Conservative support of the multiracial category was expedient for conservative color-blind goals, as they sought to curtail race-based politics. Race as a social construct, a view espoused by multiracial organizations, was used to support arguments that race in and of itself should not be used as a barometer for understanding differences in social position among different groups. Discrimination had declined, according to conservatives, and a continued focus on race would result in reverse discrimination. Many multiracial activists used the same race-as-a-social-construct argument to conclude that racism could be abated by minimizing the significance of race simply by changing how one thought about it (Dalmage, 2004).

The fact that White women initiated organizations that led the Multiracial Movement proved to be an additional criticism of the movement. In a study of local chapters of multiracial organizations between 1996 and 1999, Williams (2003) found that White middle class suburban women married to Black men were the primary leaders of the organizations. Critics of the focus and purpose of the Multiracial Movement viewed as problematic a nonminority group initiating a rights movement for minorities (Castagno, 2012).

Confronting issues of race and racism was not a primary interest of mixed-race organizations. Indeed, Williams (2003) found that racism and classism were not issues of interest for local organizations, nor did the organizations see as their responsibility to bridge racial tensions. Castagno (2012) concluded that the founding mothers approached the movement from a White, privileged position and likely sought experiences for their mixed-race children akin to those experienced by monoracial White children. Their insistence on race as social construct likely appeared a reasonable justification to ignore issues of power and privilege associated with race. The activism of the founding mothers was a reflection of their personal experiences, as they likely came to understand racism only through the experiences of their children and partners (Castagno, 2012). Still, critics have been unrelenting in their disappointment in the Movement's position on racism. As Dalmage (2004) stated:

> Positing race as social construction without further analyzing the ways race is entrenched and embedded and, indeed the very foundation of the society (social institutions and individual consciousness) is nothing short of dismissing the concept of race and by extension racism.
>
> *(p. 6)*

Nevertheless, the Multiracial Movement can be credited with increasing public awareness of a multiracial identity. The full impact of this circumstance on race and racism remains equivocal.

Concluding Thoughts

Racial ideology as espoused from both majority and minority racial group perspectives has had a profound influence on what it means to be mixed-race in the United States. At the same time, mixed-race people have had an incontrovertible impact on legal and social practices in the United States. The reality of people able to confound rigid racial boundaries set by dominant culture elites historically served to intensify attempts to reinforce and contain racial borders. The means to these ends were ruthless, cruel, and much of the time violent. Although the leaders and the aims of the Multiracial Movement faced criticism, the ability of mixed-race people to self-identify further troubled the notion of race as distinct biological categories. Even so, this event does little to change social conventions regarding race or to ameliorate the reality of the persistence racism.

The view that an increasing population of mixed-race people would eventually minimize the impact of race on social, political, and economic issues has not been realized. The tension between mixed-raceness as a mitigating force against race and the critical race perspective that race will always exist, remains. As the mothers of mixed-race children came to understand, a sense of personal identity, and indeed the ability to personally indicate one's official race/ethnicity does not change how mixed-race children will be perceived and treated by a racially stratified society. It is likely that public perceptions of race will continue to conflict with private perceptions of racial identity among mixed-race people.

Note

1. From *What are you?: Voices of mixed-race young people* © 1999 by Pearl Fuyo Gaskins. Reprinted by permission of Henry Holt Books for Young Readers. All rights reserved.

References

Asian-Nation. (n.d.). *Multiracial/Hapa Asian Americans*. From http://www.asian-nation. org/index.shtml.

Avant-Mier, R. & Hasian, M. (2002). In search of power of whiteness: A genealogical exploration of negotiated racial identities in America's ethnic past. *Communication Quarterly*, 50(3/4), 391–409.

Basson, L. (2008). *White enough to be American?: Race mixing, indigenous people, and the boundaries of state and nation*. Chapel Hill, NC: University of North Carolina Press.

Bernasconi, R. (2009). "Our duty to conserve": W.E.B. Du Bois's philosophy of history in context. *South Atlantic Quarterly*, 108(3), 519–540.

Castagno, A. (2012). *"Founding mothers:" White mothers of biracial children in the multiracial movement (1979–2000)*. From http://wesscholar.wesleyan.edu/cgi/viewcontent. cgi?article=1934&context=etd_hon_theses.

Chau, J. (1999). I'm just an object to people. In P. Gaskins (Ed.). *What are you?: Voices of mixed-race young people* (pp. 38–39). New York: Henry Holt and Company.

Crothers, A. & K'Meyer, T. (2007). "I was Black when it suited me. I was White when it suited me": Racial identity in the biracial life of Marguerite Davis Stewart. *Journal of American Ethnic History*, 26(4), 24–49.

DaCosta, K. M. (2007). *Making multiracials: State, family, and market in the redrawing of the color line*. Stanford, CA: Stanford University Press.

Dalmage, H. (2004). *The politics of multiracialism*. New York: State University of New York Press.

Daniel, R. (1992). Passers and pluralists: Subverting the racial divide. In M. P. Root (Ed.). *Racially mixed people in America* (pp. 91–107). Newbury Park, CA: Sage.

Davis, T. J. (2012). *Plessy v. Ferguson*. Santa Barbara, CA: Greenwood.

Douglass, F. (1886). The future of the colored race. *North American Review*, 142(354), 437–440. From http://etext.lib.virginia.edu/etcbin/toccer-new2?id=DouFutu.sgm& images=images/modeng&data=/texts/english/modeng/parsed&tag=public&part=1& division=div1.

Hochschild, J. L. & Powell, B. M. (2008). Racial reorganization and the United States Census 1850–1930: Mulattoes, half-Breeds, mixed parentage, Hindoos, and the Mexican race. *Studies in American Political Development*, 22(1), 59–96.

Hodes, M. (1997). *White women, black men: Illicit sex in the 19th century south*. New Haven, CT: Yale University Press.

Hollinger, D. (2003). Amalgamation and hypodescent: The question of ethnoracial mixture in the history of the United States. *American Historical Review*, 108(5), 1363–1390.

Khanna, N. (2011). *Biracial in America: Forming and performing racial identity*. New York: Lexington Books.

Leverette, T. (2009). Speaking up: Mixed race identity in Black communities. *Journal of Black Studies*, 39(3), 434–445.

Matsumoto, V. (2010). *Nikki Sawada Bridges Flynn and What Comes Naturally*. *Frontiers*, 31(3), 31–40.

Menchaca, M. (2008). The anti-miscegenation history of the American southwest, 1837–1970: Transforming racial ideology into law. *Cultural Dynamics*, 20(3), 279–318.

Middleton, R. (2008). The historical legal construction of Black racial identity of mixed Black-White race individuals: The role of state legislatures. *Jackson State University Researcher: An Interdisciplinary Journal*, 21(2), 17–39.

Millward, J. (2010). "The relics of slavery": Interracial sex and manumission in the American south. *Frontiers: A Journal of Women's Studies*, 31(3), 22–30.

Montgomery, M. (2012). Identity politics: The mixed-race American Indian experience. *Journal of Critical Race Inquiry*, 2(1), 1–25. From http://library.queensu.ca/ojs/index.php/CRI/article/view/4352/4471.

Navarro, M. (2012, January 14). 'For many Latinos, racial identity is more culture than color'. *The New York Times*, p. A11.

Pack, S. (2012). What is a real Indian?: The interminable debate of cultural authenticity. *AlterNative: An International Journal of Indigenous Peoples*, 8(2), 176–188.

Pascoe, P. (2009). *What comes naturally: Miscegenation law and the making of race in America*. New York: Oxford University Press.

Perdue, T. (2003). *"Mixed blood" Indians: Racial construction in the early south*. Athens, GA: The University of Georgia Press.

Qian, Z. & Cobas, J. (2004). Latinos' mate selection: National origin, racial, and nativity differences. *Social Science Research*, 33(2), 225–247.

Ramirez, R. (2002). Julia Sanchez's story: An indigenous woman between nations. *Frontiers*, 23(2), 65–83.

Romo, R. (2011). Between Black and Brown. Blaxican (Black-Mexican) multiracial identity in California. *Journal of Black Studies, 42*(3), 402–426.

Ross, K. (2013). Racial identity and the shadow of Jim Crow in the Black Community. *(1) Drop Project*. From http://1nedrop.com/racial-identity-and-the-shadow-of-jim-crow-in-the-black-community/.

Rothman, J. (2003). *Notorious in the neighborhood: Sex and families across the color line in Virginia, 1787–1861.* Chapel Hill, NC: The University of North Carolina Press.

Spickard, P. (2001). Who is Asian? Who is Pacific Islander?: Monoracialism, multiracial people, and Asian American communities. In T. Williams-Leon & C. Nakashima (Eds.). *The sum of our parts: Mixed heritage Asian Americans* (pp. 13–24). Philadelphia: Temple University Press.

Spring, J. (1996). *The cultural transformation of a Native American family and its tribe: A basket of apples.* Mahwah, NJ: Lawrence Erlbaum Associates.

Stevenson, B. (2013). What's love got to do with it?: Concubinage and enslaved women and girls in the antebellum south. *Journal of African American History, 98*(1), 99–125.

Taylor, P., Passel, J., Wang, W., Kiley, J., Velasco., & Dockterman, D. (2010). *Marrying out: One-in-seven new U.S. marriages is interracial or interethnic.* Pew Research Center. From http://pewsocialtrends.org/files/2010/10/755-marrying-out.pdf.

Williams, K. (2003). Linking the civil rights and multiracial movements. In M. Dalmage (Ed.). *The politics of multiracialism* (pp. 77–97). New York: State University of New York Press.

Williams, K. (2006). *Mark one or more: Civil rights in multiracial America.* Ann Arbor, MI: University of Michigan Press.

Wormser, R. (2003). *The rise and fall of Jim Crow.* New York: St. Martin's Press.

Yarbrough, F. (2008). *Race and the Cherokee nation: Sovereignty in the nineteenth century.* Philadelphia: University of Pennsylvania Press.

3

RACIAL IDENTITY

Multiple Perspectives on Racial Self-Understanding

> *When I was in fourth grade I found familiarity with other Mexican kids. And I wanted to hang out with them. I was like, "I'm Mexican!" And I identified as Mexican even though I lived with my White mother. And so it was really hard for me because I wasn't accepted by kids . . . And so slowly I began to transition into, I guess I identified more as White . . .*
> —Tina (Bettez, 2012, pp. 51–52)

Educators are profoundly aware of the effect students' relationships with peers have on school experiences. Yet the influence of racial identity development on students' self-understanding and thus their sense of connection with peers are rarely addressed thoroughly in teacher education textbooks. Chapters on identity development, the primary focus for psychosocial development, minimally address the role of race and ethnicity in young peoples' choices about group affiliation. Thus, they tend to deemphasize the fact that children and youth are racial beings. Rockquemore, Laszloffy, and Noveske (2006) stated that understanding children's racial identity is best approached from perspectives that ". . . recognize that children are embedded in a complex web of structural, institutional, and interpersonal relationships shaped by historically and culturally rooted boundaries, group alignments, and power" (p. 204). A lack of teacher knowledge and reflection regarding students' racial self-understanding leads to a limited understanding of an important area of identity development for White, ethnic/racial minority, and mixed-race children and youth. It also invites educators to operate from private theories of the role of race in children's group affiliations and interactions that may not have been interrogated, and thus may stand on assumptions, biases, and misinformation.

The nature of schooling experiences for mixed-race children will be addressed in later chapters. The primary purpose of this chapter is to provide a knowledge base for educators to develop more accurate perceptions of how mixed-race children develop a sense of racial identity, as well as how this identity operates in their everyday life. Today, more is understood about racial identity development processes for mixed-race children and how these processes differ from monoracial youths' routes to identity development. Hence, this chapter begins with a review of racial identity development in general, before consideration of racial identity development for mixed-raced children and youth. In this way, areas of similarity, as well as points of departure, between monoracial and mixed-race racial identity development can be more clearly understood.

The Meaning of Racial Identity Development

Educators continue to be guided by *age-stage* theories to support their understanding of children' growth and development from psychological perspectives. They rely, for example, on Jean Piaget's theory of cognitive development or Lawrence Kohlberg's theory of moral development to align cognitive or moral expectations (i.e., stages) respectively, to a chronological age range. Erik Erickson's (1963) age-stage theory of psychosocial development has been the foremost guide for understanding identity development and formation.

Identity development is the process of self-discovery that begins in young children and continues through adulthood. It is a primary focus during adolescence, and commitments made during the adolescent years serve as a guide for later decisions and actions related to self-identity and racial group affiliation. Generally, identity development theories propose that young people explore a number of options regarding multiple aspects of their identity (e.g., career choice, sexual identity, religious beliefs) prior to making decisions about what fits in terms of a sense of self. Erickson believed that adolescents who failed to establish a stable identity by the end of adolescence risked identity confusion. Marcia (1980) described this group of adolescents as experiencing identity diffusion (i.e., a lack of commitment to an identity); identity foreclosure (i.e., a premature commitment to an identity on the basis of the attitudes of others); or identity moratorium (i.e., exploring an identity although a commitment has not been made). Clearly, according to these theorists, commitment to an identity reflects the psychologically healthy adolescent.

Social identity is a process of identity development where children come to see themselves as part of a specific social group. Children organize their worlds into distinct categories at a very young age and subsequently attach value to differences they perceive between and among the categories they structure. Rogers et al. (2012) proposed that young children's categories include social status, personality traits, and physical characteristics such as skin color. Recognition in differences in skin color eventually translates into recognition that different races exist, especially given the continued emphasis on race in our racialized society. Indeed, when it comes to race, children as young as two years old recognize differences among racial groups (Hirschfeld, 2008), and by preschool, they may use race as a factor when including and excluding peers in play activities (Van Ausdale & Feagin, 2001).

The fact that children attend to race-related differences accounts for the inclusion of racial identity as a category of social identity development. Phinney (1996) described ethnic identity as ". . . a commitment and sense of belonging to one's ethnic group, positive evaluation of the group, interest in and knowledge about the group, and involvement in activities and traditions of the group" (p. 145). As you will note, Phinney used the term ethnic identity; however, she explained that she uses ethnic and racial identity interchangeably. Race, however, has biological connotations, whereas ethnicity refers to social and cultural aspects of a group. Helms (1990) noted the importance of an individual's perception that he or she shares a racial heritage with a group in the racial identity process. Hence, the current discussion uses the term racial identity development rather than ethnic identity development in order to describe the group affiliation process alluded to by both Phinney and Helms.

Monoracial Racial Identity Development and Formation

Although young children recognize physical differences among people from different racial groups, it is not until middle childhood that children begin to understand what it means to belong to a certain racial or ethnic group. They attach meaning to observable components in people such as skin color or other physical differences; behavioral components such as language; social components such as social status or relative social positions; and more abstract components such as cultural heritage, as these apply to race differences (Rogers et al., 2012). Judgments or evaluations of their observations and experiences are influenced by positive and/or negative images of race presented by the family, community, the media, and society-at-large (Phinney, 1996). Children's early meaning-making activities about race influence race-related decisions and experiences as they approach adolescence.

Children differ in terms of what they incorporate as meaningful content as they come to understand what it means to belong to different racial/ethnic groups. Sociocultural elements particular to the child's cultural and ethnic/racial related experiences influence their selection process. As examples, Black and White children's observations tend to focus on physical characteristics (e.g., skin color), and relative social positions seem to be important to them as well. The social emphasis on differences in experiences between Black and White people in society likely makes these observations and social components more important to these children. Minority language children tend to focus on differences in language, given the importance of language in their experiences, and Chinese children are less likely to attend to pride aspects associated with race or ethnicity, given the lack of emphasis on this attribute in some Asian cultures (Rogers et al., 2012).

Phinney (1996) believed children of color and White children have different tasks with respect to racial identity development. For example, children of color wrestle with issues of status, privilege, stereotypes, and racism in the racial identity development process, challenging issues that may not be of importance for monoracial White children. Still, it has been generally accepted that children of color who engaged the racial identity process were likely to have a more secure sense of identity. As a matter of fact, a number of racial minority–specific models for racial identity development emerged in the 1990s (e.g., models for Native Americans, Asian Americans, Hispanics) in an effort to ensure that support for the racial identity development process among racial minority young people was appropriate and reflected the cultural, political, and racial contexts in which their development took place (Kwan & Liem, 2001). Even today, a strong racial identity is believed to have a positive impact on the social, emotional, and academic well-being of monoracial minority youth (Eggen & Kauchak, 2013; Ormrod, 2014; Woolfolk, 2013).

White racial identity development has received less attention than racial identity development for monoracial minority groups. Earlier studies of race/ethnicity-based group affiliation for White people focused on the ethnic identity of European immigrants. Once immigrants were fully assimilated as White, these studies disappeared, roughly around 1990. White racial identity studies were subsequently replaced with studies of whiteness (McDermott & Samson, 2005). Many White people however believe they have no race—that they are simply American. As a result, the content of what it means to be White is often invisible and goes unexamined, save the privilege and social/cultural superiority associated with whiteness.

In an effort to provide content beyond the less than positive aspects associated with whiteness (e.g. privilege and superiority), Helms (1990) proposed an often-referenced model of White racial identity. She theorized that a healthy White racial identity is a nonracist identity that rejects racism and the privileges of whiteness. Accordingly, the White person must confront their whiteness and its implications vis-à-vis the various forms of racism (e.g., personal racism, institutional racism, cultural racism). They can then work to develop a sense of self that does not rely on the superiority of one racial group over another.

Theories of racial identity development for monoracial youth, whether White youth or youth of color, have in common the notion of stages that begin with an unexplored identity that reflects beliefs and values of their parents, peers, or society. They experience a crisis that rattles their sense of complacency and motivates them to move to a different stage of development. In the case of racial identity models for monoracial minority youth, young people engage in exploration of the culture and history of the group to which they seek to connect, in response to the crisis. They subsequently arrive at a secure sense of identity (Phinney, 1996). Elements of this process are observable in models developed to explain racial identity development specific to mixed-race youth, particularly models developed in the 1990s. However, more contemporary models of racial identity development for mixed-race youth include tenets that are distinctly different from those included in models developed for monoracial youth.

Racial Identity Development for Mixed-Race Children and Youth

The discussion on monoracial identity development earlier was presented so that similarities and differences between theories of monoracial and mixed-race racial identity development can be discerned. The points of commonality and departure are also important to emphasize because too few educator-related texts address developmental issues and processes specific to mixed-race children. In a study of 12 child growth and development books published after 2004, Wardle (2007) found that only two included a discussion on the identity issues of importance for mixed-race children. In an effort to address diversity and development, the overarching tendency was to discuss issues of monoracial minority children and their developmental trajectory in both their single-race and dominant cultural contexts. The needs of the mixed-race child were often addressed as appendages to those of racial minority children in general.

More recent texts address identity development of mixed-race children, but these discussions are presented within the context of models constructed for monoracial youth. Identity development models constructed for mixed-race children and youth are not reviewed. When identity development for mixed-race children is discussed using theories developed for monoracial children, the weight of the presentation is on how challenging identity development appears to be for this group of young people (Woolfolk, 2013).

Although attention to identity development experiences of mixed-race people increased following the Multiracial Movement, a review of identity development theories reveals how perspectives on mixed-race people's racial identity processes changed over time. It is evident that sociocultural thinking around race mixing at different historical periods influenced these perspectives (see Chart 3.1). Models for mixed-race people's identity development have been generated using four different approaches: the problem approach, equivalent approach, variant approach, and the ecological approach proposed by Rockquemore, Brunsma, and Delgado, (2009). A discussion of each approach with representative theories follows.

Problem Approach

During the late nineteenth and first half of the twentieth centuries, mixed-race peoples' efforts to develop a sense of identity in relation to a specific social group were theorized as tormented and confused processes. A problem approach was the routine means for assessing mixed-race peoples' attempts toward a sense of self-understanding and acceptance. In this way, theorists focused on perceived challenges and dilemmas mixed-race people faced as a result of having parents from different races. Intermingling among the races was socially and morally vilified in most regions of the United States during this time, and racial segregation was legally sanctioned in others. According to theorists during this period, a society divided by race left mixed-race people feeling as if they had no "place," because they belonged fully neither in the White nor racial minority world.

Notions of mixed-race people as emotionally and/or socially unstable were evident in labels such as the tragic mulatto or in concepts such as the marginal man. Mixed-race people fitting either category were purportedly overwhelmed with sadness, even suicidal (as in the case of the tragic mulatto), or had psychological problems that led to a sense of social isolation (as in the case of the marginal man). Views of social and emotional deficits were joined by beliefs in hybrid degeneracy that suggested, given the unnatural nature of mixing among different "species" (i.e., races), mixed-race people were genetically inferior to either parent. Their race mixture, it was suggested, contributed to their lack of emotional fortitude. Those adhering to a problem approach for understanding racial identity development for mixed-race people proposed that the healthiest identity for mixed-race people was identification with monoracial minorities. This position, however, really became a focus during the Civil Rights and cultural nationalism movements of the 1960s and into the 1970s.

Equivalent Approach

During the 1960s, mixed-race people were expected to choose a minority race identity as a sign of solidarity with minority groups' heightened sense of race pride and as an expression of loyalty to the fight for social and political equality during the 1960s. Theorists like Cross (1971, 2001) added a psychological well-being component to this sociopolitical expectation by suggesting that a minority identity (in this case a Black identity) was needed to understand the impact of race and racism on people of color.

Cross's views fit an equivalent approach to ethnic identity development where it is proposed that there was really little difference between mixed-race people and monoracial Black people. Given their history, it was proposed, most Black people were mixed-race anyway. Thus, there was really no practical difference between mixed-race and monoracial minority people, and both should travel the same path to a racial identity (Renn, 2004). A minority monoracial identity seemed the healthiest outcome for mixed-race people.

Cross believed African American identity development was a multistep, multistage process that involved working through stages to deconstruct and analyze an old troubled self, with the aim of developing a new self that ". . . typically reconfigured elements of the old self with fresh insights and modest infusion of new elements" (Cross, 2001, p. 32). Accordingly, Black people (and, by implication, mixed-race people) needed to rid themselves of any self-hatred caused

	Sociohistorical Influences	Perceptions of Mixed-race People	Conceptions of Identity Development	Anticipated Outcomes of Development
Problem Approach	Laws during the late nineteenth and first half of the twentieth centuries required separation by race. People with any nonwhite ancestry were considered to be people of color, according to hypodecent – one-drop rule legislation.	Mixed-race people were viewed as problematic, owing to a racially divided society. They internalized conflicts from the racial divide as a personal problem.	Development was understood by studying mixed-race people's deficits, dilemmas, and negative experiences.	Life will be marked by tragic episodes. Mixed-race people will find it difficult to reconcile the race-based cultural conflict that consumes their identity. Mixed-race people eventually will accept their position as mixed-race in a racially divided world. Still, given social realities, they will own a Black identity, even though they may prefer a White identity. They will experience feelings of rejection and isolation.
Influential Theories	Robert Park Marginal Man Concept: Describes an individual who lives on the margin of two cultures/societies, where he or she is involved in the culture/traditions of both. He/she is unable or unwilling to break with the traditions either and is fully accepted by neither one. Everett Stonequist Internalized Cultural Conflict: Extension of the marginal man concept into the notion that psychological problems develop as a result of marginalized social positions.			
Equivalent Approach	During the Civil Rights Movement and Cultural Nationalism of the 1960s, people of color championed racial pride and fought for equal rights in society.	Most Black people are mixed-race. There is no need to make distinctions between mixed-race people of current and previous generations' interracial unions.	Mixed-race people should develop a healthy Black identity and avoid internalized racist views of Black people.	Mixed-race people develop a meaningful Black identity that will help them understand race and racism.
Influential Theories	Eric Erickson Eight Stages of Man Psychosocial Developmental Theory: Individuals proceed through eight stages of psychosocial development that include a stage where adolescents are expected to develop a stable sense of identity. Individuals experience a conflict at each stage and develop either a positive or negative psychosocial characteristic based on the resolution of the conflict. In the case of identity development, adolescents either develop a secure identity or suffer from role confusion. William Cross Nigrescence Stage Model: Individuals move from a preference for dominant culture identity to an internalized Black self and an expression of a Black identity. During an encounter stage, they have an overt or covert experience with racism, a racial crisis or epiphany that helps them realize the importance of race in their lives. They are motivated to learn more about their racial heritage, which leads to a connection to, and subsequently commitment to, Black culture.			
Variant Approach	The Multiracial Movement of the 1980s & 1990s focused on the rights of mixed-race people.	Mixed-race people are a distinct group, different from monoracial minority and White groups.	Mixed-race people construct stable personal and racial identities that integrate the racial heritages that comprise their racial makeup.	Mixed-race people internalize a biracial or multiracial identity that is recognized and legitimized by society.

Influential Theories	Christine Kerwin & Joseph Ponterotto Model of Biracial Identity Development: Mixed-race individuals proceed through an age-stage racial identity development process that culminates in their ability to reject pressures to choose one racial group over another as they accept a biracial heritage. They see both the advantages and disadvantages of being biracial. Carlos Poston Biracial Identity Development Model (BIDM): Mixed-race individuals are able to move beyond feelings of guilt and disloyalty that develop as a result of feeling pressured to select one aspect of their racial background over another. They develop multiracial identities that integrate the cultural backgrounds of both parents.		
Ecological Approach	Beginning in 2000, mixed-race people were able to select more than one race/ethnicity designation on the U.S. Census.	Mixed-race people are highly diverse, and able to choose or construct a racial identity based on the way they see themselves in society.	Mixed-race development is influenced by the context in which individuals develop. Racial identity cannot be predicted. The intersectionality of multiple influences (e.g., gender, class, community location and attitudes, family influences, personality traits, etc.) must be considered.	No one racial identity is better or worse than another (i.e., monoracial or multiracial)—indeed no racial identification at all is possible. Varied, complex, and flexible identities are possible.
Influential Theories	Urie Bronfenbrenner Ecological Systems Development: Development has multiple levels of influence, to include the microsystem, mesosystem, exosystem, macrosystem, and chronosystem. Representative contexts for the various levels begin with those closest to the individual (e.g., family), and extend to those within society-at-large during different sociohistorical periods. Maria P.P. Root Ecological Framework for Understanding Multiracial Identity: Racial identity for mixed-raced people will be based on personal, sociocultural, and contextual influences. Mixed-race people may claim a monoracial identity based on hypodescent; self-identified monoracial identity; blended identity; biracial or multiracial identity; or White/symbolic identity.		

CHART 3.1 Theoretical Approaches to Mixed-Race Identity Development over Time

Based on Rockquemore, Brunsma, and Delgado's (2009) review and expansion of Thornton & Watson's (1995) framework of research on mixed-race identity, using Black–White mixed-race people as the example for the overview.

by being Black. They needed to experience Nigrescence, a racial epiphany that would allow them to move from being a Negro (which implied a more power-less, negative self-concept) to a Black person (which implied a more empowered, positive self-concept) (Cross, 2001). The process of becoming Black could be enhanced through education, immersion in Black culture, and through an emotional connection with being Black.

Variant Approach

Thinking in the 1980s and 1990s about mixed-race children's racial identity development built on previous work in the field of identity development. At the same time, ideas and frameworks specific to the experiences of mixed-race children emerged. In this way, the variant approach to racial identity develop-ment aligned with concepts of mixedness reflected in the Multiracial Move-ment, which positioned mixed-race people as a distinct group different from monoracial minorities and monoracial Whites.

In an effort to show that mixed-race youth were just as psychologically healthy as their monoracial peers, studies emerged to compare monoracial and mixed-race adolescents on identity-related well-being constructs (e.g., self-worth, self-concept, and self-esteem). For example, Grove (1991) conducted a study of Asian-White adolescents who were presumed to be at risk because of the assump-tion that mixed-race youth felt socially marginalized as a result of belonging to neither White nor Asian monoracial groups. Grove concluded that Asian-White adolescents appeared to have identity statutes (i.e., identity diffusion, identity foreclosure, premature commitment to an identity, or stable identity) similar to monoracial White and Asian adolescents. Further, although their values were similar to monoracial Asian adolescents, issues around race appeared to be less a factor to Asian-White adolescents in the identity development process. In fact, some Asian-White participants felt more freedom to choose an identity, which resulted in a positive as opposed to negative outcome of being mixed-race.

Field's (1996) study compared the self-esteem levels of monoracial Black and biracial (Black-White) adolescents. She used two constructs developed by Cross as the framework for her study: personal identity (i.e., aspects of the self outside of racial identity, such as self-esteem or self-worth), and reference group orienta-tion (RGO) (i.e., factors associated with a particular racial/ethnic group such as racial identity or racial ideology). Both constructs were theorized to be associ-ated with self-concept.

Fields concluded that Black-White biracial and monoracial Black adolescents had comparable levels of positive self-concepts—although biracial children who had adopted a White RGO had a more challenging time of developing a positive self-concept than did monoracial Black adolescents who had a Black RGO or bira-cial adolescents who had a Black or bicultural RGO. Rejecting Black culture and having internalized racism negatively impacted biracial adolescents' self-concept.

Despite outcomes of her study, Fields questioned whether single-race identity development models were appropriate to assess identity-related constructs for mixed-race children. Subsequently, Root (2003b) proposed that mixed-race youth might exhibit behaviors based on efforts to make meaning of race from a mixed-race perspective that could be misunderstood as poor adjustment, should their efforts be viewed from a monoracial context. In support of these positions, Poston (1990) argued that monoracial identity development models were limited when applied to mixed-race people for a number of reasons, to include the implication that mixed-race people were required to choose values of one racial group that constituted their heritage over the other. He also believed an additional shortcoming was the fact that monoracial models were unable to accommodate an integrated identity that incorporated the culture and values from multiple groups into a single identity.

Poston's (1990) Biracial Identity Development Model and Kerwin and Ponterotto's (1995) Model of Biracial Identity Development are variant approaches to mixed-race people's racial identity development and, to some degree, respond to perceived limitations and shortcomings of monoracial models of identity development when applied to mixed-race people. As with previous racial identity theories, both biracial theories are structured around stages of development, and the Kerwin-Ponterotto model more explicitly aligns proposed stages with specific ages (i.e., preschool through adulthood).

Also, like monoracial theories, both biracial theories of racial development include a crisis that must be overcome. The content of the crisis, however, surrounds the pressure felt by mixed-race youth to choose an identity on the basis of one aspect of their racial heritage over the other, and in the process, reject the culture of one parent. In the Poston model, this situation becomes a burden that results in confusion, guilt, and feelings of disloyalty to the parent whose racial background is not chosen. Feelings of self-hatred are possible as well. The crisis is resolved when the adolescent learns to appreciate cultures of both parents. The crisis subsides in the Kerwin-Ponterotto model when the more mature young adult is able to reject expectations of others and accept their biracial heritage. In both the Poston and Kerwin-Ponterotto models, the mixed-race person is able to integrate cultures into a more holistic multiracial or biracial race identity.

Ecological Approach

According to Rockquemore et al. (2009), analysis of data about identity development journeys of mixed-race people collected over time suggests ". . . (a) racial identity varies, (b) racial identity often changes over the life course, (c) racial identity development is not a predictable linear process with a single outcome, and (d) social, cultural, and spatial contexts are critical [in the identity development process]" (pp. 20–21). These ideas are clearly represented in the ecological approach to racial identity development for mixed-race people.

The notion that multiple factors (e.g., family, community, social supports, physical characteristics) influence mixed-race children's choices about racial identity had been addressed prior to the emergence of this final approach for studying racial identity development (see Poston, 1990). The ecological approach to understanding racial identity development relies heavily on Bronfenbrenner's (1994) ecological system of human development. Bronfenbrenner explicitly illustrated that development does not occur in a vacuum, and that a number of factors influence development. Further, his model of human development represents a departure from age-stage based theories.

Bronfenbrenner believed that the developing individual acts on and is acted upon by their immediate environment. These reciprocal and enduring interactions, labeled proximal processes, are progressively more complex over the lifespan. Moreover, the

> . . . form, power, content, and direction . . ." [of these processes will vary and be influenced by the] ". . . characteristics of the developing person . . . the environments in which the processes take place . . . and the nature of the developmental outcomes under consideration.
>
> *(p. 38)*

Development is influenced by environmental elements beyond those most immediate to the individual. Bronfenbrenner's (1994) model of human development can be visualized as five concentric circles that surround the developing child, which represent the most immediate to the most remote systems of influence on the child's development. The systems summarized as follows are organized beginning with influences closes to the child, proceeding outward:

- Microsystem: represents interaction in settings such as the family, school, or peer group that invite, prohibit, or permit different activities or social roles.
- Mesosystem: links and processes between various settings in the microsystem (e.g., interactions between teachers and families).
- Exosystem: interactions and processes between two settings, one of which does not directly include the developing person, but nonetheless influences process in their immediate environment (e.g., the relationship between the home and a parent's workplace).
- Macrosystem: the "societal blueprint" (p. 40) of a giving culture or subculture that is embedded in the microsystem, mesosystem, and exosystem. The macrosystem includes the knowledge, customs, and beliefs of the culture or subculture; however, entities such as hazards and opportunities structures are included as well.
- Chronosystem: addresses the impact of time on development—time as represented by the lifespan of developing individuals and historical time. Consideration is given to consistency and change over time for the individual and

within the environment. As a result of the latter, a sociohistorical context for human development over an individual's lifespan is important.

Root's Ecological Framework for Understanding Racial Identity

Bronfenbrenner's model of human development is evident in models of racial development where the intersection of multiple personal factors and environmental influences are overtly included to explain racial identity. To date, Root's

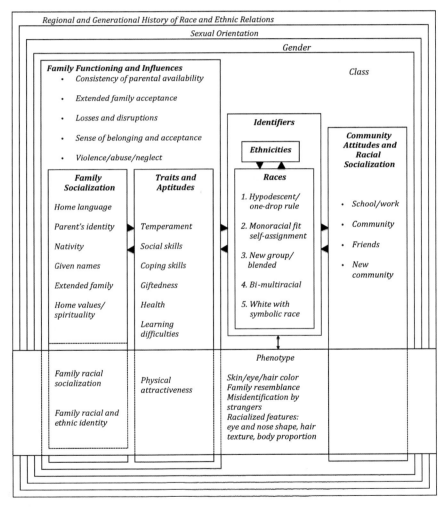

FIGURE 3.1 Root's Ecological Framework for Understanding Racial Identity

From Root, M.P.P. (2003). Multiracial families and children: Implications for educational research and practice. In J. A. Banks & C. A. McGee Banks (Eds.), *Handbook of research on multicultural education* (2nd ed., pp. 110–124). San Francisco, CA: Jossey-Bass. Copyright 2003 by Jossey-Bass. Reprinted with permission.

(2003a, 2003b) Ecological Framework for Understanding Racial Identity is the most comprehensive model of racial identity development for mixed-race people. The framework, which includes personal, sociocultural, and contextual influences on racial identity development, is structured as multiple systems of "screening lenses" (Root, 2003b, p. 117) mixed-race persons use to interpret experiences and situations that subsequently influence racial identity construc-tions. The positions of these systems shift in importance in racial identity devel-opment over the individual's lifespan. Root's model is discussed in detail in the following section, along with ideas generated from other research studies that are related to and/or support concepts proposed in the framework.

Generational and Geographical History of Race

In Root's model, generational and geographical history of race, sexual orientation, gender, and class operate as a macrosystem or macro lens influence on racial iden-tity development. Considering generational influences, Root (2003a) explicitly proposed that the intricacies of historical context require that past and current experiences of mixed-race people be viewed separately when it comes to under-standing racial identity development. Moreover, mixed-race individuals' options for racial identity are influenced by the generation into which they were born.

This notion is clearly evidenced by the "check all that apply" option on the census currently available to young people and their families, as opposed to previous generations where choice, in terms of race, was not available—race was defined for them. No longer constrained by a federally dictated racial identifica-tion, the percent of individuals reporting more than one race on the 2000 Census edged even higher with the 2010 Census. Individuals indicating a White-Black identity increased 134 percent, and White-Asian and White-American Indian/ Alaska Native–identified persons increased 87 percent and 32 percent respec-tively (Jones & Bullock, 2013).

The history of race interacts with different geographical regions to influ-ence racial identity claims as well. Root (2003a), for example, suggested that the association of racial mixing with slavery resulted in reduced numbers of people reporting more than one race on the 2000 Census in southern states. In fact, of the five states with less than 1 percent of the population reporting more than one race, four were southern states (i.e., Alabama, Mississippi, South Carolina, and West Virginia—Maine was the fifth state). By 2013, all but Mississippi had at least 1.5 percent of their population identifying as more than one race (for Mississippi, 1.1. percent identified as mixed-race on the census) (Jones & Bull-ock, 2013). Of the ten states with the highest number of people reporting more than one race (i.e., California, New York, Texas, Florida, Hawaii, Washington, Illinois, New Jersey, Pennsylvania, and Ohio) only three were southern states, which could support the notion of the impact of geographical race history on racial identity as well.

The influence of geographical race history was clearly apparent in Khanna's (2011) study of racial identity among 40 mixed-race people (nine males and 31 females). Khanna proposed that a limitation of her study was the fact that all participants, who were Black-White mixed-race people, lived in the south. The prominent history and continued influence of the one-drop rule (i.e., hypo-descent) in the south likely influenced the fact that a majority of the study's participants (24, or 60 percent) strongly identified as Black. On the other hand, Bettez's (2012) racial identity study included women from several regions of the United States, and more variation in terms of racial identity was reported (it should also be noted that Bettez's study included women from a variety of mixed-race backgrounds, which could have influenced their reported racial identity as well).

Sexual Orientation and Racial Identity Development

Racial/ethnic communities differ in terms of their position on sexual orienta-tion. Some communities of color, for example, are not as accepting of lesbian, gay, bisexual, transgender (LGBT) or exploring youth. Mixed-race people who wish to integrate their sexuality and racial identities will seek a safe and accept-ing community in which to develop both. The development of a gay identity and racial identity, however, may have competing paths, as effort to grow in one may be impeded by attempts to grow in the other (Bing, 2004). This is particularly so in many communities of color where a homosexual identity is discouraged. Although cultural factors do not impede formation of a lesbian, gay, or bisexual identity for monoracial minority youth, Black and some Latino youth are less comfortable sharing their sexual identity with others, more so than White youth (Rosario, Schrimshaw, & Hunter, 2004). Monoracial Asian American/Pacific Islander LGBT youth who feel openness about their sexual orientation may bring shame to their families (Advocates for Youth, n.d.). Mixed-race youth seeking to claim a monoracial minority identity may take their cues from their monora-cial peers in determining how receptive a community might be to their sexual orientation.

Root (2003a) proposed that the intersection of race and sexual orientation could push a LGBT mixed-race person toward White communities where they might find more acceptance and, subsequently, toward a White racial identity. Alternately, acceptance in a White LGBT community may be prohibited by perceptions of the mixed-race person as a person of color in groups that are racist and/or who wish to remain racially homogeneous (Bing, 2004).

Gender Influences on Identity Development

Cultural norms around gender intersect with race to produce different lived experiences for males and females, which in turn impact their racial identity claims. Referencing Storrs (1999), Khanna and Johnson (2010) argued that race has more salience in the racial identity construction process for mixed-race females than mixed-race males. In their view, the self-concept for males may be more connected to other identity areas. Although Rockquemore and Brunsma (2004) found that gender was not a major factor in the racial identity chosen by mixed-race participants of their study, they did conclude that males and females have different interactional experiences, which in turn influence the structure of the racial identity process.

Unlike their male counterparts, Black-White females who identified as biracial reported negative experiences during their adolescence that were perpetrated exclusively by monoracial Black females. Adverse interactions primarily focused on mixed-race girls' physical attributes (i.e., skin color, hair texture, eye color). Black-White girls were scorned for having nonblack features and accused of thinking they were "better than," simply because they possessed these physical characteristics. The fact that mixed-race males' physical characteristics were not the target for race-based hazing pointed to differentiated experiences on the basis of gender. For women participating in the Rockquemore and Brunsma (2004) study, negative interactions with monoracial peers affected their sense of belonging to a specific racial group and, subsequently, influenced their racial identity choices.

The effect of gender on identity claims is also evident when selection of a particular partner becomes the means by which some mixed-race persons accentuate their chosen identity. According to Root (2003a), the race of a male partner appears to make a more overt statement about racial identity for females than it does for males. As a result, mixed-race girls/women select partners from the racial group with which they wish to affiliate as a way of publically affirming their racial identity. A male partner of color, for example, allows them to emphasize a connection to their minority ancestry (Khanna & Johnson, 2010).

An additional gendered implication for racial identity construction relates to parents' gender and the nature of their interaction with the child. Root (2003a) highlighted the importance of children's ethnic, racial, and cultural socialization and stated that this role is traditionally assumed to be the mother's responsibility. Although socialization will be addressed in more detail in the next chapter, it is important to note here the impact of parents' gender and race on racial identity development. Bratter and Heard (2009) studied racial identity claims among mixed-race adolescents in order to determine if they leaned more toward their mother's or father's racial background for identity claims. They concluded that identity claims differed on the basis of different race categories. Asian-White adolescents, for example, tended to identify with their mother's race, regardless of whether the mother was White or Asian. Based on a small population of White-Black adolescents, the researchers concluded that White-Black adolescents with White fathers tended to identify with their father's race.

Specific to their research agenda, Bratter and Heard found that parental involvement in certain activities influenced identity claims adolescents make and that gender matters when parental involvement is considered. For example, fathers' involvement in school-related activities influenced youths' tendency to identify with the father's race. Mothers' involvement, however, resulted in adolescents' tendency to shy away from single-race claims.

Class Influences

Socioeconomic class influences the context in which racial identities develop. Different resources, experiences, and networks that potentially influence identity choices exist at various socioeconomic locations. Mixed-race children from middle to upper class interracial families are more likely to live in White communities. They attend schools where the majority of students are White and, as a result, may have more in common with their like social class peers than with mixed-race children of a lower socioeconomic status. Children from a lower socioeconomic background are more likely to live and develop in monoracial minority communities and, similar to mixed-race middle class children, may identify more with their like social class peers (Khanna & Johnson, 2010).

Mixed-race individuals from different class background draw upon their White ancestry differently (Khanna & Johnson, 2010). Mixed-race individuals who are part White and who develop in White middle class contexts may be "culturally White" and may benefit from experiences and knowledge acquired in that context as cultural capital, regardless of their racial identity (Bettez, 2012, p. 51). In some situations, mixed-race youth living in a low socioeconomic context may downplay their White heritage in order to gain favor with monoracial minority peers with the same socioeconomic background. However, they are more likely than their middle class mixed-race peers to use White privilege as means for improving their socioeconomic location (Khanna & Johnson, 2010).

Family and Community Influences

The family and community are designated as middle lens clusters in Root's framework, and are located within the macro lens influences (see Figure 3.1). Family socialization is a major influence on identity processes, along with the manner in which families function. The lack of family stability caused by circumstances listed under Family Functioning may lead the child to make sense of his or her problematic home life by associating the problems exhibited by a parent with the parent's racial group. Thus, a parent who is verbally abusive, for example, may lead the child to believe that all people of his or her racial group are verbally abusive (Root, 2003a). This thinking may lead the child to reject this aspect of their racial makeup as part of their racial identity.

In Root's (2003a) model, family dynamics can affect a child's access to networks and resources that inform his or her racial identity choices. A bitter divorce or other family disruptions, for example, could determine the nature of access both to parents as well as extended family members. Children lacking intimate access to their racial ancestry risk not having access to the knowledge, values, and behaviors to support a particular racial identity claim. They may, for example, have only superficial knowledge of their minority race ancestry and engage in performing race (i.e., acting in ways stereotypically attributed to a racial group), rather than engaging in behavior that emanates from authentic interaction with a particular racial group.

In addition to the family, the community also socializes and influences identity issues for both the child and his or her family. The community is made up of personal and group relationships in the neighborhood, church, and school, and with peers. As children begin to interact with adults and peers outside the home, they encounter information that could influence their self-perception. This information may or may not reflect family attitudes about race. Children who live in homes where race and racism are not discussed may have difficulty negotiating their racial identity. They may not know how to deal with the diverse perspectives people outside the home have about mixed-race children or, in fact, interracial families.

The degree of acceptance, rejection, or oppressive situations experienced by young people determines the salience of different community categories at any given time. In other words, if one community category communicates racial messages the child perceives as negative, the child may seek solace or acceptance in another category (e.g., the child attempts a stronger connection with peers, as opposed to the church where they had a negative race-based experience) as means for continuing the racial identity construction process. If, however, negative messages persist in a different community category, the identity construction process may continue to be negatively influenced. Root (2003b) also pointed out that as circumstances change and the child encounters new communities, he or she will need to renegotiate a racial identity.

Individual Influences

Some mixed-race children receive positive attention on the basis of personal characteristics, whereas others receive attention that makes for a longer, more difficult path to racial identity. Personal characteristics (e.g., academic aptitude, social skills, coping skills, athleticism [see Figure 3.1]) affect how a child experiences and negotiates family functioning and community relationships (Root, 2003a). Clearly, some mixed-race children will be better able to handle race-based taunts or hazing encountered outside the home than others. Inside the home, differences in physical appearance among mixed-race children from the same family (e.g., difference in skin color, eye color, hair texture, or shape of facial features) interact with all aspects of Root's framework and can result in different experiences within the family (Root, 2003a). Colorism persists in some families, and in some families, there may be a preference for lighter skinned children with more White-like physical features. These children may receive more positive interactions and feedback in both the immediate and extended family.

Untowardly attention to mixed-race children's physical characteristics by people outside the home influences both the children and their interracial families. Differential treatment of siblings from their multiple publics could result in siblings claiming different racial identities, and these affiliations may be based, to some extent, on reactions to physical characteristics (Smith, 2012). Inordinate attention to skin color from family outsiders could predominate to the point that family resemblances go unnoticed if the child's skin color does not match that of a family member (Root, 2003a). Failure to observe family resemblances lead to thoughtless and intrusive questions by outsiders, such as *"Are they yours?"* to parents of mixed-race children (Henry, 2013). Children who witness this type of insensitive behavior by outsiders will likely need to find ways to process comments that dis-integrate their families on the basis of physical differences between them and their parents.

Sometimes, mixed-race children are mistaken for children of race/ethnicities that are not a part of their racial heritage (e.g., a Black-White child may be mistaken as Latino). Ambiguously raced children may be targets for *"What are you?"* questions and in general may be subjected to more complicated feedback and social interactions that might influence their racial identity claims. They may also be subjected to negative and hurtful experiences, particularly from minority race communities. Members of minority groups may not trust ambiguously mixed-race people as being authentically minority, because the mixed-race person, in their opinion, has a choice about identity. Thus, the status of a mixed-race person as a true minority is sometimes called into question by monoracial minorities (Smith, 2012).

Multiple and Diverse Racial Identities

Racial identifiers are included in Root's (2003b) model as middle lens clusters. Assumptions that individuals with one Black parent and one White parent can understand themselves only as "Black" or "biracial" were socially, culturally, and politically promoted, and thus served as a misguided foundation for understanding racial identity among mixed-race people (Rockquemore & Brunsma, 2004). Indeed, Root (2003a) made the point that monoracial identity theories buttressed the one-drop rule by concluding that individuals could be of only one race. For these reasons, the possibility of multiple racial identities for mixed-race people is a hallmark of mixed-race racial identity theories and represents the most pronounced difference between racial identity theories for monoracial and mixed-race people. Root (2003a, 2003b) proposed that five racial identities were possible for mixed-race people: monoracial identity based on hypodescent; self-identified monoracial; blended identity; biracial or multiracial identity; and White with symbolic identity.

Mixed-race people who adopt monoracial identities may accept assigned identities that are based on hypodescent or the one-drop rule. In this instance, a White-nonwhite mixed-race person accepts the identity of the parent from the lower status monoracial minority race. A monoracial identity can be self-assigned, however. A mixed-race person may claim a monoracial minority identity based on exploration that a particular identity "fits" his or her sense of self and personal experiences. Unlike the monoracial identity claim based on hypodescent, a self-assigned monoracial claim of racial identity may not concur with how others perceive the mixed-race person. In other words, the self-assigned identity claim may not necessarily fit the mixed-race person's physical characteristics (Root, 2003b).

A third identity option in Root's framework is the blended identity, which reflects a biracial or multiracial identity. The mixed-race person claims an identity based on all ancestries that are part of his or her racial makeup. The salience of one aspect of his or her racial makeup may shift depending on the situation. A multiracial identity also incorporates all of an individual's racial heritages; however, there is no attempt on the individual's part to separate the different racial ancestries (Root 2003a, 2003b).

The final racial identity option in Root's framework is the symbolic race option. Mixed-race people adopting this option claim a White identity, and the choice is closely aligned with a preference for a specific class lifestyle or values (Root, 2003a). Although the individual makes no attempt to deny his or her mixedness or to denigrate the minority race group that is a part of his or her heritage, he or she is drawn toward whiteness. Phenotypically, it may be clear to observers that the person is mixed-race. According to Root (2003b), individuals who adopt a symbolic race identity may lack a sense of attachment to their minority heritage because they may not have had close associations with minority family members or minority communities while growing up. It is also possible that they have been repeatedly rejected by a minority community and simply decided to discontinue attempts to be a part of that community.

The notion of multiple racial identity options is also consistent with the racial identity patterns that emerged from Renn's (2004) research on mixed-race college students. Renn's identity patterns are Monoracial Identity (e.g., African American), Multiple Monoracial Identities (e.g., half White, half Chinese), Multiracial Identity (i.e., biracial, mixed-race), Extraracial Identity (e.g., refusing to identify any race), and Situational Identity (e.g., identities that shift depending on the situation).

All of Renn's patterns align with Root's racial identity options, with the exception of the Extraracial and Situational Identities. In the case of Extraracial Identities, students refused to use federally dictated race categories, albeit for different reasons. Some, who appeared White physically, chose not to adopt a culturally based identity. Others refused to respond to questions about race (either face-to-face or on forms) because they wanted to resist external definition of race categories. Still others had more intellectually based reasons for the extraracial status—they viewed race as a social construction and thus not a valid means for categorizing people. Students who adopted Situational Identities claimed monoracial White or minority or biracial identities depending on the situations in which they found themselves. Members of race-based groups who erect strict racial boundaries and who use authenticity and legitimacy in order to determine who can rightfully claim group membership may challenge young people choosing this identity option (Renn, 2004).

As a third example of frameworks that describe multiple identities among mixed-race people, Rockquemore and Brunsma (2004) presented four racial identity options based on their research: singular identity, border identity, protean identity, and transcendent identity. A singular identity in this framework could be monoracial Black or monoracial White. The latter identity is similar to Root's symbolic race in that in both instances, the mixed-race persons consider themselves to be White and not "passing" for White. The border identity is exclusively biracial and corresponds to Root's blended identity and Renn's multiracial identity. Protean identities present sometimes as monoracial White, sometimes as monoracial Black, and sometimes as biracial—similar to Renn's situational identity. Lastly, individuals who moved beyond race categories all together, believing that race has no meaning, exhibited a transcending identity. This identity category is similar to Renn's extraracial identities.

Mixed-Race Youth Navigating a Racial Identity

Unlike previous beliefs that mixed-race people should claim a single minority race identity, today it is understood that one racial identity location is no better or worse or more appropriate or healthier than any other. Rather, the pathway or process by which one arrives at an identity is more important (Rockquemore et al., 2006).

Given the multiple identity choices discussed earlier, clearly diverse categories of racial identities exist for mixed-race youth as they grow from adolescence into young adulthood. The identity construction process however is neither linear nor static. In fact, racial identity development for mixed-race adolescents is fluid and changes over time (Hitlin, Brown, & Elder, 2006; Terry & Winston, 2010).

Based on their longitudinal study of adolescent identity, Hitlin et al. found that among six possible pathways to identity development, mixed-race youth exhibited two: consolidation and divergence. Youth consolidate their identity by removing racial categories from their identity claims and incorporate divergence as part of their racial identity journey by adding race categories to their identity. As an example, White-Asian youth consolidate their racial categorization to solely White over time, which was fairly common in the Hitlin et al. study. White youth with Indian ancestry diversify to claim a White-Indian identity, which was also common in the study.

Hitlin et al. made the point that self-categorization is a more significant adolescent task for mixed-race youth than monoracial youth because of the choice factor involved. For example, regardless of different meanings monoracial Black youth might attribute to being Black, identifying their race as Black is uncontested. Mixed-race youth, however, possess different, and sometimes conflicting, frames of reference that they must make sense of in order to categorize their race.

Claiming a Racial Identity

At least some of our understanding of the impetus for consolidation and divergence processes can be drawn from Khanna's (2004, 2010, 2011) work on the effect of reflected appraisals on racial identity. Reflected appraisals are choices made about a sense of identity based on one's beliefs about how one is seen by others. Said another way, response to a mixed-race individual during social interactions influences his or her racial identity claim. Adolescence, which is an active period for racial identity work, is also a period of physical changes that may lead to an appearance indicative of membership in one aspect of mixed-race youths' racial heritage over the other, as well as a heightened sensitivity by youth as to how others perceive them. Abstract thinking is also a hallmark of adolescence. Young people are better able to make sense of abstract constructs such race/racism, sexism, and classism (Phillips, 2004). The physical and cognitive changes that occur during adolescence make reflected appraisals that could lead to consolidation and divergence processes plausible for this period of a young person's life.

According to Khanna (2010, 2011) an individual can think about his or her racial identity from two separate identity locations—which may not necessarily align with each other. A public identity reflects the label used to describe one's self to others. A mixed-race person may describe himself or herself as biracial, multiracial, or mixed race, for example. An internalized identity is the race a person identifies with most strongly, hence a person may identify himself or herself as biracial (public identity) but Black (internalized identity). This latter identity location is influenced by reflected appraisals, where phenotype plays an important role. If physical appearances reflect a minority heritage, then the mixed-race person is more likely to internalize a minority race identity because others see and treat him or her as such. In her study of mixed-race Asian-White individuals, Khanna (2004) found that study participants with more Asian physical characteristics were perceived as Asian and thus tended to claim an Asian identity. Similarly, in a subsequent study of Black-White mixed-race people, those with Black physical characteristics were perceived as Black and thus internally strongly identified with being Black (Khanna, 2010,

2011). However, the connection between phenotype and reflected appraisals is more complex for Black-White mixed-race people than it is for other mixed-race people.

Both White and Black observers may perceive Black-White mixed-race people who are phenotypically Black as Black. In fact, Black observers may judge Black-White mixed-race people to be Black regardless of phenotype. However, some Black-White participants in the Khanna's study who were initially perceived as White by White observers were reclassified as Black, once the mixed-race person's ancestry became known. Thus, Khanna argued that the one-drop rule could have more importance than phenotype in reflected appraisals for Black-White mixed-race people. Although it appears that most participants in Khanna's study arrived at a monoracial identification based on hypodescent, an identity category described by Root (2003b), other race categories for Black-White mixed-race people are possible. They may, for example, claim a symbolic White identity or blended identity. When this happens, an identity claim will likely not be validated (see following validation discussion), particularly if the one-drop rule predominates for the observer.

In earlier work, Khanna (2004) explored how cultural knowledge and exposure also played a role in reflected appraisals. The reaction among others to mixed-race persons' cultural exposure and knowledge influenced their sense of belonging to a particular racial/ethnic group. Cultural exposure and knowledge include the ability to speak the language associated with an ethnic group, knowledge gained through interaction with people in racial/ethnic communities, and knowledge of an ethnic/racial group's values, cultural events, and celebrations. Mixed-race people evaluated as having an understanding of the culture of a group will likely be perceived as belonging to that group and thus experience increased acceptance by group members.

Validation and Legitimacy of Racial Identity Claims

Rockquemore and Brunsma (2004) define validation as ". . . the social process whereby a particular racial identity is considered legitimate and accepted by others, or deemed illegitimate and ignored" (p. 86). Like reflected appraisals, validation is a process of social interaction where mixed-race people acquire information that contributes to their understanding of self. In essence, reflected appraisals either validate or invalidate young people's identity claims. As an example, Tina, a mixed-race participant in Bettez's (2012) study, initially claimed a Mexican identity because of cultural exposure within a Mexican-identified extended family. She was phenotypically White, however, and did not speak Spanish. As a result, other Latinas did not validate her Mexican identity and rejected her as a member of their community. As indicated in the opening quote to this chapter, Tina subsequently adopted a White identity. Khanna (2011) provided an example of a Black-White mixed-race person, Kate, who over time developed both a public and internalized White identity. Kate described the lack of validation as a Black person among her White friends in this way:

> . . . I would say I am black. And they were like, "You are not black. You are a white girl." . . . I would think, I have black in me . . . I mean I would think, yeah I am part black, but then again I would be like, "Yeah, you are right. I am a white girl.
>
> *(p. 51)*

The process of having one's identity claims accepted and validated by peers can be a traumatic one for adolescents and place some in positions of being rejected, as was the case for Tina. Monoracial minority peers expose some mixed-race youth who wish to be accepted by a minority community to authenticity tests. "Testing" may range from challenges to mixed-race youths' cultural knowledge to pressure to conform to tastes in clothing or music particular to a racial group, and even to choice of friends (Root, 1998). Although some mixed-race youth avoid these situations, others seek to pass the "test" by exhibiting behaviors that are stereotypically associated with a monoracial group, hiding family members that might confirm their mixed-race status, or by becoming a caricature of the way people of color are perceived (Root, 2003b).

Some identity choices are less likely to be validated than others. In some situations, biracial identities are not validated, although this is not always the case. Rockquemore and Brunsma (2004) concluded that some White communities accept and validate biracial identities. They concur with Khanna (2010, 2011), however, that some Black and White communities view mixed-race people who self-identify as biracial as monoracial Black. In addition, mixed-race youth who identify as White may not be validated either and may be accused of passing as White. This notion of passing reflects a one-drop rule rationale for racial identities and implies that mixed-race persons fraudulently appropriate an identity to which they have no right (Khanna, 2011).

Mixed-race people who claim a White identity view themselves as White despite the lack of validation for this claim (Rockquemore & Brunsma, 2004). Others may assume a monoracial White identity, most often sporadically, for social and/or economic advantages, and some mixed-race people may present themselves as monoracially Black (i.e., passing as Black) for opportunistic reasons as well (Khanna, 2011). Opportunism is not the motivation however for mixed-race people who claim a self-identified monoracial White, symbolic White identity, or a singular race identity (Rockquemore & Brunsma, 2004; Root, 2003b).

Negotiating Spaces to Belong

Mixed-race youths' racial identity experiences are based on the nature of their racial makeup and the sociocultural and personal circumstances discussed in this chapter. Collectively, however, their experiences are more complex than the identity work of monoracial youth. In addition, as surmised by Phillips (2004), the physical and behavioral ambiguity of mixed-race young people makes the route to a sense of identity more complicated for some mixed-race youth than others. Some mixed-race youth are not interested in passing as monoracial, performing race, and/or passing authenticity tests. Alternative nonmainstream groups, however, may be the choice of some mixed-race youth in order to experience a sense of belonging to a peer group (Phillips, 2004). Still others are able to develop relationships with multiple groups, and there is evidence that youth able to establish relationships with more than one racial group have a better sense of well-being. This latter group identification option may be part and parcel of the development process—that is, youth at higher levels of development may not feel pressured to relate to only one group (Binning, Unzueta, Huo, & Molina, 2009).

Although the impact of monoracial peers' acceptance or rejection remains a factor in mixed-race youths' racial identity work, the possible positive outcomes from attaching to other mixed-race youth for a sense of belonging and well-being is explored less well. Some mixed-race adolescents may seek out other mixed-race youth to find peers with whom they have much in common (Giamo, Schmitt, & Outten, 2012). Monina, a mixed-race (Black-Latina) high school student, experienced connection with a mixed-race peer in this way:

> . . . I met another Blatina . . . We were very close friends and that was really good for me because finally there was someone who completely understood. When I was with her, it was totally okay to be these two things.
> *(Diaz, 1999, p. 57)*[1]

Even with a strong bond with another mixed-race peer, Monina laments the fact that they do not have one group with which to connect, and fears that one day, they will have to choose one monoracial group (either Black or Latino) over the other.

Concluding Thoughts

The multidimensional nature of racial identity among mixed-race youth should disrupt tendencies among teachers and other school personnel to adopt essentialist notions of what it means to be mixed-race and adolescent. Indeed, the fact that very young children are aware of race differences suggests that racial self-understanding is a developmental task for the P-12 schooling years and an area of development that warrants more attention and support from educators.

Ecological frameworks for explaining racial identity development for mixed-race youth enhanced our understanding of the multiple influences on racial self-understanding and self-identification. The event of racial self-designation resulted in increased numbers of studies on the intricacies of identity work among mixed-race youth. A tremendous number of these studies focus on Black-White mixed-race youth, which is interesting given that there are fewer Black-White interracial marriages and bonds than other minority race-White liaisons. Such a focus might speak to the tremendous impact Blacks and Whites crossing the color line to marry or form other liaisons has made on society. Still, the need to understand more about the experiences of mixed-race youth from a variety of heritage backgrounds, to include those from minority-minority racial heritages, suggests a need for expanded research.

Further, most studies tend to be monoracial-centric. As such, there is a great deal of discussion on how mixed-race youth are influenced by their monoracial peers—but not as much on how mixed-race youth impact and influence monoracial peers and the environments in which they interact, as mixed-race youth seek to understand race and their racialized selves. As a result, mixed-race youth, particularly those claiming something other than a single minority racial identity, too often appear to be in subordinate positions, with little agency in their social interactions.

Although a later chapter is devoted to peer interactions, it is important to mention here the need for additional research that places mixed-raced youth at the center of social interactions. This suggestion is made not to promote the reification of race as something more than a social construct. Rather, it emanates from the critical race tenet that race and racial differences are deeply embedded in society and in social institutions like schools. As such, knowledge of the social interactions among youth from different racial/ethnic backgrounds and from multiple perspectives can only provide educators with important information to support their creation of safe and supportive learning environments for all children and youth.

Note

1. From *What are you?: Voices of mixed-race young people* © 1999 by Pearl Fuyo Gaskins. Reprinted by permission of Henry Holt Books for Young Readers. All rights reserved.

References

Advocates for Youth. (n.d.). *The impact of homophobia and racism on GLBTQ youth of color.* From http://www.lgbt.ucla.edu/documents/ImpactofHomophobiaandRacism_000.pdf.

Bettez, S.C. (2012). *But don't call me White: Mixed race women exposing nuances of privilege and oppression politics.* Boston: Sense Publishers.

Bing, V. (2004). Out of the closet but still in hiding. *Women & Therapy,* 27(1–2), 185–201. doi:10.1300/J015v27n01_13.

Binning, K., Unzueta, M., Huo, Y., & Molina, L. (2009). The interpretation of multiracial status and its relation to social engagement and psychological well-being. *Journal of Social Issues,* 65(1), 35–49.

Bratter, J. & Heard, H. (2009). Mother's, father's, or both? Parental gender and parent-child interactions in the racial classification of adolescents. *Sociological Forum,* 24(3), 658–688. doi:10.1111/j.1573–7861.2009.01124.x.

Bronfenbrenner, U. (1994). *Ecological models of human development.* From http://www.psy. cmu.edu/~siegler/35bronfebrenner94.pdf.

Cross, W. (1971). The Negro-to-Black conversion experience. *Black World*, 20(9), 13–27.

Cross, W. (2001). Encountering nigrescence. In J. Ponterotto, J. Casas, L. Susuki, & C. Alexander (Eds.), *Handbook of multicultural counseling* (pp. 30–44). Thousand Oaks, CA: Sage Publications.

Diaz, M. (1999). Race doesn't exist. In P. Gaskins (Ed.), *What are you?: Voices of mixed-race young people* (pp. 53–58). New York: Henry Holt and Company.

Eggen, P. & Kauchak, D. (2013). *Educational psychology: Windows on classrooms.* Boston: Pearson.

Erickson, E. (1963). *Childhood and society* (2nd ed.). New York: W.W. Norton.

Field, L. (1996). Piecing together the puzzle: Self-concept and group identity in biracial Black/White youth. In M. Root (Ed.), *The multiracial experience: Racial borders as the new frontier* (pp. 211–226). Thousand Oaks, CA: Sage Publications.

Giamo, L., Schmitt, M., & Outten, H. (2012). Perceived discrimination, group identification, and life satisfaction among multiracial people: A test of the rejection-identification model. *Cultural Diversity and Ethnic Minority Psychology*, 18(4), 319–328.

Grove, K. (1991). Identity development in interracial, Asian/White late adolescents: Must it be so problematic? *Journal of Youth and Adolescence*, 20(6), 617–628.

Helms, J. (1990). Introduction: Review of racial identity terminology. In J. Helms (Ed.), *Black and White racial identity: Theory, research, and practice* (pp. 3–8). Westport, CT: Praeger.

Henry, D. (2013). *What I've discovered as the mother of biracial kids.* From http://www. huffingtonpost.com/denise-henry/mothers-of-biracial-kids_b_3105615.html.

Hirschfeld, L. A. (2008). Children's developing conceptions of race. In S. M. Quintana & C. McKown (Eds.), *Handbook of race, racism, and the developing child* (pp. 37–54). Hoboken, NJ: John Wiley & Sons.

Hitlin, S., Brown, J. S., & Elder, G. H., Jr. (2006). Racial self-categorization in adolescence: Multiracial development and social pathways. *Child Development*, 77(5), 1298–1308.

Jones, N. & Bullock, J. (2013). Understanding who reported multiple races in the U.S. decennial census: Results from census 2000 and the 2010 census. *Family Relations*, 62(1), 5–16. doi:10.1111/j.1741–3729.2012.00759.x.

Kerwin, C. & Ponterotto, J. (1995). Biracial identity development: Theory and research. In J. Ponterotto, J. Casas, L. Suzuki, & C. Alexander (Eds.), *Handbook of multicultural counseling* (pp. 199–217). Thousand Oaks, CA: Sage.

Khanna, N. (2004). The role of reflected appraisals in racial identity: The case of multiracial Asians. *Social Psychology Quarterly*, 67(2), 115–131.

Khanna, N. (2010). "If you're half Black, you're just Black": Reflected appraisals and the persistence of the one-drop rule. *The Sociological Quarterly*, 51(1), 96–121.

Khanna, N. (2011). *Biracial in America: Forming and performing racial identity.* Lanham, MD: Lexington Books.

Khanna, N. & Johnson, C. (2010). Passing as Black: Racial identity work among biracial Americans. *Social Psychology Quarterly*, 73(4), 380–397.

Kwan, K. & Liem, K. (2001). Counseling applications of racial and ethnic identity models: An introduction to the special issues. *Journal of Mental Health Counseling*, 23(3), 185–192.

Marcia, J. (1980). Identity in adolescence. In J. Adelson (Ed.), *Handbook of adolescent identity* (pp. 159–187). New York: Wiley.

McDermott, M. & Samson, F. (2005). White racial and ethnic identity in the United States. *Annual Review of Sociology*, 31(1), 245–261. doi:10.1146/annurev.soc.31.041304.122322.

Ormrod, J. (2014). *Educational psychology: Developing learners* (8th ed.). Boston: Pearson.

Phillips, L. (2004). Fitting in and feeling good. *Women & Therapy*, 27(1–2), 217–236. doi:10.1300/J015v27n01_15.

Phinney, J. (1996). Understanding ethnic diversity: The role of ethnic identity. *American Behavioral Scientist*, 40(2), 143–153.

Poston, W. (1990). The Biracial Identity Development Model: A needed addition. *Journal of Counseling & Development*, 69(2), 152–155.

Renn, K. (2004). *Mixed race students in college: The ecology of race, identity, and community on campus*. Albany, NY: State University of New York Press.

Rockquemore, K. A. & Brunsma, D. (2004). Negotiating racial identity: Biracial women and interactional validation. *Women & Therapy*, 27(1–2), 85–102. doi:10.1300/J015v27no1–06.

Rockquemore, K. A., Brunsma, D., & Delgado, D. (2009). Racing to theory or retheorizing race?: Understanding the struggle to build a multiracial identity theory. *Journal of Social Issues*, 65(1), 13–64.

Rockquemore, K. A., Laszloffy, T., & Noveske, J. (2006). It all starts at home: Racial socialization in multiracial families. In D. Brunsma (Ed.), *Mixed messages: Multiracial identities in the "color-blind" era* (pp. 203–216). Boulder, CO: Lynne Rienner Publishers, Inc.

Rogers, L., Zosuls, K., Halim, M., Ruble, D., Hughes, D., & Fuligni, A. (2012). Meaning making in middle childhood: An exploration of the meaning of ethnic identity. *Cultural Diversity and Ethnic Minority Psychology*, 18(2), 99–108.

Root, M.P.P. (1998). Experiences and processes affecting racial identity development: Preliminary results from the biracial sibling project. *Cultural Diversity and Mental Health*, 4(3), 237–247.

Root, M.P.P. (2003a). Racial identity and development and persons of mixed race heritage. In M.P.P. Root & M. Kelley (Eds.), *Multiracial child resource book: Living complex identities* (pp. 34–41). Seattle: Mavin Foundation.

Root, M.P.P. (2003b). Multiracial families and children: Implications for educational research and practice. In J. A. Banks & C. A. McGee Banks (Eds.), *Handbook of research on multicultural education* (2nd ed., pp. 110–124). San Francisco: Jossey-Bass.

Rosario, M., Schrimshaw, E., & Hunter, J. (2004). Ethnic/racial differences in the coming-out process of lesbian, gay, and bisexual youths: A comparison of sexual identity development over time. *Cultural Diversity & Ethnic Minority Psychology*, 10(3), 215–228.

Smith, S. (2012). *"What Are You?": Racial ambiguity and the social construction of race in the US.* Denton, TX: UNT Digital Library. From http://digital.library.unt.edu/ark:/67531/metadc115163/.

Storrs, D. (1999). Whiteness as stigma: Essentialist identity work by mixed-race women. *Symbolic Interaction*, 22(3), 187–212.

Terry, R. & Winston, C. (2010). Personality characteristic adaptations: Multiracial adolescents' patterns of racial self-identification change. *Journal of Research on Adolescence*, 20(2), 432–455.

Thornton, M. & Wason, S. (1995). Intermarriage. In D. Levinson (Ed.), *Encyclopedia of marriage and the family* (pp. 396–402). New York: Macmillan Publishing.

Van Ausdale, D. & Feagin, J.R. (2001). *The first R: How children learn race and racism*. Lanham, MD: Rowman & Littlefield.

Wardle, F. (2007). Multiracial children in child development textbooks. *Early Childhood Educational Journal*, 35(3), 253–259. doi:10.1007/s10643-007-0157-8.

Woolfolk, A. (2013). *Educational psychology* (12th ed.). Boston, MA: Pearson.

PART II

Family, Community, and Peers

Most educators have a general understanding of the role family, community, and peers play in the social development of children and youth. The primary purpose of Part II is to place mixed-raceness at the center of this knowledge so that educators develop a clear understanding of how being mixed-race mediates interactions with people in the child's most immediate environment. Thus, rather than a broad discussion of family influences on children's growth and social development, Chapter 4 explores the family content, structure, and circumstances that are unique to interracial and multiracial families. The goal is to highlight influences and experiences that come about as a result of being raised in an interracial/multiracial home accompany mixed-race youth as they go to school.

In Chapter 5, interracial families' choices of communities in which to raise their children is the major focus. Whereas some families have limited choice when it comes to choosing a place to live, others choose communities that align with their conception of family. They prefer to live in neighborhoods that include the social and cultural resources they desire as supports for their child-rearing efforts. Social class clearly impacts living choices, which accounts to some extent for differences in capital (social, cultural, and economic) available to mixed-race youth. Central to discussions in Chapter 5 are the multiple influences interracial families have on communities and, conversely, the influences communities have on interracial families.

The final chapter of Part II, Chapter 6, addresses friendship formation and group affiliation among mixed-race youth. Although it is known that peers play an important role in the lives of young people, less attention is paid to the fact that peer groups tend to be bounded by race. This situation requires an additional set of skills in the friendship formation process for mixed-race youth, as they must learn how to situate race in their interactions with peers. The race-related issues they face and strategies they adopt to address them are the focus for this chapter.

4

STRUCTURES, PRACTICES, AND SOCIALIZATION IN INTERRACIAL AND MULTIRACIAL FAMILIES

> . . . The truth is we raise all of our children for worlds we don't, won't, and can't inhabit . . . Families will always find themselves made up of all kinds of people, overlapping all kinds of communities, straddling all kinds of lines. One way or another, by birth or by adoption, by accident or by design, as long as the color line exists, families will find themselves straddling it.
>
> —B. Rothman (2004, p. 200)

The rapid growth of interracial families was discussed in previous chapters (see Chapter 1). Many families, however, are multiracial, in that they consist of members from different racial backgrounds (e.g., White mother and father, with adopted monoracial minority children). Interracial and multiracial families are unique, given their diverse makeup and the strategies they use to ensure the well-being of their children and the family unit as whole. Like all families, they are expected to engage in practices that support the growth and development of their children. Yet they proceed with the business of being a family in a racialized society where resistance to their family form persists.

In the past, and perhaps still in some cases, the interracial family was stereotyped as dysfunctional and rife with difficulties. Further, it was speculated that children born to interracial unions would experience a life of confusion and would be unable to "fit in" with other children. It is unlikely that interracial families totally embrace the day-to-day family functioning familiar to either differently raced parent as they take care of their children. Rather, interracial couples often exhibit a family form that is a blend of understandings of family from the two partners. Still, like all families, they engage in specific tasks they believe will protect, nurture, and support their children.

This chapter begins with an overview of interracial bonds and the diverse family structures that evolve from these unions. Attention is given to stressors on interracial couples' relationships, as well as events and situations that make for strains on the family unit once children are born. A primary responsibility of all families is the socialization of children and youth. Raising children in racialized societies makes racial socialization an area of heightened importance for interracial families with mixed-race children and for multiracial families with monoracial children of color. Parents, however, approach this task differently, on the basis of their racial ideology and other personal and family characteristics. Following a brief discussion of social racialization practices of families with monoracial minority children, the chapter concludes with review of the various racial socialization practices adopted by interracial and multiracial families.

Interracial Couples

Interracial couples are diverse and include multiple relationship arrangements, as well as different racial background configurations and sexual orientations. In 2008, 14.6 percent of newlyweds married someone outside their race (see Chart 4.1). When it comes to White-nonwhite marriages, Asian Americans more frequently married a White partner, more so than members of any other minority group. Black-White liaisons were the least frequent, although there was a substantial increase in the number of Black-White marriages. When gender is considered among these unions, Black males were more apt to marry a White partner, with 22 percent of newly married males entering a Black-White interracial marriage, whereas 9 percent of African American females married White partners. In contrast, 40 percent of Asian American females married White partners, compared with 20 percent of Asian American males. There were no gender differences among Hispanic/Latino males and females in terms of marriage to White partners.

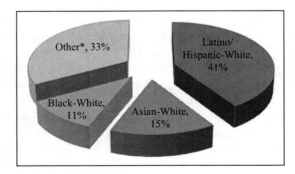

CHART 4.1 New Interracial Marriages—2008

*Other includes minority-minority, American Indian-white, or mixed/multiple races-White marriages.

From Taylor et al. (2010). *Marrying out: One-in-seven new U.S. marriages is interracial or interethnic.* Pew Research Center. http://pewsocialtrends.org/files/2010/10/755-marrying-out.pdf

Not all interracial marriages are White-nonwhite partnerships. As noted in Chart 4.1, some minorities marry members from another minority category (e.g., Latino-African American partnership) (Taylor et al., 2010). When it comes to mixed-race people, some will marry White partners. This is particularly true for mixed-race Native American-White and Asian American-White people. Higher percentages of African American mixed-race individuals marry African Americans, however (Qian & Licther, 2007).

The 2000 Census that allowed for self-identification among mixed-race individuals made documenting interracial marriages a more difficult task, because mixed-race people may identify as monoracial (person of color or White) or as more than one race. Other discernible and important factors are apparently impacting how we understand intermarriage as well. First, the increasing number of Asian and Hispanic immigrants to the United States is resulting in more native-born American and immigrant marriages. Immigration has increased the pool of potential partners for Asian Americans and Hispanics/Latinos, with the effect of a decrease in marriages between Whites and native-born Asian Americans and Whites and native-born Hispanics/Latinos. At the same time, immigrants are subject to the same racist perceptions from Whites that are directed toward native-born members of these groups. Hence, the increased pools of immigrants will not likely result in more White-immigrant liaisons (Qian & Licther, 2007).

Educational attainment (i.e., the number of years of education acquired) impacts intermarriage as well. In fact, a high level of educational attainment is a predictor for White-nonwhite intermarriage for Asian American-White and Hispanic-White marriages. Highly educated members from these groups are less impacted by increases in immigration when it comes to choosing marriage partners, because they may separate themselves both culturally and socially from immigrants who arrive with less education (Qian & Licther, 2007). Educational attainment has little impact on African American-White and Native American-White interracial marriages, however. In the case of the former, prejudice and discrimination continues to result in physical (e.g., residential) and social segregation between Whites and African Americans. As a result, highly educated African Americans are not more likely to marry a White person. Educational attainment does not influence Native American-White marriages either, as this liaison has historically been tolerated and large numbers of mixed-race Native-White individuals exist at various education completion levels.

Some different-sex interracial couples cohabit rather than marry. The number of interracial marriages will be influenced by cohabitation, which has increasingly become the choice of partnering among all young adults but is also a popular choice for interracial couples. Cohabitation may be attractive for some interracial couples because it does not require the blending of families and other social networks that usually occur with marriage (Qian & Licther, 2007).

It is important to consider that some interracial couples are same-sex adults. According to the 2010 Census, same-sex interracial couples are outpacing different-sex interracial couples. These liaisons included same-sex married couples and couples who were connected through civil unions or registered domestic partnerships, as well as partnerships that were not legally recognized. One in five same-sex couples was interracial or interethnic, a higher level of interracial partnering than either different-sex married or cohabiting couples. There were regional differences in the number of same-sex interracial/interethnic couples with the largest numbers living in Hawaii, California, and New Mexico and the lowest numbers living in Maine, Mississippi, Vermont, West Virginia, New Hampshire, and Alabama (Gates, 2012).

The Impact of Race and Gender Locations on Interracial Marriages

Race and race-gender locations in interracial marriages make for different levels of stability in and stress on these marriages, as well as varying experiences with race and racism. Here the reference is to different racial combinations of couples, as well as the racial location of partners by gender (e.g., Native American wife, White husband). Most interracial relationship stability research has focused on married couples, and even this research has been relatively limited and narrow in scope. Studies primarily examine marriages in particular regions (e.g., Hawaii) or marriages of Black-White couples (Zhang & Van Hook, 2009). As a matter of fact, the Black-White racial combination is overwhelmingly represented in interracial and mixed-race research. Even so, there is enough evidence available to suggest that gender and race configurations matter in the stability of all interracial marriages.

In their study of marriage stability among Black, Asian American, Hispanic, and White individuals who entered interracial marriages, Zhang and Van Hook found that, overall, interracial marriages tended to be less stable than marriages of people of the same race. However, separation and divorce rates differed on the basis of the racial makeup of the couple. Asian American-White interracial marriages tended to be the most stable among White-nonwhite marriages, followed by Hispanic-White interracial marriages. Black male-White female marriages tended to be the least stable, even more so than Black female-White male marriages. The researchers proposed that the racism and mistrust by society toward Black men likely results in additional marital and family stress for Black male-White female marriages.

Yancy's (2007) research corroborated these findings. The elevated race-related actions against Black males, however, led to direct experiences with racism for their White partners, which in turn led to changed racial attitudes. Although all White partners in White-nonwhite interracial marriages in Yancy's study experienced changed racial attitudes, changes made by those with nonblack partners (i.e., Asian American, Latino) tended to occur on the basis of interactions with their partners, as opposed to experiences with overt racism directed toward them or their families. An exception was White men married to Black women. Changes in racial attitudes for this partnership configuration were not precipitated by direct experiences of racism. Despite the probability that racist attitudes toward race-mixing will extend beyond couples to their offspring, many, but not all, interracial couples still decide to form families with children.

Stress on Interracial Couples

Interracial couples face a number of pressures originating from outside the relationship that impacts the stability and well-being of the union. Stress experienced by couples differs, however, depending on the racial configuration of the couple. When compared with monoracial couples, interracial couples with a Black or Native American spouse and women with a Hispanic husband appear to experience more psychological distress. Native American men and Hispanic men or women with nonwhite spouses of a different race also appear to have increased levels of stress (Bratter & Eschbach, 2006)

One source of stress for interracial couples emanates from the continued disapproval of interracial marriages among the general public (Bratter & Eschbach, 2006; Schlabach, 2013). Despite the legal right to marry and improved positive attitudes toward interracial marriages, interracial couples and their families continue to face social and legal disadvantages. According to Dalmage (2006), interracial unions cross historical "racial borders" that are ". . . contested, patrolled, and often hostile spaces near the color line." Further, racial borders have been maintained through "laws, language, cultural norms, and images," among other cultural elements (p. 306). Once racial borders became institutionalized and internalized, they provided the parameters through which people came to understand their worlds. Border incursion threatens goods and power, and for this reason there is a desire to patrol and preserve them (Dalmage, 2006).

A social expression of the desire to maintain racial borders is through microaggressions (i.e., intentional or unintentional verbal or nonverbal slights, snubs, or insults directed toward people of marginalized groups that communicate negative, hostile, or derogatory messages). The particular configuration of the interracial couple matters in terms of negative attitudes and actions directed toward their interracial status. For example, a Latino husband and White wife may be exposed to different types of microaggressions than, say, an Asian American wife and White husband. Gender and racial stereotypes account for these differences (Onwuachi-Willig & Willig-Onwuachi, 2009).

Public reactions to Black-White marriages range from microaggressions (e.g., stares of contempt) to discrimination and hostility and physical violence. Extant superiority claims over Black people could be at the root of White hostility toward Black-White interracial couples (Kenney & Kenney, 2012). However, people of color also express disapproval of interracial marriages. Black men, for example, may have their continued membership in the Black community challenged and may be perceived as disloyal to Black people for marrying out (Byrd & Garwick, 2006). Although Latino men and women are equally likely to marry out, Latino men may view a Latina's decisions to date outside the race as disruptive to traditional social arrangements of the Latino community (i.e., an arrangement with men in dominant positions). From a race-based perspective, however, Latino men are more likely to have less favorable views of Latina-Black couples than Latina-White couples. This reaction may reflect the high opinions Latinos have of Whites in general. They may see themselves as more like White people, or they may aspire to be more like White people (Garcia, Riggio, Pala-vinelu, & Culpepper, 2012).

Legally, it may be difficult for interracial couples to take advantage of certain statutes, such as those applicable to fair housing. Given that these laws do not explicitly delineate interracial couple as a protected category, it would not be unthinkable that a couple would have to split the family/couple into individuals in order to improve their claim of discrimination. In this way, a Black husband/father would have a better claim of discrimination, even when it is clear that the discriminatory act was directed at the interracial couple and not separate individuals (Onwuachi-Willig & Willig-Onwuachi, 2009).

Discriminatory practices in housing such as racially restrictive covenants are not illegal and continue to be a part of property deeds even though the practice is discouraged. An inability to legally restrain property owners from engaging in this practice places racial minorities and interracial couples in situations where property owners may choose to prevent them from purchasing or leasing available property. Dalmage (2006) recalls the experience when she and her Black husband viewed a home they considered purchasing in a neighborhood where racially restrictive covenants were known to exist. Upon initially viewing a home, the realtor told them that the house was as good as sold because she was expecting an offer on that day. Dalmage viewed the house a second time two months later (because it was still on the market), accompanied by her White realtor. The listing realtor had a completely different attitude, a difference Dalmage attributed to the fact that she was with a White man, rather than her Black husband.

Extended Family as a Source of Stress

Some interracial couples experience distress from extended family behaviors and attitudes. In some cases, a couple's parents may be disappointed or ambivalent about interracial marriages, and they may out-and-out reject the partner their son or daughter has chosen to marry and the family-with-children the couple later establishes. Blacks and Whites differ in terms of their attitudes toward interracial marriage, however. Whites generally approve of interracial marriage but not for their family members, whereas Blacks more generally disapprove of interracial marriages but are more tolerant when it comes to their family members who marry out (Rockquemore & Henderson, 2009).

In their study of Black-White interracial couples, Byrd and Garwick (2006) reported that Black mothers tended to criticize their sons marrying out, and White fathers objected to an interracial marriage for their daughters. Black mothers were disappointed that their sons were not marrying a Black woman, primarily for racial cohesion reasons. White fathers tended to be concerned about how the marriage and any children born to the union would be received. On this latter point, many White fathers came to accept the union and the family unit once the first child was born.

The lack of acceptance and support from the extended family could lead to a type of isolation that denies the interracial couple needed family support (Byrd & Garrick, 2006). When faced with this type of rejection, some couples are driven closer together and learn to rely on each other for support. Alternately, the tension and conflict that results from estrangement of an extended family negatively impacts the interracial couple's relationship and has them focus on racial differences rather than ways to integrate different racial perspectives into the family they will build. Either way, the relationship with the extended family likely influences the family identity and the family structures for the family unit.

Diverse Structures of Interracial and Multiracial Families

Interracial and multiracial families exist among the diversity of family arrangements, similar to monoracial families. These include families headed by two heterosexual adults (married or cohabitating), two same-sex adults, and families headed by a single adult, gay or straight. Interracial and multiracial families also include two adults (different-sex or same-sex) with nonbiological children (through adoption, for example) who may be mixed-race or monoracial children of color. In the latter case, children will not share a racial background with either parent (e.g., White parents adopt monoracial Asian American child). Lastly, an increased number of grandparents raise their grandchildren (Winn Tutwiler, 2005), and it is reasonable to assume that some of these grandchildren are mixed-race.

Two-Parent Interracial Families

In most cases, heterosexual parents in two-parent interracial families entered relationships with differences in terms of racial identity, affiliation groups, and experiences with race (Rockquemore, Laszloffy, & Noveske, 2006). On the basis of their backgrounds, individuals in an interracial union may have different beliefs about parenting and may lean toward family practices and customs on the basis of their upbringing (Lorenzo-Blanco, Bares, & Delva, 2013;

Winn Tutwiler, 2005). Differences exist among monoracial White and various monoracial minority families when it comes to caring for children. The extent to which couples are able to resolve these points of departure and structure a supportive and cohesive unit determines the health of the union and the well-being of children born to the union.

Children living in same-sex couple households may be adopted, a result of a prior different-sex relationship, or from artificial insemination or other reproductive technologies (Gates, 2012; Winn Tutwiler, 2005). Although the percent of same-sex couples with children declined since 2006, the decrease was likely influenced by fewer LGBT people entering a same-sex relationship with children from a prior different-sex relationship. As the stigma of being gay diminishes, fewer LGBT people feel they need to couple and have children with a different-sex individual in order to hide their sexual orientation. Hence, fewer LGBT people enter same-sex relationships with children.

Single-Parent Households

Single parents also head interracial or multiracial families, although this family structure has received little attention in the interracial/multiracial family literature (Harris, 2013; Harris, Henrikson, & Onwuegbuzie, 2013). We do know, however, that a single-parent interracial family takes the form of a mother or a father raising mixed-race children alone. The number of households headed by a single mother or father has steadily increased since 1970. A single adult raising children may be divorced from the children's mother or father, never married, widowed, or the children's grandparent and may be a straight or LGBT person. Single parents may also head a household where the parent and the child are not biologically related and do not share a racial/ethnic background (e.g., multiracial household with a White mother raising monoracial Latino/Hispanic child).

Single parents raising mixed-race children share some characteristics with single parents raising monoracial children. For example, there are more female than male heads of single-parent households, and these households live in poverty more often than their two-parent household counterparts. Further, interracial families headed by a single parent will find more acceptance by minority groups than monoracial White groups. On the basis of their review of literature related to mixed-race children in single family households, Bratter and Damaske (2013) concluded that mixed-race children of single White women whose fathers are men of color live in family situations that parallel those of monoracial Black children. Even though children in interracial single-parent households face the same stereotypes as children from monoracial single-parent households (e.g., their home is "broken," or their home life results in poor school performance), they also encounter stereotypes associated with being mixed-race. For example, they may be marginalized from a racial group with which they feel some affiliation, or they may be raced as a person of color regardless of their racial self-identity (Harris, 2013).

Gender is an additional factor that influences how interracial/multiracial single-parent families go about their everyday lives. Generally, men raising children alone, especially those who parent alone as a result of divorce, experience more community support and fewer stigmas than a woman in a similar situation. Race intersects with gender to impact the experience of single parenting in interracial/multiracial families, influenced in part by the social status of different racial groups. As an example, a White male single parent raising mixed-race White-Asian children will be viewed more favorably than a White female parent raising mixed-race Black-White children (Harris, 2013).

Interracial/Multiracial Adoptive Families

A final family configuration is the adoptive family. As mentioned earlier, parent(s) and children in adoptive interracial/multiracial families are not biologically related (the exception is a family with same-sex parents, where one parent is biologically related to children in the family, and the other parent legally adopts the children). These adoptive families often have a structure where the parents' race differs from that of monoracial children or monoracial parents adopt mixed-race children. It is also conceivable that an interracial couple could adopt a mixed-race child with the same racial heritages as the parents. Transracial adoptions, that is, adoptions that cross racial boundaries (Samuels, 2010) may be either domestic or international.

Disagreement persists about whether White families should adopt monoracial minority or White-nonwhite mixed-race children. The point of contention is whether a timely adoption (which is more likely when the adopting parents are White because there are limited numbers of adoptive parents of color) or children's cultural needs (i.e., opportunities for children to develop a healthy sense of self and skills to cope with racism in a racist society) are more important (Samuels, 2009; Winn Tutwiler, 2005). Suffice it to say, parents who adopt across racial lines may confront issues related to racial socialization and support for racial identity development for their child(ren). This family responsibility is addressed in the later racial socialization section of this chapter.

Extant racial hierarchy and colorism are evident in transracial adoptions, as some White potential adoptive parents will not adopt U.S.-born Black children. When they are unable to adopt White children, they prefer to adopt mixed-race children. Further, some White potential adoptive parents are not interested in mixed-race children who would be assumed to be Black by observers. White parents cite as a reason for their choice an inability to adequately address the Black child's eventual identity needs, believing that they would not have sufficient resources (e.g., social networks) to support the child's identity development

(Sweeney, 2013). To this degree, they align with others who believe the cultural needs of children of color should outweigh the availability of an adoptive home.

Some potential adoptive parents may use "coded concerns" (e.g., not knowing how to care for a Black child's hair) as rationales for overlooking a Black child in the adoptive process. Still, White families willingly adopt some mixed-race children because they believe they will be better able to integrate the child into their family and community, because in their view, the child will not be perceived as Black. The resistance to adopting a Black child does not transfer to all children of color, as some families will accept a Hispanic or Asian child but not a Black child, for example. In fact, some parents are willing to adopt a Black child from another country, but not an U.S.-born Black child. When this occurs, the child's unique nationality becomes the highlight—one that distinguishes the child from African American children (Sweeney, 2013).

Family Dynamics and Relationships in Interracial Families

The well-being of children is associated with a number of family factors, including the practices and processes families adopt as part of their everyday life and child-parent relationships (Lorenzo-Blanco et al., 2013; Schlabach, 2013). Family practices involve family approaches to parenting, communications processes, and family routines, for example. They comprise actions taken by parents they believe are in the best interests of their mixed-raced children. Child-parent relationships focus on both the ways parents relate to and interact with their children and the response children have to these efforts. In the best of circumstances, the nature of established practices and relationships informs the family's identity. Families with internal diversity establish a family brand of sorts that shapes how the family constructs a supportive and cohesive space for children to live and grow in the face of a society that continues to struggle with racial boundaries. Clearly, not all families are able to accomplish this ideal. Although internal family dynamics may interfere with development of a family environment conducive to children's healthy growth and development, people and situations outside the home also interfere with families' efforts on behalf of their mixed-race children and youth.

Family Practices

Racial differences between parents do not necessarily always act as barriers to family practices that lead to positive family functions. In fact, evidence suggests that race may not be the central operating factor that reflects how interracial families function. Rather, understanding how race interacts with other parental identity categories (e.g., worldview, religion, political affiliation) is pivotal to understanding how different interracial families (based on different racial configurations) perceive themselves as a family unit and how they go about daily life. In cases where race differences interfere with family functioning, it is likely that adults in the family need to reconceptualize family interactions and relationships so that a shared family identity emerges—one that goes beyond family differences (Soliz, Thorson, & Rittenour, 2009).

Parenting

Approaches to parenting in all families normally reflect the social and cultural backgrounds of the parents and may well incorporate parenting practices modeled to them when they were children (Winn Tutwiler, 2005). Parents in interracial families potentially bring differing parenting strategies to the family, some of which have cultural influences. For example, parents of color in interracial families, particularly those with African American or Hispanic/Latino racial/ethnic backgrounds, may be familiar with strategies their parents used to protect them from the racism and prejudice children of color often encounter. These strategies may have more controlling elements and potentially conflict with the independence often valued in monoracial White families.

Parents in interracial families likely resolve potential conflicts in parenting strategies by negotiating parenting approaches that do not totally reflect the previous parenting knowledge and values of either partner. Rather, a parenting approach emerges that is a blend of the two experiences and works for the family given the parents' personalities and the context (e.g., neighborhood, family identity) in which they parent (Lorenzo-Blanco et al., 2013).

Family Identity and Race Identification of Children

Family identity exists when family members feel they are a cohesive group, and belonging to this group is a source of pride. Establishing a family identity is enhanced by family self-disclosure (the ability to express one's feelings and when personal feelings of others are received) and supportive communication (the ability to turn to others for support and advice). On the other hand, identity accommodation (i.e., the extent to which differently raced family members communicate recognition, appreciation, and affirmation of each other's racial heritage) does not appear to be predictive of a shared family identity (Soliz et al., 2009).

In addition to a family identity, children have identities, which are communicated to publics outside the home, initially by parents. For example, parents designate identities for their children on institutional forms, such as those required by schools. The act of racially identifying children is a statement by parents of who their children are racially, as well as the race they wish for their children to embrace (Holloway, Wright, & Ellis, 2012). Parents may designate their children as monoracial minority, multiracial/biracial, or White.

Based on his analysis of parental identification patterns of parents of mixed-race 4- to 6-year-olds, Brunsma (2005) concluded there are a number of factors that influence parents' decisions regarding racial identification of their children.

These include the race and gender location of the parents (especially the father), socioeconomic status of the family, the racial makeup of the school the child attends, and even the region of the country where the family lives. Overall, the multiple ways these factors could intersect make for highly diverse possibilities in terms of how parents designated the race of their mixed-race children.

Generally, White-nonwhite interracial couples followed the one-drop rule and designated their children as a minority race. However, Brunsma (2005) pointed out that some parents were less inclined to designate monoracial identification for their mixed-race children, White or minority, preferring instead to take a more neutral stance such as multiracial. There was evidence that the parents of minority-minority mixed-race children (e.g., Black-Hispanic) were similarly moving in this direction. Prior to the 2000 Census, parents selected "some other race" as means for circumventing a monoracial race designation for their mixed-race children (Holloway, Wright, Ellis, & East, 2009).

With respect to socioeconomic status, higher income parents with Hispanic-White and Asian-White mixed-race children were more likely to designate their children as multiracial or White. Socioeconomic status did not factor into race designation decisions for parents of Black-White mixed-race children, however. The racial makeup of the school mixed-race children attended also seemed to have a slight impact on parents' race designation decisions. The higher the minority population of the school, the more likely parents were to choose a nonwhite identification for their children, such as a multiracial or a minority identification. Regional differences were evident in parents' race designation decisions for their mixed-race children as well. Parents of Hispanic-White children in southern regions of the United States were more likely to list a White identification for their children, whereas parents of Black-White children in the same region selected a Black racial designation. Parents of mixed-race Black-White children who lived in the northeast or western United States frequently chose a White race designation for their children, whereas parents of Asian-White mixed-race children who lived in western states selected a multiracial identification.

Lastly, gender may also play a role in how some families identify their mixed-race children, with the father's race influencing designation decisions. In cases of a Hispanic father, children were designated as Hispanic. If the father was White, then the children were designated as White. Black-White mixed-race children with a Black father tended to be designated as Black over White or multiracial. Children in Asian-White interracial families with an Asian father followed patterns similar to Black-White families, in that the child was likely to be designated Asian rather than White or multiracial.

Talking Race with Interracial/Multiracial Families

All families potentially serve as resources to schools and other agencies they partner and interact with on behalf of their children. They provide information and insight into family customs and beliefs that are invaluable to other adults who work in support of the family and children within the family (Winn Tutwiler, 2005). Given that parents in interracial families raise children in a racially polarized society, they are often acutely aware of and proactive about family issues that involve race. As a result, they are in the best position to provide information on issues that are best addressed through the unique lens interracial families possess (Kenney & Kenney, 2012). Some parents, however, may be hesitant to initiate conversations around race when working with schools and other agencies. Thus, it is important that parents sense an openness to discussions about race with other adults who interact with their children (Byrd & Garwick, 2006). Children, regardless of their racial background, are always advantaged when they perceive that their home and the schools they attend are on the same page and are working collaboratively for their well-being (Winn Tutwiler, 2005).

Family Dynamics that Compromise Children's Well-Being

A number of situations have a negative influence on the growth and development of children, regardless of the racial makeup of the family. Some of these situations play out differently in interracial families, however. Family divorce, substance abuse, death or other losses, for example, have the potential to negatively affect children's development. For children in interracial families, lack of access to parents from the different sides of the children's racial heritage potentially limits information they need as part of the racial identity development process (Root, 2003). Further, a family's stability and the availability of emotional support from parents will influence the ability of a child to handle at least some of the situations they face that are specific to their status as mixed-race children.

Microaggressions within the Family

Earlier, the impact of microaggressions on interracial couples emanating from outside of the home was discussed. Microaggressions can also appear within the family directed at mixed-race children, with extended family members most often the perpetrators. Nadal, Sriken, Davidoff, Wong, and McClean's (2013) study of microaggressions experienced by mixed-race people focused on adults as participants. Their findings are discussed here, however, because children can also be targets of microaggressions from adults (Allen, 2010; Kohli & Solorzano, 2012; Meeks, 2010). The imprints left by these experiences are lasting and consequential for mixed-race people's sense of self, as many of the experiences described by participants of the study occurred during childhood.

Nadal et al. identified five major areas of microaggressions as described by their participants: isolation, favoritism, questioning of authenticity, denial of identity and experiences, and lack of information about family heritage and culture. These areas or domains do not necessarily operate independently of each other, as experience in one domain may precipitate feelings on the part of mixed-race people in another. For example, a mixed-race child at the negative end of favoritism in the family may also feel a sense of isolation from the family member(s) who communicates in various ways that they like or love a sibling more.

Physical appearance of the mixed-race child is often at the center of several microaggression domains. Extended family members may engage in favoritism, for example, by expressing preference for a lighter skinned mixed-race family member. Favoritism brings about negative feelings for either the one being favored or the one who is less favored. Physical characteristics may also lead mixed-race family members to feel excluded when their authenticity as a family member is questioned (e.g., they may not be recognized as belonging during large family gatherings). Alternately, an extended family member may focus on physical characteristics to a fault, which leads to feelings of objectification. In other words, one's mixed-race appearance becomes the major point of interaction rather than the individual, himself or herself. Although objectification was not a major microaggression area in the Nadal et al. study, some participants experienced it.

As mentioned earlier, supportive communication is essential for family identity formation. When family members are unwilling to listen to and/or minimize the fact that a microaggression experience has taken place, the identity and experiences of the mixed–race person (child) are denied. Consequently, the mixed-race person feels misunderstood and unsupported by his or her family. In addition, sometimes families are unwilling to discuss the mixed-race child's mixed heritage. Nadal et al. stated that although this last category is not a microaggression per se, it could lead to sadness and feelings of regret as the child matures and could interfere with his or her ability to identify with one parent's racial background.

Grandparent-Grandchildren Relationships

The difficulties some extended family members have with interracial marriages or bonds affect relationships between extended family members and children born to interracial couples. The situation is especially distressing when the opposing family member is a grandparent. Extended family separation from the interracial family interferes with grandparent-grandchildren relationships and disrupts the role played by grandparents in the lives of grandchildren. Grandparents potentially offer nurturance, support, and emotional security to grandchildren and establish bonds with them that are important to identity development.

Evidence suggests that mixed-race adolescents do not experience as much grandparent closeness as do monoracial White children. They are closer, however, to grandparents than are monoracial minority adolescents (Schlabach, 2014). Still, public support and recognition of the interracial family unit by the extended family is important to the family identity formation process the inter-racial family will undergo and facilitates the ability of children in the family to integrate worldviews from both parents' racial backgrounds into that process.

Circumstances that Interfere in Interracial Families' Well-Being

There are a number of overt and subtle objectionable social situations that seek to dismiss interracial families as stable and well-functioning units. Further, Onwuachi-Willig and Willig-Onwuachi (2009) maintained that interracial families are made invisible, juxtaposed with monoracial families when they are not represented in the media and when children in interracial families do not see reflections of their family configuration in textbooks they read in school. With respect to the media, a case in point is the reaction to a recent Cheerios commercial featuring an interracial family.

In an effort to celebrate all types of families, General Mills chose an interracial family (i.e., Black father, White mother, and mixed-race daughter) to communicate the health benefits of the cereal from a child's perspective. The commercial generated a number of online racist and insulting comments, even though a majority of the observers "liked" the ad. Still, it was surprising to the company that the participants in the ad were such an "issue" (Stuart, 2013). Wortham (2013), relieved that reactions to the commercial were more positive when it aired during the 2014 Super Bowl football game, wondered why presentation of the everyday lives of interracial families were not featured more frequently in the media, when multiple examples existed as possibilities.

It is also common for interracial families to directly experience insults in public that undermine their status as a family unit. These may include assumptions by others in public places that the parents are not together and/or not a couple, or that the children and parents are not part of a family unit when either parent appears alone with the children in public. Unfortunately, these situations become indelible childhood memories, as children often witnesses insolent adult behavior. Nissel (2006) recalls:

> . . . Our family vacation photo album actually has a section called Star-ing White Women . . . I remember a few black women coming right out asking if my father was white. The white women never did that; they said nothing with their lips; their eyes would say it all: *How in the world did that happen?*
>
> (p. 45)

Nissel, of course, is an adult now; however, rude race-based reactions to the racial background of mixed-race children persist. Callahan (2013), for example, recounted situations where she had been confronted with comments about her children's physical characteristics (i.e., how White or Korean they looked) and asked whether she anticipated the children's physical characteristics would change over time. Thoughtless actions, both those grounded in impudence and those meant to protest the right of interracial families to exist, are sources of irritation for interracial couples. Yet many find ways to socialize their children (see racial socialization in this chapter) in ways that protect them from the potentially harmful effects of these intrusions.

Child-Parent Relationships

Despite their desire to develop close relationships with their children, most parents experience periods of strained child-parent bonds, especially as children reach adolescence. In many ways, relationships between mixed-race youth and their parents do not differ from those of monoracial youth and their parents (Radina & Cooney, 2000). Still, racial diversity in interracial and multiracial families makes for an additional element to child-parent relationships that are not experienced by relationships in monoracial families. Parent-initiated discussions about race are often the first time mixed-race children hear about tensions around race differences. They also learn that some people may have difficulty with the fact that their family is interracial or multiracial. Although race discussions with children may be difficult for some parents, talking about race appears to have a positive influence on mixed-race children's sense of identity (Sechrest-Ehrhardt, 2012).

Some parents may not understand the importance of race discussions for the child's sense of emotional and social well-being. Minority-minority mixed-race youth, for example, rarely have discussions about being mixed-race with their parents. Parents in minority-minority interracial families may prepare their children for discrimination and rejection from Whites. However, they do not consider the fact that their children may also experience rejection from monoracial minorities, even though parent and children alike consider the children to be minorities as well (Talbot, 2008). Hence minority-minority mixed-race children are left without support and strategies for addressing these situations.

Parents' understanding of the role race plays in their children's peer interactions influences child-parent relationship in ways not apparent in many monoracial families. For example, parents in interracial families may be more protective of girls in the family and may feel the need to shelter them from discrimination and prejudice from outsiders. As discussed elsewhere in the text, some mixed-race girls are more likely to have negative peer interactions with monoracial girls than mixed-race boys have with either other boys or girls. Consequently, mixed-race girls often have more contact with both their mothers and fathers than do their monoracial counterparts. This is not the case for mixed-race boys, who are less a target for race-based hazing from peers (Radina & Cooney, 2000).

Mixed-race boys, however, may be more emotionally vulnerable than their monoracial peers and may wish to connect with their fathers on an emotional level. Some fathers are not comfortable interacting with their sons in this way. When this is the case, the relationship between the mixed-race boy and his father can be strained. Boys in these circumstances develop closer relationships with their mothers, partly because mothers have a tendency to be more relationship focused—this in addition to mothers' desires to minimize their children's anxiety. An additional father-son interaction is important to note between mixed-race boys and their White fathers. Mixed-race boys may feel they will not be able to match their father's academic and career accomplishments. In their estimation, their fathers did not face the race-based barriers to education that boys of color (as some may be perceived and as they may perceive themselves) experience. This circumstance also results in emotional distance between father and son (Radina & Cooney, 2000).

In some families, the mother-child relationships may be more strained than father-child relationships. Mothers continue to play a central role in parenting children. They spend more time with and more time taking care of children (Stephens, 2009). Further, mothers provide a majority of the socialization for their children (Rockquemore et al., 2006; Root, 2003). White mothers of mixed-race children may not encounter the deleterious impact of race and racism until their children experience racially tinged situations. When mothers—and fathers, actually—lack the experience of dealing with race-based issues experienced by their mixed-race children, the children may feel unsupported. Children may direct more of these feeling toward mothers, given the role played by mothers in the family (Lorenzo-Blanco et al., 2013; Schlabach, 2013).

A perception of lack of support is potentially at issue for all mixed-race youth, regardless of their gender and racial makeup. In most cases, mixed-race children grow up in families where they will not have a mixed-race parent. In families where both parents are monoracial, neither has experienced growing up mixed-race. Hence, they may not completely understand how their mixed-race children experience being more than one race (Rockquemore et al., 2006) and, in fact, children may sense this shortcoming in their parents. Sometimes, parents feel uncertain when addressing issues faced by mixed-race children. In these instances, parent education programs offered by schools and other agencies could be of great support, particularly if they are able to address this parenting challenge (Lorenzo-Blanco et al., 2013).

In other instances, the parent may not need to be mixed-race in order to provide their children with needed support. They may be able to rely on their cultural background and experiences, along with authentic communication, to relate to issues their mixed-race children face. The following parent-child interaction between a mixed-race son and his monoracial father is an example. The son lived on the Quinault Indian Reservation with his family. He wrote:

> . . . I may be part Mexican, and part white and part Indian, but in my heart I am just Indian. I'm probably the lightest person in my family . . . I

felt ashamed that I didn't look more like how I felt inside . . . It was a hard thing to deal with . . .

(Ogemageshig, 1999, pp. 41–43)[1]

Ogemageshig recounted the importance of his relationship with his father, who communicated to his son that being mixed race was "a gift . . . a strength" that would lead to "power" to "walk in two worlds" (Ogemageshig, 1999, p. 43). At age 17, the essence of his father's teachings became clearer. Without necessarily naming the experience, the father in this situation presented to his son the circumstance of border crossing, a capability viewed as a positive outcome of being mixed-race. Given the experience of having parents from different racial backgrounds, mixed-race people are better able to traverse borders that often separate people from different racial and cultural backgrounds (Root, 1996). Sometimes they will need the support of parents to feel invited to do so, however.

Racial Socialization

Socialization is the process by which young people learn the norms, values, attitudes, and customs of a given culture, along with appropriate behaviors required to participate in that culture. Racial socialization is a different matter, however. Rollins and Hunter (2013) identified dimensions of racial socialization that included teaching and learning around social position associated with race, providing information about racial cultural heritage, and allowing for individual development juxtaposed to racial group membership and solidarity.

For parents of color, racial socialization also involves processes and practices used that teach children how to navigate life in a racialized society. The primary goal is to protect youth of color by teaching them how to negotiate life in a society where children of color are not always valued. It also promotes ethnic–racial identity formation and enhances positive social-emotional and cognitive outcomes (Csizmadia, Rollins, & Kaneakua, 2014). It would be a mistake, however, to assume that monoracial White children are not racially socialized. To the contrary, all parents, whether directly or indirectly, teach their children about race, racial differences, and who they are racially. The messages between monoracial White and monoracial parents of color may be different, but racial socialization is taking place nonetheless (Rockquemore et al., 2006).

According to Rockquemore et al. (2006), racial socialization in interracial families is complicated by circumstances specific to particular family configurations. Further, most interracial families lack a model with which the child might identify, because most interracial families do not include a mixed-race parent. Indeed, parents may feel they too lack models to emulate and may perceive there is no clear community of mixed-race people from which they can garner information to guide them in the racial socialization process.

Even so, Rockquemore & Laszloffy (2005) concluded that racial socialization is not optional for parents of mixed-race children. It is a parental responsibility that must be pursued in order to ensure that mixed-race children too will understand and be able to effectively navigate life within contexts permeated by the intricacies of race. Mixed-race children who experience racial socialization in the home ". . . develop a stronger sense of self-esteem, have higher rates of academic achievement, and lower rates of disciplinary problems, and appear to be more psychologically well adjusted . . . (p. 60).

Types of Racial Socialization

Rockquemore et al. (2006) identified three types of racial socialization that parents may embrace as they racially socialize their children: preparation for bias, cultural socialization, and racial group membership. Parents' racial ideology, however, influences their approach to racial socialization, regardless of the type racial socialization they confront. Some parents take a color-blind approach to racial socialization, where they minimize the impact of race and racism on the lives of their mixed-race children. Other parents are guided by a racial ideology that challenges the racial status quo and are more apt to adopt a proactive stance against racism in strategies used for racial socialization of the their children (Rockquemore et al., 2006).

Racial Bias

The approach parents of mixed-race children take to teach about racial bias influences the child's ability to respond to discrimination they may encounter. Parents of color tend to believe that it is important for children to understand that racism exists and that discrimination and bias are the likely outcomes of racism. Consequently, children of color are taught how to recognize and respond to bias based on race. Parents who adopt a color-blind approach tend to believe it is best to address discrimination only after the child experiences it. Whether they intentionally take a color-blind approach, Rollins and Hunter (2013) suggested that mothers whose mixed-race children are not part Black tend to underestimate the role discrimination will play in their children's experiences.

Other parents take a more preemptive approach and teach their children about discrimination as an event they will likely face, whether the child has yet to experience bias. They intend to equip their children with skills to identify that bias has taken place and strategies of how best to deal with instances of discrimination. The reticence on the part of parents taking a color-blind approach to address race-based bias leaves children, especially adolescents, feeling defenseless when they actually experience bias (Rockquemore & Laszloffy, 2005).

Cultural Socialization

The goal of cultural socialization is to promote a positive disposition toward a group's cultural history and heritage in order to mitigate negative perspectives society might hold against the group (Rockquemore & Laszloffy, 2005). Elsewhere, I described this as an enculturation process, where ethnic/minority parents adopt practices to ensure their children acquire beliefs, knowledge, and behaviors that allow them to function among specific ethnic/cultural groups (Winn Tutwiler, 2005). Minority parents employ a number of strategies to accomplish this end, including exposing children to racial/ethnic group cultural events and reading materials, as well as celebrating racial group specific holidays. They may also communicate their value for the ethnic/racial group through lifestyle choices (e.g., neighborhood location, organization memberships) (Rockquemore et al., 2006).

Some parents of mixed-race children choose to downplay cultural differences. Both parents who are biologically related to their mixed-race children and White parents of adopted of mixed-race children may take a color-blind approach to cultural socialization (Samuels, 2010). They communicate to their children that they are members of the human race and, in the process, dismiss the importance of the child's minority race heritage (Rockquemore et al., 2006). These actions on the part of parents are tantamount to socializing the child as White.

Alternately, some parents of mixed-race children embrace cultural socialization practices similar to those of minority race parents. They adopt enculturation as means to ensure that their children are not marginalized from members of their minority heritage group (Rollins & Hunter, 2013). Some White parents of adopted monoracial Black children, for example, seek cultural socialization that would allow their children to identify with and connect to the Black community (Butler-Sweet, 2011; Samuels, 2010). Yet, they may not understand the complexities of Black culture enough to place their children in situations that reflect their class related values. Butler-Sweet (2011) found that middle class White adoptive parents, who embraced many of the same values as middle class Black parents, mistook *urban culture* to be *Black culture* and directed their children toward experiences in the former, rather than experiences typical of the Black middle class.

Their inclinations were accurate; however, they selected a means to an end that likely contradicted other goals they had for their children. As a matter of fact, parents of mixed-race children who adopt cultural socialization practices seeking outcomes overtly similar to those of minority parents must take care that their efforts are not compromised by the absence of meaningful and ongoing interactions with communities of color appropriate for the child's racial makeup. For example, some of the mixed-race adults in Samuels's (2010) study who were raised by two White parents stated that their parents' efforts to expose them to Black culture included race-related toys, race-related reading materials, and attendance at Black cultural events. Yet, for some, cultural events and artifacts did not enable them to develop a sense of racial kinship, as they felt the cultural symbols to which they were exposed were "disconnected from the communities and people" (p. 32) with whom they shared a racial heritage.

Obama (2004) described his mother's cultural socialization efforts, when she decided he should understand and embrace his blackness:

> . . . She would come home with books on the civil rights movement, recordings of Mahalia Jackson, the speeches of Dr. King . . . she told me stories of schoolchildren in the South who were forced to read books handed down from wealthier white schools but who went on to become doctors and lawyers and scientists . . . Every black man was Thurgood Marshall or Sidney Poitier; every black woman Fannie Lou Hamer or Lena Horne. To be black was to be the beneficiary of a great inheritance, a special destiny, glorious burdens that only we were strong enough to bear.
>
> *(pp. 50–51)*

These painstaking efforts notwithstanding, the lack of interactions with Black people and communities during his youth left Barack Obama feeling a sense of bewilderment about the meaning of being a Black person. His kinship journey to blackness was undertaken as an adult and included both a trip to Africa to connect with his father's family and a stint as a community organizer in a Black community in Chicago. Kinship journeys are common projects for mixed-race people who lacked experiences with their minority heritage communities as children. They seek these experiences as adults in order to develop a more authentic connection and sense of kinship to the heritage communities to which they wish to affiliate.

White-minority mixed-race people are not always seeking connections to their minority heritage in their kinship journeys. McBride (1996), for example, sought a sense of connection with his Jewish heritage. His mother raised him in Black communities, although she sent him to public schools outside the neighborhood that were predominantly attended by Jewish children. Her reasoning was apparently less about McBride acquiring experiences about what it meant to be Jewish, and more about him receiving an education better than the one available at neighborhood schools. Although a sense of affiliation with Black people and communities was established, it is also apparent that McBride was influenced by his mother's Jewish values and worldview. She did not, however, provide McBride experiences with the Jewish community that would facilitate a sense of kinship with his nonblack heritage. McBride initiated this connection himself, as an adult. He wrote:

> . . . I was standing in front of the only synagogue in downtown Suffolk . . . My long search for the Shilsky family ended here . . . I wanted

to see the inside of the synagogue. I wanted see it, then later tell my black wife and my two children about it—because some of my blood runs there, because my family has history there, because there is a part of me in there whether I, or those that run the synagogue, like it or not.

(pp. 219–221)

Racial Identification

A final type of racial socialization is racial identification. Racial identity theories were discussed in depth in previous chapters. Here we review parental input into racial identification as part of their racial socialization practices. Rockquemore et al. (2006) believed efforts by parents of monoracial children and those of mixed-race children differed most in this particular area of racial socialization. Monoracial Black parents endeavor to ensure that their children develop positive Black identities, regardless of any negative messages society might convey about being Black.

Parents with a color-blind approach to socialization want their children to believe that race is not important. Although they encourage their children to embrace a mixed-race identity, they emphasize whiteness and, in essence, socialize the children as White. These parents erroneously believe their children will be perceived as White, and so they treat them as such as they neglect racial socialization. They are convinced that they are shielding their children from the hardships associated with being a person of color. In reality, they are in denial regarding the role race will likely play in their children's lives (Csizmadia et al., 2014).

Parents who embrace racial socialization encourage a mixed-race identity that emphasizes blackness or may encourage a monoracial Black identity. They do so on the basis of their belief that society will view and treat their child as a Black person (Rockquemore et al., 2006). Parents who approach racial socialization in this way want their children to feel a sense a pride in being Black but also want them to be able to navigate racial boundaries (Csizmadia et al., 2014).

Parental Factors and Racial Socialization

Parents' racial ideology is but one factor that influences their racial socialization approaches and practices. Using Black-White interracial couples as examples, Rockquemore and Laszloffy (2005) identified additional personal factors that influence parents' socialization practices: the racial socialization experienced by parents when they were children, their racial experiences, and their personal sense of racial identity.

Being married or in partnership does not guarantee that an interracial couple possesses the same views on race and racism and how children should be socialized around these issues. Undoubtedly, in most cases, White parents and parents of color were exposed to different socialization practices when they were children. White families tend to raise children so that they believe race it not their issue, but rather an issue for people of color. They tend not to explicitly discuss White privilege; thus, some White parents of mixed-race children will not clearly understand the role race plays in their lives or the social inequities precipitated by race differences as experienced by people of color. It is likely that many White parents of mixed-race children will not have a model for addressing issues of race as they parent their mixed-race children (Rockquemore et al., 2006; Rockquemore & Laszloffy, 2005).

Most Black parents of mixed-race children have some understanding of race and racism and have been exposed to a possible model for socializing their children around issues of race. It should not be assumed, however, that all Black people have been socialized about race in the same way. Rockquemore and Laszloffy (2005) suggested that some monoracial Black children are socialized to accept an oppressed location for Black people, believing they should not confront this position. Others have been socialized to confront racism, either covertly or overtly, in everyday life. Still others adopt an internalized racism position, and align with whiteness. Thus, they may adopt the same negative beliefs about Black people that are held by some White people. The multiple possibilities of racial socialization experienced by parents in interracial families account for the myriad of possibilities of how they will approach socialization of their children.

The experiences of parents with different racial groups also influence their racial socialization practices. Both the frequency and quality of contact are important. It is more likely that the parent of color—in this case, the Black parent—has had more frequent interactions with his or her own heritage community and with White people than his or her White partner, who likely interacted more or exclusively with White communities. The very nature of social and economic arrangement of institutions in the United States heightens this possibility.

Alternately, it possible that some Black or other parents of color were raised in White neighborhoods and/or attended predominantly White schools and, as a result, have less-than-expected interactions with people of color. Also, some White parents could have lived in a diverse neighborhood, and/or attended very diverse schools, thus resulting in more frequent interactions with people of color. In all cases, frequency of interaction combines with the quality or nature of those interactions (e.g., positive or negative) to influence parents' decisions about the type of interactions they wish their mixed-race children to have with different racial communities (Rockquemore & Laszloffy, 2005).

Finally, parents' sense of their racial identity matters when it comes to their approach to racial socialization. Parents who understand the effects of their racial identity on their worldview and who are comfortable with their racial selves are in the best position to racially socialize their mixed-race children. Optimally, White parents have reached Helms's (1990) final stage of White identity development and thus are able to provide their mixed-race children with a healthy model of whiteness. Recall Helms's view that a nonracist racial identity rejects all forms of racism and rests on the belief that one racial group is not superior to another. White parents who have not confronted the effects of whiteness on their life risk transmitting the underlying values of whiteness to their children (Rockquemore & Laszloffy, 2005).

Like White parents, Black parents of mixed-race children may also be at different stages of racial identity development. Their thinking about race can range from internalized racism, where they reject positive aspects of Blackness, with a complete acceptance of White beliefs, values, and culture, to a sense of rage about White culture that locates all White people into a monolithic group responsible for Black oppression. A healthy Black identity is one where the individual has pride in being Black, while at the same time is able to critically evaluate White culture and whiteness for it negative impact on Black people without generalizing this understanding to all White people (Rockquemore & Laszloffy, 2005).

Other parental factors associated with the inclination of parents to engage in racial socialization and the frequency with which they do so are parental age and socioeconomic status and the geographic location of the family (Csizmadia et al., 2014). Older parents are less inclined to engage in racial socialization and/or to discuss race issues with their mixed-race children. They are likely less comfortable talking about race than their younger counterparts. Also, parents living in lower socioeconomic situations are less likely to engage in racial socialization than parents living in higher socioeconomic situations. Parents in lower socioeconomic situations have fewer resources and less time to devote to racial socialization efforts. On the other hand, parents living in higher socioeconomic situations feel more control over their lives and feel better positioned to draw on resources to support their racial socialization efforts. Further, because they are more likely to live in White neighborhoods, they are more motivated to prepare their children for race-related questions and situations they feel are probable, given their residential location.

Related to residential locations, parents living in certain geographic regions tend more toward racial socialization than parents in other regions. Parents raising mixed-race children in the south or in small towns are less likely to discuss race or racially socialize their children as mixed-race. However, parents living in the northeast or west, as well as those who live in urban areas, more frequently engage racial socialization practices. Parents who live in the west and urban areas have support from more diverse communities for their racial socialization efforts (Csizmadia et al., 2014).

There are two final parental factors to consider as parents racially socialize their mixed-race children. The importance of family dynamics on children's well-being has already been addressed. Negative family dynamics that become racialized affect children's understanding of race as it applies to their racial identity. When parents intentionally insert race into their conflicts and disagreements with each other, children are placed in a position to take sides. A parent, for example, may overtly attribute a problematic situation between the parents to the differently raced parent's race. Children may also infer messages about race not overtly communicated. They assume one parent's negative feelings about a differently raced parent came about as a result of the differently raced parent's actions or behavior that caused a difficult family situation. The parent's problematic behaviors and actions are generalized to the parent's race as a whole and not a characteristic attributable solely to the problematic parent. In either case, children may develop closer connections to the parent with whom they align and, subsequently, to that parent's race. In the process, they distance themselves from the race of the other parent (Rockquemore & Laszloffy, 2005).

Lastly, parents can insert practices based on colorism into the family environment. They do so by communicating preference for a sibling with more White-like physical characteristics that sends a message to all children in the family that one race is more valued over another. Colorism also becomes a factor in racial socialization when mothers of color are assumed to be nannies and not the mothers of their phenotypically White-looking children. As Rockquemore and Laszloffy (2005) pointed out, White mothers of mixed-race children (regardless of the children's appearance) are not assumed to be their children's nannies. Locating women of color as servants sends messages about race to children who witness these encounters. In the case of favoritism, parents must be resolutely committed to not showing race-based preferences for one child over another. They must also be prepared to explain situations of misperceptions by outsiders that disintegrate their family, as part of the racial socialization process.

Concluding Thoughts

Children and youth arrive at school from tremendously diverse home experiences. The call for parental involvement in the education of children and youth that escalated in the late 1990s into the twenty-first century focused educators' attention on family differences. They were challenged to think about multiple influences on how families function, including family structure, the race/ethnicity and socioeconomic status of the family, as well as parental educational attainment, for example. This information ostensibly supported their interactions with parents, and as well how best to work with children in their classrooms.

Although interracial and multiracial families share many characteristics with other families, the unique race/ethnicity attributes of these families and their children present an additional layer of diversity for educators to consider. It is clear from the literature that some parents in interracial/multiracial families wrestle with how best to prepare their children to negotiate their mixedness in racialized contexts. Given the amount of time children spend in schools, this particular location is likely a primary focus for their efforts.

Like all families, the amount of support needed by families from schools will vary. In the best of circumstances, a reciprocal relationship between schools and families will be established, with an agreed-upon recognition that race will often play a role in information shared by each institution (i.e., the family and the school). This is the best way for teachers to gain information about how to support interracial/multiracial parents and children given the work of the school, and for parents to assess how their racial socialization and overall support for development of their children is working in school environments.

Note

1. From *What are you?: Voices of mixed-race young people* © 1999 by Pearl Fuyo Gaskins. Reprinted by permission of Henry Holt Books for Young Readers. All rights reserved.

References

Allen, Q. (2010). Racial microaggressions: The schooling experiences of middle class males in Arizona's secondary schools. *Journal of African American Males in Education*, 1(2), 125–143.

Bratter, J. & Damaske, S. (2013). Poverty at a racial crossroads: Poverty among multiracial children of single mothers. *Journal of Marriage and Family*, 75(2), 486–502.

Bratter, J. & Eschbach, K. (2006). 'What about the couple?': Interracial marriage and psychological distress. *Social Science Research*, 35(4), 1025–1047.

Brunsma, D. (2005). Interracial families and the racial identification of mixed-race children: Evidence from the Early Childhood Longitudinal Study. *Social Forces*, 84(2), 1131–1157.

Butler-Sweet, C. (2011). "A healthy Black identity" Transracial adoption, middle class families, and racial socialization. *Journal of Comparative Family Studies*, 42(2), 193–212.

Byrd, M. & Garwick, A. (2006). Family identity: Black-White interracial family health experience. *Journal of Family Nursing*, 12(1), 22–37.

Callahan, N. (2013, August 19). 'Mixed kids are always so beautiful'. *New York Times*. From http://parenting.blogs.nytimes.com/2013/08/19/mixed-kids-are-always-so-beautiful/?_php=true&_type=blogs&_r=0.

Csizmadia, A., Rollins, A., & Kaneakua, J. (2014). Ethnic-racial socialization and its correlates in families of Black-White biracial children. *Family Relations*, 63(2), 259–270.

Dalmage, H. (2006). Finding a home: Housing the color line. In D. Brunsma (Ed.), *Mixed messages: Multiracial identities in the "color blind" era* (pp. 301–312). Boulder, CO: Lynne Rienner Publishers.

Garcia, A., Riggio, H., Palavinelu, S., & Culpepper, L. (2012). Latinos' perceptions of interethnic couples. *Hispanic Journal of Behavioral Sciences,* 34(2), 349–362.

Gates, G. (2012). *Same sex couples in the census 2010: Race and ethnicity*. From http://williamsinstitute.law.ucla.edu/wp-content/uploads/Gates-CouplesRaceEthnicity-April-2012.pdf.

Harris, H.L. (2013). Counseling single-parent multiracial families. *The Family Journal*, 21(4), 386–395.

Harris, K., Henrikson, R., & Onwuegbuzie, A. (2013). Counseling single mothers of multiple heritage children: What is the difference? *The Family Journal*, 21(4), 396–401.

Helms, J. (1990). Introduction: Review of racial identity terminology. In J. Helms (Ed.), *Black and White racial identity: Theory, research, and practice* (pp. 3–8). Westport, CT: Praeger.

Holloway, S. R., Wright, R., & Ellis, M. (2012). *Constructing multiraciality in U.S. families and neighborhoods.* From http://caligari.dartmouth.edu/~geospace/mixedmetro/Publications/constructing_multiraciality_text.pdf.

Holloway, S. R., Wright, R., Ellis, M., & East, M. (2009). Place, scale and the racial claims made for multiracial children in the 1990 US Census. *Ethnic and Racial Studies, 32*(3), 522–547.

Kenney, K. & Kenney, M. (2012). Contemporary US multiple heritage couples, individuals, and families: Issues, concerns, and counseling implications. *Counseling Psychology Quarterly, 25*(2), 99–112.

Kohli, R. & Solorzano, D. (2012). Teachers, please learn our names!: Racial microaggressions and the K-12 classroom. *Race, Ethnicity, and Education, 12*(4), 441–462.

Lorenzo-Blanco, E., Bares, C., & Delva, J. (2013). Parenting, family processes, relationships, and parental support in multiracial and multiethnic families: An exploratory study of youth perceptions. *Family Relations, 62*(1), 125–139.

McBride, J. (1996). *The color of water: A Black man's tribute to his White mother.* New York: Riverhead Books.

Meeks, M. (2010). *Racial microaggressions by secondary school teachers against students of color.* From http://digitalcommons.georgiasouthern.edu/cgi/viewcontent.cgi?article=1355&context=etd.

Nadal, K., Sriken, J., Davidoff, K., Wong, Y., & McClean, K. (2013). Microaggressions within families: Experiences of multiracial people. *Family Relations, 62*(1), 109–201.

Nissel, A. (2006). *Mixed: My life in Black and White.* New York: Villard Books.

Obama, B. (2004). *Dreams from my father: A story of race and inheritance.* New York: Three River Press.

Ogemageshig, T. G. (1999). The color of my skin is not the color in my heart. In P. Gaskins (Ed.), *What are you?: Voices of mixed-race young people* (pp. 40–44). New York: Henry Holt and Company.

Onwuachi-Willig, A. & Willig-Onwuachi, J. (2009). A house divided: The invisibility of the multiracial family. *Harvard Civil Rights-Civil Liberties Law Review, 44*(1), 231–253.

Qian, Z. & Lichter, D. (2007). Social boundaries and marital assimilation. Interpreting trends in racial and ethnic intermarriage. *American Sociological Review, 72*(1), 68–94.

Radina, M. & Cooney, T. (2000). Relationship quality between multiracial adolescents and their biological parents. *American Journal of Orthopsychiatry, 70*(4), 445–454.

Rockquemore, K. & Henderson, L. (2009). Interracial families in post-civil rights America. In B. J. Risman (Ed.), *Families as they really are* (pp. 99–111). New York: W. W. Norton and Co.

Rockquemore, K. & Laszloffy, T. (2005). *Raising biracial children.* New York: Rowman & Littlefield Publishers, Inc.

Rockquemore, K. A., Laszloffy, T., & Noveske, J. (2006). It all starts at home: Racial socialization in multiracial families. In D. Brunsma (Ed.), *Mixed messages: Multiracial identities in the "color-blind" era* (pp. 203–216). Boulder, CO: Lynne Rienner Publishers, Inc.

Rollins, A. & Hunter, A. (2013). Racial socialization of biracial youth: Maternal messages and approaches to address discrimination. *Family Relations, 62*(1), 140–153.

Root, M.P.P. (1996). *The multicultural experience: Racial borders as the new frontier.* Thousand Oaks, CA: Sage Publications.

Root, M.P.P. (2003). Multiracial families and children: Implications for educational research and practice. In J. A. Banks & C. A. McGee Banks (Eds.), *Handbook of research on multicultural education* (2nd ed., pp. 110–124). San Francisco: Jossey-Bass.

Rothman, B. (2004). Transracial adoption: Refocusing upstream. In H. Dalmage (Ed.), *The politics of multiracialism: Challenging racial thinking* (pp. 193–201). Albany, NY: State University of New York.

Samuels, G. (2009). "Being raised by White people": Navigating racial difference among adopted multiracial adults. *Journal of Marriage and Family, 71*(1), 80–94.

Samuels, G. (2010). Building kinship and community: Relational processes of bicultural identity among adult multiracial adoptees. *Family Process, 49*(1), 26–42.

Schlabach, S. (2013). The importance of family, race, and gender for multiracial adolescent well-being. *Family Relations, 62*(1), 154–174.

Schlabach, S. (2014). *Does race matter for grandparent-grandchild relationships?: Grandparent closeness in the biracial context.* From http://paa2014.princeton.edu/papers/140667.

Sechrest-Ehrhardt, L. (2012). *Understanding the racial identity development of multiracial young adults through their family, social, and environment experiences.* From SechrestEhrhardt_ cua_0043A_10339display.pdf.

Soliz, J., Thorson, A., & Rittenour, C. (2009). Communicative correlates of satisfaction, family identity, and group salience in multiracial/ethnic families. *Journal of Marriage and Family, 71*(4), 819–832.

Stephens, M. (2009). *Gender differences in parenting styles and effects on the parent child relationship.* From https://digital.library.txstate.edu/bitstream/handle/10877/3300/fulltext.pdf.

Stuart, E. (2013, June 1). 'Vitriol online for Cheerios ad with interracial family'. *New York Times*, p. B4.

Sweeney, K. (2013). Race-conscious adoption choices, multiraciality, and color-blind racial ideology. *Family Relations, 62*(1), 42–57.

Talbot, D. (2008). Exploring the experiences and self-labeling of mixed-race individuals with two minority parents. *New Directions for Student Services, 123*, 23–31.

Taylor, P., Passel, J., Wang, W., Kiley, J., Velasco, G., & Dockterman, D. (2010). *Marrying out: One-in-seven new U.S. marriages is interracial or interethnic.* Pew Research Center. http://pewsocialtrends.org/files/2010/10/755-marrying- out.pdf

Winn Tutwiler, S. (2005). *Teachers as collaborative partners: Working with diverse families and communities.* Mahwah, NJ: Lawrence Erlbaum Associates, Publishers.

Wortham, J. (2013, February 8). "Where is my family on TV?" *New York Times.* From http://www.nytimes.com/2014/02/09/opinion/sunday/where-is-my-family-on-tv. html?_r=0.

Yancy, G. (2007). Experiencing racism: Differences in the experiences of Whites married to Blacks and Non-Black racial minorities. *Journal of Comparative Family Studies, 38*(2), 197–213.

Zhang, Y. & Van Hook, J. (2009). Marital dissolution among interracial couples. *Journal of Marriage and Family, 71*(1), 95–107.

5

COMMUNITY, SOCIAL CLASS, AND SOCIOCULTURAL INTERACTIONS

Communities, like clothes, are held together at the seams . . . social seams are the places where people come together . . .

—H. Dalmage (2006, p. 301)

If you want to know how well an outfit is made, look at the seams. Metaphorically, the social seams of communities are the schools, streets, parks, and other community spaces one might call "public," because they are presumably open to everyone who lives within the community (Dalmage, 2006). When interracial families leave their homes, these are the places they expect to commune and associate with people in a climate where they and their children will not encounter race-based frictions. Given this line of thinking, experiences in the seams of communities help parents in interracial families gain clarity about the appropriateness of a neighborhood or community as a place to live, especially as their children begin to have experiences beyond the home.

Teachers have access to information about mixed-race children along one community seam: schools. However, they are advantaged in their educational efforts when they have knowledge of mixed-race youths' experiences in the broader community, because it is understood that children's experiences outside of school influence their experiences inside of school. A primary goal of this chapter is to address the different places mixed-race youth live and how the nature of those places affects multiple aspects of their lives. Conversely, interracial families influence their communities, and the impact of this phenomenon on the environment in which mixed-race children grow will be explored as well.

I take the position in this chapter that interracial families, regardless of their racial configuration, contribute to the diversity of their communities. Yet, although living spaces are increasingly diverse in terms of race and ethnicity, where families live continues to, for the most part, reflect their socioeconomic status. Socioeconomic status, the composition of youths' mixedness, and the context of the community in which they grow combine to make for different life experiences among mixed-race youth. They emerge from these circumstances with differently constituted knowledge, dispositions, and skills that contribute to differences in their interactions with their social worlds. This chapter, as has been evident in previous chapters, will explore diversity among mixed-race youth, with more emphasis on differences created by social class status.

Interracial Families' Neighborhoods and Communities

Many interracial families choose communities that support the family's goals for a decided-upon family identity, as well as the family's chosen approach for the socialization of children. It must be remembered, however, that not all families with mixed-race children have the same flexibility and level of choice when it comes to where the family resides. Any number of circumstances (e.g., affordability, proximity to work locations, availability of transportation, community resources) influence where families live. Both individual family and community characteristics factor into decisions interracial families make about where to live.

Because many monoracial group members continue to prefer racially segregated neighborhoods, communities that are primarily racially homogeneous continue to exist. Some interracial families choose to live in these communities, and their decisions may be influenced to some extent by the gender locations of partners in the interracial couple. As discussed earlier, Native American, Latina, and Asian American women are more likely than Black women to marry a White man. In a study of residential location of more recent interracial couples, Wright, Holloway, and Ellis (2013) found that a White male as a partner tended toward residence in Whiter neighborhoods. Thus, White-nonwhite couples where the male is White are less likely to live in diverse neighborhoods than other interracial couples.

Black-White interracial couples may choose to live in predominantly Black communities. Acceptance of mixed-race youth, and as an extension, interracial liaisons within Black communities continues to be equivocal. To be sure, mixed-race people who identify as monoracial Black, and/or who are assumed to be so, are more accepted. The notion of mixed-race individuals being biracial (or mixed-race) but Black persists in many Black communities, which fosters mixed-race youths' acceptance in Black communities. There are gender issues to consider, however, especially related to the acceptance of mixed-race girls by their Black female peers (Khanna, 2011), and these are addressed in more detail in subsequent chapters. Nonetheless, issues of solidarity that impact the political presence and power of the broader Black community makes full embrace of mixed-race identities problematic (Leverette, 2009).

Socioeconomic status also influences interracial couples' residential decisions (Holloway, Ellis, Wright, & Hudson, 2005). Some White-nonwhite interracial couples who are able to own their homes and have higher household incomes and higher levels of educational attainment prefer predominantly White neighborhoods. Holloway et al. refer to residential attainment theory to explain this phenomenon. Basically, once members of a minority group reach socioeconomic levels similar to a dominant group, they tend to want to live among those with whom they have socioeconomic parity. In this instance, White-nonwhite couples may behave in ways similar to other monoracial minority group couples.

Income levels play out differently for minority-minority interracial couples, however, and these families are not likely to choose predominantly White neighborhoods. Further, their residential patterns also differ from monoracial minority families. Black-Latino households, regardless of income, are more likely to live in the same neighborhoods with Latinos more so than same-race Black couples, and are more apt to live in a Black neighborhood more so than same-race Latino couples. Asian-Latino interracial households with high incomes live in neighborhoods where they have more contact with Whites than do same-race Latino or Asian couples. Low income interracial couples with this interracial configuration live in neighborhoods where they come into contact with Blacks more than same-race Latino or same-race Asian households (Holloway et al., 2005).

Many interracial couples prefer diverse neighborhoods, most often in cities, more so than their same-race couple counterparts (Clark & Maas, 2009; Holloway et al., 2005). City neighborhoods are dynamic places, however. Through gentrification, for example, it is possible for city neighborhoods to shift from places of relative diversity (both cultural and socioeconomic) to predominantly White and middle class (Dalmage, 2006; Winn Tutwiler, 2005). Interracial couples looking to these areas may be attracted to what was ostensibly a diverse location. However, it is possible for an area to appear to be "diverse," yet have "seams" that remain predominantly White as a White perspective dominates (Dalmage, 2006). For this reason, some interracial couples seek living spaces that are diverse in terms of internal individual household diversity (e.g., interracial families such as themselves) and community diversity (e.g., community made up of different racial/ethnic groups throughout the neighborhood). They may perceive the family will be less a target for race-based hassles in diverse living spaces than they would in a predominantly monoracial neighborhood (Holloway et al., 2005).

A Sense of Belonging

Beyond safety concerns associated with a living place, many interracial families seek a feeling of belonging to the community in which they reside. They seek what Neal and Neal (2014) conceptualized as a sense of community—a person's perception of ". . . belongingness, cohesion, and bond*(ing)* with a group" (p. 2). However, a number of scholars have proposed that diverse neighborhoods are not likely to promote the sense of belonging some interracial families seek. They suggested that increased diversity corresponds to a diminution in trust and social cohesion among community members (Neal & Neal, 2014; Portes & Vickstrom, 2011; Putnam, 2007; Townley, Kloos, Green, & Franco, 2011).

Putnam (2007), for example, argued that a lack of trust in diverse communities, at least in the short run, negatively impacts social cohesion within that community. Basing his comments on the integration (and assimilation) of immigrants, Putnam believed it was possible and necessary for societies to address the negative influence of increased diversity on trust and social solidarity by developing broader and more inclusive identities. A new sense of community would emerge in which tendencies of diverse groups to own their difference would not cause community members to retreat at the sight of diversity. The notion of redefining what is meant by community was also suggested by Neal and Neal (2014), who concluded that the negative influence of diversity on community could be ameliorated by changing the meaning of community so that community ties become more important than community trust and cohesion.

Others determined that the social and economic condition of a community impact community ties more so than its diversity (Letki, 2008; Phan, Blumer, & Demaiter, 2009; Sturgis, Brunton-Smith, Read, & Allum, 2011). Diversity alone does not appear to erode trust in any significant way (Phan et al., 2009). Views that diversity has a negative effect on community trust were also countered by Stolle, Soroka, and Johnston (2008), who contended that the more people in diverse communities interact with each other, the less threatening diversity is when it comes to neighbors trusting each other. Stolle et al.'s analysis reflected a "contact hypothesis" approach to the impact of diversity on social cohesion. In this sense, the more differently raced people are around each other, the more they learn to tolerate and feel a sense of connection with each other. Glanville and Andersson (2013) echoed this perspective when they concluded that informal ties (e.g., socializing with neighbors) enhanced trust.

Given the nature and level of diversity sought by some interracial families, they are likely more interested in communities where they share a desire for diversity with other community residents. They would be less interested in living places where nonwhite people are perceived as "integrating" the living space, and thus to be tolerated or not tolerated by their dominant group neighbors. Chai's (2007) family integrated a community when her family relocated for her father to take a new position at a local university. In addition to being the only interracial family (mixed-race children with a White mother and Chinese father) in a small, rural South Dakota community, the family did not conform to community race-based ways. For example, they hired Indians to do work in their home (her mother had even prepared tea and sandwiches to share with them) and refused to be a part of the hysteria and mistrust directed toward the Indian population in the area. Chai was stunned by the community's reaction (and actions) when her family decided to relocate to a different (and more diverse) living place.

> It had been an awful selling process . . . We'd return home to find the drawers of our dressers pulled out, our clothes rifled through. Boxes of

food were removed from our cabinets and displaced on the counter . . . one professor bragged that he'd lain on the carpet in our living room and listened to our "aura" . . . Our house became a curiosity . . . simply because we lived in it . . . every loan application for our house would fail at the local bank . . . We would sell at a loss, nearly a decade later only because the buyer . . . paid cash . . . If people disliked us so much . . . why didn't they let us leave? It felt as if we were being punished for crimes we hadn't realized we committed: arrogance, urbanity, miscegenation, failure to conform to norms that we hadn't known existed.

(pp. 114–115)

Putnam's study has been replicated enough to suggest some credence to his findings. Still, the wisdom of decisions among interracial families to locate in diverse neighborhoods where neighbors are ostensibly socially isolated seems dubious. There are, however, two incentives to consider. First, there are no homogeneously raced communities for interracial families. At least one partner and possibly children in the family would be considered differently raced from the overall community. Putnam (2007) offers a second caveat that might lead interracial couples to diverse communities. There appears to be a positive correlation between community resources, the "seams" where people interact (e.g., schools, libraries, sport facilities, day-care facilities), and diversity. Interracial couples with the capability and flexibility to choose their residential location may be attracted to communities with abundant resources and the fact that they and their children will interact with people from different racial/cultural backgrounds in these places.

The Influence of Place on Identity and Socialization

Some interracial families choose to raise their children in communities they deem to be more progressive, which for some means communities where their children will be valued. Moreover, they sense their mixed-race children will receive the type of support from their schools and neighborhoods that provides a "safe haven" for them to explore and develop their sense of identity (Sechrest-Ehrhardt, 2012, p. 95). For these parents, diverse communities are perceived as more progressive (Wieling, 2003). In addition, diverse communities potentially include the type of explicit nondominant cultural and language experiences parents of mixed-race children seek in order to ensure that their children have meaningful familiarity with all aspects of their racial/ethnic heritage (Sechrest-Ehrhardt, 2012).

Parents' school and community involvement are very important to a child's sense of self and belonging in diverse environments. Not only are mixed-race children able to interact with children from a variety of backgrounds, they also perceive that both they and their family are connected to the community. Mixed-race youth who live in environments that lack diversity, combined with a lack of parental participation in that environment, develop ambivalent feelings about how the environment affirms or disaffirms their status as mixed-race persons (Sechrest-Ehrhardt, 2012).

Earlier, a number of influences on interracial couples' race designations for their mixed-race children on various official forms were discussed (see Chapter 4). Holloway, Wright, Ellis, and East (2009) found that families' neighborhood locations also influenced parents' race designations for their children. Families located in White neighborhoods listed their children as White, whereas families living in a nonwhite neighborhood listed children as nonwhite. In the latter case, parents often used "some other race" as a race designation for their children.

Holloway, Wright, and Ellis (2012) extended this line of research in order to determine the influence of living in a diverse community on parents' decision to indicate more than one specific race designation (rather than "some other race") for their mixed-race children. They concluded that both diversity and the configuration of diversity in communities matter in interracial couples' race designation decisions for their children. Although Black-White interracial couples who live in segregated White neighborhoods tend to designate their children as White only, Black-White interracial couples living in neighborhoods with other interracial families are likely to designate their children as both Black and White. This probability increases with the percentage of mixed-race individuals living in the area.

The percentage of mixed-race individuals also influences the race designations Asian-White interracial couples make for their children. Asian-White couples are likely to designate both White and Asian for their children when White-Asian mixed-race individuals share a noticeable percentage of people living in the neighborhood. However, they are likely to designate the children as White only when the proportion of Asian individuals in the neighborhood increases.

Mixed-Race Children in Rural Communities

Most studies on the influence of residential location on mixed-race youths' identity concentrate on metropolitan areas, as mixed-race people generally tend to locate in central cities and suburbs (Clark & Maas, 2009). However, racially diverse small towns exist that exhibit patterns in racial segregation similar to some metropolitan areas. For example, there was a decline in racial segregation for both cities and rural areas in the 1990s for both Blacks and Hispanics. Black people are more heavily represented in rural places than Hispanics and Native Americans and are also more segregated. Where racial segregation exists, there is a corresponding limited participation in community affairs for people of color and limited interaction with other racial groups (Lichter, Parisi, Grice, & Taquino, 2007).

Rural communities take on a number of different forms. Exurbs, for example, are rural living spaces located beyond suburbs that are the residential choices of fairly high-income families who seek to escape the hassles of city living (and sometimes its diversity). Many rural areas are farming communities, and some attract companies engaged in corporate farming. This latter circumstance increases diversity in rural communities when inexpensive immigrant labor is hired to work in the companies' plants (Winn Tutwiler, 2005). Mixed-race youth also live in rural communities, and some live in interracial families, which have been place-bound in rural areas for generations.

Mixed-Race Children on Native Homelands

Liebler (2004, 2010) studied Native American parents (some of whom were mixed-race) who lived on or near reservations to determine their race designations for their mixed-race children. Residential places for these families were described as "homelands" or "culturally meaningful physical places" (Liebler, 2010, p. 596). Liebler (2004) hypothesized that the nature of a person's ties to the individual family *and* to the community influenced racial identity (i.e., how an individual perceives himself or herself) and racial identification (i.e., how an individual is perceived by others). Moreover, the "thickness" of ties to a racial group influenced major life decisions (or actions) such as marriage, friendship, religious proclivities, and norm-based behaviors (p. 703).

Liebler's (2004) study focused on families who, on the basis of responses on the 1990 Census, lived in a nonmetropolitan area where a family member had a tribal affiliation, and where a Native American language was spoken in the home. These families were identified as having thick ties to the Native American community. Despite opportunities to do otherwise, parents with mixed-race children living in families that met Liebler's criteria for "thickness" reported their children as Native American only on the 1990 Census. This tendency was especially true for children in families who lived in nonmetropolitan areas and/or families where a parent reported a tribal affiliation.

Liebler's (2010) conclusions in a subsequent study of influences on race designations of mixed-race Native American children supported Holloway et al. (2005) findings that contextual influences on identity designations for mixed-race children include both the nature of diversity within families living in the community and the racial/ethnic makeup of the overall community. She expanded on this notion by suggesting that the social, cultural, and political characteristics of the physical place are also important. For example, the location of reservations in rural, geographically bounded places create spaces where ". . . intergenerational transmission of a strong indigenous identity . . ." can occur (Liebler, 2010, p. 596). The stories, ceremonies, language, and traditions that constitute the cultural knowledge used to facilitate this process are tied to physical places.

In addition to a location separated by boundaries from other communities, Liebler (2010) discussed place characteristics that contributed the likelihood of "homelands" being places to engender a Native American identity for mixed-race children. Unlike the level of diversity sought by some parents of mixed-race children, homeland places usually lack diversity, which limits connections with other racial/ethnic groups, while increasing the likelihood of connections with other Native American families. In addition, the level of poverty existing in homeland places supports a minority identity, because there appears to be a connection between a low socioeconomic status and minority race identification. Thus, while the influence of community on race designation and identity are clear, Native American homeland places are used to solidify a single-race designation and identity as opposed to the "more than one" tendency of a number of interracial families.

White and Nonwhite Triracial Isolates

Triracial isolates represent a second example of mixed-race youth living in rural communities. Starcher (2005) studied triracial isolates living in rural Appalachia, in order to determine the impact of being minority in a poor rural community on social experiences, and subsequently social identities. Starcher pointed out that triracial isolates, who are people of White, African American, and Native descent, live in 175 small rural communities located in 16 states in the eastern United States. Approximately one third of these "triracial enclaves" (p. 17) are located in rural Appalachia. Participants for Starcher's study were mixed-race youth who lived in families with relatively stable residency over several generations. Like the Native American homelands, these rural communities were characterized by geographic remoteness, close-knit relationships among inhabitants, a long-standing connection to and respect for the land, and resistance to change and/or interference from outsiders.

Based on the 2000 Census, only 21 percent of the community's residents reported themselves as nonwhite, with 15 percent listing themselves as Black and the remaining 6 percent indicating "some other race." Some residents of the community self-identified as White, and others were identified as White on the basis of phenotype when someone other than the individual completed the census form. The one-drop rule predominated in this community, which meant the mixed-race-but-Black mind-set prevailed.

Given the numbers on the census, it is clear that some residents were racially assigned as Black even though they may not describe themselves in this way. Racial identification in day-to-day interactions appeared to be based more on how one socially identified (as opposed to racial lineage) and where one lived. Phenotypically, youth in Starcher's study spanned possible inherited physical characteristics of their lineage and some youth with more White physical characteristics "passed for White." Other youth socially identified as Black and were perceived as Black.

Mixed-race youth in the community attended county-operated schools with youth from other communities. Both mixed-race and monoracial poor White youth living in the area were stigmatized by their more well-to-do-peers. However, being identified as socially Black, poor, and a resident of the triracial enclave exacerbated differentiated school experiences that included peer interactions ranging from contempt to physical and verbal attacks. Whites, both those who fared better economically and those who were poor, and some mixed-race youth passing for White, disassociated themselves from triracials.

Based on findings of neighborhood characteristics that factor into parental decisions about where to live (e.g., Holloway et al., 2005; Sechrest-Ehrhardt, 2012; Wieling, 2003), where there is flexibility in terms of choice, interracial families will not likely choose to live in communities described in the foregoing discussions. Middle class and higher interracial families have more choice about where to live and can more easily locate in communities that serve their conception of family and support the racial identity designations they choose for their children.

Families with less income may not be able to afford the type of diverse communities they would like for their children to grow. Contrary to their wishes, they may end up in monoracial neighborhoods (Dalmage, 2006) that do not necessarily reflect the racial designations they prefer for their children or the children's own sense of racial identity. Mixed-race youth living in place-bound rural areas point to the certainty that some mixed-race youth lack agency when it comes to their racial identity, as their choices are constrained by place. The notion of lack of agency when it comes to racial identity as limited by place could apply as well to mixed-race youth living in nonrural locations.

Mixed-Race Youth: Class and Socialization

A number of studies locate mixed-race children in one or more of the social positions identified in a framework proposed by Bratter and Damaske (2013) when attempting to understand how social position variables such as race, class, and gender influence a number of socially produced experiences (e.g., racism, prejudice, privilege). To this degree, the proposed the framework is useful for examining the intersection of race, class, and gender in the family and community lives of mixed-race youth.

Bratter and Damaske suggested that mixed-race children's social status could be explained through monoracial effects, which means the dynamics shaping the lives of monoracial children of color influence mixed-race children as well. Alternately, given the racial stratification evident in interracial unions (i.e., experiences of Asian American–White unions are different from Black–White unions), experiences for some mixed-race youth reflect an in-between status, because the family is able to access some of the privileges available to White families that are not as available to many monoracial minority families. As a result, the social status of the mixed-race youth does not fully correspond to that of advantaged monoracial White youth but is higher than that of monoracial youth of color.

Finally, mixed-race children may experience marginalization owing to their mixed-race status and the fact that their home environment (e.g., living in an interracial household) is still considered unconventional. As result, they and their families are disconnected from family supports and resources that could be helpful to the family's social and economic well-being. It is also possible that youth located in this position experience mixed-race bias from individuals or agencies beyond the family, which means they are subject to treatment different from that of children in other racial and/or social class groups. Clearly, these positionalities do not necessarily operate independently of each other, and it is conceivable that mixed-race youth are simultaneously located in more than one, depending on the nature and context of the social situation under discussion.

Mixed-Race Youth Living in Poverty

The current increase in and attention to the mixed-race population is sometimes accompanied by a tendency to glamorize what it means to be mixed-race. The number of mixed-race youth living in poverty with a single parent reveals a far different reality for many mixed-race youth. It has been established that children living in single-parent households are more likely to live in poverty. The vast majority of single-parent households continue to be headed by women, although single men raising children represent approximately 8 percent of households with children (Pew Research, 2013). Women raising children alone are vulnerable to poverty, given that they often lack child support payments from a divorced or estranged partner, and many possess education and training that lands them in minimum wage jobs. Even single mothers with more education are disadvantaged in the labor market as women continue to garner lower wages than men performing similar work (Bratter & Kimbro, 2013; Winn Tutwiler, 2005).

In 2012, 53 percent of American Indian children lived in a single-parent home, and 67 percent of African American children and 42 percent of Hispanic/Latino children lived in this type of household. During the same year, 43 percent of mixed-race children (i.e., those designated as having two or more races) lived in a home with a single parent (Annie E. Casey Foundation, 2012). The rate of mixed-race children living in a home headed by a single mother is influenced by the tendency of interracial couples to cohabit rather than marry, which in some situations makes for a less stable family arrangement. Further, some combinations of interracial unions have a higher incidence of divorce. Women who have children with Black men are more likely to remain single parents than women who have children with White or Hispanic men. Thus, White female single parents with Black-White mixed-race children are more at risk for living in poverty (Bratter & Kimbro, 2013).

Despite the number of mixed-race children living in single-parent homes, they have poverty rates below all monoracial minority children with the same family structure. Poverty rates in 2013 were 27 percent for American Indian children, 39 percent for Black children, and 33 percent for Hispanic/Latino children, but 23 percent for children of two or more races (Annie E. Casey Foundation, 2013). Children born as a result of an interracial union are located in an "in-between" poverty position between monoracial White and monoracial children of color. This is true for both children of minority-minority (e.g., Black-Latino) and White-nonwhite lineages, although minority-minority children have higher incidences of poverty than White-nonwhite children. The poverty rate is reduced even further, however, for minority-minority mixed-race youth who live with both parents.

Overall, the racial hierarchy is evident when it comes to poverty status of mixed-race youth. Thus it is not surprising that an exception to the in-between poverty status for mixed-race youth is Asian American-White youth, who have poverty rates very similar to monoracial Whites (Bratter & Kimbro, 2013). The race of the mother appears to matter in female-headed households with mixed-race children, and having a White mother in the case of White-Indian/Alaska Native and Black-White mixed-race children reduces the possibility of living in poverty (Bratter & Damaske, 2013).

Experiences with Social Welfare Agencies

The in-between status of mixed-race youth with respect to poverty suggests that interracial families likely have access to support and resources not available to monoracial minority families that act as a safety net to reduce their risk of poverty. Moreover, the social and economic variables that land monoracial minority youth in poverty (e.g., living in a mother-only home) do not similarly effect mixed-race youth (Bratter & Damaske, 2013; Bratter & Kimbro, 2013). Still, even though the poverty status of mixed-race youth is primarily positioned in an in-between location, this status is not static and may shift in different social situations. The interaction with social welfare agencies is discussed here as a case in point.

Children living in poverty and in single-parent homes are at a higher risk for child abuse and neglect, and some of these children end up in foster care situations. Children of color, especially Black and Native American children, are overrepresented in the child welfare system given their numbers in the general population, even though race is not a predictor of child maltreatment. Black children made up 30 percent of children in foster care in the United States in 2008. Although American Indian/Alaskan Native children made up only 2 percent of youth in foster care nationally for the same period, the percentage was much higher in areas of the country with larger Native American populations (e.g., Minnesota, Hawaii, South Dakota). Disparity may also be evident in outcomes for children and families who are a part of the child welfare system. For example, Black children spend more time in foster homes when compared with White children (Child Welfare Information Gateway, 2011).

Mixed-race children are not always treated as an independent group in the system, thus their experiences are not clearly reported. This is an oversight, especially given the number of mixed-race youth living in poverty. Because poverty is a predictor of child abuse and neglect, it is likely that some of the children who are reported as monoracial children of color are actually mixed-race children. Fusco, Rautkis, McCrae, Cunningham, and Bradley-King (2010) conducted an exploratory study in order determine if mixed-race children, when viewed as a stand-alone category, were also overrepresented in child welfare service referrals and investigations. They concluded that mixed-race children, like Black children, were disproportionately referred to child welfare services, given their proportion of the population studied. Further, mixed-race children were investigated at rates higher than either Black or White children.

The level of risk for children referred to welfare agencies was assessed in three areas: risk for the child (e.g., severity of abuse/neglect or prior abuse or neglect), caregiver (e.g., age, parenting skills, substance abuse, or intellectual, physical, or emotional status of person caring for the child), and the family (e.g., condition of the home, presence of support or stress in the home environment) (Fusco et al., 2010, p. 444). Mixed-race children were rated at the moderate-to-high risk level in the caregiver area (i.e., age; physical, intellectual, emotional status; parenting; and skills and knowledge of the caregiver). These rating were significantly higher than either Black or White children.

Mixed-race children's experiences with child welfare services can be explained simultaneously through monoracial effects and marginalization. In the case of the former, mixed-race children were referred to child welfare agencies at rates not so unlike those of Black children. They are marginalized, however, given the rate at which referrals led to investigations. Moreover, the outcomes of those investigations suggested mixed-race children were at moderate-to-high risk in caregiver areas, at rates higher than either Black or White children. Fusco et al. (2010) proposed that racial bias could be at the root of referral and investigations experienced by mixed-race youth and their families. Elevated risk levels in caregiver areas could be a statement of disapproval of White women who crossed racial boundaries to engage in relationships with men of color. Thus, mixed-race children are placed in a marginalized location as a result of bias precipitated by the intersection of race, class, and gender. This positionality, however, is not experienced by mixed-race youth in interracial households that are middle class and/or those headed by two parents.

Social Class and Identity Claims

The fact that low socioeconomic mixed-race youth have experiences different from their middle class counterparts is also evident in how they racially self-identify. Evidence suggests social status influences not only how individuals racially perceives themselves, but also how others racially perceive them. Thus, mixed-race individuals with a lower socioeconomic status are believed to be members of lower status racial groups (e.g., Black, Latino) (Penner & Saperstein, 2008). Mixed-race youth from middle class backgrounds identify as biracial more so than mixed-race youth from a low socioeconomic background. They likely feel more encouraged to choose a racial identity than youth from a lower or working class backgrounds (Townsend, Wilkins, Fryberg, & Markus, 2012). At least part of this tendency could be related to the independence and individualism that is characteristic of middle class homes (Winn Tutwiler, 2005).

Social, Cultural, and Economic Capital

The final section of this chapter is organized around social theorist Pierre Bourdieu's (1986) three forms of capital, in order to expand on the effect of place and social status on the life circumstances of mixed-race youth and their families. Bourdieu described social capital as the resources possible through association or membership in a network where members provide each other with capital or resources ostensibly shared by group members. A second form of capital, cultural capital, is presented in three states. Cultural capital exists as the acquisition or incorporation of dispositions or ways of being driven by life experiences (embodied state); as cultural artifacts or goods such as books, art, and so forth (objectified state); or as objectified knowledge recognized in the form of academic credentials or qualifications (institutionalized state). The final form, economic capital, is the money or property rights that are differently possessed, despite assertions of its possibility for anyone in a given society. Bourdieu maintained that economic capital was at the root of all other types of capitals; thus, in his view, social and cultural capitals are merely converted forms of economic capital.

Social Capital

Bourdieu's thesis concentrated on the *content* of social capital. In contrast, Putnam (2007), in recent discussions on the topic, focused more on how social capital is influenced by community diversity. He defined social capital as ". . . social networks and the associated norms of reciprocity and trustworthiness" (p. 137).

Social networks are based on trust among people that leads to cooperation that benefits those who are part of the network. The norms for reciprocity and trust existing in different communities are reflected in social networks. According to Putnam (2000, 2007), social networks may be bonding (i.e., inwardly focused connections that reinforce the exclusivity and homogeneity of a group) and/or bridging (i.e., outwardly focused and more inclusive). Social networks may also extend beyond community boundaries, as people may feel connected to and provide benefits to each other, even when they are separated by physical distance (Winn Tutwiler, 2005).

Earlier discussions of the impact of diversity on community are especially relevant to social capital when it comes to interracial families who live in diverse communities. Recall that Putnam (2007) concluded that increased diversity in communities is associated with mistrust among neighbors. Accordingly, in the face of diversity in their living space, people "hunker down" and, in the process, retreat from not only their neighbors but also collective life beyond the neighborhood. Given this line of thinking, social networks both within and outside the neighborhood would be compromised by diversity in a given the community. In short, according to Putnam, diversity undermines social networks, and thus social capital.

Laurence (2013), like other scholars, agreed with Putnam that as diversity increases, trust in neighbors decline. Further, Laurence concluded that in diverse settings, neighbors connect with each other less frequently, do not have close friends who are neighbors, and do not rely on other neighbors in crisis situations. Based on a study of British communities, Laurence, like Putnam, concluded that fewer strong ties exist in diverse communities. He could not, however, corroborate Putnam's findings that the lack of connectivity extends beyond the neighborhood. In his view, social networks beyond the neighborhood were not influenced by neighborhood diversity.

Also mentioned earlier, a number of scholars are far less convinced about the adverse effect of diversity on community ties and trust, and thus do not concur with the premise that diversity alone is the primary driver for reduced social capital in a community. They point to the fact that social capital tends to be lower in deprived areas and that low-income people are not as likely to help others as are people with higher incomes (Phan et al., 2009). Moreover, the nature of social capital differs in different communities; thus, a generalized definition does not capture the nature of social capital in some communities or how it is affected by characteristics particular to a given community. Even trust, which is instrumental to development of social networks and thus social capital, may have different meanings in different communities.

Despite the debate regarding diversity's influence on communities' ties and trust, to date, the influence of interracial families as a component of community diversity and their potential influence on community ties have not been explicitly determined. It is probable, however, that in two-parent interracial families, parents' experiences and expectations of social networking may differ because of their different racial backgrounds. For example, Black partners in Black-White liaisons may expect instrumental interactions with neighbors (e.g., information exchange, different types of support and/or assistance) more so than their White partners (Phan et al., 2009). It is probable, however, that once the interracial family is formed, parents create approaches to social networks and social capital that fit the perceived needs of the family.

By way of illustration, Cheng and Powell (2007) presented evidence that interracial couples as a unit actually approach social capital in ways that are different from their same-race family counterparts. The researchers determined that parents in interracial families were better able than their monoracial counterparts at providing economic and cultural resources to their young children. However, they were less able to engage the type of social relations necessary for development of social networks that would lead to social capital for their children. In this sense, interracial couples might exhibit the "hunkering down" inclinations believed to be true of all neighbors in diverse communities. This possibility should be considered, however, along with the possibility that social interactions with neighbors may be constrained by the stigma associated with being in an interracial relationship. Even so, interracial couples' focus on cultural and economic capital leads to a concentration on education as a major investment. Cheng and Powell concluded that parents' attention to this area might be motivated by a propensity to compensate for any actual or potential disadvantage or marginality their children might experience as a result of being mixed-race.

Interracial families living in communities that lack strong ties may also rely on social networks beyond the community. Racial minorities who are part of interracial families may continue to rely on networks accessed by people of color in monoracial unions. Political organizations for monoracial groups (e.g., NAACP, National Council of La Raza) as well as those addressing the social and political needs for mixed-race people and interracial families (e.g., MAVIN Foundation, AMEA) are potential sources for network building. Social media adds a layer of social networking beyond the neighborhood and provides opportunities for interracial families to connect with other interracial families for information and resources to support this particular family configuration.

Social Capital within Families

Schlabach (2013) identified family structure, cohesion, relationships, and educational expectations as social capital located within the home. In fact, the interracial family itself may serve as a form of social capital, given that parents of mixed-race youth often develop behaviors and practices specific to the needs of their children (Cheng & Powell, 2007). Children may have more or less access to family social capital beyond the immediate family, based on certain family characteristics.

Children in Black-White interracial families headed by White mothers may have fewer external social networks because of the stigma White women face for marrying Black men (Schlabach, 2013). Further, although the extended family potentially serves as social capital for some families, as discussed before, some interracial couples are estranged from their extended families. With respect to interracial family networks, at least for some, the immediate family is apparently a stronger source of social capital than either the extended family or the community. In fact, Schlabach proposed that the level of social capital in the home diffuses observed overall differences between mixed-race and White adolescents when it comes to social and emotional well-being.

Children develop networks beyond those established by their parents. Young people, especially adolescents, may actually play important roles in the development of social networks within their neighborhoods, thus are instrumental in building social capital for both themselves and their families. Their efforts take place at the "seams" of communities (e.g., schools, parks, other local public places) depending to a great extent on the amount of autonomy parents are willing to extend to them. In the process of developing their own social networks, children improve the social networking opportunities for and among parents and may also contribute to stronger ties overall within a community (Weller & Bruegel, 2009). Although the benefits of parents' community involvement has been noted, it appears that children and youths' involvement in the community has family benefits as well.

Cultural Capital

What counts as cultural capital, incorporating all states proposed by Bourdieu (i.e., embodied, objectified, or institutionalized), depends on the context in which it is developed and subsequently expected to gain advantage. Although this fact is a conundrum for some mixed-race youth, it allows for flexibility in multiple social situations for others. Recall Khanna's (2004) notion of reflected appraisals and the role played by cultural capital (likely both embodied and objective capital) in how mixed-race youth were perceived by others and the extent to which they were accepted or not accepted by minority monoracial peers. Lacking specific cultural capital (e.g., knowledge, behaviors, or ways of being in general) excludes some mixed-race youth from groups in which they seek membership.

On the other hand, as a result of having a White parent, White-nonwhite mixed-race youth may acquire the cultural capital that permeates all of society, thus allowing them to navigate dominant culture situations regardless of whether they identify as White. Here we pay attention to the fact that for mixed-race youth, cultural capital and racial identity alignment does not always have to exist. A related point to be made about cultural capital and mixed-race youth is clearly illustrated by Chua (2011) who, with her Jewish husband, decided that their children would be bicultural, drawing from both Chinese and Jewish cultures:

> The deal that Jed and I struck when we got married was that our children would speak Mandarin Chinese and be raised Jewish . . . I hired a Chinese nanny to speak Mandarin constantly to Sophia, and we celebrated our first Hanukkah when Sophia was two months old.
>
> *(pp. 7–8)*

Children growing up in homes where biculturality is intentionally and authentically inculcated not only possess cultural capital for social situations that reflect two different cultural perspectives, but also develop a level of comfort when interacting across multiple culturally different social settings. Biculturality as cultural capital depends on the social context, however, as Samuels (2010) made clear in her work with mixed-race adoptees. Being bicultural could be problematic for some mixed-race youth as they attempt to establish relationships in racialized social contexts (e.g., with homogenous monoracial groups). It is necessary for bicultural mixed-race youth to develop a certain level of cultural savvy in order know how to use cultural capital to negotiate various social situations.

Mixed-race youths' cultural affinity (and hence what they accept as cultural capital) may depend on their beliefs about race and how they identify racially. When mixed-race adults talk about childhood socialization, they refer to the community their parents chose to live in and the racial composition of their social networks as sending powerful messages about race (Rockquemore, Laszloffy, & Noveske, 2006). Where mixed-race youth live, at least in part, provides them with information and inclinations used for social comparisons, where they evaluate themselves juxtaposed with monoracial people in order to gain clarity about racial self-identity. Essentially, they make judgments about how they are similar and/or dissimilar to monoracial people as a means for declaring who they are racially. Racial differences in family values, along with dress, language, and tastes in food and music are among the possible categories mixed-race youth use to distinguish between racial groups (Khanna, 2011).

Khanna (2011) described several dimensions mixed-race people might use for comparisons, including phenotype, culture, and experiences. Here I focus primarily on social comparisons using culture as the basis for discussing Bourdieu's cultural capital as an embodied state. Mixed-race youth with limited authentic information and experiences with communities of color could perceive themselves as culturally White (Rockquemore et al., 2006) because their social comparisons lead them to believe they are more like White people than people of color. The same could be true for mixed-race youth with limited interactions with White communities (i.e., the lack of contact could lead to a monoracial minority racial self-identity). In both circumstances, stereotypical perceptions about culture based on race could emerge because of limited authentic interactions with communities on either side of mixed-race youths' racial lineage (Khanna, 2011).

Differences in social comparisons exist, even when the mixed-race lineage is the same as illustrated by two narratives from Khanna's (2011) study of mixed-race Black-White people paraphrased as below. The first are views expressed by a Black-White mixed-race male who identifies as White, and the second, a Black-White mixed-race female who identifies as Black.

Mixed-race male:

> . . . When I go and try to hang out with [black people], I feel a bit of a culture shock. The Ebonics talking, the dialect—I guess a lot of it has to do mainly with that.

Mixed-race female:

> I haven't been around [whites] so much . . . For a short time, I went to a private middle school, which was mostly white . . . I didn't associate with them at all, and it was kind of awkward . . . Different styles of dress . . . Different manners of talk. . . . but when I see friends at black schools, I give them high fives . . . At [white] schools they shake hands . . . it was all kind of awkward. It just didn't fit.
>
> *(pp. 91–92)*

Cultural Capital within Families

As discussed in Chapter 4, parents culturally socialize their children. Mixed-race youth may develop cultural whiteness, which serves as a form of cultural capital learned from being raised by a White parent. A participant in Bettez's (2012) study aptly described cultural whiteness as ". . . access to and implicit understanding of mainstream culture that permeates all aspects of *[dominant]* culture including music, knowledge, language, and leisure time activities . . ." (p. 166). In far too many instances in literature related to mixed-race youth and their families, reference to *parents* focuses on families with a White mother and a father of color, with much less attention to interracial families with a mother of color (except to discuss how mixed-race youth are disadvantaged by having a mother of color).

Mothers of color raising mixed-race children also provide their mixed-race children with cultural capital, albeit not in the form of cultural whiteness. Nevertheless, the capital gained as result of being raised by a mother of color serves mixed-race children well in dominant culture social situations. For example, Chua (2011) championed the benefits of raising her Chinese-Jewish daughters according to Chinese traditions over the more permissive Western parenting adopted by many U.S. families. Even though her views on how to best raise children were met with criticism, her children were able to achieve in school settings and to become accomplished in other areas in predominantly White settings.

Nissel (2006), mixed-race with a White father and a Black mother, was raised by her mother in a single-parent home for a good portion of her childhood. She spent many hours in a Black beauty salon listening to Black women discuss the realities of being Black in a racialized society. These experiences, along with modeling from her mother, likely influenced Nissel's ability to read and react to racialized situations from the perspective of a Black person. As a younger child, she proclaimed her hatred for Black people and believed her "half-white side" would protect her from being "lumped with black people" (p. 39). She moved from that position to one of adopting a Black identity, with an ability to use cultural knowledge (sometimes for ulterior motives) to negotiate in dominant culture social situations. The following paraphrased excerpt was based on her experience as a mixed-race high school student in a predominantly White, upper class private high school for girls:

> "Don't be like them girls and not eat," the salad-bar tender told me. "I won't, Miss Betty," I said. "I haven't had one these students call me *Miss* yet," she said. Your mother raised you right."
>
> *(p. 120)*

Here Nissel exhibits respect for elders, regardless of the context and any class differences that might exist—a behavior taught to many Black children. Later, as she attempted to irritate school personnel to point of getting kicked out of the school, she made a series of race-related demands, such as a request that non-European languages be taught and that the release of Nelson Mandela receive attention similar to that of the fall of the Berlin Wall. At one point, she used the cultural knowledge of the treatment of elders as part of her campaign to be removed from the school (although this is not to imply that her request was completely disingenuous). She stated to school officials: "It makes me sick to my stomach that third-graders are allowed to call the cleaning women by their first names!" (Nissel, 2006, p. 122). Her declaration led to a rule that the name of all adults in the school (i.e., faculty and staff) should be preceded with Mr. or Ms. Still, her requests did not lead to her being expelled from the school!

The extended family also serves as source of cultural capital. Another participant in Bettez's (2012) study was a Filipina-White mixed-race woman raised in a working class environment, who was initially estranged from her White grandmother. The grandmother detached herself from the family because she disapproved of her son's choice for a wife. According to Bettez, the grandmother provided the study participant ". . . with cultural capital by teaching her aspects of middle class, White culture" (p. 113). The study participant shared the following with Bettez:

> . . . When we were kids, she would take us up to Boston and bring us to museums and the symphony and just all these cultural things that I don't think—if it weren't for her we would never have gotten that, which is important.
>
> *(p. 113)*

An additional type of cultural capital within the interracial family is the parents' knowledge about education and schooling. As mentioned earlier, education appeared to be a major focus for interracial couples (Cheng & Powell, 2007). When thinking about education as cultural capital, the focus is both on the extent to which interracial couples value education, and the information, resources, and possible dispositions they possess that supports the eventual acquisition of academic credentials by their mixed-race children. Parents of color in White-nonwhite interracial unions lean toward the instrumental value of education where their children become educated to acquire credentials needed for economic status and security. Although their White partners view education as a vehicle for self-knowledge and expression, couples tend to be guided by a co-created perspective for education constructed between spouses to navigate the educational lives of their children (Lawton, Foeman, & Brown, 2013).

Cultural capital in this vein crosses family socioeconomic status and family configuration. The interracial couples in the Lawton et al. (2013) study were married, with middle to upper socioeconomic status. On the other hand, both Obama (2004) and Nissel (2006) lived in single-parent homes, but their mothers placed them in prestigious educational settings with children from homes having higher socioeconomic statuses than theirs. It should be stated, however, that in both cases, the mothers had education beyond the secondary level (Nissel's mother was a nurse, and Obama's mother eventually received a PhD.). Still, more research is needed about cultural capital as it relates to education among less educated parents of mixed-race children.

Economic Capital

Economic capital, or the financial assets interracial families have, influences where the family can afford to live and the resources they can access to support their children's education and overall well-being. Clearly, family income influences community location choices and, as will be discussed in more detail in later chapters, where children live often influences the quality of their education and schooling. To be sure, parents with more money (and education) simply have more resources to support goals they have for their mixed-race children. Although parents of mixed-race youth may use their economic location to place their children in in the best social position possible, they still wrestle with how their children will be received outside the safety of the home and the status of their well-being as a result of these interactions. It is likely for this reason that parents with resources attempt to arm their children with tools and strategies available through social and cultural capital to deal with social situations related to their mixedness.

Parents of mixed-race youth who lack economic capital may experience a level of stress that interferes with their ability to adequately care for their children. This is especially true for parents of mixed-race youth who are estranged from family members and friends who disapproved of their liaison with a person of a different race. The combination of isolation from family members and friends, living in poverty, and social disapproval places these parents in vulnerable positions. These families may benefit from community-based resources to alleviate the type of stress that interferes with their ability to care for their children and construct scenarios to facilitate their overall well-being. In this sense, community resources create supportive networks that supplant family and friends as a primary source of support (Fusco et al., 2010).

Concluding Comments

Socioeconomic differences among interracial families speak to yet another aspect of intragroup diversity among mixed-race children and youth. One manifestation of these differences is the variety of communities where mixed-race youth live. Communities can be a form of advantageous cultural capital for some youth but a source of distress for others. Parents vary in their ability to respond to the impact of living spaces on their mixed-race children. To be sure, differences exist in the support and resources parents are able to provide in order to facilitate life goals they may have for their mixed-race children.

Many educators live in communities with the children and youth they teach. Surely they have a sense of the diversity of their neighborhoods, and whether that diversity is collectively valued by community members. Teachers, both those who live within the community and those who do not, should take note of attitudes toward mixedness in the communities where their schools are located. Despite notions that education takes place only in schools, educators must be acutely aware of how their reactions to community (and classroom) diversity influences attitudes toward differences, for both their students and adults in their communities. Their position on diversity allows them to serve as both educators and advocates for building the type of trust and social cohesion necessary for community members to strengthen community ties. The community and its school can only benefit from their efforts.

References

Annie E. Casey Foundation. (2012). *Children in single-parent families by race.* From http://data center.kidscount.org/data/tables/107-children-in-single-parent-families-by#detailed/1/any/false/868,867,133,38,35/10,168,9,12,1,13,185/432,431.

Annie E. Casey Foundation. (2013). *Children in poverty by race and ethnicity.* From http://datacenter.kidscount.org/data/tables/44-children-in-poverty-by-race-and-ethnicity?loc=1&loct=1#detailed/1/any/false/36,868,867,133,38/10,11,9,12,1,13,185/324,323.

Bettez, S. C. (2012). *But don't call me White: Mixed race women exposing nuances of privilege and oppression politics.* Boston: Sense Publishers.

Bourdieu, P. (1986). The forms of capital. In J. Richardson (Ed.), *Handbook of theory and research for the sociology of education* (pp. 241–258). New York: Greenwood.

Bratter, J. & Damaske, S. (2013). Poverty at a racial crossroads: Poverty among multiracial children of single mothers. *Journal of Marriage and Family,* 75(2), 486–502.

Bratter, J. & Kimbro, R. T. (2013). Multiracial children and poverty: Evidence from the Early Childhood Longitudinal Study of kindergartners. *Family Relations,* 62(1), 175–189.

Chai, M. (2007). *Hapa girl: A memoir.* Philadelphia: Temple University.

Cheng, S. & Powell, B. (2007). Under and beyond constraints: Resource allocation to young children from biracial families. *American Journal of Sociology,* 112(4), 1044–1094.

Child Welfare Information Gateway. (2011). *Addressing racial disproportionality in child welfare.* From www.childwelfare.gov/pubs/issue_briefs/racial_disproportionality.

Chua, A. (2011). *Battle hymn of the tiger mother.* New York: Penguin Books.

Clark, W. & Maas, R. (2009). The geography of a mixed-race society. *Growth and Change,* 40(4), 565–593.

Dalmage, H. (2006). Finding a home: Housing the color line. In D. Brunsma (Ed.), *Mixed messages: Multiracial identities in the "color blind" era* (pp. 301–312). Boulder, CO: Lynne Rienner Publishers.

Fusco, R., Rauktis, M., McCrae, J., Cunningham, M., & Bradley-King, C. (2010). Aren't they just black kids?: Biracial children in the child welfare system. *Child and Family Social Work,* 15(4), 441–451.

Glanville, J. & Andersson, M. (2013). Do social connections create trust?: An examination using new longitudinal data. *Social Forces,* 92(2), 545–562.

Holloway, S., Ellis, M., Wright, R., & Hudson, M. (2005). Partnering 'out' and fitting in: Residential segregation and the neighborhood contexts of mixed-race household. *Population, Space, and Place,* 11(4), 299–324.

Holloway, S. R., Wright, R., & Ellis, M. (2012). *Constructing multiraciality in families and neighborhoods.* From http://caligari.dartmouth.edu/~geospace/mixedmetro/Publications/constructing_multiraciality_text.pdf.

Holloway, S. R., Wright, R., Ellis, M., & East, M. (2009). Place, scale and the racial claims made for multiracial children in the 1990 US Census. *Ethnic and Racial Studies,* 32(3), 522–547.

Khanna, N (2004). The role of reflected appraisals in in racial identity. The case of multiracial Asians. *Social Psychology Quarterly,* 67(2), 115–131.

Khanna, N. (2011). *Biracial in America: Forming and performing racial identity.* New York: Lexington Books.

Laurence, J. (2013). "Hunkering down or hunkering away?": The effect of community ethnic diversity on residents' social networks. *Journal of Elections, Public Opinions and Parties,* 23(3), 255–278, doi:10.1080/17457289.2013.808641.

Lawton, B., Foeman, A., & Brown, L. (2013). Blending voices: Negotiating educational choices for upper/middle class well-educated interracial couples' children. *Howard Journal of Communication*, 24(3), 215–238.

Letki, N. (2008). Does diversity erode social cohesion? Social capital and race in British neighborhoods. *Political Studies*, 56(1), 99–126.

Leverette, T. (2009). Speaking up: Mixed race identity in Black communities. *Journal of Black Studies*, 39(3), 434–445.

Lichter, D., Parisi, D., Grice, S., & Taquino, M. (2007). National estimates of racial segregation in rural and small-town America. *Demography*, 44(3), 563–581.

Liebler, C. (2004). Ties on the fringes of identity. *Social Science Research*, 33(4), 702–723.

Liebler, C. (2010). Homelands and indigenous identities in a multiracial era. *Social Science Research*, 39(4), 596–609.

Neal, Z. & Neal, J. (2014). The (in)compatibility of diversity and sense of community. *American Journal of Community Psychology*, 53(1–2), 1–12.

Nissel, A. (2006). *Mixed: My life in Black and White*. New York: Villard Books.

Obama, B. (2004). *Dreams from my father: A story of race and inheritance*. New York: Three River Press.

Penner, A. & Saperstein, A. (2008). How social status shapes race. *Proceedings of the National Academy of Sciences of the United States of America*, 105(50), 19628–19630.

Pew Research. (2013). *The rise in single fathers: A ninefold increase since 1960*. From http://www.pewsocialtrends.org/2013/07/02/the-rise-of-single-fathers/.

Phan, M. B., Blumer, N., & Demaiter, E. (2009). Helping hands: Neighborhood diversity, deprivation, and reciprocity of support in non-kin networks. *Journal of Social and Personal Relationships*, 26(6–7), 899–918.

Portes, A., & Vickstrom, E. (2011). Diversity, social capital, and cohesion. *Annual Review of Sociology*, 37, 461–479.

Putnam, R. (2000). *Bowling alone: The collapse and revival of American community*. New York: Simon and Schuster.

Putnam, R. (2007). E Pluribus Unum: Diversity and community in the twenty-first century. *Scandinavian Political Studies*, 30(2), 137–174.

Rockquemore, K. A., Laszloffy, T., & Noveske, J. (2006). It all starts at home: Racial socialization in multiracial families. In D. Brunsma (Ed.), *Mixed messages: Multiracial identities in the "color-blind" era* (pp. 203–216). Boulder, CO: Lynne Rienner Publishers, Inc.

Samuels, G. (2010). Building kinship and community: Relational processes of bicultural identity among adult multiracial adoptees. *Family Process*, 49(1), 26–42.

Schlabach, S. (2013). The importance of family, race, and gender for multiracial adolescent well-being. *Family Relations*, 62(1), 154–174.

Sechrest-Ehrhardt, L. (2012). *Understanding the racial identity development of multiracial young adults through their family, social, and environment experiences*. From SechrestEhrhardt_cua_0043A_10339display.pdf.

Starcher, D. (2005). *The triracial experience in a poor Appalachian community: How social identity shapes the school lives of rural minorities*. From https://etd.ohiolink.edu/!etd.send_file?accession=ohiou1126296583&disposition=inline.

Stolle, D., Soroka, S., & Johnston, R. (2008). When does diversity erode trust? Neighborhood diversity, interpersonal trust and the mediating effect of social interactions. *Political Studies*, 56(1), 57–75.

Sturgis, P., Brunton-Smith, I., Read, S., & Allum, N. (2011). Does ethnic diversity erode trust?: Putnam's 'hunkering down' thesis reconsidered. *British Journal of Political Science*, 41(1), 57–82.

Townley, G., Kloos, B., Green, E. P., & Franco, M. M. (2011). Reconcilable differences? Human diversity, cultural relativity, and sense of community. *American Journal of Community Psychology*, 47(1–2), 69–85.

Townsend, S., Wilkins, C., Fryberg, S., & Markus, H. (2012). Being mixed: Who claims a biracial identity? *Cultural Diversity and Ethnic Minority Psychology*, 18(1), 91–96.

Weller, S. & Bruegel, I. (2009). Children's 'place' in the development of neighborhood social capital. *Urban Studies*, 46(3), 629–643.

Wieling, E. (2003). Latino/a and White marriages: A pilot study investigating the experiences of interethnic couples in the United States. *Journal of Couple & Relationship Therapy*, 2(2/3), 41–55.

Winn Tutwiler, S. (2005). *Teachers as collaborative partners: Working with diverse families and communities.* Mahwah, NJ: Lawrence Erlbaum Associates, Publishers.

Wright, R., Holloway, S., & Ellis, M. (2013). Gender and the neighborhood location of mixed-race couples. *Demography*, 50(2), 393–420.

6

PEER RELATIONS AND FRIENDSHIP FORMATIONS

When we arrived, the party [given by Black friends] was well on its way . . . I could tell right away that the scene had taken my white friends by surprise. They kept smiling a lot. They huddled together in a corner. After maybe an hour, they asked me if I'd take them home.

—B. Obama (2004, p. 84), age 16, circa 1979

"You like Joshua? You can't be serious, Rain. He likes Jewish girls, and like, duh, I'm Jewish and you're not . . . there's no such thing as a black Jew."

—R. Pryor (2006, p. 134), age 14, circa 1983

It's going to be interesting when I . . . start dating. I'm not supposed to want to date white people, I'm not supposed to want to date black people. I don't know what people expect.

—A. Holzhauer (1999, p. 216), age 16, circa 1999[1]

Black people see me like I'm Black. But . . . you have some complexities inside of that too. I'm the light skinned Black girl which has its own issues . . . 'she's light skinned . . . oh, she thinks she's all that . . . who does she think she is with her hair and all that' . . . I've probably dealt more with racism with the Black culture.

—Young Mixed-Race Girl #1 (Cochrane, 2013)

For many mixed-race youth, race is a consequential issue in their relationships and friendships. Many parents in interracial families are very active in their young children's friendships, and are thus able to approve their children's playmates. This involvement allows parents to make sure, as much as possible, that early friendships do not act as countervailing influences on the family's identity goals or to intervene should their child's mixedness become the basis for conflict between children (or a problem for playmates' parents). Protective tendencies by parents are challenged, however, as children get older and seek relationships with peers of their own choosing. At this point, family influence lessens as peer relationships become important in the life of the adolescent.

Peers, like the family, are instrumental in socialization processes, especially during adolescence. Indeed, in many circumstances, peer relationships become more significant to youth than their relationships with other social institutions (e.g., the family or the church). The importance of peers in the lives of young people is evidenced by the influence of peer relationships on educational outcomes, social behaviors (e.g., smoking, substance abuse), and acceptable attitudes toward and interactions with other peers. It is almost impossible to capture all the different ways adolescent peer groups find to distinguish themselves from each other. We do know, however, that peer groups differ in the rules, language, customs, tastes in music, and dress they adopt, for example.

Peer groups tend to be racially homogenous (Doyle & Kao, 2007), and as evident from the introductory quotes, this phenomenon has existed for decades. Even when young people from different racial backgrounds are in social situations that facilitate their interaction (in school, for example), peer groups often reflect the racial stratification existing in society. Consequently, friendship choices for mixed-race youth become a more challenging event, one that is characterized by strains, conflicts, and dilemmas not experienced by their monoracial counterparts.

Chapter 6 focuses on the social interactions between mixed-race youth and their peers in school and in their communities. Given the salience of race in peer group formations and interactions, the manifestations of attitudes toward racial differences in the form of racism, monoracism, prejudice, and discrimination, as they are enacted and experienced by the nation's young, is critical to our understanding of friendships among mixed-race youth. This information serves as a backdrop for discussing issues faced by mixed-race youth as they select peer groups and friendships.

Young People and Racism, Monoracism, Prejudice, and Discrimination

Understanding the relationship among racism, monoracism, prejudice, and discrimination is important, because children and youth can engage and/or experience all four. Racism is generally understood to be the belief that differences in human abilities and character are based on race, and that one race is superior in these areas to others. It sustains the distinct racial boundaries that precipitate monoracism, which is a form of systematic and/or interpersonal oppression directed toward people who do not fit into a single racial category. Monoracism is often at the root of pressure for mixed-race youth to attach to one monoracial group (Jackson, Wolven, & Aguilera, 2013).

Racism is animated in prejudice and discrimination. Prejudice has been defined in many ways; however, a common theme is the adverse orientation toward all members of a racial group that includes affective (e.g., disliking), cognitive (e.g., believing unfavorable stereotypes), and behavioral (e.g., ostracizing others) components (Raabe & Beelmann, 2011). Discrimination, on the other hand, is defined as the unjust treatment of people as a group, based on their race (but could also include unjust treatment based on other characteristics such as age or gender).

Race, Racism, and Monoracism

That children become aware of race at an early age was discussed in Chapter 3, along with the fact that children's ability to make meaning about racial differences changes as they develop cognitively (Hirschfeld, 2008; Rogers et al., 2012). Relatedly, it has been noted that peer inclusion and exclusion based on race begins as early as preschool (Van Ausdale & Feagin, 2001). According to Risman and Banerjee (2013), methods used to understand children and youths' racial knowledge and attitudes changed over time. Initial information-gathering approaches included children's responses to cultural artifacts. Clark and Clark's (1947) often-referenced and replicated study using Black dolls and White dolls is a renowned example. Other research methods focused on children's attitudes toward race-related issues, race-related research on children in their natural social settings (e.g., schools, families), children's understanding of race and racism and, more recently, information gleaned from how children talk about race. Children's understanding of race has long been of interest to psychologists, sociologists, and others interested in child growth and development.

Youths' conceptual understanding of race is more complex than previously believed. Some White youth, for example, understand race well enough to use it as a mediating tool in their everyday interactions (Lewis, 2010). Indeed, White children understand the power (and privilege) associated with race, as early as preschool (Van Ausdale & Feagin, 2001). Even when interacting with peers who are racially ambiguous (which might be the case when interacting with mixed-race youth), White children use other characteristics to locate youth they perceive as nonwhite as others, and thus deserving subordinate positions and/or exclusion (Risman & Banerjee, 2013).

Black children's understanding of race most often links race with the historical and the prevailing lower social status of Black people. This is evidenced, for example, by replications of the Clark and Clark study where even today, Black children have more positive views of a White or lighter skinned doll or drawing of a doll over a Black or darker skinned doll or drawing (Cooper, 2010; Davis, 2007). This understanding of race is not common to all children of color, however. Hispanic children, especially immigrant children with social experiences and roots from Latin America, are often mixed-race. They may not recognize the Black-White binary as manifested by racism in U.S. culture, where people of color are positioned at a lower or marginalized status. They eventually learn about the low status of people of color from interaction with others (Dulin-Keita, Hannon, Fernandez, & Cockerham, 2011), and soon they, like the Black children referenced earlier, may also engage in a type of colorism that elevates the status of those believed to be closer to White.

Even though all children make distinctions based on race, White children, more so than children of color, learn early on to engage a color-blind rhetoric (i.e., we are all the same regardless of race). As a result, some children are uncomfortable talking about race because to them, such talk implies they are racist or prejudiced (Lewis, 2010; Risman & Banerjee, 2013). In fact, they lack the language and confidence to talk about anything they perceive as racial (which can range from skin color to politics) believing they risk insulting a peer of color (Lewis-Charp, 2003).

White adolescents are also influenced by "public scripts" (Lewis, 2010, p. 403) that suggest that race no longer matters. When addressing differences among their peers, children may turn to other personal characteristics (e.g., personality), proposing that these differences are more important than race. Still, stated positions that minimize the role of race in peer-to-peer interactions conflict with actual social experiences, such as those that take place at school, among young people.

According to Lewis (2010), White children's feelings about racial differences are often constrained by a "culture of silence" (p. 410) around race as part of a color-blind perspective learned in the home and/or at school. This response to race actually feeds racial difference as a reason for conflict, rather than racial difference as a social reality that can be openly discussed with the goal of acceptance for diversity. A color-blind position is also evident when young people suggest that race does not matter to them personally, but appears to be important to their peers, especially their Black peers. In this instance, youth are hesitant to speak frankly about their personal belief system on issues of race, a position that can be adopted by both White and Black children (Lewis, 2010).

Children of color experience racism from both adults and their peers in their schools and communities (Pachter, Bernstein, Szalacha, & Coll, 2010). Racism by educators will be addressed in a subsequent chapter. Here we discuss racism among children, which is often evident in the way children view others who are different from them. In the study conducted by Risman and Banerjee (2013), for example, White children distinguished themselves from Black children on the basis of cultural stereotypes (e.g., Black boys are gangsters or aggressive). Race as cultural difference was also understood through dress and self-presentation, and this type of racial difference through culture was common among girls in the study. Girls, more so than boys, normalized beauty and dress on the basis of White standards. The fact that children acknowledge differences is less at issue than the evaluative emphasis placed on difference that elevates one's race location over another. Here is yet another instance of a culture of silence around race, where attitude and dress rather than race become the reason for White superiority as expressed by children.

Mixed-race youth are susceptible to both racism and monoracism. When they are believed to be children of color by White peers (or teachers), they are positioned to experience racism not so unlike that experienced by their non-white, minority race peers. On the other hand, they can experience monoracism at the hands of their monoracial minority peers (or teachers), who have difficulty with their claims of being more than one race. Jackson et al. (2013) explained that monoracism among mixed-race Mexican Americans takes the form of ethnic discrimination, where mixed-race people face pressure to prove they are authentically a member of a racial/ethnic group. For example, mixed-race youth conceivably face situations where they have to answer for their lack of an ability to speak the language of their minority race heritage, which for some could be two non-English languages (e.g., the expectation that mixed-race Mexican American/Native Americans be able to speak Spanish by Mexican-Americans and a Native American language by Native Americans). Having one's membership to either side of one's heritage questioned is particularly stressful and requires strategies by the mixed-race person to keep his or her sense of well-being intact (Jackson et al., 2013).

Prejudice among Children and Youth

Based on a meta-analysis of 113 research studies on the trajectory of the development of prejudice in children and youth, Raabe and Beelmann (2011) found prejudice increases as children reach preschool age (2–4-year-olds) and during early elementary school age (5–7-year-olds). Prejudice decreases beyond age 7, but no general trend on prejudice could be discerned from the studies reviewed for adolescents. The researchers suggested that the development of prejudice in children follows a predictable inverted U-curve path, with the caveat that the ways in which prejudice was operationalized in various studies likely masks differences in outcomes of age-related changes in prejudice.

Baron and Banaji (2006) concluded that not only do young White children exhibit prejudice, but also, in their view, prejudice remains relatively stable throughout elementary school. While they were interested in confirming that pro-White/anti-Black bias existed at an early age for White children, they were also interested in when children consciously expressed these attitudes. Baron and Banaji found that by age 6, children had developed pro-White/anti-Black attitudes and were candid about their preferences. Ten-year-olds' racial preferences were similar to those of 6-year-olds; however, the 10-year-olds were less inclined to openly self-report their preferences. Adults in the study had the same preferences as did the children, but *reported* equal Black/White preferences. Baron and Banaji also surmised that preferences for social groups appear to be influenced by the status of the group in the broader society. For example, young Hispanic children have preferences for Hispanic people over Black people, but not Hispanic people over White people.

Aboud (2003) questioned if the pro-White/anti-Black bias observed in young children was about in-group preference, more so than out-group prejudice. He concluded that even though significant levels of in-group preferences existed by age 5, and even though out-group prejudice subsided, in-group preference persisted. The diversity of the contexts where children spend time (e.g., schools) apparently influences racial attitudes according to Aboud, because there was a reciprocal relationship between in-group favoritism and out-group bias in more homogeneous schools. In fact, children in school settings with less diversity and where there are no opportunities to interact with minority peers view minorities less positively and cannot envision themselves in friendships with peers of color (McGlothlin & Killen, 2006).

How Youth Experience and Enact Discrimination

Although it is true that children of color experience discrimination as a result of actions from White youth, discrimination occurs between minority group youth (e.g., between Blacks and Latinos) and within minority groups (between Black and Black youth) (Pachter et al., 2010; Risman & Banerjee, 2013). Discrimination for mixed-race youth can be described as a monoracial effect in that the rate of discrimination experienced is similar to that of monoracial minorities, and this is particularly the case for mixed-race Black-White youth (Herman, 2004). In fact, mixed-race participants in a study conducted by Khanna (2011) experienced discrimination from White people who "raced" (p. 66) them as Black rather than biracial or mixed-race. However, unlike other monoracial groups (White or minority), mixed-race people experience discrimination not only in public and in their neighborhoods, but also within their families (Campbell & Herman, 2010; Jackson et al., 2013).

The Pachter et al., (2010) study is useful for understanding how discrimination takes place among and between children. The researchers wanted to determine the frequency of discrimination and the settings in which discrimination took place, as perceived by 277 children of color between the ages of eight and 16. Discrimination was operationalized as being ". . . treated badly, not given respect, or are considered inferior because of the color of their skin, because they speak a different language or have an accent, or because they come from a different country or culture" (p. 62).

Of the children surveyed, 88 percent reported they had an experience they would describe as racial discrimination. Even though 53, or 20 percent, of the participants self-identified as multiracial or multicultural, the researchers did not conduct analysis for this subgroup. Given these data, it's likely that the discrimination experiences of the multiracial or multicultural children can be understood through monoracial effects, where dynamics that influence the experiences of monoracial children of color similarly influenced mixed-race youth.

Racialized remarks and insulting names were the more common forms of discrimination experienced by youth in the Pachter et al. (2010) study. Discriminatory experiences reported by children of color (i.e., Black and Hispanic) between the ages of seven and 12 in a similar study conducted by Dulin-Keita et al. (2011) included being perceived as less smart than other children, an awareness that one's race precipitated fear in others, and being perceived as dishonest because of one's race. These studies substantiate the fact that children are clearly aware of when they are being disparaged because of their racial group membership.

In addition to exposure to discrimination as pejorative remarks and/or the attribution of undesirable behaviors or attitudes based on racial group location, peer-to-peer race-based discrimination can also be understood through acts of inclusion and exclusion. Inclusion and exclusion is a product of racial categorization that structures social groups and the boundaries that separate them (Lewis, 2003). Mixed-race youth are at risk for exclusion from one or both of the racial groups that represent their racial heritage. Even so, their ability to negotiate boundaries between these groups allows them to better manage the discrimination they may encounter (Herman, 2004).

Discrimination as exclusion is understood differently by children, on the basis of the individual(s) responsible for barring others from inclusion. In a study of fourth graders, Lewis (2010) observed that both Black and White children spoke of peers' exclusionary behavior along racial lines. It should be mentioned parenthetically that some participants in the study were likely mixed-race, because some reported themselves *as* whole or partially White or Black. Unfortunately, the experiences of children who self-identified in these ways were not explicitly included in the study analysis.

When children who identified themselves as White discussed exclusionary practices of Black peers, they generally attributed this characteristic to all Black children (e.g., the Black kids are . . .). When White children and Black children discussed exclusionary practices of White peers, the attribution was attached to an individual or an isolated event (e.g., Joey is . . .). Lewis proposed that this phenomenon is consistent with whiteness, where White racial group identity is invisible. As a result, exclusionary behavior among White children became an individual trait, but when instigated by Black children became a behavior typical of Black children as a group. It is plausible that mixed-race youths' beliefs about discrimination by exclusion were consistent with that of their monoracial peers. Evidenced here is the fact that even among the young, differentiated meanings of discrimination for different racial groups suggests discrimination becomes a choice by individual White people rather than a practice inextricably linked to the pervasiveness of racism. This circumstance is important to consider when attempting to discern how mixed-race youth make sense of their inclusion in and exclusion from certain groups.

Group Acceptance and Membership

Like all adolescents, mixed-race youth are concerned about how they are evaluated by their peers. They want to be accepted by the peer group they wish to join. Some mixed-race youth are relatively confident in their claim to a biracial or multiracial identity and are skilled at frame switching. As such, the compatibility they perceive between the different aspects of their racial identity allows them to skillfully negotiate differently raced homogenous monoracial contexts, as well as heterogeneous diverse contexts (Binning, Unzueta, Huo, & Molina, 2009). Mixed-race youth who live in diverse communities are often able to interact with youth from several different racial backgrounds, as was the case with the young Barack Obama (see introductory quote). This does not mean, however, that their acquaintances from different racial groups will necessarily desire to, or interact comfortably with each other. Further, Putnam's (2007) notion that community diversity restricts trust and cohesion among neighbors could translate into a lack of interest among the community's young in interacting socially with peers of a different race. Mixed-race youth living in this type of diverse community will not be advantaged in their friendship formation efforts. Rather, the lack of cohesion will likely feel like a burden.

Other mixed-race youth present monoracial minority or White behaviors depending on the social situation, expecting that they will be more acceptable to a monoracial peer group at a given time. Their self-presentation is not always consistent with a sense of racial identity, which for many is still developing. In fact, mixed-race youth may mingle with both groups of their racial heritage as part of the identity selection process. Hence, observable behaviors should not be taken as necessarily representative of the youth's sense of racial identity. When mixed-race youth have peer groups of separate racial backgrounds, they may feel pressure to act in ways that are acceptable to one group over another at different times. In reality, their behaviors are likely neither exclusively non-white nor White but a combination of both (Ruebeck, Averett, & Bodenhorn, 2008). Nonetheless, the various and diverse behaviors possible among mixed-race youth influence the peer groups they are able to join and feel comfortable joining.

Acting White and Acting Black

According to Burrell, Winston, and Freeman (2012) "race acting" is based on young peoples' beliefs about ". . . what it means to act like a member of a racial group . . ." (p. 97). They proposed that the process by which young people learn and embrace what it means to be a certain race is diverse and complex. Without a doubt, the circumstances in which young people grow and develop will influence their beliefs and behaviors around race. Acting White and acting Black are two ways, but certainly not the only ways, that young people engage race acting.

Young people *accuse* each other of acting White or acting Black. This indictment can be directed toward a person of any race, and the accuser can be of any race as well. However, when a Black peer states that another Black peer or a mixed-race peer is acting White, it is meant as an insult. It is a jab of sorts—and a charge that a peer's behaviors are not in keeping with what it means to be Black. This accusation can be very distressful to the young person on the receiving end of the condemnation (Murray, Neal-Barnett, Demmings, & Stadulis, 2012). Alternately, an accusation of acting Black from one Black peer to another can also be meant as an insult. In this case, the person on the receiving end of the insult is charged with displaying behaviors that represent negative and stereotypical constructions of Black people.

Acting White has historically had different meanings when attributed to Black people. For example, prior to emancipation, acting White meant that slaves behaved in ways expected by Whites, which were not behaviors representative of White people themselves. Rather, they were behaviors that reflected Whites peoples' construction of Black people's culture and speech. These behaviors were engaged as a matter of survival—Blacks who overtly acted in ways not meeting White's expectations risked punishment or even death. Black people neither behaved nor talked in ways expected by Whites when they were only with each other and away from the gaze of White slave owners. However, over time, and with emancipation and other freedoms, Blacks who wanted to assimilate into White culture, and even later, those who wanted to advance educationally, economically, and socially actually emulated White behaviors and speech (Ogbu, 2004).

Acting White and acting Black are generally believed to be divergent behaviors, with acting White positioned as more socially acceptable behavior in the wider society. In reality, the positive or negative evaluation of behaviors believed to be race related depends on the social context in which the behaviors are enacted. Based on a study of 115 Black adolescents, Burrell et al. (2012) concluded acting White and acting Black are not necessarily polar opposites, and affirmative and nonaffirmative attributions could be made for both, at least from the perspectives of participants in their study. When asked to define acting White and acting Black in multiple ways, participants' responses resulted in broad thematic descriptions that were applied across each racial group, some with shared descriptors.

For example, *Academic Intelligence* was a theme applied to both racial groups, and descriptions such as being smart or stupid appeared for each race-acting category (i.e., acting White and acting Black). Similarly, an *Authenticity* theme emerged from analysis of participants' definitions, and being yourself was a term applicable to both acting White and acting Black. *Style* was an example of a theme that crossed race-acting categories, albeit with different meanings. Sagging pants was attributed to acting Black, whereas wearing your pants high was attributed to acting White. The two themes with no crossover were *Superiority* (i.e., "acting like they are superior") and *Ghetto* (i.e., "ghetto mentality"), with the former attributed to acting White and the latter to acting Black (Burrell et al., 2012, p. 104).

Mixed-race youth and monoracial youth raised in interracial and multiracial homes may view race acting differently from the Black youth in the study cited earlier. Based on interviews conducted by Butler-Sweet (2011), young people with these racial and family backgrounds believed that acting White was, in fact, the opposite of acting Black. Interviewees, reflecting on their adolescence, distinguished between the two using cultural markers and, interestingly, all respondents had the same view of what acting White and acting Black meant. They distinguished between the two in areas such as dress, speech, and tastes in music. Academic achievement was viewed as characteristic of acting White, although some respondents did not believe academic mediocrity was a Black trait.

Identity claims and social contexts play a major role in how mixed-race youth perceive and experience race acting. Those who claim to be White and enact White behaviors and attitudes are seen as culturally familiar (i.e., White culture) to their White friends, yet they can still be viewed as nonwhite. Hence, the mixed-race person may be treated in the same way a White peer might treat a Black peer. This does not remove the expectation that the mixed-race person's behaviors remain culturally White (Samuels, 2010). It is highly probable the situation described by Nissel (2006) when she was eight years old is played out in multiple and different ways in mixed-race youths' peer interactions:

> I made the mistake of bringing a black Barbie out to play with the White girls . . . they treated her like dirt . . . "Ewww! That's not Barbie,". . . . With Michelle and the gang looking on . . . I had Skipper tell Black Barbie she couldn't play with the group.
>
> *(pp. 37–38)*

On the other hand, Black peers may view mixed-race peers as racially familiar, especially for those who phenotypically look Black, however their behavior (acting White) leads to questions about their authenticity as a Black person (Samuels, 2010). Mixed-race youth who are charged with acting White by Black peers may be expected to prove their authenticity as a member of the monoracial minority group. Efforts toward that end lead some mixed-race youth to engage in behaviors stereotypically attributed to a monoracial minority group, rebuff family members, or become caricatures of general perceptions of people of color (Root, 2003). A clear example was reported by a mixed-race youth to Butler-Sweet (2011). The young man wanted closer ties to the Black community. After being hurt by accusations of acting White, he developed strategies he believed would result in closer ties to Black peers:

> . . . I would study the music of black hip-hop culture and learn the dance, I learned the dialect too, I would wear the bigger clothes and jeans under my butt and all that kind of stuff . . .
>
> *(p. 204)*

Although authenticity tests for mixed-race Black-White youth are often emphasized, the situation for minority-minority mixed-race youth (e.g., Asian and Mexican) can be even more complex and more daunting. Dual minority mixed-race youth may be pushed to prove authenticity to both groups that constitute the racial/ethnic lineage (Romo, 2011). Some mixed-race youth simply avoid situations where authenticity is an issue. The following reflection by a young girl aptly summarizes how mixed-race youth who claim a biracial identity experience the race-acting conundrum:

> . . . There really is no way to be Black or White . . . that's the problem with being mixed . . .
>
> *(Cochrane, 2013, Young Mixed-Race Girl #2)*

In situations where race acting and authenticity challenges are an issue, the potential outcome is the self-exclusion by mixed-race youth and/or their rejection and marginalization from communities of colors to which they may wish to be a part (Root, 2003).

The Nature of Friendships

Friendships are important, especially in adolescence. They contribute to identity development and provide an avenue for autonomy from parents while providing connections with peers (McGill, Way, & Hughes, 2012). Having friends both of the same and different racial backgrounds contributes to children and youths' sense of well-being. In the case of the former, similarities promote a sense of safety and closeness, whereas the latter leads to expanded frames of reference for understanding others. Even so, friendships among adolescents tend to be highly segregated by race (Quillian & Redd, 2009).

Cultural differences influence the meaning and nature of friendships, which may in turn affect friendships across racial lines. For example, Black children are more likely to choose friends from racial groups other than their own, and Black and Latino children tend to remain friends with the same peers for long periods of time. Further, Black and Latino youth may have a higher tolerance for confrontation in relationships than White youth, which impacts the stability of the friendship. In other words, an argument or disagreement between friends who are Black or Latino does not mean they intend to no longer be friends. Asian American youth are least likely to choose friends from other racial groups, and some tend to have friendships of shorter duration (McGill et al., 2012).

Communities where children live and the schools they attend influence friendships across racial lines as well. Young children are generally more likely to have a friend of a different race than older children. This may be due in part to the instability of adolescent relationships. Connections young people make during this period in life must withstand the emotional, physical, and cognitive changes that occur during adolescence. The organization of schools may also contribute to the sometime tenuous nature of friendships during adolescence. The transition from elementary to middle school, for example, with the onset of departmentalized class schedules makes maintaining former connections more difficult. Generally friendships that are based on similarities beyond race, such as a friendship based on shared interests, tend to be more stable over time (McGill et al., 2012).

Mixed-Race Youths' Approaches to Friendship Formation

The extent to which friendships are encouraged or discouraged in the home appears to affect how children pursue friendships in general, as well as whether friendships are sought across racial lines (McGill et al., 2012). This is especially important to note for mixed-race youth who share the same racial lineage but may be racially socialized differently in their respective homes. For example, a White-nonwhite mixed-race child socialized in ways akin to his or her minority heritage might develop friendship proclivities similar to those of monoracial minority youth. An alternate approach to friendships might be observed in youth who are socialized as White or as color-blind. The cultural content of families' socialization practices also affect how and with whom young people form friendships. The fact that mixed-race Asian-White and Asian-Black youth, particularly those with Asian mothers, tend to select Asian best friends is an example. This is believed to be the case because Asian culture is often emphasized in interracial Asian households (Doyle & Kao, 2007).

Acceptance by individuals one wishes to befriend or the group in which one seeks to be a part is extremely important to all children, especially as they enter adolescence. The question becomes how are mixed-race youth situated in friendships within a culture where friendships remain overwhelmingly segregated? Quillian and Redd (2009) organized their research on mixed-race youth friendship networks around an "axes of variation" (p. 283) that reflects the ways in which friendships for mixed-race youth have been discussed in the literature (see Figure 6.1). As such, competing possibilities for the development and nature of friendships are described.

Isolation vs. Popularity

A number of studies on mixed-race youths' friendships focus on the rejection experienced by mixed-race youth from peers that leads to isolation. Still others contend that the acceptance of multiraciality makes youths' mixed-race status less a factor in their acceptance by peers. Based on their study of mixed-race adolescent friendship networks, Quillian and Redd (2009) did not find evidence that mixed-race youth were any less popular than their monoracial peers of color. They concluded that peers did not reject mixed-race youth in ways that led

Isolation vs. Popularity

- **Isolation** – Mixed-race youth experience rejection from monoracial peers that leads to low popularity.
- **Popularity** – Mixed-race youth are as popular as their monoracial peers because multiraciality is more acceptable.

Diversity vs. Homogeneity

- **Diversity** – Because of their multiracial backgrounds, mixed-race youth develop more diverse friendships than their monoracial peers.
- **Homogeneity** – Because of the continued racial segregation of friendships, mixed-race youth seek connections with a monoracial peer group that results in more homogeneous friendship networks.

Background Bridging vs. Polyracialism

- **Background Bridging** – Mixed-race youth use their mixed backgrounds to form friendships with peers from both sides of their racial lineage.
- **Polyracialism** – Race is not a major barrier to friendships, thus mixed-race youth form friendships with peers from several racial groups.

FIGURE 6.1   Axes of Variations in Mixed-Race Youths Friendship Relations

Based on Quillian, L. & Redd, R. (2009). The friendship networks of multiracial adolescents. *Social Science Research*, 38(2), 279–295.

to social isolation. This is not to suggest, however, that monoracial peers never reject their mixed-race peers. On the contrary, Quillian and Redd pointed out that mixed-race adolescents might have concerns about how they fit with their monoracial peers.

Still other studies concluded that mixed-race youth often experience rejection from their monoracial peers. Some of these studies proposed that the event of mixed-race youth feeling less social acceptance with monoracial peers appeared to be race specific (Campbell & Eggerling-Boeck, 2006). Herman (2004) maintained that rejection by monoracial peers was a certainty in mixed-race youths' peer interactions. However, as mentioned earlier, experiences of discrimination in the form of exclusion facilitated development of racial boundary crossing skills that aided mixed-race youths' ability to manage discrimination.

Diversity vs. Homogeneity

Doyle and Kao (2007) explored peer group attachments among mixed-race youth and concluded that mixed-race youth could be located at either point along the diversity/homogeneity axes, and in some ways exhibited aspects of both. Because friendship groups continued to be predominantly racially segregated, mixed-race youth are given to form friendships with monoracial peers that reflect their more than one race backgrounds. Doyle and Kao determined that blending and amalgamation were two friendship patterns observed among mixed-race youth. Accordingly, some mixed-race youth develop friendships that do not quite reflect either group that makes up their racial lineage, and thus exhibit a friendship formation pattern that is "in-between" those of their monoracial peers. This friendship pattern was labeled blending. As an example, Doyle and Kao found that Black-White mixed-race youth are more likely to choose a best friend who is White more so than a monoracial Black peer and to choose a Black friend more frequently than a monoracial White peer. Consequently, their friendships could be described as more diverse than their monoracial peers.

Mixed-race youth may also exhibit a friendship pattern of amalgamation, as they choose friendships in one racial group over another. For example, Doyle and Kao found that Native American-Black mixed-race youth tended to merge with monoracial Black peers for friendships, whereas Native American-White youth merged with White peers. These friendships may appear to be more homogeneous, because mixed-race youth may be viewed as belonging to a single-race group that makes up their mixed heritage. In other words, Native American-White youth may be perceived as monoracial White. When they enter a friendship group of White peers, appearances suggest a monoracial White peer group, thus supporting homogeneity in friendships.

Both patterns of amalgamation and blending were observed among Black-White, Asian-White, and Asian-Black youths (Doyle & Kao, 2007). Mixed-race youth with Black lineage (e.g., Black-White and Black-Asian) tended to amalgamate with Black peers. On the other hand, mixed-race youth with White lineage, with the exception of Black-White youth (e.g., White-Asian mixed-race youth) tended to amalgamate with White peers. Blending is also observable, given that the friendship choices still differ from monoracial peers (e.g., a Black-Asian youth would select a Black friend, or a White-Asian youth would select a White friend more so than an Asian peer would choose a Black or a White friend, respectively).

Background Bridging vs. Polyracialism

Related to diverse friendships, mixed-race youth may use/bridge their mixed-race status to develop friendships from both sides of their racial heritage or may form friendships with peers from multiple racial groups.

Mixed-race youth who form friendships based on blending patterns as described by Doyle and Kao (2007) clearly exhibit bridging behavior, in that they may seek friendships from either side of their racial heritage. Friendship homophily (see following section) is an example of polyracialism, especially when mixed-race youth seek out other mixed-raced youth, regardless of their racial mixture.

Homophily and Mixed-Race Youths' Peer Relations

The lack of a mixed-race peer community leaves some mixed-race youth feeling alienated. Although they may erect flexible boundaries that allow them to fit into more than one racial peer group, they may feel that they do not fully belong to any one group with which they may interact (Miville, Constantine, Baysden, & So-Lloyd, 2005). As a result, some mixed-race youth exhibit friendship homophily, where they seek out other mixed-race youth as friends. Friendship homophily may occur for a number of reasons. Selection of a best friend is tied to a sense of identity, thus mixed-race youth who identify as biracial or multiracial, for example, may seek out others who similarly identify. Being mixed-race will suffice—the racial configuration does not have to be the same (e.g., a Black-White mixed-race youth may befriend a mixed-race Latino-White peer). Mixed-race youth who befriend other mixed-race youth may find more acceptance in those relationships. To be sure, friendship homophily by mixed-race youth may be driven by the exclusion and/or rejection perpetrated by monoracial peers (Doyle & Kao, 2007).

Homophily occurs by race, but socioeconomic status influences the character of friendships among mixed-race youth as well. Black-White youth, for example, may have limited opportunity to mingle with monoracial minority children if their families live in predominantly middle class White neighborhoods. They may also attend schools with a population of middle class White students. Hence, fewer monoracial Black middle class neighbors and schoolmates limits opportunities to select a Black best friend. As a result, race and class can intersect to bring about friendship homophily (Doyle & Kao, 2007).

The Intersection of Race and Gender in Friendship Formation

As noted in previous chapters, the interaction of race and gender influences mixed-race girls' relationships in ways that do not affect peer relationships for mixed-race boys.

Physical appearance is central when friction surfaces between mixed-race girls and their female minority monoracial peers, with colorism as a primary source for tension (Rockquemore & Laszloffy, 2005). Friction also exists between mixed-race girls and their monoracial White female peers, but the cause of tension is different.

The strained relationship between the young mixed-race girl in the quote at the beginning of this chapter (see Young Mixed-Race Girl #1) and her Black female peers is due to her physical characteristics that do not reflect those of many monoracial Black girls. In contrast, the marginalization of Rain Pryor as illustrated in the opening quote was not due to her physical appearance, but simply because she was perceived as not White. This is not an uncommon occurrence, as mixed-race participants in Khanna's (2011) study of Black-White biracial/mixed-race people also experienced exclusion from interactions (e.g., close friendships, dating) deemed by White adolescent peers as events for monoracial Whites only. Thus a number of possibilities characterize the relationships between mixed-race girls and their peers, including derision and selected exclusion, but could also include threats of physical abuse. As mixed-race Nissel (2006) remembers of her initial interaction with Black girls at a new school:

> The bullying at school worsened. Tascha would threaten to cut my hair . . . Christina would force girls to throw me against my locker . . . Every day, I'd hear a new rumor about when I was going to get my ass kicked.
>
> *(p. 95)*

Exclusion Based on Physical Appearance

As so fittingly pointed out by Gordon (2008), "adolescent girls become aware that their bodies are increasingly looked at and evaluated by others . . ." (p. 245). At the same time, they internalize views others have of their physical appearance. Women and girls continue to be sexually objectified in society to the point that their sense of value is caught up in physical beauty, most often as defined by White standards. According to Gordon (2008), the media is an important source of information all girls use as they come to understand that women are expected to be attractive and are often valued because of their physical appearance. Given the prevalence of young, White, and thin women in the media, it is no surprise that many girls (of any race) come to believe this prototype is the benchmark to use in order to determine how they measure up in terms of attractiveness.

The standards of beauty may be shifting, however, as women of more than one race/ethnicity are often viewed as more attractive than monoracial White women, and those without White race mixture (e.g., Black-Asian or Black-Native American) are regarded as the most attractive (Sims, 2012). Model Naomi Jones (African-Jamaican and Chinese-Jamaican decent) and *Avatar* star Zoe Saldana (Puerto Rican and Dominican) are examples. Even so, nonwhite women in the media who are considered attractive often present with physical characteristics (e.g., hair texture, facial features) that approximate White standards of beauty.

Beyoncé, Rihanna, Alicia Keys, and Nicki Minaj (a group that includes light-skinned Black, mixed-race, or otherwise ambiguously raced women) are among the women of color considered to be beautiful and sexually desirable. Moreover, many Black women in film who receive romantic attention from their male co-stars have physical characteristics similar to these performers and are likewise viewed as sexually desirable. Some Black women in popular culture who do not naturally possess physical characteristics that meet White standards of beauty attempt to approximate this look by wearing contact lenses to change their eye color and using hair treatments to transform their hair color, length, or texture. Some women of color have been accused of using skin-lighters to change the color of their skin (Wilson, 2013).

Studies are split on the impact media images of White and Black women have on young Black girls' perceptions of beauty. One group of studies, however, suggests that Black girls likely use images of Black and non-White women in the media to compare themselves. Like other girls, they are exposed to media images that ". . . emphasize women's appearance, sexuality, and desirability to men . . . (Gordon, 2008, p. 253). Further, Gordon (2008) states that these media images are so pervasive,

> . . . that it is virtually impossible for girls to avoid them. Consequently, girls whose self-worth and attitudes did not initially emphasize the importance of beauty and appearance may come to adopt the dominant media perspective over time because they are bombarded with these portrayals.
>
> *(p. 254)*

Mixed-race girls are closer to White standards of beauty than are many, but certainly not all Black girls. The closer mixed-race females approximate the skin color, facial features, and/or hair texture of White females, the more beautiful they are deemed to be, and thus more valued. Both dark-skinned Black and darker skinned mixed-race girls are less valued (Rockquemore & Laszloffy, 2005). Townsend, Neilands, Thomas, and Jackson (2010) speculated that most Black girls recognize they cannot meet colorism-based beauty standards that require White-like physical characteristics. As a result, their self-evaluations may be more negative when it comes to judging their physical appearance.

The overemphasis on the physical appearance of mixed-race children and youth both within and outside their families has already been discussed. For the most part, mixed-race children are perceived as being good-looking. There are benefits to being judged as attractive. These include perceptions of being more capable academically, being rated higher in performance situations, and just being treated more favorably whether the individual extending the treatment is an acquaintance (Sims, 2012). Sims coined the term Biracial Beauty Stereotype to encapsulate references to mixed-race people in both popular media and scholarly literature as ". . . 'exotic', 'fascinating', and 'exquisitely beautiful' . . ." (p. 64). Some mixed-race youth internalize the notion that mixed-race people are simply more beautiful. In fact, some mixed-race girls embrace a position of being more attractive as a result of their mixed-race status to the point of having difficulty accepting their Black physical features, which they may not find attractive (Ahnallen, Suyemoto, & Carter, 2006).

Some Black girls feel devalued as a result of their physical appearance, which can lead to feelings of powerlessness and rage that are expressed toward girls who more closely approximate White standards of beauty (Rockquemore & Laszloffy, 2005). Light-skinned Black girls receive some hazing from their darker skinned peers, but not as much as mixed-race girls who are known to have a parent who is not Black. One way of understanding how Black girls may come to reject or even harass mixed-race girls is through stereotype threat. Referencing Steele (1997), Townsend et al. (2010) suggested that Black girls with a strong Black identity might be susceptible to stereotype threats, which occur when they act out a negative stereotype of Black girls. As this possibility relates to the present discussion, Black girls might mistreat, threaten, and physically challenge mixed-race girls on the basis of the negative stereotype that Black girls are loud and aggressive (Fordham, 1993).

Competition for attention from boys is another area that exacerbates the ill will some Black girls may feel toward mixed-race Black-White girls. Black girls may feel boys prefer lighter skinned girls and that Black boys can seek relationships with girls from a number of racial groups (e.g. White, Asian, or Latina), as well as with mixed-race girls. On the other hand, the pool of boys for romantic liaisons for Black girls is limited, as most will likely have a boyfriend who is Black, more so than a boyfriend from another racial group. Even though Black girls may believe mixed-race girls have an advantage of being preferred by all boys, including Black boys and boys of other races (especially given the Biracial Beauty Stereotype), in reality, mixed-race girls too are often rebuffed by White boys who do not seek them for dates at the middle school and high school levels (Khanna, 2011).

Approaches to Contest Exclusion Threats

Mixed-race youth face competing demands and dilemmas when it comes to friendship formation and peer group participation. These include the intersection of racial self-identification and group membership and relationships, as well as conflicting cultural expectations and in some cases pressures to choose one racial peer group over another. Often, they are unable to discuss these issues with their families or with peers facing similar predicaments (Phillips, 2004). Still, mixed-race youth attempt to engage a range of strategies in order to avoid being excluded from a desired friendship or peer group.

According to Binning et al. (2009), mixed-race youth who are comfortable with a biracial/multiracial identity are better able to navigate diverse racial contexts and less susceptible to feeling a need to "pass" as one race over another. Other mixed-race youth may feel their multiracial inclinations will not be acceptable (to either family or peers), and thus end up seeking connections with a single race group. Even in these situations, youth risk being rejected by their chosen monoracial group. How mixed-race youth think about their connections with peers, as well as the relationship pathways they experience, have been the focus of a number of studies.

Racial Self-Identification and Peer Affiliations

Racial self-identification plays a significant role in peer relationships for many mixed-race youth. According to Khanna (2011), mixed-race people in general engage in "identity work," which refers to the ". . . strategies . . . to highlight, downplay, or conceal particular racial identities with others" (p. 80). Mixed-race youth engage identity work in the process of affiliating or attempting to affiliate with peers. Alternately, peer affiliations play a role in helping mixed-race youth present and/or solidify a chosen racial identity.

Strategies such as verbally identifying (i.e., I am . . .) or disidentifying (i.e., I am not . . .) a racial identity were among the identity work strategies used by participants in Khanna's study of Black-White mixed-race adults. Jackson et al. (2013) too noted this process of defending self as an interpersonal process used among mixed-race Mexican Americans in the face of monoracism or, contrastingly, in situations where their legitimate membership in a chosen monoracial group was questioned. Other strategies related to issues of group affiliation and racial identity included changing physical appearance to more closely align looks with a chosen racial identity, consciously displaying cultural symbols of a racial group (i.e., wearing a particular style of clothing or using language associated with a particular race), and being selective with identity disclosure (i.e., hiding aspect of their racial lineage) (Khanna, 2011).

Making friends was one reason mixed-race people were motivated to use strategies outlined by Khanna, many of which were enacted during adolescence and early adulthood. Having a particular friendship network reinforces youths' sense of who they are racially but also sends a message to others about the youths' chosen racial positionality. Any or all of strategies such as altering physical appearances, embracing cultural symbols, and being less than forthcoming about a racial makeup may combine with the act of consciously selecting friends of a particular racial background. In short, mixed-race youth send messages about who they are racially by peers they call friends and peer groups they seek to join. Actions taken around racial identity are meant to ensure inclusion as member of their chosen group.

Fitting In

Mixed-race youth in middle school through college may experience a form of "racial hazing" and may have to engage in authenticity test (Root, 2003). Their status as a mixed-race person is at the center of acceptance or nonacceptance among their peers, and some will need to prove who they are racially by their chosen group. Although Binning et al. (2009) concluded that mixed-race youth with biracial/multiracial identities were able to get along with a diversity of peers given their facility in diverse racial contexts, the researchers did not expound on mixed-race youths' day-to-day actions and experiences that led to development of this skill.

Such was the focus of Waring's (2013) study. Based on interviews with 60 Black-White mixed-race adults, Waring concluded that some mixed-race people are able to gain in-group membership in two racially disparate worlds, given their ability to navigate differently raced contexts. Recall from Chapter 3 that mixed-race people with blended identities as described by Root (2003), border identities as discussed by Rockquemore and Brunsma (2004), and situational identities as proposed by Renn (2004) had in common the fact that they accepted all aspects of a racial heritage, and that situations dictated the salience of a particular aspect of their heritage at a given time. It is likely that mixed-race people with identities such as these seek membership status in all communities that represent their racial heritage.

According to Waring (2013), in-group membership in Black and White communities was due to use of "racial capital," defined as the ". . . repertoire of racial resources (knowledge, experience, meaning, and language) that biracial Americans draw upon to negotiate or cope with racial boundaries in a highly racialized society" (p. 67). As such, some mixed-race people have insight into the cultural frames possessed by racially different groups (e.g., White people and Black people) even though members of these groups have two different and distinct ways of making sense of the world. Mixed-race people possess "racialized tool kits" (p. 76) that enable them to interact in the racially coded ways required to be acceptable in both Black and White settings. As part of this process, they are able to make one group or the other feel comfortable, and as such gain membership as one of them—either Black or White—depending on the situation.

To be sure, this is a fairly sophisticated way of interacting with peers, and one that likely begins in adolescence. It also requires the type of socialization that allows for a significant amount of access to both Black and White cultures. Indeed, according to Waring (2013), the knowledge, experiences, language, and meanings required for this practice are acquired over time through authentic interaction with both communities. The ability to stand upright in two racial communities is not, however, a fail-safe practice that guarantees protection against exclusion from a peer group.

Mixed-race young people who desire in-group membership in two separate racial worlds risk "getting caught in the act" (Waring, 2013, p. 78). A member of one race or the other could witness the mixed-race person acting in ways believed to be characteristic of the other race. In this instance, the mixed-race person could be accused of race acting, and their authenticity may be questioned. Remember, some groups have strict racial boundaries and are more apt to reject racial claims of a mixed-race person on authenticity grounds (Renn, 2004).

There is also the question of how to behave in the presence of both races. Undoubtedly, it would be difficult to meet expectations (e.g., behavioral, language) each group may have of the mixed-race person in the same space (e.g., a school dance). Lastly, the mixed-race person may not effectively negotiate racial boundaries, and may speak or act in ways that do not clearly reflect what normally transpires in a given race-based setting. At risk is exclusion from one group or the other, based on perceptions of not been authentically or fully a member of that group.

Conformity and Risky Behaviors

All adolescents encounter pressure to conform to certain peer group parameters, the nature of which is often determined by the racial makeup of the peer group. In some communities, mixed-race youth have a great deal of choice when it comes to friendships and peer group membership. However, the advantage of more choice comes with a high cost of acceptance in some situations, which could lead to riskier behaviors in order to increase the possibility that peer group membership will occur (Fryer, Kahn, Levitt, & Spekkuch, 2008). It is possible that the challenges some mixed-race youth encounter when attempting to attach to a peer group leads to either withdrawal or overconformity. The case of the latter may lead to engagement in risky behaviors (Cheng & Klugman, 2010).

There are other reasons for risky behavior among mixed-race youth, however. According to Choi, Haraich, Gillmore, and Catalano (2006), the prejudice and discrimination experienced by mixed-race youth in their communities and schools correlated with increased involvement in risky behaviors. They found that mixed-race youth were more likely than monoracial peers (White, Black, or Asian) to have smoked and drank and more likely to have tried marijuana than White or Asian peers. Moreover, Choi et al. reported that mixed-race youth were more likely to have engaged in certain types of violent behavior than White and Asian peers but, again, not so much their Black peers.

In addition to experiences of prejudice and discrimination, the researchers suggested that a lack of ethnic identity development correlated with problematic behavior among mixed-race youth. However, the ethnic identity measure used to determine the impact of ethnic identity development on risky behaviors was designed for monoracial youth. As discussed in Chapter 3, and as presented as a limitation of the study by the researchers, these measures may not be appropriate for mixed-race youth. As a result, additional research is needed to determine the nature of influences on the notion that mixed-race engage in riskier behaviors than their monoracial peers.

Concluding Comments

Adolescence can be challenging for all young people, given the cognitive, physical, and emotional changes that take place during that period, along with the cultural practice in the United States that youth begin making friendship decisions for themselves. As noted in earlier chapters, adolescence is also the period when young people develop a sense of self through identity and racial identity development. The importance of peers during adolescence has been noted, and it is clear that peer relations influence not only the social and emotional well-being of youth, but also extends to their academic "health." Given the interrelatedness of these statuses, schools ought to pay attention to the individual and group experiences of young people during this period.

Race plays a unique role in the lives of mixed-race youth as they seek friends and peer group membership during adolescence. It is important to recognize that mixed-race youth will adopt diverse, complex, and flexible strategies to manage the social implications of race during this period in their lives. These tendencies should not be characterized as deficiencies or viewed as signs of unhealthy development owing to their mixed-race status. Rather, they should be looked at as a reflection of the ubiquitous nature of race, of the continued attempts to separate people into race-based bounded categories, and how even our children are obligated to find ways to navigate the hurdles our construction of race presents.

Note

1. From *What are you?: Voices of mixed-race young people* © 1999 by Pearl Fuyo Gaskins. Reprinted by permission of Henry Holt Books for Young Readers. All rights reserved.

References

Aboud, F. (2003). The formation of in-group favoritism and out-group prejudice in young children: Are they distinct attitudes? *Developmental Psychology*, 39(1), 48–60.

Ahnallen, J. M., Suyemoto, K., & Carter, A. S. (2006). Relationship between physical appearance, sense of belonging and exclusion, and racial/ethnic self-identification among multiracial Japanese European Americans. *Cultural Diversity and Ethnic Minority Psychology*, 12(4), 673–686.

Baron, A. S. & Banaji, M. R. (2006). The development of implicit attitudes: Evidence of race evaluations from ages 6 and 10 and adulthood. *Psychological Science*, 17(1), 53–58.

Binning, K., Unzueta, M., Huo, Y., & Molina, L. (2009). The interpretation of multiracial status and its relation to social engagement and psychological well-being. *Journal of Social Issues*, 65(1), 35–49.

Burrell, J. O., Winston, C. E., & Freeman, K. E. (2012). Race-acting. The complex affirmative meaning of "acting Black" for African-American adolescents. *Culture and Psychology*, 19(1), 95–116.

Butler-Sweet, C. (2011). "A healthy Black identity" transracial adoption, middle-class families, and racial socialization. *Journal of Comparative Family Studies*, 42(2), 193–212.

Campbell, M. E. & Eggerling-Boeck, J. (2006). What about the children? The psychological and social well-being of multiracial adolescents. *The Sociological Quarterly*, 47(1), 147–173.

Campbell, M. E. & Herman, M. R. (2010). Politics and policies: Attitudes toward multiracial Americans. *Ethnic and Racial Studies*, 33(9), 1511–1536.

Cheng, S. & Klugman, J. (2010). School racial composition and biracial adolescents. *The Sociological Quarterly*, 51(1), 150–178.

Choi, Y., Harachi, T., Gillmore, M. R., & Catalano, R. F. (2006) Are multiracial adolescents at greater risk? Comparisons of rates, patterns, and correlates of substance use and violence between monoracial and multiracial adolescents. *American Journal of Orthopsychiatry*, 76(1), 86–97.

Clark, K. B. & Clark, M. P. (1947). Racial identification and preference among Negro children. In E. L. Hartley (Ed.), *Readings in Social Psychology* (pp. 169–178). New York: Holt, Rinehart, and Winston.

Cochrane, C. B. (2013, December 7). *Bi-Racial kids/people hate being called black* [Video file]. From http://youtu.be/rV7pXEVvO0U.

Cooper, A. (2010, May 16). *Skin color: The way kids see it* [Video file]. From http://youtu.be/JcAuO0PNnrs.

Davis, K. (2007, April 16). *A girl like me*. From http://youtu.be/z0BxFRu_SOw.

Doyle, J. M. & Kao, G. (2007). Friendship choices of multiracial adolescents: Racial homophily, blending, and amalgamation? *Social Science Research*, 36(2), 633–653.

Dulin-Keita, A., Hannon, L., Fernandez, J., & Cockerham, W. (2011). The defining moment: Children's conceptualization of race and experiences with racial discrimination. *Ethnic and Racial Studies*, 34(4), 662–682.

Fordham, S. (1993). Those loud Black girls: (Black) women, silence, and passing in the academy. *Anthropology and Education Quarterly*, 30(3), 272–293.

Fryer, R. G., Kahn, L., Levitt, S. D., & Spekkuch, J. L. (2008). The plight of mixed race adolescents. *NBER Working Paper Series*. From http://www.nber.org/papers/w14192.pdf.

Gordon, M. (2008). Media contributions to African American girls' focus on beauty and appearance: Exploring the consequences of sexual objectification. *Psychology of Women Quarterly*, 32(3), 245–256.

Herman, M. (2004). Forced to choose. Some determinants of racial identification in multiracial adolescents. *Child Development*, 75(3), 730–748.

Hirschfeld, L. A. (2008). Children's developing conceptions of race. In S. M. Quintana & C. McKown (Eds.), *Handbook of race, racism, and the developing child* (pp. 37–54). Hoboken, NJ: John Wiley & Sons.

Holzhauer, A. (1999). People want me to choose. In P. Gaskins (Ed.), *What are you?: Voices of mixed-race young people* (p. 216). New York: Henry Holt and Company.

Jackson, K. R., Wolven, T., & Aguilera, K. (2013). Mixed resilience: A study of multiethnic Mexican American stress and coping in Arizona. *Family Relations*, 62(1), 212–225.

Khanna, N. (2011). *Biracial in America: Forming and performing racial identity*. New York: Lexington Books.

Lewis, A. E. (2003). Everyday race-making: Navigating racial boundaries in schools. *American Behavioral Scientist*, 47(3), 283–305.

Lewis, R. L. (2010). Speaking the unspeakable: Youth discourses on racial importance in school. In H. B. Johnson (Ed.), *Sociological studies of children and youth, Vol. 13: Children and youth speak for themselves* (pp. 401–421). Bingly, UK: Emerald Group Publishing Ltd.

Lewis-Charp, H. (2003). Breaking the silence: White students' perspectives on race in multiracial schools. *Phi Delta Kappan*, 85(4), 279–285.

McGill, R., Way, N., & Hughes, D. (2012). Intra- and interracial friendships during middle school: Links to social and emotional well-being. *Journal of Research on Adolescence*, 22(4), 722–738.

McGlothlin, H. & Killen, H. (2006). Intergroup attitudes of European American children attending ethnically homogeneous schools. *Child Development*, 77(5), 1375–1386.

Miville, M., Constantine, M., Baysden, M., & So-Lloyd, G. (2005). Chameleon changes: An exploration of racial identity themes of multiracial people. *Journal of Counseling Psychology*, 52(4), 507–516.

Murray, M.S., Neal-Barnett, A., Demmings, J.L., & Stadulis, R.E. (2012). The acting White accusation, racial identity, and anxiety in African American adolescents. *Journal of Anxiety Disorders*, 26(4), 526–531.

Nissel, A. (2006). *Mixed: My life in Black and White*. New York: Villard Books.

Obama, B. (2004). *Dreams from my father: A story of race and inheritance*. New York: Three River Press.

Ogbu, J. (2004). Collective identity and the burden of "acting White" in Black history, community, and education. *The Urban Review*, 36(1), 1–36.

Pachter, L.M., Bernstein, B.B., Szalacha, L., & Coll, C. (2010). Perceived racism and discrimination in children and youths: An exploratory study. *Health & Social Work*, 35(1), 61–70.

Phillips, L. (2004). Fitting in and feeling Good. *Women & Therapy*, 27(1–2), 217–236, doi:10.1300/JO15v27n01_15.

Pryor, R. (2006). *Jokes my father never taught me: Life, love, and loss with Richard Pryor*. New York: Harper-Collins Publishers.

Putnam, R. (2007). E Pluribus Unum: Diversity and community in the twenty-first century. *Scandinavian Political Studies*, 30(2), 137–174.

Quillian, L. & Redd, R. (2009). The friendship networks of multiracial adolescents. *Social Science Research*, 38(2), 279–295.

Raabe, T. & Beelmann, A. (2011). Development of ethnic, racial, and national prejudice in childhood and adolescence: A multinational meta-analysis of age differences. *Child Development*, 82(6), 1715–1737.

Renn, K. (2004). *Mixed race students in college: The ecology of race, identity, and community on campus*. Albany, NY: State University of New York Press.

Risman, B.J. & Banerjee, P. (2013). Kids talking about race: Tween-agers in a post-civil rights era. *Sociological Forum*, 28(2), 213–235.

Rockquemore, K.A. & Brunsma, D. (2004). Negotiating racial identity: Biracial women and interactional validation. *Women & Therapy*, 27(1–2), 85–102. doi:10.1300/J015v27no1–06.

Rockquemore, K.A. & Laszloffy, T. (2005). *Raising biracial children*. New York: Rowman and Littlefield Publishers, Inc.

Rogers, L., Zosuls, K., Halim, M., Ruble, D., Hughes, D., & Fuligni, A. (2012). Meaning making in middle childhood: An exploration of the meaning of ethnic identity. *Cultural Diversity and Ethnic Minority Psychology*, 18(2), 99–108.

Romo, R. (2011). Between Black and Brown: Blaxican (Black-Mexican) multiracial identity in California. *Journal of Black Studies*, 42(3), 402–426.

Root, M.P.P. (2003). Multiracial families and children: Implications for educational research and practice. In J.A. Banks & C.A. McGee Banks (Eds.), *Handbook of research on multicultural education* (2nd ed., pp. 110–124). San Francisco: Jossey-Bass.

Ruebeck, C., Averett, S., & Bodenhorn, H. (2008). Acting white or acting black: Mixed-race adolescents' identity and behavior. From http://www.nber.org/papers/w13793.

Samuels, G. (2010). Building kinship and community: Relational processes of bicultural identity among adult multiracial adoptees. *Family Process*, 49(1), 26–42.

Sims, J.P. (2012). Beautiful stereotypes: The relationship between physical attractiveness and mixed race identity. *Identities: Global Studies in Culture and Power*, 19(1), 61–80.

Steele, C. (1997). A threat in the air: How stereotypes shape intellectual identity and performance. *American Psychologist*, 52(6), 613–629.

Townsend, T.G., Neilands, T.B., Thomas, A.J., & Jackson, T.R. (2010). I'm no Jezebel: I am young, gifted, and Black: Identity, sexuality, and Black girls. *Psychology of Women Quarterly*, 34(3), 273–285.

Van Ausdale, D., & Feagin, J. R. (2001). *The first R: How children learn race and racism.* Lanham, MD: Rowman & Littlefield.

Waring, C. (2013). *Beyond "code switching:" The racial capital of Black/White biracial Americans.* From http://digitalcommons.uconn.edu/cgi/viewcontent.cgi?article=6276&context=dissertations.

Wilson, J. (2013, March). *India Arie accused of lightening skin, singer looks very different 'Cocoa Butter' cover.* From http://www.huffingtonpost.com/2013/03/29/india-arie-accused-of-lightening-skin-cocoa-butter-cover_n_2980852.html.

PART III
Education and Schooling
People, Places, and Practices

In Part III, we shift from experiences mixed-race youth have outside of school to a more concentrated explication of their experiences inside of schools. Teachers mixed-race youth encounter, the places where schooling takes place, and the policies and practices that guide the day-to-day functioning of schools combine to shape mixed-race youths' schooling experiences. The first chapter in Part III, Chapter 7, emphasizes the impact teachers have on the schooling experiences of mixed-race youth, with a focus on how teachers' personal belief systems and praxis around race interact to profoundly impact their approach to educating differently race youth.

Teachers' personal beliefs about race in general and the ways in which they approach the education of mixed-race youth are expressed within school contexts having varying amounts of diversity, when diversity is viewed as percentages of students from different racial backgrounds attending the same school. The primary focus of Chapter 8 is to explore the extent to which different school contexts, diverse or not diverse, impact the education and development of mixed-race youth. Although the numbers with respect to the racial representation of youths in school settings provide some insight regarding how schools operate as racialized contexts, the policies and practices that undergird the organizational logic of schools are more telling.

The final chapter of Part III, Chapter 9, draws upon major themes discussed throughout the text, to construct a framework of elements of schooling that are of particular importance to the education of mixed-race youth. A number of existing school strategies, polices, and practices are reframed to illustrate how they relate to the schooling of mixed-race youth. A renewal to a commitment to address the schooling needs of all children is emphasized, one that overtly includes those who straddle more than one race.

7

TEACHERS' (MIXED) RACE CONSTRUCTIONS AND TEACHING IN MULTIRACIAL CLASSROOMS

What I'd like teachers to know about ethnicity and race is that it needs to be an open con-versation on an ongoing basis; political correctness that requires a moratorium on the subject of race is not working.

K. Notarainni
Mother of Mixed-Identity Child
(Davis, 2009, p. 117)

Teachers play a pivotal role in the lives of students and can communicate affirm-ing and/or disaffirming messages on a daily basis over a given period of time. To be sure, youths' interactions with some teachers provide lasting memories of their schooling experiences. Teachers may or may not be aware of how presentation of their personal and professional selves influences students. Still, what they teach, how they teach it, and the tone they set in the classroom that governs teacher-student and student-student interactions conceivably leaves some students with indelible memories about their experiences with particular teachers.

Numerous elements of teaching involve issues of race, which teachers may attend to or avoid. In some instances, teachers may not be aware of the racial connotations of what takes place in schools. Still, how teachers consciously or unconsciously incorporate race as a system of beliefs into their professional lives provides insight into their notions of how race ought to be situated as a part of the schooling process. In order to capture this phenomenon, this chapter begins with a brief overview of the role race has played and continues to play in how teachers conceive of their positions as teachers. It explores how teacher practice based on monoracial constructions of race is disturbed when mixed-raceness becomes part of the teaching and learning environment.

Educational theorists, teacher educators, and educational activists continue to seek strategies and approaches to education that address the different social experiences students bring to school. Strategies including multicultural education, culturally relevant pedagogy, and teacher-student racial congruence are among approaches meant to address the schooling needs of public schools' diverse student population. This chapter includes discussion of these approaches with a focus on how schooling of mixed-race youth is impacted or not impacted by these efforts.

The vast amount of literature addressing how teachers relate to students who share their race and students whose race is different from theirs is instructive for exploring teachers' relationships with mixed-race students as well. Racial backgrounds of teachers and students affects not only teachers' perceptions of students' ability and performance, but also teacher attitudes in affective areas such as caring. According to Nieto (2010), teaching is essentially about the relationships teachers develop with their students, families, and professional colleagues. Caring, which has different meaning among teachers, is an essential factor in these relationships. The race of the caregiver and the cared for (Noddings, 2005) should be given consideration as we attempt to understand caring relationships. The final section of this chapter addresses the importance of teachers' caring relationships with mixed-race students and their families, along with barriers that interfere with this process.

Perspectives on Race and Teacher Practice

Teachers have used prevailing meanings of race in given historical periods to guide both their praxis and their interactions with children and youth from different racial backgrounds (Burkholder, 2012). The project of separating groups of people by race for social, political, and economic purposes relied on the institution of education as an essential support for a racialized social agenda. As the social focus ostensibly changed to one of integrating racial groups and facilitating equal opportunity in society regardless of race, schools once again were central to this undertaking as well. Shifting aims related to how racial difference was to be situated in society were reflected in teacher practices that sometimes accommodated and perpetuated, and at other times challenged, the expected use of education to accomplish racialized social goals and purposes. Not surprisingly, the manifestation of race in the teaching profession differs, often depending on teachers' racial backgrounds.

White Teachers' Racial Perspectives

Historically, most White teachers overtly leaned toward dominant culture White-nonwhite constructions of race, which for the most part supported White hegemonic racial ideologies in force at given times. For example, race as ethnicity (Omi & Winant, 2015) predominated understandings of race in the early 1900s, and differences among White ethnic groups were expressed as racial differences. This conception of race guided White teachers' Americanization efforts during early twentieth century that were based on the social perception that children of White racial minorities (i.e., southern and eastern European immigrants) were inferior to, and less capable and less intelligent than U.S.-born White children. Nonetheless, assimilation was believed possible, if children of the new immigrants could learn and adopt American behaviors, values, customs, and beliefs.

White teachers have supported superior/inferior positions based on race, even when they ostensibly appeared not to. Prior to *Brown v. Board of Education,* for example, schools in the south served as one of many social structures needed to solidify White supremacy and ensure that Black people remained in subordinate social and economic positions (Fairclough, 2007). Although liberal White teacher organizations in the 1930s supported the idea of White teachers teaching White students the notion of "fair play" by teaching racial tolerance, they at the same time supported racial subordination of Black people and segregation in all areas of public life. White students accepted these teachings about race as part and parcel of being an educated person, whether their lived experience of race were reflected in those teaching (Burkholder, 2012).

All teachers arrive at the teaching profession with beliefs about race garnered over their lifetime that they apply to their relationships with students and students' families. Given the current demographics of the teaching profession (i.e., a teaching force predominated by White, middle class, monolingual females), students of color will most likely be taught by a teacher who does not share their race, home culture, and/or language (Dickar, 2008) at some point during their P-12 education. Most White teachers, however, have limited exposure to and interactions with people of color. Hence their relationships with students of color are susceptible to stereotypes and prejudicial attitudes formed prior to entering the teaching profession. White teachers will continue to have misconceptions about race and the culture of their students of color if they never have experiences to problematize long-held, erroneous, and stereotypical beliefs about people of color (Bell, 2002).

Some White teachers continue to understand race as ethnicity (Sleeter, 2005), a theory of race that supported the notion of White racial minorities in the late eighteenth and early nineteenth centuries. This view presupposes race as synonymous with culture. As such, cultural differences that interfere with school performance can be eliminated by change in language, values, and/or behaviors, for example. Along this line of thinking, there are presumably no restrictions in society for individuals wanting to benefit from opportunities available in society. In this sense, race does not matter.

Understanding race as ethnicity is consistent with a color-blind perspective. An individualistic view of racial differences is adopted, where merit, and not one's race, is believed to be the primary factor when it comes to success or failure (Sleeter, 2005). As Chapman (2013) explained, this perspective essentially reinforces patterns of White dominance, and ". . . allows school adults to disregard the racial identities of students by solely viewing them as individuals who are divorced from the social, economic, and cultural factors that shape their past and present experiences " (p. 614).

Color-Blind Ideology at Work

White teachers who accept a color-blind ideology are able to minimize the significance of race, while at the same time engage in evasive strategies that prevent and protect them from owning up to the link between race and privilege (Dickar, 2008). Ruling out race as an instrumental factor in the school performance of children of color opens the door for teachers to turn to other aspects of students' lives in order to account for the lack of progress. A problematic family life, lack of motivation, and/or the lack of ability are common areas for explanation. Some teachers of color also adopt a color-blind ideology, even as they acknowledge, experience, and witness racial inequality in their schools. They determine that it is in their best interest and that of their students to act as if race and extant racism do not exist, as they pursue goals that might in the long run lead to a different social position for their students of color (Stoll, 2014).

A color-blind perspective insulates White teachers, especially those who have little to no understanding of racism and White privilege, from engaging a structural analysis of race, racism, and privilege, and how these impact the lives of their students (Sleeter, 2005). In fact, a color-blind ideology is tantamount to color-blind racism because inequities are ignored and privilege remains unchanged (Bonilla-Silva, 2014). Some White teachers continue to believe that White privilege does not exist—and even if it did, it does not reflect who they are personally or professionally. In addition, teachers in majority-minority schools may believe White privilege does not exist in their schools, given the racial makeup of the student population. They have little understanding of the pervasiveness of White privilege and how it impacts children of color, even in settings where White children are in the minority (Vaught & Castagno, 2008). As a result, they resist professional development and programs designed to improve their understanding of racism and race privilege (Sleeter, 2005).

Teachers who view White privilege in this way are not likely to comprehend or challenge the structural nature of White privilege existing in their schools or their districts. Vaught and Castagno (2008) concluded that the education of teachers around issues of race must include experiences where teacher candidates are compelled to view White privilege not from individualistic frameworks (as something that exists or does not exist for them), but rather as the deeply embedded social advantages and benefits that create structural and systemic circumstances that privileges some children while disadvantaging others.

Teaching around Race

White teachers are also less likely to incorporate conversations about race in what they teach. The silence about race is often based in fear of saying something offensive to students of color that might lead to accusations that they are racist. White teachers might also be evasive when it comes to talking about race as a way of distancing themselves from the realities of the consequences of race in their schools. For example, they may discuss the impact of socioeconomic class on challenging school situations, when all or most students fitting into the group referenced are students of color. Speaking in code when it comes to race allows teachers to keep whiteness as the school norm, because problematic school issues can be attributed to something other than race (Dickar, 2008).

Not only are teachers silent about race, but they also teach children to be silent on issues of race as well, by teaching public scripts to children and youth (of all racial backgrounds) that minimize the importance of race and race differences. Youth often follow these teachings, even when their personal or private experiences of race contradict what they are learning (Lewis, 2010). In essence, some youth are taught to accept a color-blind racial ideology that is popular among many White teachers today, even though they may witness (or experience) prejudice and discrimination based on race both inside and outside of their schools and classrooms.

Black Teachers Striving for Racial Uplift

Early in the twentieth century, Black teachers, like White teachers, held binary (i.e., Black and White) perspectives on race. Indeed, this view of race was the foundation for Black teachers' educational goals for Black children. Black teachers' understanding of race served not only to highlight the injustices promulgated by a privileged and segregated White race, but also to remind Black people of the necessity to coalesce and to work together in order to improve the social position of the Black race (Burkholder, 2012). Education was believed to be the primary vehicle for racial uplift, thus in many communities, Black teachers held exalted positions and were viewed as community leaders (Fairclough, 2007). In fact, there was a belief among some Black people that the "destiny of the race" (p. 8) was in the hands of Black teachers.

Black teachers' approach to this charge fluctuated throughout much of the early part of the twentieth century. Early on, their teaching was guided by a belief in racial egalitarianism and the eventuality of Black peoples' cultural assimilation. This perspective gave way to teaching focused on racial pride and racial identity, as beliefs that White people would ever accept Black people as equals waned. Further, the project of counteracting negative racial stereotypes about Black people through teaching Negro History became part of Black teachers' practice, especially for teachers in southern states. Teachers subsequently began to pay more attention to racial discrimination and the fact that separate was not equal in areas such as teaching resources, facilities, and teacher compensation (Burkholder, 2012).

Teaching for Social Justice

Although Black teachers had willingly engaged in accommodationism (e.g., outward subservient and ingratiating behavior toward White people in order to obtain needed resources for Black schools), teaching for social justice was evident as part of their teaching about democracy and patriotism through and beyond the period of World War II (Burkholder, 2012; Fairclough, 2007). Post–World War II, Black teachers held more steadfast beliefs that democracy and racial superiority should not be able to thrive side-by-side. They, more so than their White counterparts, embraced social justice through education as part of what is meant to teach Black students. According to Murtadha and Watts (2005), Black educators

> . . . linked the struggle for education with social justice, [and that they were] acting within a moral imperative. Educational leadership for African Americans meant fighting to overcome the social barriers of poverty and class, slavery, and institutionalized racism's inequities within a democratic society.
>
> *(p. 592)*

Again, like liberal White teachers in the early 1930s, Black teachers supported teaching about racial tolerance—but not as a disposition where prejudice and racial segregation could be maintained outside of the classroom. Rather, they sought a reduction in racial prejudice that would allow for a racially integrated society. Bolstered by a growing Civil Rights movement, Black educators moved from positions of accommodationism to one of demanding racial justice and educational opportunities and resources for Black children similar to those enjoyed by White children.

Construction of the Black Teacher

It would be misleading to suggest that there was no conflict between Black teachers and the communities they served. Although there was no separation by race, a superior-inferior divide existed in some Black communities. A social distance of sorts separated Black teachers and the much less educated people in Black communities. Some teachers took on an air of superiority in their assessment of the uneducated parents of their students. Alternately, parents mocked teachers for behaviors (especially their speech) believed to imitate White people. Evidence also suggested that teachers and families did not always value education in the same way, and this was especially true for families in rural areas who often did not appreciate the practical value of education. These class-based conflicts between teacher and community persisted over time (Fairclough, 2007).

Still, a conceptualization of the Black teacher emerged that was grounded in the Black social and cultural experience. Teachers perceived teaching sometimes as a religious duty (Fairclough, 2007), at other times as service or as part of a cultural tradition (Ware, 2002), and most consistently as central to racial uplift efforts. Elements of these perceptions of teaching are evident among some Black teachers today. For example, in Dixson and Dingus's (2008) qualitative study of Black female teachers' reasons for entering the teaching profession, themes emerged that included teaching as a family tradition, teaching as an opportunity to be in service to and connected to the Black community, and teaching as a spiritual mission. On the other hand, some Black teachers appear to be disconnected from the historical and cultural importance of teaching to the Black community as a motivation for entering the profession. In a separate study of reasons Black female teachers chose teaching as a profession, Farinde, LeBlanc, and Otten (2015) arrived at emergent themes from participants that hardly reflected the traditional beliefs about being a teacher that were born of the experiences of Black people in society. Reasons such as ". . . a love of school, students, and teaching . . ." (p. 44), although important, do not carry the depth of racial responsibility once expressed by Black teachers.

Supporters of racial congruence between Black students and Black teachers rely, to some degree, on the historic successes Black teachers were able to realize with Black students. Advocates base their support on the belief that Black teachers understand from whence Black students come (e.g., their family and community life) and what is needed to move them to their next station in life. Moreover, it is believed that like Black teachers of the past (see Siddle Walker, 1996, for example), today's Black teachers will serve as mentors and role models for Black students and make use of tacit knowledge of what is necessary for their educational success. However, in 2012, Black teachers made up only 7 percent of the teaching force nationally (Hispanic teachers were 8 percent of the teaching force) (U.S. Department of Education, n.d.). Further, Black teachers no longer teach Black students only in tightly knit Black communities. They are often dispersed in communities with varying levels of diversity throughout the nation, and many find themselves pursuing racial uplift goals in isolation of other Black teachers.

Even so, Black students have expectations of the Black teachers they encounter that are different from expectations of their White teachers. They expect racial solidarity with Black teachers, and as a result of their shared racial background, they look for both moral and general support and advocacy. Further, Black students may trust what Black teachers teach about certain subjects, such as Black History, more than they trust a teacher of a different race. The expectations Black students have of Black teachers can place teachers at odds with their professional roles. Students may want teachers to take actions that are beyond the power or position of the teacher, and which do not fit with what teachers deem appropriate for the profession. When Black teachers can't deliver, their relationships with Black students may suffer. Black teachers stand to be viewed as disloyal. It is also possible that Black teachers will have their authenticity as Black persons questioned if they do not act or talk in ways students expect (Dickar, 2008).

Race-Based Teacher-to-Teacher Interactions

Race related issues not only affect interactions and relationships between teacher and students, but can also shape professional relationships between teachers. A color-blind ideology held by an individual teacher and/or as an overarching approach to education among most teachers in a particular school setting interferes with the ability of teachers to have meaningful conversations about race with each other that might benefit the environment in which they teach. Moreover, conflict arises between Black and White teachers when the cultural knowledge Black teachers have about Black students that could contribute to more positive learning experiences go unrecognized by their White colleagues (Dickar, 2008).

How monoracial teachers of any race interact with mixed-race teachers is an area ripe for research. At this point, however, insufficient data exist on the mixed-race sector of the teaching force. There is some indication, however, that mixed-race teachers experience being raced in ways similar to mixed-race students. Assumptions might be made about a mixed-race teacher's racial background, and thus who he or she is socially and culturally. Expectations of tacit cultural knowledge could lead to tension and misunderstanding between both mixed-race and monoracial teachers (Janis, 2012).

Teachers' One-Drop Rule Racial Identifications

I presented the forgoing overview on ways in which race was inserted into and many ways shaped the goals of teacher practice as a framework for discussing interactions between monoracial White and Black teachers and mixed-race youth. I propose that teacher practice in these relations will reflect, at least in part, elements of the historical ways that race was understood and approached by teachers from different racial backgrounds. The intersection among the historical incursion of race into education, teachers' personal racial biography, and the approach to race taken in various school settings serve as a foundation for understanding teachers' interactions with mixed-race students.

Despite exclamations to the contrary, teachers not only see race, but also begin to have expectations of students based on their perceptions of students' race at the initial moment of social contact (Herman, 2010; Williams, 2011). Generally, people observe characteristics used to determine social status the moment social interaction begins. Their expectations of an individual's behaviors are made at that instant, based on stereotypes of the characteristics they observe (Herman, 2010).

Where observations of mixed-race people are concerned, recognition of racial ambiguity leads to conclusions that the mixed-race person is nonwhite. This conclusion, however, is followed by a decision based on hypodescent (one-drop rule) that the person is a minority race individual (Herman, 2010). It is also true that with additional information (for example, cultural information), the perception of race may change to mixed-race. However, there must be some interest and motivation on the part of the observer in going beyond the physical characteristics most immediately available. Even with a mixed-race identification, the individual may still be viewed the same as a monoracial minority person (i.e., mixed-race but Black) (Peery & Bodenhausen, 2008).

Incongruence occurs when teachers' perceptions of a student's race does not match how the student self-identifies. Mixed-race youth experience stress, not only when they are misidentified on the basis of physical characteristics, but also when incongruence exists between how they are perceived racially and how they self-identify. In the case of the latter, a teacher may recognize that a student is mixed-race Asian and White, but view the student as Asian only, when the student may self-identify as White. Williams (2011) found that teachers are often guided by the one-drop rule and view mixed-race Black-White students as Black. As important, they assume mixed-race students have the same background and experiences as their monoracial Black peers. As a result, some mixed-race students believe their teachers are not interested in their experiences as mixed-race individuals. Teachers also assume students racial background on the basis of phenotype and will, for example, determine that mixed-race students who look White are White, regardless of the racial self-identity the student might possess.

Teachers' perception of race is important to note because teachers continue to treat students differently on the basis of race. Educational literature is replete with evidence of race bias perpetrated by teachers. Stoll (2014) summarized areas where race bias is in effect to include low performance expectations of students of color, differences in the application of discipline to differently raced students, more frequent use of minimizing labels assigned to one racial group (e.g., at-risk) over another, and teacher-student interactions and communications that are more positive with students from one racial group than others. Teachers' academic performance expectations of students on the basis of race impact students' achievement (Williams, 2011). Indeed, as Sleeter (2005) pointed out, some White teachers automatically assume children of color will not perform as well academically as White children, thus the achievement gap becomes a taken-for-granted fact of teaching.

Teachers also make assumptions not directly tied to academic performance about mixed-race students, which they express through silence when race-related incidents occur in their classrooms. On the other hand, some teachers give voice to their race-related assumptions about mixed-race youth, both as statements directly to mixed-race youth and through communication to the class in general. In either event, teachers' verbal and nonverbal behaviors model how to race mixed-race youth, which in turn impacts how peers race mixed-race youth in peer-to-peer relations.

McBride (1996), who is mixed-race with a Black father and White mother, for example, attended a school that was predominantly attended by Jewish students. He recalled an experience where classmates presumably believed the stereotype that all Black people could dance, and they wanted him to dance like James Brown. Despite protests that he could not dance, they routinely pestered him to dance for them. He finally acquiesced, placing in himself in a position where he performed race, a situation witnessed by his teacher. He described the event this way:

> . . . I found myself standing in front of the classroom . . . I slid around the way I had seen him [James Brown] do . . . They were delighted . . . I sat down with their applause ringing in my ears, . . . knowing I had pleased them . . . happy to feel accepted . . .
>
> *(p. 105)*

McBride recognized immediately following his dance that his classmates were motivated by a desire to ridicule rather than accept him. Although McBride clearly stood out as phenotypically Black among his White classmates, his mixed-race status was essentially erased. Even though he identified as Black, it was not lost to him that peers who were the same race as his mother did not accept him. In fact, as he reflected on the incident, he was reminded that he too had felt some of the same disdain he observed in his peers' faces when he thought of himself as part White and part Black.

Teachers similarly force mixed-race youth into race-performing situations motivated by the one-drop rule. This occurs when they for example, persuade youth to take on a topic or project with a nonwhite or monoracial minority focus, where there are multiple options of topics from which to choose. Given both the location (i.e., where they happen to be) in the racial self-identity developmental process and the trajectory (direction of their affiliation) of the student's self-racial identity journey, a different focus for a topic of the student's choosing might be more appropriate.

It is plausible to conclude that McBride's experience was based on use of the one-drop rule as means for separating by race (through ridicule) with the end goal of positioning one group in a more favorable light or position than another. Teachers of color also evoke the one-drop rule when interacting with mixed-race youth; however, it is conceivable that this is sometimes done from a collective or protective position rather than a pejorative one. Their actions may be based on the belief that a mixed-race student will be perceived and treated as a person of color, and so mixed-race youth should accept that identity as well. The following experience of a fifth grader is a case in point, as she responded to her Black teachers' question of why she checked "other" for race on a form she was required to complete.

> She was like, "Why did you do this?" I said, "'Cause my mom's white and my dad's black." She said, "Change this to black. You're black because your father's black . . . So forget the white side."
>
> *(Barner, 1999, p. 58)*[1]

The student in this scenario, however, did not perceive the teacher's actions as protective or instructive. In fact, she expressed an intense dislike for her teacher. Mixed-race individuals who are older, and perhaps more secure in their racial identity claims, may actually confront teachers who race them in ways that conflict with their self-racial identity. A mixed-race graduate student-teacher interaction in Khanna's (2011) study of biracial identity unfolded as follows:

> . . . Our teacher was black and she made reference to the black students in the class and lumped me in with them. And I raised my hand and I was, like, "I'm not black." And she almost wanted to argue with me, like, "Yes, you are." And no, no I'm not . . .
>
> *(p. 115)*

In both situations, teachers used their positions of authority to race their mixed-race students using the one-drop rule. Suffice to say that the relationships between both the younger and older students and their teachers were strained. Clearly, and rightly so, mixed-racial students do not appreciate having their racial identity claims challenged by their teachers.

Other Black teachers may invalidate mixed-race students' racial identity claims, not because they wish to embrace or protect mixed-race youth. Some Black teachers hold views of racial solidarity that make it difficult for them to wholly accept mixed-race youths, especially those who claim a Black racial identity, but who are phenotypically more White than Black. They also exhibit monoracist attitudes when they have difficulty with mixed-race people who want to equally claim all aspects of their racial heritage. A mixed-race (Black-White) high school student described the following experience with a Black teacher, who was also the advisor for the school's Black Student Association.

> . . . He was insistent that only Hispanics and Blacks be allowed in the club. He had a very hard time letting me in because I am not Black . . . I just really wasn't welcomed there . . . He knew that I was Black and White, and I looked too White for him, I guess.
>
> *(Howard, 2004, p. 61)*

Situating Race into Teacher Praxis

Race has been and continues to be a primary student characteristic that attracts the type of bias that leads to inequity. Schools have been a primary edifice to house practices that produce and sustain schooling experiences that contribute to the disparity in life chances among differently raced children and youth. For this reason, it is important to review how race continues to inform teacher practice, with a primary goal of understanding how these practices shape schooling experiences for mixed-race youth.

Teachers entrenched in whiteness have a difficult time understanding children of color, their families, and how societal structural elements precipitate difficulties in the lives of children of color in general, but also in their school performance. In fact, White teachers describe a lack of efficacy when teaching students of a race different from their own. Limited to no interaction with differently raced people, at least in part, is the reason (Henfield & Washington, 2012). More important, however, both pre-service and practicing teachers have limited understanding of race and racism and how power is related to the two (Castagno, 2013). These race-related areas of knowledge and experiences potentially surface with mixed-race youth who identify fully or in part as persons of color. They are also important to note in situations where mixed-race youth are raced by their teachers as persons of color, regardless of how they racially self-identity.

Many White teachers are reticent to change long-held race-related beliefs, a fact that is evident even during teacher education courses designed to have pre-service teachers interrogate their beliefs about race. They rely on what Picower (2009) contended are "tools of Whiteness" that allow them to ". . . deny, evade, subvert, or avoid . . ." issues related to race (pp. 204–205). In a study that analyzed pre-service teachers' reactions to race-related course content, Picower observed that White pre-service teachers actively engaged emotional tools of whiteness (e.g., " I never owned slaves"), race ideological tools of whiteness (e.g., color blindness), and performative tools of whiteness (e.g., silence) (pp. 205–209). Teacher education programs unable to disrupt use of these tools ensure a population of teachers who will create classrooms based on racial ideologies that support White hegemony as taken-for-granted structural elements of schooling (Picower, 2009).

The implications for mixed-race youth are clear. Inclinations by some White teachers to maintain beliefs and practices based on White hegemony compel them to engage in deficit evaluations of some of their students. Mixed-race youth who are perceived as nonwhite by their teachers will be susceptible to devaluing experiences similar to those of some monoracial minorities. Evidence suggests, however, that evaluation of mixed-race youth will differ on the basis of their location along a socially entrenched racial hierarchy that arranges social groups by race into high and low social status positions.

Teacher-Student Racial Congruence Revisited

Teacher-student racial congruence appears to matter when it comes to teacher evaluation of students' performance. Egalite, Kisida, and Winters (2015) suggested that racial congruence between teacher and student had a positive impact on all monoracial students, White and nonwhite. Literature that addresses the negative outcomes of racial incongruence between teacher and student is substantial; however, most of this literature reports on the White teacher-Black student dyad. In this instance, White teachers are consistently more negative toward Black students than White students as they evaluate behavior and academic performance. McGrady and Reynolds (2013) extended this line of research, however, to include the impact of racial congruence on performance by students from different racial backgrounds (White, Black, Latino, and Asian) and the perceptions of both White and nonwhite teachers of students' ability and behavior.

White teachers, more so than nonwhite teachers, were swayed by racial stereotypes in their evaluations of Asian, Black, and Latino students. Based on the model minority stereotype, Asian students were evaluated more positively, and based on a host of negative stereotypes about Black and Latino students, they were evaluated less favorably when it came to ability and performance. Nonwhite teachers who shared the same racial background as their students tended to evaluate Black and Hispanic students more positively; however, they evaluated Asian students less favorably. Although the authors of this study could not fully explain the latter phenomena, they maintained their primary thesis that racial incongruence between student and teacher resulted in less favorable evaluations.

Mixed-race teachers' and mixed-race students' racial self-identities and racial affiliations complicate determining the impact of racial congruence between mixed-race teacher and mixed-race student. Just as mixed-race students who share the same racial heritage have different racial identities and racial affiliations, mixed-race teachers who share a racial lineage with their mixed-race students might not share their racial identity or racial affiliation. Important to consider also is the fact that just as not all teachers of color are committed to social justice and may incorporate whiteness into their belief systems and professional practice, the same is true for mixed-race teachers.

It is plausible that mixed-race teachers may have commitments similar to those of many White teachers, based on their racial identity and racial affiliation. Still, when mixed-race teachers connect with students around a shared mixed-race identity, the possibility exists for a teacher-student relationship that has a positive effect on the student's schooling experience. A mixed-race student (Black, White, and Native American) in Davis's study (2009) shared how she experienced schooling with teachers who looked like her:

> I loved my little country school where all the children looked like me and where the teachers who looked like me told me I could grow up to become

a teacher or anything else I set my mind to becoming . . . My teachers were warm, friendly, cared about me, maintained high expectations, and knew me well.

(p. 115)

Scholars, teacher educators, and policymakers seek situations where educational experiences for most children resemble the one just described. Perceptions of the enormity of the task of transforming White teachers' belief systems leave some believing teacher-student racial congruence for nonwhite students is the best option. As a result, they turn their attention to increasing the numbers of teachers of color in order to address the persistent performance gap between White and nonwhite students. It is assumed, however, that a match in race presupposes a match in culture (Achinstein & Aguirre, 2008).

Teachers of color are expected to be more effective with culturally relevant teaching than their White professional peers when it comes to teaching students of color (Achinstein & Aguirre, 2008). They are believed to be in a better position to structure classroom environments that are both culturally congruent and responsive to students' home cultures. Indeed, among the pillars of culturally relevant pedagogy is the expectation of cultural competence, where teachers are able to use their understanding of students' cultural experiences to facilitate students' learning in various academic areas (Ladson-Billings, 1995). It is also believed that teachers who share the same race, language, culture, and/or class backgrounds as their students can better serve as role models for success and provide images that counter negative stereotypes students learn from society about their racial and cultural backgrounds.

Achinstein and Aguirre (2008) pointed out that the assumed match in culture may be mediated by differences in areas such as ". . . class, language, color, educational opportunities, regionalism, cultural capital, and schooling experiences . . ." (p. 1508). Further, they suggested that the value of racial congruence is based on a belief that teachers of color will be able to effectively access and use cultural resources in their praxis. Ladson-Billings (2014) advised that closer attention needs to be paid to the fluid and dynamic and thus ever-changing nature of culture. She also expressed concern that educators' understanding of culturally relevant teaching had become superficial, as reflected by rather surface notions of culture that did not capture within-group diversity among groups.

Proponents of student-teacher racial congruence also assume that students will accept teachers of color as suitable representatives of culture as perceived and experienced by students. In reality, students may view teachers of color as "culturally suspect" (Achinstein & Aguirre, 2008, p. 1513) and question teachers' cultural authenticity. In these situations, teachers' "racial credentials" will be challenged, and this is true for both monoracial and mixed-race teachers. Even so, just as monoracial students may still have specific expectations of teachers of the same race, the same would likely be true for mixed-race youth as well.

Mixed-race youth might feel a special kinship to a mixed-race teacher, based on their assumptions about the teacher's racial identity. In fact, both mixed-race and monoracial White or students of color may make racial assumptions about mixed-race teachers based on phenotype and have expectations of racial solidarity or understanding based on those assumptions (Janis, 2012). Tension and misunderstanding are possible when student expectations are based on faulty racial background and affinity assumptions. Unmet expectations could have an adverse effect on teacher-student relationships.

The Mixed-Race Experience and Multicultural Education

Clearly, teacher-student racial congruence as an educational strategy will not fully address the goals to improve the educational experiences of students of color. If for no other reason, the sheer imbalance of the majority-minority public school student population, juxtaposed with the limited diversity in the public school teaching force, makes it improbable that nationally, even a reasonable number of students of color will to be taught by a teacher of color. Multicultural education as a strategy meant to ensure that students of color have a more culturally connected schooling experience by focusing teacher efforts on issues of cultural inclusion and more equitable educational outcomes.

The Inception of Multicultural Education

As she reflected on the current status of culturally relevant teaching, Ladson-Billings (2014) warned that the sociopolitical aspects of this approach was being neglected. The notion of a sociopolitical element to teacher practice with a goal of minimizing inequities in students' schooling experiences in some ways triggered the educational activism and theorizing that is the basis for multicultural education. The oppression of African Americans in society in general prompted attention to schooling experiences as a source of inequities; however, the focus was on culture and not race. As a result, the call for ethnic studies following the Civil Rights Movement was based on a desire to include the history, experiences, and contributions of minority racial groups in the United States (e.g., African Americans, Asian Americans, Mexican Americans, and Native Americans) in textbooks and the school curriculum (Banks, 2013). However, the inclusion of content from nonwhite groups into the curriculum proved to be an additive component to the curriculum, more so than a transformative one with the possibility of students learning to challenge White hegemony based on the content to which they were exposed.

Early multiethnic education did not include the social and cultural experiences of students and how these impacted school performance. Thus even as aspects of multiethnic education morphed in multicultural education, early theorists (e.g., Geneva Gay, James Banks, Lisa Delpit) raised concerns about other schooling elements that impacted the education of children of color. These included school policy and politics, school culture and the hidden curriculum, learning styles, community participation and input, and instructional materials and teaching styles and strategies (Banks, 2013, p. 77).

Still other scholars were more exacting about the need for a sociopolitical perspective for multicultural education and linked this educational approach to social justice goals. Further, more explicit references to teacher practice and race surfaced, along with attention to other social characteristics (e.g., class, gender, and language) in both content and pedagogical perspectives (Chapman & Grant, 2010). Nieto (2004) noted that as multicultural education became inclusive, teachers were more apt to avoid discussions of race by directing attention to social characteristics (e.g., class) with which they were more comfortable.

In fact, based on an analysis of multicultural education courses taught in teacher preparation programs across the nation, Gorski (2009) concluded that the focus appeared to be on skills and cultural awareness as a means for preparing future teachers to work with diverse student populations. Social justice commitments were not observed, as most courses did not appear focused on teaching teachers how to create learning environments based on equity. Moreover, diversity-related courses did not include content and experiences that would assist future teachers with development of a critical consciousness needed to address issues of equity from sociopolitical perspectives. Issues of power and privilege as they relate to persistent education inequities were not addressed.

Avoiding Race in Multicultural Education

The tendency to ignore race as central to teaching goals related to diversity has resulted in limited attention to mixed-raceness in multicultural education. Recently, Picower (2009) proposed that there is a sense that White teachers needed to develop a "racialized critical conscience" (p. 199) that would not only shape their relationships with students, but also inform their praxis and curriculum-building activities. Nonetheless, although some multicultural theorists positioned multicultural education to be counter-hegemonic, teachers have been able to use it to perpetuate and sustain whiteness. According to Castagno (2013), overtime, multicultural education has come to mean ". . . something that has to do with "diversity" and "equality" in educational contexts but which fails to challenge whiteness" (p. 107). Further, teachers may use multicultural education as a vehicle for assimilationist goals, which is consistent with a race-as-ethnicity perspective discussed earlier in this chapter. Behavior, attitudes, values, and language, and not race, then become the cause for differences in students' schooling experiences.

Proponents of the anti-racist approach to education claim that the implementation of multicultural education is too often an event of celebrating differences over explicit incorporation of racial ideology and racism as the reasons for differences in peoples' experiences (DiAngelo, 2012; Niemonen, 2007). It must be mentioned, however, that anti-racist education as a remedy for this shortcoming is not without its critics. According to Niemonen (2007), even though anti-racist approaches confront whiteness and criticize color blindness, the approach is more a moral based than theoretically based explanation of the significance of race on society. As such, in practice, anti-racist theories focus on raising awareness of racism and racial privilege awareness for White people, but according to Blackwell (2010), provides limited opportunities for students of color to explore these issues in any meaningful way.

Teachers who neglect to include race as significant to groups' social experiences miss a social characteristic that is salient to many mixed-race students—one that is critical to how they experience their worlds, both inside and outside of schools. Nonetheless, some teachers prefer to focus on other student characteristics in the name of multicultural education, all of which, of course, are important to consider, and all of which contribute to student diversity. A both/and rather than either/or approach, which considers the intersection of multiple social characteristics, facilitates a more holistic view of students and their educational needs.

One way that teachers engage multicultural education is by attention to students' different learning styles. Accordingly, they employ multiple pedagogical strategies to respond to the different ways students approach learning. Human relations is another common interpretation of multicultural education that teachers willingly adopt. Educators believe students learn to accept and respect differences when they are exposed to content from multiple cultures and have opportunities to interact with students from backgrounds different from their own (Castagno, 2013).

Educators may be unaware of how issues of power relate to multicultural education. Thus, they are inclined to be indifferent to disparities in power experienced by students in the same classroom and/or school setting. Students' sense of power, gained from perceptions of their value juxtaposed with that of a differently raced peer, influences peer-to-peer relationships. Moreover, students recognize the advantages or disadvantages they experience in school, when compared with those of students with a different racial background. The sense of power of the advantaged is enhanced, whereas the lack thereof is emphasized for the disadvantaged, as their sense of a lowered status in school is accentuated. Castagno (2013) described teachers' tendency to ignore differences in power students possess as powerblind sameness. Teachers adopting this position are able to interact with students on the basis of meritocratic and equality perspectives, where all students supposedly have the same opportunity to advance and to be successful in school. The power advantage experienced by some students, given how they are valued, supported, and positioned within the context of school, is overlooked.

Teachers are also able to mask and avoid the sociopolitical goals of multicultural education by conflating race with class. Ruby Payne's (2005) framework, for example, may serve as knowledge base for teachers' understanding of students living in poverty. Recall, however, that Payne overused examples of people of color to explain tenets of how poverty influences behavior. When teachers think of multicultural education as an educational approach that addresses the needs of children living in poverty, they ostensibly ignore race. In reality, their conception of poverty actually applies to children having a particular racial background. They focus on class without a critical analysis of how race intersects with class to locate youth of some racial backgrounds in poverty locations, in numbers disproportionate to the representation of the racial group in society.

Teachers who ignore race in their content, pedagogy, and classroom environment arrangements as they apply multicultural education in practice leave out an essential area of diversity for mixed-race youth (indeed for all of their students). In fact, "sameness" and color-blind perspectives fly in the face of many mixed-race youths experiences, as many of their interactions with peers, teachers, and within their communities (both White and nonwhite) remind them that they are different because of their mixed-race status. This occurs, for example, when they are required to define who they are racially with "what are you" questions, when their racial self-identity claims are challenged because of phenotype or beliefs in the one-drop rule, and when they are rejected by peers (either monoracial minority or White) because of monoracism.

Mixed-race youth are made to feel different because of the sociopolitical meanings of race in society. The very presence of mixed-race youth in classrooms, however, screams the role race has played in society—because there is no place to easily locate them in a society stratified by race. White teachers committed to whiteness are forced to decide where to place mixed-race youth along a racial hierarchy. Similarly, teachers of color must decide how to locate children who racially are nonwhite but who are not monoracial minority either. Add to this conundrum the complex and multiple ways mixed-race youth racially self-identify. Many teachers, White and teachers of color, decide to locate mixed-race youth on the basis of the one-drop rule, which is a race-based concept with enormous sociopolitical connotations.

Acknowledgment of mixed-race youth as a group challenges teachers' goals of multicultural education as human relations. There is no specific "cultural" understanding attached to mixed-race youth as a group, and so the goal of having students interact with someone of a different culture becomes a problematic project when it comes to monoracial and mixed-race student interactions. Teachers would have to impose a monoracial group's culture onto mixed-race youth and assume that there is a shared worldview between the mixed-race youth and that particular monoracial group that makes up part of their racial lineage. The within-group diversity among mixed-race youth, in terms of racial lineage, racial self-identity, and socialization from the home that influences their worldview, makes the goal of facilitating interaction by culture alone a chancy endeavor.

Caring Relationships with Mixed-Race Youth and Their Families

The focus on social and political implications of teaching may appear to over-shadow a fundamental truth about teachers and teaching—teachers who care about their students, and as an extension, students' families, are better positioned to create conditions that lead to positive schooling experiences for children and youth. Children and youth are acutely aware of differences in their relationships with teachers who care about them and those who do not. Parents, in general, expect teachers to care about their children and their unique needs. Further, as Davis (2009) stated about teacher-family relationships, "if parents don't think we first care about their children, they often choose not to engage in meaning-ful communication with us" (p. 97). Some teachers undoubtedly hold outdated beliefs about interracial families, because four in ten adults still have difficulty with interracial marriages (Taylor et al., 2010). Moreover, this number likely includes teachers of any racial background, depending on their beliefs and per-spectives about race.

Many teachers, White and nonwhite, quite possibly harbor resentment and/ or disdain for interracial families. Their beliefs and attitudes about marriages and partnerships that cross racial boundaries are infused into how they approach caring relationships with mixed-race students and their families. Many White teachers are ". . . dysconscious about the influences of their cultural identities and ideologi-cal commitments" on their teaching and their notion of caring relationships with their students, however (Parsons, 2006, p. 31). Renowned scholar Joyce E. King coined the term dysconsciousness to describe a habit of thinking that results in limited or narrow perceptions of reality (Brandon, 2006; King, 1991).

Even with narrow-minded views of race-related diversity, some teachers are able to create classrooms that exude warmth and caring, regardless of negative and stereotypical views they may have about their students' families. They may believe that students' socialization at home does not adequately support children's education and development. As an example, a teacher may believe that a White single parent who chooses to socialize a mixed-race child to adopt a White iden-tity is not acting in the best interest of the child. Teachers may present an attitude of "benevolently saving" students where they assume they know what is best for students (Pennington, Brock, & Ndura, 2012, p. 767), even when their views are in opposition to families' wishes.

Teachers, whether monoracial White or teachers of color, may have differ-ent notions of caring than those accepted as caring by mixed-race youth and their families. Tosolt (2010) studied the influence of race and gender on fifth through eighth graders' perception of caring teachers. Academic caring (i.e., providing feedback on academic performance) over interpersonal caring may be a preference for some mixed-race students. This is consistent with the instru-mental value of education often preferred by nonwhite parents in interracial families (Lawton, Foeman, & Brown, 2013). White students may perceive a teacher as caring when the teacher combines interpersonal caring (e.g., compliments about personal appearance) with academic caring. A White single parent and her mixed-race child might acknowledge these teacher actions as caring, based on Lawton et al.'s thesis that White parents appreciate the self-knowledge opportunities through education.

Most teachers are underprepared by their education programs to communicate with parents or to understand and empathize with children from families that are different from their own. Wardle (2014) maintained that this is particularly true when it comes to teacher preparation to work with interracial families. Still, many teachers insist caring about children was a primary motivation for entering the teaching profession. As Noddings (2005) has pointed out, the one cared for needs to perceive actions on the caregivers' part as caring. When it comes to mixed-race youth and their families, teachers will need an open mind to the diversity they will surely encounter among interracial families and a willingness to understand what counts as caring for the family enhances the possibility of a productive and caring teacher-student-family relationship.

Concluding Comments

Earlier in this text, I discussed the heightened emphasis many parents of mixed-race youth place on the education of their children. They do so to provide children with a buffer against any negative social experiences their children might experience as a result of being mixed-race. Parents in interracial families are likely to play close attention to teacher interactions with their children. They understand the possibility of teachers bringing to the classroom attitudes and beliefs that might contradict perspectives the family inculcates at home around issues of race and mixed-raceness.

Conflating race and culture is just a problematic as conflating race and class. Rather than substitute social characteristics for each other, we should interrogate how the intersection of each influences the experience of schooling for children and youth. Ignoring and/or avoiding race as a distinct contributing social characteristic to youths' lived experiences is no longer defensible. Given the growing population of mixed-race youth in schools, teachers of all cultural, racial, and ethnic backgrounds ought to feel compelled to learn more about this population of students and their families. This effort necessarily involves understanding how race has been infused into educational aims and practices as a means for restricting social groups to different social locations and experiences based on monoracial notions of race. It also requires knowing how mixed-race children confound those goals.

In a clear sense, information and exposure to mixed-race children and interracial families will expand teachers' knowledge around race. Most teachers understand that youth find it particularly disconcerting when they believe their teachers out-and-out reject them because of a personal characteristic (e.g., being mixed-race) and/or are not interested in knowing who they are. Overcoming the resistance to addressing race allows teachers to develop more authentic relationships with their mixed-race students.

Note

1. From *What are you?: Voices of mixed-race young people* © 1999 by Pearl Fuyo Gaskins. Reprinted by permission of Henry Holt Books for Young Readers. All rights reserved.

References

Achinstein, B. & Aguirre, J. (2008). Cultural match or culturally suspect: How new teachers of color negotiate sociocultural challenges in the classroom. *Teachers College Record*, 110(8), 1505–1540.

Banks, J. A. (2013). The construction and historical development of multicultural education, 1962–2012. *Theory into Practice*, 52(1), 73–82.

Barner, M. (1999). Black dominates. In P. Gaskins (Ed.), *What are you?: Voices of mixed-race young people* (pp. 58–60). New York: Henry Holt and Company.

Bell, L. A. (2002). Sincere fictions: The pedagogical challenges of preparing White teachers for multicultural classrooms. *Equity & Excellence in Education*, 35(3), 236–244.

Blackwell, D. (2010). Sidelines and separate spaces: Making education anti-racist for students of color. *Race, Ethnicity, & Education*, 13(4), 473–494.

Bonilla-Silva, E. (2014). *Racism without racists: Color-blind racism and the persistence of racial inequality in the United States*. Lanham, MD: Rowman & Littlefield.

Brandon, L. (2006). On dysconsciousness: An interview with Joyce E. King. *Educational Studies*, 40(2), 196–208.

Burkholder, Z. (2012). "Education for citizenship in a bi-racial civilization": Black teachers and the social construction of race, 1929–1954. *Journal of Social History*, 46(2), 335–363.

Castagno, A. E. (2013). Multicultural education and the protection of whiteness. *American Journal of Education*, 120(1), 101–128.

Chapman, T. (2013). You can't erase race! Using CRT to explain the presence of race and racism in majority white suburban schools. *Discourse: Studies in the Cultural Politics of Education*, 34(4), 611–627.

Chapman, T. & Grant, A. (2010). Thirty years of scholarship in multicultural education. *Race, Gender, & Class*, 17(1–2), 39–46.

Davis, B. M. (2009). *The biracial and multiracial student experience: A journey to racial literacy*. Thousand Oaks, CA: Corwin.

DiAngelo, R. (2012). Nothing to add: A challenge to White silence in racial discussions. *Understanding and Dismantling Privilege*, 2(1), 1–17.

Dickar, M. (2008). Hearing the silenced dialogue: An examination of the impact of teacher race on their experience. *Race Ethnicity and Education*, 11(2), 115–132, doi:10.1080/12613320802110233.

Dixson, A. D. & Dingus, J. (2008). In search of our mothers' gardens: Black women teachers and professional socialization. *Teachers College Record*, 110(4), 805–837.

Egalite, A. J., Kisida, B., & Winters, M. A. (2015). Representation in the classroom: The effect of own-race teachers on student achievement. *Economics of Education Review*, 45, 44–52.

Fairclough, A. (2007). *A class of their own: Black teachers in the segregated south*. Cambridge, MA: The Belknap Press of Harvard University Press.

Farinde, A., LeBlanc, J. K., & Otten, A. (2015). Pathways to teaching. An examination of Black females' pursuits of careers as K-12 teachers. *Educational Research Quarterly*, 38(3), 32–51.

Gorski, P. (2009). What we're teaching teachers: An analysis of multicultural teacher education coursework syllabi. *Teaching and Teacher Education*, 25(2), 309–318.

Henfield, M. S. & Washington, A. R. (2012). I want to do the right thing but what is it?: White teachers' experiences with African American students. *Journal of Negro Education*, 81(2), 148–161.

Herman, M. (2010). Do you see what I am? How observers' backgrounds affect their perceptions of multiracial faces. *Social Psychology Quarterly*, 73(1), 58–78.

Howard, L. (2004). Unless you're mixed, you don't know what it's liked to be mixed. In S. Nieto (Ed.), *Affirming diversity: Sociopolitical context of multicultural education* (pp. 57–65). Boston: Pearson Education, Inc.

Janis, S. (2012). Am I enough?: A multi-race teacher's experience in-between contested race, gender, class, and power. *Journal of Curriculum Theorizing*, 28(3), 128–141.

Khanna, N. (2011). *Biracial in America: Forming and performing racial identity*. New York: Lexington Books.

King, J. E. (1991). Dysconscious racism. Ideology, identity, and miseducation of teachers. *The Journal of Negro Education*, 60(2), 133–146.

Ladson-Billings, G. (1995). But that's just good teaching: The case for culturally relevant pedagogy. *Theory into Practice*, 34(8), 159–165.

Ladson-Billings, G. (2014). Culturally relevant pedagogy 2.0: A.k.a. the remix. *Harvard Educational Review*, 84(1), 74–84.

Lawton, B., Foeman, A., & Brown, L. (2013). Blending voices: Negotiating educational choices for upper/middle class well-educated interracial couples' children. *Howard Journal of Communication*, 24(3), 215–238.

Lewis, R. L. (2010). Speaking the unspeakable: Youth discourses on racial importance in school. In H. B. Johnson (Ed.), *Sociological studies of children and youth, Vol. 13: Children and youth speak for themselves* (pp. 401–421). Bingly, UK: Emerald Group Publishing Ltd.

McBride, J. (1996). *The color of water: A Black man's tribute to his White mother*. New York: Riverhead Books.

McGrady, P. B. & Reynolds, J. R. (2013). Racial mismatch in the classroom: Beyond black-white differences. *Sociology of Education*, 86(1), 3–17.

Murtadha, K. & Watts, D. M. (2005). Linking the struggle for education and social justice: Historical perspectives of African American leadership in schools. *Educational Administration Quarterly*, 41(4), 591–608.

Niemonen, J. (2007). Antiracist education in theory and practice: A critical assessment. *The American Sociologist*, 38(2), 159–177.

Nieto, S. (2004). *Affirming diversity: Sociopolitical context of multicultural education*. Boston: Pearson Education, Inc.

Nieto, S. (2010). Preface. In W. Ayers (Ed.), *To teach: The journey of a teacher* (pp. ix–x). New York: Teachers College Press.

Noddings, N. (2005). *The challenge to care in schools: An alternative approach to education*. New York: Teachers College Press.

Omi, M. & Winant, H. (2015). *Racial formation in the United States* (3rd ed.). New York: Routledge.

Parsons, E. C. (2006). From caring as a relation to culturally relevant caring: A White teacher's bridge to Black students. *Equity & Excellence in Education*, 38(1), 25–34.

Payne, R. (2005). *A framework for understanding poverty: A cognitive approach.* Highland, TX: aha! Process, Inc.

Peery, D. & Bodenhausen, G. V. (2008). Black + White = Black: Hypodescent in reflexive categorization of racially ambiguous faces. *Psychological Science,* 19, 973–977.

Pennington, J. L., Brock, C., & Ndura, E. (2012). Unraveling the threads of white teachers' conceptions of caring: Repositioning white privilege. *Urban Education,* 47(4), 743–775.

Picower, B. (2009). The unexamined Whiteness of teaching: How White teachers maintain and enact dominant racial ideologies. *Race Ethnicity and Education,* 12(2), 197–215.

Siddle Walker, V. (1996). *Their highest potential: An African American school community in the segregated south.* Chapel Hill, NC: The University of North Carolina Press.

Sleeter, C. E. (2005). How White teachers construct race. In C. McCarthy, W. Crichlow, G. Dimitradis, & N. Dolby (Eds.), *Race, identity, and representation in education* (pp. 243–256). New York: Routledge.

Stoll, L. C. (2014). Constructing the color-blind classroom: Teachers' perspectives on race and schooling. *Race Ethnicity and Education,* 17(5), 688–705, doi:10.1080/13613324.2014.885425.

Taylor, P., Passel, J., Wang, W., Kiley, J., Velasco, G., & Dockterman, D. (2010). *Marrying out: One-in-seven new U.S. marriages is interracial or interethnic.* Pew Research Center. From http://pewsocialtrends.org/files/2010/10/755-marrying-out.pdf.

Tosolt, B. (2010). Gender and race differences in middle school students' perceptions of caring teacher behaviors. *Multicultural Perspectives,* 12(3), 141–151.

U.S. Department of Education. (n.d.) *National Center for Education Statistics: Fast facts.* From https://nces.ed.gov/fastfacts/display.asp?id=55.

Vaught, S. & Castagno, A. (2008). "I don't think I'm a racist": Critical race theory, teacher attitudes, and structural racism. *Race Ethnicity and Education,* 11(2), 95–113.

Wardle, F. (2014). *Future teachers are not prepared to work with multiracial students.* The Center for the Study of Biracial Children. From http://csbchome.org/?p=49.

Ware, F. (2002). Black teachers' perceptions of their professional roles and practices. In J. J. Irving (Ed.), *In search of wholeness: African American teachers and their culturally specific classroom practices* (pp. 33–45). New York: Palgrave.

Williams, R. M. (2011). When gray matters more than Black or White: The schooling experiences of Black-White biracial students. *Education and Urban Society,* 42(2), 175–207.

8

THE RACIAL CONTEXT OF SCHOOLING AND MIXED-RACE YOUTH

[At school] . . . *not a day goes by that I'm not reminded about my race.*
(OhKeiSyd, 2013)

Whether overtly attended to, race permeates school environments, even those with seemingly homogeneous student populations. Race is evident in school's organization, curriculum, what is celebrated, and in the administrators and teachers chosen to work at schools. School environments are racialized when children and youth are treated differently because of their race, in ways that affect their educational experiences and school success. Research on race-related factors in schools that explicitly influence the schooling of mixed-race youth is still evolving, as most research in this area has focused on monoracial youth. Even so, it is important to understand how various educational elements around race influence the schooling of monoracial youth, because in many ways, these same elements impact the education of mixed-race youth. It is also significant to note, however, that race-related schooling issues will influence mixed-race youth differently, depending on their racial self-identity and the way they are raced by peers and school personnel.

This chapter is first and foremost concerned with the settings where mixed-race youth attend school and the racial climate that exists within those schools. Schools differ in terms of geographic location, diversity of student population, available resources, teacher quality, and the organization of learning activities, among other factors. Different school climates have considerable influence on children and youth within schools, including their academic achievement. As such, this chapter begins with a discussion of how policies and practices in various schools create climates that affect the educational experiences and outcomes of mixed-race youth.

The various ways mixed-race youth are made invisible or visible in schools settings are explored in this chapter, as well as the extent to which they are perceived as contributing or not contributing to a school's diversity. Relatedly, the degree to which mixed-race youth are considered a distinct group disserving inclusion in school curricula, as schools attempt to address diversity, will be explored. The final section of this chapter examines school-family relations, with a focus on how the interracial status of families influences school-related decisions for mixed-race children, and the interaction of interracial families with school personnel.

The Impact of School Climate on Differently Raced Youth

School climates depend on the organization of learning activities within a school, the academic and nonacademic policies and practices that determine how a school functions, and the attitudes toward students projected by school personnel. Schools differ, however, in terms of the norms and values that undergird school processes, as well as opinions held about school student populations. The nature of the structuring elements of individual schools potentially facilitates racialized learning environments. In fact, Lasley and Ronnkvist (2007), expanding on Feagin's (2001) ideas, determined that the organizational logic of schools can result in both the creation and maintenance of "white spaces" (p. 1519) where whiteness is built into how schools function, both formally and informally. As a result, some children and youth attend schools organized in ways that predictably places some at an educational advantage and others at a disadvantage.

Schools Organized to Advantage White Youth

Disparities by race continue to exist in the nation's public schools in a number of areas critical to the educational success of all children. For example, some schools have policies and practices that result in youth of color having far less access to a rigorous curriculum in schools than their White peers. At the same time, children of color are disproportionately affected by school discipline policies, and this is especially true for Black and Latino boys (U.S. Department of Education, 2014). The structure of learning activities in schools organized as white space contributes to differences in academic expectations among differently raced children in ways that produce unequal educational outcomes. This phenomenon is clearly illustrated by school policies and practices for enrollment in advanced placement and honors courses, juxtaposed with enrollment in lower level or general courses.

High- and Low-Level Course Enrollment

According to Kelly (2009), Black students in majority White schools enroll in low-level math courses more frequently than their White peers by the time they reach their sophomore year in high school. Given school policies and practices around tracking, students are rarely placed in a single low-level course. Rather, they tend to be placed in low-level courses across multiple subject areas, so that their course schedule reflects a total program of less challenging coursework. Multiple factors influence students' enrollment in lower level courses, including previous academic performance and prior course-taking activities, as well as structural factors such as the student's socioeconomic status. However, "collective action" (p. 50) among school personnel that favors high status groups (e.g., White students) over lower status groups (e.g., Black students) in recommendations for higher level courses further contributes to placement of students of color in lower track courses.

Even though schools may have open enrollment in advanced courses, students of color attending predominantly White schools may view these courses as existing primarily for White students. Indeed, students may view advanced courses as "white space" even when these classes have a relatively balanced enrollment by race, as might be the case in more diverse schools (Nunn, 2011). Students of color enrolled in higher level courses in majority White populated schools feel a sense of isolation when they find fewer peers of color in their classes. Moreover, they often feel distant from their teachers and White peers in the classroom and may even feel alienated from the content that is being taught (Corra, Carter, & Carter, 2011; Kelly, 2009). For these reasons, some students of color who are capable of handling the work required in higher level courses actually choose to enroll in a lower level course.

Even so, too many youth of color who attend schools organized as white spaces are stripped of a sense of agency and feel they have limited choice over school decisions (e.g., level of course enrollments) that are ostensibly made in their best interest (Lasley & Ronnkvist, 2007). The separation of students by race, class, or gender into particular learning situations and opportunities not only keeps students physically separated, but also influences students' perceptions of where they and other students ought to be located academically, based on social characteristics such as race (Carter, 2010).

Disproportionality in Application of Discipline Policies

Uneven application of school discipline polices not only negatively affects the social and emotional well-being of children and youth more frequently disciplined, but also contributes to the academic failure of the affected students (Winn Tutwiler, 2007). Black and Latino students are removed from the classroom through in-school and external suspension more frequently than their White peers, often because of minor offenses (e.g., disrespect, classroom disruption). This practice continues, even when it is obvious that these solutions do not eliminate the offending behaviors (Christle, Nelson, & Jolivette, 2007). Although disparity in the application of discipline polices by race has been noted

for years, some scholars suggest that inequitable policies and practices are
likely to occur in schools with a majority of White students and where a ⌐
centric climate predominates. Scholars suggest, for example, that differenc ⌐⌐
the behavioral and communication styles of White and Black cultures lead to
a misunderstanding of Black youth, which subsequently results in them being
singled out for discipline (Ferguson, 2001; Hilberth & Slate, 2014)

The treatment of youth of color when it comes to discipline is not lost to their
White peers. White youth in schools organized as white space develop racial
and cultural stereotypes regarding youth of color, and view them as problematic
elements in the school environments (Risman & Banerjee, 2013). In this way,
unequal treatment of youth of color supports a school climate that aids and abets
unequal power in relations between White and students of color. Students of
color do not miss occasions when they are treated pejoratively in both academic
and nonacademic circumstances either. Consequently, they often self-segregate
as a means for protection from both covert and overt acts of racism directed
toward students of color (Tatum, 1997).

[handwritten: Is a school with 97% white students automatically a white space?]

Hidden Privilege in Schools Organized as White Space

Hidden privileges are preserved in school settings where a color-blind ideology
is embedded in the organizational logic of the school. Earlier, I discussed color-
blind ideology as an approach to race adopted by some teachers, and that for
Bonilla-Silva (2014) their stance was tantamount to color-blind racism. It follows,
then, that schools that operate on the basis of color blindness engage in institutionalized color-blind racism, which permeates the total school (Bonilla-Silva,
2014; Chapman, 2013). Where it exists, it touches all sectors of the school context,
including school policies, curriculum, and academic and nonacademic programs.

Even when they appear to be race neutral, school policies and practices work
to the advantage of White over nonwhite students and their families, in schools
organized as white space. School attendance policies are a case in point. A middle
class White parent seeking permission to remove his or her child from school
for a few days to attend an out-of-town family event would not face the same
hurdles as a non–middle class parent of color requesting that his or her child
miss a few days of school to watch other children in the home, because of an
unforeseen child-care crisis (Lasley & Ronnkvist, 2007).

Extracurricular activities are an additional area of hidden privilege. Participation in these activities are often race based because students make connections and friendships in classes that are segregated by race and then extend these
relationships into shared interests in school-sponsored activities outside of the
classroom. Differentiated participation in extracurricular activities can also be
attributed to the status of certain racial groups within the school and the control they have over certain activities (e.g., student government or cheerleading)
(Carter, 2010).

Finally, instructional approaches elevate the position of whiteness in some schools and subsequently in classrooms as well. Nunn (2011) observed an advanced-level course where the vast majority of students were White, even though the school was diverse. She noted that the ". . . styles of interaction, modes of humor, and general sensibilities that dominate[d] the classroom space . . . [were] aligned with White and middle-class values" (p. 1234). This type of classroom environment is not insignificant when it comes to hidden privilege in the classrooms. Indeed, White students have a higher level of comfort in these classrooms than their peers of color. They also exhibit a sense of entitlement when it comes to advanced class enrollment, with the implication that although they belong in these classes their peers of color may not. A White participant in Nunn's study who was enrolled in an honors English course shared the following about a Latina peer:

> Honestly, like I have a Latino girl in . . . my English honors class . . . she is very quiet; she doesn't say anything in the class. And I don't know if she really belongs there or if they didn't have room for her somewhere else . . .
> *(p. 1245)*

While the foregoing discussion focused on white space created in schools with predominantly White student populations, white space can exist in majority-minority schools as well. Some teachers in majority-minority schools believe a White student school population in the minority makes it impossible for white privilege to exist in their schools. However, the actual school student and staff demographics become secondary to the organizational logic of the school in producing white space (Lasley & Ronnkvist, 2007; Vaught & Castagno, 2008). Teachers who teach in schools organized as white space may or may not subscribe to racial prejudice. However, the school's organizational logic normalizes racialized practice. Differential treatment of students in these schools is systemic, thus teachers engage in racialized practices as matter of following school policy.

School Diversity and School Climate

There are alternatives to creating and sustaining racialized school spaces. Learning environments with diverse student populations potentially promote interactions and social cohesion among students who differ racially, culturally, and socioeconomically. As a result, schools with diverse student populations can contribute to development of sociocultural skills that will be needed to participate in economic and cultural opportunities of the broader society, which is becoming more diverse. In the process, these schools enhance students' cultural flexibility, which Carter (2010) defined as ". . . the propensity to value and move across different cultural and social peer groups and environments . . ." (p. 1529).

Development of cultural flexibility skills and dispositions facilitates students' ability to cross social boundaries (race, class, cultural, etc.) not only within school, but also in students' future work and community interactions. Diversity in student population alone does not ensure cultural flexibility among students, however. School contextual factors, especially the ways in which student learning and other school-related activities are organized, can have a negative or positive effect on development of cultural flexibility among students. Differentiated access to learning opportunities and extracurricular activities by race and class contributes to a school climate where more distinct racial boundaries among students exist, making cultural flexibility more difficult to accomplish. Diverse schools organized in this way are more likely to be schools where the majority of students are White, rather than majority-minority schools. When school are organized to facilitate diversity in learning and other school activities, the potential for interactions among differently raced youth increases, which in turns advances development of cultural flexibility (Carter, 2010).

Mixed-Race Youth in White Space and Diverse Schools

The number of mixed-race children and youth in the nation's P-12 public schools is increasing (see Chart 8.1). There are, however, regional differences with more mixed-race youth attending public schools in the Midwest and West than in the South and Northeast areas of the country. Regardless of their location, schools operating as "white space" and schools that embrace diversity impact schooling experiences of mixed-race youth, sometimes in ways similar to their

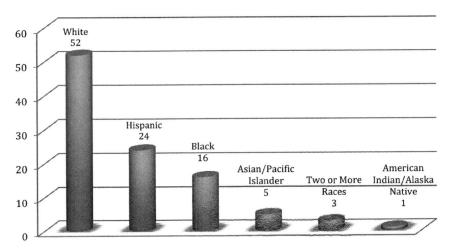

CHART 8.1 Percentage of P-12 Students in Public Schools by Race—2011

From National Center for Education Statistics. (2014). *Racial/ethnic enrollment in public schools.* https://nces.ed.gov/programs/coe/indicator_cge.asp

monoracial peers, and other times in ways that are unique to the fact that the child is mixed-race.

Schools that facilitate and support the division of youth by race in course-work, extracurricular activities, and in positions of power are a conundrum for some mixed-race youth. As discussed earlier, however, schools that create environments where students develop the flexibility to cross racial boundaries present more opportunities for mixed-race youth to interact with peers in ways that align with their sense of racial self-identity. I focus here more closely on school climate and how peers and school personnel race mixed-race youth and how mixed-race youth view themselves racially in different school climates.

Being Raced by Others

How mixed-race children and youth are raced potentially affects their experience both in schools organized as white space, and those where student diversity factors into how schools operate. A Black-White mixed-race youth in a predominantly White school, for example, may be raced as monoracial Black. In this case, he or she is susceptible to the same prejudice and discrimination as a monoracial minority peer that potentially includes exposure to unfair discipline practices and more frequent placement in lower level classes. They may also experience rejection by White peers, and even when youth are known to be mixed-race they may still be treated the same as monoracial minorities (Khanna, 2011). Although Sydney, a Black-White mixed-race student in a predominantly White school, did not experience rejection from White peers, they did not accept her as White or a mixed-race person. Their lack of awareness of and insensitivity to race and related issues made them oblivious to the fact that their race-related teasing was disturbing to Sydney. Of her interactions in high school, Sydney stated:

> . . . People expect you to be one or the other, you can't be both . . . they don't understand the whole mixed thing . . . they expect me to be Black . . . the stereotypical Black girl . . . I can't do that, I'd feel like . . . I'm posing almost . . . going to school, people teased me . . . 'oh you should be Black, have a Black girl attitude, ha, ha' . . . and I go wow, I don't know *how* . . . I'm just as White as you are . . . not a day goes by that I'm not reminded about my race.
>
> *(OhKeiSyd, 2013)*

Mixed-race youth may find more acceptance in diverse schools where there are more students of color. Khanna (2011) pointed out, however, that the one-drop rule may predominate in these situations and mixed-race youth may be viewed as Black (i.e., mixed-race but Black). Further, as has been pointed out elsewhere in this book, mixed-race girls' acceptance among Black girls is often strained, especially when the Biracial Beauty Stereotype acts as a wedge to separate the two groups of young people.

As alluded to by Lewis (2003), children and youth learn what it means to be of a certain race inside of school walls. These lessons can take place in predominantly White or majority-minority schools. Lasley and Ronnkvist (2007), for example, reported the experiences of Josie, a fair-skinned Puerto Rican who moved to the mainland with her family during her middle school years. Josie was considered White in Puerto Rico, but when she attended middle school on the mainland, her peers and adults in the school made sure she understood that she was not White. The purpose of this "education," which took place in a majority-minority school, was for Josie to understand that she was not eligible for privileges available to White students. This experience led Josie to engage in identity work that resulted in a racial self-identity change from White to nonwhite.

Undoubtedly, mixed-race youth have similar experiences where they are raced at school as either White or nonwhite, which may or may not align with their chosen identity. According to Binning, Unzueta, Huo, and Molina (2009), children who adopt a multiracial identity (i.e., neither White nor student of color) tend to associate with multiple groups more so than mixed-race peers who are monoracially identified, White or minority. They tended to be more actively involved in school activities than their mixed-race peers with a monoracial minority identity and to feel less alienated from school than their peers who adopted a monoracial high-status group identity (e.g., White or Asian). Mixed-race youths' social interaction proclivities are inhibited when they attend schools where they are continuously raced. This is especially true when the race designation by peers and others in the school environment contradicts their racial self-identity (Sydney's school experience is an example).

The Impact of School Climate on Racial Self-Identification

Middle and high school years are important ones for the identity work mixed-race youth perform. In Binning et al.'s (2009) study of the relationship between self-identity and overall well-being, mixed-race youth who identified as White (or Asian) felt that school rules were unimportant and that rules were made to control but not protect students like them. School diversity influences the racial self-identity of mixed-race youth. School environments where cultural flexibility is valued support the identity work of many mixed-race adolescents. The possibility of interacting with peers from multiple racial and cultural backgrounds supports the fluid nature of mixed-race youths' racial self-identity process. Further, the act of crossing social boundaries that is a goal of cultural flexibility allows mixed-race youth to make a transition from one identity location to another, based on interaction with peers at a particular school. They may adopt, at any given time, any of the identities available to them (e.g., monoracial minority or White, situational identity, biracial identity).

Cheng and Klugman (2010) studied the impact of schools' racial diversity on the sense of belonging among mixed-race students. They surmised that belonging had both psychological (feeling of satisfaction in life) and affective (connecting with peers) dimensions that potentially affected students' motivation, social competence, and adherence to school norms. School diversity, specifically the population of Black and White students, appeared to affect a sense of belonging for minority-minority (e.g., Asian-Black, Hispanic-Black) mixed-race youth, who tended to have stronger school attachments in majority-minority schools. On the other hand, White-nonwhite mixed-race youth appeared able to adapt to school environments, regardless of the school's racial makeup. Recall that some mixed-race youths' friendship formation patterns can be described as background bridging, where they use their mixed-race status to form friendships with peers from multiple racial backgrounds (Doyle & Kao, 2007).

Cheng and Klugman (2010) further concluded that White-nonwhite youth appeared to be unaffected by divisions between Black and White students in their schools. Their study, however, was based on analysis of the large database from the National Longitudinal Study of Adolescent Health collected during 1994–1995, which allowed the researchers to determine racial identification but not racial affiliation among mixed-race youth. The distinction is an important one, however, and one they listed as a limitation of their study. They suggested, and critically so, that racial affiliation (e.g., whether a White-nonwhite adolescent affiliates more with White or nonwhite peers) could affect how the racial makeup of a school influences mixed-race youths' sense of school attachment.

The Invisibility of Mixed-Race Youth in Schools

Mixed-race youths' racial self-identity is often misunderstood or ignored. Sydney's experience, once again, is an instructive example. Although she was accepted as being mixed-race, she identified as White. Her sense of identity did not matter to her peers, as evidenced by the thoughtless teasing that challenged her to "act" like their stereotypical notions of how Black girls behave. To this degree, the essence of mixed-race youths' mixedness becomes invisible sometimes in student-to-student interactions.

Prior to recent changes in the way student race data are collected, mixed-race youth were essentially invisible in school databases as well. This situation will change based on new student race data collection guidelines published by the Department of Education (DOE) (U.S. Department of Education, 2007). Despite a call by increased numbers of educational activists and policymakers for "race neutral" (McDermott, Frankenberg, & Diem, 2015, p. 507) policies and practices, school districts will have to pay even closer attention to the racial and ethnic makeup of students in their schools (Renn, 2009; U.S. Department of Education, 2007). The new guidelines for collecting, aggregating, and reporting student race and ethnicity data were expected to be implemented by the

2010–2011 school year. An anticipated outcome of the DOE's requirement will be the increased visibility of mixed-race youth in the nation's schools.

Two DOE requirements are of particular interest when considering the visibility of mixed-race youth in schools. First, the DOE advised that ". . . when collecting racial and ethnic data at the elementary and secondary school level, the identification of a student's race and ethnicity is to be primarily made by the parents or guardians . . ." (U.S. Department of Education, 2007, p. 59267). As a result, parents of mixed-race children are now able to officially report that their children are of any race parents want them to be. On the other hand, if parents do not supply racial identification information to schools, then the DOE allows school districts to use "observer identification" (p. 59268) as a last resort in order to collect racial data. This aspect of the guidelines potentially invites identification by physical characteristics and thus use of the one-drop-rule to identify mixed-race youth as monoracial minority.

Secondly, the DOE adopted race categories structured and implemented by the Equal Employment Opportunity Commission, which included a category for two or more races (Renn, 2009; U.S. Department of Education, 2007). Hence, parents who want to identify their children as neither White nor monoracial minority are no longer limited to the ambiguous category of "other race." At the same time, parents who wish to identify their mixed-race children as monoracial of any race are able to do so as well.

The DOE now expects student race data in the following categories:

- Hispanic/Latino of any race

  (Or one of the following categories for individuals who are not Hispanic/Latino only)

- American Indian or Alaska Native
- Asian
- Black or African American
- Native Hawaiian or Other Pacific Islander
- White
- Two or more races

In many ways, the two or more race category is comparable to the multiracial category desired by some multiracial organizations during the height of the Multiracial Movement in the 1990s. However, recall that some groups wanted a multiracial category that would allow for self-identification of the distinctive aspects of mixed-race people's racial heritage (e.g., Black-White or Asian-White) (Castagno, 2012). The new guidelines did not go that far although the potential exists for a parent to determine that his or her child is Asian, White, and two or more races.

The inclusion of a two or more race category potentially has additional positive effects. Like it or not, children and youth are separated from regular academic programs into special programs ostensibly designed to meet their educational needs (e.g., gifted programs, special education program and services). Special education programs and services, for example, provide an illustrative example of the importance of mixed-race youth being identifiable as a separate group of children. It is known, for example, that Black and Latino youth are disproportionately represented in special education classes (Ford, 2012). What is less clear is how often mixed-race youth have been raced as monoracial minorities and counted as Black or Latino when it comes to representation in special education classes.

Information about the participation of mixed-race youth in special education classes is important, not simply to separate them from monoracial minority youth as perfunctory educational exercise. Rather, it would be an action taken to understand the extent and nature of mixed-race youths' participation, so that educators, policymakers, and educational researchers can determine how mixedness factors into the evaluation and placement of mixed-race youth for special education classes and related services. Recall, for example, that Fusco, Rautkis, McCrae, Cunningham, and Bradley-King (2010) found that separating the child welfare experiences of mixed-race youth and their families from those of monoracial minority youth and their families resulted in an understanding that mixed-race youth and their families had experiences both similar to and different from their monoracial peers.

The requirement that school districts include data on mixed-race youth for reporting purposes to the DOE is one step toward acknowledging the fact that this particular group of students exists apart from other groups of students. Even though national figures of special needs mixed-race youth had previously been reported, these data were based on the percentage of children listed under the ambiguous category of "other," which has not always been a reliable category consisting only of mixed-race youth. The new reporting guidelines, along with parents' right to racially identify their mixed-race youth, should provide schools an opportunity to determine the schooling experiences of mixed-race youth with more confidence and more clarity. This prospect can occur not only in special education classes and services, but also in all areas that are a part of the academic and nonacademic components of schools.

On an additional positive note, performance data for mixed-race students will now be included on national reports, such as the Annual Yearly Progress report required by No Child Left Behind. Thus, national data will now be available for mixed-race youth, which allows them to be part of the conversation about achievement specific to racial groups that is of interest to educators, scholars, and education policymakers. Still, identifying academic performance among mixed-race youth becomes more challenging when consideration is given to the diversity of mixedness among mixed-race youth and the multiple ways students racially self-identify (Campbell, 2009; Herman, 2009). Renn (2009) found it problematic that data for mixed-race youth will not include a clear delineation of the racial heritage of mixed-race students. While aggregate achievement data will be available for mixed-race youth, more precise data based on race combinations will not be available. As a result, policies and programs that might support the education and development of a particular group of mixed-race youth may not be available.

Invisibility in School Integration and Diversity

Using integration and diversity interchangeably is fairly common in today's discourses on youths' race-related schooling experiences. As suggested by Welton (2013), both are meant to focus on ". . . policies to design and practices to implement racially heterogeneous communities, districts, and schools" (Welton, 2013, p. 1). As established earlier, diverse schools are believed to be more positive environments for mixed-race youths' learning and development. Indeed, as Thompson Dorsey (2013) concluded, "integrated schools benefit all students of all races and ethnicities socially, emotionally, and academically" (p. 543). Moreover, students who attend more diverse schools are better able to interact with people of diverse backgrounds once they complete their formal education. Welton (2013) argued, however, that it is not enough to measure diversity solely by the number or percentage of students from diverse racial and socioeconomic backgrounds attending the same school. Diversity by the number, so to speak, will not accomplish the underlying goals and intent of school integration or diversity. In fact, without intervention, a number of school structures, attitudes, and practices will continue to relegate students to segregated schooling experiences, albeit under the same roof.

Nonetheless, when educators and policymakers focus on diversity by the number, young people continue to have schooling experiences separated by race, and socioeconomic segregation has become an area of concern as well. Demographic shifts, however, have led to a different racial makeup in the nation's public school population. It was projected that by 2014, public schools would be a majority minority, primarily because of increases in the Hispanic and Asian populations (Krogstad & Fry, 2014). As the nation's public schools become populated with fewer monoracial White students, it becomes clear that the student population of segregated schools of the past, those for whom the ruling in *Brown v. Board of Education* was designed to intervene, have changed substantially (Diem & Frankeberg, 2013).

Mixed-race youth were included in the increased percentage of "minority" students that is leading to majority-minority public schools. School diversity discourse, however, is most often approached from a monoracial-centric perspective, with little discussion of the impact mixed-race youth have on school integration or diversity. Even so, mixed-race youth contribute to the multiracial, multiethnic diversity that characterizes the nation's student population today. The diversity within the mixed-race population (both race designation and

-identity) makes them a more challenging group to pinpoint, result-
1ore challenging task of determining their impact on school diversity.
⌐⌐⌐⌐ ⌐⌐ ⌐ome indication this may be changing, however, at least when it comes
to analyzing student racial data (Krogstad & Fry, 2014) (see also Chart 8.1).

Thompson Dorsey (2013) reiterated a well-known fact—Black and Latino students are more segregated today than they were 55 years ago. Frankenberg (2013)
pointed out that there continues to be a reciprocal relationship between residential
and school segregation. When coupled with reduced legal pressure on school districts to pursue segregation policies and legal challenges to voluntary desegregation,
the possibility of young people from different racial and social class backgrounds
interacting with other both during and after school hours has attenuated. This is
especially true for Latino youth who are the most segregated group in schools, and
for all students in the nation's urban schools (Diem & Frankeberg, 2013). The latter point is important, because many interracial families choose to locate in urban
areas where they are more likely to find more diversity in all of its forms.

The lack of more precise data generated from the two or more race category potentially impacts the reliability of reported diversity in different learning environments. For example, although data collected to report schools' racial
composition potentially include information for mixed-race youths, the actual
racial makeup of individual schools will be imprecise given the multiple combinations of racial mixture possible. This circumstance has important implications for information regarding the status of integration and diversity in schools.
For example, schools where the "two or more" population is predominantly
minority-minority mixed-race youth who also identify as minority can hardly
claim a diverse or integrated status as a result of their mixed-race students. By the
same token, schools where the "two or more" population is made up of White-
Asian mixed-race youth who identify as White begs the question of whether the
school is truly diverse and whether the intent of school integration is being met.

In both instances, students have may have cultural similarity to the majority
population in their respective schools, even though they are racially dissimilar.
What counts in terms of diversity, it seems, is the extent to which youth with a
diversity of perspectives and worldviews owing to their day-to-day lived experiences interact with each other in ways that stretch their understanding of the
human experience.

well
said

The Complexity of Race-Neutral School Policy

Some White communities are not interested in diverse schools, regardless of the
makeup of the racial groups that would lead to school diversity. School districts
face pressure from White and middle class families to make district-level school
attendance decisions where they are advantaged. In most cases, these decisions are
presented as race neutral, although, in effect, they act to disadvantage students
of color and those living in low socioeconomic homes. Diverse schools are not

always the primary concern of some communities of color either. Some communities of color may also prefer race-neutral policies. They may, for example, desire policies that result in school improvements over the more race-conscious policy of school integration (McDermott et al., 2015). Still other parents may agree with the concept of diversity in principle but will not support district diversity policies, the implementation of which they believe would result in situations not in the best interest of their children (e.g., a diversity policy that would result in busing their children outside the neighborhood) (Diem, Frankenberg, Cleary, & Ali, 2014).

School districts that are guided by race-neutral approaches to school policy ignore the realities of demographics of public schools today (Wells, 2014). McDermott et al. (2015) explained how one district-level policy could simultaneously create what they referred to as enclave schools and default schools. Enclave schools are schools in a district attended by more White and affluent students than other schools in the district. Default schools are attended by substantially fewer White and affluent students. Some enclave schools are neighborhood schools located in communities that price out families with less money and/or resources. Other enclave schools may come about as a result of social networks where families that are alike in race and/or class share information about certain schools in school choice districts, schools with admissions requirements that are merit based, or schools with transportation requirements that exclude families who are unable to transport their children to the school's location.

Wells (2014) recommended that schools adopt a "color conscious" approach to educational policies that will not only result in more racially diverse schools, but also attend to the curriculum, teaching, and assessment practices needed to address diverse school environments. Although not always included as part of the diverse student population discourse, mixed-race youth contribute to multiracial, multiethnic diversity that is sweeping the United States today. It is unfortunate that some parents of mixed-race youth are sometimes faced with choosing between the social and emotional benefits of a school (e.g., more diverse schools that support mixed-race youths' social and identity development), juxtaposed with its academic benefits (less diverse resource rich majority White schools). School choice, which is often described as a race-neutral approach to school assignment policy, does not have to result in less diverse and less integrated schools. The policies that give parents the flexibility to choose from schools within the district could be used to facilitate, rather than impede, the development of more diverse schools (McDermott et al., 2015; Wells, 2014).

Mixedness in the Curriculum and Related Academic Programs

Chapman (2013) maintained that the curriculum is often a manifestation of White privilege existing in some schools. She stated that schools ". . . reinstantiate White privilege through the absence of racially diverse content and critical stances used to examine power and privilege . . ." (p. 616). The history and experiences of mixed-race people are invisible in the curriculum and other programs in both diverse schools and those organized as white space. It is evident from earlier chapters in this book that mixed-race people have a long-standing presence and have contributed much to the history of the United States. However, when people of note in politics, the arts, or the sciences among other areas are discussed in classrooms, their mixed-raced backgrounds are rarely mentioned. Moreover, when schools attempt to improve race relations through the curriculum or other programs, the focus is on monoracial groups, often leaving the experiences of mixed-race youth untouched (Fernandes Williams, 2011).

This is likely as much a circumstance of lack of knowledge as it is of disinterest among curriculum developers and teachers. Further, there are few explicit and overt representations of mixed-race people and their experiences in the textbooks and other materials to which mixed-race youth are exposed in their classrooms (Cruz-Janzen & Wardle, 2004). And, even though the number of books with mixed-race characters and themes could benefit from continued growth, existing books do not routinely appear in classrooms and libraries.

The result is that mixed-raced children and youth rarely have opportunities to read (and have others read) about people like them who are respected and honored for their accomplishments. While Homer Plessey and W.E.B. Du Bois may be mentioned in middle school or high school classrooms, they are most likely presented as Black men, when in reality both were mixed race. One chose to honor his mixedness (Plessey) whereas the other identified as monoracial Black (Du Bois), which is not so unlike the identity choices faced by many mixed-race youth today. As another example, there is a rich history of differently raced men and women who resisted negative attitudes toward interracial relationships and miscegenation laws in order to form interracial families. The Supreme Court ruling in *Loving v. Virginia* may be discussed in classrooms but not within the context of contributions those seeking to form interracial families made to civil rights efforts in general.

Multicultural education encourages educators to align curriculum, instruction, and other school practices to the needs of diverse student populations (Dickar, 2008). The impetus to include the history and experiences of those who live "in-between races" (Janis, 2012, p. 129) is lacking, however. Moreover, multicultural education that ignores the existence and experiences of a particular group serves only to further marginalize those discounted and/or overlooked (Janis, 2012). When mixed-race youth are not exposed to mixed-race people who have made noteworthy contributions, they potentially come to believe that mixed-race people have had little to do with the content they learn in school (Fernandes Williams, 2011). Gay (2005) suggested that academic injustice is committed when youth (her reference was to monoracial minority youth) are not taught about the history and achievements of their people. Educators are committed to social justice when they develop curriculum that makes the ". . . invisible visible, and teaching the truth about historical records" (p. 35).

Academic Achievement and Educational Attainment

The notion that mixed-race youth have low academic achievement as a result of low self-esteem emanating from the marginalized status of mixed-race people has been debunked. Nonetheless, Herman (2009) proposed a number of relevant factors when considering the academic performance of mixed-race youth, some of which have previously been addressed as important to understanding the overall social experiences of mixed-race people. First, youths' racial self-identity and its location along the extant racial hierarchy appear to matter. In Herman's study of academic performance of mixed-race youth, participants who were part Black or part Hispanic and who racially self-identified with their minority racial heritage tended to have lower achievement as measured by grade point averages than their mixed-race peers who identified as White or Asian. Herman cautioned that a connection between ancestry and achievement should not be made with this finding because some youth with Black ancestry could self-identify as White.

Burke and Kao (2013) also found a connection between racial self-identity and school achievement. In contrast to the Herman study, Burke and Kao found that mixed-race Black-White and Asian-White youth who identified as White had significantly lower grades than mixed-race youth who did not identify as White. They suggested that the contested nature of a White identity for mixed-race youth, especially those who are not phenotypically White, could have a negative impact on a range of school-related experiences including achievement. In fact, both Burke and Kao (2013) and Herman (2009) agreed that a White identity might have negative school-related outcomes for mixed-race youth in a number of developmental areas other than academic achievement. These finding are consistent with Binning et al. (2009), who suggested that a White identity was consistent with a sense of alienation from the school attended.

The stark differences in the outcomes of the Herman and the Burke and Kao studies on academic performance, although disconcerting, in many ways reflect the challenges researchers face when attempting to categorically situate mixed-race youth into specific achievement locations. Campbell (2009) noted that generalizations about educational outcomes for mixed-race youth are difficult, given the differences across outcomes (e.g., grade point averages, college attendance patterns) between and among different race combinations. This sentiment was echoed by Herman (2009), who acknowledged that it is ". . . challenging to develop theory that is simultaneously broad enough to encompass achievement across all racial groups and detailed enough to explain much of the variation" (p. 39).

In addition to the importance of mixed-race youths' racial self-identity, how others race them matters in their academic performance as well. Although there was no significant difference in achievement between monoracial Black and Hispanic students, minority-minority mixed-race Black-Hispanic students in

Herman's (2009) study had grade point averages lower than all other mixed-race youth and monoracial Black and monoracial Hispanic study participants. One could speculate that the low achievement evident among Black-Hispanic mixed-race youth is due to a Black achievement orientation, which aligns with Ogbu's (1978) oppositional culture theory. Accordingly, mixed-race youth with a strong identity with an involuntary ethnic group (Black or Latino) would have low academic performance as a reaction in opposition to White culture. Herman found little empirical support for this hypothesis. She suggested that there was no relationship between the value youth may place on their ethnic identity and peer affiliation and academic performance.

Alternately, how mixed-race youth are raced could be a factor in educational outcomes, because assumptions about race could lead to discrimination and bias similar to that experienced by monoracial Black or Latino youth. Teachers who treat all mixed-race youth as if they are monoracial minority may potentially have a negative impact on the academic performance of these youth. To be sure, all youth, regardless of their racial background and racial self-identity, deserve the type of teacher feedback and encouragement that is known to have a positive impact on students' academic performance and achievement. That mixed-race youths' achievement may be influenced by a monoracial minority effect is just another indication of how our understanding of mixed-race youths' schooling experiences furthers our understanding of the overall pervasive and negative impact of race on the educational experiences of our children.

School behavior, previous academic performance, and beliefs about achievement all appear to influence academic achievement, along with youths' peer groups and the racial makeup of schools (Herman, 2009). Burke and Kao (2013) added that feeling a sense of belonging at school also influences academic achievement. Campbell (2009) concluded that the number one predictor of educational outcomes for mixed-race youth is their parents' income and level of educational attainment. Thus, it appears important to attend to multiple factors when attempting to understand achievement among mixed-race youth.

Trends in Academic Performance

Large-scale databases that describe academic trends and performances of the nation's youth are beginning to include mixed-race youth as a category; however, this is not done consistently in all reports and across all areas. For example, in its national report on mathematics and reading performance, the National Assessment of Educational Progress (2013) did not include a category to describe the progress or performance of mixed-race youth. That said, meaningful inclusion of data on mixed-race youths' performance will be complicated by the in-group diversity of mixed-race youth. Even so, mixed-race youth overall compare favorably in terms of academic attainment when compared with their monoracial peers (see Chart 8.2).

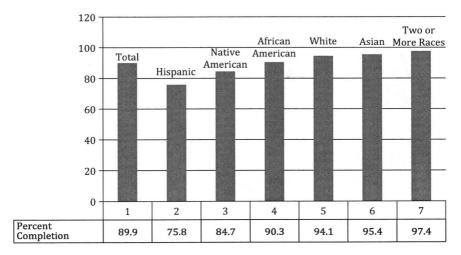

CHART 8.2 High School Completion or Higher by Race—2013

From National Center for Education Statistics. (2013). *Digest of education statistics*. http://nces.ed.gov/programs/digest/d13/tables/dt13_104.20.asp

Interracial Families' Interactions with Schools

The family culture of interracial families is diverse and is influenced by a number of characteristics, including the socioeconomic status of the family, the racial backgrounds of the parent or parents in the family, and family configuration (e.g., single-parent family, married couple family). As discussed earlier, education is often the vehicle used by parents of mixed-race youth to compensate for any marginality (real or anticipated) their mixed-race youth might experience outside the home (Cheng & Powell, 2007). As they make decisions about the education of their mixed-race children, interracial couples bring perspectives related to schools and schooling both from their individual cultural backgrounds as well as from the family culture they create as an interracial family.

School Attendance Decisions

Asian, Latino, and African American partners in interracial marriages often embrace the instrumental value of education as the way to ensure the social and economic well-being of their children's future. This perspective appears to be a value for parents of color with mixed-race children of various family structural configurations and socioeconomic backgrounds (Chua, 2011; Lawton, Foeman, & Brown, 2013; Nissel, 2006; Obama, 2004). On the other hand, White partners in interracial families lean toward education as a means for self-exploration and affirmation. Parents of mixed-race youth appear able to develop a co-created perspective to address the needs of their mixed-race children that incorporates the views of each differently raced partner (Lawton et al., 2013).

The diversity of schools presents a dilemma for some parents of mixed-race youth. In reality, either enclave or default schools may be more or less diverse. Enclave schools supported by parents of monoracial White youth are more likely to operate as white space, which is probably acceptable to and promoted by White and affluent parents. Although these schools encourage the resegregation of public schools, they are likely to be acceptable to some interracial couples of like socioeconomic status as well. Education as cultural and social capital ranks high among some parents of mixed-race children. Those with resources may be willing to exchange the social and emotional benefits ostensibly found in more diverse schools for the educational benefits available in enclave schools. Herman (2009), for example, found that mixed-race youth had higher academic performance in schools that were whiter, even though the lack of diversity had negative consequences for other areas of development for mixed-race youth.

Recall from Chapter 5 that many interracial couples prefer residing in diverse neighborhoods. Similarly, many parents of mixed-race youth prefer diverse schools for their children, believing that their children will benefit most in these learning environments (Fernandes Williams, 2011). Diversity does not necessarily mean majority-minority schools where a single minority racial group predominates. Like their preferences in the racial makeup of their communities, some interracial couples seek schools attended by children of multiple racial and ethnic backgrounds, including mixed-race youth. In some cases, diversity becomes secondary to school quality (Fernandes Williams, 2011). Nissel's (2006) mother's decision to place her in a predominantly White private school and McBride's (1996) mother's decision for him to attend a school of predominantly Jewish children rather the neighborhood school of predominantly Black children are examples.

Interracial Family-School Relationships

Schools will most likely interact with parents of mixed-race children where the mother has the more dominant role concerning children's education. Further, given the nature of child well-being perspectives developed within interracial families, schools may encounter mothers who advocate for their children using diverse and complex strategies designed to ensure the needs of their children are met (Lawton et al., 2013). White mothers of mixed-race children are probably familiar with the way schools organized as white space work, information they are able to use for the benefit of their children. At the same time, more educated women of color who mother mixed-race children will also have some information about how schools organized for White children work, as many have learned how to negotiate these environments when they were students.

Even so, given that parents of mixed-race youth in most interracial families have not experienced what it means to be a mixed-race child in school environments, they still may have a need to address issues of race with schools. I noted earlier the resistance of some teachers to incorporate race into their instructional content. In too many schools, especially those with a predominantly White student population, race is rarely addressed as a school-wide issue, especially in schools where color-blindness predominates. When teachers and/or administrators view race from purportedly color-blind perspectives and/or believe race is primarily an issue of students of color (which is how some may view mixed-race youth) this particular need of some interracial families and their mixed-race children becomes invisible (Rockquemore & Laszloffy, 2005).

Rockquemore and Laszloffy (2005) further suggested that personnel at these schools lack both racial awareness and racial sensitivity. Racial awareness is ". . . the ability to recognize that race exists and that it shapes reality in inequitable and unjust ways . . ." (p. 91). Correspondingly, racial sensitivity is the ability to ". . . translate . . . awareness into action because . . . [of a] capacity to anticipate how others may think and feel, and adjust . . . behavior accordingly" (p. 91). There is a connection between school climate and the existence of racial awareness and sensitivity among school personnel (Rockquemore & Laszloffy, 2005). Consequently, it is improbable that parents of mixed-race youth (and indeed the children themselves) attending schools organized as white spaces will find a climate where they feel invited to discuss issues of race that might be affecting the education of their children.

The communities in which interracial families live will also influence how they interact with schools. Interracial families may not have a large presence in their communities, which affects the extent to which they benefit from school-community connections. Said another way, schools that are a part of predominantly White communities may not reflect the presence or needs of interracial families. The same is true, however, for interracial families in communities that are predominantly people of color. For the most part, interracial families may not have a larger "community" per se that reflects their interracial family form, with which they can coalesce to address the specific needs of mixed-race youth in schools. This is not to insinuate that interracial couples will not find common ground with other families in their communities to collectively address educational issues. Nonetheless, they are likely to find themselves addressing race-related issues specific to their mixed-race youth in isolation of the community of school families.

Concluding Comments

The experiences of mixed-race youth in schools advance our understanding of school diversity as both a layered and complex phenomenon. School diversity and school integration, when used to mean the same thing, begins when students with different life perspectives (owing to the intersection of their racial, socioeconomic, language, and sexual orientation backgrounds, for example) are placed together under the same roof to learn. Almost without further interrogation, mixed-race youth are "counted" in diversity literature as part of the monoracial minority population when schools assess diversity. In fact, mixed-race youth do contribute to schools' diversity, however, in ways that are different from monoracial youth, either White or student of color. As a result, they often require support from school settings that differ in some ways from their monoracial peers.

Schools that operate from a color-blind ideology are less able to meet the multiple needs of mixed-race youth. Moreover, schools that ostensibly embrace race-neutral policies and practices disappear mixed-race students. At the same time, diverse schools that operate as white space, and/or those unable to take a multiracial approach to the multiple aspects of schooling, miss opportunities to serve the needs of mixed-race youth as well. Some school districts, school policymakers, and individual schools have decided to view school diversity simply as the percentage of students from different backgrounds located in the same school. They are oblivious to the possibilities of what could take place in diverse contexts for children and youth. Lack of an organizational logic in schools, with accompanying policies, practices, and curricular and other programmatic supports that facilitate learning in and from diverse contexts, ignores the tremendous benefits of these environments for children and youth and the broader society.

It has been known for some time that the racial contexts of schools influence the learning and educational experiences and outcomes of children from all racial backgrounds. The pervasive and persistent nature of race as an ingrained component of our system of education is made even more visible by some of the educational experiences of mixed-race youth. In many instances, the notion of race is accentuated in the schooling experiences of mixed-race youth. It becomes an issue for their sense of self when peers and school personnel race them in ways that do not align with their racial identity claims. They are often made invisible, even in schools where attempts are made to pay attention to diversity in the school curriculum and programs. And they often experience the monoracial effect in terms of perceptions and expectations of school personnel, which ignores their mixed-race status. Their experiences provide insights into how schools as racialized institutions continue to be focused on separation by race as a means for sustaining a racial hierarchy and its associated race privilege.

References

Binning, K., Unzueta, M., Huo, Y., & Molina, L. (2009). The interpretation of multiracial status and its relation to social engagement and psychological well-being. *Journal of Social Issues*, 65(1), 35–49.

Bonilla-Silva, E. (2014). *Racism without racists: Color-blind racism and the persistence of racial inequality in America*. New York: Rowman & Littlefield Publishers, Inc.

Burke, R. & Kao, G. (2013). Bearing the burden of whiteness: The implications of racial self-identification for multiracial adolescents' school belonging and academic achievement. *Ethnic and Racial Studies*, 36(5), 747–773.

Campbell, M. E. (2009). Multiracial groups and educational inequality: A rainbow or a divide? *Social Problems*, 56(3), 425–446.

Carter, P. (2010). Race and cultural flexibility among student in different multiracial schools. *Teachers College Record*, 112(6), 1529–1574.

Castagno, A. (2012). *"Founding mothers": White mothers of biracial children in the multiracial movement (1979–2000)*. From http://wesscholar.wesleyan.edu/cgi/viewcontent. cgi?article=1934&context=etd_hon_theses.

Chapman, T. K. (2013). You can't erase race! Using CRT to explain the presence of race and racism in majority white suburban schools. *Discourse: Studies in the Cultural Politics of Education*, 34(4), 611–627.

Cheng, S. & Klugman, J. (2010). School racial composition and biracial adolescents. *The Sociological Quarterly*, 51(1), 150–178.

Cheng, S. & Powell, B. (2007). Under and beyond constraints: Resource allocation to young children from biracial families. *American Journal of Sociology*, 112(4), 1044–1094.

Christle, C., Jolivette, K., & Nelson, M. (2007). School characteristics related to high school dropout rates. *Remedial and Special Education*, 28, 325–339.

Chua, A. (2011). *Battle hymn of the tiger mother.* New York: Penguin Books.

Corra, M., Carter, J. S., & Carter, S. K. (2011). The interactive impact of race and gender on high school advanced course enrollment. *The Journal of Negro Education*, 80(1), 33–46.

Cruz-Janzen, M. I. & Wardle, F. (2004). *Meeting the needs of multiethnic and multiracial children in schools.* Boston: Pearson.

Dickar, M. (2008). Hearing the silenced dialogue: An examination of the impact of teacher race on their experience. *Race Ethnicity and Education*, 11(2), 115–132. doi:10.1080/12613 320802110233.

Diem, S. & Frankenberg, E. (2013). The politics of diversity: Integration in an era of political and legal uncertainty. *Teachers College Record*, 115(11), 1–30.

Diem, S., Frankenberg, E., Cleary, C., & Ali, N. (2014). The politics of maintaining diversity policies in demographically changing urban–suburban school districts. *American Journal of Education*, 120(3), 351–389.

Doyle, J. & Kao, G. (2007). Friendship choices of multiracial adolescents: Racial homophily, blending, or amalgamation? *Social Science Research*, 36, 633–653.

Feagin, J. R. (2001). *Racist America: Roots, current realities, & future reparations.* New York: Routledge.

Ferguson, A. (2001). *Bad boys: Public schools in the making of Black masculinity.* Ann Arbor, MI: University of Michigan Press.

Fernandes Williams, R. M. (2011). When gray matters more than Black and White: The schooling experiences of Black-White biracial students. *Education and Urban Society*, 45(2), 175–207.

Ford, D. (2012). Culturally different students in special education. Looking backward to move forward. *Exceptional Children*, 78(4), 392–405.

Frankenberg, E. (2013). The role of residential segregation in contemporary school segregation. *Education and Urban Society*, 45(5), 548–570.

Fusco, R., Rauktis, M., McCrae, J., Cunningham, M., & Bradley-King, C. (2010). Aren't they just black kids?: Biracial children in the child welfare system. *Child and Family Social Work*, 15(4), 441–451.

Gay, G. (2005). Afterthought: The imperative of learning about legacies. *Black History Bulletin*, 68(1), 35–37.

Herman, M. R. (2009). The black-white-other achievement gap: Testing theories of academic performance among multiracial and monoracial adolescents. *Sociology of Education*, 82(1), 20–46.

Hilberth, M. & Slate, J. R. (2014). Middle school Black and White student assignment to disciplinary consequences. A clear lack of equity. *Education and Urban Society*, 46(3), 312–328.

Janis, S. (2012). Am I enough?: A multi-race teacher's experience in-between contested race, gender, class, and power. *Journal of Curriculum Theorizing*, 28(3), 128–141.

Kelly, S. (2009). The Black-White gap in mathematics course taking. *Sociology of Education*, 82(1), 47–69.

Khanna, N. (2011). *Biracial in America: Forming and performing racial identity*. Lanham, MD: Lexington Books.

Krogstad, J. & Fry, R. (2014). *Department of Education projects public schools will be majority-minority this fall*. From http://www.pewresearch.org/fact-tank/2014/08/18/u-s-public-schools-expected-to-be-majority-minority-starting-this-fall/.

Lasley, H. & Ronnkvist, B. (2007). Racialized space: Framing Latino and Latina experience in public schools. *Teachers College Record*, 109(6), 1517–1538.

Lawton, B., Foeman, A., & Brown, L. (2013). Blending voices: Negotiating educational choices for upper/middle class well-educated interracial couples' children. *Howard Journal of Communication*, 24(3), 215–238.

Lewis, A. (2003). *Race in the schoolyard: Negotiating the color line in classrooms and communities*. New Brunswick, NJ: Rutgers University Press.

McBride, J. (1996). *The color of water: A Black man's tribute to his White mother*. New York: Riverhead Books.

McDermott, K. A., Frankenberg, E., & Diem, S. (2015). The "post-racial" politics of race: Changing student assignment policy in three school districts. *Educational Policy*, 29(3), 504–554.

National Assessment of Educational Progress. (2013). *The nation's report card: 2013 mathematics and reading*. From http://www.nationsreportcard.gov/reading_math_2013/#/.

National Center for Education Statistics. (2013). *Digest of education statistics*. http://nces.ed.gov/programs/digest/d13/tables/dt13_104.20.asp.

National Center for Education Statistics. (2014). *Race/ethnic enrollment in public schools*. From https://nces.ed.gov/programs/coe/indicator_cge.asp.

Nissel, A. (2006). *Mixed: My life in Black and White*. New York: Villard Books.

Nunn, L. M. (2011). Classrooms as racialized spaces. Collaboration, tension, and student attitude in urban and suburban high schools. *Urban Education*, 46(6), 1226–1255.

Obama, B. (2004). *Dreams from my father: A story of race and inheritance*. New York: Three River Press.

Ogbu, J. (1978). *Minority education and caste: The American system in cross-cultural perspective*. New York: Academic Press.

OhKeiSyd. (2013, March 26). *Being biracial in school* [Video file]. From https://youtu.be/Sl8emlHju0Y.

Renn, K. (2009). Educational policy, politics, and mixed heritage students in the United States. *Journal of Social Issues*, 65(1), 165–183.

Risman, B. J. & Banerjee, P. (2013). Kids talking race: Teenagers in a post-civil rights era. *Sociological Forum*, 28(2), 213–235.

Rockquemore, K. & Laszloffy, T. (2005). *Raising biracial children.* New York: Rowman & Littlefield Publishers, Inc.

Tatum, B.D. (1997). *"Why are all the black kids sitting together in the cafeteria?": And other conversations about race.* New York: Basic Books.

Thompson Dorsey, D. (2013). Segregation 2.0: The new generation of school segregation in the 21st century. *Education and Urban Society,* 45(5), 533–47.

U.S. Department of Education. (2007). *Final guidance on maintaining, collecting, and reporting racial and ethnic data to the U.S. Department of Education.* From http://www.gpo.gov/fdsys/pkg/FR-2007–10–19/pdf/E7–20613.pdf.

U.S. Department of Education. (2014). *Expansive survey of America's public schools reveals troubling racial disparities.* From http://www.ed.gov/news/press-releases/expansive-survey-americas-public-schools-reveals-troubling-racial- disparities.

Vaught, S. & Castagno, A. (2008). "I don't think I'm a racist": Critical race theory, teacher attitudes, and structural racism. *Race, Ethnicity, & Education,* 11(2), 95–113.

Wells, A.S. (2014). *Seeing past the "Colorblind" myth: Why education policymakers should address racial and ethnic inequality and support culturally diverse schools.* Boulder, CO: National Education Policy Center. From http://nepc.colorado.edu/publication/seeing-past-the-colorblind-myth.

Welton, A.D. (2013). Even more racially isolated than before: Problematizing the vision for "diversity" in a racially mixed high school. *Teachers College Record,* 115(11), 1–42.

Winn Tutwiler, S (2007). How schools fail African American boys. In S. Books (Ed.), *Invisible children in the society and its schools* (pp. 141–156). New York: Routledge.

9

SCHOOLING SUPPORTIVE
OF MIXED-RACE YOUTH

. . . As I have watched my daughter develop her own racial awareness, I have been surprised that too many of her experiences are like mine, despite the passage of time.

Ann
Biracial Teacher/Mother
(Singleton & Linton, 2006, p. 116)

As the numbers of mixed-race youth in public schools continue to rise, educators will be compelled to pay closer attention to the social experiences and educational needs of this group of students. A number of themes related to mixed-race youths' experiences within and outside of school point to an initial framework of practices, policies, and programs that would contribute to supportive schooling for mixed-race youth. The framework includes the following elements: race-focused educator professional development, educator advocacy, multiracial/multicultural education, authentically diverse school environments, and interracial family-school-community relations. The primary purpose of this final chapter is to explore how these elements facilitate supportive schooling for mixed-race youth.

Race-Focused Educator Professional Development

Teachers have the closest and most frequent contact with the children and youths in schools. Although their classroom practices are influenced by the context in which they teach, teachers are able to influence teaching and learning contexts as well. Still, teachers may feel the need to follow school and/or district dictated policies that guide instructional practices, even those they believe are not in the best interest of mixed-race youths in their classrooms. On the other hand, some teachers possess a sense of agency that propels them into action in order to effectively address the learning and developmental needs of their students. This disposition is often the impetus for teachers to seek professional (and sometimes personal) development opportunities in order to improve their ability to meet the learning needs of students they teach. Teacher actions on behalf of mixed-race students are enhanced when they develop the ability to pay attention to, and critically assess, how race-related issues and events impact the teaching and learning environments where young people arrive daily to learn.

Teacher Education about Race

Discussions of race-related topics are very difficult for many teachers. Yet race is often the proverbial "elephant in the room" as teachers plan what to teach, act on beliefs about students' capabilities, and arrange their classrooms in ways they believe are conducive to teaching and learning. Teachers who are silent about race teach their students to be silent as well. Further, young people in these classrooms who eventually become teachers often continue a cycle of silence around race. Without intervention, they replicate what they were taught when race-related issues surface in their classrooms. As important, another generation of young people enter the adult world with limited understanding and/or mis-information about how certain ideological perspectives on race shaped our past and continues to affect social institutions and interactions today.

The effects of racial (and sometimes class) differences on teaching and learn-ing are at the center of educators' deliberations as they wrestle with how to eradicate a persistent achievement gap between White and nonwhite students. Achievement, as influenced by race, is an important issue for mixed-race youth as well, because the achievement of some mixed-race youths mirrors that of monoracial minority youth. An underlying concern is the extent to which edu-cators' beliefs about the racial backgrounds of children and youth are infused into their practices in ways that negatively affect student performance.

Educators' beliefs about race have an additional implication for mixed-race youth. The racial ideology that guides educators' beliefs about race potentially portend a host of beliefs that lock mixed-race youth into rigid racial categories, often in ways that ignore youths' feelings about themselves and which may con-flict with what is taught about mixed-raceness in the home. Teacher education and professional development about race that affect teachers' views about mixed-raceness are needed to problematize long-held beliefs about race. This event necessarily begins with teachers acknowledging ". . . their own misconceptions and discomforts when addressing racial issues and identity in their classrooms" (Baxley, 2008, p. 231). In the process, they confront their thinking about race, racism, whiteness, and privilege. Teachers who are willing to be introspective about reasons for holding onto long-held, often erroneous beliefs about people of different races may gain insight into their beliefs about and attitudes toward mixed-raceness as well.

King (1991) noted that teachers may not intentionally engage in racism (or monoracism for that matter). Rather they are given to dysconscious racism, which is an impaired way of thinking about diversity and inequity, primarily caused by misinformation and miseducation (Brandon, 2006; King, 1991). The good news is that teachers can learn to think differently through education and exposure to information and experiences that transform their ways of thinking about race (King, 1991). Most educators are passionate about teaching and care not only about what they teach, but also who they teach (Nieto, 2005; Singleton & Linton, 2006). It is unfortunate when inaccurate information, lack of experiences with diverse communities, and lack of understanding and acceptance of people with diverse worldviews intrude upon teachers' ability to serve the needs of students they teach.

Upon reflection, it appears that dysconscious racism is at the heart of White teachers' (and pre-service teachers') use of tools of whiteness to reject information about race and privilege that challenge long-held beliefs about race. Avoidance to professional development (or teacher education content) that addresses these issues is often the result. Teachers committed to addressing the schooling needs of mixed-race youth must be committed as well to interrogating their beliefs about race. It is possible that development of a racial critical consciousness that nurtures curiosity for accurate information and motivates teachers to seek transformative race-related experiences can override dysconsciousness.

As they approach the project of addressing the social and learning needs of mixed-race youth, teachers should actually feel a sense of disequilibrium about their practice. Said another way, they should feel uncomfortable with at least some of the strategies used in the past, in order to address the student diversity they encounter in schools. These feelings should prevent them from adopting pact responses and action as they teach and develop relationships with students. It is more likely that teachers who attend to the diversity among mixed-race youth (e.g., race mixture, racial self-identification, race affiliation) will engage in ongoing reflection on how to best structure learning opportunities that include these students.

Deliberate Race-Informed Relationships

As discussed in foregoing chapters, teachers, especially White teachers, tend to not only avoid race as a topic for inclusion in what they teach, but also sidestep race-related matters in their interactions with students and colleagues. At the same time, many teachers adopt color-blind perspectives, which guide their interactions with students. In the process, they model a color-blind perspective to students as an effective way to address race.

Teachers who acknowledge racial differences are better positioned to be aware of how an extant racial hierarchy operates to segment mixed-race youth on the basis of the specifics of their racial heritage. To this degree, they become more cognizant of within-group diversity among mixed-race youth and the extent to which students' racial heritage affects aspects of their schooling. Teachers who are astute about how racial hierarchical arrangements work in the lives of mixed-race youth pay attention to varying perceptions about capabilities, placement in certain classes and programs, and peer-to-peer associations and relationships, all based on the nature of mixedness. Relatedly, they become more aware of how and when colorism and the one-drop rule sneaks into their interactions with, beliefs about, and evaluations of mixed-race children and youth, as well as when these beliefs are at the center of peer-to-peer relations. Color-blind perspectives interfere with teachers' ability to reflect on how their practices are detrimental to the learning and development of mixed-race youth and prevents them from interceding on behalf of mixed-race youth who are treated poorly in the classroom or, indeed, school-wide.

As teachers pursue race-informed relationships with students, they are likely to approach teaching in ways that benefit the classroom environment not only for mixed-race youth, but for all students. The skills and habits of mind they develop contribute to the making of an authentically diverse learning environment. In the process of preparing teachers to use a critical multicultural approach to teaching, DiAngelo and Sensoy (2010) delivered instruction to help future teachers recognize the complex nature of constructs such as diversity, racism, and privilege. Their goal was to facilitate an understanding that formulaic approaches to teaching diverse student populations are often more harmful than helpful.

Practicing teachers too should understand that prescriptive approaches for teaching mixed-race youth are often not effective. Teaching to address the needs of mixed-race youth begins with the recognition that relationships are dynamic and influenced by context in which they develop. Teachers who are open to developing meaningful relationships with students who are different from them on the basis of any number of social characteristics (e.g., race, class, gender) will be in the best position to create learning opportunities for diverse students (DiAngelo & Sensoy, 2010). In short, teachers must engage in the type of social and racial boundary crossing we expect of our young people who will as adults assuredly enter a society that is increasingly more diverse.

Race-Conscious Classroom Environments

Major themes addressed in the preceding chapters also pointed to a number of important issues to consider when structuring supportive classroom environments for mixed-race youth. Teachers' awareness of student-to-student relationships in their classrooms is necessary for structuring classrooms environments where all students feel welcomed and safe. Mixed-race students experience a number of peer interactions both inside and outside of the classroom around race that are unique to the fact that they are mixed-race. Experiences of racism and/or monoracism at the hands of peers marginalize mixed-race youth. In fact, depending on the diversity of the classroom, it is possible that mixed-race youth experience both simultaneously, which could lead to ostracization from both monoracial White and students of color.

Children are always learning in schools—not only what is taught from subject matter, but also from the racial climate of the classroom and the school. Students learn how to think about race and which behaviors are acceptable when it comes to race and racial differences. If a student spat on the floor in the middle of a lesson, teachers would be outraged and immediately confront the student about his or her action. With increased racial awareness and sensitivity, teachers will be just as incensed with students' racially insensitive comments or acts, especially those taking place in racially diverse classrooms, and will be moved to act. A response that is less punitive and more instructive benefits all students in the learning environment.

The practice of peers racing mixed-race youth, sometimes in ways that do not align with mixed-race youths' self-racial identity, can lead to tension in the classroom. Recall also that mixed-race girls may particularly encounter challenging interactions. When it is clear that race is at least one of the social characteristics at the center of contentious peer-to-peer relations, teachers can take action. It is possible that young people, like adults, also are given to dysconscious racism and monoracism. Just as information can transform teachers' habits of the mind, so too can it impact the ways students think about race and mixed-raceness. Color-blind ideology and silence around issues of race interfere with students' opportunity to learn about race as a social construct that has been interjected into society as a tool to separate people into hierarchical social arrangements, with accompanying beliefs about acceptable ways to treat them.

Singleton and Linton (2006) determined the value of educators learning to address the impact of race on schooling by engaging in what they labeled as courageous conversations about race. Their strategy involves all members of an educational community (i.e., educators, parents, and the members of the surrounding community) and is structured to engage even those who were reticent and uncomfortable talking about race. According to Singleton and Linton, entering into discussions about race and remaining in the conversations through discomfort results in ". . . authentic understanding and meaningful action" (p. 16). Arguably, teachers able to converse about race are better able to structure race-conscious classrooms.

Educator Advocacy

Advocacy for mixed-race youth is one way to heighten their visibility in schools. It begins with a clear understanding of issues associated with the schooling of mixed-race youth within a given educational context. In the process of serving as advocates, teachers take action for or against policies, practices, or attitudes both inside and outside of their schools (Winn Tutwiler, 2005). Teachers often advocate for improved schooling experiences of students who share a single social or educational characteristic (e.g., language minority students or students with disabilities). Although the impetus for advocacy may differ, there are common attitudes and approaches teachers employ as they advocate *for* students (de Oliveira & Athanases, 2007; Haneda & Alexander, 2015; Peters & Reid, 2009). For example, advocates show a sense of agency and are proactive as they engage in action meant to improve the learning environment for students sharing a characteristic that might be overlooked or not well addressed by existing school policy or practices. Also, they are committed to working both inside and outside of schools to support their efforts on behalf of a group of students, and often for students' families as well.

The importance of becoming informed about the mixed-race experience in the United States from both historical and contemporary perspectives cannot be minimized as a responsibility of teachers advocating for mixed-race students. Although interacting with mixed-race youth and their families is tremendously helpful, educator advocates are also able to gain insight from a number of sources focused on mixedness, mixed-race youth, and interracial and multiracial families. A number of informative texts currently exist about mixed-race youth and their families (e.g., Cruz-Janzen & Wardle, 2004; Davis, 2009; Khanna, 2011; Rockquemore & Laszloffy, 2005). In addition, reading historical and contemporary autobiographies/biographies and fiction written by and about mixed-race people deepens advocates understanding of mixed-race peoples' social experiences. Organizations' websites and information blogs dedicated to exploring and explaining experiences of mixed-race people (e.g. MAVIN, SWIRL, Project RACE) are also excellent sources of information about mixed-race people in general, as well as mixed-race youth and their families. Advocates for mixed-race youth who are well informed not only become resources for their colleagues at the school or district levels, but may also be able to refer parents to resources of which they were unaware.

Teacher advocates seek sustained and ongoing improvements in schooling experiences of mixed-race youth. The nature of advocacy automatically implies a goal of affecting change in educational practices and policies that become part of the organizational logic of schools. To be sure, not all practicing teachers have the knowledge and dispositions to become student advocates on their own, even when they are aware that support for a group of students is needed. Peters and Reid (2009) proposed that teacher preparation programs at the graduate and undergraduate levels could actually develop teacher advocates during the teacher preparation process. Based on their analysis of programs offering this type of learning experience, they recommended programs that attended to the ". . . historical, legal, cultural, and social contexts of education . . . offer alternative representations [of schooling] through strong grounding in counter-hegemonic narratives . . . stress continual reflection . . . and promote individual and collective advocacy . . ." (p. 557), among other program components. These knowledge and attitudinal areas appear especially pertinent to advocacy for mixed-race youth. Collaborative advocacy is also possible. In this instance, teachers work together to develop the knowledge needed to promote schooling environments supportive of mixed-race youth.

Multicultural Education

On the surface, multicultural education seeks to address student diversity in learning settings, based on strategies grounded in beliefs of equity and the democratic ideal ostensibly valued in society. There are many approaches to multicultural education with different aims and practices for attending to student diversity. In practice, teachers apply principles associated with one or more of these approaches, either of their own accord or in response to school- and/or district-wide diversity-related directives. Multicultural education is by no means a panacea to all challenges faced by public schools today. However, I argue that the most frequently applied multicultural education is lacking to some degree when it comes to the schooling of mixed-race youth.

Sleeter and Grant (2009) developed a typology of multicultural education that includes the following five approaches, which are very briefly discussed:

1. *Teaching exceptional and culturally different students.* This approach views student differences from deficit locations. Teachers apply specific strategies that are believed to ameliorate, remediate, or compensate for negative influences on academic achievement caused by student differences (e.g., race, class, abilities).
2. *Human relations.* Teachers engage in instruction and classroom practices in order to facilitate positive interpersonal relationships among students from different social and cultural backgrounds.
3. *Single-group studies.* Education is focused on an isolated social characteristic (e.g., gender, ethnicity, disability) in order to increase awareness of specific groups. Ethnic studies or women's studies are good examples.
4. *Multicultural education.* This approach attends to the entire educational process, with the goal of effecting equity, improving student achievement, and promoting acceptance of cultural diversity.
5. *Multicultural social justice education.* Students are taught critical skills that enable them to determine the extent to which democracy, justice, and equality are available for all social groups in society, and to take action on the basis of what they have learned.

There are two additional approaches for working with diversity not included in the Sleeter and Grant typology that are important to consider. Proponents of anti-racist education consider this approach to be an improvement to multicultural education, which they believe pays scant attention to racism. A primary aim of this approach is to improve students' awareness of whiteness and white privilege, and to problematize color blindness (Niemonen, 2007). Lastly, the critical multicultural education approach, which may also be referred to as critical pedagogy, transgressive pedagogy, or liberatory pedagogy, for example, is concerned with the uneven distribution of power in society that inevitably transfers into unequal power in schools. Critical multiculturalists also reject the routinization and standardization of teacher practice and the curriculum. A primary aim is for teachers to possess an understanding of the long-standing and deeply embedded racism and power imbalances in society and the effect of these on educational practices today (DiAngelo & Sensoy, 2010; The South Shore Journal, 2011).

Multiracial/Multicultural Education

I propose a multiracial/multicultural approach to education that borrows from existing approaches to addressing diversity, while at the same time addresses obvious shortcomings when it comes to including the experiences of mixed-race people. The term multiracial/multicultural is used to distinguish race from culture. To be sure, no one culture captures the range of cultural perspectives adopted by mixed-race people. The primary aim of a multiracial/multicultural approach is to foster school practice that creates and sustains equitable, supportive, and inclusive learning environments for all students. The heightened attention to race and mixed-raceness, however, is meant to ensure that these constructs are not overlooked in the process of delivering education that is multicultural.

Banks's (2008) framework for the dimensions of multicultural education is especially useful for exploring elements of multiracial/multicultural education. The dimensions are comprehensive in that they address multiple elements that are important to the day-to-day schooling of mixed-race youth.

Content integration primarily addresses school curriculum and is usually explained as the act of teachers incorporating information from a variety of groups, as they teach key concepts, theories, and ideas in various content areas. Most approaches to multicultural education include reference to what is taught. Approaches with a content integration component advise teachers to include information from monoracial groups with no reference to the inclusion of information related to the experiences of mixed-race people. A multiracial/multicultural approach reminds teachers that mixed-race people have experiences that are similar to people of other races people, as well as experiences that are unique to the fact that they are mixed-race. Hence, their experiences contribute to the richness of a diverse society; thus, they should be included in the curriculum.

Knowledge construction refers to the notion that knowledge is not culture and value free. Attitudes, beliefs, and social positions of knowledge producers must be taken into consideration as students consume information. Students should view information and ideas as suspect when certain groups are excluded. Approaching this dimension from a multiracial/multicultural perspective allows for critical examination of the extent to which either monoracial minorities and/or mixed-raced people are excluded as producers of knowledge, not so unlike the approach to multicultural education proposed by supporters of critical multicultural education. Further, as teachers embrace the notion of the import of worldview on knowledge production, they would be less likely to ignore and/or omit the multiple and diverse worldviews of mixed-race people as they determine which knowledge is worthy of being a part of the content they teach.

Prejudice reduction stresses the importance of modifying racial attitudes through instruction and related materials. Most approaches to multicultural education and teaching for diversity (with the exception of teaching exceptional and culturally different students) address this dimension in some way. The prejudice reduction dimension as reframed for a multiracial/multicultural approach to multicultural education goes beyond modification of racial attitudes. It borrows from anti-racist and critical multicultural approaches, where more direct and dynamic positions are taken with respect to the influence of race and racism on the principles of equity and democracy valued by society. Transformation, rather than modification, is the goal.

Prejudice reduction in this sense calls for explicit instruction around race as a social construct, as well as instruction about ideological perspectives on race that led to disparate social locations and opportunities for differently raced people. Further, students will be exposed to information and experiences that facilitate an understanding of the relationship between racial prejudice and efforts by social elites to keep differently raced people separate (e.g., through social segregation and anti-miscegenation laws). A multiracial/multicultural approach to multicultural education is based on the belief that prejudice reduction can occur only when students have sound learning experiences around issues of race that allow them to critically analyze the role of race in the building of a nation historically, and how race continues to intervene at micro and macro levels in everyday contemporary life. This type of education requires abandonment of public scripts that support silence around issues of race and color blind ideologies that suggest race no longer matters.

Finally, a multiracial/multicultural approach departs from other multicultural education approaches in that it explicitly includes monoracism as an area of concern, when racial prejudice is addressed. According to Hamako (2014), monoracism may be dismissed by anti-racists, even though mixed-race people are susceptible to oppression and marginalization as a result of their mixed-race status. Further, he noted that in the past, academia "pathologized and vilified" (p. 98) mixed-race people in ways that contributed to their marginalization. A multiracial/multicultural approach to diversity recognizes the systemic nature of monoracism and that it stands distinct from racism because of ". . . the systemic privileging of things, people, and practices that are racialized as "single race," and or "racially pure," (e.g., monoracial) . . ." (p. 81).

Equity pedagogy as described by Banks concerns teaching methods used to teach children and youth from different race, class, language, and cultural backgrounds. Culturally responsive or culturally relevant pedagogical approaches might be applied, and attention to different learning styles is another way to embrace this dimension. The overall goal is to apply instructional strategies that connect to characteristics students bring to the learning environment in ways that aid students' academic achievement. A multiracial/multicultural approach requires teachers to pay attention to the multiple identities and racial affiliations among mixed-race youth. Consideration of the intersection of mixed-raceness, class, gender, and race group affiliation is essential when thinking about effective pedagogical approaches for mixed-race youth.

A multiracial/multicultural approach to equity pedagogy most closely aligns with critical multicultural approaches, where discursive rather than formulaic approaches to teaching are valued (DiAngelo & Sensoy, 2010). Teachers would be given to rely on practices that are counter-hegemonic and inclusive. Further, their professional practices would be influenced by both reflection on self and the context in which they teach, in order to remain diligent in their efforts to resist giving in to pact practices that essentialize how young people learn, and thus how they are supposed to be taught.

Empowering school culture and social structure requires educators to evaluate the extent to which the structure and organization of the learning environment allow for equitable participation of all students in all programs and activities, both academic and nonacademic, as well as the extent to which students feel empowered to do so. Aspects of this dimension will be discussed more closely in the following section of this chapter. Suffice it to say here that a multiracial/multicultural approach to multicultural education urges educators to examine the extent to which schools operate from monocultural or monoracial perspectives in ways that interfere with a sense of belonging to the school for some students.

As discussed in previous chapters, the position of powerblind sameness adopted by some educators results in some students feeling disempowered in their schools (Castagno, 2013). Schools organized so that isolated racial groups predominate in various school-sponsored events and programs disappear mixed-race youth, who may not feel invited to join program or activities of interest to them.

Authentically Diverse School Environments

As noted earlier, the nature of diversity in schools influences a number of school-related areas for mixed-race youth, including their sense of belonging, racial self-identity journeys, and development of social boundary crossing skills. School diversity can be viewed from a number of perspectives, however. Clearly, the social characteristics of the student population represent one way of determining whether a school is diverse. Schools with limited numbers of students from different racial, cultural, and/or social class backgrounds can hardly claim to be diverse—and as discussed in previous chapters, some parents and communities do not view diversity as a necessary or desired characteristic for their schools. On the other hand, some schools may appear to be diverse because of the percentages of students from different backgrounds attending the school. Nonetheless, the policies and practices that guide the day-to-day functioning of the school render them less so.

Little in the way these schools operate, the school curriculum presented, or the predominant school climate suggest interest in or energy toward the social justice and democratic goals of schooling Welton (2013) suggested as clearly linked to diversity in education. Some schools adopt multicultural education as human relations to encourage positive interactions among students from different racial and class backgrounds. The ultimate goal in this instance, of course, is to reduce negative and stereotypical beliefs youth attach to peers from race and class background different form their own. The lack of change in school practices that would lead to consideration of the diversity of needs and worldviews of students who make up the student population suggest that these schools are not authentically diverse.

The extent to which mixed-race youth contribute to diversity remains equivocal in too many schools, and this is true for both majority White and majority-minority schools. Clearly, a first step in the deciding how or if mixed-race youth contribute to school diversity is to recognize them as a distinct group of students who view their raciality in diverse ways. A second and very important step is to accurately determine the number of mixed-race students in the school (or district) population. To do less renders the mixed-race student population and their unique schooling needs invisible. In fact, the visibility of mixed-race students in some schools may be so ambiguous that the school (or district) is unable to accurately communicate (to teachers, parents, and the community-at-large) a true accounting of the mixed-race student population.

Changes in the U.S. Department of Education student data collection procedures presents tremendous opportunity for schools and school districts to have more exact information about mixed-race students and their families who are part of the school community. No longer hindered by the "other" category on school forms, schools and districts can collect data that allow for the creation of policies, practices, and programs that ensure the inclusion of the mixed-race student population in the life of the school community. As schools disaggregate data by race, they become aware of how mixed-race students are faring in their schools. They will be able to discern, for example, the placement of mixed-race students in special programs (e.g., special education, gifted programs), the extent to which mixed-race youth are tracked in high- or low-level courses, and even their involvement in extracurricular activities. This information allows schools to examine policies and practices that possibly contribute to limited participation of mixed-race youth in some schooling components and overrepresentation in others.

Schools and districts committed to understanding and addressing the schooling needs of mixed-race youth are further advantaged when they drill deeper into mixed-race student data to ascertain the within-group diversity among the mixed-race students attending their schools. When combined with other information about students (e.g., parental racial heritage), schools become aware of how the nature of students' racial mixture influence or does not influence the schooling experiences of mixed-race students. For example, they will be able to determine if White-minority mixed-race students have different schooling experiences from minority-minority mixed-race students at their schools. Mixed-race students' peer associations and racial group affiliation patterns are also telling and provide additional information about how mixed-race students experience schooling a particular school sites.

Race-Conscious Policies, Programs, and Practices

School diversity can also be determined in terms of the organizational logic of the school, which relates to the empowering school culture and social structure dimension of multicultural education discussed earlier. When educators and policymakers are intent on becoming more knowledgeable about students who attend their schools, they are able to generate policies and practices to ensure that all students receive the support they need to be successful. Welton (2013) pointed to the improbability of students' and educators' ability to take advantage of diversity in places where school systems and structures have not changed to keep up with changes in student diversity in their schools. The degree to which students feel that policies and practices foster a sense of equity among students, as noted by the empowerment dimension discussed earlier, determines the extent to which they feel they belong to the school (and that the school belongs to them).

Depending on their racial self-identity and racial affiliation, mixed-race students may not feel they totally belong in either schools organized as white space or those that are majority-minority. In these schools, mixed-race youth actually contribute to the diversity of one school or the other, in that they may have needs for social, emotional, or academic support that differs from the schools' dominant student population. Policies, practices, and programs in either predominantly White or majority-minority schools should be examined to ensure that they attend not only to single-race students, but also mixed-race students.

Race-conscious policies, practices, and programs should not be solely for the benefit of monoracial youth in schools, even when schools are diverse as a result of a student population that includes monoracial White and monoracial students of color from multiple racial backgrounds. Educators and policymakers, for example, may mistakenly believe that practices, programs, and celebrations generated to address the belonging and inclusion needs of monoracial minority youth address these same needs for mixed-race youths as well. This is not necessarily the case. Race-conscious policies and practices must go beyond single-race practices to find ways to include mixed-race youth that are unique to their mixed-race status. Celebrations and activities that intentionally include individuals from multiple racial backgrounds (including those who straddle races) more clearly signal inclusion of mixed-race youth in the school community. Further, at least some mixed-race students might be interested in activities or clubs that facilitate interaction with other mixed-race students. This possibility can be explored without assuming this type of activity would of interest to all mixed-race students attending the school.

Support for Racial Identity Development

A final way to look at diversity in schools is the extent to which the learning environment has support for the multiple and diverse developmental tasks students undertake. Mixed-race youth, like many monoracial minority youth, are in the midst of a racial identity journey during adolescence that becomes a big part of their overall sense of self. Unlike monoracial youth of color, however, mixed-race youth have multiple possibilities for racial identity, which makes racial identity development a more daunting task for some. Also, race likely has more, if not a different, meaning for mixed-race youth than it does for monoracial youth of color. It is important, for example, to mixed-race youth that they are accurately perceived racially by people with whom they interact. For them, race is more like a personality characteristic, and so accurate racial identification is a means for self-verification (Remedios & Chasteen, 2013).

Schools that ignore the mixed status of mixed-race youth may actually contribute to difficulties they might encounter with racial self-identity (Baxley, 2008). Knowing the importance and complexity of racial self-identity for some mixed-race youth allows schools to ensure appropriate support is available. For example, school counselors who are aware of the issues associated with racial identity development, and who are cognizant of strategies and techniques to address the unique issues faced by the mixed-race adolescents, are important school personnel to consider (Maxwell & Henrikson, 2012). Counselors may also understand the nature of tensions that sometimes arise in peer-to-peer interactions between mixed-race and monoracial youth and will be able to make recommendations to teachers and other school personnel about how to best address these situations. In this sense, they serve not only as support for mixed-race youth, but also as resources for teachers who want to understand more about the mixed-race youth experience around race.

Interracial Family-School/Community Relations

The evidence is clear when it comes to the positive effect parental involvement has on the education of children and youth (Winn Tutwiler, 2005). Thus, as a matter of policy, schools should foster productive relations between the school and students' homes. Interracial families are not universally accepted in society-at-large, and so the total community of educators will not likely accept this family form either. Outdated views on racial boundary crossing continue to inform opinions on the appropriateness of marriage across races. Educator professional development around issues of race, racism, and monoracism is necessary to help educators develop different ways of viewing and interacting with these families and their children, both in schools where there are sizeable numbers of youth in interracial homes and in those where the numbers are small. The possibility of a sense of isolation in the latter case makes reaching out to these families even more important.

It is critical for educators to have a genuine understanding not only of the unique challenges interracial families face, but also the strengths this family form brings to bear on both the positive development and school performance of mixed-race youth. Increasing teacher and administrator knowledge, skills, and positive attitudes toward diverse family arrangements reduces stumbling blocks and barriers to strong home–school relationships. Clearly, parents are more eager to work collaboratively with schools where they feel they and their family are welcomed and respected.

Educators should also be prepared for the fact that the within-group diversity that characterizes mixed-race youth is true as well for their families. As addressed earlier in this book, there are a number of racial combinations possible for parents in interracial families. The intersection of parental racial backgrounds, family configurations (e.g., same sex or different sex; two parent or single parent), and social class location, among other characteristics, make for a highly diverse family group. Hence, educators should be prepared for the multiple perspectives parents in interracial families bring to school-family interactions. Moreover, parents of mixed-race youth will have concerns that differ from single-race families and may even view their roles in the education of their children differently from monoracial families as well (Brown, 2009).

Educators will also find difference among parents in interracial families in terms of the race designation decisions they make on behalf of their children. This is true even when parents in one family share the same racial configuration as parents in a different family (e.g., Asian American mother, African American father). Similarly, differences exist in terms of how families racially socialize their children. Teachers' initial perceptions of students' racial identification does not always align with the racial designation made by parents. Still, race designation is important information for educators to know.

Teachers have a number of options for inviting parents to share this information. Classroom surveys where parents can discreetly share race-related information is one possibility. Face-to-face communication during parent conference, for example, is another. Teachers can openly ask about a student's racial heritage. Many parents of mixed-race youth are not resistant to discussing race issues with educators. Indeed, many may welcome the opportunity, especially if they sense that their child is encountering race-related issues that interfere with the child's education and social well-being (Byrd & Garwick, 2006).

Just as parents of monoracial youth have child-rearing questions for educators, so may be the case for parents of mixed-race youth, albeit the nature of some of the questions may differ. Remember, most parents of mixed-race youth did not have the mixed-race student experience in school. Although parents serve as sources of information about their mixed-race children for educators, educators too can be sources of information for parents. If resource centers exist, information that addresses the experiences of interracial families and raising mixed-race youth should be available. Relatedly, if information is posted on school or district websites, information of interest to parents of mixed-race youth should be included as well. To this latter point, information displayed for and about interracial families increase their visibility as members of the school community.

Parents of mixed-race youth may also serve as a source of information for curriculum and appropriate classroom activities (Baxley, 2008) and may even be appropriate speakers for topics addressed in the classroom. However, teachers should be sensitive to the fact that some mixed-race youth do not want to "show off" their parents to peers, regardless of the parents' accomplishments. Mixed-race students may feel uncomfortable with a parent (monoracial White or monoracial minority) appearing in their classroom, because the parents' racial location may not be in keeping with the racial self-identity the youth is attempting to develop. Similarly, perceptions peers may have about a mixed-race student's racial background will be contradicted once the youth's parent appears at school. Peers who thought the student was White, for example, are now aware that the child has a parent of color (Baxley, 2008).

Checking with mixed-race students before inviting a parent to the classroom is a relatively simple way to make sure the student's sense of self will not be disturbed by the presence of a parent in the classroom. Issues of race are complex for mixed-race youth, and some need more time to figure race related issues than others. A teacher who overrides a student's wishes on the basis of a belief of what the student should feel or how he or she should relate to his or her parents interferes in ways that are not in the best interest of the student or the parent. This issue between parent and children may best be resolved within the home. Additional support from the school can be given, only if requested by the parent.

Nissel's (2006) path to a racial identity provides an instructive example. The fact that her mother was Black was not an issue for her. However, during her elementary school years, Nissel was committed to a White identity. Inviting her mother to her classroom to speak would have contradicted the place where she happened to be in her racial developmental journey by emphasizing the nonwhite aspect of her heritage to her White friends. Nissel ended up with a solid Black identity, given time to complete her racial developmental journey. Educators who are sensitive to the complexity of the relationship between mixed-race youth and their parents will be better positioned to understand when to take advantage of parents' possible contributions to the classroom and when to defer to students wishes.

As a final point, it is important for schools to have the pulse of the community outside of schools, in terms of community attitudes toward race, mixed-raceness, and diversity in general. To be sure, many attitudes related to these issues will find their way into the school environment, either overtly or covertly. Instruction related to prevailing negative attitudes would be appropriate for the classroom and could result in the adoptions of more inclusive perspectives in both the school and wider community.

Knowing the community has the added benefit of educators being aware of resources that might be needed by some interracial families. Some families may turn to schools when they face problematic issues. Schools' ability to make referrals and/or point families to helpful resources in many cases deepens the sense of connection between the home and the school. Schools and districts can also be instrumental in helping interracial families build community networks, particularly those with other interracial families. They may, for example, bring families of mixed-race youth together through workshops or other school-related events focused on this population of students. Schools should present themselves as institutions at the center of building community, both inside of schools and in the broader community. Indeed, they should model the merits of diversity as they work to serve the needs all students and families, not just those from a particular family arrangement.

Final Comments on the Schooling of Mixed-Race Youth

Although this final chapter was concerned with actions educators can take to create schools supportive of mixed-race youth, actions taken in earnest potentially support schooling of all youth. It is inconceivable, for example, that an educator who critically assesses the impact of race and racism on the education of mixed-race youth would not be able to also see the impact of these constructs on the education of monoracial children, both White and nonwhite. To this degree, at least a seed of the expectation that increased attention to a growing mixed-race population would signal changes in race relations in the United States has been planted.

Change happens slowly. It is unlikely that the impact of racial divisions will be eliminated as a result of a single social event. Whether hopes were placed on the Multiracial Movement or the election of the first Black president to rid the nation of the role race plays in life circumstances, the significance of race persists, and the coming of a post-racial society has not been realized. Still, there is a possibility that as schools attend to the schooling needs of mixed-race youth, the improbability of avoiding the impact of race on schooling will result in improved schooling situations for children of differently raced backgrounds.

Finally, I attempted throughout the text to reflect the current school-related experiences of mixed-race youth in the United States as it is portrayed in existing literature. Nevertheless, the schooling of mixed-race youth is ripe for additional research, in all areas related to the education of this population of students. It is my hope that scholars continue to observe and analyze the experiences of this group of students, not instead of monoracial youth, but as an additional means for understanding how race operates within the institution of education for all students. A number of research areas stand out. These include the experiences of mixed-race youth in diverse and more racially homogenous school contexts, academic performance of mixed-race youth as data on this event becomes more available, continued research on educational experiences of mixed-race youth as informed by within-group diversity, and school-interracial family relations, just to pinpoint a few areas. Finally, international comparisons of schooling experiences of mixed-race youth throughout the world will serve only to enrich this area of scholarship.

References

Banks, J. A. (2008). *An introduction to multicultural education* (4th ed.). Boston: Allyn & Bacon.

Baxley, T. (2008). What are you?: Biracial children in the classroom. *Childhood Education*, 84(4), 230–233.

Brandon, L. (2006). On dysconsciousness: An interview with Joyce E. King. *Educational Studies*, 40(2), 196–208.

Brown, M. (2009). A new multicultural population: Creating effective partnerships with multiracial families. *Intervention in School and Clinic*, 45(2), 124–131.

Byrd, M. & Garwick, A. (2006). Family identity: Black-White interracial family health experience. *Journal of Family Nursing*, 12, 22–37.

Castagno, A. E. (2013). Multicultural education and the protection of whiteness. *American Journal of Education*, 120(1), 101–128.

Cruz-Janzen, M. & Wardle, F. (2004). *Meeting the needs of multiethnic and multiracial children in schools*. Boston: Pearson.

Davis, B. M. (2009). *The biracial and multiracial student experience: A journey to racial literacy*. Thousand Oaks, CA: Corwin.

de Oliveira, L. & Athanases, S. (2007). Graduates' reports of advocating for English language learners. *Journal of Teacher Education*, 58(3), 202–215.

DiAngelo, R. & Sensoy, O. (2010). "Ok, I get it! Now tell me how to do it!": Why we can't just tell you how to do critical multicultural education. *Multicultural Perspectives*, 12(2), 97–102.

Hamako, E. (2014). *Improving anti-racist education for multiracial students*. From http://scholarworks.umass.edu/cgi/viewcontent.cgi?article=1079&context=dissertations_2.

Haneda, M. & Alexander, M. (2015). ESL teacher advocacy beyond the classroom. *Teaching and Teacher Education*, 49, 149–158.

Khanna, N. (2011). *Biracial in America: Forming and performing racial identity*. Lanham, MD: Lexington Books.

King, J. E. (1991). Dysconscious racism. Ideology, identity, and miseducation of teachers. *The Journal of Negro Education*, 60(2), 133–146.

Maxwell, M. J. & Henriksen, R.C. (2012). Counseling multiple heritage adolescents: A phenomenological study of experiences and practices of middle school counselors. *Professional School Counseling*, 16(1), 18–28.

Niemonen, J. (2007). Antiracist education in theory and practice: A critical assessment. *The American Sociologist*, 38(2), 159–177.

Nieto, S. (2005). *Why we teach*. New York: Teachers College Press.

Nissel, A. (2006). *Mixed: My life in Black and White*. New York: Villard Books.

Peters, S. & Reid, D. (2009). Resistance and discursive practice: Promoting advocacy in teacher undergraduate and graduate programmes. *Teaching and Teacher Education*, 25(4), 551–558.

Remedios, J. D. & Chasteen, A. L. (2013). Finally, someone who "gets" me!: Multiracial people value others accuracy about their race. *Cultural Diversity and Ethnic Minority Psychology*, 19(4), 453–460.

Rockquemore, K. A. & Laszloffy, T. (2005). *Raising biracial children*. New York: Rowman & Littlefield Publishers, Inc.

Singleton, G. & Linton, C. (2006). *Courageous conversations about race: A field guide for achieving equity in schools*. Thousand Oaks, CA: Corwin Press.

Sleeter, C. & Grant, C. (2009). *Making choices for multicultural education: Five approaches to race, class and gender* (6th ed.). New York: John Wiley & Sons, Inc.

The South Shore Journal. (2011). *Curriculum and schooling. Multiculturalism, critical multiculturalism and critical pedagogy*. From http://www.southshorejournal.org/index.php/about-us/84-journals/vol-4-2011/78-curriculum-a-schooling-multiculturalism-critical-multiculturalism-and-critical-pedagogy.

Welton, A. D. (2013). Even more racially isolated than before: Problematizing the vision for a racially mixed high school. *Teachers College Record*, 115(11), 1–42.

Winn Tutwiler, S. (2005). *Teachers as collaborative partners: Working with diverse families and communities*. Mahwah, NJ: Lawrence Erlbaum Associates, Publishers.

INDEX

Note: Page numbers with *f* indicate figures; those with *c* indicate charts.